# EU Private International Law

ELGAR EUROPEAN LAW

**Founding editor:** John Usher, *formerly Professor of European Law and Head, School of Law, University of Exeter, UK*

European integration is the driving force behind constant evolution and change in the laws of the member states and the institutions of the European Union. This important series will offer short, state-of-the-art overviews of many specific areas of EU law, from competition law to consumer law and from environmental law to labour law. Whilst most books will take a thematic, vertical approach, others will offer a more horizontal approach and consider the overarching themes of EU law.

Distilled from rigorous substantive analysis, and written by some of the best names in the field, as well as the new generation of scholars, these books are designed both to guide the reader through the changing legislation itself, and to provide a firm theoretical foundation for advanced study. They will be an invaluable source of reference for scholars and postgraduate students in the fields of EU law and European integration, as well as lawyers from the respective individual fields and policymakers within the EU.

Titles in the series include:

EU Consumer Law and Policy
*Stephen Weatherill*

EU Private International Law
Harmonization of Laws
*Peter Stone*

EU Public Procurement Law
*Christopher H. Bovis*

EU Criminal Law and Justice
*Maria Fletcher and Robin Lööf with Bill Gilmore*

Judicial Review in EU Law
*Alexander H. Türk*

EU Intellectual Property Law and Policy
*Catherine Seville*

EU Private International Law
Second Edition
*Peter Stone*

# EU Private International Law

## Second Edition

Peter Stone

*Professor, School of Law, University of Essex, UK*

ELGAR EUROPEAN LAW

**Edward Elgar**
Cheltenham, UK • Northampton, MA, USA

Published by
Edward Elgar Publishing Limited
The Lypiatts
15 Lansdown Road
Cheltenham
Glos GL50 2JA
UK

Edward Elgar Publishing, Inc.
William Pratt House
9 Dewey Court
Northampton
Massachusetts 01060
USA

A catalogue record for this book is available from the British Library

Library of Congress Control Number: 2009941137

ISBN 978 1 84844 083 8 (cased)

Typeset by Cambrian Typesetters, Camberley, Surrey
Printed and bound by MPG Books Group, UK

# Contents

# Preface

The European Union legislation in the sphere of private international law has undergone considerable development since the publication of the first edition of this work in 2006. The case-law on existing EU measures (the Brussels I Regulation on civil jurisdiction and judgments; the Rome Convention 1980 on the law applicable to contractual obligations; the Brussels IIA Regulation on matrimonial matters and parental responsibility; and the Regulation on insolvency proceedings) has continued to expand, and several new EU regulations have been adopted. Thus choice of law in respect of civil obligations is now governed by the Rome I Regulation on contractual obligations, and by the Rome II Regulation on non-contractual obligations. In the sphere of family law, a Regulation on jurisdiction, choice of law and judgments in respect of maintenance obligations has been adopted and will become applicable in 2011. The European Union has become a member of the Hague Conference on Private International Law, and is in the process of giving effect, in relation to external countries, to the Hague Convention 1996 on parental responsibility and child protection, and to the Hague Convention 2005 on choice of court agreements. With regard to the EFTA countries, a revised Lugano Convention on civil jurisdiction and judgments has been concluded by the European Union and brought into operation in relation to Norway. Consideration has also begun of a proposal for an EU regulation dealing with succession on death.

In general, the present author continues to welcome the harmonisation of private international law at European Union level. Since private international law seeks to co-ordinate the operation of private law in the interests of justice and certainty for persons involved in transnational activities or relationships, and the achievements of these goals can be obstructed by divergencies between the rules adopted in different countries, the establishment of a harmonised system of private international law, operative throughout most of Europe, seems an appropriate activity for the EU institutions. Thus the recent willingness of British governments to give way to pressure from certain commercial interests and their level advisers, and accordingly to play an obstructive role in relation to this harmonisation project, seems entirely regrettable.

On the other hand, there are features of the current approach adopted by the European institutions in this sphere which appear to merit fundamental reconsideration. In particular, the enthusiasm of the EU Commission to eliminate the need, in the context of the enforcement of one Member State of a judgment given in another Member State, for an enforcement order made by a court of the State of enforcement, seems unjustified and, indeed, dangerous. Apart from the practical difficulties which may arise, the idea of automatic enforceability gives far too little consideration to the need to ensure that (at least) private individuals and small businesses receive a minimum of essential procedural protection from the courts of the country in which they reside or are based. Even the suppression of jurisdictional review in the State addressed goes beyond what has been found acceptable between sister States in the United States of America, and has obvious dangers, especially in relation to proceedings brought in bad faith. There is a real risk that excessive enthusiasm for 'the free movement of judgments' may eventually discredit the whole process of harmonisation in this sphere.

In general the manuscript of this work was completed in January 2010. But major developments (such as rulings given by the European Court) up to September 2010 have been incorporated.

Peter Stone
Colchester
England

PART I

Introduction

# 1. Introduction

## PRIVATE INTERNATIONAL LAW AND ITS HARMONISATION

The area of law known as private international law, or the conflict of laws, addresses three kinds of problem which arise, in connection with legal relationships governed by private law, where a factual situation is connected with more than one country. Rules of private international law may conveniently be referred to as conflict rules.

Such a situation may arise from the connections of persons, of acts or events, or of property involved. Thus relevant connections may include an individual's domicile, residence, or nationality; the place of incorporation, or the location of the headquarters, or of a branch, of a company; the place of conclusion or performance of a contract; the place where an accident giving rise to a tort claim occurred; or the location of property.

Three kinds of problem are dealt with by conflict rules. They relate to direct jurisdiction; to choice of law; and to foreign judgments. Rules on direct jurisdiction define the circumstances in which the courts of one country are competent, and should be willing, to entertain proceedings in respect of disputes which have some connection with another country. Such rules are applicable by a court for the purpose of determining its own jurisdiction to entertain proceedings instituted before it. Rules on choice of law select from the connected countries the one whose law is to supply the substantive rules to be applied in determining the merits of the dispute. Rules on foreign judgments define the circumstances in which a judgment given by a court of one country is to be recognised or enforced in another country.

In the modern world, every country having a developed legal system has its own set of conflict rules, which form part of its private law. Such rules differ from one country to another, and these differences tend to undermine the purposes of the rules. For such purposes include the achievement of legal security (by way of certainty, predictability and uniformity of results, regardless of which country's courts are involved) for the persons involved. Like any other rules of a country's private law, its conflict rules may be harmonised with those of other countries by means of international treaties, and in this respect much has been achieved by the conventions negotiated at the Hague Conference on Private International Law.[1] Especially in recent years, further harmonisation has been achieved at European level by measures adopted within the framework of the European Community or Union, and it is on such harmonisation that the present work is focused.

---

[1] On 3rd April 2007, the European Community became a member of the Hague Conference on Private International Law, by accession pursuant to EC Council Decision 2006/719, [2006] OJ L297/1. See pp. 13–14 et seq. below.

## HARMONISATION AT EUROPEAN COMMUNITY LEVEL

Since the entry into force of the Treaty of Lisbon on 1st December 2009, the adoption at European level of measures for the harmonisation of conflict rules is now governed by Title V (Articles 67–89) of Part III of the Treaty on the Functioning of the European Union. These provisions have replaced Title IV (Articles 61–9) of the EC Treaty, under which many important measures had been adopted in the sphere of private international law, mainly in the form of EC regulations adopted either by the Council alone, or jointly by the Council and the Parliament. By the Treaty of Lisbon, the European Union has replaced and succeeded to the European Community.

Article 67(1) of the Treaty on the Functioning of the European Union declares that the Union constitutes an area of freedom, security and justice with respect for fundamental rights and the different legal systems and traditions of the Member States. Article 67(4) adds that the Union is to facilitate access to justice, in particular through the principle of mutual recognition of judicial and extrajudicial decisions in civil matters.

Within Title V of the Treaty on the Functioning of the European Union, Chapter 3 (Article 81) is entitled Judicial Co-operation in Civil Matters.[2] Article 81(1) requires the Union to develop judicial co-operation in civil matters having cross-border implications, based on the principle of mutual recognition of judgments and of decisions in extrajudicial cases; and specifies that such co-operation may include the adoption of measures for the approximation of the laws and regulations of the Member States. Then Article 81(2) authorises the adoption of measures for these purposes, particularly when necessary for the proper functioning of the internal market,[3] aimed at ensuring the following results:

(a)  the mutual recognition and enforcement between Member States of judgments and of decisions in extrajudicial cases;
(b)  the cross-border service of judicial and extrajudicial documents;
(c)  the compatibility of the rules applicable in the Member States concerning conflict of laws and of jurisdiction;
(d)  co-operation in the taking of evidence;
(e)  effective access to justice;
(f)  the elimination of obstacles to the proper functioning of civil proceedings, if necessary by promoting the compatibility of the rules on civil procedure applicable in the Member States;
(g)  the development of alternative methods of dispute settlement; and
(h)  support for the training of the judiciary and judicial staff.

Thus it seems clear that all aspects of private international law may be subjected to harmonisation by measures adopted under Title V.

Article 81(2) also specifies that measures under Article 81 are to be adopted by the Parliament and the Council, acting in accordance with the ordinary legislative procedure.[4]

---

[2]   Article 81 replaces Articles 65 and 67 of the EC Treaty.
[3]   The insertion of 'particularly' in Article 81(2) seems designed to weaken the requirement of connection with the internal market, as compared with Article 65 of the EC Treaty.
[4]   This corresponds to the co-decision procedure under the EC Treaty.

But an exception is made by Article 81(3) in respect of measures concerning family law with cross-border implications. Measures on family law are to be established by the Council, acting in accordance with a special legislative procedure, under which the Council will act unanimously after consulting the European Parliament.[5]

The power of the European Court to give preliminary rulings on the validity or interpretation of acts of the European institutions at the request of national courts, now conferred by Article 267 of the Treaty on the Functioning of the European Union, now has full application to measures adopted under Article 81 of that Treaty or under its predecessor, Articles 61(c) and 65 of the EC Treaty. Prior to the entry into force of the Treaty of Lisbon, Article 68 of the EC Treaty enabled preliminary rulings on the interpretation of measures adopted under Title IV thereof to be requested only by national courts of last resort, but this restriction has now been eliminated by the Treaty on the Functioning of the European Union. Thus a reference for the interpretation of a provision of, for example, the Brussels I Regulation may now be made by any court of a Member State, whether the referring court is a court of first instance, a court of intermediate appeal, or a court of final appeal.[6]

By Protocol 21 to the Treaty on European Union and the Treaty on the Functioning of the European Union, as amended by the Treaty of Lisbon, measures adopted under Title V of Part III of the Treaty on the Functioning of the European Union apply to the United Kingdom or Ireland only if they elect to participate in the adoption of, or after its adoption to accept, the measure in question. By Protocol 22, as so amended, measures adopted under Title V do not apply to Denmark, unless and until it elects wholly or partly to abandon this opt-out. These provisions conferring options on the relevant Member States resemble those formerly made by Article 69 of the EC Treaty, along with associated Protocols, in relation to measures adopted under Title IV of that Treaty. But Protocol 22 now enables Denmark to substitute a regime giving it an option in relation to each individual measure, similar to that enjoyed by the United Kingdom and Ireland.

So far Ireland has chosen to participate in the adoption of all of the measures which have been adopted under Title IV of the EC Treaty in the sphere of private international law, and with one exception[7] the United Kingdom has chosen either to participate in the adoption of, or after adoption to accept, all of these measures. Accordingly, almost all of the existing measures in this sphere are applicable to the United Kingdom and to Ireland. But these measures have not become applicable to Denmark except where a special agreement on their extension to Denmark has been concluded between the European Community and Denmark.

---

[5]   Article 81(3) also permits the Council to adopt a decision transferring aspects of family law with cross-border implications to the ordinary legislative procedure. Such a decision may be adopted by the Council, acting unanimously on a proposal from the Commission and after consulting the European Parliament. But the proposal must also be notified to the national Parliaments, and if a national Parliament makes known its opposition within six months of the notification, the decision cannot be adopted.

[6]   In principle, a national court of last resort has an obligation to refer relevant questions, but this is subject to the limited exception relating to clear and obvious points admitted by the European Court in Case 283/81: *CILFIT v Ministry of Health* [1982] ECR 3415. For a sound application of the *acte clair* principle in the sphere of private international law, see *T v L* [2008] IESC 48 (Irish Supreme Court). For a rejection of a reference by a lower court, relating to the Brussels I Regulation, as inadmissible under Article 68 of the EC Treaty, see Case C-278/09: *Martinez v MGN*, 20th November 2009.

[7]   The exception relates to EC Council Decision 2009/941, on the Hague Protocol 2007 on the Law Applicable to Maintenance Obligations.

Before 1999, measures designed to secure the harmonisation of conflict rules at EC level had taken the form of conventions, signed and ratified by the Member States. Conventions in this sphere could be concluded on the basis of Article 220 of the EEC Treaty, or its successor, Article 293 of the EC Treaty, which required the Member States, so far as is necessary, to enter into negotiations with each other with a view to securing for the benefit of their nationals (inter alia) the simplification of formalities governing the reciprocal recognition and enforcement of judgments of courts or tribunals and of arbitration awards. Conventions could also be based on a voluntary choice by the Member States to go beyond the requirements of that provision. After the entry into force of the Treaty of Maastricht on European Union, such conventions could also be drawn up by the Council, and recommended to the Member States for adoption in accordance with their respective constitutional requirements, on the basis of Title VI (Article K) of that Treaty, which dealt with co-operation in the fields of justice and home affairs, including judicial co-operation in civil matters. After the entry into force of the Treaty of Amsterdam, Title VI of the Treaty of Maastricht ceased to be available; and after the entry into force of the Treaty of Lisbon, Article 293 of the EC Treaty has also ceased to be available. Thus future measures at European level within the sphere of private international law must now be based on Article 81 of the Treaty on the Functioning of the European Union.

The measures of European harmonisation of conflict rules, currently adopted or proposed, may be classified under five headings: civil jurisdiction and judgments; the law applicable to civil obligations; family matters; insolvency; and procedural co-operation.

## CIVIL JURISDICTION AND JUDGMENTS

### The Brussels I Regulation

The most important Community instrument in the sphere of private international law is Regulation 44/2001 on Jurisdiction and the Recognition and Enforcement of Judgments in Civil and Commercial Matters, which is commonly referred to as the Brussels I Regulation.[8] The Regulation was adopted by the EC Council on 22nd December 2000. It entered into force on 1st March 2002 for the fourteen then existing Member States other than Denmark; on 1st May 2004 for the ten then acceding Member States;[9] on 1st January 2007 for Bulgaria and Romania;[10] and on 1st July 2007 for Denmark.[11] It has replaced the Brussels Convention of 27th September 1968 on Jurisdiction and the Enforcement of Judgments in Civil and Commercial Matters, which is commonly referred to as the Brussels Convention.[12]

---

[8]    For its text, see [2001] OJ L12/1. The Brussels I Regulation is examined in Chapters 2–11 and 18 of the present work.

[9]    See the Athens Act of Accession 2003, Article 2. For minor adjustments, see its Annex II, Part 18(A)(3).

[10]    See the Luxembourg Act of Accession 2005, Articles 2 and 56; [2005] OJ L157.

[11]    See the Agreement between the European Community and Denmark, approved by EC Council Decisions 2005/790 and 2006/325; [2005] OJ L299/61 and [2006] OJ L120/22.

[12]    For the latest version of its text, see [1998] OJ C27/1. The Convention was based on Article 220 of the EEC Treaty.

The Regulation lays down rules on direct jurisdiction, applicable by the court seised of the original action in determining its own jurisdiction, as well as rules on the recognition and enforcement of judgments given in other States to which the Regulation applies. It applies to most types of civil matter. But certain matters (such as most family matters; and insolvency proceedings) are excluded from its scope.

On 21st April 2009, the EC Commission issued a Report on the Application of the Brussels I Regulation,[13] together with a Green Paper on the Review of the Regulation.[14] These documents launched a consultation, designed to lead eventually to a proposal for the amendment of the Regulation.

**The Lugano Conventions**

The Brussels I Regulation is supplemented by the Lugano Convention of 16th September 1988 on Jurisdiction and the Enforcement of Judgments in Civil and Commercial Matters, which may conveniently be referred to as the Lugano Convention 1988.[15] This was designed in substance to extend the Brussels Convention to the EFTA countries, and its substantive provisions largely accord with those of the 1989 version of the Brussels Convention. It remains in force between the fifteen pre-2004 EC Member States, and Switzerland, Iceland and Poland.

A revised version, which may conveniently be referred to as the Lugano Convention 2007, has been signed and concluded by the European Community.[16] This entered into force between the Community, Denmark and Norway on 1st January 2010, but it has not yet entered into force for Switzerland and Iceland. Its contents largely reflect the Brussels I Regulation.

**The Hague Convention 2005**

A Convention on Choice of Court Agreements was adopted at the Hague Conference on Private International Law on 30th June 2005. This Convention was signed by the European Community on 1st April 2009,[17] and has also been signed by the United States of America, and acceded to by Mexico; but it has not yet entered into force.

**Uncontested Claims**

As regards judgments, the Brussels I Regulation is now supplemented by EC Regulation 805/2004, creating a European Enforcement Order for Uncontested Claims.[18] This

---

[13]    COM(2009) 174 final.

[14]    COM(2009) 175 final.

[15]    For its text, see [1988] OJ L319/9. See also the Jenard and Möller Report, [1990] OJ C189/57.

[16]    See EC Council Decisions 2007/712 and 2009/430; [2007] OJ L339/1 and [2009] OJ L147/1. The revised Convention was signed at Lugano on 30th October 2007. For its text, see [2009] OJ L147/5.

[17]    See EC Council Decision 2009/397; [2009] OJ L133/1. For the text of the Convention, see [2009] OJ L133/3. The Convention is examined at pp. 181–6 and 252–4 below.

[18]    This will be referred to as the Uncontested Claims Regulation. For its text, see [2004] OJ L143/15. For discussion, see Chapters 10 and 11 below.

Regulation was adopted by the Parliament and Council on 21st April 2004. It became applicable on 21st October 2005 in the twenty-four then Member States other than Denmark, and on 1st January 2007 in Bulgaria and Romania.[19] It enables the court of origin to issue a European Enforcement Order in respect of a judgment on an uncontested claim, with the result that the judgment becomes enforceable in other Member States without the need to obtain an enforcement order there.

Further provision in relation to uncontested claims has been made by EC Regulation 1896/2006, creating a European Order for Payment Procedure.[20] This Regulation became applicable in the Member States other than Denmark on 12th December 2008. It creates a procedure which involves an ex parte application to a court of a Member State for a European payment order. When made by the court, the order is served on the defendant. If he lodges a statement of opposition, the case proceeds as an ordinary civil proceeding. If he fails to lodge a statement of opposition, the court declares the order for payment enforceable, and it then becomes enforceable throughout the Member States, without the need for a declaration of enforceability in the State of enforcement.

**Small Claims**

EC Regulation 861/2007, establishing a European Small Claims Procedure,[21] became applicable on 1st January 2009 in the Member States other than Denmark. It establishes a European procedure for small claims intended to simplify and speed up litigation concerning small claims in cross-border cases, and to reduce costs. The procedure is available to litigants as an alternative to the procedures existing under the laws of the Member States. The Regulation also eliminates the intermediate proceedings necessary to enable recognition and enforcement, in other Member States, of judgments given in a Member State under the European small claims procedure.

## THE LAW APPLICABLE TO CIVIL OBLIGATIONS

### The Rome I Regulation

In the sphere of choice of law, EC Regulation 593/2008 on the Law Applicable to Contractual Obligations, which is commonly referred to as the Rome I Regulation,[22] lays down choice of law rules for most types of contract. The Regulation became applicable in the Member States other than Denmark on 17th December 2009, in respect of contracts concluded after that date.

The Rome I Regulation has replaced the Rome Convention of 19th June 1980 on the Law Applicable to Contractual Obligations, which may conveniently be referred to as the Rome Convention 1980.[23] The Convention was not based on any particular Treaty provision, but on the desire of the Member States 'to continue in the field of private international law the work

---

[19]   See the Luxembourg Act of Accession 2005, Articles 2 and 56; [2005] OJ L157.
[20]   For its text, see [2006] OJ L399/1. For discussion, see Chapter 11 below.
[21]   For its text, see [2007] OJ L199/1. For discussion, see Chapter 11 below.
[22]   For its text, see [2008] OJ L177/6. The Regulation is examined in Chapters 12 and 13 below.
[23]   For its text, see [1998] OJ C27/34.

of unification of law which has already been done within the Community, in particular in the field of jurisdiction and enforcement of judgments'.

The Rome Convention had entered into force on 1st April 1991. Prior to the entry into operation of the Rome I Regulation, the Rome Convention 1980 had been in force in all twenty-seven Member States.[24] It remains in force in Denmark, and also remains applicable elsewhere in relation to contracts concluded before 17th December 2009.

### The Rome II Regulation

EC Regulation 864/2007, on the Law Applicable to Non-contractual Obligations, which is commonly known as the Rome II Regulation,[25] lays down choice of law rules for torts and restitutionary obligations. It became applicable in the Member States other than Denmark on 11th January 2009, in respect of events occurring after that date.

## FAMILY MATTERS

### The Brussels IIA Regulation

In the sphere of family law, jurisdiction and judgments in respect of matrimonial proceedings and of proceedings concerning parental responsibility for children are now governed by EC Regulation 2201/2003, concerning Jurisdiction and the Recognition and Enforcement of Judgments in Matrimonial Matters and the Matters of Parental Responsibility, which may conveniently be referred to as the Brussels IIA Regulation.[26] The Regulation became applicable on 1st March 2005 in the twenty-four then Member States other than Denmark, and on 1st January 2007 in Bulgaria and Romania.[27]

The Brussels IIA Regulation deals with jurisdiction and judgments (but not choice of law) in respect of matrimonial proceedings (divorce, separation and annulment of marriage), and also of proceedings concerning parental responsibility for children, regardless of whether a marriage or divorce is involved. It replaces EC Regulation 1347/2000 on Jurisdiction and the Recognition and Enforcement of Judgments in Matrimonial Matters and in Matters of Parental Responsibility for Children of Both Spouses, which is commonly referred to as the Brussels II Regulation.[28] This in turn had replaced a Convention, commonly referred to as the Brussels II Convention,[29] based on Article K.3(2)(c) of the Treaty on European Union, which had been adopted and signed on 28th May 1998, but had not entered into force.

---

[24]  See the Luxembourg Accession Convention of 14th April 2005, [2005] OJ C169/1; the Luxembourg Act of Accession 2005, Article 3(3)–(4) and Annex 1, para 1, [2005] OJ L157; and EC Council Decision 2007/856, [2007] OJ L347/1.

[25]  For its text, see [2007] OJ L199/40. The Regulation is examined in Chapters 14 and 15 below.

[26]  For its text, see [2003] OJ L338/1. The Brussels IIA Regulation is examined in Chapters 16 and 17 below.

[27]  See the Luxembourg Act of Accession 2005, Articles 2 and 56; [2005] OJ L157.

[28]  For its text, see [2000] OJ L160/19. The Brussels II Regulation had entered into force on 1st March 2001 for the fourteen then Member States other than Denmark, and on 1st May 2004 for the ten Member States which joined the European Community on that date. See the Athens Act of Accession 2003, Article 2; and for minor adjustments, see its Annex II, Part 18(A)(2).

[29]  For its text, see [1998] OJ C221/1.

As regards matrimonial proceedings, the Brussels IIA Regulation consolidates the provisions of the Brussels II Regulation without substantial alteration. As regards parental responsibility, the Brussels IIA Regulation is much wider than its predecessor, since it extends to all children, regardless of whether a marriage or divorce is involved.

## The Hague Convention 1996

By its Decisions 2003/93 and 2008/431,[30] the EC Council has authorised the Member States, in the interest of the Community, to sign and to ratify or accede to the Hague Convention of 19th October 1996 on Jurisdiction, Applicable Law, Recognition, Enforcement and Co-operation in respect of Parental Responsibility and Measures for the Protection of Children.[31] The Member States are also authorised to make declarations that, as between Member States, recognition and enforcement of judgments relating to parental responsibility and child protection will be governed by Community law. The intention is that the Hague Convention 1996 will govern the relations between the Member States and non-member countries in regard to proceedings and judgments concerning parental responsibilty for children. It was hoped that the ratifications or accessions would take place by 6th June 2010, but this deadline has not been met.

## The Maintenance Regulation

On 18th December 2008, the EC Council adopted Regulation 4/2009 on Jurisdiction, Applicable Law, Recognition and Enforcement of Decisions and Co-operation in Matters relating to Maintenance Obligations, which may conveniently be referred to as the Maintenance Regulation.[32] The Regulation will become applicable in the Member States other than Denmark on 18th June 2011. As regards jurisdiction and judgments concerning familial maintenance, it will replace the Brussels I Regulation.

As regards choice of law, the Maintenance Regulation is designed to operate in conjunction with the Hague Protocol of 23rd November 2007 on the Law Applicable to Maintenance Obligations (which may conveniently be referred to as the Hague Protocol 2007).[33] Accordingly, on 30th November 2009 the EC Council adopted Decision 2009/941,[34] approving the conclusion of the Protocol by the European Community and making the Protocol applicable within the Community from 18th June 2011. But the Protocol will not be applicable in Denmark or the United Kingdom.

On 23rd November 2007, the Hague Conference on Private International Law also adopted a Convention on the International Recovery of Child Support and Other Forms of Family Maintenance (which may conveniently be referred to as the Hague Convention 2007). On 28th July 2009 the EC Commission presented a Proposal for a Council Decision on the conclusion by the European Community of the Hague Convention 2007.[35]

---

[30]   See [2003] OJ L48/1 and [2008] OJ L151/36.
[31]   For the text of the Hague Convention 1996, see [2003] OJ L48/3. For discussion, see Chapter 17 below.
[32]   For its text, see [2009] OJ L7/1. The Maintenance Regulation is examined in Chapter 18 below.
[33]   For its text, see [2009] OJ L331/19. The Protocol is examined in Chapter 18 below.
[34]   See [2009] OJ L331/17.
[35]   See COM(2009) 373 final. See also JUSTCIV 235, of 6th November 2008.

**Matrimonial Property and Succession**

On 17th July 2006, the EC Commission presented a Green Paper on Conflict of Laws in Matters concerning Matrimonial Property Regimes, including the question of Jurisdiction and Mutual Recognition.[36] But no European measure on matrimonial property has yet been adopted or even proposed.

On 14th October 2009, the EC Commision presented a Proposal for a Regulation of the European Parliament and the Council on Jurisdiction, Applicable Law, Recognition and Enforcement of Decisions and Authentic Instruments in Matters of Succession and the Creation of a European Certificate of Succession.[37] The Proposal followed a consultation process initiated by a Green Paper presented on 1st March 2005.[38]

**Various Hague Conventions**

After joining the Hague Conference on Private International Law, the European Community has considered its stance in regard to existing Hague Conventions. In a letter of 14th October 2008 from the EC Commission to the Hague Conference, signed jointly by the EC Commission's Director in the Directorate-General for Justice, Freedom and Security, and the Chairman of the EC Council's Civil Law Committee,[39] the Community has indicated that there are several Conventions relating to family or similar matters whose adoption is for the time being to be left to the Member States individually, because they deal with matters which are of low priority for the Community. These are the 1961 Convention on the Form of Testamentary Dispositions; the 1978 Convention on the Validity of Marriages; the 1978 Convention on Matrimonial Property; the 1989 Convention on Succession to the Estates of Deceased Persons; the 1993 Convention on Inter-country Adoption; and the 2000 Convention on the Protection of Adults.

# INSOLVENCY PROCEEDINGS

EC Regulation 1346/2000 on Insolvency Proceedings, which may conveniently be referred to as the Insolvency Regulation,[40] entered into force on 31st May 2002 for the fourteen then Member States other than Denmark; on 1st May 2004 for the ten States which joined the Community on that date;[41] and for Bulgaria and Romania on 1st January 2007.[42] It deals with jurisdiction, choice of law, and the recognition and enforcement of judgments, in relation to insolvency proceedings. The Insolvency Regulation replaced a Convention, based on the

---

[36]   See COM(2006) 400 final.
[37]   See COM(2009)154 final. The Proposal is examined in Chapter 18 below.
[38]   See COM(2005) 65 final.
[39]   See JUSTCIV 235, of 6th November 2008.
[40]   For its text, see [2000] OJ L160/1. The Insolvency Regulation is examined in Chapter 19 below.
[41]   See the Athens Act of Accession 2003, Article 2. For minor adjustments, see its Annex II, Part 18(A)(1).
[42]   See the Luxembourg Act of Accession 2005, Articles 2 and 56; [2005] OJ L157.

Article 293 of the EC Treaty, which had been opened for signature on 23rd November 1995,[43] but had not entered into force.


## PROCEDURAL CO-OPERATION

### Service of Documents

In the sphere of procedural co-operation, the service in a Member State of documents originating in other Member States is now governed by EC Regulation 1393/2007, on the Service in the Member States of Judicial and Extrajudicial Documents in Civil or Commercial Matters.[44] Regulation 1393/2007 entered into application for all the Member States except Denmark on 13th November 2008.

Regulation 1393/2007 has replaced Regulation 1348/2000,[45] which had entered into force on 31st May 2001 for the fourteen then Member States other than Denmark; on 1st May 2004 for the ten States which joined the Community on that date;[46] for Bulgaria and Romania on 1st January 2007;[47] and for Denmark on 1st July 2007.[48] Regulation 1348/2000 remains in force in respect of service in Denmark, and of documents originating in Denmark. Regulation 1348/2000 had in turn replaced a Convention, based on Article K.3(2)(c) of the Treaty of Maastricht, which had been signed on 26th May 1997 but had not entered into force.

### Taking Evidence

Also in the sphere of procedural co-operation, EC Regulation 1206/2001, on Co-operation between the Courts of the Member States in the Taking of Evidence in Civil or Commercial Matters,[49] provides for a procedure whereby a court of a Member State requests a court of another Member State to take evidence for use in judicial proceedings. It also provides for a procedure whereby a court of a Member State requests permission to take evidence directly in another Member State. The Regulation entered into force on 1st January 2004 for the four-

---

[43]    See (1996) 35 ILM 1223.

[44]    For its text, see [2007] OJ L324/79. Regulation 1393/2007 is examined at pp. 62–6 below.

The European Community envisages that further reflection is necessary on whether it should adopt the Hague Convention of 15th November 1965 on the Service Abroad of Judicial and Extrajudicial Documents in Civil or Commercial Matters; see JUSTCIV 235, of 6th November 2008.

[45]    For its text, see [2000] OJ L160/37.

[46]    See the Athens Act of Accession 2003, Article 2.

[47]    See the Luxembourg Act of Accession 2005, Articles 2 and 56; [2005] OJ L157.

[48]    See the Agreement between the European Community and Denmark, [2005] OJ L300/55, approved by the EC Council in Decisions 2005/794 and 2006/326, [2005] OJ L300/53 and [2006] OJ L120/23.

[49]    For its text, see [2001] OJ L174/1. Regulation 1206/2001 is examined at pp. 217–21 below. Along with Regulation 1206/2001, the EC Council adopted Decision 2001/470, establishing a European judicial network in civil and commercial matters; [2001] OJ L174/25.

The European Community envisages that further reflection is necessary on whether it should adopt the Hague Conventions of 18th March 1970 on the Taking of Evidence Abroad in Civil or Commercial Matters, and of 25th October 1980 on International Access to Justice; see JUSTCIV 235, of 6th November 2008.

teen then Member States other than Denmark; on 1st May 2004 for the ten States which joined the Community on that date;[50] and for Bulgaria and Romania on 1st January 2007.[51]

## THE EUROPEAN UNION AND THE HAGUE CONFERENCE

On 3rd April 2007, the European Community became a member of the Hague Conference on Private International Law, by depositing its instrument of acceptance of the Statute of the Hague Conference. This followed the amendment of the Statute of the Hague Conference to enable the admission of Regional Economic Integration Organisations, and the adoption by the EC Council of Decision 2006/719, on the accession of the Community to the Hague Conference on Private International Law.[52] By the Treaty of Lisbon, the European Union has now replaced and succeeded to the European Community.

Now that the European Union has become a member of the Hague Conference, it is able to participate in the negotiations within the Conference leading to the conclusion of new conventions, or the revision of existing conventions. It is also able, under certain conditions and by various procedures, to sign and ratify, and thereby become a party to, conventions adopted by the Conference.

The ability of the European Union to become a party to a Hague Convention depends primarily on its competence under EU law to legislate in relation to the subject-matter of the Convention. Since Article 81 of the Treaty on the Functioning of the European Union empowers the Union to legislate on all aspects of private international law, the Union now has at least non-exclusive competence to become party to any of the Hague Conventions. Where the European Union has already adopted internal legislation whose operation would be affected by the adoption of the relevant Hague Convention, the competence of the Union to become party to the Convention is exclusive of the competence of the Member States.[53]

The manner in which the European Union may become a party to a Hague Convention depends on whether the relevant Hague Convention provides for its adoption by a Regional Economic Integration Organisation. Recent conventions often do so, and it is then possible for the Union to sign and ratify the convention, either on its own (where its competence under Union law is exclusive) or along with the Member States (where its competence is concurrent). Thus EC Council Decision 2009/397, on the signing by the European Community of the Hague Convention of 30th June 2005 on Choice of Court Agreements,[54] declares that the Community has exclusive competence in all matters governed by the Convention, and that the Member States will not sign, ratify, accept or approve the Convention, but will be bound by the Convention by virtue of its conclusion by the Community.

Earlier conventions often contain no provision for their adoption by a Regional Economic Integration Organisation. Thus, in the absence of renegotiations for the amendment of the convention by the addition of such a provision, it is not possible to utilise the straight-forward

---

[50]   See the Athens Act of Accession 2003, Article 2.
[51]   See the Luxembourg Act of Accession 2005, Articles 2 and 56; [2005] OJ L157.
[52]   [2006] OJ L297/1. The text of the Statute of the Hague Conference is attached to the Decision as Annex IV.
[53]   See Opinion 1/03 [2006] ECR I-1145, on the revision of the Lugano Convention.
[54]   [2009] OJ L133/1.

method of signature and ratification by the European Union itself. In such cases, an alternative procedure may be used, whereby the EU Council adopts decisions authorising the Member States to sign and ratify the convention in the interest of the Union. This procedure has been used in respect of the Hague Convention of 19th October 1996 on Parental Responsibility and Child Protection.[55]

The current stance of the European Union as to its possible adoption of various existing Hague Conventions has been clarified by a letter of 14th October 2008 from the EC Commission to the Hague Conference, signed jointly by the EC Commission's Director in the Directorate-General for Justice, Freedom and Security, and the Chairman of the EC Council's Civil Law Committee.[56] This classifies the existing Hague Conventions as follows:

(i)     Conventions on which no action by the European Union is envisaged, because all the Member States are already party to them. This applies to the 1961 Convention on Legalisation for Foreign Public Documents, and the 1980 Convention on Child Abduction.

(ii)    Conventions which the European Union intends to adopt. This applies to the 1996 Convention on Parental Responsibility and Child Protection; the 2005 Convention on Choice-of-Court Agreements; the 2007 Convention on Child Support; and the 2007 Protocol on the Law Applicable to Maintenance Obligations.

(iii)   Conventions on which further reflection is envisaged. This applies to the 1965 Convention on Service Abroad of Documents; the 1970 Convention on the Taking of Evidence Abroad; the 1970 Convention on Divorces and Legal Separations; the 1980 Convention on Access to Justice; and the 2006 Convention on Securities held with an Intermediary.

(iv)    Conventions which the European Union intends not to adopt, because existing European legislation is regarded as adequate. This applies to the 1971 Convention on Traffic Accidents; the 1973 Convention on Products Liability; and the 1978 Convention on Agency.

(v)     Conventions whose adoption is for the time being to be left to the Member States individually, because they deal with matters which are of low priority for the Union. This applies to the 1961 Convention on the Form of Testamentary Dispositions; the 1978 Convention on the Validity of Marriages; the 1978 Convention on Matrimonial Property; the 1985 Convention on Trusts; the 1989 Convention on Succession to the Estates of Deceased Persons; the 1993 Convention on Inter-country Adoption; and the 2000 Convention on the Protection of Adults.

---

[55]   See EC Council Decisions 2003/93 and 2008/431; [2003] OJ L48/3 and [2008] OJ L151/36.
[56]   See JUSTCIV 235, of 6th November 2008.

# PART II

# Civil Jurisdiction and Judgments

# 2. History, outline and scope

## HISTORY

### The Brussels I Regulation

The most important Community instrument in the sphere of private international law is Regulation 44/2001 on Jurisdiction and the Recognition and Enforcement of Judgments in Civil and Commercial Matters, which is generally known as the Brussels I Regulation.[1] The Regulation has replaced the Brussels Convention of 27th September 1968 on Jurisdiction and the Enforcement of Judgments in Civil and Commercial Matters, which is generally known as the Brussels Convention. It is on the Brussels I Regulation that this part (Chapters 2–11) of the present work is mainly focused.

The Brussels I Regulation was adopted by the EC Council on 22nd December 2000. It entered into force on 1st March 2002 for the fourteen then Member States other than Denmark;[2] on 1st May 2004 for the ten States which joined the Community on that date;[3] on 1st January 2007 for Bulgaria and Romania;[4] and on 1st July 2007 for Denmark.[5] Thus the Regulation now applies in and between all the EC Member States. It extends to the French overseas departments, which are treated as part of France, and to Gibraltar, which is treated as part of the United Kingdom.[6] It also extends to fixed or floating installations positioned on

---

[1]    For its text, see [2001] OJ L12/1. See also EC Council doc 14139/00, JUSTCIV 137, 14th December 2000, containing various statements to be minuted in connection with the adoption of the Regulation.

[2]    See Recitals 20–21 and Article 1(3) of the Regulation.

[3]    See the Athens Act of Accession 2003, Article 2 and (for minor adjustments) Annex II, Part 18(A)(3). The ten acceding States were Poland; Hungary; the Czech Republic; Slovakia; Slovenia; Latvia; Lithuania; Estonia; Malta; and Cyprus.

Protocol 10 on Cyprus, which is annexed to the Act of Accession 2003, suspends the application of the existing Community law in the areas of Cyprus in which the Government of the Republic of Cyprus does not exercise effective control. In Case C-420/07: *Apostolides v Orams* [2009] ECR I-3571, the European Court ruled that this does not preclude the application of the Brussels I Regulation to a judgment which is given by a Cypriot court sitting in the area of the island effectively controlled by the Cypriot Government, but which concerns land situated in areas not so controlled.

[4]    See the Luxembourg Act of Accession 2005, Articles 2 and 56; [2005] OJ L157. See also Regulation 1791/2006; [2006] OJ L363/1.

[5]    The extension of the Brussels I Regulation to Denmark, in the face of Article 69 of the EC Treaty, was effected by means of an Agreement between the European Community and Denmark, [2005] OJ L299/62, which was approved by the EC Council in its Decisions 2005/790 and 2006/325, [2005] OJ L299/61 and [2006] OJ L120/22.

[6]    See Article 355 of the Treaty on the Functioning of the European Union, and Annexes II and III of the Regulation. See also the Statement by the United Kingdom, [2001] OJ C13/1, that judgments of Gibraltar courts will be certified by the Foreign and Commonwealth Office in London with a view

or above the part of the continental shelf adjacent to a Member State, in the context of the prospecting or exploitation of its natural resources; these are treated as part of its territory.[7] But it does not apply to the French overseas territories.[8]

By Article 68(1), as between the Member States bound by the Regulation, it supersedes the Brussels Convention. Article 68(2) adds that, insofar as the Regulation replaces the provisions of the Brussels Convention between Member States, any reference to the Convention must be understood as a reference to the Regulation. This applies, for example, to references to the Convention made by other Community legislation dealing with trade marks, designs or insolvency proceedings. The Regulation followed negotiations on the revision of the Convention, which were completed in April 1999, when the Working Party involved reached agreement on a revised text.[9] Recital 5 to the Regulation explains that continuity in the results achieved in the revision of the Convention should be ensured. Hence in the present work cases decided under the Brussels Convention will be described as if decided under the corresponding provisions of the Brussels I Regulation, where there is no textual or other change indicating that the relevant provisions have a different effect.

**The Brussels Convention**

Since, during its operation, the Brussels Convention was amended at various times by four accession conventions,[10] five versions of the Convention have come into existence: the original 1968 version;[11] the 1978 version;[12] the 1982 version;[13] the 1989 version;[14] and the 1996 version.[15] Important amendments affecting all Contracting States were made by the accession conventions of 1978 and 1989. In contrast, those of 1982 and 1996 only made minor technical adjustments.

At the entry into force of the Brussels I Regulation on 1st March 2002, the 1996 version of the Convention was in force in the fourteen then Member States other than Belgium. In Belgium the 1989 version was then in force, and it was not superseded by the 1996 version until August 2004.[16] Although upon its entry into force the Regulation replaced the

---

to enforcement under the Regulation. (Earlier the United Kingdom had chosen to apply provisions corresponding to those of the Brussels Convention as between itself and Gibraltar; see s 39 of the Civil Jurisdiction and Judgments Act 1982, and the Civil Jurisdiction and Judgments Act 1982 (Gibraltar) Order 1997 (SI 1997/2602)).

[7] See Case C-37/00: *Weber v Universal Ogden Services* [2002] ECR I-2013.

[8] See Article 68(1) of the Regulation, and Article 355 of the Treaty on the Functioning of the European Union.

[9] For the April 1999 draft, see Council doc 7700/99, JUSTCIV 60, 30th April 1999.

[10] The four accession conventions are: the Luxembourg Convention of 9th October 1978 on Danish, Irish and British accession, [1978] OJ L304/1; the Luxembourg Convention of 25th October 1982 on Greek accession, [1982] OJ L388/1; the San Sebastián Convention of 26th May 1989 on Spanish and Portuguese accession, [1989] OJ L285/1; and the Brussels Convention of 29th November 1996 on Austrian, Finnish and Swedish accession, [1997] OJ C15/1.

[11] See [1978] OJ L304/36. See also the Jenard Report, [1979] OJ C59/1.

[12] See [1978] OJ L304/77. See also the Schlosser Report, [1979] OJ C59/71.

[13] See [1983] OJ C97/2. See also the Evrigenis and Kerameus Report, [1986] OJ C298/1.

[14] See [1990] OJ C189/2. See also the Cruz, Real and Jenard Report, [1990] OJ C189/35.

[15] See [1998] OJ C27/1.

[16] The commencement dates for each Member State and each version are shown in Table 2.1 at the end of this chapter.

Convention as between the fourteen then Member States other than Denmark, the Convention remained in force between Denmark and the other fourteen Member States[17] until 1st July 2007, when the Regulation was extended to Denmark by means of an Agreement between the European Community and Denmark[18] and EC Council Decisions 2005/790 and 2006/325.[19]

At present, the Brussels Convention continues to apply between the French overseas territories, on the one hand, and the fourteen pre-2004 Member States other than France, on the other.[20] The Convention also remains applicable in some transitional cases; for example, where recognition or enforcement is sought of a judgment given before the entry into force of the Brussels I Regulation for both of the States involved.[21]

## The Lugano Convention 1988

The Brussels I Regulation is supplemented by the Lugano Convention of 16th September 1988 on Jurisdiction and the Enforcement of Judgments in Civil and Commercial Matters, which may conveniently be referred to as the Lugano Convention 1988.[22] This was designed in substance to extend the Brussels Convention to the EFTA countries. Other States which were not members of the European Community nor of EFTA could (with the unanimous agreement of all the EC and EFTA Member States) be invited to accede to the Lugano Convention 1988,[23] and (before joining the European Community) Poland had so acceded.[24] At present, the Lugano Convention 1988 is in force between nineteen countries: the fifteen pre-2004 EC Member States, and Switzerland, Norway, Iceland, and Poland,[25] except insofar as it has been superseded by the Lugano Convention 2007.[26] The substantive provisions of the Lugano Convention 1988 largely accord with those of the 1989 version of the Brussels Convention.

The relationship between the Brussels I Regulation and the Lugano Convention 1988 within an EC Member State which is a Contracting State to the Lugano Convention 1988 ('a dual State'; such as the United Kingdom) is governed by Article 54B(1)–(2) of the Lugano Convention 1988 and Article 68(2) of the Brussels I Regulation. The general rule is that the Brussels I Regulation prevails. But, as regards direct jurisdiction, the courts of a dual State must apply the Lugano Convention 1988 where the defendant is domiciled in a State which is not an EC Member State but is a Contracting State to the Lugano Convention 1988 ('a Lugano only country'; such as Iceland), or where Article 16 (on exclusive jurisdiction on

---

[17]   See the Brussels I Regulation, Recitals 9, 21 and 22, which also indicated that the jurisdiction of the courts of the other Member States over a defendant domiciled in Denmark remained governed by the Brussels Convention.

[18]   For its text, see [2005] OJ L299/62.

[19]   [2005] OJ L299/61 and [2006] OJ L120/22.

[20]   See the Brussels I Regulation, Recital 23 and Article 68(1), and the Treaty on the Functioning of the European Union, Article 355.

[21]   See *T v L* [2009] ILPr 5 (Irish Supreme Court).

[22]   For its text, see [1988] OJ L319/9. See also the Jenard and Möller Report, [1990] OJ C189/57.

[23]   See Articles 60(c) and 62–3 of the Lugano Convention 1988.

[24]   See the Preamble to (UK) SI 2000/1824, recognising that Poland acceded on 1st February 2000.

[25]   The commencement dates are shown in Table 2.1 at the end of this chapter.

[26]   See pp. 20–23 below.

account of subject-matter) or Article 17 (on jurisdiction clauses) of the Lugano Convention 1988 confers jurisdiction on the courts of a Lugano only country. As regards concurrent actions, the courts of a dual State must apply Articles 21 and 22 of the Lugano Convention 1988 when one of the proceedings is instituted in a Lugano only country, and the other in a dual State. Similarly, as regards recognition and enforcement, the courts of a dual State must apply the Lugano Convention 1988 where either the State of origin or the State addressed is a Lugano only country.

An important institutional difference between the Brussels I Regulation and the Lugano Convention 1988 concerns the role of the European Court in giving preliminary rulings on interpretation. Since the Brussels I Regulation is an act of a Community institution, the preliminary ruling procedure under Article 267 of the Treaty on the Functioning of the European Union applies to its interpretation.[27] In contrast, the European Court has no power to interpret the Lugano Convention 1988, and there is no other body empowered to give internationally binding rulings on its interpretation. Instead, the Second Protocol to the Lugano Convention 1988, and the Second and Third Declarations made on its signature, merely recognise that the negotiations which led to the conclusion of the Lugano Convention 1988 were based on the Brussels Convention in the light of the rulings given by the European Court up to the signature of the Lugano Convention 1988; and encourage the courts of each Contracting State (and the European Court) to pay due account to the principles laid down by decisions of other courts.[28] They also set up a system of exchange of information concerning judgments via the Registrar of the European Court; and establish a Standing Committee for the purpose of exchanging views on the functioning of the Lugano Convention 1988 and making recommendations for its revision in particular respects.

**The Lugano Convention 2007**

The negotiations on the revision of the Brussels Convention extended to the Lugano Convention, and the Working Party included members from the Lugano only countries. Thus in April 1999 a revised text of the Lugano Convention was also agreed on by the Working

---

[27]    Since the entry into force of the Treaty of Lisbon, the restriction imposed by Article 68 of the EC Treaty, by which the power to request a ruling on the interpretation of measures based on Title IV of the EC Treaty was confined to courts of last resort, has ceased to apply.

As regards the interpretation of the Brussels Convention, the Luxembourg Protocol of 3rd June 1971 (as amended by the accession conventions), [1990] OJ C189/25, empowers the European Court to give preliminary rulings at the request of appellate courts of Contracting States, and a large body of authoritative decisions has resulted. This procedure closely resembles the procedure under Article 267 of the Treaty on the Functioning of the European Union, the principal difference being that under the 1971 Protocol a court sitting at first instance has no power to request a preliminary ruling. On this restriction, see Case 80/83: *Habourdin v Italocremona* [1983] ECR 3639; Case 56/84: *Von Gallera v Maitre* [1984] ECR 1769; Case C-24/02: *Marseille Fret v Seatrano Shipping* [2002] ECR I-3383; Case C-69/02: *Reichling v Wampach* [2002] ECR I-3393; and Case C-18/02: *Danmarks Rederiforening, acting on behalf of DFDS Torline v LO Landsorganisationen i Sverige, acting on behalf of SEKO Sjöfolk Facket för Service och Kommunikation* [2004] ECR I-1417.

[28]    See Case C-394/07: *Gambazzi v DaimlerChrysler* [2009] ECR I-2563, where the European Court, dealing with a reference relating to the public policy proviso under Article 27(1) of the Brussels Convention, considered a Swiss judgment on Article 27(1) of the Lugano Convention 1988.

Party.[29] Subsequently, in October 2002, the EC Council authorised the Commission to enter into negotiations with the Lugano Convention countries with a view to the adoption of an amended Lugano Convention.[30] But in February 2003, the Council decided to request an opinion of the European Court as to whether the conclusion of a new Lugano Convention fell within the exclusive competence of the Community, or within the sphere of shared competence of the Community and the Member States.[31] The completion of the negotiations was delayed while the opinion of the Court on the request was awaited.[32] Eventually, on 7th February 2006, the Court ruled that the conclusion of a new Lugano Convention fell entirely within the sphere of exclusive competence of the European Community.[33]

The negotiations on the revision of the Lugano Convention were completed in March 2007. The revised Convention may conveniently be referred to as the Lugano Convention 2007.[34] Pursuant to EC Council Decision 2007/712,[35] the Lugano Convention 2007 was signed on behalf of the European Community, along with Denmark, Switzerland, Norway and Iceland, at Lugano on 30th October 2007. On 27th November 2008 the EC Council adopted Decision 2009/430, approving the conclusion of the Lugano Convention 2007.[36] The Convention entered into force between the European Union, Denmark and Norway on 1st January 2010, but it has not yet entered into force for Switzerland or Iceland.[37]

The contents of the Lugano Convention 2007 largely reflect the Brussels I Regulation. A Recital to the Convention recognises that the extension of the principles laid down in the Brussels I Regulation to the Contracting Parties to the Convention will strengthen legal and economic co-operation. The parties to the Convention are or will be the European Union, Denmark, Norway, Switzerland, and Iceland. But its provisions on connecting factors (such as domicile) refer to 'a State bound' by the Convention, and thus treat each EU Member State as a separate unit.

By Article 69(6), the Lugano Convention 2007 replaces the Lugano Convention 1988, and any reference to the Lugano Convention 1988 in other instruments is to be understood as a reference to the Lugano Convention 2007. By Articles 69(7), 70(1)(b), 71 and 73(2), the Lugano Convention 2007 may be extended by accession to non-European territories which are part of the territory of an EU Member State or for whose external relations an EU Member State is responsible, and will then, as between the other EU Member States and such territories, replace the Brussels Convention (if previously applicable).[38] By Articles 70(1)(a) and 71, the Lugano Convention 2007 will also be open to accession by any State which subsequently

---

29    For the April 1999 draft, see Council doc 7700/99, JUSTCIV 60, 30th April 1999.
30    See Commission doc COM(2002) 738 final, 16th December 2002; and Council doc 6220/03, JUSTCIV 20, 24th June 2003.
31    See Council doc 5852/03, JUSTCIV 12, 30th January 2003.
32    See Commission doc COM(2003) 291 final, 22nd May 2003.
33    Opinion 1/03, [2006] ECR I-1145.
34    For its text, see [2009] OJ L147/5. See also the Pocar Report, JUSTCIV 179 of 6th October 2009.
35    [2007] OJ L339/1.
36    [2009] OJ L147/1.
37    By Article 69, the Convention will enter into force for Switzerland or Iceland on the first day of the third month after its ratification.
38    At present the Brussels Convention is applicable as between the French overseas territories and the fourteen pre-2004 EC Member States other than France.

joins EFTA. By Article 70(1)(c) and 72, accession by any other State is also possible, but only with the unanimous agreement of existing parties, and only in relation to parties which do not object to the accession.[39]

The relationship between the Lugano Convention 2007 and the Brussels I Regulation and other relevant EU measures (the Brussels Convention, the Luxembourg Protocol, the Accession Conventions, and the Agreement with Denmark) is dealt with by Article 64(1) and (2) of the Lugano Convention 2007. Article 64(1) lays down a general rule that the Lugano Convention 2007 is not to prejudice the application by the EU Member States of the Brussels I Regulation and the other EC measures. But, by way of exception, Article 64(2)(a) insists that the Lugano Convention 2007 must in any event be applied, in matters of jurisdiction, where the defendant is domiciled in a Lugano only country (a State where the Lugano Convention 2007 applies, but none of the EU measures applies), or where Articles 22 or 23 of the Lugano Convention 2007 (on exclusive jurisdiction by reference to subject-matter, and on jurisdiction clauses) confer jurisdiction on the courts of a Lugano only country. In addition Article 64(2)(b) insists that, in relation to concurrent actions, Articles 27 and 28 of the Lugano Convention 2007 must in any event be applied when one of the proceedings is instituted in a Lugano only country and the other in an EU Member State. Article 64(2)(c) insists further that the Lugano Convention 2007 must in any event be applied in matters of recognition and enforcement, where either the State of origin or the State addressed is a Lugano only country. These provisions closely resemble Article 54B(1)–(2) of the Lugano Convention 1988.

The interpretation of the Lugano Convention 2007 is addressed by its Second Protocol.[40] Article 1(1) of the Protocol requires any court applying and interpreting the Lugano Convention 2007 to pay due account to the principles laid down by any relevant decision rendered by the courts of the States bound by the Convention and by the Court of Justice of the European Communities in respect of the same provisions of the Convention, or in respect of similar provisions of the Lugano Convention 1988, the Brussels I Regulation, or the Brussels Convention. For the courts of the EU Member States, this obligation is qualified by Article 1(2), which gives priority to their obligations in relation to the European Court under the Treaty on the Functioning of the European Union or the Agreement between the European Community and Denmark.[41] As the second and third Recitals to the Protocol recognise, the European Court has jurisdiction to give rulings on the interpretation of the provisions of the

---

[39]    See also Article III(2)–(4) of the First Protocol, for certain reservations available in relation to such acceding States.

[40]    Protocol 2 on the uniform interpretation of the Convention and on the Standing Committee, which (by Article 75) forms an integral part of the Convention.

[41]    Article 2 of the Protocol enables a Lugano only country to submit statements of case or written observations to the European Court in proceedings on a reference by a court of an EU Member State for a preliminary ruling on the interpretation of the Lugano Convention 2007, the Brussels I Regulation, or the Brussels Convention. Article 3 provides for the setting up by the EC Commission of a system of exchange of information concerning judgments delivered under the Lugano Convention 2007, the Lugano Convention 1988, the Brussels I Regulation and the Brussels Convention. Article 4 provides for the establishment of a Standing Committee, composed of the representatives of the Contracting Parties, for consultation on matters relating to the Lugano Convention 2007. Article 5 provides for meetings of experts to exchange views on the functioning of the Convention, in particular on the development of the case-law and on new legislation which may influence the application of the Convention.

Brussels I Regulation and the Brussels Convention; and since the Lugano Convention 2007 becomes part of the European Union rules, the European Court also has jurisdiction to give rulings on the interpretation of its provisions as regards their application by the courts of the EU Member States.

Other Recitals to the Protocol emphasise the substantial link between the Lugano Convention 2007, the Lugano Convention 1988, the Brussels I Regulation and the Brussels Convention; refer to the rulings delivered by the European Court on the interpretation of the Brussels I Regulation and the Brussels Convention up to the time of signature of the Lugano Convention 2007, and to the rulings delivered by the courts of the Contracting Parties to the Lugano Convention 1988 on that Convention up to the time of such signature; explain that the parallel revision of the Lugano Convention 1988 and the Brussels Convention, which led to the conclusion of a revised text for those Conventions, was substantially based on the said rulings on those Conventions; note that the revised text of the Brussels Convention has been incorporated, after the entry into force of the Treaty of Amsterdam, into the Brussels I Regulation; emphasise that this revised text also constituted the basis for the text of the Lugano Convention 2007; and explain that the Protocol is designed to prevent divergent interpretations and to arrive at an interpretation as uniform as possible of the provisions of the Lugano Convention 2007 and of those of the Brussels I Regulation which are substantially reproduced in the Lugano Convention 2007, and of the Brussels Convention.

## OUTLINE

The Brussels I Regulation consists of a Preamble, followed by 76 Articles arranged in eight Chapters, and six Annexes. Both in substance[42] and in structure[43] the Regulation closely resembles the Brussels Convention.

Chapter I (Article 1) defines the material scope of the Regulation. It applies to civil or commercial matters, as distinct from public or criminal matters, but with certain exceptions, such as individual status, matrimonial property, succession on death, insolvent liquidation, and arbitration. The core of the Regulation is contained in Chapter II (Articles 2–31) on direct jurisdiction, and Chapter III (Articles 32–56), on the recognition and enforcement of judgments. Chapter II deals with direct jurisdiction, laying down rules applicable by a court of a Member State, when seised of an action on the merits, for the purpose of deciding its own

---

[42]  The principal substantive changes are in Article 5(1), on jurisdiction over ordinary contracts; Articles 9 and 14 (ex Articles 8 and 12A) on insurance; Articles 18–21 (ex Articles 5(1) and 17(6)), on employment; Article 22(1) (ex Article 16(1)), on tenancies; Article 23 (ex Article 17) on jurisdiction clauses; Article 30, on the time of seisin; Article 34 (ex Article 27), on grounds for refusal of recognition; Article 46 (ex Article 38), on the powers of an appellate court in enforcement proceedings; Articles 53–5, on documentation in enforcement proceedings; Article 60 (ex Article 53), on the domicile of companies; Article 71 (ex Article 57), on specialised conventions; and Article 72 (ex Article 59), on agreements with a third country.

[43]  The Brussels Convention consists of a Preamble, followed by 68 Articles arranged under eight Titles, and an Annexed Protocol. The Protocol annexed to the Convention has been incorporated into the body of the Regulation, mainly in Chapter V. The Annexes to the Regulation contain lists of national legislation, rules, courts and procedures, taken from the body of the Convention, and standard forms for use in connection with enforcement.

jurisdiction to entertain the action. In order to strengthen the legal protection of persons estab-lished in the Community, it establishes a general rule that a defendant domiciled in a Member State must be sued in that State, and harmonises the exceptional cases in which a defendant domiciled in one Member State can be sued in another Member State. Chapter III seeks to establish the 'free movement of judgments', by strictly limiting the grounds on which a judg-ment given in one Member State can be refused recognition or enforcement in another Member State, and establishing a swift procedure for obtaining a declaration of enforceabil-ity or a decision establishing recognition. In view of the harmonisation of direct jurisdiction achieved by Chapter II, a court in which recognition or enforcement is sought under Chapter III is in most cases precluded from reviewing the jurisdiction of the original court.

In Chapter II, the basic rules on the existence of direct jurisdiction are specified by Articles 2–4. Where the defendant is domiciled in a Member State, Article 2 confers jurisdiction to entertain actions against him on the courts of that State, and Article 3 deprives the courts of the other Member States of jurisdiction to entertain actions against him. Where the defendant is not domiciled in any of the Member States, the jurisdiction of the courts of each Member State is referred to the law of that State. These basic rules are subject to exceptions defined by the remaining provisions of Chapter II.

Articles 5–7 derogate from Article 3 by specifying a number of cases in which they confer jurisdiction on courts of one Member State over a defendant domiciled in another Member State. In such a case, the plaintiff has the choice of suing at the defendant's domicile, in accor-dance with Article 2, or in another Member State, in accordance with Articles 5–7. The bases of jurisdiction used by Article 5 involve a connection between the cause of action and the territory of the court on which jurisdiction is conferred. For example, as the place of perfor-mance of a relevant contractual obligation; as the place where a tortious event occurred; or as the location of a branch of the defendant undertaking, from whose activities the dispute has arisen. The bases used by Article 6 involve a connection between the claim and another claim pending in same court. It deals with co-defendants, third-party proceedings, counterclaims, and related contractual and proprietary claims involving land. Article 7 deals with admiralty limitation actions. None of these provisions applies where the defendant is not domiciled in any of the Member States.

Articles 8–14, 15–17, and 18–21 lay down particular jurisdictional rules for (respectively) insurance contracts, certain consumer contracts, and employment contracts. They are based on the assumption that the policy-holder, consumer or employee is in a weaker bargaining position than the insurer, supplier or employer, and thus merits special protection. Accordingly a policy-holder, consumer or employee is given a choice of places in which to sue the insurer, supplier or employer. These include the policy-holder's or the consumer's own domicile or the place where the employee habitually works. In contrast, actions by the insurer, supplier or employee must usually be brought at the defendant's domicile. Contrary agreements, concluded before the dispute has arisen, are usually rendered invalid. But all these provisions apply only where the defendant is domiciled in a Member State, or where the defendant insurer, supplier or employer has a branch in a Member State and the dispute has arisen from the operations of the branch.

Article 22 provides for exclusive jurisdiction over certain disputes on account of their subject-matter. For example, as regards proprietary rights to land, on the courts of the Member State in which the land in question is situated; or, as regards the validity of a patent or registered trade mark, on the courts of the Member State in which the patent or mark was granted or registered. This provision is overriding: it applies regardless of domicile, agreement or appearance; and even where the defendant is not domiciled in any of the Member States.

Articles 23 and 24 provide for submission by agreement or appearance. Article 23 enables parties, by an express and sufficiently formal agreement, to choose a court of a Member State which will have jurisdiction to determine disputes concerning a particular legal relationship. This freedom is restricted by Articles 13, 14, 17 and 21 in relation to insurance, consumer and employment contracts, and by Article 22 in relation to disputes which are subject to exclusive jurisdiction on account of their subject-matter. By Article 24, a court before which the defendant enters an appearance without contesting its jurisdiction becomes competent, unless the dispute falls within Article 22.

The foregoing provisions of Chapter II define the connecting factors on which the existence of jurisdiction depends. They are followed by a group of provisions concerned with the exercise of jurisdiction. Articles 25 and 26(1) require a court to decline its jurisdiction of its own motion, where it is rendered incompetent by Articles 3 or 22. Article 26(2)–(4) requires a court to stay its proceedings until appropriate steps have been taken to notify a defendant who is domiciled in another Member State. Articles 27–30 deal with the situation where similar or related proceedings are pending in courts of different Member States. They require or permit the court subsequently seised to decline jurisdiction or stay its proceedings in favour of the court first seised. Finally Article 31 enables a court to grant provisional relief even if it lacks jurisdiction to determine the substance of the dispute.

Chapter III provides for the recognition and enforcement in each Member State of judgments given by the courts of the other Member States. The obligation to recognise is subject to very limited exceptions relating to public policy, insufficient service, or irreconcilability with another judgment. Only in exceptional cases is the court addressed permitted to review the jurisdiction of the original court, and it is never allowed to review the substance or merits of the judgment. A judgment which qualifies for recognition also qualifies for enforcement, provided that it is enforceable in the original country. The procedure for obtaining a declaration of enforceability is elaborated in detail, and the same procedure may be used to obtain a decision establishing recognition, though recognition may also be invoked incidentally whenever it is relevant. Chapter IV (Articles 57–8) provides for the enforcement in a Member State of authentic instruments drawn up or registered, and court settlements approved, in other Member States.

Chapter V (Articles 59–65) lays down rules for the determination of domicile for the purpose of the Regulation. By Article 59, whether an individual is domiciled in a Member State is governed by the law of that State. By Article 60, corporate domicile is given a substantive definition referring alternatively to the registered office, central administration, and principal place of business. Chapter V also incorporates a miscellany of minor supplementary or exceptional provisions.

Chapter VI (Article 66) contains transitional provisions. Chapter VII (Articles 67–72) deals with the relationship between the Regulation and other Community legislation or international conventions. Chapter VIII (Articles 73–6) deals with entry into force and amendments. The Annexes to the Regulation contain lists of relevant national legislation, rules, courts and procedures, and standard forms for use in connection with enforcement.[44]

---

[44]    For amendments to the Annexes, see Regulation 1496/2002, [2002] OJ L225/13; the Athens Act of Accession 2003, [2003] OJ L236/33; Regulation 1937/2004, [2004] OJ L334/3; Regulation

# MATERIAL SCOPE

The material scope of the Brussels I Regulation is defined by Article 1(1) and (2).[45] By Article 1(1), the Regulation applies in civil and commercial matters, whatever the nature of the court or tribunal, but it does not extend, in particular, to revenue, customs or administrative matters. By Article 1(2), it does not apply to: (a) the status or legal capacity of natural persons, rights in property arising out of a matrimonial relationship, wills and succession; (b) bankruptcy, proceedings relating to the winding-up of insolvent companies or other legal persons, judicial arrangements, compositions and analogous proceedings; (c) social security; and (d) arbitration.

## Civil and Commercial Matters

The purpose of Article 1(1) is to confine the scope of the Regulation to claims under private law, as distinct from public law.[46] Since the distinction between public law and private law is not drawn in precisely the same way in all the Member States, the European Court has ruled that the concept of civil and commercial matters, used in Article 1, must be given an autonomous meaning, derived from the objectives and scheme of the instrument and the general principles underlying the national legal systems as a whole. Accordingly, the Regulation does not apply to a dispute between a private person and a public authority, where the dispute arises out of acts done by the public authority in the exercise of its powers as such,[47] or where the relevant legal relationship between a public authority and a private person involves the exercise by the State of powers going beyond those existing under the rules applicable to relations between private persons.[48] Conversely, the Regulation is applicable where neither party to the dispute is a public body,[49] even if the dispute relates to ownership of land and the defendant's title is derived from an act of a public authority.[50] Moreover,

---

2245/2004, [2004] OJ L381/10; the Agreement between the European Community and Denmark, [2005] OJ L299/62; and Regulation 1791/2006, [2006] OJ L363/1.

[45] These provisions echo Article 1 of the Brussels Convention in its 1978 and subsequent versions, and of the Lugano Convention 1988.

[46] This reflects the approach traditionally adopted by treaties dealing with aspects of private international law. In contrast, both the Hague Convention of 19th October 1996 on Jurisdiction, Applicable Law, Recognition, Enforcement and Co-operation in respect of Parental Responsibility and Measures for the Protection of Children, (1996) 35 ILM 1391, and the Brussels IIA Regulation (considered in Chapters 16 and 17 below) have broken new ground by including public measures of child protection within their scope.

[47] See Case 29/76: *LTU v Eurocontrol* [1976] ECR 1541; Case 814/79: *Netherlands v Rüffer* [1980] ECR 3807; and Case C-172/91: *Sonntag v Waidmann* [1993] ECR I-1963. Cf. *Schmidt v Home Secretary* [1995] 1 ILRM 301 (Geoghegan J); and see also *Short v Ireland* [1997] 1 ILRM 161 (Irish Supreme Court).

[48] See Case C-271/00: *Gemeente Steenbergen v Baten* [2002] ECR I-10489; Case C-266/01: *Tiard* [2003] ECR I-4867; and Case C-433/01: *Freistaat Bayern v Blijdenstein* [2004] ECR I-981.

[49] See Case C-167/00: *VKI v Henkel* [2002] ECR I-8111, which involved an action brought by a consumer protection organisation for the purpose of preventing a trader from using allegedly unfair terms in contracts with private individuals. The European Court explained that a consumer protection organisation is a private body, and such proceedings did not in any way involve the exercise of powers derogating from the legal rules applicable to relations between private individuals.

[50] See Case C-420/07: *Apostolides v Orams* [2009] ECR I-3571.

the Regulation is applicable where the dispute is between a public authority and a private person, but the relevant legal relationship between them does not involve the exercise by the State of powers going beyond those existing under the rules applicable to relations between private persons.[51]

Thus, the Regulation does not apply where a public authority created by international treaty (such as the European Organization for the Safety of Air Navigation) seeks to recover from a private person charges for the use of its equipment and services, where such use is obligatory and exclusive and the charges and collection procedures are fixed unilaterally by the authority.[52] Similarly, the Regulation does not apply where an authority responsible for administering a public waterway sues a shipowner responsible for a maritime collision for the costs incurred by the authority in the removal of a wreck.[53] Nor where a government department (such as the UK Department of Trade and Industry) seeks the winding up of a foreign company which is running locally an illegal 'snowball' lottery.[54] Nor where a public body, acting under statutory powers whose objective is to deprive beneficiaries of criminal conduct of the proceeds of such conduct, claims payment of sums by which the defendant had been corruptly enriched.[55] Similarly, the Regulation does not apply to an action for libel, brought against a foreign central bank and its officers, in respect of a letter sent in the exercise of its supervisory functions as regulator of financial institutions.[56]

Nor, as the European Court ruled in *Lechouritou v Germany*,[57] does the Regulation apply to claims for compensation brought against a Member State by individuals as victims or successors of the victims of acts perpetrated by its armed forces in the course of warfare, even if the acts complained of were contrary to the law of war and amounted to crimes against humanity. For operations conducted by armed forces are one of the characteristic emanations of State sovereignty, especially as they are decided upon in a unilateral and binding manner by the competent public authorities and are inextricably linked to foreign and defence policy; and unlawful acts carried out in the exercise of public powers retain their public character.

On the other hand, the Regulation does apply to an action for damages brought against a teacher in a state school who caused injury to a pupil through negligent supervision during a school trip.[58] For the conduct of a teacher in a state school, in his function as a person in charge of pupils during a school trip, does not entail the exercise of powers going beyond those applicable in relations between private individuals. He assumes the same functions vis-à-vis his

---

[51] See Case C-266/01: *Tiard* [2003] ECR I-4867.

[52] See Case 29/76: *LTU v Eurocontrol* [1976] ECR 1541. Such judgments may, however, continue to be enforceable under bilateral conventions; see Article 70(1) and Cases 9–10/77: *Bavaria Fluggesellschaft Schwabe v Eurocontrol* [1977] ECR 1517.

[53] See Case 814/79: *Netherlands v Rüffer* [1980] ECR 3807.

[54] See *Re Senator Hanseatische Verwaltungsgesellschaft* [1996] 2 BCLC 562 (Scott V-C); affirmed on other issues, [1996] 4 All ER 933 (CA).

[55] See *Criminal Assets Bureau v JWPL* [2007] IEHC 177 (Feeney J).

[56] See *Grovit v De Nederlandsche Bank NV* [2008] 1 All ER (Comm) 106 (CA).

[57] Case C-292/05, [2007] ECR I-1519. The case involved claims brought against Germany in a Greek court by the children of victims for compensation for loss suffered as a result of acts perpetrated by the German armed forces at the time of the occupation of Greece during the Second World War. The claims arose from a massacre of 676 civilian inhabitants of the municipality of Kalavrita (Greece) by German soldiers on 13th December 1943.

[58] See Case C-172/91: *Sonntag v Waidmann* [1993] ECR I-1963.

pupils as those assumed by a teacher in a private school, and it is immaterial that insurance cover may be provided under a scheme governed by public law.

The Regulation also applies to a claim by a State against a private person for customs duties, if the claim is based on a guarantee contract governed by private law, and the legal relationship between the creditor and the guarantor, under the guarantee contract, does not entail the exercise by the State of powers going beyond those existing under the rules applicable to relations between private persons.[59] For, even if the guarantor may raise pleas in defence which necessitate an investigation into the existence and content of the customs debt, that would amount only to a preliminary issue, and the specific exclusion of customs matters is designed merely to clarify the concept of civil and commercial matters. A *fortiori*, the Regulation is applicable where an action for the recovery of sums paid to discharge customs duties is brought by a guarantor who has paid the duties against the importer as principal debtor, by way of subrogation under a provision of civil law, since the relationship between the importer and the guarantor is governed by private law.[60]

Where a public body seeks to recover from a private person sums paid by the body by way of social assistance to a member of his family (such as his spouse, divorced spouse or child), the Regulation applies if the basis and the detailed rules relating to the claim are governed by the rules of the ordinary law in regard to maintenance obligations, but not if the action for recourse is founded on provisions by which the legislature has conferred on the public body a prerogative of its own. Thus, the Regulation does not apply to a claim for recourse under Dutch legislation which enables the public body to disregard an otherwise binding maintenance agreement lawfully entered into between former spouses and approved by a judicial decision.[61] On the other hand, the Regulation applies to actions by a German public body against parents of recipients of education grants under the German Act on Educational Support, by way of a statutory subrogation governed by civil law.[62]

Although the Regulation does not apply to criminal proceedings themselves, it does apply to a civil claim in tort, even when it is made ancillarily to a prosecution in a criminal court.[63]

---

[59]   See Case C-266/01: *Tiard* [2003] ECR I-4867. This appears to overrule the earlier English decision in *QRS v Frandsen* [1999] 3 All ER 289 (CA) that the exclusion of revenue matters extends to an action which in form appears to involve an ordinary civil claim between private parties, but in substance seeks the indirect enforcement of a tax claim; as where a company in liquidation sues a former director or shareholder for restitution of misappropriated assets or damages for their misappropriation, but the sole creditor is a tax authority, and the whole object and potential result of the action is to collect the tax for the authority.

[60]   See Case C-265/02: *Frahuil v Assitalia* [2004] ECR I-1543.

[61]   See Case C-271/00: *Gemeente Steenbergen v Baten* [2002] ECR I-10489.

[62]   See Case C-433/01: *Freistaat Bayern v Blijdenstein* [2004] ECR I-981.

[63]   See Article 5(4), which confers jurisdiction on a court of a Member State to entertain a civil claim for damages or restitution against a defendant who is domiciled in another Member State, where the civil claim is based on an act giving rise to criminal proceedings, the court is seised of such criminal proceedings, and the court has jurisdiction under its own law to entertain civil proceedings; Case C-172/91: *Sonntag v Waidmann* [1993] ECR I-1963; and Case C-7/98: *Krombach v Bamberski* [2000] ECR I-1935. See also Article 61 (ex Article II of the Protocol annexed to the Brussels Convention), which entitles a defendant to appear and defend through a qualified representative, without appearing in person, in certain situations of this kind; and Case 157/80: *Rinkau* [1981] ECR 1391, which confines this right to criminal proceedings in which civil liability is in question, or on which civil liability could subsequently be based.

Thus, where the relatives of a deceased victim join as civil plaintiffs in a prosecution for manslaughter, seeking compensation from the alleged offender, the Regulation applies to the civil claim. This form of procedure is common in many of the Member States, especially in the case of road accidents, though not in England, where there is rigorous procedural separation between criminal and civil aspects of the same incident.

## The Excluded Matters

For a variety of reasons, a number of matters (individual status or capacity, matrimonial property, succession, insolvency, social security, and arbitration) are excluded from the scope of the Brussels I Regulation by Article 1(2).[64] In *Marc Rich v Impianti (The Atlantic Emperor),*[65] which involved the exclusion of arbitration, the European Court emphasised that, in order to determine material scope, reference must be made solely to the principal subject-matter of the dispute, and not to any preliminary, subsidiary or incidental issue which the court may have to resolve in order to determine the dispute.[66] Thus, for example, the Regulation would apply to an action founded on a breach of contract, even if minority were raised as a defence, since the principal subject-matter of the action would be the contract, and the defendant's capacity would only be a subsidiary issue.

A preliminary, subsidiary or incidental issue must be distinguished from an ancillary claim. For, as the European Court emphasised in *De Cavel v De Cavel (No 2),*[67] whether ancillary claims come within the scope of the Regulation depends on their own subject-matter, and not on the subject-matter involved in the principal claim. Thus, the Regulation applies to an application for maintenance, even when made ancillarily in divorce proceedings, which are themselves excluded from the scope of the Regulation as concerning individual status.[68]

Ancillary claims must be distinguished from provisional measures (such as orders for the freezing of assets, or the delivery up of documents to prevent their use in evidence). As regards the scope of the Regulation, provisional measures follow the nature of the rights which they serve to protect.[69]

## Family Matters

The exclusion from the scope of the Brussels I Regulation by Article 1(2)(a) of 'the status or legal capacity of natural persons, [and] rights in property arising out of a matrimonial relationship' covers most (but not all) matters falling within family law.

---

64    For a further exclusion, relating to the recognition of external judgments, see Case C-129/92: *Owens Bank v Bracco* [1994] ECR I-117, considered at p. 43 below.

65    Case C-190/89, [1991] ECR I-3855.

66    See also the Jenard Report, at p 10; the Schlosser Report, at p 89; and Case C-129/92: *Owens Bank v Bracco* [1994] ECR I-117, at para 34.

67    Case 120/79, [1980] ECR 731. See also Article 5(2).

68    See also *Martin*, 3rd April 1990 (French Court of Cassation), enforcing under the Brussels Convention a German maintenance order made ancillarily to a declaration of paternity.

69    See Case 143/78: *De Cavel v De Cavel (No 1)* [1979] ECR 1055; Case 120/79: *De Cavel v De Cavel (No 2)* [1980] ECR 731; Case 25/81: *CHW v GJH* [1982] ECR 1189; and Case C-391/95: *Van Uden v Deco-Line* [1998] ECR I-7091.

The exclusion of individual status covers proceedings for divorce, judicial separation or annulment of marriage, and proceedings in respect of parental responsibility for children, but such proceedings are now governed by EC Regulation 2201/2003 concerning Jurisdiction and the Recognition and Enforcement of Judgments in Matrimonial Matters and the Matters of Parental Responsibility, which may conveniently be referred to as the Brussels IIA Regulation.[70] The exclusion by Article 1(2)(a) of the Brussels I Regulation also covers proceedings concerning the adoption of children, and at present there is no Community measure on adoption.

While Article 1(2)(a) of the Brussels I Regulation excludes matrimonial property from the scope of the Regulation, it is clear from Article 5(2)[71] and the European Court's ruling in *De Cavel v De Cavel (No 2)*[72] that the Regulation does apply to maintenance claims under family law, and does so even when the maintenance claim is made ancillarily in proceedings in which the principal claim is excluded from the Regulation as a matter of status, such as divorce proceedings. So the Regulation insists on a tiresome necessity to distinguish between matrimonial property and maintenance.

In *De Cavel v De Cavel (No 1)*,[73] the European Court made clear that 'matrimonial property' is not confined to property arrangements specifically and exclusively envisaged by certain national legal systems in the case of marriage, but extends to any proprietary legal relationships between spouses resulting directly from the matrimonial relationship or its dissolution, though not to proprietary legal relations existing between spouses which have no connection with the marriage. On the other hand, in *De Cavel v De Cavel (No 2)*,[74] the European Court construed 'maintenance' as covering periodical payments between former spouses after divorce, where such payments are designed to compensate for the disparity in their living standards arising from the breakdown of the marriage, and are fixed on the basis of their respective needs and resources. Eventually, in *Van den Boogaard v Laumen*,[75] the Court faced the problem of an English 'clean-break' divorce settlement. Its ruling established that a decision rendered in divorce proceedings ordering payment of a lump sum and transfer of ownership in certain property by one former spouse to the other falls within the Regulation, as relating to maintenance, if its purpose is to ensure the recipient's maintenance. Where a provision awarded is designed to enable the recipient former spouse to provide for herself, or the needs and resources of each of the spouses are taken into consideration in the determina-

---

[70]   For its text, see [2003] OJ L338/1. For discussion, see Chapters 16 and 17 below.

[71]   Article 5(2) specifies that: 'A person domiciled in a Member State may, in another Member State, be sued ... in matters relating to maintenance, in the courts for the place where the maintenance creditor is domiciled or habitually resident or, if the matter is ancillary to proceedings concerning the status of a person, in the court which, according to its own law, has jurisdiction to entertain those proceedings, unless that jurisdiction is based solely on the nationality of one of the parties'. In Case C-295/95: *Farrell v Long* [1997] ECR I-1683, the European Court ruled that the reference in Article 5(2) to a maintenance creditor covers anyone applying for maintenance, including a person making a maintenance application for the first time.

[72]   Case 120/79, [1980] ECR 731. See also *T v L* [2009] ILPr 5 (Irish Supreme Court), affirming *DT v FL* [2007] ILPr 56 (McKechnie J).

[73]   Case 143/78, [1979] ECR 1055. See also Case 25/81: *CHW v GJH* [1982] ECR 1189.

[74]   Case 120/79, [1980] ECR 731.

[75]   Case C-220/95, [1997] ECR I-1147. See also *Fournier v Fournier* [1998] 2 FLR 990 (CA); and *DT v FL* [2007] ILPr 56 (McKechnie J in the Irish High Court).

tion of its amount, the decision is concerned with maintenance. But where the provision awarded is solely concerned with dividing property between the spouses, the decision is concerned with matrimonial property, and is therefore not enforceable under the Regulation. A mixed decision may, under Article 48, be enforced in part if it clearly shows the aims to which the different parts of the order correspond.

In view of this ruling, and of the provisions of the (English) Matrimonial Causes Act 1973 (as amended), it might have been concluded that any English order for financial provision or property adjustment, made ancillarily in divorce proceedings, would count as maintenance and not matrimonial property for the purpose of the Regulation, since all such orders take account of the needs and resources of each of the spouses. But in *Cartwright v Cartwright*,[76] the English Court of Appeal, invoking the reasoning in *Van den Boogaard v Laumen*[77] by analogy in the context of an order for both periodical payments and a lump sum payment made in Hong Kong, considered that, in view of the separate provision for periodical payments, the lump sum payment should be regarded not as capitalised maintenance but as property division.

The effect of the ruling in *Van den Boogaard v Laumen*[78] was more fully considered by the English Court of Appeal in *Moore v Moore*,[79] which involved the characterisation of a prior Spanish application, made in connection with Spanish divorce proceedings, in the context of a subsequent English application for financial relief after a foreign divorce under Part III of the Matrimonial and Family Proceedings Act 1984. The Court of Appeal concluded that whether a claim is for maintenance depends upon an autonomous interpretation of the term, and the label given to the claim by national law is not decisive. Payment of a lump sum or transfer of property may be in the nature of maintenance if it is intended to ensure the support of a spouse. But payment of a lump sum or transfer of property which serves only the purpose of a division of property or compensation for non-material damage is not in the nature of maintenance, and a payment or transfer of property intended as a division of assets concerns matrimonial property. Whether a claim relates to maintenance will depend on its purpose, and in particular whether it is designed to enable one spouse to provide for himself or herself, or if the needs and resources of each of the spouses are taken into consideration in the determination of its amount, or where the capital sum set is designed to ensure a predetermined level of income. But where the provision is solely concerned with dividing property between the spouses, the decision will be concerned with matrimonial property, and will therefore not be enforceable under the Brussels I Regulation.[80]

English proceedings under s 17 of the Married Women's Property Act 1882 appear to fall within the Regulation as ordinary civil matters, involving neither maintenance nor matrimonial property, since in such proceedings existing proprietary rights, arising from the ordinary law of property applicable regardless of any marital relationship, are dominant. The same applies to proceedings between spouses under the Trusts of Land and Appointment of Trustees Act 1996, in which one spouse seeks a declaration establishing his entitlement to an equitable interest in property owned by the other.[81]

---

[76]   [2002] 2 FLR 610.
[77]   Case C-220/95, [1997] ECR I-1147.
[78]   Case C-220/95, [1997] ECR I-1147.
[79]   [2007] EWCA Civ 361 (CA); especially at para 80.
[80]   See also *C v C* [2007] CSOH 191 (Outer House).
[81]   See *Prazic v Prazic* [2006] 2 FLR 1128 (CA).

On 18th December 2008, the EC Council adopted Regulation 4/2009 on Jurisdiction, Applicable Law, Recognition and Enforcement of Decisions and Co-operation in Matters relating to Maintenance Obligations, which may conveniently be referred to as the Maintenance Regulation.[82] This Regulation will become applicable on 18th June 2011. It deals with the direct jurisdiction of courts and equivalent authorities, as well as choice of the applicable substantive law and the recognition, enforceability and enforcement of decisions, in respect of maintenance obligations arising from a family relationship, parentage, marriage or affinity. Subject to transitional provisions, the Maintenance Regulation will replace the provisions of the Brussels I Regulation in respect of matters relating to maintenance obligations.[83] But it will still be necessary to distinguish between maintenance and matrimonial property, since matrimonial property will remain excluded from the scope of the Brussels I Regulation and will not fall within the scope of the Maintenance Regulation, and indeed will remain exempt from all EU measures designed to harmonise rules of private international law.

## Succession

As regards the exclusion from the Brussels I Regulation by Article 1(2)(a) of 'wills and succession' (on death), a narrow approach to the exclusion was adopted by Rattee J in *Re Hayward*.[84] The proceedings were brought by a trustee in bankruptcy, claiming property as having belonged to the bankrupt and accordingly vested in the trustee by virtue of the bankruptcy. The bankrupt had died and the defendant had acquired the property from a person who claimed it by succession. The exclusion was held inapplicable on the ground that the proceedings were not principally concerned with succession, since the trustee's claim was based simply on the deceased's ownership and the effect of his bankruptcy.

It also seems appropriate, in interpreting Article 1(2)(a) of the Brussels I Regulation, to take account of the distinction drawn by Article 4 of the Hague Convention of 1st July 1985 on the Law Applicable to Trusts and on their Recognition, which is transposed in the United Kingdom by the Recognition of Trusts Act 1987, between issues concerning a trust and preliminary issues relating to the validity of wills or other acts by virtue of which assets are transferred to the trustee. Thus the exclusion of succession from the Brussels I Regulation should not extend to proceedings concerning a testamentary trust which has been perfected by transfer of the assets to the trustees, unless the action is based on a claim involving a challenge to the validity or propriety of such transfer.

## Insolvency

By Article 1(2)(b), the Brussels I Regulation does not apply to 'bankruptcy, proceedings relating to the winding-up of insolvent companies or other legal persons, judicial arrange-

---

82    For its text, see [2009] OJ L7/1. For examination of its provisions, see Chapter 18 below.
83    See the Maintenance Regulation, Recital 44 and Articles 68(1) and 75(2). In its Green Paper of 21st April 2009, the EC Commission envisages that maintenance matters should be added to the list of exclusions from the scope of the Brussels I Regulation, in view of the adoption of the Maintenance Regulation; see COM(2009) 175 final, at question 8.
84    [1997] Ch 45.

ments, compositions and analogous proceedings'. Parallel negotiations initiated under Article 293 (ex Article 220) of the EC Treaty eventually led to the adoption on 29th May 2000, and the entry into force on 31st May 2002, of EC Regulation 1346/2000 on Insolvency Proceedings, which may conveniently be referred to as the Insolvency Regulation.[85]

The bankruptcy exclusion from the Brussels I Regulation was construed by the European Court in *Gourdain v Nadler*[86] as referring primarily to proceedings based on the debtor's suspension of payments, insolvency or inability to raise credit, and involving judicial intervention for the purpose either of compulsory and collective liquidation of assets, or simply of supervision. But now that the Insolvency Regulation has entered into force, it seems clear, in view especially of Article 67 of the Brussels I Regulation,[87] that the exclusion specified in Article 1(2)(b) of the Brussels I Regulation must be construed as referring primarily to the collective insolvency proceedings entailing the total or partial divestment of a debtor and the appointment of a liquidator which fall within the scope of the Insolvency Regulation as defined by its Articles 1(1) and 2 and listed in its Annex A. The exclusion from the Brussels I Regulation must no doubt be construed as also extending to collective insolvency proceedings which would have fallen within the scope of the Insolvency Regulation but for the exclusion by Article 1(2) of that Regulation of insolvency proceedings in respect of certain undertakings which provide financial services. However, in *Re DAP Holding NV*,[88] Lewison J held that the reference in Article 1(2)(b) of the Brussels I Regulation to 'judicial arrangements' has the effect that such proceedings as an application under s 899 of the Companies Act 2006 for judicial sanction of a scheme of arrangement are outside the scope of both the Brussels I Regulation and the Insolvency Regulation. In any event the Brussels I Regulation does apply to a dispute between a creditor and a solvent company which is in members' voluntary liquidation.[89]

In *Gourdain v Nadler*,[90] the European Court also ruled that the bankruptcy exclusion from the Brussels I Regulation extends to proceedings which derive directly from a bankruptcy or insolvent liquidation and are closely connected with the primary insolvency proceedings. Thus the Regulation does not apply to an application by a liquidator, made under a provision of insolvency law (such as Article 99 of the French Bankruptcy Act 1967) and in the interest of the general body of creditors, to a court seised of corporate liquidation proceedings, for an

---

[85]    For its text, see [2000] OJ L160/1. For discussion, see Chapter 19 below.

The entry into force of the Insolvency Regulation has rendered obsolete the European Court's ruling in Case C-267/97: *Coursier v Fortis Bank*, [1999] ECR I-2543, that the effects in one Member State of an insolvency judgment given in another Member State are to be determined in accordance with the conflict rules of the State addressed, even as regards the effect of the insolvency judgment on the enforcement under Chapter III of the Brussels I Regulation of an ordinary judgment given before the insolvency proceedings.

[86]    Case 133/78, [1979] ECR 733 at 744; following the Jenard and Schlosser Reports at pp. 11–12 and 90.

[87]    Article 67 specifies that the Brussels I Regulation does not prejudice the application of provisions governing jurisdiction and the recognition and enforcement of judgments in specific matters which are contained in other Community instruments. See further at pp. 46–7 below.

[88]    [2006] BCC 48. See also *Re Sovereign Marine and General Insurance Co Ltd* [2007] 1 BCLC 228 (Warren J).

[89]    See *Re Cover Europe Ltd* [2002] BPIR 931.

[90]    Case 133/78, [1979] ECR 733.

order against a manager of the company in liquidation, requiring him to pay a sum into the company's assets with a view to making good a deficiency presumed to be due to his misman-agement. This ruling clearly covers English proceedings under sections 213–15 of the Insolvency Act 1986. In view of this ruling, it is rather surprising that in *Ashurst v Pollard*[91] the English Court of Appeal held that the exclusion did not apply to proceedings consequen-tial upon a bankruptcy, such as proceedings aimed at requiring the debtor and a co-owner to co-operate with the liquidator in the realisation of foreign assets.

It seems that the crucial question in this context is whether the claim made in the proceed-ings is based on insolvency law, or is based on ordinary law, with the bankruptcy amounting merely to an incidental feature. Thus a claim by a liquidator to recover property belonging to the debtor, or a debt owing to the debtor, falls within the Brussels I Regulation, since the debtor's title is based on the ordinary law and the bankruptcy merely has the incidental effect of transferring it to the liquidator.[92] On the same principle, the bankruptcy exclusion does not apply to an action brought by a creditor against the insolvent debtor to determine the amount owing under their contract.[93] Similarly, the Brussels I Regulation applies where an insolvent foreign company brings an action in England against its former directors and professional advisors for conspiracy to defraud and breaches of fiduciary duty and to establish construc-tive trusts, for the claims are based on ordinary law, rather than insolvency law, and the foreign insolvency proceedings are purely collateral.[94] On the other hand, the bankruptcy exclusion applies to a claim for payment of a guaranteed debt against a guarantor which is in liquidation abroad, where the claim as framed relies on the decision opening the liquidation and a decision of the liquidator as accelerating and capitalising sums otherwise payable at a later date.[95]

Despite the entry into force of the Insolvency Regulation, the Brussels I Regulation remains applicable to cases where, although an insolvency proceeding has been opened, the claim in question is based on the ordinary law, and the bankruptcy amounts merely to an inci-dental feature. Thus, in *German Graphics Graphische Maschinen GmbH v Van der Schee*,[96] the European Court ruled that the Brussels I Regulation applies to an action brought by a seller of goods against an insolvent buyer, seeking recovery of the goods on the basis of a reservation of title clause, since the claim to ownership is not based on insolvency law and does not require the opening of insolvency proceedings or the involvement of a liquidator, even if the goods are situated in the Member State of the opening of insolvency proceedings in respect of the buyer at the time of opening of the insolvency proceedings, and even if the buyer's liquidator is in fact a party to the action brought by the seller.

---

[91] [2001] Ch 595 (CA), affirming [2000] 2 All ER 772 (Jacob J).

[92] See *Re Leyland DAF Ltd* [1994] 2 BCLC 106 (CA); *Re Hayward* [1997] Ch 45 (Rattee J); *QRS v Frandsen* [1999] 3 All ER 289 (CA); and *Oakley v Ultra Vehicle Design Ltd* [2005] EWHC 872 (Lloyd LJ). See also Case 288/82: *Duijnstee v Goderbauer* [1983] ECR 3663; and Case C-214/89: *Powell Duffryn v Petereit* [1992] ECR I-1745.

[93] See *UBS v Omni Holding* [2000] 1 WLR 916 (Rimer J).

[94] See *Grupo Torras v Al-Sabah* [1995] 1 Lloyd's Rep 374 (Mance J); affirmed without consid-eration of the bankruptcy exclusion, [1996] 1 Lloyd's Rep 7 (CA).

[95] See *Firswood v Petra Bank* [1996] CLC 608 (CA).

[96] Case C-292/08, [2009] ECR I-8421.

But new provision is now made by the Insolvency Regulation for cases which fall within the bankruptcy exclusion from the Brussels I Regulation as derived and connected proceedings under the ruling in *Gourdain v Nadler*. By Article 25 of the Insolvency Regulation, judgments which derive directly from and are closely linked with insolvency proceedings are made enforceable in other Member States in accordance with Chapter III of the Brussels I Regulation. In such cases, the usual exceptions to enforcement specified in Article 34 of the Brussels I Regulation are replaced by the exceptions relating to public policy, personal freedom and postal secrecy, specified in Articles 25 and 26 of the Insolvency Regulation.[97] Moreover, in *Seagon v Deko Marty*,[98] the European Court ruled that Article 3(1) of the Insolvency Regulation confers on the courts of the Member State within which insolvency proceedings have been opened jurisdiction to decide actions which are derived directly from the insolvency proceedings and are closely connected to them, such as an action to set a transaction aside by virtue of insolvency, even where the action is brought against a person resident in another Member State.

**Social Security**

The exclusion of 'social security' from the Brussels I Regulation by Article 1(2)(c) was clarified by the European Court in *Gemeente Steenbergen v Baten*,[99] where it ruled that the exclusion does not apply to an action under a right of recourse by which a public body seeks from a person governed by private law recovery in accordance with the rules of the ordinary law of sums paid by it by way of social assistance to the divorced spouse and the child of that person. More generally, the Court explained that the concept of 'social security' in Article 1(2)(d) encompasses the matters covered by EC Regulation 1408/71, as defined in Article 4 thereof and clarified in the Court's case-law; and in any event that the exclusion of social security by Article 1(2)(d) is confined to disputes arising out of the relationship between the administration and employers or employees.

**Arbitration**

Article 1(2)(d) of the Brussels I Regulation provides laconically that the Regulation does not apply to 'arbitration'. This exclusion has given rise to enormous difficulties, especially in England, but many of these problems have now been resolved by the ruling of the European Court in *Allianz v West Tankers*.[100]

---

[97] The ruling of the European Court in Case C-111/08: *SCT Industri v Alpenblume* [2009] ECR I-5655, that the exclusion specified by Article 1(2)(b) of the Brussels I Regulation applied to a judgment which invalidated a transfer of local assets by a foreign liquidator on the ground that the law of the country of origin did not recognise his power to dispose of local assets, was given in the context of a situation in which the Insolvency Regulation was not applicable because the insolvency proceedings were opened before its entry into force.

[98] Case C-339/07, [2009] ECR I-767.

[99] Case C-271/00, [2002] ECR I-10489.

[100] Case C-185/07, [2009] ECR I-663.

## The relevance of the New York Convention 1958

The New York Convention of 10th June 1958 on the Recognition and Enforcement of Foreign Arbitral Awards[101] provides for the recognition and enforcement of both arbitration agreements and arbitration awards. But it does not deal with all judicial proceedings which are ancillary to arbitration proceedings. For example, it does not deal with applications to a court for the appointment of an arbitrator. The parties to the New York Convention include all twenty-seven EU Member States, and all the Lugano Convention countries.

It seems clear that, even apart from Article 1(2)(d), Article 71 of the Brussels I Regulation would ensure that, in the case of conflict, the New York Convention would prevail over the Regulation. But in *Marc Rich v Impianti (The Atlantic Emperor)*,[102] the European Court, while recognising that one of the purposes of Article 1(2)(d) is to prevent conflict with the New York Convention, ruled that Article 1(2)(d) extends to arbitration in its entirety, and is not limited to aspects covered by the Convention.

## The test of principal subject-matter

In *Marc Rich v Impianti (The Atlantic Emperor)*,[103] the European Court established that Article 1(2)(d) extends to judicial proceedings whose principal subject-matter is arbitration, such as an application to a court for an order appointing an arbitrator. Such an application is excluded from the Regulation by Article 1(2)(d), regardless of any preliminary issue involved in the proceedings, including one relating to the existence or validity of an arbitration agreement.

Subsequently, in *Van Uden v Deco-Line*,[104] the European Court approved a statement in the Schlosser Report[105] that the Regulation does not apply to judgments determining whether an arbitration agreement is valid or not or, because it is invalid, ordering the parties not to continue the arbitration proceedings; nor to proceedings and decisions concerning applications for the revocation, amendment,[106] recognition and enforcement of arbitration awards;[107] nor to proceedings ancillary to arbitration proceedings, such as the appointment or dismissal of arbitrators,[108] the fixing of the place of arbitration, or the extension of the time-limit for making awards. Similarly it was accepted by Aikens J in *The Ivan Zagubanski*[109] and by Clarke LJ in *The Hari Bhum*[110] that the Regulation does not apply to any court proceedings or judgments in which the principal focus of the matter is arbitration, and this includes

---

[101]   [1958] JBL 396.
[102]   Case C-190/89, [1991] ECR I-3855.
[103]   Case C-190/89, [1991] ECR I-3855. The reference had been made by an English court which had been requested by one party to appoint an arbitrator after an Italian court had been requested by the other party to determine the substantive dispute.
[104]   Case C-391/95, [1998] ECR I-7091, at para 32.
[105]   [1979] OJ C59/71, at pp. 92–3.
[106]   Thus the Regulation does not apply to proceedings for the remission or setting aside of an arbitral award, or by way of appeal from an arbitral award; see *Marc Rich v Impianti* [1989] ECC 198 (Hirst J).
[107]   See also *ED & F Man Sugar Ltd v Lendoudis* [2008] 1 All ER 952 (Christopher Clarke J).
[108]   Thus the Regulation does not apply to an application for a declaration that an arbitrator has been validly appointed in accordance with an arbitration agreement; see *The Lake Avery* [1997] 1 Lloyd's Rep 540 (Clarke J).
[109]   [2002] 1 Lloyd's Rep 106.
[110]   [2005] 1 Lloyd's Rep 67 (CA).

proceedings concerning the validity or existence of an arbitration agreement; the appointment of arbitrators; ancillary assistance to arbitration proceedings;[111] and the recognition and enforcement of awards. Thus, as Waller J held in *ABCI v Banque Franco-Tunisienne*,[112] a French judgment authorising enforcement of a French award is not enforceable in England under the Regulation, though the award itself may be enforceable under the New York Convention. Similarly, in *A v B*,[113] Colman J held that Article 1(2)(d) of the Regulation applies to proceedings seeking the avoidance of an arbitration agreement and the setting aside of orders made by the arbitrator.

On the other hand, as the European Court ruled in *Van Uden v Deco-Line*,[114] Article 31 of the Regulation, which enables a court which lacks substantive jurisdiction to order provisional measures, such as an order freezing the defendant's assets pending determination of the substantive claim in a competent forum, extends to cases where the court's lack of jurisdiction arises from an arbitration agreement and the provisional measures are intended to support arbitration proceedings, provided that the nature of the substantive claim is such that it otherwise falls within the scope of the Regulation. For such provisional measures are not in principle ancillary to arbitration proceedings, but are ordered in parallel to such proceedings and are intended as measures of support. Thus they concern not arbitration as such, but the protection of the substantive rights.[115]

### Judicial proceedings principally concerned with an arbitration agreement

It is now clear from the rulings of the European Court in *Van Uden v Deco-Line*[116] and *Allianz v West Tankers*[117] that Article 1(2)(d) extends to judicial proceedings whose principal subject-matter is the existence, validity or binding force of an arbitration agreement, such as proceedings seeking a declaration on that very point, or claiming damages for breach of the arbitration agreement. The same view has been adopted in England by Clarke J in *The Lake Avery*;[118] by Colman J in *Toepfer v Cargill*;[119] by Aikens J in *The Ivan Zagubanski*;[120] and by the Court of Appeal (per Clarke LJ) in *The Hari Bhum*.[121] But Article 1(2)(d) does not apply where the claim is against a person who is not a party to the arbitration agreement, such as a broker whose authority to conclude the contract containing the arbitration clause on behalf of his principal is in dispute.[122]

---

[111]   For example, judicial proceedings for the obtaining of evidence for use in arbitration proceedings.

[112]   [1996] 1 Lloyd's Rep 485; affirmed on other issues, [1997] 1 Lloyd's Rep 531 (CA).

[113]   [2007] 1 All ER (Comm) 591.

[114]   Case C-391/95, [1998] ECR I-7091.

[115]   See also *Re Q's Estate* [1999] 1 Lloyd's Rep 931, where Rix J held that, as a matter of construction, a normally worded English arbitration clause is not intended to prevent the grant by an English court of ancillary relief in support of arbitration, such as a freezing order.

[116]   Case C-391/95, [1998] ECR I-7091, at para 32.

[117]   Case C-185/07, [2009] ECR I-663. See also per Darmon AG in Case C-190/89: *Rich v Impianti* [1991] ECR I-3855.

[118]   [1997] 1 Lloyd's Rep 540.

[119]   [1997] 2 Lloyd's Rep 98.

[120]   [2002] 1 Lloyd's Rep 106.

[121]   [2005] 1 Lloyd's Rep 67 (CA); affirming [2004] 1 Lloyd's Rep 206 (Moore-Bick J).

[122]   See *Vale do Rio doce Navegacao v Shanghai Bao Steel* [2000] 2 Lloyd's Rep 1 (Thomas J).

In *The Hari Bhum*,[123] the Court of Appeal held further that Articles 27–30 of the Regulation, on concurrent actions, do not apply where a court of a Member State is seised of a proceeding to which Article 1(2)(d) applies, such as an application for a declaration as to the validity of an arbitration agreement, after a court of another Member State has been seised of an action for determination of the substantive dispute in defiance of the arbitration agreement. It distinguished the ruling of the European Court in *Gasser v MISAT*,[124] that the provisions of the Regulation on concurrent actions apply even if there is a jurisdiction clause selecting the second court in accordance with Article 21, on the ground that in that case the second action falls within the scope of the Regulation. On this point, the ruling of the Court of Appeal seems compatible with the ruling of the European Court in *Allianz v West Tankers*.[125]

### Judicial proceedings brought in defiance of an arbitration agreement

In *Van Uden v Deco-Line*,[126] the European Court accepted that a valid arbitration agreement has the effect of excluding the substantive jurisdiction of all courts to determine the merits of a dispute under Chapter II (Articles 2 and 5–24) of the Brussels I Regulation. On the other hand, as the European Court explained in *Allianz v West Tankers*,[127] the Regulation does apply where a court of a Member State is seised of an action on the merits, but the defendant requests it to decline jurisdiction in order to give effect to an arbitration agreement (perhaps invoking Article II of the New York Convention). For in this situation the principal subject-matter of the judicial proceedings is the substantive claim, and the validity and effect of the arbitration clause is merely an incidental issue.[128]

*Allianz v West Tankers*[129] involved a tort claim brought in an Italian court by a charterer's loss insurer against a shipowner for damage to an Italian jetty. The charterparty was governed by English law and contained a London arbitration clause. After the English High Court had granted to the shipowner an anti-suit injunction against the Italian action on the ground that the claim fell within the arbitration clause, the House of Lords referred a question as to the proprietary of such an injunction. In responding, the European Court explained that the Italian action claiming damages in tort fell within the Regulation, and consequently a preliminary issue concerning the applicability of an arbitration agreement, raised as an incidental question to contest the jurisdiction of the Italian court, also fell within its scope. Thus, the objection of lack of jurisdiction, raised by the shipowner before the Italian court on the basis of the existence and validity of an arbitration agreement, fell within the scope of the Regulation, and it was therefore exclusively for that court to rule on that objection and on its own jurisdiction, pursuant to Articles 1(2)(d) and 5(3) of the Regulation.

Where Article II of the New York Convention requires the court seised to decline jurisdiction in accordance with the arbitration agreement, Article 71 of the Regulation ensures that

---

123    [2005] 1 Lloyd's Rep 67 (CA).
124    Case C-116/02, [2003] ECR I-14693.
125    Case C-185/07, [2009] ECR I-663.
126    Case C-391/95, [1998] ECR I-7091, at para 24.
127    Case C-185/07, [2009] ECR I-663.
128    See also the Schlosser Report, at pp. 92–3; the Evrigenis and Kerameus Report, at para 35; and the opinion of Léger AG in Case C-391/95, *Van Uden v Deco-Line* [1998] ECR I-7091.
129    Case C-185/07, [2009] ECR I-663.

this obligation prevails over any conflicting provision of the Regulation.[130] But it is now clear from the reasoning of the European Court in *Allianz v West Tankers*[131] that if the court seised holds (even erroneously) that the arbitration agreement relied on is invalid or ineffective, and therefore proceeds to accept jurisdiction and to determine the substantive claim, its decision on the substantive claim qualifies for recognition and enforcement in the other Member States under Chapter III of the Regulation. For the validity and effect of the arbitration agreement constituted only a preliminary issue, and one which was relevant only to the jurisdiction of the original court, and Article 35 of the Regulation prevents review of the jurisdiction of the original court by the court addressed.

It also seems reasonably clear from the reasoning of the European Court in *Allianz v West Tankers*[132] that the same applies where the original court, seised in defiance of an alleged arbitration agreement, has merely made a decision accepting jurisdiction on the ground that the agreement is invalid or ineffective, and has not yet proceeded to determine the substantive claim. The courts of the other Member States must accord recognition under Chapter III of the Regulation to the decision that the agreement is invalid or ineffective. For Chapter III extends to interlocutory decisions, and it requires incidental recognition to be accorded by the courts of a Member State to a judgment given in another Member State in all proceedings in which the decision is relevant, including in proceedings which are themselves otherwise excluded from the scope of the Regulation by Article 1(2).

Unfortunately, in this scenario, a contrary view is at present adopted by the English courts. Before the ruling in *Allianz v West Tankers*,[133] the English Court of Appeal had in *The Hari Bhum*[134] refused to recognise in an English application principally concerned with arbitration (such as an application for a declaration that an arbitration agreement is valid and binding) a judgment of a court of another Member State accepting jurisdiction over a substantive claim on the ground that the arbitration agreement is invalid or ineffective. Clarke LJ accepted that the foreign proceedings were within the scope of the Regulation, but considered that recognition of the judgment was somehow irrelevant to the declarations sought in the English proceedings.

Similarly, in *National Navigation Co v Endesa Generacion SA*,[135] Gloster J accepted that a judgment of a Spanish court, upholding its jurisdiction to determine an action on the merits in the face of an alleged agreement for arbitration, fell within the scope of the Regulation. But she also held that the Regulation did not require the Spanish judgment to be recognised in English proceedings which fell outside the scope of the Regulation, such as an application for a declaration that the arbitration clause had been validly incorporated into the contract and was bind-

---

[130]  In England, the remedy for a party who claims that English proceedings are brought in breach of an arbitration agreement is to seek a stay under s 9 of the Arbitration Act 1996; see *Youell v La Reunion Aerienne* [2009] EWCA Civ 175.

[131]  Case C-185/07, [2009] ECR I-663. See also *The Hari Bhum* [2005] 1 Lloyd's Rep 67 (CA). Cf. *CMA CGM v Hyundai Mipo Dockyard* [2009] 1 All ER (Comm) 568, where Burton J ruled that the findings of the foreign court on the merits were irrelevant in a claim in an English arbitration for damages for breach of the arbitration agreement.

[132]  Case C-185/07, [2009] ECR I-663.

[133]  Case C-185/07, [2009] ECR I-663.

[134]  [2005] 1 Lloyd's Rep 67 (CA). Cf. *The Heidberg* [1994] 2 Lloyd's Rep 287 (Judge Diamond QC).

[135]  [2009] EWHC 196 (Comm).

ing on the parties. She further held in the alternative that recognition of the Spanish judgment in relation to the issues relating to arbitration would be manifestly contrary to the public policy of the United Kingdom, under Article 34(1) of the Regulation. Accordingly, she proceeded to make declarations that the arbitration clause had been validly incorporated and was binding.

It is submitted that there is no justification for limiting the obligation imposed by the Regulation to recognise a judgment which falls within the Regulation to cases where the proceedings in which recognition is sought themselves fall within the Regulation. On the contrary, it seems natural to read Article 33 as requiring that a judgment which falls within the Regulation must be recognised whenever it is relevant to proceedings in the State addressed, whatever the nature or subject-matter of those proceedings may be. The contrary view, adopted by Gloster J, would seem to entail that, for example, a French divorce which is entitled to recognition in England under the Brussels IIA Regulation may be ignored in English proceedings which are concerned with matrimonial property. Moreover, the suggestion that recognition of the Spanish judgment could be refused on grounds of public policy under Article 34(1) disregards the prohibition specified by Article 35(3), which prevents the application of public policy under Article 34(1) to rules relating to jurisdiction.

### Anti-suit injunctions

Until recently, the English courts had for some years asserted, and readily exercised, a power to grant an anti-suit injunction restraining a party from commencing or continuing an action on the merits in a court of another Member State in breach of an English arbitration agreement.[136] But, on 10th February 2009, the European Court ruled in *Allianz v West Tankers*,[137] on a reference from the House of Lords, that it is incompatible with the Brussels I Regulation for a court of a Member State to make an order to restrain a person from commencing or continuing proceedings before the courts of another Member State on the ground that such proceedings would be contrary to an arbitration agreement. Earlier, in *Turner v Grovit*,[138] the European Court had ruled in general terms that the Regulation precludes the grant of an injunction whereby a court of a Member State prohibits a party to proceedings pending before it from commencing or continuing proceedings before a court of another Member State. But, until the ruling in *Allianz*, the English courts had persisted in granting anti-suit injunctions against actions brought in courts of other Member States in breach of arbitration agreements, on the ground that the applicability of Article 1(2)(d) to the English application for the anti-suit injunction somehow immunised the injunction from the ruling in *Turner v Grovit*.[139] The

---

[136]    See *The Angelic Grace* [1995] 1 Lloyd's Rep 87 (CA); *Toepfer v Cargill* [1997] 2 Lloyd's Rep 98 (Colman J); *The Ivan Zagubanski* [2002] 1 Lloyd's Rep 106 (Aikens J); *The Hari Bhum* [2005] 1 Lloyd's Rep 67 (CA); and *The Front Comor* [2005] EWHC 454 (Colman J). Cf. *Toepfer v Molino* [1996] 1 Lloyd's Rep 510 (Mance J); and *Toepfer v Cargill* [1998] 1 Lloyd's Rep 379 (CA).

One argument for the compatibility of such intervention with the Brussels I Regulation invoked the analogy of the supposedly overriding effect of Article 23 of the Regulation in respect of choice of court agreements, asserted in *Continental Bank v Aeakos* [1994] 1 WLR 588 (CA), but that supposed effect was resolutely rejected by the European Court in Case C-116/02: *Gasser v MISAT* [2003] ECR I-14693. See pp. 198–9 below.

[137]    Case C-185/07, [2009] ECR I-663.

[138]    Case C-159/02, [2004] ECR I-3565.

[139]    See *The Hari Bhum* [2005] 1 Lloyd's Rep 67 (CA); and *The Front Comor* [2005] EWHC 454 (Colman J).

ruling in *Allianz* has now definitively established that the Brussels I Regulation prevents a court of a Member State from granting an anti-suit injunction in relation to proceedings in a court of another Member State in respect of a dispute concerning a matter which falls within the scope of the Regulation, even if the ground for the anti-suit injunction is an arbitration agreement in respect of the matter in question.

The *Allianz* case involved a tort claim brought in an Italian court by a charterer's loss insurer against a shipowner for damage to an Italian jetty. The charterparty was governed by English law and contained a London arbitration clause. After the English High Court had granted to the shipowner an anti-suit injunction against the Italian action on the ground that the claim fell within the arbitration clause, the House of Lords referred a question as to the proprietary of such an injunction.[140]

In response, the European Court accepted that the English proceedings giving rise to the anti-suit injunction were outside the scope of the Brussels I Regulation, since their subject-matter and the rights which they served to protect were covered by the exclusion for arbitration. Nonetheless, the European Court explained that such proceedings had consequences which undermined the effectiveness of the Regulation, by preventing the attainment of the objectives of unification of the rules of conflict of jurisdiction in civil and commercial matters and the free movement of decisions in those matters, in particular by preventing a court of another Member State from exercising the jurisdiction conferred on it by the Regulation. For the Italian action claiming damages in tort fell within the Regulation, and consequently a preliminary issue concerning the applicability of an arbitration agreement, raised as an incidental question to contest the jurisdiction of the Italian court, also fell within its scope.[141] Thus, the objection of lack of jurisdiction, raised by the shipowner before the Italian court on the basis of the existence and validity of an arbitration agreement, fell within the scope of the Regulation, and it was therefore exclusively for that court to rule on that objection and on its own jurisdiction, pursuant to Articles 1(2)(d) and 5(3) of the Regulation. Accordingly, the use of an anti-suit injunction to prevent a court of a Member State, which normally had jurisdiction to resolve a dispute under Article 5(3) of the Regulation, from ruling, in accordance with Article 1(2)(d) of the Regulation, on the very applicability of the Regulation to the dispute brought before it, necessarily amounted to stripping that court of the power to rule on its own jurisdiction under the Regulation.

Thus, such an anti-suit injunction was contrary to the general principle established by the Court's decisions that under the Regulation every court seised itself determines, under the rules applicable to it, whether it has jurisdiction to resolve the dispute before it, and that the Regulation does not authorise the jurisdiction of a court of a Member State to be reviewed by a court in another Member State. Since jurisdiction is determined directly by the rules laid down by the regulation, including those relating to its scope of application, in no case is a court of one Member State in a better position to determine whether the court of another Member State has jurisdiction. Moreover, in obstructing the court of another Member State in the exercise of the powers conferred on it by the Regulation, to decide, on the basis of the rules defining its material scope, including Article 1(2)(d), whether the Regulation is applicable, such an

---

140    See *The Front Comor* [2005] EWHC 454 (Colman J) and [2007] UKHL 4.

141    See also *Youell v La Reunion Aerienne* [2009] EWCA Civ 175 (CA); and *DHL GBS v Fallimento Finmatica* [2009] EWHC 291 (Comm) (Tomlinson J).

anti-suit injunction also runs counter to the trust which the Member States accord to one another's legal systems and judicial institutions and on which the system of jurisdiction under the Regulation is based.

The European Court added that if by means of an anti-suit injunction the Italian court were prevented from examining itself the preliminary issue of the validity or the applicability of the arbitration agreement, a party could avoid the proceedings merely by relying on that agreement, and the claimant, who considered that the agreement was void, inoperative or incapable of being performed, would thus be barred from access to the court before which it brought proceedings under Article 5(3) of the Regulation, and would therefore be deprived of a form of judicial protection to which it was entitled. The Court also considered that its conclusion was supported by Article II(3) of the New York Convention, by which it is the court of a Contracting State which is seised of an action in a matter in respect of which the parties have made an arbitration agreement that will, at the request of one of the parties, refer the parties to arbitration, unless it finds that the said agreement is null and void, inoperative or incapable of being performed.

But, as was recognised by Cooke J in *Shashoua v Sharma*,[142] the ruling in *Allianz* does not prevent the English court from granting an anti-suit injunction against proceedings in a non-member country which are designed to challenge or otherwise interfere with an English arbitration.

**Possible reform**

With regard to arbitration, in its Report and Green Paper of 21st April 2009,[143] the EC Commission adopts a radical approach to the interface between the Regulation and arbitration. The Commission accepts that the New York Convention 1958 should remain the basic starting point, but it also suggests that the exclusion of arbitration from the scope of the Brussels I Regulation by Article 1(2)(d) should be deleted, and various specific points relating to arbitration should be addressed in the Regulation.

Thus court proceedings in support of arbitration would come within the scope of the Regulation, and legal certainty could be enhanced by the adoption of a special rule allocating exclusive jurisdiction over such proceedings to the courts of the Member State of the place of arbitration. Moreover, all the jurisdictional rules of the Regulation would apply to the issuance of provisional measures in support of arbitration.

Further, the deletion of the exception would allow the recognition of judgments deciding on the validity of an arbitration agreement, and clarify the recognition and enforcement of judgments merging an arbitration award. It could also ensure the recognition of a judgment setting aside an arbitral award. This could prevent parallel proceedings between courts and arbitral tribunals where the agreement is held invalid in one Member State and valid in another.

In addition, the co-ordination between proceedings concerning the validity of an arbitration agreement before a court and an arbitral tribunal could be addressed. Thus, priority could be given to the courts of the Member State where the arbitration takes place to decide on the existence, validity, and scope of an arbitration agreement, and a uniform conflict rule

---

[142]   [2009] EWHC 957 (Comm).
[143]   COM(2009) 174 final, at section 3.7, and COM(2009) 175 final, at question 7.

concerning the validity of arbitration agreements, referring to the law of the State of the place of arbitration, could reduce the risk that an agreement is considered valid in one Member State and invalid in another.

Further, arbitral awards which are enforceable under the New York Convention could benefit from the adoption of a rule allowing the refusal of enforcement to a judgment which is irreconcilable with such an award. Another possible provision could grant to the Member State where an arbitral award was given exclusive competence to certify the enforceability of the award as well as its procedural fairness, after which the award would freely circulate in the Community.

It remains to be seen how far the radical suggestions made by the Commission will obtain support.

## External Judgments

A further exclusion was created by the decision of the European Court in *Owens Bank v Bracco*,[144] where it established that the Brussels I Regulation does not apply to proceedings, or issues arising in proceedings, in Member States concerning the recognition and enforcement of judgments given in non-member States. It made clear that Brussels I Regulation as a whole is inapplicable to such proceedings. Thus Articles 27–30, on simultaneous proceedings in different Member States concerning similar or related claims, did not apply to concurrent proceedings in Italy and England seeking enforcement of a judgment given in St Vincent, even though fraud in obtaining the St Vincent judgment was relied on as a defence in both the Italian and the English proceedings seeking its enforcement. In reaching this (perhaps surprising) conclusion, the European Court did not rely on Article 1 of the Regulation, but on inferences from Articles 33–5 and 38 and the Jenard Report.[145]

## Ordering Costs against a Non-party

In *The Ikarian Reefer (No 2)*,[146] Rix J held that an English application for the costs of litigation, made under s 4 of the Courts and Legal Services Act 1990 against a non-party to the litigation (such as a controlling shareholder of a plaintiff company), is outside the scope of Chapter II of the Brussels I Regulation, in view of its incidental character. The Court of Appeal (per Waller LJ) were inclined to agree that such a proceeding does not involve 'suing' the non-party, so as to fall within the scope of Chapter II, since it does not involve the pursuit of a substantive cause of action, but only the making of orders ancillary to substantive proceedings already pending before the court. This seems very doubtful, especially in view of the definition of a judgment, in Article 32, as including a determination of costs. However, Waller LJ held, in the alternative, that if Chapter II does apply to such an application, it counts as a third-party proceeding, within Article 6(2).

---

[144] Case C-129/92, [1994] ECR I-117.
[145] At p. 15.
[146] [2000] 1 WLR 603 (CA), affirming [1999] 2 Lloyd's Rep 621 (Rix J).

## SPECIALISED CONVENTIONS AND COMMUNITY MEASURES

### Specialised Conventions

Article 71 of the Brussels I Regulation governs its relationship with international conventions which regulate civil jurisdiction or judgments in respect of particular matters ('specialised conventions'). There are many existing specialised conventions, especially in relation to international carriage[147] or transport,[148] nuclear incidents,[149] familial maintenance,[150] and arbitration.[151]

Article 71 of the Brussels I Regulation replaces Article 57(1)–(2) of the Brussels Convention. But while Article 57 of the Brussels Convention applied even where a Member State became a party to a specialised convention after it had become a party to the Brussels Convention, Article 71 of the Regulation is confined to existing specialised conventions, to which Member States are already party. In future, the negotiation of specialised conventions is a matter for the Community institutions.[152] Article 57(1) of the Lugano Convention 1988, and Article 67(1) of the Lugano Convention 2007, accord with the Brussels Convention in including future specialised conventions within their scope.

By Article 71 of the Brussels I Regulation, where one or more of the Member States is also a party to a specialised convention, then, insofar as there is conflict between the provisions of the Regulation and the specialised convention, the specialised convention prevails over the Regulation. As regards direct jurisdiction, the effect of Article 71(1) and (2)(a)[153] is that, in

---

[147]    See, for example, on carriage by air, the Warsaw Convention (1929), the Hague Protocol (1955), the Guadalajara Convention (1961), and the Montreal Protocols (1975); on carriage by rail, the Berne Convention (1980); and on carriage by road, the Geneva Convention on the Contract for the International Carriage of Goods by Road (1956), which is commonly referred to as the CMR Convention, and the Geneva Convention on the Contract for the International Carriage of Passengers and Luggage (1973), which is commonly referred to as the CVR Convention. As regards jurisdiction to entertain claims arising out of carriage by road, Article 31(1) of the CMR Convention enables claims by or against an assignee (such as a cargo-insurer) to be brought at the same place as corresponding claims by or against his assignor, but claims against an assignee cannot be brought at its own ordinary residence or principal place of business as such; see *Hatzl v XL Insurance* [2009] EWCA Civ 223.

[148]    See, for example, the Brussels Convention on Certain Rules concerning Civil Jurisdiction in Matters of Collision (1952); the Brussels Convention relating to the Arrest of Seagoing Ships (1952); the Brussels Convention on Civil Liability for Oil Pollution Damage (1969) and amending Protocol (1976); and on employment of crew of ships or aircraft, the European Convention on Consular Functions (1967).

[149]    See the Paris, Supplementary and Vienna Conventions (1960–3) and the Joint Protocol (1988).

[150]    See the Hague Convention of 2nd October 1973 on the Recognition and Enforcement of Decisions relating to Maintenance Obligations, to which nineteen of the thirty EU Member States or Lugano Convention countries are party.

[151]    See the New York Convention on the Recognition and Enforcement of Foreign Arbitral Awards (1958).

[152]    See also para 2 of the First Joint Statement of the EC Council and Commission, made on the adoption of the Regulation, which declares that, since it may sometimes be useful to draw up specific rules on particular matters, the Council and Commission will pay particular attention to the possibility of engaging in negotiations with a view to the conclusion of international agreements in some of these areas; see Council doc 14139/00, JUSTCIV 137, of 14th December 2000.

[153]    These provisions of the Brussels I Regulation correspond to Article 57(1) and (2)(a) of the

a Member State which has become party to a specialised convention, in the event of conflict the provisions of the specialised convention prevail over Chapter II of the Regulation, even where the defendant is domiciled in another Member State which is not a party to the specialised convention.[154] By way of exception, Article 71(2)(a) makes Article 26 of the Regulation applicable in any event. Article 26 requires a court in certain cases to examine its jurisdiction of its own motion and to stay its proceedings until adequate steps have been taken to notify the defendant of them. But, when verifying its jurisdiction of its own motion under Article 26(1) over a defendant who is domiciled in another Member State and has failed to enter an appearance, a court must take account of the rules of jurisdiction laid down by specialised conventions to which the forum State is a party.[155]

Moreover, in *The Maciej Rataj*,[156] the European Court emphasised that Article 71 precludes the application of the Regulation only in relation to issues which are actually governed by a specialised convention, and accordingly ruled that Articles 27 and 28 of the Regulation, on concurrent actions in different Member States in respect of similar or related claims, remain applicable in cases where the existence of jurisdiction is governed by a specialised convention (such as the Brussels Convention of 1952 on the Arrest of Seagoing Ships), but the specialised convention contains no provision dealing with concurrent actions.[157] Similarly, as Simon J held in *Sony v RH Freight Services*,[158] where a specialised convention (such as the CMR Convention) contains a provision dealing with similar actions, but contains no provision dealing with related actions, Article 28 of the Brussels I Regulation remains applicable to related actions.

As regards recognition and enforcement, the effect of Article 71(1) and (2)(b) of the Brussels I Regulation[159] is as follows. A judgment given by a court of a Member State in the exercise of jurisdiction provided for in a specialised convention must be recognised and enforced in the other Member States in accordance with Chapter III of the Regulation. Thus,

---

Brussels Convention; Article 57(1) and (2) of the Lugano Convention 1988; and Article 67(1) and (2) of the Lugano Convention 2007.

[154]    In *The Po* [1991] 2 Lloyd's Rep 206, the English Court of Appeal held that the effect of Article 71 is to preserve English jurisdiction in cases where it is conferred on one ground by an unimplemented provision of a specialised convention, and on another ground by a provision of traditional English law; as was the case, in connection with the Brussels Convention of 10th May 1952 on Civil Jurisdiction in Matters of Collision, where the action was in respect of a maritime collision and the ship was served but was not arrested because security was given.

[155]    See Case C-148/03: *Nürnberger Allgemeine Versicherungs v Portbridge Transport International* [2004] ECR I-10327.

[156]    Case C-406/92, [1994] ECR I-5439.

[157]    Cf. *The Bergen* [1997] 1 Lloyd's Rep 380, where Clarke J held that conflict does exist between Article 7 of the Arrest Convention, which enables jurisdiction to be founded on the arrest of a vessel, and Article 23 of the Regulation, by which an agreement on jurisdiction excludes the jurisdiction of courts of other Member States than that of the chosen court(s). See also, as regards the loss of goods in the course of carriage by road, *Merzario v Leitner* [2001] 1 Lloyd's Rep 490, where the Court of Appeal (overruling *Frans Maas Logistics v CDR Trucking* [1999] 2 Lloyd's Rep 179) held that Article 31(2) of the CMR Convention applies even if one of the actions is for a declaration of non-liability, and that it uses the same concepts of pendency and of similarity of claims as Article 21 of the Brussels Convention.

[158]    [2007] All ER (D) 310 (Feb).

[159]    These provisions correspond to Article 57(1) and (2)(b) of the Brussels Convention; Article 57(1), (3) and (5) of the Lugano Convention 1988; and Article 67(3) and (5) of the Lugano Convention 2007.

if a specialised convention deals only with direct jurisdiction, or if it has been adopted only by the State of origin and not by the State addressed, Chapter III of the Regulation applies to judgments given in pursuance of the specialised convention in the same way as it applies to other judgments, and the specialised convention has no effect at the stage of recognition and enforcement. But the situation is more complex if a specialised convention dealing with recognition and enforcement has been adopted both by the State of origin and by the State addressed. Then, insofar as there is conflict in respect of the substantive requirements for recognition and enforcement, those laid down by the specialised convention prevail over those contained in Chapter III of the Regulation. As regards the procedure for obtaining recognition or enforcement, the applicant is entitled to use the procedure provided for by Chapter III, unless the specialised convention insists on a different procedure which it defines. Even if the specialised convention also provides for a procedure, the applicant normally has the option of using either the procedure provided for by Chapter III or that provided for by the specialised convention.[160]

In *TNT v AXA*,[161] the European Court restricted the operation of specialised conventions under Article 71 in cases internal to the European Union, by insisting, as conditions for the application in such cases of the rules on jurisdiction and judgments laid down by a specialised convention, that such rules must be highly predictable, facilitate the sound administration of justice, and enable the risk of concurrent proceedings to be minimised, and that they must ensure, under conditions at least as favourable as those provided for by the Brussels I Regulation, the free movement of judgments in civil and commercial matters and mutual trust in the administration of justice in the European Union. The case involved a contract for the carriage of goods by road, within the scope of the CMR Convention, and an argument that under Article 31 of the CMR Convention a German judgment should not be enforced in the Netherlands because it had been given in the face of similar proceedings pending in the Netherlands. Such an objection is not admissible under Chapter III of the Brussels I Regulation.

Under the Lugano Convention 1988, Article 57(4) provides an additional ground for refusal of recognition and enforcement of judgments given in the exercise of jurisdiction provided for in a specialised convention. This ground applies where the State addressed is not a contracting party to the relevant specialised convention, and the person against whom recognition or enforcement is sought is domiciled in the State addressed, and the judgment is not otherwise recognisable or enforceable under any rule of law in the State addressed. This ground is retained by Article 67(4) of the Lugano Convention 2007, and is extended to cases where the State addressed is an EU Member State, and the relevant specialised convention would have to be concluded by the European Union, and the person against whom recognition or enforcement is sought is domiciled in any EU Member State.

**Specialised European Union Instruments**

Article 67 of the Brussels I Regulation specifies that the Regulation does not prejudice the application of provisions governing jurisdiction and the recognition and enforcement of judg-

---

[160]    See the Schlosser Report at pp. 139–41.
[161]    Case C-533/08, [2010] All ER (D) 47 (May).

ments in specific matters which are contained in European Union instruments or in national legislation harmonised pursuant to such instruments. This echoes Article 57(3) of the Brussels Convention, and ensures that, in the event of conflict between the Brussels I Regulation and provisions as to jurisdiction or judgments in respect of particular matters contained in other, existing or future, acts of European Union institutions (such as regulations or directives), the provisions of the other European Union act will prevail.

Such a provision is contained in Article 6 of Directive 96/71, on the posting of workers in the framework of the provision of services,[162] which enables proceedings designed to enforce the terms and conditions of employment guaranteed by the Directive to be instituted in the Member State to which the worker in question was posted. There are also such provisions in Regulation 207/2009 on the Community trade mark,[163] in Regulation 2100/94 on the Community plant variety right,[164] and in Regulation 6/2002 on Community designs.[165]

As regards proceedings concerning the winding-up or reorganisation of an insurance undertaking which is regulated by an EC Member State or an EEA country under EC Directive 2001/17, on the reorganisation and winding-up of insurance undertakings,[166] the Directive confers exclusive jurisdiction on the courts of the regulating State. The Directive applies whether the insurance undertaking is solvent or insolvent; and accordingly, where the insurance undertaking is solvent, the Directive prevails over the Brussels I Regulation in accordance with Article 67 of the Regulation, so that Article 22(2) of the Regulation does not apply.[167]

For the purposes of the Lugano Convention 1988, its Third Protocol assimilates provisions on jurisdiction or judgments in respect of particular matters contained in existing or future acts of European Union institutions to specialised conventions within Article 57 of the Convention. It adds, however, that if a Contracting State considers that such a provision is incompatible with the Lugano Convention 1988, the Contracting States will promptly consider amending the Convention under Article 66. For the purposes of the Lugano Convention 2007, corresponding rules are specified by its Third Protocol, which also extends their operation to national legislative provisions which transpose acts of European Union institutions.

## TEMPORAL SCOPE

The main rule on the temporal scope of the Brussels I Regulation is laid down by Article 66(1), which provides that the Regulation applies only to legal proceedings instituted, and to documents formally drawn up or registered as authentic instruments, after its entry into force.[168] The commencement date of the Regulation is 1st March 2002 for the fourteen then

---

[162]  [1997] OJ L18/1.
[163]  [2009] OJ L78/1; replacing Regulation 40/94, [1994] OJ L11/1. See pp. 157–60 below.
[164]  [1994] OJ L227/1. See pp. 160–61 below.
[165]  [2002] OJ L3/1. See pp. 161–2 below.
[166]  [2001] OJ L110/28.
[167]  See *Re Sovereign Marine and General Insurance Co Ltd* [2007] 1 BCLC 228 (Warren J).
[168]  In the Brussels Convention, corresponding provision is made by Article 54(1), which provides that the Convention applies only to legal proceedings instituted, and to documents formally drawn up

Member States other than Denmark; 1st May 2004 for the ten States which joined the European Community on that date; 1st January 2007 for Bulgaria and Romania; and 1st July 2007 for Denmark. Probably, proceedings are to be regarded for this purpose as instituted on the date of seisin, determined in accordance with the rules laid down by Article 30 for the determination of priority between concurrent proceedings, and thus usually on the date on which the instituting document is lodged with the court.[169]

Accordingly, as regards direct jurisdiction, Chapter II of the Regulation applies only to proceedings instituted in a court of a Member State after its entry into force in that State.[170] But it applies even if the cause of action sued on arose before that date.[171] Moreover, in applying Chapter II (which discriminates in favour of defendants domiciled in a Member State), a court must treat as Member States those for which the Regulation had entered into force by the date on which the proceedings in question were instituted.

As regards the recognition and enforcement of judgments between Member States, Chapter III of the Regulation is limited by Article 66 to judgments given after its entry into force for both the Member State of origin and the Member State addressed.[172] By Article 66(1) and (2)(a), Chapter III has full operation where the judgment was given after the entry into force of the Regulation for both of the States involved, and the original proceedings were instituted after the entry into force of either the Regulation itself, or the Brussels Convention, or the Lugano Convention 1988, for each of those States.[173]

Where the judgment was given after the entry into force of the Regulation for both of the States involved, but at the institution of the original proceedings neither the Regulation itself, nor the Brussels Convention, nor the Lugano Convention 1988, had entered into force for both of the States, Chapter III applies, but it operates subject to a transitional provision laid down by Article 66(2)(b). This makes recognition and enforcement subject to a further requirement, that the jurisdiction of the original court should have been founded upon rules which accorded with those provided for either in Chapter II of the Regulation, or in a convention concluded between the Member State of origin and the Member State addressed which was in force when the proceedings were instituted.[174] As regards the United Kingdom, this

---

or registered as authentic instruments, after its entry into force in the State of origin and, where recognition or enforcement of a judgment or authentic instruments is sought, in the State addressed. Similar provision is also made by Article 34(1) of the 1978 Convention; Article 12(1) of the 1982 Convention; Article 29(1) of the 1989 Convention; Article 13(1) of the 1996 Convention; Article 9(1) of the Agreement between the European Community and Denmark; Article 54(1) of the Lugano Convention 1988; and Article 63(1) of the Lugano Convention 2007.

[169]    On Article 30, see pp. 196–7 below.

[170]    Chapter II extends to a counterclaim, made after the relevant commencement date, in an action instituted before that date; see *Aiglon v Gau Shan* [1993] 1 Lloyd's Rep 164 (Hirst J). On the problem of concurrent actions in courts of different Member States, one commenced before, and the other after, the relevant commencement date, see Case C-163/95: *Von Horn v Cinnamond* [1997] ECR I-5451, considered at p. 198 below.

[171]    See Case 25/79: *Sanicentral v Collin* [1979] ECR 3423.

[172]    If the judgment was given before that date, the Brussels Convention, the Lugano Convention 1988, and the earlier bilateral conventions listed in Article 69 of the Regulation, continue to apply. See Articles 68–70 of the Regulation, and *T v L* [2009] ILPr 5 (Irish Supreme Court), affirming *DT v FL* [2007] ILPr 56 (McKechnie J).

[173]    Similar provision is made by Article 9(1) and (2)(a) of the Agreement between the European Community and Denmark; and Article 63(1) and (2)(a) of the Lugano Convention 2007.

[174]    See pp. 236–7 below. For similar provisions, see Article 54(2) of the Brussels Convention;

provision is likely to be of importance in relation to judgments from the Member States which joined the European Community in 2004 or 2007, other than Poland.

As regards the enforcement of authentic instruments and court settlements, Chapter IV of the Regulation applies only to documents formally drawn up or registered as authentic instruments, and settlements approved by a court, after its entry into force in both the State of origin and the State addressed.[175]

---

Article 34(3) of the 1978 Convention; Article 12(2) of the 1982 Convention; Article 29(2) of the 1989 Convention; Article 13(2) of the 1996 Convention; Article 9(2)(b) of the Agreement between the European Community and Denmark; Article 54(2) of the Lugano Convention 1988; and Article 63(2)(b) of the Lugano Convention 2007.

[175] See Article 66(1). See also the provisons mentioned in note 168 above.

*Table 2.1   Commencement dates of the Brussels Convention, the Lugano Convention 1988, and the Brussels I Regulation*

| Country | Brussels Convention, 1968 version | Brussels Convention, 1978 version | Brussels Convention, 1982 version | Brussels Convention, 1989 version | Brussels Convention, 1996 version | Lugano Convention, 1988 | Brussels I Regulation | Lugano Convention, 2007 |
|---|---|---|---|---|---|---|---|---|
| France | Feb 1973 | Nov 1986 | Oct 1989 | Feb 1991 | Aug 2000 | Jan 1992 | March 2002 | Jan 2010 |
| Germany | Feb 1973 | Nov 1986 | Oct 1989 | Dec 1994 | Jan 1999 | March 1995 | March 2002 | Jan 2010 |
| Italy | Feb 1973 | Nov 1986 | Oct 1989 | May 1992 | June 1999 | Dec 1992 | March 2002 | Jan 2010 |
| Belgium | Feb 1973 | Nov 1986 | Oct 1989 | Oct 1997 | Aug 2004 | Oct 1997 | March 2002 | Jan 2010 |
| Netherlands | Feb 1973 | Nov 1986 | Oct 1989 | Feb 1991 | Dec 1998 | Jan 1992 | March 2002 | Jan 2010 |
| Luxembourg | Feb 1973 | Nov 1986 | Oct 1989 | Feb 1992 | May 2000 | Feb 1992 | March 2002 | Jan 2010 |
| Denmark | – | Nov 1986 | Oct 1989 | March 1996 | Dec 1998 | March 1996 | March 2002 | Jan 2010 |
| United Kingdom | – | Jan 1987 | Oct 1989 | Dec 1991 | Jan 2001 | May 1992 | July 2007 | Jan 2010 |
| Ireland | | June 1988 | Oct 1989 | Dec 1993 | Dec 1999 | Dec 1993 | March 2002 | Jan 2010 |
| Greece | | – | Oct 1989 | July 1992 | Oct 1999 | Sept 1997 | March 2002 | Jan 2010 |
| Spain | | – | – | Feb 1991 | April 1999 | Nov 1994 | March 2002 | Jan 2010 |
| Portugal | | – | – | July 1992 | Oct 1999 | July 1992 | March 2002 | Jan 2010 |
| Austria | | – | – | – | Dec 1998 | Sept 1996 | March 2002 | Jan 2010 |
| Finland | | – | – | – | April 1999 | July 1993 | March 2002 | Jan 2010 |
| Sweden | | – | – | – | Jan 1999 | Jan 1993 | March 2002 | Jan 2010 |
| Switzerland | | – | – | – | – | Jan 1992 | – | – |
| Norway | | – | – | – | – | May 1993 | – | Jan 2010 |
| Iceland | | – | – | – | – | Dec 1995 | – | – |
| Poland | | – | – | – | – | Feb 2000 | May 2004 | Jan 2010 |
| Hungary | | – | – | – | – | – | May 2004 | Jan 2010 |

| Country | | | | | | | | | May 2004 | Jan 2010 |
|---|---|---|---|---|---|---|---|---|---|---|
| Czech Republic | — | — | — | — | — | — | — | — | May 2004 | Jan 2010 |
| Slovakia | — | — | — | — | — | — | — | — | May 2004 | Jan 2010 |
| Slovenia | — | — | — | — | — | — | — | — | May 2004 | Jan 2010 |
| Latvia | — | — | — | — | — | — | — | — | May 2004 | Jan 2010 |
| Lithuania | — | — | — | — | — | — | — | — | May 2004 | Jan 2010 |
| Estonia | — | — | — | — | — | — | — | — | May 2004 | Jan 2010 |
| Malta | — | — | — | — | — | — | — | — | May 2004 | Jan 2010 |
| Cyprus | — | — | — | — | — | — | — | — | May 2004 | Jan 2010 |
| Bulgaria | — | — | — | — | — | — | — | — | Jan 2007 | Jan 2010 |
| Romania | — | — | — | — | — | — | — | — | Jan 2007 | Jan 2010 |

*Note*: In each case, the relevant date is the beginning of the month stated.

# 3. Domicile

## THE GENERAL RULES ON DIRECT JURISDICTION

The principal connecting-factor used by Chapter II of the Brussels I Regulation is the defendant's domicile at the institution of the proceedings. The basic rules on direct jurisdiction are laid down by Articles 2–4 of the Regulation, which echo Articles 2–4 of the Brussels Convention without substantial alteration.[1] Where the defendant is domiciled in a Member State, Article 2 of the Regulation confers jurisdiction on the courts of that State,[2] and Article 3 deprives the courts of the other Member States of jurisdiction.[3] Where the defendant is not domiciled in any Member State, Article 4 remits the jurisdiction of the courts of each Member State to the law of the State whose court is seised.[4] These basic rules are subject to the exceptions specified in the remaining provisions of Chapter II.

In this context, Recitals 8 and 9 to the Regulation explain that common rules on jurisdiction should, in principle, apply when the defendant is domiciled in a Member State; and that a defendant not domiciled in a Member State is in general subject to national rules of jurisdiction applicable in the Member State of the court seised. Recitals 11 and 12 add that the rules of jurisdiction must be highly predictable and founded on the principle that jurisdiction is generally based on the defendant's domicile; that jurisdiction must always be available on this ground save in a few well-defined situations in which the subject-matter of the litigation or the autonomy of the parties warrants a different linking factor; and that, in addition to the defendant's domicile, there should be alternative grounds of jurisdiction based on a close link between the court and the action or in order to facilitate the sound administration of justice.

---

[1]    In the revision negotiations which eventually led to the Brussels I Regulation, the Council Working Party considered a proposal to substitute habitual residence for domicile throughout the Convention, but ultimately rejected the proposal. Compare the final draft of April 1999 (Council doc 7700/99, JUSTCIV 60) with the earlier draft of January 1999 (Council doc 5202/99, JUSTCIV 1).

[2]    Article 2 provides: '(1) Subject to this Regulation, persons domiciled in a Member State shall, whatever their nationality, be sued in the courts of that Member State. (2) Persons who are not nationals of the Member State in which they are domiciled shall be governed by the rules of jurisdiction applicable to nationals of that State'.

[3]    Article 3(1) provides: 'Persons domiciled in a Member State may be sued in the courts of another Member State only by virtue of the rules set out in Sections 2 to 7 of this Chapter'. Article 3(2) adds: 'In particular the rules of national jurisdiction set out in Annex I shall not be applicable as against them'.

[4]    Article 4 provides: '(1) If the defendant is not domiciled in a Member State, the jurisdiction of the courts of each Member State shall, subject to Articles 22 and 23, be determined by the law of that Member State. (2) As against such a defendant, any person domiciled in a Member State may, whatever his nationality, avail himself in that State of the rules of jurisdiction there in force, and in particular those specified in Annex I, in the same way as the nationals of that State.'

The rationale of the general rule in favour of the defendant's domicile was considered by the European Court in *Handte v TMCS*.[5] It explained that the rule reflects the purpose of strengthening the legal protection of persons established within the Community, and rests on an assumption that normally it is in the courts of his domicile that a defendant can most easily conduct his defence. The Court added that the provisions enabling a defendant to be sued in a Member State other than that of his domicile must be interpreted in such a way as to enable a normally well-informed defendant reasonably to predict the courts before which he may be sued.[6]

This preference for defendants over plaintiffs, which has deep historical roots, may, however, have a rationale which goes beyond mere convenience in the conduct of litigation. It appears to be linked with such general rules as that which places on the plaintiff the burden of proving his claim, and to reflect a primordial legal assumption that complaints should be presumed to be unjustified. It is considered better, where the truth cannot be ascertained with reasonable certainty, that the courts should not intervene. Failure to rectify injustice is regarded as more tolerable than positive action imposing injustice. In the present context, such considerations give rise to a general rule that the plaintiff must establish his case to the satisfaction of the court in whose goodwill towards him the defendant would presumably have most confidence. Another reason for the rule is that it is presumably at his domicile that the defendant keeps most of his assets and that enforcement against his person or property can most easily be effected. Thus the rule tends to concentrate both adjudication of the merits and enforcement of the judgment in the same country, thereby avoiding unnecessary procedural complications.

Although the Regulation is not explicit on the point, it is clear that the references in Chapter II are to the defendant's domicile at the institution of the proceedings in question; more precisely, at the date of the issue (rather than the service) of the claim form which originates the action.[7]

It seems regrettable, however, that in the unusual case where the defendant changes his domicile between the time when the cause of action arises and that of the institution of the proceedings, the Regulation declines to offer the plaintiff the choice of suing at either of those domiciles. Provision of such an option might have enabled it to dispense with some of the less obviously appropriate options sometimes offered to a plaintiff, such as to sue at the place of performance of a contractual obligation under Article 5(1).

In contrast, the domicile of the plaintiff is of minor importance under Chapter II of the Brussels I Regulation. In *Group Josi v UGIC*,[8] which involved a claim by a Canadian insurer against a Belgian reinsurer, the European Court ruled that Chapter II of the Regulation is applicable where the defendant is domiciled in a Member State, even if the plaintiff is domiciled in a non-member country; and that where the defendant is domiciled in a Member State,

---

5    Case C-26/91, [1992] ECR I-3967.

6    See also Case C-440/97: *Groupe Concorde v 'The Suhadiwarno Panjan'* [1999] ECR I-6307.

7    See *Canada Trust v Stolzenberg (No 2)* [2002] 1 AC 1 (HL); *Petrotrade v Smith* [1998] 2 All ER 346 (Thomas J); *Grupo Torras v Al-Sabah* [1995] 1 Lloyd's Rep 374 (Mance J); and *Cherney v Deripaska* [2007] 2 All ER (Comm) 785 (Langley J). See also Article 30, on the date on which a court is regarded as seised for the purpose of priority between concurrent actions; considered at pp. 196–7 below.

8    Case C-412/98, [2000] ECR I-5925.

the operation of Chapter II is affected by the plaintiff's domicile only in the exceptional cases where it expressly so provides. Such express provisions are found only in Articles 5(2), 9(1)(b), and 16(1), which refer respectively to the domicile of a maintenance claimant, an insurance policy-holder, and a consumer.

Where the defendant is not domiciled in a Member State, a casual dictum of the European Court in *Von Horn v Cinnamond*[9] suggests that Article 4 of the Regulation, which remits jurisdiction to the lex fori, does not apply unless the plaintiff is domiciled in a Member State. But this extraordinary suggestion seems incompatible with the Court's subsequent reasoning in *Owusu v Jackson*[10] that, although the application of Chapter II of the Regulation is dependent on the existence of an international element, such an element may arise from a connection with a non-member country; and in Opinion 1/03 (on the new Lugano Convention)[11] that Article 4(1) of the Brussels I Regulation forms part of the system implemented by the Regulation, since it resolves the situation envisaged by reference to the legislation of the forum State.

## LOCAL DEFENDANTS

The general rule laid down by Article 2 of the Brussels I Regulation, conferring jurisdiction on the courts of the Member State in which the defendant is domiciled,[12] is subject to very limited exceptions. The rule applies even if the dispute has no other connection with the State in question.

Three exceptions are specified by Chapter II of the Regulation. Firstly, jurisdiction based on the defendant's domicile is excluded where, by reason of its subject-matter (such as proprietary rights in land), the dispute falls within Article 22, which confers exclusive jurisdiction on the courts of another Member State (such as the State in which the land in question is situated). Secondly, jurisdiction based on domicile may be excluded under Article 23 by an agreement between the parties, conferring exclusive jurisdiction on a designated court or courts of another Member State. Thirdly, the exercise of jurisdiction based on domicile may be prevented by Articles 27 and 28, where the court of the defendant's domicile is seised of an action after a court of another Member State has been seised of a similar or related action.

### Internal Allocation

Where the defendant is sued in the Member State in which he is domiciled, Chapter II of the Regulation is indifferent as to the allocation of jurisdiction between the courts for the various territories or districts within that State. Such allocation is left to the law of the State in question, except that Article 2(2) prevents it from taking the defendant's nationality into account.

---

[9]    Case C-163/95, [1997] ECR I-5451, at para 25. The case involved concurrent actions in Portugal and England against a defendant domiciled in England.

[10]    Case C-281/02, [2005] ECR I-1383.

[11]    [2006] ECR I-1145, at para 148.

[12]    Similarly, in the case of insurance, consumer and employment contracts, Articles 9(1)(a), 12(1), 16, 19(1) and 20(1) confer jurisdiction on the courts of the defendant's domicile.

Accordingly, in the United Kingdom, s 16 and Schedule 4 of the Civil Jurisdiction and Judgments Act 1982 (as amended)[13] provide for the allocation of jurisdiction over defendants domiciled in the United Kingdom between the English, Scottish and Northern Irish courts by means of a modified version of Chapter II of the Brussels I Regulation.[14] These provisions are designed largely to treat each part of the United Kingdom as if it were a separate Member State, and thus to assimilate English jurisdiction over a defendant domiciled in Scotland to English jurisdiction over a defendant domiciled in France. But such assimilation is less than total, since (for example) Schedule 4 omits any provisions corresponding to Articles 8–14 of the Regulation (on insurance), or to Articles 27–30 (on similar or related actions), and rule 3(a) of the Schedule (on jurisdiction based on the place of performance of a contractual obligation) continues to echo Article 5(1) of the Brussels Convention rather than Article 5(1) of the Brussels I Regulation. It is also permissible for an English court, when competent under Schedule 4, to decline jurisdiction in its discretion on grounds of forum non conveniens in favour of a Scottish or Northern Irish court which is also competent under the Schedule, even if the English court is the court first or solely seised.[15]

In *Kleinwort Benson v Glasgow City Council*,[16] the European Court refused to rule on a reference from an English court for interpretation in a case where the applicable provisions were those of the modified version contained in Schedule 4. However, on reference back,[17] the House of Lords emphasised that a provision of Schedule 4 will rarely bear a materially different meaning from the corresponding provision in Chapter II of the Regulation; and in cases arising under Schedule 4 the relevant decisions of the European Court must be taken fully into account.

**Forum Non Conveniens**

As the Schlosser Report makes clear,[18] Chapter II of the Brussels I Regulation is based on the principle, generally accepted in the laws of the Continental European countries, that a competent court, properly seised of an action, is bound to determine the substantive dispute to which the action relates, and has no discretion to decline jurisdiction in favour of a foreign court which it considers to be a more appropriate forum for the determination of the dispute.

In contrast, traditional English law (apart from the Brussels Convention and the Brussels I Regulation) contains a doctrine of forum non conveniens, often referred to as the *Spiliada*

---

[13] Especially by the Civil Jurisdiction and Judgments Order 2001 (SI 2001/3929), which was made in the light of the Brussels I Regulation.

[14] Although Gibraltar counts as part of the United Kingdom for the purpose of the Brussels I Regulation, it is not treated as a part of the United Kingdom for the purpose of s 16 and Schedule 4. Instead, by the Civil Jurisdiction and Judgments Act 1982 (Gibraltar) Order 1997 (SI 1997/2602), for this purpose Gibraltar is treated in England, Scotland and Northern Ireland as if it were another Member State.

[15] See *Cumming v Scottish Daily Record* [1995] EMLR 538 (Drake J); *Lennon v Scottish Daily Record* [2004] EMLR 18 (Tugendhat J); and *Sunderland Marine Mutual Insurance Co Ltd v Wiseman* [2007] 2 All ER (Comm) 937 (Langley J).

[16] See Case C-346/93, [1995] ECR I-615.

[17] [1999] AC 153.

[18] At paras 76–81. The mandatory character of Article 2 was clearly recognised by the French Court of Cassation (Social Chamber) in *Grimal v Ameliorair*, 30th April 1997.

doctrine.[19] Under this doctrine, a competent English court has a discretionary power to decline jurisdiction in favour of a foreign court, if it is satisfied that the foreign court is also competent and that it is a more appropriate or suitable forum for the trial of the action, in the light of the interests of all the parties and the ends of justice. It is clear that the traditional English doctrine is in general incompatible with, and therefore displaced by, the Brussels I Regulation. This has been readily accepted by the English courts in cases where the defendant is domiciled in England and the alternative forum is a court of another Member State.[20]

Unfortunately, however, for a long period commencing with its decision in *Re Harrods (Buenos Aires) Ltd*,[21] the English Court of Appeal maintained that the Regulation did not prevent an English court, seised of an action against a defendant domiciled in England, from declining jurisdiction in its discretion in favour of a more appropriate forum, being a court of a non-member country. The Court of Appeal persisted in this view in a series of cases,[22] and even extended the claimed discretion to decline jurisdiction in favour of a court of a non-member country to cases where a defendant domiciled in another Member State was sued in England on the basis of a jurisdiction clause under Article 23,[23] and to cases where a defendant domiciled in another Member State was sued in England under Article 5(1), as the place of contractual performance, or under Article 24, on submission by appearance.[24]

Two of the Court of Appeal decisions declining jurisdiction over an English defendant on grounds of forum non conveniens were reversed by the House of Lords in the exercise of the supposed discretion.[25] In the later of these, *Lubbe v Cape*,[26] Lord Bingham emphasised that, if it had been necessary to decide whether Article 2 prevents the English court from declining jurisdiction over an action brought against an English defendant by a South African plaintiff in respect of injuries received in South Africa, he would have thought it necessary to seek a ruling from the European Court, since he did not consider the answer to be clear. Subsequently, in *Owusu v Jackson*,[27] the Court of Appeal requested a ruling from the European Court as to whether it is inconsistent with the Brussels I Regulation, where a

---

19    The leading case is *The Spiliada* [1987] 1 AC 460. The 1982 Act, by s 49, seeks to preserve the doctrine, insofar as its application is not inconsistent with the Brussels Convention or the Lugano Convention.

20    See *Grupo Torras v Al-Sabah* [1995] 1 Lloyd's Rep 374 (Mance J); *Lafi v Meriden* [2000] 2 Lloyd's Rep 51 (Symons QC); and *Mahme Trust Reg v Lloyds TSB Bank* [2004] 2 Lloyd's Rep 637 (Morritt V-C). See also, in Scotland, *Bank of Scotland v Banque Nationale de Paris* [1996] SLT 103; and, in Ireland, *The Turquoise Bleu* [1996] 1 ILRM 406, and *DC v WOC*, 5th July 2000 (Finnegan J).

21    [1992] Ch 72 (CA).

22    See *The Po* [1991] 2 Lloyd's Rep 206 (CA); *The Nile Rhapsody* [1994] 1 Lloyd's Rep 382 (CA); *Nike v Parker*, 31st October 1994 (CA); *Connelly v RTZ* [1996] QB 361 (CA); *Sarrio v Kuwait Investment Authority* [1997] 1 Lloyd's Rep 113 (CA); *Lubbe v Cape* (No 1) [1999] ILPr 113 (CA), and (No 2) [2000] 1 Lloyd's Rep 139 (CA); *Re Polly Peck International* [1998] 3 All ER 812 (CA); and *Ace Insurance v Zurich Insurance* [2001] 1 Lloyd's Rep 618 (CA). The Court of Appeal's approach was doubted by Lloyd J in *Pearce v Ove Arup* [1997] 3 All ER 31. Cf. *Milor v British Airways* [1996] 3 All ER 537, where the Court of Appeal accepted that the Warsaw Convention on carriage by air excludes any doctrine of forum non conveniens.

23    See *Eli Lilly v Novo Nordisk* [2000] ILPr 73 (CA).

24    See *Ace Insurance v Zurich Insurance* [2001] 1 Lloyd's Rep 618 (CA).

25    See *Connelly v RTZ* [1997] 4 All ER 335 (HL); and *Lubbe v Cape* [2000] 1 WLR 1545 (HL).

26    [2000] 1 WLR 1545 (HL).

27    [2002] ILPr 45 (CA).

claimant contends that jurisdiction is founded on Article 2, for a court of a Member State to exercise a discretionary power, available under its national law, to decline to hear proceedings brought against a person domiciled in that State in favour of the courts of a non-member State, if the jurisdiction of no other Member State is in issue, and the proceedings have no connecting factors to any other Member State. The case involved claims by an English holiday-maker against an English lessor of premises in Jamaica and against Jamaican companies in respect of a beach accident in Jamaica.

In *Harrods*, the Court of Appeal had rejected the views of Hobhouse J in *Berisford v New Hampshire Insurance*,[28] and Potter J in *Arkwright v Bryanston*,[29] that since (apart from Article 4) the Regulation is designed to achieve uniformity and to harmonise the jurisdictional rules of the courts of the Member States, it leaves no room for the application of any discretion to decline jurisdiction by the English courts. The availability of such a discretion would destroy the framework of the Regulation and create lack of uniformity in its interpretation and implementation. The Court of Appeal preferred the assertion of Lawrence Collins[30] that the Member States had no interest in requiring a Member State to exercise a jurisdiction where the competing jurisdiction was in a non-member country. But, as Cheshire and North pointed out,[31] the text of the Regulation shows that it is not simply concerned with jurisdiction as between Member States; and the discretion asserted would undermine uniformity, since English courts would decline jurisdiction in circumstances where most other Member States would accept jurisdiction. One might add that the effect of such a discretionary rejection of jurisdiction would in some cases be to deprive a plaintiff domiciled in another Member State of the only available forum within the Member States, and in all cases to deprive the courts of the other Member States of the opportunity of recognising a decision given by the court which the Regulation regards as the primary appropriate forum. Moreover, the suggestion that the burden of defending himself in an English court might cause serious injustice to a defendant domiciled in England amounts to a grave insult to the English courts, laws and procedures. Thus Cheshire's conclusion that the decision in *Harrods* was 'misguided, if not downright wrong' seemed unduly cautious. Indeed, it was difficult to see any basis for the Court of Appeal's approach in the wording, the scheme or the purposes of the Regulation.

On 1st March 2005, the European Court ruled in *Owusu v Jackson*[32] that the Regulation precludes a court of a Member State from declining the jurisdiction conferred on it by Article 2 on the ground that a court of a non-member State would be a more appropriate forum for the trial of the action, even if the jurisdiction of no other Member State is in issue and the proceedings have no connecting factors to any other Member State.

The European Court accepted that, for the jurisdiction rules of the Regulation to apply at all, the existence of an international element is required. But the involvement of a Member State and a non-member State, for example because the plaintiff and one defendant are domiciled in the first State and the events at issue occurred in the second, makes the legal relationship international in nature and raises questions in the Member State relating to the

---

[28]   [1990] QB 631.

[29]   [1990] 2 QB 649.

[30]   (1990) 106 LQR 535.

[31]   *Cheshire & North's Private International Law*, 13th edition by North and Fawcett (Butterworths, 1999), at pp. 264–6.

[32]   Case C-281/02, [2005] ECR I-1383.

determination of international jurisdiction. Thus Article 2 extends to cases involving relationships between the courts of a single Member State and those of a non-member State, as well as cases involving relationships between the courts of a number of Member States.

The European Court emphasised that Article 2 is mandatory in nature. Respect for the principle of legal certainty would not be fully guaranteed if the court having jurisdiction under the Regulation were allowed to apply the doctrine of forum non conveniens. Application of the doctrine would be liable to undermine the predictability of the rules of jurisdiction laid down by the Regulation, in particular that of Article 2, and consequently to undermine the principle of legal certainty. The legal protection of persons established in the Community would also be undermined. Moreover, to allow use of the doctrine would be likely to affect the uniform application of the rules of jurisdiction contained in the Regulation, since the doctrine is recognised only in a limited number of Member States, and the objective of the Regulation is to lay down common rules to the exclusion of derogating national rules. The Court dismissed as irrelevant various difficulties said to arise from rejection of the doctrine. These related to the expense of the proceedings; the possibility of the defendants recovering their costs in England if the plaintiff's action were dismissed; the logistical difficulties resulting from the geographical distance; the need to assess the merits of the case according to Jamaican standards; the enforceability in Jamaica of a default judgment; and the impossibility of enforcing cross-claims against the other defendants. Such difficulties could not be allowed to override the mandatory nature of the fundamental rule of jurisdiction contained in Article 2.

Thus it is now established that the Regulation precludes a court of a Member State from declining the jurisdiction conferred on it by Article 2 on the ground that a court of a non-member country would be a more appropriate forum for the trial of the action, even if the jurisdiction of no other Member State is in issue and the proceedings have no connection with any other Member State. But, in the United Kingdom, minor controversies remain alive. Thus in *Pacific International Sports Clubs Ltd v Soccer Marketing International Ltd*,[33] Blackburne J asserted that, despite the ruling in *Owusu*, the English court retains a power to grant, on case management grounds, a temporary stay of an action against an English defendant to await the result of proceedings in a non-member country. But he accepted that such stays should be granted only in rare and compelling circumstances.[34]

### Reflexive Effect

The rejection by the European Court in *Owusu v Jackson*[35] of the Court of Appeal's view that the Regulation permits the retention of the *Spiliada* doctrine whenever the more appropriate forum is a court of a non-member country does not entail that no implied exceptions to Article 2

---

[33]   [2009] EWHC 1839 (Ch).

[34]   See also *A v B* [2007] 1 All ER (Comm) 591, where Colman J granted a temporary stay of claims against an English defendant on case management grounds, pending determination of related claims in a Swiss arbitration; and *AG of Zambia v Meer Care & Desai* [2006] EWCA Civ 390, where the Court of Appeal accepted the possibility of staying English civil proceedings until the conclusion of criminal proceedings abroad, but emphasised that this power must be exercised with great care and only where there is a real risk of serious prejudice which may lead to injustice.

[35]   Case C-281/02, [2005] ECR I-1383.

exist at all. As Georges Droz, an observer from the Hague Conference on Private International Law at the negotiating committee which drafted the original version of the Brussels Convention, pointed out as long ago as 1972,[36] it would be reasonable to construe Articles 22, 23, and 27–30 of the Regulation (on exclusive jurisdiction by virtue of subject-matter; on jurisdiction clauses; and on concurrent actions) as having a reflexive effect. In other words, the Regulation should be construed as impliedly permitting a Member State to apply these provisions analogistically in favour of a non-member country. This interpretation would enable a Member State to require or permit its courts to accord a respect equivalent to, or more limited than, that provided for by those provisions in relation to connections with other Member States, where a corresponding connection exists with a non-member country.

Acceptance of the principle of reflexive effect would enable the United Kingdom to preserve the discretion of the English courts to decline jurisdiction in favour of a court of a non-member country, despite the defendant's English domicile, in three situations. Firstly, where the subject-matter of the dispute falls within Article 22, on exclusive jurisdiction by virtue of subject-matter, but the connection envisaged by Article 22 is with a non-member country; for example, where the dispute concerns proprietary rights in land situated in New York. Secondly, where there is an agreement between the parties which would be effective to create exclusive jurisdiction under Article 23 but for the fact that the designated court is in a non-member country. Thirdly, where a court of a non-member country had been seised of a similar or related action (within the meaning of Articles 27–30) before the English court was seised of the English action.

In *Owusu v Jackson*,[37] the European Court declined to rule on the possible reflexive effect of the provisions on exclusive jurisdiction by virtue of subject-matter, jurisdiction clauses, and concurrent actions, since such issues did not arise from the facts of the instant case. It must be admitted that some of the reasoning of the European Court in Opinion 1/03 (on the new Lugano Convention)[38] may be regarded as inimical to acceptance of the principle of reflexive effect. But it is submitted that acceptance of the principle is desirable, as a means of accommodating the Regulation to the global context of civil litigation, without sacrificing the essential features and objectives of the Regulation.

In relation to Article 23, on jurisdiction clauses, the principle of reflexive effect was in substance accepted by the European Court in *Coreck Maritime v Handelsveem*.[39] The case involved an action brought in a Dutch court by cargo interests under bills of lading for damage to cargo during a voyage from China to Rotterdam. The action was brought against a German company, which was the time-charterer of the vessel and the issuer of the bills of lading, and also against the shipowner, a Russian company. The bills contained a jurisdiction clause in favour of the 'the country where the carrier has his principal place of business' and another clause specifying that the contract was between the merchant and the owner of the vessel. The European Court, in ruling that Article 23 applies only if the parties agree to

---

[36]   See Droz, *Compétence Judiciaire et Effets des Jugement dans le Marché Commun* (Librairie Dalloz 1972), at paras 165–8, 216–18, and 329–30. See also Gaudemet-Tallon, *Les Conventions de Bruxelles et de Lugano*, 2nd edition (Montchrestien 1996), at paras 75, 84, 111 and 281. Cf. the Jenard and Möller Report, at para 54, and the Cruz, Real and Jenard Report, at para 25.

[37]   Case C-281/02, [2005] ECR I-1383.

[38]   [2006] ECR I-1145, especially at paras 153 and 158.

[39]   Case C-387/98, [2000] ECR I-9337, especially at para 19.

submit disputes to a court or the courts of a Member State, explained that Article 23 does not apply to clauses designating a court in a third country. But it added, most significantly, that a court of a Member State must, if it is seised notwithstanding such a jurisdiction clause, assess the validity of the clause according to the law applicable under the conflict rules of its own country.[40] This can only mean that if the Dutch court were to find that the jurisdiction clause referred to the Russian courts, and that the clause was valid under the Dutch conflict rules, it would be entitled to decline jurisdiction in accordance with the jurisdiction clause, even though one of the defendants was domiciled in Germany and the Dutch court was otherwise competent under Article 5(1) as the place of discharge. Accordingly, in the context of jurisdiction clauses, the principle of reflexive effect is now accepted and applied by the English courts, so that an otherwise competent English court will usually, in the exercise of its discretion, decline jurisdiction in favour of a court of a non-member country whose exclusive jurisdiction has been agreed on by the parties.[41]

If the principle of reflexive effect is accepted in relation to Article 23 on jurisdiction clauses, it can hardly be rejected in relation to Article 22, on exclusive jurisdiction by virtue of subject-matter, and the principle is indeed accepted by the English courts in this situation.[42] Admittedly, in *Apostolides v Orams*,[43] Kokott AG rejected the view that Article 22(1) produces a reflexive effect in favour of non-member countries, but in ruling on this case the European Court found it unnecessary to consider the question of reflexive effect.

The possible reflexive effect of Articles 27–30, on concurrent actions, is much more doubtful. The matter was the subject of the questions which the Irish Supreme Court decided to refer to the European Court in *Goshawk Dedicated Ltd v Life Receivables Ireland Ltd*.[44] The questions concerned whether, when a defendant is sued in its country of domicile, it is inconsistent with the Brussels I Regulation for the court of a Member State to decline jurisdiction or to stay proceedings on the basis that proceedings between the same parties and involving the same cause of action are already pending in the courts of a non-member country and are therefore first in time; and (if there is no such inconsistency) what criteria should be applied by a Member State coming to a decision whether to stay its pending proceedings. Unfortunately the reference was not proceeded with. Earlier Clarke J, in the Irish High Court, had ruled against any such reflexive effect, on the grounds that the implication of an excep-

---

40 Citing the Schlosser Report, [1979] OJ C59/71, at para 176.
41 See *Berisford v New Hampshire Insurance Co* [1990] 2 QB 631 (Hobhouse J); *Arkwright v Bryanston* [1990] 2 QB 649 (Potter J); *Konkola Copper Mines v Coromin* [2005] 2 All ER (Comm) 637 (Colman J), affirmed [2006] 1 All ER (Comm) 437 (CA); and *Winnetka Trading Corp v Julius Baer* [2008] EWHC 3146 (Ch) (Norris J). See also *The El Amria* [1981] 2 Lloyd's Rep 119 (CA); *Ace Insurance v Zurich Insurance* [2001] 1 Lloyd's Rep 618 (CA); and *Donohue v Armco* [2002] 1 All ER 749 (HL). See also *Europa Carton v Cifal*, 19th December 1978, where the French Court of Cassation gave effect to an agreement between a French company and a German company choosing a Swiss court.
42 See *Arkwright v Bryanston* [1990] 2 QB 649 (Potter J); *Konkola Copper Mines v Coromin* [2005] 2 All ER (Comm) 637 (Colman J); *Masri v Consolidated Contractors (No 2)* [2008] 2 All ER (Comm) 1099 (CA), per Lawrence Collins LJ, at paras 125–7; and *Catalyst Investment Group v Lewinsohn* [2009] EWHC 1964 (Ch) (Barling J).
43 Case C-420/07, [2009] ECR I-3571. The case involved the enforcement in England of a Cypriot judgment in favour of the Greek Cypriot original owner of land situated in Northern Cyprus against an English purchaser of the land from a vendor deriving title from the Turkish Cypriot authority there. The judgment ordered delivery of the land and payment of damages to the original owner.
44 [2009] IESC 7 (Irish Supreme Court); on appeal from [2008] ILPr 50 (Clarke J).

tion by analogy is incompatible with the ruling in *Owusu v Jackson*;[45] and that there is no real analogy with Article 27, since an external court would not determine its own jurisdiction in accordance with the Regulation but in accordance with its own principles of private international law. Subsequently, in *Catalyst Investment Group v Lewinsohn*,[46] Barling J (in the English High Court) has reached the same conclusion, and for the same reasons, as Clarke J.

In its Report and Green Paper of 21st April 2009,[47] the EC Commission envisages the possibility of an amendment which would explicitly permit the courts of Member States to decline jurisdiction in favour of courts of external countries in cases where the parties have concluded an exclusive choice of court agreement in favour of the courts of an external country, or where the dispute otherwise falls within the exclusive jurisdiction of the courts of an external country, or where parallel proceedings have already been brought in an external country.

## OTHER EUROPEAN DEFENDANTS

The general rule laid down by Article 3 of the Brussels I Regulation deprives the courts of a Member State of jurisdiction over defendants domiciled in the other Member States. The exclusion of jurisdiction by Article 3 is supplemented by Article 26(1), which requires a court to consider its jurisdiction of its own motion where the defendant is domiciled in another Member State and does not enter an appearance.[48]

The exclusion of jurisdiction by Article 3 is, however, subject to numerous important exceptions, laid down by Articles 5–24 and 31. Indeed, one of the main purposes of Chapter II is to harmonise the grounds on which a defendant domiciled in one Member State may be sued in a court of another Member State. To this end, Article 3(1) establishes the general rule against such jurisdiction, and Article 3(2) specifically prohibits the assumption of such jurisdiction on the basis of various national provisions or rules which are listed in Annex I. The bases specifically prohibited involve excessive jurisdiction, based on grounds which do not involve a substantial connection between the defendant or the events giving rise to the claim and the territory of the court seised. The excessive bases referred to include the defendant's nationality[49] or temporary presence;[50] the plaintiff's nationality,[51] domicile or residence;[52] and the presence or arrest of property unconnected with the subject-matter of the dispute.[53]

---

[45]   Case C-281/02, [2005] ECR I-1383.

[46]   [2009] EWHC 1964 (Ch). See also *Arkwright v Bryanston* [1990] 2 QB 649 (Potter J).

[47]   COM(2009) 174 final, at section 3.2, and COM(2009) 175 final, at question 2.

[48]   Article 26(1) provides: 'Where a defendant domiciled in one Member State is sued in a court of another Member State and does not enter an appearance, the court shall declare of its own motion that it has no jurisdiction unless its jurisdiction is derived from the provisions of this Regulation'. For this purpose, a court must take account of the rules of jurisdiction laid down by specialised conventions to which the forum State is a party; see Case C-148/03: *Nürnberger Allgemeine Versicherungs v Portbridge Transport International* [2004] ECR I-10327.

[49]   Used in France, Belgium, Luxembourg, and Italy.

[50]   Used in England, Northern Ireland, Ireland, and Denmark.

[51]   Used in France and Luxembourg.

[52]   Used in Belgium and the Netherlands.

[53]   Used in Germany, Belgium, Scotland, Denmark, and Greece.

But the exclusion by Article 3(1) extends beyond the excessive bases referred to and listed in Article 3(2) and Annex I, and covers any jurisdictional ground provided for by national law, including reasonable bases involving a substantial connection between the defendant or the events giving rise to the claim and the territory of the court seised. For Chapter II endeavours to create a unified regime of reasonable bases of jurisdiction over defendants domiciled in the Member States, completely displacing any bases of jurisdiction (whether excessive or reasonable) provided for by national laws. Thus, for example, in contractual matters, Article 5(1) confers jurisdiction on the courts for the place of performance, but not on the courts for the place at which the contract was concluded. Accordingly, the traditional English rule utilising the place of contracting no longer applies where the defendant is domiciled in another Member State.

In many cases (especially those specified in Articles 5 and 6), the harmonised rules laid down by the Regulation give the plaintiff a choice of forum in which to sue a defendant who is domiciled in a Member State. For example, he may sue either at the defendant's domicile (under Article 2) or, in another Member State, at the place of performance of a contractual obligation or the place at which a tortious event occurred (under Article 5(1) or (3)). In such cases, the choice belongs to the plaintiff, and a competent court in which he chooses to sue has no discretion to decline jurisdiction on grounds such as forum non conveniens in favour of an equally competent court of another Member State.[54]

Before the ruling of the European Court in *Owusu v Jackson*,[55] the English Court of Appeal had asserted a discretion to decline jurisdiction on grounds of forum non conveniens in favour of a court of a non-member country in cases where the defendant was domiciled in another Member State and the English court was competent under such provisions as Article 5(1), on the place of contractual performance, or Article 23, on jurisdiction clauses, or Article 24, on submission by appearance.[56] But it is clear that this assertion is incompatible with the European Court's decision in *Owusu*.

### Service in Another Member State

As well as requiring a court to consider its jurisdiction of its own motion where the defendant is domiciled in another Member State and does not enter an appearance, Article 26 seeks to ensure that a defendant who is domiciled in another Member State receives the document instituting the proceedings in sufficient time to enable him to arrange for his defence. Thus Article 26(2) requires the court to stay the proceedings so long as it is not shown that the defendant has been able to receive the document instituting the proceedings or an equivalent document in sufficient time to enable him to arrange for his defence, or that all necessary steps have been taken to this end. But in most cases where the defendant is domiciled in another Member State, the instituting or equivalent document will have to be transmitted in

---

54    See the Schlosser Report, at paras 76-8; *Mercury Publicity v Loerke* [1993] ILPr 142 (CA), on Article 5(1); *Aiglon v Gau Shan* [1993] 1 Lloyds Rep 164 (Hirst J), on Article 6(1); *Grupo Torras v Al-Sabah* [1995] 1 Lloyd's Rep 374 (Mance J), on Articles 2, 5(3) and 6(1); and *Boss Group v Boss France* [1997] 1 WLR 351 (CA), on Article 5(1).
55    Case C-281/02, [2005] ECR I-1383.
56    See *Eli Lilly v Novo Nordisk* [2000] ILPr 73 (CA), and *Ace Insurance v Zurich Insurance* [2001] EWCA Civ 173 (CA).

accordance with EC Regulation 1393/2007, on the Service in the Member States of Judicial and Extrajudicial Documents in Civil or Commercial Matters,[57] from the forum State to the State of the defendant's domicile for service there. In such cases, Article 26(3) of the Brussels I Regulation substitutes for Article 26(2) the more detailed requirements specified by Article 19 of Regulation 1393/2007. It is not permissible for an English court to subvert the provisions of Regulation 1393/2007 on service by authorising alternative service on a defendant domiciled in another Member State by way of service on its English solicitors.[58]

Regulation 1393/2007 applies in civil and commercial matters where a judicial or extrajudicial document has to be transmitted from one Member State to another for service there.[59] It applies in and between all the Member States except Denmark. By Articles 20 and 25, it replaces Article IV of the Protocol to the Brussels Convention, the Hague Convention of 15th November 1965 on the Service Abroad of Judicial and Extrajudicial Documents in Civil or Commercial Matters, and EC Regulation 1348/2000.[60] Regulation 1393/2007 requires each Member State to designate a transmitting agency, competent for the transmission of judicial or extrajudicial documents to be served in another Member State, and a receiving agency, competent for the receipt of judicial or extrajudicial documents from another Member State.

Section 1 (Articles 4–11) of Chapter II of Regulation 1393/2007 provides for the transmission and service of judicial documents through the transmitting and receiving agencies. By Article 4, judicial documents are to be transmitted directly and as soon as possible between the designated agencies. Transmission of documents may be carried out by any appropriate means, provided that the content of the document received is true and faithful to that of the document forwarded and that all information in it is easily legible. The document to be transmitted must be accompanied by a request using a standard form. By Article 6, on receipt of a document, a receiving agency must, as soon as possible and in any event within

---

57    [2007] OJ L324/79.

58    See *Knauf UK v British Gypsum* [2001] EWCA Civ 1570 (CA).

59    In *Re Anderson Owen Ltd* [2009] EWHC 2837 (Ch), Norris J suggested that Regulation 1393/2007 does not apply to insolvency proceedings which fall within the scope of EC Regulation 1346/2000; but it is difficult to see any basis for this suggestion. He also held that service which is defective because it does not comply with Regulation 1393/2007 can be cured in the exercise of the court's discretion under rule 7.55 of the Insolvency Rules 1986.

60    Transmission to or from Denmark continues to be governed by Regulation 1348/2000 on the Service in the Member States of Judicial and Extrajudicial Documents in Civil or Commercial Matters, [2000] OJ L160/37; and Article 26(3) of the Brussels I Regulation then substitutes for Article 26(2) the more detailed requirements specified by Article 19 of Regulation 1348/2000.

With regard to transmission to or from Switzerland, Norway or Iceland, Article IV of the First Protocol to the Lugano Convention 1988, and Article I of the First Protocol to the Lugano Convention 2007, echo Article IV of the Protocol to the Brussels Convention, by providing for transmission in accordance with the procedures laid down in the conventions and agreements concluded between the relevant States, and also for direct transmission by a public officer of the State of origin to a public officer of the receiving State. Where there is another convention on service in force between the relevant States, use of one of methods indicated by Article IV is mandatory; see Case C-522/03: *Scania v Rockinger* [2005] ECR I-8639. But it seems that where there is no other convention on service in force between the States in question (as in the case of the United Kingdom and Iceland), direct transmission between public officers is not required, and any method of service which complies with the law of the State of origin is sufficient; see *Olafsson v Gissurarson (No 2)* [2008] 1 All ER (Comm) 1106 (CA).

seven days of receipt, send a receipt to the transmitting agency by the swiftest possible means of transmission using a standard form.

By Article 7, the receiving agency must itself serve the document or have it served, either in accordance with the law of the Member State addressed or by a particular method requested by the transmitting agency, unless that method is incompatible with the law of the Member State addressed. The receiving agency must take all necessary steps to effect the service of the document as soon as possible, and in any event within one month of receipt. If it has not been possible to effect service within one month of receipt, the receiving agency must immediately inform the transmitting agency by means of a certificate in a standard form, and must also continue to take all necessary steps to effect the service of the document, unless indicated otherwise by the transmitting agency, where service seems to be possible within a reasonable period of time.

By Article 8, the addressee may refuse to accept a document at the time of service or by returning the document to the receiving agency within one week, if it is not written in, or accompanied by a translation into, either a language which the addressee understands or an official language of the Member State addressed.[61] Where the addressee has refused to accept the document on this ground, the service of the document can be remedied through the service on the addressee in accordance with the Regulation of the document accompanied by an appropriate translation.[62] In *Weiss v Industrie- und Handelskammer Berlin*,[63] the European Court ruled that, as regards documents instituting judicial proceedings, the right to a translation is limited to the documents which are necessary to enable the defendant to assert his rights in the proceedings. Such documents must make it possible to identify clearly the subject-matter and basis of the claim, as well as containing the summons to appear before the court or, where relevant, indicating the possibility of an appeal. In contrast, there is no right to a translation of documents which have a purely evidential function and are not necessary for the purpose of understanding the subject-matter and basis of the claim. By Article 10, when the formalities concerning the service of the document have been completed, a certificate of completion of those formalities must be drawn up in a standard form and addressed to the transmitting agency.

Section 2 (Articles 12–15) of Chapter II of Regulation 1393/2007 permits certain other means of transmission and service of judicial documents. Article 12 permits a Member State in exceptional circumstances to use consular or diplomatic channels to forward judicial documents, for the purpose of service, to a receiving agency or a central body of another Member State. Article 13 permits a Member State to effect service of judicial documents on persons residing in another Member State, without application of any compulsion, directly through its diplomatic or consular agents, unless the Member State of service has declared that it is opposed to such service within its territory on persons other than nationals of the Member State in which the documents originate. Article 14 permits a Member State to effect service of judicial documents directly by postal services on persons residing in another Member State by registered letter, with acknowledgement of receipt or equivalent. Article 15 permits any

---

[61]   See also *Heidland Werres Diederichs v Flexiquip Hydraulics Ltd* [2006] NIQB 100 (Higgins J).

[62]   See also Case C-443/03: *Leffler v Berlin Chemie AG* [2005] ECR I-9611, on Regulation 1348/2000.

[63]   Case C-14/07, [2008] ECR I-3367.

person interested in a judicial proceeding to effect service of judicial documents directly through the judicial officers, officials or other competent persons of the Member State addressed, where such direct service is permitted under the law of that Member State.

In *Plumex v Young Sports NV*,[64] the European Court ruled that there is no hierarchy between the method of transmission and service through the transmitting and receiving agencies under Articles 4–11 of the Regulation and the method of transmission and service by post under Article 14. Thus, it is possible to serve a judicial document by one or other or both of those methods. Where transmission and service are effected both through the transmitting and receiving agencies and by post, then in order to determine vis-à-vis the person served the point from which time starts to run for the purposes of a procedural time-limit linked to effecting service, reference must be made to the date of the first service validly effected.

Article 16 of Regulation 1393/2007 specifies laconically that extrajudicial documents may be transmitted for service in another Member State in accordance with the Regulation. In *Roda Golf*,[65] the European Court ruled that the Regulation extends to the service of extra-judicial documents between private persons in the absence of legal proceedings. It applies, for example, to a letter, drawn up by a notary and executed by a party to a contract for the sale of land, designed unilaterally to terminate the contract which had been concluded between the notifying party and the recipient, even though no legal proceedings were in progress and the document was not connected with the commencement of legal proceedings.

Article 19 of Regulation 1393/2007 offers some protection to a defendant who has not entered an appearance. Article 19(1) applies where a writ of summons or an equivalent document has had to be transmitted to another Member State for the purpose of service under the Regulation and the defendant has not appeared. In that case, judgment must not be given until it is established either that the document was served by a method prescribed by the internal law of the Member State addressed for the service of documents in domestic actions upon persons who are within its territory, or that the document was actually delivered to the defendant or to his residence by another method provided for by the Regulation; and also that the service or delivery was effected in sufficient time to enable the defendant to defend.

The protection given by Article 19(1) is qualified by Article 19(2), which enables a Member State to declare that the judge may give judgment even if no certificate of service or delivery has been received, if all of the following conditions are fulfilled: (a) that the document was transmitted by one of the methods provided for in the Regulation; (b) that a period of time of not less than six months, considered adequate by the judge in the particular case, has elapsed since the date of the transmission of the document; and (c) that no certificate of any kind has been received, even though every reasonable effort has been made to obtain it through the competent authorities or bodies of the Member State addressed. In any event, Article 19(3) enables a judge to order any provisional or protective measures in case of urgency.

Article 19(4) provides an additional protection to a defendant who has not entered an appearance. It applies where a writ of summons or an equivalent document has had to be transmitted to another Member State for the purpose of service under the Regulation, and a judgment has been entered against a defendant who has not appeared. It enables the judge to relieve the defendant from the effects of the expiry of the time for appeal from the judgment

---

[64] Case C-473/04, [2006] ECR I-1417.
[65] Case C-14/08, [2009] ECR I-5439.

if the following conditions are fulfilled: (a) that the defendant, without any fault on his part, did not have knowledge of the document in sufficient time to defend, or knowledge of the judgment in sufficient time to appeal; and (b) that the defendant has disclosed a prima facie defence to the action on the merits. An application for this relief must be filed within a reasonable time after the defendant has knowledge of the judgment, and each Member State may specify a period of not less than one year following the date of the judgment within which such an application must be made. Moreover Article 19(4) does not apply to judgments concerning the status or capacity of persons.

## EXTERNAL DEFENDANTS

Under the general rule laid down by Article 4 of the Brussels I Regulation, where the defendant is not domiciled in any Member State, the courts of each Member State determine their jurisdiction over him in accordance with the law of their own State. Both the reasonable and the excessive bases of jurisdiction contained in the lex fori apply, and one of the excessive grounds is slightly extended by Article 4(2), under which a Member State (such as France or Luxembourg) which uses the plaintiff's local nationality as a basis of jurisdiction must give similar effect to the plaintiff's local domicile.[66] However, a Member State is not precluded from amending its law so as to bring the jurisdictional grounds available against external defendants into line with those which the Regulation makes applicable against defendants domiciled in other Member States. Moreover the reference by Article 4 to the lex fori includes any judicial discretion conferred thereby to decline jurisdiction on grounds such as forum non conveniens, even in favour of a court of another Member State.[67]

Although Article 4 makes an express saving only for Article 22 (on exclusive jurisdiction by reason of subject-matter) and Article 23 (on jurisdiction clauses), it seems clear that Article 4 also gives way to a number of other provisions of Chapter II. While Articles 5 and 6 (on alternative jurisdiction, based on such factors as the place of performance of a contractual obligation, or the domicile of a co-defendant) apply only where the defendant is domiciled in another Member State, the sections on insurance, consumer and employment contracts contain provisions whereby an insurer, supplier or employer who is not domiciled in any Member State but has a branch situated in a Member State is treated, for the purpose of disputes arising out of the operations of the branch, as domiciled in the State in which the branch is situated.[68] Moreover, as regards submission by appearance, the European Court established in *Group Josi v UGIC*[69] that Article 24 applies even if the defendant is not domiciled in any Member State.

---

[66]    For an example of the operation of Article 4(2), see *Guggenheim v Helion* (1998) 37 ILM 653 (French Court of Cassation), which involved a French action against a New York entity brought by a British citizen domiciled in France.

[67]    See *Grupo Torras v Al-Sabah* [1995] 1 Lloyd's Rep 374 (Mance J); *Sarrio v Kuwait Investment Authority* [1996] 1 Lloyd's Rep 650 (Mance J) and [1997] 1 Lloyd's Rep 113 (CA); *The Xin Yang* [1996] 2 Lloyd's Rep 217 (Clarke J); *Solani Bank v Bank Austria*, 15th January 1997 (CA); *Haji-Ioannou v Frangos* [1999] 2 Lloyd's Rep 337 (CA); and *Berezovsky v Michaels* [2000] 1 WLR 1004 (HL).

[68]    See Articles 9(2), 15(2) and 18(2).

[69]    Case C-412/98, [2000] ECR I-5925, at paras 44–5.

As regards concurrent proceedings in courts of different Member States, the European Court established in *Overseas Union Insurance Ltd v New Hampshire Insurance Company*[70] that Article 27 (on similar claims) applies irrespective of the domicile of the parties to the two sets of proceedings. Its reasoning, based on the need to reduce the risk of irreconcilable judgments, is equally applicable to Article 28 (on related claims) and Article 29 (on claims whose subject-matter gives rise to conflicting exclusive jurisdiction). Thus where an English court is seised of an action against a defendant not domiciled in any Member State after a court of another Member State has been seised of a similar or related action, Articles 27 and 28 prevail over the English doctrine of forum non conveniens.[71]

## Service Abroad

It is uncertain whether Article 26(2) of the Brussels I Regulation, which requires the court to stay its proceedings so long as it is not shown that the defendant has been able to receive the document instituting the proceedings or an equivalent document in sufficient time to enable him to arrange for his defence, or that all necessary steps have been taken to this end, extends to cases where the defendant is not domiciled in any Member State. Such a restriction is certainly indicated by the French text, which speaks of 'ce défendeur' and thus refers back to the Article 26(1), which explicitly contemplates a defendant who is domiciled in another Member State.

In any event, Article 26(4) of the Regulation makes applicable Article 15 of the Hague Convention of 15th November 1965 on the Service Abroad of Judicial and Extrajudicial Documents in Civil or Commercial Matters, in cases where EC Regulations 1348/2000 and 1393/2007 are not applicable, and the document instituting the proceedings or an equivalent document had to be transmitted under that Convention. The parties to the Hague Convention 1965 now include all the EU Member States and the Lugano Convention countries, with the exception of Austria and Malta, and there are 31 other parties to that Convention, including the United States, Canada, Japan, China and Russia.[72] Thus, in many cases where the defendant is domiciled in a country which is not an EU Member State, the document instituting proceedings in a court of an EU Member State will have to be transmitted for service under the Hague Convention 1965, and the defendant will receive the protection specified by Article 15 of the Convention. It is not permissible for an English court to subvert the provisions of the Hague Convention on service by authorising alternative service on the defendant's English solicitors.[73]

The provisions of the Hague Convention 1965 closely resemble those of EC Regulation 1393/2007. The Convention establishes a procedure whereby an authority or judicial officer competent under the law of the State of origin forwards to a Central Authority designated by

---

[70]   Case 351/89, [1991] ECR I-3317.

[71]   See *Sarrio v Kuwait Investment Authority* [1996] 1 Lloyd's Rep 650 (Mance J), restored [1999] AC 32 (HL); and *The Xin Yang* [1996] 2 Lloyd's Rep 217 (Clarke J).

[72]   The thirty-one other parties are Monaco, San Marino, Bosnia and Herzegovina, Croatia, FYR Macedonia, Albania, Turkey, Russia, Belarus, Ukraine, Israel, Egypt, Kuwait, the United States, Canada, Mexico, Argentina, Venezuela, India, Pakistan, Sri Lanka, China, Korea, Japan, Seychelles, Botswana, Malawi, Antigua and Barbuda, Barbados, Bahamas, and Saint Vincent and the Grenadines.

[73]   See *Knauf UK v British Gypsum* [2001] EWCA Civ 1570 (CA).

the State addressed a request for service, along with a copy of the document to be served. Service is then effected or arranged by the Central Authority, and a certificate of service is forwarded directly to the applicant. Other methods of service (for example, by diplomatic or consular agents of the State or origin, or by postal channels) are also permitted. As regards the protection of a defendant who has not entered an appearance, Article 15 of the Convention closely resembles Article 19(1)–(3) of Regulation 1393/2007, and Article 16 of the Convention closely resembles Article 19(4)–(5) of the Regulation.

**Possible Reform**

In its Report and Green Paper of 21st April 2009,[74] the EC Commission favours the amendment of the Brussels I Regulation so as to include harmonised rules on jurisdiction over external defendants. It argues that the absence of such harmonised rules causes an unequal access to justice for Community citizens, especially in situations where a party would not get a fair hearing or adequate protection before the courts of third States. Moreover, the absence of such common rules may jeopardise the application of mandatory Community legislation, for example on consumer protection (including time share), employment, commercial agents, competition, data protection or product liability, and deprive Community claimants of the protection offered to them by the Community rules. The Commission envisages the extension of provisions of the Regulation, such as Articles 5 and 6, which currently apply to internal defendants, so as to apply also to external defendants, and also the possible addition of further bases of jurisdiction over external defendants, such as the carrying out of activities related to the claim, the location of assets related to the claim, and situations where there would otherwise be no access to justice.

## THE CONCEPT OF DOMICILE

Despite the central importance of domicile under Chapter II, it is only in the case of corporations and associations that the Brussels I Regulation establishes a uniform substantive definition of the concept for its purposes. By Article 60(1), for the purposes of the Regulation, a company or other legal person or association of natural or legal persons is domiciled at each place where it has: (a) its statutory seat, or (b) its central administration, or (c) its principal place of business. This provision replaces Article 53(1) of the Brussels Convention, by which a corporation or association was domiciled at its seat, determined under the law of the country whose court was seised. In the case of an individual, Article 59 of the Regulation echoes Article 52 of the Brussels Convention, in specifying a choice-of-law rule whereby it is for the law of each Member State to determine whether an individual is domiciled in that State.[75]

It is clear from the wording of Article 59 and the structure of Chapter II that a court of a Member State, in determining its jurisdiction under Chapter II of the Regulation, must

---

[74]    COM(2009) 174 final, at section 3.2, and COM(2009) 175 final, at question 2.
[75]    Article 59 provides: '(1) In order to determine whether a party is domiciled in the Member State whose courts are seised of a matter, the court shall apply its internal law. (2) If a party is not domiciled in the Member State whose courts are seised of the matter, then, in order to determine whether the party is domiciled in another Member State, the court shall apply the law of that Member State'.

proceed as follows. The court must first determine whether the defendant is domiciled in the forum State, so that Article 2 applies. If it concludes that he is domiciled in the forum State, it applies Article 2 (and any relevant exceptions thereto), and ignores any other possible domicile of his elsewhere. Secondly, if the court has concluded that the defendant is not domiciled in the forum State, it proceeds to determine whether he is domiciled in another Member State, so that Article 3 applies. If the court concludes that the defendant is not domiciled in the forum State but is domiciled in at least one other Member State, it applies Article 3 (and the exceptions thereto), under which it is immaterial whether the defendant is domiciled in only one other Member State or in several other Member States,[76] and also immaterial that the defendant may also be domiciled in a non-member country.[77] Finally, if the court has concluded that the defendant is not domiciled in any Member State, it applies Article 4 (and the exceptions thereto),[78] under which it is immaterial whether he is domiciled in any, or any particular, non-member country or nowhere at all.[79]

**Individuals**

In the case of an individual, Article 59 of the Regulation refers to the lex fori the determination of whether he is domiciled in the forum State. If he is not domiciled in the forum State, it refers to the law of each of the other Member States the determination of whether he is domiciled in that other Member State.

As regards the domicile of an individual, the laws of the Member States share a common core, in seeking a stable establishment or substantial residence. They differ, however, in important details, especially as to whether an individual can have more than one domicile at a given time, and whether a commercial or a domestic establishment should be preferred. Thus French and Luxembourg laws refer to the person's principal establishment, and prefer

---

[76]  But it seems from Article 54B(2)(a) of the Lugano Convention 1988, Article 64(2)(a) of the Lugano Convention 2007, and Article 68 of the Brussels I Regulation, that where a court of an EU Member State in which a Lugano Convention is applicable (such as the United Kingdom) finds that the defendant is not domiciled in the forum State but is domiciled both in another EU Member State (such as Germany) and also in a non-member country which is a party to the relevant Lugano Convention (such as Switzerland, in the case of the the Lugano Convention 1988; or Norway, in the case of the Lugano Convention 2007), it must apply Article 3 and the exceptions thereto under Title II of the relevant Lugano Convention, rather than Article 3 and the exceptions thereto under Chapter II of the Brussels I Regulation.

[77]  See *The Rewia* [1991] 2 Lloyd's Rep 325 (CA).

[78]  This situation may arise where an individual defendant's residential connections are divided between two Member States, but neither regards him as domiciled in its own territory. See *Buchmann v Steiner*, 4th January 1984, where the French Court of Cassation applied Article 4 and upheld French jurisdiction on the basis of the defendant's non-domiciliary residence in France, since his business establishment in the Netherlands did not constitute a domicile under Dutch law.

[79]  However, the defendant's domicile in a particular non-member country is relevant under Article 72, which restricts the recognition and enforcement between Member States under Chapter III of judgments given against defendants domiciled or habitually resident in certain non-member countries. For this purpose, whether an individual defendant is domiciled in a relevant non-member country is determined in accordance with the law of the Member State in which recognition or enforcement is sought; see the (UK) Civil Jurisdiction and Judgments Order 2001 (SI 2001/3929), Schedule 1, para 9(7). On Article 72, see pp. 235–6 below.

a business to a domestic establishment. Similarly, Italian law refers to the principal seat of his business and interests. On the other hand, Dutch law refers to his dwelling-place, and Belgian law to the place at which he is registered on the population registers. All these laws contemplate a single domicile at a given time, but German law recognises multiplicity of domicile and refers to any stable establishment.[80]

The traditional English concept of domicile, in terms of origin or permanent residence, differs radically from the Continental (and, indeed, American) concepts, and amounts in substance to nationality in disguise. Since this concept would have been totally unsuitable for the purposes of the Brussels Convention and the Brussels I Regulation, the British implementing legislation has adopted a different concept of domicile for this purpose, though the traditional concept remains applicable in family matters and succession where the Brussels I Regulation does not apply.[81]

The British concept of individual domicile for the purpose of the Brussels I Regulation is specified by paragraph 9 of Schedule 1 to the Civil Jurisdiction and Judgments Order 2001 (SI 2001/3929).[82] By paragraph 9(2) and (3), an individual is domiciled in the United Kingdom, or in a particular part of the United Kingdom, if he is resident therein and the nature and circumstances of his residence indicate that he has a substantial connection therewith. By paragraph 9(6), there is a rebuttable presumption that an individual who has been resident in the United Kingdom, or in a particular part of the United Kingdom, for the last three months or more, has a substantial connection therewith. By paragraph 9(5), an individual is also domiciled in a particular part of the United Kingdom if he is resident in that part and has a substantial connection with the United Kingdom as a whole, but not with any particular part.

Perhaps surprisingly, these provisions seem to have created little difficulty. In *Bank of Dubai v Abbas*,[83] Saville LJ emphasised that for this purpose 'residence' requires a settled or usual place of abode with a substantial degree of permanence or continuity, and that the presumption of substantial connection from three months' residence provides no guidance as to whether the person has become resident. Moreover the significance of the existing duration of a person's stay in England varies according to the circumstances of the case. A person who comes to England to retire and who buys a house for that purpose and moves into it, selling all his foreign possessions and cutting all his foreign ties, probably becomes resident here immediately. In other circumstances, it may be necessary to balance the length of time that the person has been here with his connections abroad.

---

[80]   See Droz, at paras 344–9. See also *Haji-Ioannou v Frangos* [1999] 2 Lloyd's Rep 337 (CA), applying Article 51 of the Greek Civil Code, whereby for business purposes an individual is domiciled at his place of business.

[81]   The traditional English concept of domicile plays a role under the Brussels IIA Regulation in relation to matrimonial jurisdiction, and under the Maintenance Regulation in relation to jurisdiction over maintenance claims. See Chapters 16 and 18 below.

[82]   The concept specified by para 9 echoes that laid down by s 41 of the Civil Jurisdiction and Judgments Act 1982 for the purpose of the Brussels Convention and the Lugano Convention 1988.

[83]   [1997] ILPr 308 (CA). See also *High Tech International AG v Deripaska* [2006] All ER (D) 330 (Dec) (Eady J), and *Foote Cone & Belding Reklam Hizmetleri AS v Theron* [2006] EWHC 1585 (Ch) (Patten J).

Somewhat similarly, Sheriff Palmer in *Daniel v Foster*[84] and Mance J in *Grupo Torras v Al-Sabah*[85] equated 'residence' in paragraph 9 of the Schedule with ordinary residence, as defined by Lord Scarman in *Shah v Barnet LBC*.[86] There Lord Scarman explained that the intention necessary for ordinary residence must not be confused with that required under the traditional English concept of domicile. Ordinary residence does not require an intention to reside permanently or indefinitely. Rather it refers to an abode in a particular country which the person has adopted voluntarily and for settled purposes as part of the regular order of his life for the time being, whether of short or long duration; to a regular, habitual mode of life in a particular country, whose continuance has persisted despite temporary absences, and which has been adopted voluntarily and for a settled purpose. The residence must be voluntarily adopted, in the sense of not resulting from overwhelming compulsion (for example, by reason of kidnapping or imprisonment), and there must be some degree of settled purpose. But the duration of the purpose may be limited, and purposes relating to education, employment, health or family will suffice. No deep examination of the person's state of mind is required.

Thus, as in the case of ordinary residence, an individual can have more than one domicile under paragraph 9 of the Schedule at a given time. It is enough to make a person domiciled in a part of the United Kingdom under paragraph 9 that he has a place of business or a dwelling-place therein, which he frequently visits (perhaps for short periods) on a continuing basis, even though his main residence is in another part of the United Kingdom or abroad.[87] Accordingly, a man is domiciled in England if he owns a house in England, in which his wife lives, and at which he spends at least a week in each month, even though he spends a considerable amount of time abroad.[88] But one who visits England for a few days, during which he is arrested and then released on bail on conditions preventing his leaving the country, and then remains in England for next few weeks because he is prevented by the bail conditions from leaving, will not have acquired an English domicile.[89] Nor will a person be domiciled in England if he spends the majority of his time in Russia, even though he owns a house in England which he uses for infrequent, intermittent and fleeting visits, amounting to fewer than thirty nights each year.[90]

---

[84]   [1989] SCLR 378.

[85]   [1995] 1 Lloyd's Rep 374.

[86]   [1983] 2 AC 309 (HL). See also Stone, 'The Concept of Habitual Residence in Private International Law' [2000] Anglo-American Law Review 342.

[87]   See *Daniel v Foster* [1989] SCLR 378, and *Grupo Torras v Al-Sabah* [1995] 1 Lloyd's Rep 374. See also *Ikimi v Ikimi* [2001] 2 FCR 385 (CA), holding before the Brussels II Regulation that for purposes of matrimonial jurisdiction an adult could have two habitual residences simultaneously, as where a spouse had two marital homes, at each of which he or she spent substantial periods; and *Armstrong v Armstrong* [2003] 2 FLR 375 (Butler-Sloss P). Cf. *Marinos v Marinos* [2007] 2 FLR 1018 (Munby J), and *Munro v Munro* [2007] EWHC 3315 (Fam), [2008] All ER (D) 316 (Feb) (Bennett J), holding that, for the purpose of matrimonial jurisdiction under the Brussels IIA Regulation, a person cannot have more than one habitual residence at the same time; and that where a person divides his or her time between two countries, the real focus of his or her life will be decisive.

[88]   See *Foote Cone & Belding Reklam Hizmetleri AS v Theron* [2006] EWHC 1585 (Ch) (Patten J).

[89]   See *Petrotrade v Smith* [1998] 2 All ER 346 (Thomas J).

[90]   See *Cherney v Deripaska* [2007] 2 All ER (Comm) 785 (Langley J). See also *High Tech International AG v Deripaska* [2006] All ER (D) 330 (Dec) (Eady J).

Similarly in *Yugraneft v Abramovich*,[91] Christopher Clarke J held that a Russian oligarch was not domiciled in England, although he owned an English football club and a substantial house in England, which he used while making short visits to England, mainly to watch the club's matches. In the most relevant year, he had spent 56 full days in England, with an average length of stay of 1.47 and a longest stay of 11 full days; and in the previous year 110 full days in England, with an average length of stay of 2.68 and a longest stay of 20 full days. These few (or at least intermittent) and (on average) brief visits to England did not indicate sufficient permanence, continuity, or settlement to constitute residence.

Somewhat similarly, in Ireland, reg 11(1)(a) of the European Communities (Civil and Commercial Judgments) Regulations 2002 (SI 52/2002) specifies that for the present purpose an individual is domiciled in Ireland if and only if he is ordinarily resident therein. In *Deutsche Bank v Murtagh*,[92] Costello J held that a couple were ordinarily resident, and thus domiciled, in Ireland because they had been living there for about a year.

In its Report and Green Paper of 21st April 2009,[93] the EC Commission contemplates the possibility of introducing an autonomous concept of domicile in respect of individuals.

## Corporations and Associations

By Article 60(1) of the Brussels I Regulation, a company or other legal person or association of natural or legal persons is domiciled at each of the places where it has: (a) its statutory seat; or (b) its central administration; or (c) its principal place of business. In addition, Article 60(2) defines 'statutory seat' for British and Irish purposes as the registered office; or where there is no such office anywhere, the place of incorporation; or where there is no such place anywhere, the place under whose law the formation took place. Recital 11 explains that the domicile of a legal person is defined autonomously so as to make the common rules more transparent and avoid conflicts of jurisdiction.

Article 60 of the Regulation replaces Article 53(1) of the Brussels Convention, under which a corporation was domiciled at its seat, determined under the law (including the private international law) of the court seised. In the United Kingdom, Article 53(1) was supplemented by s 42 of the 1982 Act, under which in general a corporation or association had its seat in a State if either it had been incorporated or formed under the law of that State and had its registered office or some other official address therein, or its central management and control was exercised therein.

The concept of central administration, used in Article 60(1)(b), appears equivalent to that of the place of central management and control, used in s 42, which was clarified by the Court of Appeal in *The Rewia*.[94] The case involved a one-ship company which was incorporated and had its registered office in Liberia, but whose directors were resident in Germany and held their meetings there, and whose ship was managed by agents in Hong Kong. The Court of Appeal held that the company was domiciled, for the purpose of the

---

91    [2008] EWHC 2613 (Comm); especially at paras 440-87.
92    [1995] 1 ILRM 381.
93    COM(2009) 174 final, at section 3.8.2, and COM(2009) 175 final, at question 8.
94    [1991] 2 Lloyd's Rep 325. See also *Latchin v General Mediterranean Holidays* [2002] CLC 330 (Andrew Smith J); and *Royal & Sun Alliance Insurance v MK Digital* [2006] 2 Lloyd's Rep 110 (CA).

Brussels Convention, both in Liberia, as the place of its incorporation and registered office, and in Germany, as the place of its central management and control. Although in practice the company's agents in Hong Kong had a free hand in the day-to-day management of the vessel, their activities were subject to the control of the directors in Hamburg, which was the centre from which instructions were given when necessary, and ultimate control was exercised.

It seems probable, however, that in such a case the company would now be regarded as domiciled also in Hong Kong under Article 60(1)(c), on the basis that its principal place of business was located there. For Article 60 requires that the principal place of business should be distinguished from the central administration, and this suggests that the principal place of business is the place at or from which the most important and numerous of the company's dealings with third parties are conducted. But the English case-law has tended to equate the concepts of central administration and principal place of business, and to apply the approach used in *The Rewia*[95] to both concepts. Thus, in *King v Crown Energy*,[96] Chambers QC considered that there can be a considerable overlap between what constitutes the central administration of a company and the carrying on of its principal business, and that *The Rewia* remains an essential tool in deciding what constitutes the principal place of business.

A similar approach was adopted in *Iranian Ministry of Defence v Faz Aviation Ltd*,[97] where Langley J explained that the central administration and the principal place of business of a company will frequently be in the same country. He considered that the focus, in matters of jurisdiction, is on the country rather than any more particular location; that the principal place of business is likely to be the place where the corporate authority is to be found (in the form of the shareholders and directors), and from which the company is controlled and managed; and that the place where the day-to-day activities of the company are carried out may not be the principal place of business if those activities are subject to the control of senior management located elsewhere. He added that a company can cease to have any principal place of business, and that the principal place of business can change as the business changes. Ultimately, he concluded that the English court lacked jurisdiction over a company incorporated in Cyprus which, well before the date of the issue of the claim form, had ceased to have any real business to administer or operate, and whose agents who by then remained at all active were substantially to be found in Cyprus.

In contrast, in *889457 Alberta Inc v Katanga Mining Ltd*,[98] Tomlinson J concluded that a holding company had its central administration in England, where the entirety of its administration took place and both of its managers resided, even though it was incorporated in Bermuda, it owned mining interests in the Democratic Republic of Congo, and its board meetings were co-ordinated from Canada.

Article 60 does not apply to the determination of the location of a company's seat for the purpose of Article 22(2) of the Regulation, which provides for exclusive jurisdiction over certain disputes governed by company law. For Article 22(2) specifies that for its

---

95    [1991] 2 Lloyd's Rep 325.
96    [2003] ILPr 28.
97    [2008] 1 All ER (Comm) 372.
98    [2008] All ER (D) 61 (Nov).

purposes the seat must be determined by the court in accordance with its own rules of private international law, and in the United Kingdom for this purpose the seat is defined by paragraph 10 of Schedule 1 to the Civil Jurisdiction and Judgments Order 2001 (SI 2001/3929).[99]

---

[99]    On Article 22(2) and para 10, see pp. 149–52 below.

# 4.  Alternative jurisdiction

## INTRODUCTION

In Chapter II of the Brussels I Regulation, Section 2 (Articles 5–7)[1] specifies a variety of cases in which, by way of derogation from Article 3, a defendant who is domiciled in one Member State may be sued in another Member State. In such cases, the Regulation gives the plaintiff a choice of suing in the State of the defendant's domicile in accordance with Article 2, or in a court of another Member State in accordance with Articles 5–7. The choice is given to the plaintiff, and it is not open to any of the courts involved to override the plaintiff's choice on such grounds as the relative appropriateness or convenience of such courts.[2]

In contrast with Article 2, which confers jurisdiction on the courts in general of the Member State in which the defendant is domiciled, and leaves to the law of the State in question the allocation of jurisdiction between its courts, Articles 5–7 usually confer jurisdiction on a particular court of another Member State.

The bases of jurisdiction used by Article 5 involve a connection between the cause of action and the territory of the court on which jurisdiction is conferred. As the European Court has frequently emphasised, this freedom of choice was introduced in view of the existence in certain well-defined cases of a particularly close relationship between a dispute and the court which may be most conveniently called upon to take cognisance of the matter.[3] Thus, for example, Articles 5(1), 5(3) and 5(5) respectively confer jurisdiction on the courts for the place of performance of a contractual obligation; those for the place where a tortious event occurred; and those for the place in which the defendant has a secondary establishment from whose operations the dispute has arisen. In full Article 5 provides:

> A person domiciled in a Member State may, in another Member State, be sued:
> (1)(a) in matters relating to a contract, in the courts for the place of performance of the obligation in question;
> (b) for the purpose of this provision and unless otherwise agreed, the place of performance of the obligation in question shall be:
> – in the case of the sale of goods, the place in a Member State where, under the contract, the goods were delivered or should have been delivered,

---

[1]    These provisions replace Articles 5–6A of the Brussels Convention. There are major changes in Article 5(1) and minor changes in Articles 5(3) and 6(1). The former Article 6A is renumbered as Article 7.

[2]    See the Schlosser Report, at paras 76–8. This has been readily accepted even in the United Kingdom; see *Mercury Publicity v Loerke* [1993] ILPr 142 (CA), on Article 5(1); *Aiglon v Gau Shan* [1993] 1 Lloyd's Rep 164 (Hirst J), on Article 6(1); *Grupo Torras v Al-Sabah* [1995] 1 Lloyd's Rep 374 (Mance J), on Articles 2, 5(3) and 6(1); *Boss Group v Boss France* [1997] 1 WLR 351 (CA), on Article 5(1); and *Ferguson Shipbuilders v Voith Hydro* [2000] SLT 229 (Outer House), on Article 5(1).

[3]    See, for example, Case 12/76: *Tessili v Dunlop* [1976] ECR 1473.

– in the case of the provision of services, the place in a Member State where, under the contract, the services were provided or should have been provided,
(c) if subparagraph (b) does not apply then subparagraph (a) applies;
(2) in matters relating to maintenance, in the courts for the place where the maintenance creditor is domiciled or habitually resident or, if the matter is ancillary to proceedings concerning the status of a person, in the court which, according to its own law, has jurisdiction to entertain those proceedings, unless that jurisdiction is based solely on the nationality of one of the parties;[4]
(3) in matters relating to tort, delict or quasi-delict, in the courts for the place where the harmful event occurred or may occur;
(4) as regards a civil claim for damages or restitution which is based on an act giving rise to criminal proceedings, in the court seised of those proceedings, to the extent that that court has jurisdiction under its own law to entertain civil proceedings;
(5) as regards a dispute arising out of the operations of a branch, agency or other establishment, in the courts for the place in which the branch, agency or other establishment is situated;
(6) as settlor, trustee or beneficiary of a trust created by the operation of a statute, or by a written instrument, or created orally and evidenced in writing, in the courts of the Member State in which the trust is domiciled;
(7) as regards a dispute concerning the payment of remuneration claimed in respect of the salvage of a cargo or freight, in the court under the authority of which the cargo or freight in question:
(a) has been arrested to secure such payment, or
(b) could have been so arrested, but bail or other security has been given;
provided that this provision shall apply only if it is claimed that the defendant has an interest in the cargo or freight or had such an interest at the time of salvage.[5]

In contrast, Articles 6 and 7 are designed to concentrate jurisdiction over related disputes; for example, by enabling several defendants to be sued at the domicile of one of them. In full, Article 6 provides:

A person domiciled in a Member State may also be sued:
(1) where he is one of a number of defendants, in the courts for the place where any one of them is domiciled, provided the claims are so closely connected that it is expedient to hear and determine them together to avoid the risk of irreconcilable judgments resulting from separate proceedings;
(2) as a third party in an action on a warranty or guarantee or in any other third party proceedings, in the court seised of the original proceedings, unless these were instituted solely with the object of removing him from the jurisdiction of the court which would be competent in his case;
(3) on a counter-claim arising from the same contract or facts on which the original claim was based, in the court in which the original claim is pending;
(4) in matters relating to a contract, if the action may be combined with an action against the same defendant in matters relating to rights in rem in immovable property, in the court of the Member State in which the property is situated.

Article 7 specifies:

Where by virtue of this Regulation a court of a Member State has jurisdiction in actions relating to liability from the use or operation of a ship, that court, or any other court substituted for this purpose by the internal law of that Member State, shall also have jurisdiction over claims for limitation of such liability.

---

[4]   On maintenance, see Chapter 18 below.
[5]   In its Report and Green Paper of 21st April 2009, the EC Commission contemplates the possibility of introducing a non-exclusive jurisdiction based on the situs of movable assets, as far as rights in rem or possession with respect to such assets are concerned. See COM(2009) 174 final, at section 3.8.2, and COM(2009) 175 final, at question 8.

The European Court has frequently emphasised that the bases of jurisdiction specified by Section 2 constitute exceptions to the general rule in favour of the defendant's domicile, laid down by Section 1 (Articles 2–4). Accordingly, it has usually insisted that concepts used in Section 2 should be given an independent meaning, based principally on the system and objectives of the Regulation, and should not be construed unduly widely. In particular, it emphasised in *Handte v TMCS*[6] that the objective of strengthening the legal protection of persons established in the Community, mentioned in the Preamble to the Brussels Convention, requires that Section 2 should be interpreted in such a way as to enable a normally well-informed defendant reasonably to predict the courts, other than those of the State of his domicile, before which he may be sued. Similarly, Recitals 11 and 12 to the Regulation explain that the rules of jurisdiction must be highly predictable and founded on the principle that jurisdiction is generally based on the defendant's domicile; and that, in addition to the defendant's domicile, there should be alternative grounds of jurisdiction based on a close link between the court and the action or in order to facilitate the sound administration of justice.

In *Van Uden v Deco-Line*,[7] the European Court ruled that a court which has substantive jurisdiction under Section 2 also has jurisdiction to order provisional or protective measures, without that jurisdiction being subject to any further conditions, such as that the provisional measure must be capable of enforcement within its territory.

Section 2 does not apply unless the defendant is domiciled in a Member State. If he is not so domiciled, the possible use of similar connections is remitted by Article 4 to the law of the Member State whose court is seised. As regards English jurisdiction, there are some resemblances between the provisions of paragraph 3.1 of Practice Direction B supplementing Part 6 of the Civil Procedure Rules 1998 (as amended), which apply to such external defendants, and those of Articles 5–7 of the Brussels I Regulation, which apply to defendants who are domiciled in other Member States.[8]

In the United Kingdom, the jurisdiction over defendants domiciled in the United Kingdom, which is conferred on the courts of the United Kingdom in general by such provisions of the Brussels I Regulation as Article 2, is allocated between the courts for the various parts of the United Kingdom by Schedule 4 to the Civil Jurisdiction and Judgments Act 1982 (as amended by the Civil Jurisdiction and Judgments Order 2001, SI 2001/3929). Rules 3–6 of Schedule 4 largely echo Articles 5–7 of the Regulation,[9] and thus offer to a plaintiff, for actions against a defendant who is domiciled in the United Kingdom, a choice between courts of different parts of the United Kingdom which is similar to the choice offered by the Brussels I Regulation between courts of different Member States. But in cases where Schedule 4 confers jurisdiction on the courts for several parts of the United Kingdom, a court for one part of the United Kingdom retains its traditional discretionary power to decline jurisdiction on

---

6 Case C-26/91, [1992] ECR I-3967.

7 Case C-391/95, [1998] ECR I-7091.

8 For example, there are some resemblances between Article 5(1) and para 3.1(7); between Article 5(3) and para 3.1(9); between Article 6(1) and para 3.1(3); and between Article 6(2) and para 3.1(4).

9 But, as regards the place of performance of an ordinary contract, rule 3(a) of Schedule 4 continues to echo Article 5(1) of the Brussels Convention, rather than of the Regulation.

grounds of perceived relative appropriateness in favour of a court for another part of the United Kingdom.[10]

### Establishing Jurisdiction

Problems concerning the manner in which, and the extent to which, a court must satisfy itself as to the existence of its jurisdiction under Chapter II of the Brussels I Regulation may arise in relation to any of the provisions which confer jurisdiction. Such problems appear, however, to give rise to particular difficulty in relation to Article 5, where jurisdiction often depends on facts which are also relevant to the substantive dispute.

Limited guidance on such problems is offered by Articles 25 and 26(1) of the Regulation. By Article 25, where a court of a Member State is seised of a claim which is principally concerned with a matter over which the courts of another Member State have exclusive jurisdiction by virtue of subject-matter under Article 22, it must declare of its own motion that it has no jurisdiction. By Article 26(1), where a defendant domiciled in one Member State is sued in a court of another Member State and does not enter an appearance, the court must declare of its own motion that it has no jurisdiction unless its jurisdiction is derived from the provisions of the Regulation. It seems clear that, in the context of these provisions, it is for the lex fori to determine whether the court should simply call on the plaintiff to produce the appropriate evidence (as in England), or whether the court may initiate investigations of its own (as in France).[11]

In *Effer v Kantner*,[12] the European Court ruled that jurisdiction is not excluded merely because the defendant disputes the existence of facts relevant to its existence; as where a defendant, sued under Article 5(1) at the place of performance of an alleged contractual obligation, denies the existence of the contract relied on. Subsequently, in *Shevill v Presse Alliance*,[13] one of the questions referred by the House of Lords, in the context of the application of Article 5(3) to a libel contained in a newspaper article, concerned the standard of proof which a court should require of the plaintiff of facts relevant to the existence of jurisdiction under Article 5(3). The European Court responded that such problems are not governed by the Regulation, but by the substantive law determined by the conflict rules of the court seised, provided that the effectiveness of the Regulation is not thereby impaired.

Accordingly, in determining their jurisdiction under the Brussels I Regulation, the English courts use the same approach to the establishment of facts relevant to the existence of jurisdiction as that traditionally used under similar English legislation (such as paragraph 3.1 of Practice Direction B supplementing Part 6 of the Civil Procedure Rules 1998 as amended, and its predecessors, rule 6.20 of the Civil Procedure Rules, and Order 11 rule 1(1) of the Rules

---

[10]    See s 49 of the 1982 Act; *Cumming v Scottish Daily Record* [1995] EMLR 538 (Drake J); *Lennon v Scottish Daily Record* [2004] EMLR 18 (Tugendhat J); and *Sunderland Marine Mutual Insurance Co Ltd v Wiseman* [2007] 2 All ER (Comm) 937 (Langley J).

[11]    See Gaudemet-Tallon, *Les Conventions de Bruxelles et de Lugano*, 2nd edition (Montchrestien 1996), at para 275.

[12]    Case 38/81, [1982] ECR 825. See similarly Case 73/77: *Sanders v Van der Putte* [1977] ECR 2383, where the Court ruled that a dispute as to the existence of the relevant tenancy agreement does not affect the applicability of Article 22(1).

[13]    Case C-68/93, [1995] ECR I-415.

of the Supreme Court).[14] Thus jurisdiction is determined as a preliminary issue, on the basis of affidavit evidence, rather than being decided along with the merits at a full trial. The plaintiff must show that, after consideration of both parties' affidavits, it remains strongly arguable ('a good arguable case' exists) that facts which satisfy the jurisdictional requirement exist. This test of a strongly arguable case involves a standard lower than the normal civil standard of proof on a balance of probabilities, since it is inappropriate to reach a firm conclusion as to disputed facts on the basis of affidavit evidence, and improper thereby to prejudice, or appear to prejudice, the decision to be reached (in respect of facts which are relevant to both jurisdiction and merits) at a subsequent full trial of the substantive dispute. Subject to such limitations, the claimant must satisfy the court that he has the better argument as to the existence of jurisdictional facts on the material available; and where the arguments for and against the existence of the jurisdictional facts are evenly balanced, the court will decline jurisdiction. Thus the standard is higher than that of a serious issue warranting trial, which is used in interlocutory applications in relation to facts which are not relevant to the existence of jurisdiction but only to the merits.[15] In Ireland, the Supreme Court requires a plaintiff who relies on a provision such as Article 5(1) to establish that his claim unequivocally comes within the provision.[16]

# ORDINARY CONTRACTS

## Introduction

Article 5(1) of the Brussels I Regulation confers jurisdiction 'in matters relating to a contract' on 'the courts for the place of performance of the obligation in question'. This applies to contracts in general, but certain types of contract (contracts of insurance;[17] certain consumer contracts;[18] contracts of employment;[19] tenancies of land;[20] and contracts relating to matrimonial property or succession on death)[21] are excluded. Until recently, the operation of Article 5(1) was restricted by Article 63 where the defendant was domiciled in Luxembourg, but the restriction imposed by Article 63 has now expired.[22]

---

[14] See *Seaconsar v Bank Markazi* [1994] 1 AC 438 (HL); *Boss Group v Boss France* [1997] 1 WLR 351 (CA); *Canada Trust v Stolzenberg (No 2)* [2002] 1 AC 1 (HL), affirming [1998] 1 WLR 547 (CA); *Latchin v General Mediterranean Holidays* [2002] CLC 330 (Andrew Smith J); *Chellaram v Chellaram (No 2)* [2002] 3 All ER 17 (Lawrence Collins J); *Bank of Tokyo-Mitsubishi v Baskan Gida* [2004] ILPr 26 (Lawrence Collins J); *Bols Distilleries v Superior Yacht Services* [2007] 1 Lloyd's Rep 683 (PC); *Cherney v Deripaska (No 2)* [2009] 1 All ER (Comm) 333 (Christopher Clarke J); and *Deutsche Bank v Asia Pacific Broadband Wireless Communications* [2009] 2 All ER (Comm) 129 (CA).

[15] See *Chellaram v Chellaram (No 2)* [2002] 3 All ER 17 (Lawrence Collins J); and *Surzur v Koros* [1999] 2 Lloyd's Rep 611 (CA).

[16] See *Handbridge v British Aerospace* [1993] 3 IR 352 (Irish Supreme Court).

[17] See Article 8; and Chapter 5 below.

[18] See Article 15; and Chapter 5 below.

[19] See Article 18; and Chapter 5 below.

[20] See Article 22(1); and pp. 147–9 below.

[21] See Article 1(2)(a); and pp. 29–32 above.

[22] See p. 97 below.

Article 5(1)(a) of the Regulation echoes Article 5(1) of the Brussels Convention in providing that 'a person domiciled in a Member State may, in another Member State, be sued: in matters relating to a contract, in the courts for the place of performance of the obligation in question'. But Article 5(1)(b), a new provision, adds that 'for the purpose of this provision and unless otherwise agreed, the place of performance of the obligation in question shall be: in the case of the sale of goods, the place in a Member State where, under the contract, the goods were delivered or should have been delivered; [and] in the case of the provision of services, the place in a Member State where, under the contract, the services were provided or should have been provided'. Finally Article 5(1)(c) specifies that if Article 5(1)(b) does not apply, then Article 5(1)(a) applies.

## Contractual Matters

The Brussels I Regulation echoes the Brussels Convention in limiting the scope of Article 5(1) to 'matters relating to a contract'. Although the Regulation makes amendments to other aspects of Article 5(1), there is in general no obvious reason to suppose that the concept of contractual matters, as interpreted by the European Court in relation to Article 5(1) of the Convention, has been altered by the Regulation. Thus, the concept has an independent meaning, derived primarily from the objectives and general scheme of the Regulation. Positively, it extends to a relationship which involves close links of the same kind as those between the parties to a contract in the strictest sense. Negatively, it does not extend to a situation in which there is no obligation freely assumed by one party towards the other.

Thus in *Peters v ZNAV*,[23] the European Court ruled that the concept of a contract extends to a relationship (such as that between members of an association) which involves close links of the same kind as those between the parties to a contract (in the strictest sense). Obligations to pay a sum of money which have their basis in the relationship existing between an association and its members by virtue of membership are contractual matters within Article 5(1), whether the obligations arise simply from membership or also from decisions made by organs of the association.[24]

Similarly a claim by a consumer against a supplier under consumer protection legislation for a prize promised, whether on the placing of an order for goods or otherwise, counts as a contractual matter for the purposes of the Regulation. Accordingly, it falls within Article 5(1) if any of the conditions specified in Article 15 for the application of Section 4 (Articles 15–17) on certain consumer contracts is not satisfied, so that Section 4 does not apply.[25]

On the other hand, the need for an obligation freely assumed by one party towards the other has led the European Court to rule against the operation of Article 5(1) in a number of situations. Thus, in *Handte v TMCS*,[26] it ruled that, where there has been a chain of sales of

---

[23]    Case 34/82, [1983] ECR 987.
[24]    See also Case 9/87: *Arcado v Haviland* [1988] ECR 1539, where the Court solemnly ruled that proceedings seeking compensation for the wrongful repudiation of an independent commercial agency agreement, and the payment of commission due under such an agreement, are within Article 5(1), since such claims are based on contractual obligations under the agreement.
[25]    See Case C-96/00: *Gabriel* [2002] ECR I-6367; Case C-27/02: *Engler v Janus Versand* [2005] ECR I-481; Case C-180/06; *Ilsinger v Dreschers* [2009] ECR I-3961; and pp. 131–4 below.
[26]    Case C-26/91, [1992] ECR I-3967.

the same goods, Article 5(1) does not apply to an action between a sub-buyer of goods and a manufacturer who is not the direct seller to the sub-buyer, relating to defects in the goods or to their unsuitability for their intended purpose. The Court took into account the facts that the parties' contractual obligations may vary from contract to contract in the chain, that the identity and domicile of the sub-buyer may well be unknown to the manufacturer, and that in most Member States the liability of a manufacturer towards a sub-buyer for defects in the goods sold is not regarded as contractual in nature.[27]

Similarly, in *Réunion Européenne v Spliethoff's Bevrachtingskantoor*,[28] which involved an action brought by a consignee of goods which had been carried under a bill of lading contract, and had allegedly been damaged in the course of such carriage, not against the issuer of the bill of lading, but against the actual carrier, the European Court ruled that, since the bill of lading disclosed no contractual relationship freely entered into between the consignee and the actual carrier, such a claim was not a contractual matter within Article 5(1), but a tortious matter within Article 5(3). Again, in *Tacconi v Wagner*,[29] the Court ruled that Article 5(1) does not apply to an obligation to make good damage caused by the unjustified breaking off of negotiations, derived from breach of a rule requiring the parties to act in good faith in negotiations with a view to the formation of a contract. Similarly, in *Frahuil v Assitalia*,[30] the European Court ruled that Article 5(1) does not apply to a claim against the owner of imported goods, brought by a guarantor who had paid customs duties under a guarantee obtained by the forwarding agent, by way of subrogation to the rights of the customs authorities, if the owner was not a party to the contract of guarantee and did not authorise its conclusion.

Further, as the European Court ruled in *VKI v Henkel*,[31] Article 5(1) does not apply to a preventive action brought by a consumer protection organisation for the purpose of preventing a trader from using unfair terms in dealings with private individuals. For the consumer protection organisation and the trader are in no way linked by any contractual relationship. Although it is likely that the trader has already entered into contracts with a number of consumers, the consumer protection organisation is never itself a party to such contracts. The legal basis for its action is a right conferred by statute for the purpose of preventing the use of terms which the legislature considers to be unlawful in dealings between a professional and a private final consumer.

It is clear from the rulings in *Handte v TMCS*,[32] *Réunion Européenne v Spliethoff's Bevrachtingskantoor*,[33] and *Frahuil v Assitalia*,[34] that Article 5(1) requires some form of privity. But the requirement is not so strict as to prevent a claim brought by a third party to a contract against a contracting party on the basis that the contract was designed to confer rights on the third party from being regarded as contractual so as to fall thus within Article 5(1).

---

27 See also *SBCN v MB Marine*, 18th October 1994, where the French Court of Cassation applied Article 5(3) to such a claim.
28 Case C-51/97, [1998] ECR I-6511.
29 Case C-334/00, [2002] ECR I-7357.
30 Case C-265/02, [2004] ECR I-1543.
31 Case C-167/00, [2002] ECR I-8111.
32 Case C-26/91, [1992] ECR I-3967.
33 Case C-51/97, [1998] ECR I-6511.
34 Case C-265/02, [2004] ECR I-1543.

Thus, in *Atlas Shipping Agency v Suisse Atlantique*,[35] Rix J permitted a broker to utilise Article 5(1) when suing on a promise by the buyer, contained in a contract for the sale of a ship, to pay the broker's commission, the promise being made to the seller but treated under English law as held by the seller on trust for the broker. Similarly in *WPP v Benatti*,[36] the Court of Appeal accepted that a claim by a third party to a contract for breach of a contractual duty owed to him by virtue of the terms of the contract and the Contracts (Rights of Third Parties) Act 1999 falls within Article 5(1).[37]

### The Relation between the Claim and the Contract

Under the Brussels Convention, it seemed clear that a plaintiff who founded his claim on an assertion that there was no valid contract between the parties could not utilise Article 5(1). The provision was confined to cases where the plaintiff founded his claim on an assertion that there was a valid contract between the parties, and sought enforcement of the contract or other relief based on its validity. This approach was supported by the ruling of the European Court in *Tacconi v Wagner*[38] that a claim for loss caused by the unjustified breaking off of precontractual negotiations was not within Article 5(1) of the Convention, since there was no obligation freely assumed by one party towards another, and the liability was derived from a legal rule requiring the parties to act in good faith in negotiations with a view to the formation of a contract.

Thus the decision of the House of Lords (by a bare majority) in *Kleinwort Benson v City of Glasgow District Council*,[39] that English legislation corresponding to Article 5(1) of the Convention did not extend to a restitutionary claim to recover money paid under a void contract (such as an interest rate swap contract which was void ab initio on account of the defendant's incapacity as a local authority to enter into a contract of that nature), was subsequently vindicated by the ruling in *Tacconi*. On the other hand, the slightly later ruling of the House (again by a bare majority) in *Agnew v Länsförsäkringsbolagens*,[40] that Article 5(1) of the Lugano Convention 1988, which echoes Article 5(1) of the Brussels Convention, extended to an action seeking avoidance of a contract for misrepresentation or non-disclosure in the pre-contractual negotiations (such as an action brought by a reinsurer seeking avoidance of the reinsurance contract for breach of the duty to make a fair presentation of the risk, by giving full disclosure and avoiding misrepresentation, in the negotiations leading to the conclusion of the contract), was subsequently discredited by the ruling

---

35   [1995] 2 Lloyd's Rep 188.
36   [2007] 2 All ER (Comm) 525 (CA).
37   See also Case 201/82: *Gerling v Treasury Administration* [1983] ECR 2503, on Article 23.
38   Case C-334/00, [2002] ECR I-7357.
39   [1999] AC 153 (HL); reversing [1996] 2 All ER 257 (CA). The case directly involved, not Article 5(1) of the Brussels Convention, but the provision echoing Article 5(1) of the Convention contained in Schedule 4 to the Civil Jurisdiction and Judgments Act 1982, dealing with the allocation between courts for different parts of the United Kingdom of jurisdiction over a defendant domiciled in the United Kingdom. But the House did not consider that there was any relevant difference between Article 5(1) of the Brussels Convention and the corresponding provision of Schedule 4.
40   [2001] 1 AC 223 (HL); affirming [1997] 4 All ER 937 (CA); in turn affirming [1996] 4 All ER 978 (Mance J) and rejecting *Trade Indemnity v Forsakringsaktiebolaget Njord* [1995] 1 All ER 796 (Rix J).

in *Tacconi*.[41] Moreover, the slightly earlier decision of the Court of Appeal in *Boss Group v Boss France*,[42] permitting the use of Article 5(1) for an action in which the plaintiff was seeking a negative declaration that, contrary to the defendant's assertion, no exclusive distribution contract existed between the parties, also seems inconsistent with the approach adopted by the European Court in *Tacconi*, but in *Youell v La Reunion Aerienne*,[43] the Court of Appeal has regarded itself as still bound by its decision in *Boss Group*.

It is submitted that the principle underlying the ruling in *Tacconi*, that Article 5(1) does not apply where the plaintiff founds his claim on an assertion that there is no valid contract between the parties, and is confined to cases where the plaintiff founds his claim on an assertion that there is a valid contract between the parties, and seeks enforcement of the contract or other relief based on its validity, remains fully applicable under the Brussels I Regulation. It must be admitted that a different view might possibly be adopted in respect of cases to which the new rules laid down by Article 5(1)(b) of the Regulation apply, since that provision abandons the focus on the place of performance of the obligation on which the plaintiff's claim is based in favour of the place of delivery of goods sold, or the place of provision of services supplied, under the contract. But it is submitted that even in such cases there is no necessity for, or clear indication of intention in favour of, a widening of the scope of Article 5(1) in this respect.

In any event, under both the Regulation and the Convention, it is clear that, so long as the plaintiff's claim is based on a strongly arguable assertion that a valid contractual (or equivalent) obligation is owed by the defendant to the plaintiff, and that the defendant has committed or threatened to commit a breach of that obligation, the nature of the remedy sought for the breach is not material. Article 5(1) is not confined to claims for damages for breach of contract, or for specific performance of a contract, or for an injunction against a breach of a contract. It extends to a claim for a declaration that the plaintiff is not bound to perform a contract because of the defendant's breach; as where a reinsurer seeks a declaration that it is discharged from liability to indemnify the reinsured because of the reinsured's breaches in failing promptly to notify and to furnish information about losses.[44] Moreover, a plaintiff who relies on a breach by the defendant of a valid contract may utilise Article 5(1) even where he seeks a remedy which is regarded by the relevant national law as restitutionary rather than contractual in nature; for example, where a buyer who has paid the agreed price in advance seeks to recover it back on account of the seller's total failure, in breach of the contract, to deliver the promised goods.[45] It is less clear whether a plaintiff who seeks a restitutionary remedy on the basis that a contract was initially valid but has subsequently been frustrated

---

[41]   In any event, a claim for damages for a fraudulent or negligent misrepresentation which induced the plaintiff to enter into a contract with the defendant did not fall within Article 5(1) of the Brussels Convention; see *Dunhill v Diffusion Internationale de Maroquinerie de Prestige* [2002] ILPr 13 (Rokison QC).

[42]   [1997] 1 WLR 351 (CA). See also para 3.1(8) of Practice Direction B supplementing Part 6 of the Civil Procedure Rules 1998 (as amended).

[43]   See [2009] EWCA Civ 175.

[44]   See *AIG Group v The Ethniki* [2000] 2 All ER 566 (CA); affirming [1998] 4 All ER 301 (Colman J).

[45]   See per Lord Goff in *Kleinwort Benson v City of Glasgow District Council* [1999] AC 153.

may utilise Article 5(1); for example, where a supplier seeks to recover a quantum meruit for goods or services supplied by him before the frustrating event.[46]

## The Obligation in Question

With regard to Article 5(1), it is in respect of the concept of *the obligation in question*, whose place of performance is determinative, that the Brussels I Regulation has departed radically from the Brussels Convention. In the Convention, Article 5(1) merely referred to the obligation in question, without further definition, and this was consistently interpreted by the European Court as referring to the contractual obligation on which the plaintiff's sole or principal claim in the action was based.

In the Regulation, Article 5(1)(b) now offers specific definitions of the obligation in question, which apply to contracts for the sale of goods and to contracts for the provision of services. In the case of the sale of goods, it refers to the place in a Member State where, under the contract, the goods were delivered or should have been delivered. In the case of the provision of services, it refers to the place in a Member State where, under the contract, the services were provided or should have been provided. But Article 5(1)(a) and (c) of the Regulation provide for the continued operation of the Convention approach, which refers to the obligation on which the claim is based, in cases to which Article 5(1)(b) does not apply.[47]

Thus it is necessary to consider separately: (a) contracts for the sale of goods; (b) contracts for the provision of services; and (c) other types of contract to which Article 5(1) applies.

## Contracts for the Sale of Goods

Article 5(1)(b)(i) of the Regulation specifies that, for the purpose of Article 5(1) and unless otherwise agreed, in the case of the sale of goods, it is the place in a Member State where, under the contract, the goods were delivered or should have been delivered which counts as the place of performance of the obligation in question. This provision is designed to displace the Convention approach, under which reference was made to the obligation on which the plaintiff's sole or principal claim in the action was based, and to substitute a reference to the place of delivery of the goods, so that the courts for the place of delivery are rendered competent to entertain actions based on any of the obligations arising from a contract of sale.[48]

Formerly, under the Convention approach, where a buyer of goods sued the seller, complaining of defects in the quality or the fitness for purpose of the goods supplied, the relevant place of performance was the place at which the goods in question were delivered to the buyer.[49] On the other hand, where a seller or other supplier sued for the price of goods deliv-

---

[46]   See per Lord Clyde in *Kleinwort Benson v City of Glasgow District Council* [1999] AC 153.

[47]   See Case C-533/07: *Falco v Weller-Lindhorst* [2009] ECR I-3327.

[48]   See Case C-386/05: *Color Drack v LEXX International* [2007] ECR I-3699, at para 26, where the Court emphasised that Article 5(1)(b)(i) of the Regulation establishes the place of delivery as the autonomous linking factor applicable to all claims founded on one and the same contract for the sale of goods, rather than merely to claims founded on the obligation of delivery itself.

[49]   See *Thompson Hayward v Sirena* [1988] ECC 319 (French Court of Cassation); *Re a Consignment of Italian Wine* [1988] ECC 159 (German Supreme Court); and in England *Hewden Stuart v Gottwald*, 13th May 1992 (CA); *Viskase v Paul Kiefal* [1999] 3 All ER 362 (CA); and *MBM Fabri-Clad v Eisen und Huttenwerke Thale* [2000] ILPr 505 (CA).

ered or services supplied, the relevant obligation was that of the buyer or other recipient to pay the price, and the place where the goods or services were delivered or supplied was in itself irrelevant.[50]

The concept of a contract for the sale of goods seems reasonably clear. Since goods refers to tangible movables, Article 5(1)(b)(i) does not apply to sales of land or of intangible property (such as a patent or copyright). Since sale implies the transfer of ownership of goods in return for payment of a monetary price, Article 5(1)(b)(i) does not apply to contracts of barter (for example, for the exchange of guns for butter), nor to contracts for the hire of goods. But transactions similar to a sale of goods, such as hire-purchase, are probably included, even if they are regarded as a distinct category of contract under the technical rules contained in a national law. On the other hand, an exclusive distribution agreement does not count as a sale of goods for the purpose of Article 5(1).[51]

It is clear that a contract counts as a sale of goods, rather than a contract for the provision of services, even if the goods are to be manufactured by the seller in compliance with the special requirements of the buyer. Thus in *Car Trim v KeySafety Systems*,[52] which involved a contract between two manufacturers in the automobile sector for the supply of components used in the manufacture of airbag systems, the European Court ruled that a contract must be regarded as a sale of goods where its purpose is the supply of goods to be manufactured or produced, and the supplier is responsible for the quality of the goods and their compliance with the contract, even though the purchaser has specified certain requirements with regard to the provision, fabrication and delivery of the goods to be produced, unless the purchaser has supplied all or most of the materials from which the goods are manufactured.

In *Color Drack v LEXX International*,[53] the European Court ruled that Article 5(1)(b)(i) of the Regulation is applicable where there are several places of delivery under a single contract of sale; for example, where the seller has to make separate deliveries of different consignments to various customers of the buyer at their respective residences. In such a case, the court which is competent to hear all the claims based on the contract for the sale of goods is the court for the principal place of delivery, which must be determined on the basis of economic criteria. If the principal place of delivery cannot be ascertained, the plaintiff may sue the defendant in the court for the place of delivery of its choice. Although in *Color Drack* itself the Court was careful to confine its ruling to cases where there are several places of delivery within a single Member State, it has subsequently, by a dictum in *Rehder v Air Baltic*,[54] extended the principles laid down in *Color Drack* to cases where there are several places of delivery, located in different Member States.

---

[50]   See Case 56/79: *Zelger v Salinitri (No 1)* [1980] ECR 89; Case 266/85: *Shenavai v Kreischer* [1987] ECR 239; and Case C-288/92: *Custom Made v Stawa* [1994] ECR I-2913. See also *Nienaber v Impex-Euro* [1988] ECC 150 (Italian Supreme Court); *San Carlo v SNC Vico*, 6th February 1996 (French Court of Cassation); *Mercury Publicity v Loerke* [1993] ILPr 142 (English CA), which involved a claim for money due under a contract of commercial agency; and *Bateg Delta v Ward Group*, 25th February 1997 (French Court of Cassation), referring, in an action on a guarantee of payment, to the place at which the guarantor was bound to pay, and treating the place of performance of the obligation guaranteed as irrelevant.

[51]   See *Nestorway v Ambaflex* [2006] IEHC 235 (Clarke J).

[52]   Case C-381/08, [2010] All ER (D) 286 (Feb).

[53]   Case C-386/05, [2007] ECR I-3699.

[54]   Case C-204/08, [2009] ECR I-6073.

Determination of the place of delivery, in cases involving carriage of the goods, has now been addressed by the European Court in *Car Trim v KeySafety Systems*.[55] Before that decision, it seemed clear that delivery referred to the transfer of possession of the goods by the seller to the buyer or his agent; and, since the point at which such a transfer of possession would occur could depend on the meaning and effect of ambiguous or confusing terms contained in the contract of sale,[56] that it was for the law which governed the contract of sale under the Rome Convention 1980 or the Rome I Regulation[57] to determine the meaning and effect of the contractual terms for the purpose of ascertaining the place of delivery.[58] But in *Car Trim* the European Court explained that the autonomy of the connecting factors provided for in Article 5(1)(b) of the Regulation precludes application of the rules of private international law of the forum State and the substantive law which would be applicable thereunder.[59]

Before the ruling in *Car Trim*, it seemed likely that in most cases the effect of the reference by Article 5(1)(b)(i) to the place of delivery would have been to enable the seller to sue in his own country, whether he was suing for the price, for damages for non-acceptance, or for a negative declaration that he had complied with the contract and thus was not liable to return the price received or to pay damages. On the other hand, the buyer would usually have been unable to sue in his own country. This became apparent when typical examples of the four main categories of transnational sale were considered. Firstly, in the case of a sale ex-works, delivery would have taken place at the seller's factory. Secondly, in the case of an FOB (free on board) sale, delivery would have taken place at the port of loading,[60] which would usually (though not invariably) be located in the seller's country. Thirdly, in the case of a C&F (cost and freight) sale, delivery of the relevant documents (especially the bill of lading) would presumably have amounted to symbolic or constructive delivery of the goods. So the relevant place would presumably have been that at which the documents were or should have been tendered, rather than the place where the goods were located at the time of the tender; and, at least where English law applied, the documents would have had to be tendered, unless otherwise agreed, at the buyer's residence.[61] But a contrary agreement would often have existed, especially where the contract provided for payment by means of a documentary credit, usually involving tender at and payment by a bank located in the seller's country. Only in the fourth and least common case, the arrival

---

55    Case C-381/08, [2010] All ER (D) 286 (Feb).
56    See *Scottish and Newcastle International Ltd v Othon Ghalanos Ltd* [2008] 2 All ER 768 (HL).
57    On the Rome Convention 1980 and the Rome I Regulation, see Chapter 12 below.
58    See Case 12/76: *Tessili v Dunlop* [1976] ECR 1473, and Case C-440/97: *Groupe Concorde v 'The Suhadiwarno Panjan'* [1999] ECR I-6307, which dealt with the ascertainment of the place of performance under the Brussels Convention; and per Lord Bingham in *Scottish and Newcastle International Ltd v Othon Ghalanos Ltd* [2008] 2 All ER 768, at para 4, adopting a similar approach to the ascertainment of the place of delivery under the Regulation.
59    See paras 47–53. See also Case C-386/05: *Color Drack v LEXX International* [2007] ECR I-3699, at para 30.
60    See *Scottish and Newcastle International Ltd v Othon Ghalanos Ltd* [2008] 2 All ER 768 (HL).
61    See *Johnson v Taylor* [1920] AC 144 (HL); and *The Albazero* [1974] 2 All ER 906 (Brandon J), reversed on other grounds, [1977] AC 774 (HL). Cf. the view of Lord Mance in *Scottish and Newcastle International Ltd v Othon Ghalanos Ltd* [2008] 2 All ER 768, at para 52, that Article 5(1)(b)(i) of the Regulation directs attention to a place of physical delivery of goods.

contract, would Article 5(1)(b) usually have conferred jurisdiction on the courts of the buyer's country.[62]

Any such analysis, with its arguably perverse preference for the interests of the seller, has now been rejected by the European Court. In *Car Trim v KeySafety Systems*,[63] which involved a sale of components by a German manufacturer to an Italian manufacturer, it ruled that, in the case of a sale involving carriage of goods, the place of delivery must be determined primarily on the basis of the express provisions of the contract. Where it is possible to identify the place of delivery in that way, without reference to the substantive law applicable to the contract, it is the place so identified which is to be regarded as the place of delivery for the purposes of Article 5(1)(b)(i) of the Regulation. But, secondly, in the absence of such a contractual provision, it is the place where the goods were or should have been physically transferred to the purchaser at their final destination, so as to place them at the actual disposal of the purchaser, which counts as the place of delivery under Article 5(1)(b)(i). The principal effect of the ruling, in contrast with the results which might previously have been expected, is that, in the case of a C&F contract, or of a 'mixed' contract whose terms have some features usual in an FOB contract and others usual in a C&F contract, the relevant place will now be the port of discharge, as specified in the contract. In the case of an ex-works contract, an ordinary FOB contract, or an arrival contract, the express terms of the contract will unambiguously point respectively to the seller's factory, the port of loading, or the buyer's premises. Thus the ruling appears to eliminate any substantial preference for the seller's country.

Another difficulty with Article 5(1)(b) of the Regulation arises from its reference to a contrary agreement, which will apparently exclude the application of Article 5(1)(b). Presumably this is not intended merely as a reminder that Article 5 in its entirety can be overridden by a jurisdiction clause which operates under Article 23. What seems to be envisaged is an agreement that the place of delivery or service provision shall *not* be regarded as the place of performance, so as to eliminate the operation of Article 5(1)(b), and to restore the operation of the Convention approach, referring to the obligation on which the plaintiff's sole or principal claim is based, in accordance with Article 5(1)(a) and (c). It is true that in *Car Trim* the European Court accepted that under Article 5(1)(b) the parties to the contract enjoy a certain freedom in defining the place of delivery of the goods, and that the place of delivery is in principle to be that agreed by the parties, so that a term which unambiguously specifies the place of delivery will be effective. But to allow the parties, by an agreement not complying with the requirements of Article 23, to designate a fictitious place of delivery or service provision for the purposes of Article 5(1), so as to establish jurisdiction without intending actual performance at the specified place, would subvert the limitations on jurisdiction clauses imposed by Article 23.[64]

A further difficulty concerns the operation of Article 5(1) in respect of a contract for the sale of goods or the provision of services, in cases where the place of delivery or service provision is not located in a Member State, but in an external country or outside any national

---

62    For an example of an arrival contract, in the context of Article 5(1) of the Brussels Convention, see *MBM Fabri-Clad v Eisen und Huttenwerke Thale* [2000] ILPr 505 (CA).
63    Case C-381/08, [2010] All ER (D) 286 (Feb).
64    See Case C-106/95: *MSG v Les Gravières Rhénanes* [1997] ECR I-911; *Gotz v Noge*, 27th February 1996 (French Court of Cassation); and *7E Communications v Vertex Antennentechnik* [2007] 2 All ER (Comm) 798 (CA).

territory (such as on the high seas), or where the terms of the contract, along with any supplementary rules laid down by the European Court, are inadequate to enable the place of delivery or service provision to be identified. On a literal reading, in such cases Article 5(1)(b) does not apply, and the Convention approach becomes applicable under Article 5(1)(a) and (c). Such a result was envisaged by Lords Bingham and Mance in *Scottish and Newcastle International Ltd v Othon Ghalanos Ltd*.[65] But it is difficult to see any substantial justification for giving the plaintiff 'a second bite at the cherry' in this way, and it is certainly possible to read Article 5(1)(b) as 'applying', and thus excluding the Convention approach, in cases where the contract is for the sale of goods or the provision of services, even though it does not have the effect of making any court available because the place of delivery or service provision is not located within the Member States or is unascertainable.

## Contracts for the Provision of Services

Article 5(1)(b)(ii) of the Regulation specifies that, for the purpose of Article 5(1) and unless otherwise agreed, in the case of the provision of services, it is the place in a Member State where, under the contract, the services were provided or should have been provided which counts as the place of performance of the obligation in question. As in the case of the sale of goods, this provision is designed to displace the Convention approach, under which reference was made to the obligation on which the plaintiff's sole or principal claim in the action was based, and to substitute a reference to the place of provision of the services, so that the courts for the place of service provision are rendered competent to entertain actions based on any of the obligations arising from a contract for services.[66]

In *Falco v Weller-Lindhorst*,[67] the European Court explained that, for the purpose of Article 5(1)(b)(ii) of the Regulation, the concept of service implies that the party who provides the service carries out a particular activity in return for remuneration. Accordingly, it ruled that a contract under which the owner of an intellectual property right (such as a copyright) grants its contractual partner a licence to use that right in return for remuneration is not a contract for the provision of services within Article 5(1)(b)(ii), since such a contract does not involve an activity by the licensor, but only an obligation by the licensor not to challenge the use of the right by the licensee, and it is immaterial whether the licensee is obliged to use the intellectual property right licensed.

In view of this ruling that a service provider must carry out a particular activity in return for remuneration, it may be inferred that Article 5(1)(b)(ii) does not apply to contracts under which the service takes the form of a monetary payment (such as contracts of loan;[68] contracts of reinsurance; contracts of guarantee;[69] and bankers' letters of credit). It may also be inferred that Article 5(1)(b)(ii) does not apply to contracts under which *both* of the parties have oblig-

---

65    [2008] 2 All ER 768, at paras 3 and 50.
66    See Case C-204/08: *Rehder v Air Baltic* [2009] ECR I-6073; and Case C-19/09: *Wood Floor Solutions Andreas Domberger GmbH v Silva Trade SA* [2010] 1 WLR 1900. Article 5(1)(b) appears to have been overlooked by the Court of Appeal in *WPP v Benatti* [2007] 2 All ER (Comm) 525.
67    Case C-533/07, [2009] ECR I-3327.
68    See *Tavoulareas v Tsavliris* [2006] 1 All ER (Comm) 109 (Andrew Smith J).
69    See *Commercial Marine Piling Ltd v Pierse Contracting Ltd* [2009] EWHC 2241 (TCC) (Ramsey J).

ations to perform substantial activities other than the making of monetary payments (such as franchising contracts; exclusive distribution contracts; and contracts between an author and a publisher for the writing and publication of a literary work).

On the other hand, it is clear that Article 5(1)(b)(ii) applies to contracts for professional services, such as those of an architect, a lawyer, an accountant, or a tax adviser;[70] and to contracts for commercial services, such as the erection, improvement or repair of a building, or the servicing or repair of a vehicle, or the activities of a commercial agent in the negotiation or conclusion of transactions on behalf of a principal.[71]

It is also clear that Article 5(1)(b)(ii) applies to contracts for the carriage of goods or passengers. In *Rehder v Air Baltic*,[72] which involved a contract for the carriage of a passenger by air from Munich in Germany to Vilnius in Lithuania by a Latvian airline,[73] the European Court established the principle that Article 5(1)(b)(ii) confers jurisdiction on the courts for the place or places at which the main provision of services is to be carried out. Thus, in the case of a contract for the carriage of a passenger by air from one Member State to another Member State, Article 5(1)(b)(ii) confers jurisdiction both on the court for the place of departure of the aircraft, and on the court for the place of arrival of the aircraft, as specified in the contract, and gives the plaintiff the choice of suing in either of those courts. The Court explained that air transport consists, by its very nature, of services provided in an indivisible and identical manner from the place of departure to that of arrival of the aircraft, with the result that a separate part of the service which is the principal service and is to be provided in a specific place, cannot be distinguished in such cases on the basis of an economic criterion.

It seems clear that the ruling in *Rehder* applies analogistically to contracts for the carriage of goods, and to contracts for carriage of passengers or goods by other means than air (such as carriage by sea, road or rail), including voyage charterparties of ships or aircraft.[74] While Article 5(1)(b)(ii) no doubt extends to time charterparties, its precise effect on such contracts may need further elucidation. On the other hand, it seems probable that a bare-boat charterparty does not count as a contract for services, but as a contract for the hire of goods, and thus remains subject to the Convention approach, in accordance with Article 5(1)(a) and (c). Moreover, in *Rehder*, the Court was careful to confine its ruling to cases in which there is a single contracting and operating carrier. Thus the precise

---

70    See also *Barry v Bradshaw* [2000] ILPr 706, where under the Convention the English Court of Appeal accepted jurisdiction to entertain an action by an Irish client of an Irish accountant, who had been instructed to deal with the client's position in relation to United Kingdom taxation, on the ground that the principal obligation was to communicate with the United Kingdom tax authority and secure representation at a hearing in England.

71    See Case C-19/09: *Wood Floor Solutions Andreas Domberger GmbH v Silva Trade SA* [2010] 1 WLR 1900.

72    Case C-204/08, [2009] ECR I-6073.

73    The claim brought by the passenger against the airline was for compensation for cancellation of the flight under EC Regulation 261/2004, and was therefore not within the scope of the Montreal Convention 1999.

74    Cf. *Union Transport v Continental Lines* [1992] 1 WLR 15, where, under the Convention, the House of Lords held that where, in breach of a voyage charterparty, the shipowner failed both to nominate and then to provide a vessel, the more fundamental and thus the principal of these obligations was the obligation to nominate.

effect of Article 5(1)(b)(ii) in relation to contracts for multi-modal carriage (for example, by sea and then road or rail) awaits further elucidation.

As regards claims for damage to or loss of cargo under a bill of lading contract, the approach adopted by the European Court in *Rehder* has now replaced that adopted under the Brussels Convention by Rix J in *The Sea Maas*.[75] Under the Convention, everything depended on the nature of the bill of lading holder's claim. If the shipowner had misdelivered the goods at destination, the place of performance of the obligation in question would have been the port of discharge. If the ship was seaworthy, but the alleged failure of due diligence was some lack of care during the voyage, then the place of performance of the obligation in question, to carry and care for the goods with due diligence, might have been the high seas, so that there would have been no special jurisdiction under Article 5(1) and the matter would have rested with Article 2. But if the fundamental matter of complaint was that the shipowner had never provided a seaworthy vessel, then the place of performance of the obligation in question would have been the port of loading.

It may also be inferred from the ruling in *Rehder* that, in the case of a contract for the provision of code or data, to be downloaded from a website via the Internet, Article 5(1)(b)(ii) gives the plaintiff the choice of suing at the location of the server from which the code or data is provided, or at the location of the receiving computer, at least where the place in question is specified in the contract.

A further inference which may be drawn from the ruling in *Rehder* is that, in the case of a contract to inspect goods and report on their quality, Article 5(1)(b)(ii) confers jurisdiction both on the court for the place where the inspection is to be carried out, and on the court for the place where the report is to be delivered, at least where the place in question is specified in the contract. Thus the decision under the Convention of the Court of Appeal in *Source v TUV Rheinland Holding*,[76] that the obligation to carry out the inspection, rather than to provide the report, constituted the principal of those obligations, has been superseded by the Regulation.[77]

In *Wood Floor Solutions Andreas Domberger GmbH v Silva Trade SA*,[78] which involved a contract of commercial agency, the European Court confirmed that Article 5(1)(b)(ii) of the Regulation applies to cases in which services are provided in several Member States, and that in such cases it refers to the place of the main provision of services. More specifically, in the case of a commercial agency contract, it is the commercial agent who performs the obligation which characterises the contract and who provides the services. Thus where these are several places where services are provided by the agent, Article 5(1)(b)(ii) refers to the place of the main provision of services by the agent, and this place must, where possible, be identified by

---

[75] [1999] 2 Lloyd's Rep 281. See also *Royal & Sun Alliance Insurance v MK Digital* [2006] 2 Lloyd's Rep 110 (CA). Cf. the proposal made by Colomer AG, but rejected by the European Court, in Case C-440/97: *Groupe Concorde* [1999] ECR I-6307, that in the case of a bill of lading contract, the port of destination as specified in the bill should be regarded under the Convention as the place of performance of all the obligations under the contract.

[76] [1998] QB 54 (CA).

[77] In any event, the decision in *Source* to decline jurisdiction over claims, not only for negligently inspecting goods in China and Taiwan, but also for submitting the resulting inaccurate reports in England, overlooked the enabling (rather than restrictive) character of the reference under the Convention to the principal among the obligations on which the plaintiff's claims were based.

[78] Case C-19/09, [2010] 1 WLR 1900.

reference to the provisions of the contract. If the provisions of a contract do not enable the place of the main provision of services to be determined (either because they provide for several places where services are provided, or because they do not expressly provide for any specific place where services are to be provided), but the agent has already provided such services, reference must be made to the place where he has in fact for the most part carried out his activities in the performance of the contract, provided that the provision of services in that place is not contrary to the provisions of the contract; and for this purpose account may be taken of the time spent in a place and the importance of the activities carried out there. As a last resort, where the place of the main provision of services cannot be determined on the basis of the provisions of the contract itself or its actual performance, reference must be made, in the case of services provided by a commercial agent, to the place where the agent is domiciled.

It may perhaps be inferred from the ruling in *Wood Floor Solutions* that the European Court will strive to ensure that, for each type of contract for the provision of services, there is a specific connection which must always exist and which serves as the indication of the place of service provision unless displaced by the terms of the contract or its actual performance.

In the case of contracts for services (as in the case of the sale of goods), Article 5(1)(b) of the Regulation provides for its exclusion by means of a contrary agreement, so as to restore the operation of the Convention approach. It is also possible that the Convention approach may be applicable where the place of service provision is not located in a Member State, but in an external country or outside any national territory (such as on the high seas), or where the terms of the contract, along with any supplementary rules laid down by the European Court, are inadequate to enable the place of service provision to be identified.[79]

**The Convention Approach**

The effect of Article 5(1)(a) and (c) of the Brussels I Regulation is to preserve the Convention approach, referring to the place of performance of the obligation on which the plaintiff's sole or principal claim is based, in all cases where the new approach specified by Article 5(1)(b), referring to the place of delivery or service provision, does not apply. In *Falco v Weller-Lindhorst*,[80] the European Court confirmed that the Community legislature intended, in relation to Article 5(1) of the Regulation, to maintain, for all contracts other than those concerning the sale of goods and the provision of services, the principles established by the Court in relation to the Brussels Convention, regarding the obligation to take into consideration, and the determination of the place of its execution. Thus the effect to be given to Article 5(1)(a) of the Regulation should be identical to that of Article 5(1) of the Convention, and for this purpose reference must continue to be made to the principles which result from the case-law of the European Court on Article 5(1) of the Convention.

The primary case in which the Convention approach remains applicable by virtue of Article 5(1)(a) and (c) of the Regulation is where the contract is not for the sale of goods nor for the provision of services. Thus the Convention approach remains applicable to a wide

---

[79] See pp. 87–8 above.
[80] Case C-533/07, [2009] ECR I-3327.

range of contracts. These include contracts for the sale of land, or of corporate securities or other financial instruments (such as shares or bonds), or of intellectual property rights (such as a patent, a trade mark, or a copyright); contracts for the licensing of intellectual property rights;[81] franchising contracts; exclusive distribution contracts; contracts between an author and a publisher for the writing and publication of a literary work; contracts for the exchange of goods or services (guns for butter; hotel accommodation for advertising; or beer for theatre tickets); contracts for the hire of goods; contracts for the loan of money;[82] reinsurance contracts; contracts of guarantee;[83] and bankers' letters of credit.

But there are also some situations in which, under Article 5(1)(a) and (c) of the Regulation, the Convention approach retains a supplementary role in relation to contracts for the sale of goods or for the provision of services. It seems clear this is so where the parties have agreed to exclude the operation of Article 5(1)(b), but they have not also made a valid agreement on exclusive jurisdiction in accordance with Article 23, so as to exclude Article 5(1) altogether. It may well also be so where the place of delivery or service provision is not located in a Member State, but in an external country or outside any national territory (such as on the high seas); or where the place of delivery or service provision is not ascertainable by reference to the terms of the contract, along with any supplementary rules laid down by the European Court. This may include the situation where under the contract one of the parties is given an option to designate the place of delivery or service provision, and he has not yet exercised the option.

Where the Convention approach applies, the rulings of the European Court have established that the obligation in question, now referred to in Article 5(1)(a) of the Regulation, is the contractual obligation on which the plaintiff's action is based.[84] Where in his action the plaintiff makes claims based on a number of obligations under the same contract, the obligation in question is the principal (or most important) contractual obligation among those on which the plaintiff's claims are based.[85] But where the plaintiff's claims are based on several obligations which are of equal importance, the court is competent to entertain only those claims which are based on obligations whose places of performance are within its territory.[86] Moreover, Article 5(1)(a) does not apply where the place of performance of the obligation on which the claim is based is indeterminate, because the contractual obligation at issue consists

---

81  See Case C-533/07: *Falco v Weller-Lindhorst* [2009] ECR I-3327.

82  See *Tavoulareas v Tsavliris* [2006] 1 All ER (Comm) 109 (Andrew Smith J).

83  See *Commercial Marine Piling Ltd v Pierse Contracting Ltd* [2009] EWHC 2241 (TCC) (Ramsey J).

84  See Case 14/76: *De Bloos v Bouyer* [1976] ECR 1497; Case 266/85: *Shenavai v Kreischer* [1987] ECR 239; Case C-288/92: *Custom Made v Stawa* [1994] ECR I-2913; and Case C-420/97: *Leathertex v Bodetex* [1999] ECR I-6747.

85  See Case 266/85: *Shenavai v Kreischer* [1987] ECR 239; Case C-420/97: *Leathertex v Bodetex* [1999] ECR I-6747; *Union Transport v Continental Lines* [1992] 1 WLR 15 (HL), affirming [1991] 2 Lloyd's Rep 48 (CA); and *Source v TUV Rheinland Holding* [1998] QB 54 (CA).

86  See Case C-420/97: *Leathertex v Bodetex* [1999] ECR I-6747, which involved claims by a commercial agent for compensation for the wrongful termination of the agency contract without notice, and for payment of commission earned. See also *Union Transport v Continental Lines* [1991] 2 Lloyd's Rep 48 (CA), where Lloyd LJ explained that *Shenavai* did not require the court to select a principal obligation if it would be artificial or arbitrary to do so. The decision was affirmed without consideration of this point, [1992] 1 WLR 15 (HL).

in a negative undertaking without any geographical limitation and therefore having multiple places of performance, as in the case of an obligation not to participate in a competing bid for a concession.[87] The European Court has specifically rejected arguments that any obligation under the relevant contract will do,[88] or that reference should be made to the obligation which is characteristic of the contract,[89] or that jurisdiction should belong to the court with whose territory the dispute has its closest connection.[90] It has justified this approach by emphasising the need for certainty, and for a court to be able to determine its jurisdiction without having to consider the substance of the case.

The Convention approach remains applicable to bankers' letters of credit. Thus where a beneficiary sues an issuing bank for payment under a letter of credit, it is the place of payment, and not that of presentation of the documents, which constitutes the relevant place of performance under Article 5(1)(a) of the Regulation; and if the letter entitles the beneficiary to choose the place of payment, by notifying the bank at the time of presentation, Article 5(1)(a) enables the beneficiary to sue at the place thus chosen and notified.[91] Where a contract between the issuing and confirming banks of a letter of credit provides for reimbursement through a third bank, the place of performance of the issuing bank's obligation to reimburse the confirming bank is at the specified place of business of the third bank.[92]

The Convention approach also remains applicable to contracts of loan. Thus where a loan governed by English law is repayable on demand, Article 5(1)(a) of the Regulation confers jurisdiction over a claim for repayment on the court for the creditor's residence at the time of the demand.[93]

As regards the identification of the principal obligation among those on which the plaintiff's claims are based, in *Rank Film Distributors v Lanterna*,[94] where the licensor under an exclusive film-exploitation agreement was suing for the agreed licence-fee, and also for a much smaller sum for materials (such as copies of the films) supplied, Saville J held that the principal obligation was to pay the licence-fee. In *Raiffeisen Zentralbank v National Bank of Greece*,[95] which involved an agreement between banks concerning the financing of a shipbuilding operation, Tuckey J held the defendant's principal obligation involved was its obligation to make payments to the plaintiff as work progressed, rather than its warranty that there had been no default under the existing loan agreement between the defendant and the purchaser of the vessel.

There is some doubt as to the right approach where an exclusive distributor sues the manufacturer for infringing the agreed exclusivity or repudiating the contract. The highest courts in Belgium, the Netherlands and France have held that the relevant place of performance is

---

[87] See Case C-256/00: *Besix v WABAG* [2002] ECR I-1699.
[88] See Case 14/76: *De Bloos v Bouyer* [1976] ECR 1497.
[89] See Case 266/85: *Shenavai v Kreischer* [1987] ECR 239; and Case C-420/97: *Leathertex v Bodetex* [1999] ECR I-6747.
[90] See Case C-288/92: *Custom Made v Stawa* [1994] ECR I-2913.
[91] See *Chailease Finance Corp v Credit Agricole Indosuez* [2000] 1 Lloyd's Rep 348 (CA).
[92] See *Royal Bank of Scotland v Cassa di Risparmio delle Provincie Lombard* [1992] WL 895017 (English CA).
[93] See *Tavoulareas v Tsavliris* [2006] 1 All ER (Comm) 109 (Andrew Smith J).
[94] [1992] ILPr 58.
[95] [1999] 1 Lloyd's Rep 408.

the territory in respect of which the contract granted exclusive rights to the distributor,[96] and a similar approach has been adopted in Ireland.[97] In contrast, the English Court of Appeal has looked to the obligation to give reasonable notice of termination at the distributor's place of business[98] or to the obligation to deliver the relevant goods, possibly ex works in the country of manufacture.[99]

As the Court of Appeal ruled in *AIG Group v The Ethniki*,[100] where the plaintiff seeks a declaration that he is not bound to perform a contract because of the defendant's breach of a particular term of the contract, it is that term which constitutes the obligation in question under Article 5(1)(a) of the Regulation, and not the plaintiff's obligation to perform the contract. In that case, a reinsurer was seeking a declaration that it was discharged from liability to indemnify the reinsured under the reinsurance contract on the ground that the reinsured had, in breach of the contract, failed to advise the reinsurer within 72 hours of becoming aware of a relevant loss, and to furnish the reinsurer with all information available respecting such losses.

Under the Convention approach, once the relevant obligation has been identified, the place of its performance must be determined. In this context, the rulings of the European Court in *Tessili v Dunlop*[101] and *Groupe Concorde v 'The Suhadiwarno Panjan'*[102] have established that the concept of the place of performance, unlike most of the concepts used by the Convention and the Regulation, does not have an independent meaning. Rather the place of performance must be determined in accordance with the substantive law which is applicable to the obligation under the conflict rules of the country whose court is seised.

Usually the substantive law by reference to which the place of performance of an obligation must be determined for the purpose of Article 5(1)(a) of the Regulation will be the national law which governs the contract as its proper law under the Rome Convention 1980 or the Rome I Regulation.[103] It could, however, be a uniform substantive law defined in an international treaty,[104] or a national law determined in accordance with conflict rules laid down by another international convention which prevails over the Rome Convention and the Rome I Regulation.[105]

---

[96]   See *Knauer v Callens* [1978] I Pas Belge 871; *Audi-NSU v Adelin Petit* (1979) 94 Journal des Tribunaux 625; *Hacker Kuchen v Bosma* [1993] ECC 55; and Gaudemet-Tallon, at para. 164.

[97]   See *Nestorway v Ambaflex* [2006] IEHC 235 (Clarke J).

[98]   See *Medway Packaging v Meurer Maschinen* [1990] 2 Lloyd's Rep 112.

[99]   See *Boss Group v Boss France* [1997] 1 WLR 351.

[100]   [2000] 2 All ER 566 (CA); affirming [1998] 4 All ER 301 (Colman J).

[101]   Case 12/76, [1976] ECR 1473.

[102]   Case C-440/97, [1999] ECR I-6307.

[103]   See Case C-440/97: *Groupe Concorde v 'The Suhadiwarno Panjan'* [1999] ECR I-6307; and *Raiffeisen Zentralbank v National Bank of Greece* [1999] 1 Lloyd's Rep 408 (Tuckey J). The Rome Convention and the Rome I Regulation are examined in Chapters 12 and 13 below.

[104]   See Case C-288/92: *Custom Made v Stawa* [1994] ECR I-2913. For example, insofar as the Convention approach continues to play a supplementary role in relation to contracts for the sale of goods, the Vienna Convention of 11th April 1980 on Contracts for the International Sale of Goods, which is now in force in twenty-three of the EU Member States (the exceptions being the United Kingdom, Ireland, Portugal, and Malta), as well as Switzerland, Norway and Iceland.

[105]   See Articles 21 and 23–4 of the Rome Convention; Articles 25 and 26 of the Rome I Regulation; and *San Carlo v SNC Vico*, 6th February 1996, where French Court of Cassation applied, as supplying the relevant French conflict rule, Article 3(1) of the Hague Convention of 15th June 1955

The Convention approach, applicable under Article 5(1)(a) of the Regulation, contemplates a single place of performance, at which it enables an action to be brought. Thus where the place of performance of the relevant obligation is multiple or indeterminate, no court will be competent under Article 5(1)(a).[106] This was recognised by the European Court in *Besix v WABAG*,[107] which involved a negative obligation not to participate in a competing bid for a concession offered by a Cameroon authority. The Court ruled that Article 5(1)(a) does not apply in cases (such as the instant case) where the place of performance of the relevant contractual obligation is indeterminate, because it consists of a negative undertaking without any geographical limitation and therefore has multiple places of performance.

Similarly, in *Mora Shipping v Axa Corporate Solutions Assurance*,[108] the English Court of Appeal held that the English court was not competent under Article 5(1)(a) to entertain a claim against an insurer who had undertaken to pay a general average contribution to the shipowner *or* to the average adjuster, the shipowner being domiciled abroad and the adjuster domiciled in England, since the place of payment was multiple and the option belonged to the debtor. Again, in *Gard Marine v Tunnicliffe*,[109] which involved a claim by a Bermudan insurer against a Swiss reinsurer under a reinsurance contract, Hamblen J declined jurisdiction on the ground that the claimant had failed to establish an implied term requiring the reinsurer to pay claims to the brokers in London; a practice of doing so was insufficient. Similarly, in *Montagu Evans v Young*,[110] a Scottish court declined jurisdiction under the Convention over a claim by chartered surveyors for payment by an English client of an introduction fee, since the creditor had places of businesses in both England and Scotland, some of the properties involved were situated in Scotland and others in England, and it was not established that the debtor had expressly or impliedly agreed to make payment at the creditor's Scottish place of business, so as to entitle the creditor to insist on payment there and not elsewhere. Again, in *Swan v Kall Kwik*,[111] a Scottish court insisted, in the context of a franchise agreement, that the contract must *require* that the relevant obligation should be performed in the territory of the court seised. On the other hand, as the Court of Appeal (affirming Pumfrey J) held in *Kenburn Waste Management v Bergmann*,[112] in the case of a negative obligation to produce a result in a particular country (for example, not to communicate threats of patent litigation to persons there), the place of performance will be in the country where the result is to be achieved.

In *Crucial Music v Klondyke Management*,[113] Livesey QC explained that, as regards a warranty as to an existing condition or state of affairs, the place of performance of the obligation in question, for the purpose of Article 5(1)(a), is the place where the condition or state

---

on the Law Applicable to International Sales of Goods. That Convention is in force in France, Italy, Denmark, Sweden, Finland, Norway, and Switzerland. See also the Hague Convention of 14th March 1978 on the Law Applicable to Agency, which is in force in France, the Netherlands and Portugal.

[106]   See Gaudemet-Tallon, at para 173, citing French decisions declining jurisdiction under Article 5(1) because no single place of performance could be identified.

[107]   Case C-256/00, [2002] ECR I-1699.

[108]   [2005] EWCA Civ 1069.

[109]   [2009] EWHC 2388 (Comm).

[110]   [2000] SLT 1083 (Outer House).

[111]   [2009] CSOH 99 (Outer House).

[112]   [2002] ILPr 33 (CA), affirming [2002] FSR 44.

[113]   [2008] 1 All ER (Comm) 642.

of affairs is required by the contract to exist. He concluded that, in the case of a warranty, given by a third party to a purchaser of a collection of copyrights for various countries, that the copyrights were subject to certain specified licences and no others, the place of performance of the warranty was the place where the assignment of the copyrights was effected.

In the context of the Convention approach as preserved by Article 5(1)(a) and (c) of the Regulation, the principle laid down in *Tessili* continues to have a concealed discriminatory effect. This arises despite the harmonisation of conflict rules achieved by the Rome Convention 1980 and the Rome I Regulation, because of continuing differences in the national substantive laws. For example, as regards the place where a debt is payable unless the parties have otherwise agreed, English, Scottish, Irish, Italian, Danish and Greek laws refer to the creditor's residence, while French and German laws (apart from international conventions) refer to the debtor's residence. Thus the effect of *Tessili* in the context of the residual approach to the relevant obligation is to enable an English or Irish creditor, who contracts under English or Irish law, to sue for the debt in his own country, while a French or German supplier, contracting under French or German law, has no similar right to sue for the debt in his own country.[114] Fortunately, the scope of such discrimination between creditors is now reduced by the new approach to the obligation in question established by Article 5(1)(b).

In *Zelger v Salinitri (No 1)*,[115] the European Court ruled that the substantive law applicable to the obligation under the forum's conflict rules also governs the formal requirements applicable to an express agreement as to the place of performance of the obligation for the purpose of Article 5(1)(a) of the Regulation. The formal requirements laid down by Article 23, on agreements as to jurisdiction, do not apply to an agreement specifying a place of performance. Thus an entirely informal agreement on the place of performance of an obligation will be effective under Article 5(1)(a) if the applicable substantive law imposes no formal requirements.[116] However, in *MSG v Les Gravières Rhénanes*,[117] the European Court made clear that this approach only applies to a genuine agreement, designed to determine the place of actual performance. A fictitious agreement, purporting to specify the place of performance, but in reality designed only to establish jurisdiction, is not effective under Article 5(1)(a), but must be treated as an agreement on jurisdiction governed by Article 23. No doubt the approach to formal requirements adopted in *Zelger* must now be extended to an agreement which, as is permitted by Article 5(1)(b) of the Regulation, relates to a contract for the sale of goods or the provision of services, and is designed simply to exclude the operation of the rule specified by Article 5(1)(b) in favour of the

---

[114]    See *Unidare v Scott* [1991] 2 IR 88; *Mercury Publicity v Loerke* [1993] ILPR 142 (CA); *Definitely Maybe v Marek Lieberberg* [2001] 1 WLR 1745 (Morison J); *Montagu Evans v Young* [2000] SLT 1083 (Outer House); and *Bateg Delta v Ward Group*, 25th February 1997 (French Court of Cassation). See also *Atlas Shipping Agency v Suisse Atlantique* [1995] 2 Lloyd's Rep 188 (Rix J), enabling a third-party beneficiary of a promise to pay commission to sue at his own residence.

[115]    Case 56/79, [1980] ECR 89.

[116]    In France, it has been held conversely that an agreement on the place of performance will be ineffective if it fails to comply with formal requirements imposed by the applicable substantive law, even if these are more stringent than those specified in Article 23; see *IBF v GIH*, 27th February 1996 (French Court of Cassation).

[117]    Case C-106/95, [1997] ECR I-911. See also *Gotz v Noge*, 27th February 1996 (French Court of Cassation).

place of delivery or service provision, and to restore the operation of the Convention approach in accordance with Article 5(1)(a) and (c).

## The Luxembourg Concession

By a transitional concession specified by Article 63 of the Brussels I Regulation, defendants domiciled in Luxembourg were exempted for six years from the operation of Article 5(1) in cases where the contract involved goods or non-financial services, and the final place of delivery of the goods involved, or the final place of provision of the non-financial services involved, was in Luxembourg. The exact significance of the reference to the 'final' place of delivery or service provision was far from clear. Perhaps the concession applied to an FOB sale of goods, under which the goods were to be loaded onto an aircraft at Heathrow for carriage to Luxembourg. The exemption expired on 1st March 2008, and defendants domiciled in Luxembourg are now subject to the jurisdiction of the courts of other Member States under Article 5(1) in the same way as defendants who are domiciled in other Member States. Accordingly, no provision corresponding to Article 63 of the Brussels I Regulation is included in the Lugano Convention 2007.

Article 63 of the Brussels I Regulation had replaced Article I(1) of the Protocol annexed to the Brussels Convention, which had granted a full exemption from Article 5(1) to defendants who were domiciled in Luxembourg. A similar exemption, granted by Article I(1) of the First Protocol annexed to the Lugano Convention 1988, remains for the time being in force.

## The Merits of Article 5(1)

To the present writer it seems regrettable that the Regulation failed to take the opportunity of deleting Article 5(1) altogether. Even as reformed, it remains a complex provision, requiring the court seised to examine the terms of the alleged contract, in some cases to ascertain and examine its proper law, and to reach at least tentative conclusions on factual issues which also affect the merits of the substantive claim. Thus elaborate preliminary litigation on competence is systematically encouraged. Moreover, the reform has added further issues as to the interpretation of Article 5(1) for judicial consideration.

More fundamentally, the reformed Article 5(1) continues to resolve the question of whether a plaintiff can sue in his own country in a manner and with results which are essentially arbitrary when tested against any reasonable policy considerations, such as the need to protect a party who, from a social or economic perspective or in terms of ability to litigate abroad, is in a weaker position than his opponent.

It must be borne in mind that Article 5(1) is mainly concerned with commercial contracts (for example, for the sale of goods) between companies whose headquarters are located in different Member States. There is no reason to presume that one of the parties to such a contract is in a weaker position than the other, so as to need or deserve special protection. The advantage appears to lie with a rule which confines jurisdiction to the country of the defendant's domicile and, where relevant, that of its secondary establishment involved in the transaction, in accordance with Articles 2 and 5(5). A party who finds such restrictions unacceptable is free, when entering into the contract, to insist on a contrary agreement on jurisdiction, in accordance with Article 23. Thus it is submitted that the appropriate reform, for adoption when an opportunity for amendment of the Regulation arises, is the simple deletion, without replacement, of Article 5(1).[118]

# TORTS

Article 5(3) of the Brussels I Regulation confers jurisdiction over a defendant domiciled in another Member State 'in matters relating to tort, delict or quasi-delict, [on] the courts for the place where the harmful event occurred or may occur'.[119] The reference to the place where the harmful event may occur makes explicit what was implied in the Brussels Convention, that Article 5(3) extends to a preventive action in respect of a threatened or future tort.[120] Article 5(3) also extends to an action brought by an alleged tortfeasor seeking a declaration of non-liability.[121]

## Tortious Matters

In a line of decisions,[122] the European Court has established that the reference in Article 5(3) to tortious matters ('matters relating to tort, delict or quasi-delict') has an independent meaning, and that the concept is not confined to torts in an ordinary sense, but extends to all actions which seek to establish the liability of a defendant and which are not contractual matters within Article 5(1).

Thus, in *Kalfelis v Schröder*,[123] the European Court ruled that Article 5(3) applies to a claim by way of restitution against unjust enrichment for repayment of sums which had been paid by the plaintiff to the defendant pursuant to an invalid contract. The ruling was given in the context of a German action against a Luxembourg bank arising from losses suffered by the plaintiff as a result of futures transactions in silver bullion which he had entered into with the bank. The plaintiff's claims were based on breach of a contractual obligation to provide information; on tort, in the form of conduct contrary to morality; and on unjust enrichment, in that the nature of the transactions rendered them invalid under mandatory provisions of German law, and thus entitled him to repayment of the sums which he had paid. The Court also ruled that a court which has jurisdiction under Article 5(3) over an action insofar as it is based on tort (in the enlarged sense) does not have jurisdiction over the action insofar as it is not so based. Thus Article 5(3) was not applicable to the plaintiff's

---

[118]    Gaudemet-Tallon, at para 177, also concludes that the simple deletion of Article 5(1) would perhaps be the best solution.

[119]    In the United Kingdom, similar provision is made by rule 3(c) of Schedule 4 to the Civil Jurisdiction and Judgments Act 1982 (as amended), as regards the allocation of jurisdiction between the courts for the parts of the United Kingdom over defendants domiciled in the United Kingdom.

[120]    See Case C-167/00: *VKI v Henkel* [2002] ECR I-8111.

[121]    See *Equitas v Wave City Shipping* [2005] EWHC 923 (Christopher Clarke J); and *Knorr-Bremse v Haldex* [2008] 2 All ER (Comm) 448 (Lewison J).

[122]    See Case 189/87: *Kalfelis v Schröder* [1988] ECR 5565; Case C-51/97: *Réunion Européenne v Spliethoff's Bevrachtingskantoor* [1998] ECR I-6511; Case C-334/00: *Tacconi v Wagner* [2002] ECR I-7357; and Case C-167/00: *VKI v Henkel* [2002] ECR I-8111.

[123]    Case 189/87, [1988] ECR 5565.

claim for breach of contract, but was applicable both to his claim in tort (in the ordinary sense) and to his claim in restitution based on unjust enrichment.[124]

The ruling of the European Court in *Reichert v Dresdner Bank (No 2)*[125] that Article 5(3) does not extend to a 'pauline' action under French law, whereby a creditor seeks the setting aside as against the creditor of a transfer of property by his debtor on the ground that it was made in fraud of the creditor's rights, must be regarded as based on the proprietary, as distinct from obligational, character of the claim. The Court explained that such an action is directed not only against the debtor, but also against the transferee, who is not a party to the debtor's obligation to the creditor, and is available where there is no consideration for the transfer, even if the transferee acted in good faith and committed no wrongful act. Thus such an action cannot be regarded as seeking to establish the liability of a defendant within Article 5(3).

Recent decisions of the European Court have confirmed the principle that Article 5(3) extends to all actions which seek to establish the liability of a defendant and which are not contractual matters within Article 5(1). Thus in *Réunion Européenne v Spliethoff's Bevrachtingskantoor*,[126] the Court ruled that Article 5(3) applies to an action brought by a consignee of goods which had been carried under a bill of lading contract, and had allegedly been damaged in the course of such carriage, not against the issuer of the bill of lading, but against the actual carrier, there being no contractual relationship between the consignee and the actual carrier. Similarly, in *Tacconi v Wagner*,[127] the Court ruled that Article 5(3) applies to an obligation to make good damage caused by the unjustified breaking off of negotiations, derived from the breach of a legal rule which requires the parties to act in good faith in negotiations with a view to the formation of a contract. Further, in *VKI v Henkel*,[128] the Court ruled that Article 5(3) applies to a preventive action brought by a consumer protection organisation for the purpose of preventing a trader from using terms considered to be unfair in contracts with private individuals, since it seeks to establish the defendant trader's liability in respect of its non-contractual obligation to refrain in its dealings with consumers from certain behaviour deemed unacceptable by the legislature, and the harmful event referred to in Article 5(3) extends to the undermining of legal stability by the use of unfair terms which it is the task of consumer protection associations to prevent. Moreover, in *Land Oberösterreich v ČEZ*,[129] the European Court confirmed that Article 5(3), and not Article 22(1), applies to actions in respect of a nuisance or other tort affecting land, whether the claim is for damages or for an injunction, since the existence and content of rights in rem (usually rights of ownership) are of only marginal significance in the context of a claim in tort for nuisance affecting or damage to land.

In view of these decisions (especially *Tacconi v Wagner*),[130] it is clear that the European Court stands by its ruling in *Kalfelis* on the breadth of Article 5(3); and more specifically that Article 5(3) applies to any action based on an autonomous restitutionary claim, either

---

124 See also per Darmon AG in Case C-89/91: *Shearson Lehman Hutton v TVB* [1993] ECR I-139, at para 102.
125 Case C-261/90, [1992] ECR I-2149.
126 Case C-51/97, [1998] ECR I-6511.
127 Case C-334/00, [2002] ECR I-7357.
128 Case C-167/00, [2002] ECR I-8111.
129 Case C-343/04, [2006] ECR I-4557.
130 Case C-334/00, [2002] ECR I-7357.

unconnected with any contract or arising from the initial invalidity or illegality of a contract. Thus the decision of the House of Lords in *Kleinwort Benson v City of Glasgow District Council*,[131] refusing to apply Article 5(3) to a claim for restitution of money paid under a void contract, on the ground that Article 5(3) is confined to tort in a normal sense and does not apply to restitution, must be regarded as based on a misunderstanding of the ruling in *Kalfelis*. On the other hand, it seems probable that Article 5(1) applies, and therefore that Article 5(3) does not apply, to claims seeking a remedy which is restitutionary in nature, if the claim is based on a breach by the defendant of a valid contract, and possible that the same applies if the claim is based on the frustration of an initially valid contract.

It is also clear that Article 5(3) extends to an action for what in England is regarded as an equitable wrong, such as misuse of confidential information,[132] breach of fiduciary duty by a person other than a trustee,[133] dishonest assistance in a breach of trust or other fiduciary duty,[134] or knowing receipt of trust property.[135] But Article 5(3) can never apply to a claim which is based on a breach of contract and thus falls within Article 5(1). Moreover, the analogy between Article 5(1) on contracts and Article 5(6) on certain trusts[136] makes it probable that Article 5(3) does not apply to a claim for breach of trust if the claim is between such parties and in respect of such trusts as to be capable of falling within Article 5(6). Similarly, it seems probable that the specific provisions of Articles 5(2) and 5(7) prevent a claim for familial maintenance, or for salvage of cargo or freight, from falling within Article 5(3).

It seems clear from the ruling in *Kalfelis* that where a plaintiff's claim for damages is properly pleaded both as a claim for breach of contract, and also as a claim in tort, based on the same facts except for the contract, one must determine jurisdiction over the contractual claim in the light of Article 5(1), and jurisdiction over the tort claim in the light of Article 5(3). This approach is now followed by the English Court of Appeal, which in *WPP v Benatti*[137] accepted that concurrent claims in contract and tort are to be submitted respectively to Articles 5(1) and 5(3), and thus impliedly overruled its earlier decision to the contrary in *Source v TUV Rheinland Holding*.[138]

---

[131]    [1999] AC 153. The claim was for restitution of money paid under an interest rate swap contract which was indisputably void ab initio on account of the defendant's incapacity as a local authority under the ultra vires rule to enter into such a contract.

[132]    Cf. *Kitechnology v Unicor* [1995] FSR 765 (CA), where the point was left open.

[133]    See *WPP v Benatti* [2007] 2 All ER (Comm) 525 (CA), which involved a management consultant who was engaged to devise proposals and strategies to improve the performance of a corporate group.

[134]    See *Casio Computer v Sayo* [2001] ILPr 43 (CA); and *Dexter v Harley* [2001] WL 272859, 'The Times' of 2nd April 2001 (Lloyd J).

[135]    See *Dexter v Harley* [2001] WL 272859, 'The Times' of 2nd April 2001 (Lloyd J).

[136]    On Article 5(6), see pp. 111–12 below.

[137]    [2007] 2 All ER (Comm) 525 (CA). See also *Raiffeisen Zentralbank v National Bank of Greece* [1999] 1 Lloyd's Rep 408 (Tuckey J).

[138]    [1998] QB 54 (CA). In *Source*, a plaintiff who had engaged the defendant to conduct quality control inspections of goods being purchased from a third person complained that the inspections had been carried out negligently, relying both on breach of the contract to inspect and on the tort of negligence. The Court of Appeal held that in such cases both claims must be regarded as contractual matters, within Article 5(1) and not Article 5(3). See also *Rayner v Davies* [2002] 1 All ER (Comm) 620 (Morison J), affirmed without reference to this point, [2003] 1 All ER (Comm) 394 (CA).

In *DFDS Torline v SEKO*,[139] the European Court ruled that Article 5(3) extends to an action seeking to establish the illegality of industrial action (such as 'blacking'), even where under the law of the forum State exclusive jurisdiction over such an action belongs to a court other than the court which has jurisdiction over claims for compensation for losses caused by the industrial action. The case involved an action in Denmark seeking to establish the illegality of a notice of industrial action given by a Swedish trade union acting in the interests of the Polish crew of a Danish ship operating between Sweden and England. The Court also ruled that the necessary causal connection between the damage and the wrongful act exists where the industrial action is a necessary precondition of sympathy action which may result in harm, and that the application of Article 5(3) is not affected by the fact that the implementation of the industrial action was suspended by the trade union pending a ruling on its legality.

## Harmful Events

### The general principles

In a series of decisions, the European Court has resolved the ambiguity of the reference to the place where the harmful event occurred. It has established that Article 5(3) enables a plaintiff to sue in the courts for the place where either the wrongful conduct of the defendant occurred, or the resulting initial injury to the plaintiff or an associated person occurred.

In *Bier v Mines de Potasse d'Alsace*,[140] the European Court ruled that where the place of the happening of the event which may give rise to liability in tort and the place where that event results in damage are not identical, the reference in Article 5(3) to the place where the harmful event occurred must be understood as being intended to cover both the place where the damage occurred and the place of the event giving rise to it. Accordingly, the defendant may be sued, at the plaintiff's option, either in the courts for the place where the damage occurred or in the courts for the place of the event which gives rise to and is at the origin of the damage. In other words, Article 5(3) enables a plaintiff to sue in the courts for the place where either the wrongful conduct of the defendant, or the resulting injury to the plaintiff, occurred. Thus it permitted a Dutch horticulturalist to bring an action in a Dutch court against a French mining company, complaining of the defendant's discharge of saline waste into the Rhine in France, which had caused damage to the plaintiff's plantations in the Netherlands.[141]

Subsequently, the European Court has drawn a distinction between the initial injury and consequential losses, and has refused to permit a plaintiff to sue in the courts for a place where he has merely suffered financial loss consequential on an initial injury sustained

---

[139]   Case C-18/02: *Danmarks Rederiforening, acting on behalf of DFDS Torline v LO Landsorganisationen i Sverige, acting on behalf of SEKO Sjöfolk Facket för Service och Kommunikation* [2004] ECR I-1417.

[140]   Case 21/76, [1976] ECR 1735.

[141]   See also Case C-343/04: *Land Oberösterreich v ČEZ* [2006] ECR I-4557, where the European Court confirmed that Article 5(3), and not Article 22(1), applies to actions in respect of a nuisance or other tort affecting land, whether the claim is for damages or for an injunction, since the existence and content of rights in rem (usually rights of ownership) are of only marginal significance in the context of a claim in tort for nuisance affecting or damage to land. The case involved nuisance by nuclear pollution, as did *Short v Ireland* [1997] 1 ILRM 161 (Irish Supreme Court).

elsewhere, whether by the plaintiff himself or by a person associated with the plaintiff (such as its subsidiary company). Thus in *Dumez v Hessische Landesbank*,[142] the European Court refused to permit a French company to bring an action in a French court against a German bank whose cancellation of loans to a German property-developer had led to the suspension of a building project in Germany, and thereby caused the plaintiff's German subsidiary to become insolvent, and the plaintiff itself to suffer consequential financial loss in France. Similarly, in *Marinari v Lloyd's Bank*,[143] it refused to permit a man domiciled in Italy to bring an action there against an English bank in respect of his arrest and the seizure of his promissory notes in England, despite his claim to have suffered consequential financial loss in Italy. Again, in *Réunion Européenne v Spliethoff's Bevrachtingskantoor*,[144] it refused to permit a consignee of goods, damaged in the course of a transport operation comprising carriage by sea and then by land, to bring an action against the maritime carrier at the consignee's domicile, where it received the goods at the conclusion of the transport operation and discovered the damage to them. In such circumstances, the place of injury would be the place where the maritime carrier was to deliver the goods. Similarly in *Kronhofer v Maier*,[145] which involved a financial loss sustained by an Austrian investor as a result of a speculative investment in Germany, it ruled that Article 5(3) does not confer jurisdiction on the courts for the place where the claimant is domiciled and his assets are concentrated and at which he has suffered financial loss, if that loss resulted from a loss of part of his assets which arose and was incurred in another Member State.[146]

In *DFDS Torline v SEKO*,[147] which involved an action in Denmark seeking to establish the illegality of a notice of industrial action ('blacking') given by a Swedish trade union acting in the interests of the Polish crew of a Danish ship operating between Sweden and England, it ruled that the nationality or flag of the ship is decisive only if the national court reaches the conclusion that the damage arose on board the ship.

With regard to a product liability claim against a manufacturer, the European Court ruled in *Zuid-Chemie v Philippo's Mineralenfabriek*[148] that Article 5(3) confers jurisdiction on the courts for the place of manufacture, which counts as the place of the wrongful conduct, and on the courts for the place where the initial injury to the plaintiff's person, or the initial damage to the plaintiff's other property, occurred as a result of the normal use of the product for the purpose for which it was intended, which counts as the place of injury.

---

142     Case 220/88, [1990] ECR I-49.
143     Case C-364/93, [1995] ECR I-2719.
144     Case C-51/97, [1998] ECR I-6511.
145     Case C-168/02, [2004] ECR I-6009.
146     See also *Re a Consignment of Italian Wine* [1988] ECC 159 (German Supreme Court); and *Kitechnology v Unicor* [1995] FSR 765 (CA), on non-contractual claims in respect of misuse of confidential information. Cf. *Max Mara v Galerie Kleber*, 9th April 1996, where the French Court of Cassation permitted a trader complaining of tortious refusal to supply goods to sue at the place where he would have resold.
147     Case C-18/02: *Danmarks Rederiforening, acting on behalf of DFDS Torline v LO Landsorganisationen i Sverige, acting on behalf of SEKO Sjöfolk Facket för Service och Kommunikation* [2004] ECR I-1417.
148     Case C-189/08, [2009] ECR I-6917. The case involved a claim by a manufacturer of a finished product (a fertiliser) against a manufacturer of an intermediate product used in the manufacture of the final product. See also *Grehan v Medical Inc* [1988] ECC 6 (Irish Supreme Court); and *Hewden Stuart v Gottwald*, 13th May 1992 (English CA).

Some further limitation on the scope of Article 5(3) may result from the European Court's observation in *Handte v TMCS*[149] that Article 5 must be interpreted in such a way as to enable a normally well-informed defendant reasonably to predict the courts, other than those of his domicile, before which he may be sued. Thus, although in general a personal injury action may be brought at the place of injury, even where the claim is against a manufacturer of a defective product, it seems possible that the need for predictability of forum may on occasion prevent this; for example, where the injury is sustained while the product is being used at a place where it has not been marketed through the manufacturer's chain of distribution, but to which it has been taken by the ultimate purchaser after acquisition elsewhere.[150] Moreover, as regards fatal accident actions, while Article 5(3) enables the deceased's estate and dependants to sue at the place where the deceased sustained the initial injury, it seems clear that the rejection of the place of consequential loss prevents the assumption of jurisdiction based on the place of the deceased's death,[151] as well as on the dependants' residence, at which they suffer grief and the loss of his financial support.

## Defamation

In *Shevill v Presse Alliance*,[152] the European Court considered the application of Article 5(3) to an action for libel brought against the publisher of a newspaper in respect of a defamatory article contained therein. The case involved an English libel action brought by an English woman against the publisher of a French newspaper of which a few copies (230 copies out of about 250,000) were distributed in England. The defamatory statements related to alleged money-laundering for drug-traffickers by a bureau de change in Paris at which the plaintiff was temporarily employed.

The European Court ruled that, in the context of defamation by newspaper article, the place of the wrongful conduct is that of the publisher's establishment from which the libel was issued and put into circulation. Thus Article 5(3) enables the plaintiff to sue in the courts for that place, and those courts have jurisdiction to award damages for all the harm caused anywhere by the defamation. In addition, in enabling the plaintiff to sue at the place of injury, Article 5(3) confers jurisdiction on the courts of any Member State in which the newspaper was distributed and the victim claims to have suffered injury to his reputation, but such jurisdiction is limited to the harm caused in the forum State.[153] In any event, the criteria for assessing whether an event is harmful, and the evidence required of the existence and extent of the harm alleged by the victim of the defamation, are governed by the substantive law determined by the forum's conflict rules, provided that the effectiveness of the Convention is not thereby impaired.

---

[149]  Case C-26/91, [1992] ECR I-3967.
[150]  See *World-Wide Volkswagen v Woodson* 444 US 286 (1980).
[151]  Cf. *Host v Doll*, 21st October 1981 (French Court of Cassation).
[152]  Case C-68/93, [1995] ECR I-415. See also, on reference back, [1996] AC 959 (HL); and *Murray v Times Newspapers* [1997] 3 IR 97 (Irish Supreme Court). For cogent criticism of the ruling in *Shevill*, as inhibiting legitimate investigative reporting, see Vick and MacPherson, 'Anglicising Defamation Law in the European Union', (1996) 36 Virginia Journal of International Law 933.
[153]  See also *Berezovsky v Michaels* [2000] 1 WLR 1004 (HL), applying the same principle, enabling the court for a place of distribution of a magazine to assume a jurisdiction in defamation confined to the injury to the plaintiff's local reputation, against an external defendant under the predecessor of para 3.1(9) of Practice Direction B supplementing Part 6 of the Civil Procedure Rules.

The *Shevill* principles extend to a television broadcast[154] and, no doubt, to a publication by means of a webpage on the Internet. In the latter case, the relevant establishment of the website operator[155] under the first principle will be its domicile or secondary establishment from, and by the staff attached to, which the website is maintained, rather than the place at which its website is located,[156] and jurisdiction based on the place of conduct will overlap with that conferred by Article 2 or 5(5). But the second principle will enable any court of a Member State other than the defendant's domicile to entertain a claim that material down-loaded locally from a website maintained elsewhere by a defendant domiciled in another Member State caused injury within the forum State, though its jurisdiction will be confined to the local injuries. *A fortiori*, the second principle will ensure that the courts of the Member State in which the defendant's website is located have jurisdiction to entertain a claim for libel in respect of injury to the plaintiff''s reputation in that State as a result of downloads received there.[157]

A similar approach was adopted by the High Court of Australia in *Dow Jones & Co Inc v Gutnick*,[158] where it ruled in favour of Victorian jurisdiction to entertain an action brought by a Victorian resident against a print and web publisher, incorporated in Delaware but having its editorial office in New York, for defamation in respect of information uploaded by the defendant from New York onto a web-server in New Jersey and downloaded by its subscribers in Victoria. Gleeson CJ explained that, in the case of material on the worldwide web, it is not available in comprehensible form until downloaded onto the computer of a person who has used a web browser to pull the material from the web server. It is where that person downloads the material that the damage to reputation may be done. Similarly, in *King v Lewis*,[159] the English Court of Appeal accepted jurisdiction, under the predecessor of para-graph 3.1(9) of Practice Direction B supplementing Part 6 of the Civil Procedure Rules, over a libel action brought by a plaintiff resident in Florida against a defendant resident in New York in respect of statements which had been downloaded in England from websites based in California.

### Economic torts

In the economic sphere, a number of problems arising from Article 5(3) have been addressed by English courts. As regards the tort of inducing breach of contract, jurisdiction exists at the place where under the contract the relevant payment or other benefit should have been received by the plaintiff, as the place of injury.[160] Jurisdiction also exists at the place where

---

[154]    See *Ewins v Carlton Television* [1997] 2 ILRM 223 (Barr J), permitting an action in Ireland for a libel effected by means of a television broadcast transmitted from Ulster and received in Ireland, but limited to injury to reputation in Ireland.

[155]    The website operator is the person who controls the content of the site, rather than the service provider who provides hosting facilities. See Directive 2000/31 on electronic commerce, [2000] OJ L178/1, for the immunities of a host provider.

[156]    See Directive 2000/31 on Electronic Commerce, Recital 19 and Article 2(c).

[157]    See *Olafsson v Gissurarson (No 2)* [2008] 1 All ER (Comm) 1106 (CA).

[158]    (2002) 194 ALR 433.

[159]    [2004] EWCA Civ 1329.

[160]    *Dolphin Maritime & Aviation Services Ltd v Sveriges Angartygs Assurans Forening* [2009] EWHC 716 (Comm) (Christopher Clarke J). See also *Metall und Rohstoff v Donaldson Lufkin & Jenrette* [1990] QB 391 (CA), which involved a defendant domiciled in an external country.

the inducing act was committed, as the place of the wrongful conduct.[161] As regards the tortious interference with a contract of carriage of goods by the arrest of the carrying vessel, the place of the relevant conduct is where the arrest takes place, rather than where the decision to arrest is made.[162]

A substantial English case-law deals with tortious claims in respect of false statements made by the defendant and relied on by the plaintiff, giving rise to liability for deceit, negligent misrepresentation or conspiracy to defraud.[163] This establishes that Article 5(3) confers jurisdiction on the court for the place where the statement was issued by the defendant (as the place of the wrongful conduct); and on the court for a place where goods were delivered or money was paid, as a result of the plaintiff's reliance on the statement (as the place of injury). But Article 5(3) does not confer jurisdiction on the court for a place where the plaintiff merely received the statement and/or acted in reliance on the statement by taking a decision or giving an instruction or entering into a contract leading to a delivery or payment elsewhere.

Thus in *Domicrest v Swiss Bank Corp*,[164] Rix J declined jurisdiction over a claim in respect of a false statement relevant to a buyer's credit, which had been made by a Swiss bank in a telephone conversation with an English seller, and acted on by the seller in releasing to the buyer without prior payment goods located in Switzerland and Italy. Similarly, in *Dunhill v Diffusion Internationale de Maroquinerie de Prestige*,[165] Rokison QC declined jurisdiction over a claim in respect of a false statement about the quality of goods, which had been transmitted by telephone, fax and letter from Italy to England, and had led to an order for the goods and eventually to their delivery in France. Conversely, in *London Helicopters v Heliportugal*,[166] Simon J accepted jurisdiction in respect of a claim by a buyer of a helicopter engine in respect of a false statement contained in an airworthiness certificate issued by a Portuguese repairer of the engine, since the engine was accepted in England by the buyer. Somewhat similarly, in *Crucial Music Corporation v Klondyke Management*,[167] Livesey QC held that, in the case of a misrepresentation by the defendant which induced the plaintiff to purchase a collection of copyrights for various countries from a third party, the injury occurred at the place where the plaintiff entered into and performed the contract with the third party to purchase the copyrights. Where the defendant's false statement induced the plaintiff to make a loan or enter into a financing agreement, Article 5(3) confers jurisdiction on the court for the place at or from which the money advanced by the plaintiff was paid.[168]

---

[161] See *Equitas v Wave City Shipping* [2005] EWHC 923 (Christopher Clarke J).

[162] See *Anton Durbeck v Den Norske Bank* [2002] EWHC 1173; partly reversed on other grounds, [2003] QB 1160 (CA).

[163] See *Domicrest v Swiss Bank Corp* [1999] QB 548 (Rix J); *Dunhill v Diffusion Internationale de Maroquinerie de Prestige* [2002] ILPr 13 (Rokison QC); *Raiffeisen Zentralbank v National Bank of Greece* [1999] 1 Lloyd's Rep 408 (Tuckey J); *Vilona v Delorenzi* [2002] EWHC 3016 (Comm) (Cresswell J); *ABCI v Banque Franco-Tunisienne* [2003] 2 Lloyd's Rep 146 (CA); *Bank of Tokyo-Mitsubishi v Baskan Gida* [2004] ILPr 26 (Lawrence Collins J); *London Helicopters v Heliportugal* [2006] 1 All ER (Comm) 595 (Simon J); and *Crucial Music Corporation v Klondyke Management* [2008] 1 All ER (Comm) 642 (Livesey QC).

[164] [1999] QB 548; approved in *ABCI v Banque Franco-Tunisienne* [2003] 2 Lloyd's Rep 146 (CA).

[165] [2002] ILPr 13.

[166] [2006] 1 All ER (Comm) 595.

[167] [2008] 1 All ER (Comm) 642.

[168] See *Raiffeisen Zentralbank v National Bank of Greece* [1999] 1 Lloyd's Rep 408 (Tuckey J);

As regards the tortious conversion of goods by their detention and use, Article 5(3) confers jurisdiction on the court for the place of the detention and use, and not on the court for the place at which the plaintiff suffered consequential loss because (for example) the detention of master tapes prevented his exploitation there of his copyright in the sound recordings embodied in the tapes.[169] As regards the fraudulent conversion of corporate funds by an officer of the company, where the officer diverts funds received from a customer abroad into his own bank account, the place where his bank account is kept counts as the place of injury, even if the funds are transferred from the customer's account in another country; and where the officer removes funds from a corporate bank account into his own bank account, the place where the corporate bank account is kept counts as the place of conduct, even if the funds are transferred to the officer's own account in another country.[170]

As regards passing off, jurisdiction over a manufacturer of deceptively packaged goods exists, by analogy with *Shevill*, at the place where he manufactured the goods and delivered them for export, as that of the wrongful conduct, and also at the place where the goods were subsequently sold to a deceived public, as the place of injury; but not elsewhere, such as at the plaintiff's domicile, where he ultimately suffered loss by receiving fewer orders.[171]

As regards actions for the infringement of a specific intellectual property right, such as a patent, a copyright[172] or a registered trade mark,[173] Article 5(3) confers jurisdiction on the courts for the place where the infringing act was committed. It confers jurisdiction on the courts for the place of the infringing act even in respect of a defendant who is sued for authorising the infringement by means of an act committed elsewhere.[174] It also extends to an action for a declaration of non-infringement, and confers jurisdiction on the courts for the place where the non-infringing act has been or would be committed.[175] Article 2 confers parallel jurisdiction at the defendant's domicile over infringements committed elsewhere, unless the proceedings involve a challenge to the validity of a grant or registration, and there-

---

*ABCI v Banque Franco-Tunisienne* [2003] 2 Lloyd's Rep 146 (CA); and *Bank of Tokyo-Mitsubishi v Baskan Gida* [2004] ILPr 26 (Lawrence Collins J), at paras 219–23. Cf. *Maple Leaf v Rouvroy* [2009] EWHC 257 (Comm), where Andrew Smith J (with unusual generosity to the plaintiff) allowed a financier to sue in England for deceit in inducing it to make a loan in connection with the acquisition of share warrants, on the ground that the financier had sent from England its agreement to the loan and its subscription to the relevant warrants, although it was unclear where the money had been advanced. Cf. also *Sunderland Marine Mutual Insurance Co Ltd v Wiseman* [2007] 2 All ER (Comm) 937, where Langley J held that it was insufficient to create English jurisdiction over a Scottish defendant under Schedule 4 to the Civil Jurisdiction and Judgments Act 1982 (as amended), in respect of a claim for conspiracy to defraud a hull insurer by scuttling a ship and making a false claim on the insurance, that it was from England that the payment of the claim by the insurer had been made.

[169]    See *Mazur Media Ltd v Mazur Media Gmbh* [2005] 1 Lloyd's Rep 41 (Lawrence Collins J). See also *Bank of Tokyo–Mitsubishi v Baskan Gida* [2004] ILPr 26 (Lawrence Collins J), at para 218.

[170]    See *Cronos Containers v Palatin* [2003] 2 Lloyd's Rep 489 (Morison J).

[171]    See *Modus Vivendi v Sanmex* [1996] FSR 790 (Knox J). See also *Mecklermedia v DC Congress* [1998] Ch 40 (Jacob J), accepting jurisdiction in passing off at a place to which the defendant had sent brochures advertising exhibitions elsewhere.

[172]    See *Pearce v Ove Arup* [1997] Ch 293 (Lloyd J); and *IBS v APM* [2003] All ER (D) 105 (Apr) (Briggs QC).

[173]    See *Re Jurisdiction in Contract and Tort* [1988] ECC 415 (German Supreme Court); also holding that such jurisdiction is not excluded because the defendant relies on a contractual licence.

[174]    See *ABKCO v Music Collection* [1995] RPC 657 (CA).

[175]    See *Knorr-Bremse v Haldex* [2008] 2 All ER (Comm) 448 (Lewison J).

fore fall within the exclusive jurisdiction of the State of the grant or registration under Article 22(4).[176]

Article 5(3) of the Brussels I Regulation does not apply to actions for infringement of a Community-wide intellectual property right (a Community trade mark, registered under EC Regulation 207/2009;[177] a Community plant variety right, granted under EC Regulation 2100/94;[178] or a Community design, registered or otherwise protected under EC Regulation 6/2002).[179] Instead, each of the Regulations governing the intellectual property right itself confers jurisdiction on the courts of the Member State in which an infringing act has been committed or threatened, but only in respect of infringing acts committed in that State.[180]

### Contribution between tortfeasors

A claim for contribution between joint tortfeasors under the Civil Liability (Contribution) Act 1978 falls within Article 5(3) of the Brussels I Regulation. Accordingly, the English court has jurisdiction in respect of such a claim against a foreign manufacturer which arises from an English accident involving its product; but not where the accident happened abroad, and the only English element is the litigation between the victim and the party claiming contribution.[181]

### Equitable wrongs

Where the defendant is sued for breach of a non-contractual confidence obligation in misusing confidential information in the production of goods which have not been exported, Article 5(3) does not create jurisdiction at a place other than that of the production of the goods.[182]

Where the defendant is sued for dishonest assistance in a breach of trust or other fiduciary duty, Article 5(3) creates jurisdiction at the place where money is moved into and out of a bank account, as a result of the defendant's instructions given elsewhere.[183] But in the case of equitable claims based on dishonest assistance in a breach of trust, or on knowing receipt of trust property, Article 5(3) does not create jurisdiction at the place where the original breach of trust or fiduciary duty by someone other than the defendant took place, if nothing which involved the defendant occurred there.[184] Where a non-contractual claim for breach of

---

[176]   See pp. 152–5 below. As regards claims alleging the abuse of a dominant position in connection with the licensing or enforcement of patents, see *Sandisk v Philips Electronics* [2007] EWHC 332 (Ch) (Pumfrey J).

[177]   Regulation 207/2009 on the Community trade mark, [2009] OJ L78/1; replacing Regulation 40/94, [1994] OJ L11/1.

[178]   Regulation 2100/94 on Community plant variety rights, [1994] OJ L227/1.

[179]   Regulation 6/2002 on Community designs, [2002] OJ L3/1.

[180]   See Articles 94–8 of Regulation 207/2009; Articles 101–2 of Regulation 2100/94; and Articles 79–83 of Regulation 6/2002. See further pp. 157–62 below.

[181]   See *Santa Fe v Gates*, 16th January 1991 (English CA); and *Hewden Tower Cranes v Wolfkran* [2007] EWHC 857 (TCC) (Jackson J).

[182]   See *Kitechnology v Unicor* [1995] FSR 765 (CA).

[183]   See *Casio Computer v Sayo* [2001] ILPr 43 (CA), where it was held that Article 5(3) created English jurisdiction over a Spanish defendant who assisted by giving instructions abroad enabling money to be moved into and out of a bank account in England.

[184]   See *Dexter v Harley* [2001] WL 272859, 'The Times' of 2nd April 2001 (Lloyd J), holding that the English court lacked jurisdiction over a Spanish defendant who had received money in, and transferred it from, her bank account in Alderney, one of the Channel Islands. Cf. *Nabb Brothers Ltd v*

fiduciary duty is based on the defendant's failure to declare a conflicting interest, Article 5(3) confers jurisdiction on the courts for the place at which the disclosure should have been made, as the place of the wrongful omission.[185]

### Restitutionary claims

Where the action is based on an autonomous restitutionary claim, either unconnected with any contract or arising from the initial invalidity or illegality of a contract, the reference in Article 5(3) to the harmful event must be read analogistically, as referring to an event equivalent or corresponding to a harmful event. Thus jurisdiction is conferred both on the courts for the place of the transfer (the movement of the benefit away from the plaintiff), and on those for the place of the enrichment (the receipt of the benefit by the defendant).[186]

### Possible Reform

The need for a provision having the width of the present Article 5(3) may be questioned. If full weight were to be given to the considerations of justice and certainty underlying the basic principle of Article 2 in favour of the defendant's domicile, and exceptions were to be made only on the basis of predictable inequality between the parties, Article 5(3) could be confined to cases of tort (as distinct from restitution) in which the plaintiff is an individual (as distinct from a corporate body) and is suing in respect either of personal injury, or of wrongful death, or of physical damage to property which was not being used in the course of a business.

More specifically, the potential effects of the European Court's ruling in *Shevill* warrant concern. While the decision is intelligible in a technical sense, in view of the wording of Article 5(3) and the Court's other decisions thereon, a seminal article by Vick and MacPherson[187] has convincingly demonstrated how, in the light of the character of the English substantive and procedural law applicable to civil defamation, which is unusually favourable to claimants, the ruling effectively subjects major newspaper publishers, established in European Union countries other than the United Kingdom, to substantial additional inhibitions on investigative journalism, derived from English law, in defiance of the policy of the State in which the publisher is established and most of the copies are distributed, and with potentially prejudicial effect on the right to freedom of expression conferred by Article 10 of the European Convention on Human Rights. It seems clear that the appropriate solution, in terms of the Brussels I Regulation, would be the exclusion of actions for defamation from the scope of Article 5(3).

---

*Lloyds Bank International (Guernsey) Ltd* [2005] EWHC 405 (Lawrence Collins J), on the position of external defendants under para 3.1(15) and (16) of Practice Direction B supplementing Part 6 of the Civil Procedure Rules.

[185]   See *WPP v Benatti* [2007] 2 All ER (Comm) 525 (CA).

[186]   See Peel, 'Jurisdiction under the Brussels Convention', in Rose (ed), *Restitution and the Conflict of Laws* (Mansfield Press, 1995). See also *Re Jogia* [1988] 1 WLR 484, and *Finnish Marine Insurance v Protective National Insurance* [1990] 1 QB 1078, on what has now become para 3.1(6)(a) of Practice Direction B supplementing Part 6 of the Civil Procedure Rules; and para 3.1(15) and (16) thereof.

[187]   'Anglicising Defamation Law in the European Union', (1996) 36 Virginia Journal of International Law 933.

**Criminal Proceedings**

In the Brussels I Regulation, Article 5(3) is supplemented by Article 5(4), which confers jurisdiction over a defendant domiciled in another Member State 'as regards a civil claim for damages or restitution which is based on an act giving rise to criminal proceedings, [on] the court seised of those proceedings, to the extent that that court has jurisdiction under its own law to entertain civil proceedings'.[188] Probably Article 5(4) has no operation in the United Kingdom.[189]

Article 61 of the Regulation[190] supplements Article 5(4) by ensuring that, without prejudice to more favourable provisions of national laws, persons who are domiciled in a Member State, and who are being prosecuted in the criminal courts of another Member State of which they are not nationals for an offence which was not intentionally committed,[191] may be defended by persons qualified to do so, even if they do not appear in person. But the court seised of the matter is permitted to order appearance in person. Then, in the case of failure to appear, a judgment given in the civil action without the person concerned having had the opportunity to arrange for his defence need not be recognised or enforced in the other Member States. In *Rinkau*,[192] the European Court ruled that Article 61 is confined to criminal proceedings in which civil liability is in question, or on which civil liability could subsequently be based.

## SECONDARY ESTABLISHMENTS

Article 5(5) of the Brussels I Regulation confers jurisdiction over a defendant who is domiciled in another Member State, as regards a dispute arising out of the operations of a branch, agency or other establishment, on the courts for the place in which the branch, agency or other establishment is situated.[193]

**A Branch, Agency or Other Establishment**

Although the Regulation refers verbosely to 'a branch, agency or other establishment', in substance it uses a single concept of a secondary establishment. This has been defined by the European Court as an effective place of business, which has the appearance of a permanent extension of a parent body, has a management, and is materially equipped to negotiate business with third parties, so that the latter, although knowing that there will if necessary be a

---

[188]   For examples, see Case C-172/91: *Sonntag v Waidmann* [1993] ECR I-1963, and Case C-7/98: *Krombach v Bamberski* [2000] ECR I-1935.

[189]   See *Davenport v Corinthian Motor Policies at Lloyds* [1991] SLT 774.

[190]   Article 61 echoes Article II of the Protocol annexed to the Brussels Convention.

[191]   On intentional offences, see Case C-7/98: *Krombach v Bamberski* [2000] ECR I-1935; and pp. 240–42 below.

[192]   Case 157/80, [1981] ECR 1391.

[193]   This echoes Article 5(5) of the Brussels Convention. For a wider use of the same concepts in the context of insurance, consumer and employment contracts, see Articles 9(2), 15(2) and 18(2) of the Regulation; considered in Chapter 5 below.

legal link with the parent body whose head office is abroad, do not have to deal directly with the parent body but may transact business at the extension.[194] Moreover, an essential characteristic of a secondary establishment is that it must be subject to the direction and control of the parent body, so that an independently owned exclusive distributor of a manufacturer's products is not a secondary establishment of the manufacturer.[195] Similarly, an independent commercial agent does not constitute a secondary establishment of an undertaking which he represents if he merely negotiates business, he is basically free to arrange his own work and decide what proportion of his time to devote to the interests of the undertaking represented, he cannot be prevented by that undertaking from also representing its competitors, and he merely transmits orders to the undertaking without being involved in either their terms or their execution.[196] It is clear from these rulings, and accords with Directive 2000/31 on Electronic Commerce,[197] that a merely electronic presence in the form of a website does not constitute an establishment.

On the other hand, one company within a corporate group will be regarded as a secondary establishment of another company in the same group if it acts as such, by negotiating and concluding transactions in the name and on behalf of the other company, at least if the companies have similar names and a common management.[198] Similarly, Article 5(5) may be satisfied where a director of a company uses the office of its subsidiary to negotiate a contract on behalf of the company.[199]

**Operations**

Article 5(5) is confined to disputes arising out of the operations of the secondary establishment. The European Court once adopted a very narrow definition of such operations, but has now adopted a broader approach. In *Somafer v Saar-Ferngas*,[200] it confined Article 5(5) to actions relating to: (a) rights and obligations concerning the management (in a strict sense) of the secondary establishment itself, such as those concerning the situation of the building where it is established or the local engagement of staff to work there; (b) undertakings which have been entered into at the secondary establishment in the name of the parent body and which must be performed in the Member State in which the secondary establishment is situ-

---

[194]   See Case 33/78: *Somafer v Saar-Ferngas* [1978] ECR 2183; followed on this point in Case C-439/93: *Lloyd's Register of Shipping v Campenon Bernard* [1995] ECR I-961.
[195]   See Case 14/76: *De Bloos v Bouyer* [1976] ECR 1497.
[196]   See Case 139/80: *Blanckaert & Willems v Trost* [1981] ECR 819. See also per Darmon AG in Case C-89/91: *Shearson Lehman Hutton v TVB* [1993] ECR I-139, opining that a subsidiary company which lacks authority to contract on behalf of its parent cannot be regarded as a secondary establishment of the latter for purposes such as Article 15(2).
[197]   [2000] OJ L178/1. The Directive, by Recital 19, declares that the place of establishment of a company providing services via an Internet website is not the place at which the technology supporting its website is located or the place at which its website is accessible, but the place where it pursues its economic activity; and, by Article 2(c), in defining an established service provider, specifies that the presence and use of the technical means and technologies required to provide an information society service do not, in themselves, constitute an establishment of the provider.
[198]   Case 218/86: *Schotte v Parfums Rothschild* [1987] ECR 4905.
[199]   See *Latchin v General Mediterranean Holidays* [2002] CLC 330 (Andrew Smith J).
[200]   Case 33/78, [1978] ECR 2183.

ated; and (c) non-contractual obligations arising from the activities in which the secondary establishment has engaged at its location on behalf of the parent body.

However, in *Lloyd's Register of Shipping v Campenon Bernard*,[201] the Court abandoned the *Somafer* definition of operations, and accepted that Article 5(5) extends to any contractual obligations entered into by the secondary establishment in the name of its parent body, regardless of whether they are to be performed in the Member State in which the secondary establishment is established, and even if they are to be performed by another secondary establishment of the same parent body situated in another Member State. It recognised that the former interpretation would make Article 5(5) largely overlap with Article 5(1) so as to be almost wholly redundant.

Although in *Lloyd's Register* the Court did not explicitly consider the concept of operations in relation to non-contractual obligations, its reasoning indicates by analogy that Article 5(5) now applies to any claim in tort or restitution against the parent body which arises from anything done anywhere on its behalf by members of the staff attached (solely or principally) to the secondary establishment. Thus, as the English Court of Appeal has ruled, Article 5(5) extends to claims in respect of tortious acts authorised by the secondary establishment, regardless of where they are committed.[202]

# TRUSTS

Article 5(6) of the Brussels I Regulation[203] confers jurisdiction over a defendant domiciled in another Member State, where he is sued as settlor, trustee or beneficiary of a trust created by the operation of a statute, or by a written instrument, or created orally and evidenced in writing, and the trust is domiciled in the forum State. Article 5(6) does not apply to non-statutory constructive trusts, such as those which arise from estate contracts.[204]

By Article 60(3) of the Regulation,[205] the court seised determines the domicile of a trust in accordance with its own law. In both the United Kingdom and Ireland, a trust is regarded as domiciled in the country with whose law it has its closest and most real connection.[206] It seems probable that Article 5(6) has no operation in most of the Member States, where the trust institution (as understood in the United Kingdom and Ireland) is unknown.

In *Chellaram v Chellaram (No 2)*,[207] Lawrence Collins J ruled the test of closest connection must be applied as of the date when the proceedings are instituted, and in the light of the Hague Convention of 1st July 1985 on the Law Applicable to Trusts and on their

---

201    Case C-439/93, [1995] ECR I-961.

202    See *Anton Durbeck v Den Norske Bank* [2003] QB 1160 (CA).

203    This echoes Article 5(6) of the Brussels Convention.

204    See the Schlosser Report, at para 117; and *Atlas Shipping Agency v Suisse Atlantique* [1995] 2 Lloyd's Rep 188 (Rix J).

205    This echoes Article 53(2) of the Brussels Convention.

206    For the United Kingdom, see paras 7 and 12 of Schedule 1 to the Civil Jurisdiction and Judgments Order 2001 (SI 2001/3929), which also allocate jurisdiction to the courts of the part of the United Kingdom in which the trust is domiciled. See also para 3.1(12) of Practice Direction B supplementing Part 6 of the (English) Civil Procedure Rules 1998. For Ireland, see the European Communities (Civil and Commercial Judgments) Regulations 2002 (SI 52/2002), reg 11(1)(c).

207    [2002] 3 All ER 17.

Recognition, and the Recognition of Trusts Act 1987. He also considered that it is permissible to take into account an express choice of foreign law to negate a closest connection with English law.

In *Gomez v Gomez-Monche Vives*,[208] the Court of Appeal (per Lawrence Collins LJ) explained that, in view of the primacy given to an express choice by the Hague Convention 1985 and the Recognition of Trusts Act 1987, an express choice in a trust instrument of English law as the law governing the trust will now be sufficient to ensure that, for the purpose of Article 5(6) of the Brussels I Regulation and the Civil Jurisdiction and Judgments Order 2001, the trust has its closest connection with English law and thus is domiciled in England. In such a case, the English courts will be competent under Article 5(6), even if there is no other connection between the trust and England; as in the instant case, where the trust was administered in Liechtenstein by a trustee resident there, the principal assets were shares in a company incorporated in the Cayman Islands, and the beneficiaries were resident in Spain, Portugal and the United States. On the other hand, a choice of foreign law in what would otherwise be an English trust may be disregarded where it was intended to avoid some important principle of English law. The Court of Appeal also held in *Gomez* that Article 5(6) applies to a claim by one beneficiary against another beneficiary seeking repayment of sums received in excess of the latter's entitlement under the trust, but not to a claim against a person on whom the trust instrument confers fiduciary powers but who is not (in the normal sense) a trustee.

Further provision for trusts is made by Article 23(4) of the Regulation.[209] This enables a provision contained in a trust instrument to confer exclusive jurisdiction on a designated court or courts of a Member State over proceedings against a settlor, trustee or beneficiary, involving relations between such persons or their rights or obligations under the trust. It appears to apply regardless of the defendant's domicile.[210]

In principle, Articles 5(6) and 23(4) give way to Article 22, on exclusive jurisdiction by virtue of subject-matter. But it seems that the rights of beneficiaries under an English or Irish trust can only constitute rights in rem in land, within Article 22(1), in the rare situation where they have become binding on all-comers as a result of registration.[211]

The exclusion of 'wills and succession' from the scope of the Regulation by Article 1(2)(a) seems to confine Articles 5(6) and 23(4) to trusts which are created inter vivos, rather than by will or intestacy.[212] But this would create problems, especially where a trust fund contains some assets which have been settled inter vivos and other assets which have been bequeathed by will. It is therefore suggested that the exclusion should be construed narrowly, so as to render the Regulation applicable to testamentary trusts, where the action is brought after the property has been transferred by the personal representative to the trustees, unless the action questions the validity or propriety of such transfer. For at that stage the testamentary character of the trust is of merely historical significance.

---

[208]    [2009] 1 All ER (Comm) 127 (CA).
[209]    This echoes Article 17(3) of the Brussels Convention.
[210]    Cf. rule 12(2) of Schedule 4 to the Civil Jurisdiction and Judgments Act 1982 as amended.
[211]    See pp. 144–6 below.
[212]    See the Schlosser Report, at paras 52 and 112.

# ADMIRALTY

Article 5(7) of the Brussels I Regulation[213] deals with disputes concerning the payment of remuneration claimed in respect of the salvage of a cargo or freight. It confers jurisdiction over a defendant who is domiciled in another Member State on the court under whose authority the cargo or freight in question has been arrested to secure such payment, or could have been so arrested, but bail or other security has been given. It applies only if it is claimed that the defendant has an interest in the cargo or freight, or had such an interest at the time of salvage. Article 5(7) authorises actions in personam as well as actions in rem.[214]

This rather minor provision for jurisdiction over claims for salvage of cargo or freight, based on the arrest or bailing of the cargo or freight involved, is designed to supplement the much more important provisions for jurisdiction based on the arrest or bailing of a ship made by the Brussels Convention of 10th May 1952 on the Arrest of Seagoing Ships.[215] The Arrest Convention, as a specialised convention, prevails over the Brussels I Regulation by virtue of Article 71.[216] Thus the courts of an EU Member State which is a party to the Arrest Convention have jurisdiction to entertain an action in respect of a maritime claim in accordance with the Arrest Convention if an appropriate ship has been arrested in its territory, even if the shipowner is domiciled in another Member State,[217] and even if there is an agreement on jurisdiction complying with Article 23 of the Regulation.[218] Jurisdiction also exists, without arrest, if the shipowner acknowledges the issue of the writ or provides bail;[219] but not merely because the usual undertakings designed to prevent arrest are given by the shipowner's insurers.[220] However, the traditional English view that an action in rem against a ship is not an action against a person, and accordingly that the shipowner's other assets are not at risk in the action unless he enters an appearance (usually in order to bail the ship or otherwise obtain its release against security), has no significance for the purposes of the Brussels I Regulation. Such an action must be treated for the purposes of the Regulation as an action against the shipowner (or other person interested in the ship) against whom the plaintiff would wish to proceed in personam if he entered an appearance.[221]

---

[213]  This echoes Article 5(7) of the Brussels Convention.

[214]  See *The Deichland* [1990] QB 361 (CA).

[215]  See Cmd 8954. For English provisions implementing the Arrest Convention, see s 21 of the Senior Courts Act 1981 and s 28 of the County Courts Act 1984.

[216]  On Article 71, see pp. 44–6 above.

[217]  See *The Anna H* [1995] 1 Lloyd's Rep 11 (CA). See also *Ladgroup v Euroeast Lines* [1997] SLT 916 (Scottish Outer House); and *The Turquoise Bleu* [1996] 1 ILRM 406 (Irish High Court).

[218]  See *The Bergen* [1997] 1 Lloyd's Rep 380 (Clarke J), also holding that in such a case an English court retains its traditional discretion to decline arrest jurisdiction in accordance with the agreement.

[219]  See *The Prinsengracht* [1993] 1 Lloyd's Rep 41 (Sheen J). Cf. *The Anna H* [1995] 1 Lloyd's Rep 11, where Clarke J agreed that the provision of bail amounts to submission, but the Court of Appeal left the point open.

[220]  See *The Deichland* [1990] QB 361 (CA).

[221]  See Case C-406/92: *The Maciej Rataj* [1994] ECR I-5439, on Article 27 of the Regulation; *The Deichland* [1990] QB 361 (CA), on Articles 2 and 3; and *The Indian Endurance (No 2)* [1998] AC 878, on s 34 of the Civil Jurisdiction and Judgments Act 1982.

In *The Po*,[222] the Court of Appeal ruled that Article 71 preserves English jurisdiction in cases where it is conferred both by an unimplemented provision of the Brussels Convention of 10th May 1952 on Civil Jurisdiction in Matters of Collision[223] and by a continuing provision of traditional English law. This was the case where a collision action was brought in rem, and the ship was served but not arrested because security was given. Service on the ship was sufficient under traditional English law, and under Article 1(1)(b) of the Collision Convention it was sufficient that arrest could have been effected and security had been furnished.

Article 7 of the Brussels I Regulation[224] specifies that where by virtue of the Regulation a court of a Member State has jurisdiction in actions relating to liability arising from the use or operation of a ship, that court, or any other court substituted for this purpose by the internal law of that Member State, shall also have jurisdiction over claims for limitation of such liability. This provision was considered necessary because the Convention of 10th October 1957 on Limitation of Liability of Owners of Seagoing Ships does not deal with judicial jurisdiction. The effect of Article 7 is to enable a shipowner to bring a limitation action at his own domicile.[225] As regards concurrent liability and limitation actions, the European Court ruled in *Maersk Olie & Gas v de Haan & de Boer*[226] that an application to a court of a Member State by a shipowner for the establishment of a liability limitation fund, in which the potential victim of the damage (for example, to an oil-rig) is indicated, and an action for damages brought before a court of another Member State by that victim against the shipowner, are not similar actions within Article 27 of the Regulation, but are related actions within Article 28.[227] In its Report and Green Paper of 21st April 2009,[228] the EC Commission contemplates the possibility of providing for the consolidation of proceedings aimed at setting up a liability fund with individual liability proceedings.

Article 64 of the Regulation laid down a transitional provision which was applicable for six years from the entry into force of the Regulation, and which has now expired. It applied to proceedings involving a dispute between the master and a member of the crew of a sea-going ship registered in Greece, Portugal or Denmark,[229] concerning remuneration or other conditions of service. It required a court of another Member State, when seised of such proceedings, to establish whether the diplomatic or consular officer responsible for the ship had been notified of the dispute. But it permitted the court to act as soon as that officer had been notified. There is no similar provision in the Lugano Convention 2007.

Article 64 had replaced a wider provision contained in Article VB of the Protocol annexed to the Brussels Convention. A similar provision, contained in Article VB of the First Protocol annexed to the Lugano Convention 1988, remains for the time being applicable to disputes between the master and a member of the crew of a sea-going ship registered in Iceland,

---

222    [1991] 2 Lloyd's Rep 206 (CA).
223    Cmd 8954.
224    This echoes Article 6A of the Brussels Convention.
225    See *The Volvox Hollandia* [1988] 2 Lloyd's Rep 361 (CA).
226    Case C-39/02, [2004] ECR I-9657.
227    Cf. *The Happy Fellow* [1998] 1 Lloyd's Rep 13, where the English Court of Appeal had taken the view that in such cases Article 27 probably applied.
228    COM(2009) 174 final, at section 3.8.2, and COM(2009) 175 final, at question 8.
229    See Article 2(2)(d) of the Agreement between the European Community and Denmark; [2005] OJ L299/62.

concerning remuneration or other conditions of service. The courts of other Contracting States are required, not only to establish whether the diplomatic or consular officer responsible for the ship has been notified of the dispute, but further to stay the proceedings so long as he has not been notified, and of their own motion to decline jurisdiction if the officer, having been duly notified, has exercised the powers accorded to him in the matter by a consular convention, or in the absence of such a convention has, within the time allowed, raised any objection to the exercise of such jurisdiction.

## ANCILLARY JURISDICTION

The Brussels I Regulation recognises the desirability, in the interests of the sound administration of justice and of reducing the risk of conflicting judgments, that related disputes should be decided together in a single proceeding. Article 6 gives positive effect to this principle, by providing for ancillary jurisdiction over co-defendants, third parties and counterclaims, and by enabling a court exercising exclusive jurisdiction over a right in rem in land to entertain a related contractual claim against the same defendant, even if the court would not have had jurisdiction to entertain the additional claim in its own right. The principle is also given negative effect by Articles 27–30, which endeavour to prevent concurrent actions in different Member States in respect of similar or related disputes by requiring or encouraging the court subsequently seised to decline jurisdiction or at least stay its proceedings in favour of the court first seised.[230]

But the Regulation does not ensure that in all cases a court properly seised of one claim will also be competent to entertain a related claim by the same plaintiff against the same defendant. In particular, a court may be competent to entertain a contractual claim under Article 5(1) but not to entertain a related tortious claim under Article 5(3), or conversely.[231] Moreover, Article 6 does not provide for multiple claims by the same plaintiff against the same defendant, except in the case of proprietary and contractual claims relating to land, and Article 28 has only negative effect.[232]

It is also possible for contracting parties to exclude the operation of Article 6 between themselves by means of a clearly worded agreement on jurisdiction complying with Article 23.[233] It is submitted that the presumption should be that a jurisdiction clause is not intended to exclude ancillary jurisdiction under Article 6 unless the contrary intention is clearly expressed. But the contrary presumption appears to be accepted in France, except in relation to counterclaims.[234]

---

[230]   See Chapter 8 below.

[231]   See Case 189/87: *Kalfelis v Schröder* [1988] ECR 5565.

[232]   See Case 150/80: *Elefanten Schuh v Jacqmain* [1981] ECR 1671; Case C-51/97: *Réunion Européenne v Spliethoff's Bevrachtingskantoor* [1998] ECR I-6511; and Case C-420/97: *Leathertex v Bodetex* [1999] ECR I-6747. See also *Mutuelle Parisienne de Garantie v Delfino*, 24th March 1987 (French Court of Cassation).

[233]   See Case 23/78: *Meeth v Glacetal* [1978] ECR 2133; and *Hough v P & O Containers* [1999] QB 834 (Rix J).

[234]   See *Berlit Staudt v Co d'Assurance l'Alsacienne*, 18th October 1989 (French Court of Cassation), and Gaudemet-Tallon, at paras 234–6.

## Co-defendants

By Article 6(1) of the Brussels I Regulation, a person domiciled in a Member State may be sued, where he is one of a number of defendants, in the courts for the place where any one of them is domiciled, provided that the claims are so closely connected that it is expedient to hear and determine them together to avoid the risk of irreconcilable judgments resulting from separate proceedings. The main clause echoes Article 6(1) of the Brussels Convention. The proviso reflects the decision of the European Court in *Kalfelis v Schröder*.[235]

The relevant date for ascertaining whether one of the defendants is domiciled in the forum's territory is that of the issue of the claim form initiating the proceedings against that defendant, and not that of service on him, nor that of the subsequent joinder of the other defendant.[236]

Article 6(1) extends to a counterclaim, so as to enable a defendant who counterclaims against a local plaintiff to join a foreign co-defendant to the counterclaim.[237] Similarly, it extends to a claim by a third party (joined by a defendant) against local and foreign plaintiffs,[238] or against a local defendant (who joined the third party) and a foreign plaintiff.[239] But it does not extend to separate actions brought by different plaintiffs against different defendants, even if they involve common issues.[240] Nor does Article 6(1), or any other provision of Chapter II, enable joinder of a co-defendant as such, if he is domiciled in another Member State, in an action against another defendant who is domiciled in a non-member country.[241]

The proviso, requiring that the claims against the local (or anchor) defendant and the foreign defendant must be so closely connected that it is expedient to hear and determine them together to avoid the risk of irreconcilable judgments resulting from separate proceedings, echoes the definition of related actions in Article 28(3) of the Regulation. In *Roche Nederland BV v Primus*,[242] the European Court left open whether, in relation to the proviso specified in Article 6(1), it is sufficient that there is a risk of conflicting decisions (as would be sufficient in relation to related actions under Article 28), or whether there must be a risk of decisions which give rise to mutually exclusive legal consequences (so as to satisfy the test used in respect of recognition and enforcement under Article 34). The Court explained that, even if the concept of irreconcilable judgments for the purpose of Article 6(1) must be understood in the broad sense of contradictory decisions, for decisions to be regarded as contradictory, it is not sufficient that there is a divergence in the outcome of the dispute. The divergence must also arise in the context of the same situation of law and fact. No such divergence arose in the instant case, which involved claims for infringement of parallel patents,

---

[235]    Case 189/87, [1988] ECR 5565.
[236]    See *Canada Trust v Stolzenberg (No 2)* [2002] 1 AC 1; and *Petrotrade v Smith* [1998] 2 All ER 346 (Thomas J). Cf. *Gard Marine v Tunnicliffe* [2009] EWHC 2388 (Comm) (Hamblen J), accepting jurisdiction over a foreign defendant on the basis that a co-defendant, subsequently joined, had been domiciled in England throughout.
[237]    See *Aiglon v Gau Shan* [1993] 1 Lloyd's Rep 164 (Hirst J).
[238]    See *SCOR v Eras (No 2)* [1995] 2 All ER 278 (Potter J).
[239]    See Gaudemet-Tallon, at para 223.
[240]    See *Kleinwort Benson v City of Glasgow District Council* [1994] QB 404 (CA).
[241]    See Case C-51/97: *Réunion Européenne v Spliethoff's Bevrachtingskantoor* [1998] ECR I-6511.
[242]    Case C-539/03, [2006] ECR I-6535.

granted for several Member States, against several defendants, domiciled in different Member States, each being sued for an infringement committed in the State of its domicile.[243]

In England, a broad approach is applied in the determination of the risk of irreconcilable decisions, so as to include inconsistent findings of fact, rather than one based on close analysis of the respective claims; and it is emphasised that only a risk, rather than a certainty, of irreconcilable decisions is required.[244] The test of connection is similar to that utilised in relation to 'necessary or proper parties' under the traditional English law (now found in paragraph 3.1(3) of Practice Direction B supplementing Part 6 of the Civil Procedure Rules). The liability of both defendants must depend on the same investigation, though their liabilities may be either cumulative or alternative.[245] Thus in *Gascoine v Pyrah*,[246] the Court of Appeal permitted an English purchaser of a French horse, who was suing his English agent who had acted in the purchase, to join as a co-defendant under Article 6(1) a German veterinary surgeon who had been engaged to examine and report on the condition of the horse, the claims against both defendants being for negligence in advising in favour of the purchase. Similarly, in *Casio Computer v Sayo*,[247] the Court of Appeal allowed joinder where the English and foreign defendants were both alleged to have dishonestly assisted in breaches of fiduciary duty at different stages in the operation of a fraudulent scheme to misappropriate a sum belonging to the claimant. Again, in *Latchin v General Mediterranean Holidays*,[248] Andrew Smith J allowed joinder of claims against an English individual and a foreign company, relating to similar contracts negotiated together by the individual with the plaintiff, one on his own behalf and the other on behalf of the company. Similarly, in *King v Crown Energy*,[249] Chambers QC allowed joinder of a Swiss company, sued as employer for breach of a service agreement, in an action against its English parent company, sued as guarantor of the service agreement, and on a related agreement for further remuneration, and for inducing breach of the service agreement. Again, in *FKI Engineering Ltd v De Wind Holdings Ltd*,[250] the Court of Appeal accepted that there was a sufficient connection under Article 6(1) between a claim against the local defendant for damages for breach of contract, and a claim against a foreign defendant for a declaration of non-liability under another contract, where the existence of the plaintiff's liability to the foreign defendant would affect the assessment of damages in respect of the plaintiff's claim against the local defendant. Similarly, in *Gard*

---

[243]    In its Report and Green Paper of 21st April 2009, the EC Commission contemplates (without much enthusiasm) the possibility of establishing a specific rule allowing infringement proceedings concerning certain industrial property rights against several defendants to be brought before the courts of the Member State where the defendant co-ordinating the activities or otherwise having the closest connection with the infringement is domiciled. See COM(2009) 174 final, at section 3.4, and COM(2009) 175 final, at question 4.

[244]    See *Bank of Tokyo-Mitsubishi v Baskan Gida* [2004] ILPr 26 (Lawrence Collins J), at paras 188 and 216. See also *King v Crown Energy* [2003] ILPr 28.

[245]    See *Massey v Heynes* (1881) 21 QBD 330; and *Croft v King* [1893] 1 QB 419. See also *FKI Engineering Ltd v De Wind Holdings Ltd* [2009] 1 All ER (Comm) 118 (CA), accepting that under Article 6(1) the claims may be alternative.

[246]    [1994] ILPr 82 (CA).

[247]    [2001] ILPr 43 (CA).

[248]    [2002] CLC 330.

[249]    [2003] ILPr 28.

[250]    [2009] 1 All ER (Comm) 118 (CA).

*Marine v Tunnicliffe*,[251] Hamblen J held that there was sufficient connection between claims for indemnity by an insurer against English and Swiss reinsurers, who had each reinsured part of the risk on similar terms in the context of a common reinsurance programme and by way of contracts governed by English law; and also that there was sufficient connection between the claim for indemnity against the Swiss reinsurer and an alternative claim for damages against the English broker through which the reinsurance was placed, since these claims were largely dependent on the same issue.

On the other hand, as Rix J held in *The Xing Su Hai*,[252] there is no sufficient link, or risk of irreconcilable judgments, where the claim against the local defendant is merely for disclosure of information about the location of assets of the foreign defendants. Nor, as the Court of Appeal ruled in *Messier Dowty v Sabena*,[253] where the plaintiff's claim is for declarations of non-liability, and the foreign defendant has made no claim against the plaintiff. In contrast, as the Court of Appeal recognised in *Dadourian Group v Simms*,[254] it is possible to utilise Article 6(1) in the context of a freezing order, for the purpose of joining as a co-defendant a person who is alleged to hold assets belonging to an existing defendant.

In *Freeport v Arnoldsson*,[255] the European Court ruled that the fact that claims brought against a number of defendants have different legal bases does not preclude application of Article 6(1). The Court overruled its earlier dictum in *Réunion Européenne v Spliethoff's Bevrachtingskantoor*[256] that there was no sufficient connection between claims by the same plaintiff against two defendants in respect of the same loss, if one of the claims was contractual and the other was based on tort. This extraordinary dictum had led to a reference to the European Court by the English Court of Appeal in *Watson v First Choice Holidays*,[257] but the reference was eventually abandoned, presumably because the parties had settled the claim. Subsequently, the dictum in *Réunion* had been rejected in Ireland by Kearns J in *Daly v Irish Group Travel*[258] and in England by Cooke J in *Andrew Weir Shipping v Wartsila*.[259] The ruling in *Freeport* has now eliminated this problem.

It has now been established by the rulings of the European Court in *Reisch Montage v Kiesel Baumaschinen*[260] and *Freeport v Arnoldsson*[261] that there is no requirement under Article 6(1) that, to enable joinder of a foreign defendant, the claim against the local defendant must be plausible, or seriously arguable, and not made solely for the purpose of enabling the foreign defendant to be joined. Before these rulings a requirement of this kind had been

---

251   [2009] EWHC 2388 (Comm).
252   [1995] 2 Lloyd's Rep 15.
253   [2000] 1 WLR 2040 (CA).
254   [2006] 3 All ER 48 (CA).
255   Case C-98/06, [2007] ECR I-8319.
256   Case C-51/97, [1998] ECR I-6511, at para 50.
257   [2001] 2 Lloyd's Rep 339 (CA). In *Watson*, an English tourist, who had suffered personal injuries during a holiday in Spain, brought an English action in contract against the English organiser of the package holiday, and sought to join a claim in tort against a Spanish sub-contractor in respect of the same injuries.
258   [2003] ILPr 38.
259   [2004] 2 Lloyd's Rep 377.
260   Case C-103/05, [2006] ECR I-6827.
261   Case C-98/06, [2007] ECR I-8319.

implied by both English[262] and Irish[263] courts. But in *Reisch Montage v Kiesel Baumaschinen*,[264] the European Court (rejecting the advice of Colomer AG) ruled that Article 6(1) may be relied on in the context of an action brought in a Member State against a defendant domiciled in that State and a co-defendant domiciled in another Member State, even when the action against the local defendant is regarded under a national provision as inadmissible from the time it is brought, for example by reason of insolvency proceedings. In *Freeport v Arnoldsson*,[265] the European Court went further and (rejecting both a dictum of its own in *Reisch Montage* and the advice of Mengozzi AG) ruled that Article 6(1) only requires that the claims against the defendants must be sufficiently connected (in the sense that it is expedient to hear and determine them together to avoid the risk of irreconcilable judgments resulting from separate proceedings), and that there is no further requirement that the claims must not have been brought with the sole object of ousting the jurisdiction of the courts of the Member State where one of the defendants is domiciled. It is clear that the rulings in *Reisch Montage* and *Freeport* have the potential to undermine the entire structure of Chapter II of the Regulation, by enabling joinder where the claim against the local defendant is obviously hopeless and absurd. Moreover the English Court of Appeal continues to insist that the claim against the English defendant must be seriously arguable if it is to enable the joinder of a foreign co-defendant under Article 6(1).[266]

**Third-party Proceedings**

By Article 6(2) of the Brussels I Regulation,[267] a person domiciled in a Member State may be sued in another Member State, as a third party in third party proceedings, in the court seised of the original proceedings, unless these were instituted solely with the object of removing him from the jurisdiction of the court which would be competent in his case. This extends to an application in England for the costs of litigation, made under s 4 of the Courts and Legal Services Act 1990, against a non-party to the litigation (such as a controlling share-holder of a plaintiff company).[268]

In *Hagen v Zeehaghe*,[269] the European Court made clear that this power of a defendant to join a third party applies regardless of the basis of the court's jurisdiction over the defendant.

---

[262] See *The Rewia* [1991] 2 Lloyd's Rep 325 (CA); *The Xing Su Hai* [1995] 2 Lloyd's Rep 15 (Rix J); *Holding Oil v Marc Rich* [1996] CLY 1085 (CA); *Messier Dowty v Sabena* [2000] 1 Lloyd's Rep 428 (CA); *Bank of Tokyo-Mitsubishi v Baskan Gida* [2004] ILPr 26 (Lawrence Collins J), at para. 217; and *Andrew Weir Shipping v Wartsila* [2004] 2 Lloyd's Rep 377 (Cooke J).

[263] See *Gannon v British and Irish Steampacket Co* [1993] 2 IR 359 (Irish Supreme Court). See also *Doran v Power* [1996] 1 ILRM 55 (Irish Supreme Court).

[264] Case C-103/05, [2006] ECR I-6827.

[265] Case C-98/06, [2007] ECR I-8319.

[266] See *FKI Engineering Ltd v De Wind Holdings Ltd* [2009] 1 All ER (Comm) 118 (CA). In any event, where the co-defendant is domiciled in a non-member country, the English court (applying English law in accordance with Article 4 of the Regulation) will refuse to permit joinder of the co-defendant if the claim against the English defendant is not seriously arguable; see *Yugraneft v Abramovich* [2008] EWHC 2613 (Comm) (Christopher Clarke J), especially at paras 488–97.

[267] This echoes Article 6(2) of the Brussels Convention.

[268] See *The Ikarian Reefer* [2000] 1 WLR 603 (CA).

[269] Case 365/88, [1990] ECR I-1845.

Such jurisdiction need not be based on the defendant's domicile. It may be based on Article 5(1), as in *Hagen* itself. Probably it may be based on any other provision of Chapter II, including Article 4 (on defendants domiciled in non-member countries) or Article 24 (on submission by appearance).[270]

In *Hagen*, the Court also ruled that the procedural admissibility of a third-party proceeding in non-territorial respects is governed by the law of the court seised, provided that the effectiveness of the Regulation is not impaired, but that leave to join a third party cannot be refused on the ground that the third party resides or is domiciled in another Member State. In *Réunion Européenne v Zurich España*,[271] the European Court added that Article 6(2) does not require the existence of any particular type of connection between the original claim and the third-party claim, beyond what is sufficient to establish that the choice of forum does not amount to an abuse by way of the removal of the third party from the jurisdiction of the court otherwise competent in his case. But it reiterated that the conditions for admissibility of a third party claim remain subject to the forum's procedural rules, except insofar as their application would impair the effectiveness of the Regulation by restricting the application of the rules of jurisdiction laid down therein. Thus, as Rix J recognised in *Caltex v Metro*,[272] Article 6(2) requires that there must be a proper connection between the main claim and the third-party claim, such as would be recognised by the forum's own third-party statute;[273] but it is not permissible to exercise a forum non conveniens discretion in relation to Article 6(2).[274]

As regards the proviso to Article 6(2), insisting that the original proceedings must not have been instituted solely with the object of removing the third party from the jurisdiction of the court which would be competent in his case, Rix J explained in *Hough v P & O Containers*[275] that this is confined to situations where the plaintiff and the defendant are effectively in collusion to bring a claim against a third party in an otherwise incompetent forum; or where, even without collusion, the plaintiff has no good reason to sue the defendant, but is hoping by doing so to enable the defendant to utilise Article 6(2) so as to bring the third party to such a forum.

Article 65 of the Regulation[276] adapts Article 6(2) in view of the limited character of the third-party proceedings which exist in Germany, Austria and Hungary. In those countries, such proceedings are designed to preclude the third party from disputing matters decided in the action between the plaintiff and the defendant, but the defendant cannot in the same proceedings obtain affirmative relief against the third party. Article 65 ensures that a person domiciled in another Member State may be joined as a third party in the context of the limited procedures available in Germany, Austria and Hungary; and that the effects which judgments

---

[270]    See *Veenbrink v BIAO*, 14th May 1992 (French Court of Cassation), permitting the use of Article 6(2) where jurisdiction over the main action was governed by Article 4; and Gaudemet-Tallon, at para 226.

[271]    Case C-77/04, [2005] ECR I-4509.

[272]    [1999] 2 Lloyd's Rep 724. Cf. *Waterford Wedgwood v Nagli* [1999] ILPr 9 (Aldous QC).

[273]    In England, the relevant enactment is now Part 20 of the Civil Procedure Rules, as amended.

[274]    See also *Dornoch v Westminster International* [2009] EWHC 201(Admlty) (Tomlinson J), on the English court's discretion under rule 19.2 of the Civil Procedure Rules 1998 to refuse the joinder of additional defendants on non-territorial grounds.

[275]    [1999] QB 834.

[276]    Article 65 echoes Article V of the Protocol annexed to the Brussels Convention. It is extended to Hungary by the Act of Accession 2003.

have under the law of the Member State of origin on persons joined as third parties are recognised and enforced throughout the Community under Chapter III of the Regulation. In its Report and Green Paper of 21st April 2009,[277] the EC Commission contemplates the possibility of replacing Article 65 by a uniform rule on third-party proceedings.

In the context of the Lugano Convention 1988, provision similar to Article 65 of the Regulation is made in relation to Germany, Austria, Spain and Switzerland by Article V of the First Protocol annexed to the Convention. In the context of the Lugano Convention 2007, provision similar to Article 65 of the Regulation is made in relation to Germany, Austria, Hungary, Estonia, Latvia, Lithuania, Poland, Slovenia and Switzerland by Article II of the First Protocol and Annex IX to the Convention, along with Annex II of the Council Decision approving the conclusion of the Lugano Convention 2007. In view of this breach in the parallelism between the Brussels I Regulation and the Lugano Convention 2007, the EC Commission envisages revision of the rules on third-party proceedings in the context of the Regulation.[278]

## Counterclaims

By Article 6(3) of the Brussels I Regulation,[279] a person domiciled in a Member State may also be sued in another Member State on a counterclaim arising from the same contract or facts as those on which the original claim was based, in the court in which the original claim is pending.

Probably the reference to the same contract or facts must be construed broadly, in the light of the definition of related actions provided by Articles 6(1) and 28(3). Thus Article 6(3) extends to a case where the plaintiff sues for the price of goods supplied, and the defendant counterclaims for damages for infringement or repudiation of an exclusive distribution contract, pursuant to which the contract of sale sued on by the plaintiff was entered into.[280] In any event, Article 6(3) is confined to a cross-claim made by a person sued, and does not extend to a claim made by a sister company of the defendant.[281] Article 6(3) is also limited to a counterclaim against the original claimant, and does not provide for jurisdiction over an additional party joined by counterclaim.[282]

In the context of monetary claims, the European Court ruled in *Danvaern v Otterbeck*[283] that Article 6(3) is confined to a true counterclaim, as distinct from a purely defensive set-off. It applies where the defendant, by a separate claim made in the same proceedings, seeks a judgment ordering the plaintiff to pay him a debt, possibly of an amount exceeding that claimed by the plaintiff, even if the plaintiff's claim is dismissed. In contrast, the admissibility of a purely defensive set-off, invoked solely for the purpose of wholly or partially extinguishing the plaintiff's claim, is not governed by Article 6(3), but by the law of the court seised.

---

[277] COM(2009) 174 final, at section 3.8.2, and COM(2009) 175 final, at question 8.
[278] See JUSTCIV 94, of 27th May 2008; and JUSTCIV 246, of 14th November 2008.
[279] This echoes Article 6(3) of the Brussels Convention.
[280] See *Gianotti v Montuori*, 18th February 1994 (French Court of Cassation); and Gaudemet-Tallon, at para 229. Cf. per Léger AG in Case C-341/93: *Danvaern v Otterbeck* [1995] ECR I-2053.
[281] See *Dollfus Mieg v CDW International* [2004] ILPr 12.
[282] See *Bank of Tokyo-Mitsubishi v Baskan Gida* [2004] ILPr 26 (Lawrence Collins J), at para 189.
[283] Case C-341/93, [1995] ECR I-2053.

## Claims Involving Land

By Article 6(4) of the Regulation,[284] a person domiciled in a Member State may also be sued in another Member State in matters relating to a contract, if the action may be combined with an action against him in matters relating to rights in rem in immovable property, in the court of the Member State in which the property is situated.

This is designed to enable a plaintiff who brings an action based on a proprietary right in land before a court of the Member State in which the land is situated in accordance with Article 22(1)[285] to add a contractual claim relating to the same land against the same defendant. An example would be where a mortgagee of land sues the mortgagor, seeking orders for possession and sale of the mortgaged land and also an order for payment by the mortgagor of the mortgage debt.[286] But Articles 22(1) and 6(4) do not apply to a claim for payment only, where the mortgaged land has already been sold.[287]

---

[284]   This echoes Article 6(4) of the Brussels Convention.
[285]   See pp. 144–6 below.
[286]   See Gaudemet-Tallon, at para 230.
[287]   See *Union de Credit Pour Le Batiment*, 22nd January 1999 (English CA).

# 5.  Protected contracts

## INTRODUCTION

Chapter II of the Brussels I Regulation lays down special rules on jurisdiction in respect of three types of contract: insurance contracts,[1] consumer contracts,[2] and contracts of employment.[3] As the European Court has recognised,[4] these provisions are inspired by a concern to protect the party who is expected to be economically weaker and less experienced in legal matters than the other party to the contract. Similarly, Recital 13 explains that, in relation to insurance, consumer contracts and employment, the weaker party should be protected by rules of jurisdiction more favourable to his interests than the general rules provide for.

Accordingly, these provisions offer the weaker party (the policy-holder, consumer or employee) a wide choice of fora in which to sue the stronger party (the insurer, supplier or employer), while limiting the fora in which the stronger party can sue the weaker party, and invalidating contrary agreements in respect of future disputes save in exceptional cases. Moreover, in the case of insurance and consumer contracts (though, perhaps surprisingly, not in the case of employment contracts), the protective policy is reinforced by Article 35, which prevents the recognition and enforcement of judgments under Chapter III where the original court accepted jurisdiction in contravention of the protective provisions.[5]

In general, the protective provisions apply only when the defendant is domiciled in a Member State. Thus if the defendant is not domiciled within the Member States, jurisdiction in respect of these contracts is usually remitted by Article 4 to the law of the Member State whose court is seised, in the same way as in the case of ordinary contracts.[6] However, by Articles 9(2), 15(2) and 18(2), where an insurer, supplier or employer is not (under the normal rules) domiciled in any Member State, but it has a secondary establishment in a Member State, and the dispute arises from the operations of the secondary establishment, the insurer,

---

[1]  Chapter II, Section 3, Articles 8–14.

[2]  Chapter II, Section 4, Articles 15–17.

[3]  Chapter II, Section 5, Articles 18–21.

[4]  See Case C-89/91: *Shearson Lehman Hutton v TVB* [1993] ECR I-139, at para 18.

[5]  See pp. 234–5 below. Moreover, under EC Regulation 805/2004, creating a European Enforcement Order for Uncontested Claims, [2004] OJ L143/15, the court of origin, before certifying a default judgment on an uncontested claim as a European Enforcement Order, must be satisfied, in the case of insurance, that the judgment does not conflict with the rules on jurisdiction laid down in Section 3 of Chapter II of the Brussels I Regulation; or where the claim relates to a consumer contract, and the debtor is the consumer, that the judgment was given in the Member State of the debtor's domicile within the meaning of the Brussels I Regulation. See pp. 267–71 below.

[6]  See Articles 8, 15(1) and 18(1), which explicitly save Article 4; and Case C-318/93: *Brenner v Dean Witter Reynolds* [1994] ECR I-4275. For this purpose, English law treats insurance, consumer and employment contracts in the same way as ordinary contracts; see para 3.1 of Practice Direction B supplementing Part 6 of the Civil Procedure Rules.

supplier or employer is treated as domiciled in the State in which the secondary establishment is situated. Such an insurer, supplier or employer will be referred to as 'secondarily domiciled' in a Member State. There is no similar provision in relation to a policy-holder, consumer or employee.

The protective provisions do not affect a number of important provisions of Chapter II, which apply in the normal way to protected contracts. Thus an action based on a protected contract can always be brought in the courts of the Member State in which the defendant is domiciled, and in such cases the Regulation retains its normal indifference to the allocation of jurisdiction between the courts for the various territories of the domiciliary State.[7] Similarly, it remains possible to sue at the location of the defendant's secondary establishment from whose operations the dispute arose,[8] or to make a counterclaim based on the same contract in the court seised of the original action,[9] and submission by appearance remains effective to found jurisdiction.[10] Again the provisions of Articles 26-31, on consideration of jurisdiction of the court's own motion, on service of the defendant, on concurrent actions, and on provisional measures, remain applicable.

## INSURANCE

### Scope

The protective provisions in respect of insurance are laid down by Section 3 (Articles 8–14) of Chapter II of the Brussels I Regulation.[11] No explicit definition of insurance is provided, and it seems clear that, as with most other concepts used by the Regulation in determining its scope,[12] an independent meaning of 'insurance' will in due course be announced by the European Court, derived from the scheme and purposes of the Regulation and taking account of other relevant Community legislation.[13] The independent concept of insurance will presumably involve a uniform concept of insurable interest, serving to distinguish insurance from wagering.

In any event, it is clear that all types of insurance (as generally understood) are covered, and that the Section is not confined to insurance taken out for domestic or private purposes.[14] But the Regulation has dramatically reduced the protection provided by permitting contracting-out in the case of 'large risks', which are widely defined.[15]

---

   7   See Articles 2, 9(1)(a), 12(1), 16(1)–(2), 19(1) and 20(1); and Chapter 3 above. In the United Kingdom, insurance contracts are treated for the purpose of such allocation in the same way as ordinary contracts, since Schedule 4 to the 1982 Act deliberately omits any specific provision for insurance. For a perverse result of such omission, see *Davenport v Corinthian Motor Policies at Lloyd's* [1991] SLT 774.
   8   See Articles 5(5), 8, 15(1) and 18(1).
   9   See Articles 6(3), 12(2), 16(3) and 20(2).
   10   See Articles 13(1), 17(1), 21(1) and 24; and Case C-111/09: *ČPP v Bilas* [2010] All ER (D) 203 (May).
   11   Replacing Section 3 (Articles 7–12A) of Title II of the Brussels Convention.
   12   See, for example, Case C-89/91: *Shearson Lehman Hutton v TVB* [1993] ECR I-139, on the concept of a consumer contract.
   13   Such as Article 7 of the Rome I Regulation; see Chapter 13 below.
   14   See *New Hampshire Insurance Co v Strabag Bau* [1992] 1 Lloyd's Rep 361 (CA).
   15   See Articles 13(5) and 14(5); and pp. 128–30 below.

The European Court ruled in *Group Josi v UGIC*[16] that for present purposes reinsurance does not count as insurance, so that the provisions of Section 3 do not extend to disputes between a reinsurer and a reinsured in connection with a reinsurance contract. It recognised, however, that Section 3 does apply where a policy-holder, insured or beneficiary of an insurance contract invokes his rights under the insurance contract directly against his insurer's reinsurer, for example in the event of the insurer's bankruptcy or liquidation. Somewhat similarly, in *Réunion Européenne v Zurich España*,[17] the European Court ruled that Section 3 does not apply to third-party proceedings between insurers based on multiple insurance, such as the remarkable claim for contribution apparently made available to a liability insurer against a loss insurer by the French Insurance Code. In England, the Court of Appeal has accepted that Section 3 does not extend to disputes between co-insurers, since the Section is designed to protect the weaker party to a transaction.[18]

## Actions Against an Insurer

Articles 8–10 of the Regulation offer to a plaintiff a wide choice of fora in which to bring an action against an insurer who is domiciled (or secondarily domiciled) in a Member State. The choice offered by Articles 8–10 is available not only where the action is brought by the policy-holder (the person who as principal concluded the contract with the insurer, or the universal successor to the estate of that person, such as his executor or trustee in bankruptcy); but also where the action is brought by some other insured or beneficiary under the insurance (such as, in the case of a motor liability policy, a person driving the policy-holder's vehicle with his consent; or in the case of a life policy, a person in whose favour a trust of the benefit of the policy has been declared by the policy-holder). By Article 11(2), the choice offered by Articles 8–10 is also available in relation to a direct action against a liability insurer brought by a third-party victim of a tort covered by the insurance, if such a direct action is permissible under the law governing the issue according to the conflict rules of the court seised.

The admissibility of such a direct action is now governed by Article 18 of the Rome II Regulation,[19] which enables a tort victim to bring his claim directly against the tortfeasor's liability insurer, if either the law applicable to the tort or the law applicable to the insurance contract so provides. Under traditional English law, the admissibility of such a direct action was governed by the proper law of the insurance contract.[20] In some Member States, which are party to the Hague Convention of 4th May 1971 on the Law Applicable to Traffic Accidents,[21] a rule even more favourable to the victim than that specified by the Rome II

---

16 Case C-412/98, [2000] ECR I-5925. See also *Agnew v Länsförsäkringsbolagens* [2000] 1 All ER 737 (HL).

17 Case C-77/04, [2005] ECR I-4509.

18 See *Youell v La Reunion Aerienne* [2009] EWCA Civ 182.

19 See pp. 408–9 below.

20 See *The Hari Bhum* [2005] 1 Lloyd's Rep 67 (CA), affirming [2004] 1 Lloyd's Rep 206 (Moore-Bick J); and *Maher v Groupama* [2009] EWCA Civ 1191.

21 Parties to the Hague Convention 1971 include the following EU Member States and Lugano Convention countries: France, Belgium, the Netherlands, Luxembourg, Spain, Austria, Poland, the Czech Republic, Slovakia, Slovenia, Latvia, Lithuania and Switzerland. But not the United Kingdom.

Regulation remains applicable to traffic accidents, in view of Article 28 of that Regulation. By Article 9 of the Hague Convention 1971, a traffic victim has a direct claim against a liability insurer if such a claim is recognised either by the law applicable to the victim's claim against the insured; or by the internal law of the country of the accident; or by the law which governs the insurance contract.

In accordance with the general principle in favour of the defendant's country, Article 9(1)(a) and (2) of the Brussels I Regulation confers jurisdiction over actions against an insurer on the courts of the Member State in which the defendant insurer is domiciled (or secondarily domiciled); and Articles 5(5) and 8 confer jurisdiction over such actions on the courts for the place (in a Member State other than that of the defendant insurer's domicile) at which the defendant insurer has a secondary establishment from whose operations the dispute has arisen.

But, radically departing from its usual rejection of the plaintiff's country as such, Article 9(1)(b) of the Regulation also confers jurisdiction on the courts for the place (in a Member State other than that of the defendant insurer's domicile or secondary domicile) at which the plaintiff (whether he is the policy-holder or some other insured or beneficiary) is domiciled at the institution of the proceedings.[22] Moreover, in *FBTO Schadeverzekeringen v Odenbreit*,[23] the European Court ruled that the effect of Articles 9(1)(b) and 11(2) of the Regulation is to enable a tort victim to bring an action directly against the tortfeasor's liability insurer in the courts for the place in a Member State where the victim himself is domiciled, provided that such a direct action is permitted and the insurer is domiciled in a Member State. Further, in *Vorarlberger Gebietskrankenkasse v WGV-Schwäbische Allgemeine Versicherungs AG*,[24] the European Court ruled that the benefit of suing at the plaintiff's own domicile, conferred by Articles 9(1)(b) and 11(2), extends to an indirect victim, such as the successor of a direct victim who has died, but not to a social security institution, acting as the statutory assignee of the rights of the direct victim of a motor accident, since a social security institution cannot be regarded as an economically weaker and legally less experienced party than a civil liability insurer.

The radical nature of Article 9(1)(b) is especially clear when it is borne in mind that the transaction and the risk need have no other connection with the country in which the policy-holder or other plaintiff is domiciled. If, for example, the Belgian branch of a German manufacturing company were to insure its Belgian factory with an English insurer against risks such as damage by fire, a claim under the policy could be pursued in Germany, as the plaintiff policy-holder's domicile, as well as in England, as the insurer's domicile, and in Belgium, as the place of the harmful event. Or if an individual domiciled in Italy were to take out life insurance there with an Italian company, and then to move his domicile to Sweden, he would have the option of suing on the policy in either Sweden or Italy. Or if a Portuguese pedestrian, while visiting France, were injured in a road accident there by colliding with a car driven by a French domiciliary and covered by liability insurance issued by a French insurer, he would have the option of suing the insurer in either Portugal or France.

---

[22]    See the Jenard Report, at p. 31, and Gaudemet-Tallon, at para 247. Article 9(1)(b) of the Regulation departs from Article 8(1)(2) of the Brussels Convention, which referred to the domicile of the policy-holder, rather than that of the plaintiff, and thus enabled another insured or beneficiary or a third-party victim to sue at the policy-holder's domicile, but not at his own domicile as such. The merits of this change are not obvious.

[23]    Case C-463/06, [2007] ECR I-11321.

[24]    Case C-347/08, [2010] 1 All ER (Comm) 603.

The jurisdiction normally conferred by Article 5(1) of the Regulation on the courts for the place of performance of a contractual obligation is excluded by Article 8. But in the case of liability insurance, or insurance of land, or where land and movable property are covered by the same insurance policy and adversely affected by the same contingency, Article 10 confers jurisdiction on the courts for the place (in a Member State other than that of the defendant insurer's domicile or secondary domicile) at which the harmful event occurred. It seems clear that in the case of insurance of land, or of land and movables together, the damage to the land (and perhaps movables) constitutes the relevant harmful event, so that jurisdiction is conferred on the courts of the situs. In the case of liability insurance, the concept is presumably the same as under Article 5(3).

As regards ancillary jurisdiction over co-defendants, Article 6(1) of the Regulation is excluded by Article 8, but Article 9(1)(c) confers jurisdiction over a defendant co-insurer on a court (of a Member State other than that of the defendant co-insurer's domicile or secondary domicile) in which proceedings are pending against the leading insurer. It does not appear to matter on what basis jurisdiction over the leading insurer was obtained. Thus an English co-insurer could be joined as a co-defendant in a French action against an American leading insurer, in which jurisdiction was founded on the plaintiff's French nationality under Article 4 of the Regulation and Article 14 of the French Civil Code.

Similarly, as regards third parties, Article 6(2) of the Regulation is excluded, but Article 11(1) permits third party proceedings against a liability insurer in a court (of a Member State other than that of the defendant insurer's domicile or secondary domicile) in which proceedings brought by a victim against an insured are pending.[25] As regards counterclaims, Article 12(2) enables the making of a counterclaim in a court (of a Member State other than that of the defendant insurer's domicile or secondary domicile) in which an action arising from the same policy is pending.

As regards submission by agreement, Article 13(2) of the Regulation ensures that an insurer can be sued in a court of a Member State which has been chosen by an agreement on jurisdiction which complies with the requirements of Article 23. As regards submission by appearance, Articles 13(1) and 24 ensure that a court of a Member State will become competent if the defendant insurer enters an appearance without contesting its jurisdiction.[26] The normal rules laid down by Articles 27–31 on concurrent actions and provisional measures also remain applicable in insurance cases.

## Actions Brought by an Insurer

In accordance with its protective purpose, the Regulation severely restricts jurisdiction to entertain an action brought by an insurer against a policy-holder or other insured or beneficiary who is domiciled in a Member State. By Article 12(1), in general the action must be brought in the courts of the Member State in which the defendant is domiciled.[27] But, by Articles 5(5) and 8, it may be brought in another Member State in the courts for the place at

---

[25]   See also Article 65; considered at pp. 120–21 above.

[26]   See Case C-111/09: *ČPP v Bilas* [2010] All ER (D) 203 (May).

[27]   This applies even if the plaintiff insurer is not domiciled in any Member State; see *Jordan v Baltic Insurance Group* [1999] 2 AC 127.

which the defendant has a secondary establishment from whose operations the dispute has arisen.

Ancillary jurisdiction is also recognised. Thus Article 12(2) enables the making of a counterclaim in a court (of a Member State other than that of the defendant's domicile) in which an action arising from the same policy is pending, and Article 11(3) enables a liability insurer to join a policy-holder or other insured as a third party in a direct action brought by a victim.[28] Submission by appearance remains effective under Articles 13(1) and 24,[29] but agreements on jurisdiction concluded before the dispute arises are often invalidated by Article 13. The normal rules laid down by Articles 27–31 on concurrent actions and provisional measures remain applicable.

In *Jordan v Baltic Insurance Group*,[30] the House of Lords ruled that the protection conferred by Article 12(1) extends to actions by the insurer against persons other than a policy-holder, insured or beneficiary, if the insurer's claim against them arises from the insurance; such as persons who have conspired with the policy-holder to defraud the insurer. It further ruled that Article 12(2) only permits a counterclaim against the original plaintiff, and does not enable an insurer, sued by an insured, to join additional co-defendants to its counterclaim, such as persons alleged to have conspired with the policy-holder to defraud the insurer. On the other hand, in *The Ikarian Reefer*,[31] the Court of Appeal held that an application for the costs of litigation, made under s 51 of the Supreme Court Act 1981 against a non-party to the litigation, such as a controlling shareholder of a plaintiff company, does not fall within the scope of Section 3, even where the litigation in question relates to insurance and the costs are sought against the controlling shareholder of a plaintiff corporate policy-holder.

**Agreements on Jurisdiction**

To ensure the effectiveness of the protective policy, Article 13 of the Brussels I Regulation invalidates any agreement on jurisdiction which departs from the provisions of Section 3, except in specified cases. The invalidation probably extends to clauses choosing a court of a non-member State,[32] but not to arbitration clauses.[33]

The first exception, specified by Article 13(1), permits an agreement on jurisdiction which is entered into after the dispute has arisen. At this stage, the policy-holder is presumably in possession of suitable legal advice. The second exception, specified by Article 13(2), allows an agreement insofar as it enables the policy-holder, an insured or a beneficiary to sue in additional courts. Obviously such an effect is compatible with the protective purpose.

The third exception, specified by Article 13(3), permits an agreement which is concluded between a policy-holder and an insurer who at the conclusion of the contract are domiciled

---

[28]   See also *Maher v Groupama* [2009] EWCA Civ 1191, where Moore-Bick LJ considered that Article 11(3) also enables a victim who has brought a direct action against a liability insurer to join the insured tortfeasor as a co-defendant.

[29]   See Case C-111/09: *ČPP v Bilas* [2010] All ER (D) 203 (May).

[30]   [1999] 2 AC 127.

[31]   [2000] 1 WLR 603 (CA).

[32]   See Gaudemet-Tallon, at para 252.

[33]   See Articles 1(2)(d) and 71 of the Regulation; and Article II of the New York Convention of 10th June 1958 on the Recognition and Enforcement of Foreign Arbitral Awards.

or habitually resident in the same Member State, and which has the effect of conferring juris-diction on the courts of that State, to the exclusion of the courts of a possible harmful event elsewhere (or of a subsequently acquired domicile elsewhere), unless such an agreement is contrary to the law of the chosen State. But, in view of the general requirement of privity applicable under Article 23, such an agreement will not be effective against a third-party victim who brings a direct action against a liability insurer.[34] Nor, as the European Court ruled in *Peloux v Axa Belgique*,[35] can Article 13(3) be relied on against an insured or benefi-ciary under the insurance who is not the policy-holder, and who is domiciled in a Member State other than that of the policy-holder and the insurer.

The fourth exception, specified by Article 13(4), permits an agreement which is concluded with a policy-holder who is not domiciled (presumably at the conclusion of the agreement)[36] in any Member State, except insofar as the insurance is compulsory under the law of a Member State or the insurance relates to land situated in a Member State.[37]

The last exception, specified by Article 13(5), applies to an agreement which relates to a contract of insurance insofar as it covers one or more of the risks set out in Article 14. This exception has been greatly expanded by the Regulation. Under the Brussels Convention, it covered insurance of most maritime or aviation risks, other than personal injury to passengers and loss of or damage to their baggage.[38] These remain specified by Article 14(1)–(4) of the Regulation, which refers in detail to the following risks:

1. any loss of or damage to:

   (a) seagoing ships, installations situated offshore or on the high seas, or aircraft, arising from perils which relate to their use for commercial purposes;
   (b) goods in transit other than passengers' baggage where the transit consists of or includes carriage by such ships or aircraft;

2. any liability, other than for bodily injury to passengers or loss of or damage to their baggage:

   (a) arising out of the use or operation of ships, installations or aircraft as referred to in point 1(a) in so far as, in respect of the latter, the law of the Member State in which such aircraft are regis-tered does not prohibit agreements on jurisdiction regarding insurance of such risks;
   (b) for loss or damage caused by goods in transit as described in point 1(b);

3. any financial loss connected with the use or operation of ships, installations or aircraft as referred to in point 1(a), in particular loss of freight or charter-hire;

4. any risk or interest connected with any of those referred to in points 1 to 3.

In *Charman v WOC Offshore*,[39] the English Court of Appeal held that, in view of Article 14(4), the maritime exception extends to cases where the insurance and the jurisdiction

---

34  See Gaudemet-Tallon, at para 254; and pp. 170–71 below.
35  Case C-112/03, [2005] ECR I-3707.j123
36  See Gaudemet-Tallon, at para 256.
37  On compulsory insurance, see the Schlosser Report, at para 138.
38  Article 12A of the Lugano Convention 1988 echoes the Brussels Convention, and corresponds to Article 14(1)–(4) of the Brussels I Regulation.
39  [1993] 2 Lloyd's Rep 551 (CA).

agreement cover both marine and non-marine risks, so long as the non-marine risks are not the main risks, and there is a sufficient connection between the marine and the non-marine risks. Thus they upheld an English jurisdiction clause in respect of an insurance of equipment for use in reconstructing a breakwater in Algeria. For all the property insured was being used for a single adventure, the construction of the breakwater; it all belonged to the same insured; it was all insured against the same risk, of detention in Algeria; and the land-based items (such as caterpillar tractors) amounted to little more than 20% of the whole in value. Similarly, in *Standard Steamship Owners' Protection and Indemnity Association (Bermuda) Ltd v GIE Vision Bail*,[40] Cooke J held that Article 14(3) and (4) extend to an employer's liability insurance obtained by a concessionaire of shops located on board ships in respect of claims by its employees who staff such shops.

Article 14(5) of the Regulation adds a further category of risks in respect of which agreements on jurisdiction are permitted. This represents one of the most important changes from the Brussels Convention. It applies where the agreement on jurisdiction relates to a contract of insurance insofar as it covers one or more risks which are 'large risks' as defined in EC Directives 73/239, 88/357 and 90/618 as they may be amended.[41] The definition of 'large risks' by Article 5(d) and the Annex of Directive 73/239, as amended by Article 5 of Directive 88/357 and Article 2 of Directive 90/618, is very wide.

Some transport risks are always regarded as large, regardless of the policy-holder's business character or size. This covers damage to or loss of ships, aircraft, or railway rolling stock; damage to or loss of goods in transit or baggage, irrespective of the form of transport; and liability arising out of the use of ships or aircraft, including carrier's liability. Risks relating to credit or suretyship are regarded as large if the policy-holder is engaged in and the risks relate to a business activity.

Most kinds of risk are regarded as large if the policy-holder is engaged in and the risks relate to a large or medium-sized business activity. As regards size, two of the following three conditions must be fulfilled in respect of the policy-holder or the group to which it belongs: that the balance-sheet total exceeds 6.2 million; that the net turnover exceeds 12.8 million; and that the average number of employees during the financial year exceeds 250. The risks in this category include damage to or loss of property (including motor vehicles) by natural causes (such as fire or storm) or other events (such as theft); miscellaneous financial loss of various kinds; and liability, including that arising out of the use of motor vehicles. The only kinds of risk which can never be regarded as large are accident and sickness benefits, and legal expenses.

---

[40]    [2004] EWHC 2919 (Comm).
[41]    See [1973] OJ L228/3; [1988] OJ L172/1; and [1990] OJ L330/44. On the substitution of the euro for the ecu, see EC Regulation 1103/97, [1997] OJ L162/1. In the Lugano Convention 2007, Article 14(5) simply refers to 'all large risks'. But the Pocar Report on the Lugano Convention 2007 explains, at paras 76–7, that the general reference to large risks in Article 14(5) of the Convention is to be understood to designate the same risks as those referred to in the Directives listed in Article 14(5) of the Brussels I Regulation, and is to be interpreted in the light of the Community rules, present and future, at least insofar as the Community rules do not make radical changes to the approach to the handling of large risks; see JUSTCIV 179, of 6th October 2009.

# CONSUMER CONTRACTS

## Scope

The protective provisions in respect of consumer contracts are laid down by Section 4 (Articles 15–17) of Chapter II of the Brussels I Regulation. These provisions have replaced Section 4 (Articles 13–15) of Title II of the Brussels Convention. In contrast with insurance, Article 15 of the Regulation (like Article 13 of the Convention) provides an elaborate definition of the consumer contracts to which the protective provisions apply. The European Court has ruled that in this context the concept of a consumer contract has an independent meaning, derived from the wording, system and objectives of the legislation.[42] It has also recognised that the concept has in some respects a wider scope under the Regulation than under the Convention.[43] The scope of Section 4 is determined by a combination of substantive requirements, relating to the nature of the parties and the contract, and territorial requirements, relating to the connection of the contract with the country of the consumer's domicile.

### Substantive requirements

Viewed generically, a consumer contract might be defined as a contract entered into by an individual, not acting in the course of a business, whereby he acquires goods or services, for his own private consumption, from a supplier acting in the course of a business, or whereby he obtains credit in connection with such an acquisition of goods or services. But both the Regulation and the Convention depart in various ways from this generic definition.

Article 15(1) of the Regulation (echoing Article 13(1) of the Convention) refers to 'a contract concluded by a person, the consumer, for a purpose which can be regarded as being outside his trade or profession'. But, unlike the Convention, the Regulation does not confine the scope of the protective provisions to contracts for the supply of goods or services, or of credit in connection with the sale of goods.

As regards the character of the acquirer, the European Court has emphasised, in rulings on the Brussels Convention, that Section 4 is confined to cases where the contract was entered into by a private final consumer, not engaged in trade or professional activities,[44] and it is clear that the same applies to Section 4 of the Regulation. It also seems clear that under the Regulation, as under the Convention, the acquirer must be an individual, as distinct from a corporate entity,[45] and that Section 4 does not apply where a person acquiring goods or

---

[42]  See Case C-89/91: *Shearson Lehman Hutton v TVB* [1993] ECR I-139.

[43]  See Case C-180/06: *Ilsinger v Dreschers* [2009] ECR I-3961.

[44]  See Case C-89/91: *Shearson Lehman Hutton v TVB* [1993] ECR I-139, where the Court added that Section 4 does not apply to an action brought against the supplier not by the consumer himself, but by his assignee, a company acting in pursuance of its trade or professional activity; Case C-269/95: *Benincasa v Dentalkit* [1997] ECR I-3767, where the Court added that a person who concludes a contract, such as a franchise agreement in relation to a shop to be opened, with a view to pursuing a trade or profession at a future time, cannot be regarded as a consumer; Case C-167/00: *VKI v Henkel* [2002] ECR I-8111, where it ruled that Section 4 does not apply to an action brought by a consumer protection organisation on behalf of consumers generally; and Case 150/77: *Bertrand v Ott* [1978] ECR 1431.

[45]  See Case C-269/95: *Benincasa v Dentalkit* [1997] ECR I-3767; and Article 6(1) of the Rome I Regulation.

services holds himself out as contracting for business purposes to a person who contracts in good faith on that basis.[46]

The problem of a person acting for mixed business and non-business purposes was addressed by the European Court in *Gruber v Bay Wa*,[47] which involved a contract concluded by a farmer for the purchase of roofing tiles for a farmhouse which was occupied by him partly in a private capacity as a family dwelling and partly for farming purposes to house live-stock and fodder. The Court ruled that a person who concludes a contract partly for business purposes and partly for non-business purposes does not count as a consumer unless his busi-ness purpose is of negligible importance in relation to the transaction. Moreover, in the case of a contract for mixed purposes it is for the alleged consumer to establish that the business purpose is of negligible importance. In determining whether the contract in question was concluded to a more than negligible extent for business purposes, the court seised must refer primarily to the objective facts as a whole, rather than confining itself to matters known to the supplier at the time of conclusion of the contract. But there is an exception where the alleged consumer so conducted himself as to create the impression in the supplier that he was acting for business purposes. This would be the case, for example, where an individual, in ordering goods which are capable of business use, uses notepaper with a business letter-head, has the goods delivered to his business address, or refers to the possibility of reclaiming value-added tax. In such circumstances, Section 4 would not apply even if in reality the contract did not have a more than negligible business purpose, for the consumer would be regarded as having renounced its protection in view of the impression he had created in the supplier, acting in good faith. Although this ruling was given under the Convention, there is no reason to doubt that it remains fully applicable under the Regulation.

As regards the character of the supplier, Section 4 of the Regulation (like Section 4 of the Convention) clearly requires that the other party to a consumer contract, the supplier, must be acting in the course of a trade or profession. This had been confirmed by the European Court in rulings on the Convention,[48] and is made explicit by Article 15(1)(c) of the Regulation.

Under the Convention, the European Court had also insisted that the contract must be concluded for the purpose of satisfying the acquirer's own needs in terms of private consump-tion.[49] No doubt such needs had to be understood as including those of the acquirer's family, and also as including the need to fulfil his ordinary social obligations; for example, in the making of seasonal presents to friends. But the requirement appeared to exclude a contract entered into for purposes of investment or financial speculation, such as a purchase of corpo-rate shares or commodity futures.[50] On the other hand, a contract for the provision of credit designed to enable the borrower to obtain goods or services for his private consumption was

---

[46]    See Case C-464/01: *Gruber v Bay Wa* [2005] ECR I-439; *Project XJ220 Ltd v Comte D'Uzes and Comte De Dampierre*, 19th November 1993 (Boyd QC); and the Giuliano and Lagarde Report, [1980] OJ C282 at p. 23.

[47]    Case C-464/01, [2005] ECR I-439.

[48]    See Case C-96/00: *Gabriel* [2002] ECR I-6367, at para 39; and Case C-27/02: *Engler v Janus Versand* [2005] ECR I-481, at para 34. See also the Giuliano and Lagarde Report on the Rome Convention, [1980] OJ C282/1 at p. 23; and Article 6(1) of the Rome I Regulation.

[49]    See Case C-269/95: *Benincasa v Dentalkit* [1997] ECR I-3767.

[50]    Cf. the suggestion of Darmon AG in *Shearson* that an agency contract concerning dealings in currency, security and commodity futures could count as a consumer contract.

within Section 4. Now, however, in *Ilsinger v Dreschers*,[51] the European Court has ruled that under the Regulation there is no requirement that the contract must be concluded for the purpose of satisfying the acquirer's own needs in terms of private consumption. Subject to the specific exclusion of certain transport contracts, Section 4 of the Regulation extends to all contracts, whatever their purpose, if they have been concluded by a consumer with a professional and fall within the latter's commercial or professional activities.

It follows that Section 4 of the Regulation extends not only to contracts for financial services such as banking, but also to contracts entered into for purposes of investment or financial speculation, including contracts for the acquisition of financial instruments or transferable securities (such as corporate shares, corporate or public bonds, units in an investment fund, commodity futures, or other derivative instruments).[52] However, the requirement that the alleged consumer must not be acting for business purposes prevents Section 4 from applying to a loan arranged by the managers of company for the purpose of acquiring its shares and thus enabling them to continue to manage the company.[53] Under the Convention, it was not clear whether contracts for the sale of land could fall within Section 4,[54] but under the Regulation it is now clear that Section 4 extends to cases where an individual purchases land for non-business purposes.

On the other hand, despite the wording of the ruling in *Ilsinger*, it seems impossible to suppose that Section 4 can apply where under the contract a person not acting for business purposes supplies goods or services to a trader; for example, where a widow who has no driving licence sells her deceased husband's car to a motor trader. To require a supplier to be treated as a consumer would constitute so startling a reversal of concept, as compared with earlier legislation at both Community and national levels, that the intention to do so would need to be expressed with unmistakable clarity.

Under the Regulation, Section 4 has a wider operation in relation to claims under consumer protection legislation by a consumer against a supplier for a prize promised by the supplier as a marketing device with a view to inducing the consumer to place an order for goods or services. Under the Convention, Section 4 extended to a claim by a consumer against a supplier under consumer protection legislation for a prize promised upon the placing of an order for goods;[55] but not where the prize was not made conditional on the placing of an order for goods or services, but only on a request for payment of the prize, and no order was placed.[56]

In *Ilsinger v Dreschers*,[57] the European Court ruled on the operation of Section 4 of the Regulation in cases where a consumer seeks, in accordance with protective legislation, an order requiring a mail-order company to pay a prize which the consumer has apparently won,

---

[51]   Case C-180/06, [2009] ECR I-3961. See especially at paras 48–50.

[52]   It seems impossible to import into the Brussels I Regulation by analogy the complex and obscure distinctions drawn for choice of law purposes by Article 6 of the Rome I Regulation.

[53]   See *Maple Leaf v Rouvroy* [2009] EWHC 257 (Comm) (Andrew Smith J).

[54]   Cf. Gaudemet-Tallon, at para 261.

[55]   See Case C-96/00: *Gabriel* [2002] ECR I-6367.

[56]   See Case C-27/02: *Engler v Janus Versand* [2005] ECR I-481; also holding that such a claim counted as a contractual matter within Article 5(1).

[57]   Case C-180/06, [2009] ECR I-3961. Cf. per Tizzano AG in Case C-234/04: *Kapferer v Schlank & Schick* [2006] ECR I-2585.

where the company, with the aim of encouraging the consumer to conclude a contract, had sent a letter addressed to him personally, giving the impression that he would be awarded a prize if he requested payment by returning the 'prize claim certificate' attached to the letter, but without the award of that prize depending on an order for goods offered for sale by the company. The Court ruled that such an action brought by the consumer falls within Section 4 of the Regulation where either the business seller has undertaken in law to pay the prize to the consumer, or the consumer has in fact placed an order with the business seller. The Court explained that Section 4 of the Regulation is not limited to situations in which the parties have assumed reciprocal obligations, but that the Section does require that the action relates to a contract which has been concluded between a consumer and a business. For this purpose, a contract may exist where one of the parties merely indicates its acceptance, without assuming any legal obligation to the other party, but it is necessary that the latter party should assume such a legal obligation by submitting a firm offer which is sufficiently clear and precise with regard to its object and scope as to give rise to a link of a contractual nature. In the context of a prize notification, there must have been a legal commitment contracted by the mail-order company; in other words, the latter must have expressed clearly its intention to be bound by such a commitment, if it is accepted by the other party, by declaring itself to be unconditionally willing to pay the prize at issue to consumers who so request. Accordingly, Section 4 of the Regulation cannot apply if the business did not undertake contractually to pay the prize promised to the consumer who requests its payment, unless the misleading prize notification was followed by the conclusion of a contract by the consumer with the mail-order company evidenced by an order placed with the latter.

Article 15(3) of the Regulation excludes from Section 4 a contract of transport, other than a contract which, for an inclusive price, provides for a combination of travel and accommodation.[58] But it seems likely that the exclusion will be construed restrictively, so that a contract for a combination of transport and admission to a cultural or sporting event may fall within the Section. It is clear that insurance contracts are always governed by Section 3, to the exclusion of Section 4.[59]

**Territorial requirements**

In addition to the substantive requirements discussed above, for a consumer contract to qualify for protection under Section 4 of the Regulation, Article 15(1)(c) requires that the supplier must have pursued commercial or professional activities in the Member State of the consumer's domicile, or by any means directed such activities to that Member State or to several States including that Member State, and that the contract must fall within the scope of such activities.[60]

---

[58]    Cf. Article 13(3) of the Convention, which simply excluded contracts of transport from Section 4, without any exception for combinations of travel and accommodation. See also pending Case C-585/08: *Peter Pammer v Reederei Karl Schlüter GmbH & Co KG* [2009] OJ C44/40.

[59]    See Gaudemet-Tallon, at para 261.

[60]    Cf. rule 7(1)(c) of Schedule 4 to the (UK) Civil Jurisdiction and Judgments Act 1982, as amended by the Civil Jurisdiction and Judgments Order 2001 (SI 3929/2001), which refers to a contract which is concluded with a person who pursues commercial or professional activities in the part of the United Kingdom in which the consumer is domiciled, or by any means directs such activities to that part or to other parts of the United Kingdom including that part, and which falls within the scope of such activities.

To this requirement of relevant business activities by the supplier, in or directed to the country of the consumer's domicile, exceptions are made by Article 15(1)(a) and (b) of the Regulation.[61] These exceptions eliminate any territorial requirement where the contract is for the sale of goods on instalment credit terms, or where the contract is for a loan repayable by instalments, or for any other form of credit, made to finance the sale of goods. The exceptions appear to cover any consumer contract which involves the provision of credit for the acquisition of goods.[62] But, as the European Court ruled in *Mietz v Intership Yachting Sneek*,[63] the first exception (referring to the sale of goods on instalment credit terms) is confined to situations where the seller has granted credit to the buyer by transferring possession of the goods to the buyer before the buyer has paid the full price. It does not apply where the full price had to be paid before transfer of possession, even if it was payable in several instalments.

Article 15(1)(c) of the Regulation replaces Article 13(1)(3) of the Brussels Convention, which referred to any other contract for the supply of goods or a contract for the supply of services, where the conclusion of the contract was preceded by a specific invitation addressed to the consumer, or by advertising, in the State of his domicile, and the consumer took in that State the steps necessary for the conclusion of the contract on his part. In *Gabriel*,[64] the European Court explained that the concepts of 'advertising' and 'specific invitation addressed' in Article 13(1)(3) of the Brussels Convention covered all forms of advertising carried out in the State in which the consumer was domiciled, whether disseminated generally by the press, radio, television, cinema or any other medium, or addressed directly, for example by means of catalogues sent specifically to that State, as well as commercial offers made to the consumer in person, in particular by an agent or door-to-door salesman. It added that the reference to 'the steps necessary for the conclusion of the contract' covered any document written or other step taken by the consumer in the State of his domicile which expressed his wish to take up the supplier's invitation.

Article 13(1)(3) of the Brussels Convention was also considered by Jacobs AG in *Gruber v Bay Wa*.[65] He advised that for this purpose the conclusion of a contract must be regarded as preceded by advertising in the State of the consumer's domicile where the supplier had previously advertised goods or services in that State, even if he did not mention the specific products acquired by the consumer. He also explained that where in the State of his domicile a consumer receives a specific offer by telephone from a supplier in another Member State and subsequently acquires from that supplier the goods or services thus offered, the conclusion of the contract must be regarded as preceded by a specific invitation, even if its actual terms are based on a subsequent offer not received in the State of the consumer's domicile. He added that a consumer takes the steps necessary for the conclusion of a contract in the State of his domicile when he communicates his acceptance of an offer from that State (for example, by telephone), regardless of the place where the offer was made and regardless of the means of

---

61    These echo Article 13(1)(1)–(2) of the Convention.
62    In its Report and Green Paper of 21st April 2009, the EC Commission contemplates the alignment of the wording of Articles 15(1)(a) and (b) of the Brussels I Regulation with the definition of consumer credit in EC Directive 2008/48, on credit agreements for consumers, [2008] OJ L133/66. See COM(2009) 174 final, at section 3.8.2, and COM(2009) 175 final, at question 8.
63    Case C-99/96, [1999] ECR I-2277.
64    Case C-96/00, [2002] ECR I-6367.
65    Case C-464/01, [2005] ECR I-439.

communication used. But in *Gruber* the European Court found it unnecessary to address these questions.[66]

The change made by Article 15(1)(c) of the Regulation is intended to emphasise that contracts concluded through the Internet are included,[67] but probably this was already largely achieved by the earlier provisions. Under the Regulation, there is no doubt that, in the ordinary case of a consumer ordering goods or services electronically from a website maintained by the supplier, the supplier is by means of the website directing commercial activities to all countries (including that of the consumer's domicile) from which the page is accessible, and that the order falls within the scope of such activities. The only noticeable difference seems to be that the new, but not the old, definition would be satisfied where the consumer was not in his own country when he accessed the site and placed the order. For example, if an English domiciliary placed the order from an Internet café while on holiday in France. Since the location of the terminal used by the consumer has no real significance in relation to electronic transactions, this very minor change seems well justified.

Moreover, the risk of unfair surprise to the trader is largely eliminated once it is recognised that the Regulation (like the Brussels Convention) must be construed as respecting the principles of predictability[68] and good faith.[69] Accordingly, a consumer who misleads the supplier as to the location of the consumer's domicile, as by entering on the order form an address (perhaps of a relative or friend) in a different country, will be estopped from relying on his actual domicile so as to satisfy the definition if the trader would have rejected the order (probably by setting his software in advance to do so) had he known the consumer's true domicile.

Article 15(1)(c) emerged from the Working Party's draft of April 1999, and immediately provoked an outcry from electronic traders. But their special pleading failed to obtain any concession, and the Regulation as adopted retains the wording agreed by the Working Group. In the Second Joint Statement[70] made on the adoption of the Regulation, the Council and Commission emphasised that the development of new distance marketing techniques based on the use of the Internet depends in part on the mutual confidence which may grow up between undertakings and consumers, and that one of the major elements in this confidence is the opportunity offered to consumers by the Regulation to bring possible disputes before the courts of the Member States in which they reside. They added that the mere fact that an Internet site is accessible is not sufficient for Article 15 to be applicable, although a factor will be that the site solicits the conclusion of distance contracts and that a contract has actu-

---

[66]   Cf. *Rayner v Davies* [2003] 1 All ER (Comm) 394 (CA), affirming [2002] 1 All ER (Comm) 620 (Morison J), where the English courts insisted that the initial approach or solicitation should have been made by the supplier and not by the consumer.

[67]   See Case C-180/06: *Ilsinger v Dreschers* [2009] ECR I-3961, at para 50, where the Court noted that the conditions which were specified in Article 13(1)(3)(a)–(b) of the Convention are now worded more generally in Article 15(1)(c) of the Regulation, in order to ensure better protection for consumers with regard to new means of communication and the development of electronic commerce.

[68]   See Case C-26/91: *Handte v TMCS* [1992] ECR I-3967; and Case C-51/97: *Réunion Européenne v Spliethoff's Bevrachtingskantoor* [1998] ECR I-6511.

[69]   See Case 25/76: *Segoura v Bonakdarian* [1976] ECR 1851; and Case C-464/01: *Gruber v Bay Wa* [2005] ECR I-439.

[70]   See Council doc 14139/00, JUSTCIV 137, 14th December 2000; and Recital 24 to the Rome I Regulation.

ally been concluded at a distance, by whatever means.[71] On the other hand, the language or currency which a website uses is not a relevant factor.

## Actions Against a Supplier

The Regulation offers the consumer a choice of fora in which to sue a supplier who is domiciled (or secondarily domiciled) in a Member State. In accordance with the general principle in favour of the defendant's country, Articles 15(2) and 16(1) confer jurisdiction on the courts of the Member State in which the defendant supplier is domiciled (or secondarily domiciled); and Articles 5(5) and 15(1) confer jurisdiction on the courts for the place (in a Member State other than that of the defendant supplier's domicile) at which the defendant supplier has a secondary establishment from whose operations the dispute has arisen. But, radically departing from the usual rejection of the plaintiff's country as such, Article 16(1) confers jurisdiction also on the courts for the place (in a Member State other than that of the supplier's domicile) at which the plaintiff consumer is domiciled at the institution of the proceedings.

It seems clear that, even in the case of a consumer contract not involving credit in connection with the sale of goods, where the application of Section 4 depends on the supplier pursuing business activities in or directing business activities to the State in which the consumer is domiciled at the time of the conclusion of the contract, a consumer who subsequently changes his domicile to another Member State becomes entitled under Article 16(1) to sue at his new domicile, instead of his previous domicile.

In addition, Articles 6(3) and 16(3) enable a consumer to counterclaim in the court in which a claim against him by the supplier in respect of the same contract is pending. Under Articles 17(2) and 23, a consumer may also sue in a court specified by a jurisdiction agreement; and, by Articles 17(1) and 24, the supplier's submission by appearance remains effective to found jurisdiction.[72] The normal rules laid down by Articles 27–31 on concurrent actions and interim relief also remain applicable in consumer cases.

## Actions Against a Consumer

Article 16(2) of the Regulation confines jurisdiction to entertain an action brought by a supplier against a consumer who is domiciled in a Member State to the courts of the Member State in which the defendant consumer is domiciled.

By way of exception, Article 6(3) and 16(3) enable a supplier to counterclaim in the court in which a claim against him by the consumer in respect of the same contract is pending; and, by Articles 17(1) and 24, the consumer's submission by appearance remains effective to found jurisdiction.[73] But Article 17 usually prevents a supplier from suing in reliance on a jurisdiction clause unless it was agreed on after the dispute had arisen.

---

[71]   See also pending Case C-585/08: *Peter Pammer v Reederei Karl Schlüter GmbH & Co KG* [2009] OJ C44/40.
[72]   See Case C-111/09: *ČPP v Bilas* [2010] All ER (D) 203 (May).
[73]   See Case C-111/09: *ČPP v Bilas* [2010] All ER (D) 203 (May).

**Agreements on Jurisdiction**

To ensure the effectiveness of the protective policy, Article 17 of the Regulation invalidates any agreement on jurisdiction which departs from the provision of Section 4, except in three specified cases which correspond to the first three cases in which Article 13 permits such an agreement in relation to insurance. The invalidation extends to a clause choosing a court of a non-member State.[74]

Thus the first exception, specified by Article 17(1), permits an agreement on jurisdiction which is entered into after the dispute has arisen. The second exception, specified by Article 17(2), allows an agreement insofar as it enables the consumer to bring proceedings in additional courts. The third exception, specified by Article 17(3), permits an agreement which is entered into by a consumer and a supplier who at the time of conclusion of the contract are domiciled or habitually resident in the same Member State, and which confers jurisdiction on the courts of that State, unless such an agreement is contrary to the law of the chosen State. The third exception enables the supplier to guard against the risk of the consumer moving to another Member State and then suing at his new domicile. But a clause in a contract between parties domiciled in the same country, choosing the court for the place of the supplier's domicile, may be rendered invalid by Directive 93/13, on unfair terms in consumer contracts.[75]

# EMPLOYMENT

## Scope

Chapter II of the Brussels I Regulation contains a new Section 5 (Articles 18-21) on individual contracts of employment. The original version of the Brussels Convention contained no specific provisions on contracts of employment, but the European Court nonetheless discerned a purpose of protecting employees on account of their weaker socio-economic position, and accordingly adopted a special interpretation of Article 5(1) in relation to contracts of employment.[76] Building on these rulings, the 1989 version of the Brussels Convention made specific provision for employment in the second clause of Article 5(1) and in Article 17(6). Now the Regulation deals with employment, like insurance and consumer contracts, in a semi-autonomous Section.[77]

By Article 18(1), Section 5 operates without prejudice to Article 4, on external defendants, and to Article 5(5), and on secondary establishments of internal defendants. But, by Article 18(2), an employer who is not domiciled in any Member State but has a branch, agency or other establishment in a Member State is, in regard to disputes arising out of the operations

---

[74]    See Gaudemet-Tallon, at para 264.

[75]    See Case C-240/98: *Océano Grupo Editorial v Quintero* [2000] ECR I-4941.

[76]    See Case 133/81: *Ivenel v Schwab* [1982] ECR 1891; Case 266/85: *Shenavai v Kreischer* [1987] ECR 239; and Case 32/88: *Six Constructions v Humbert* [1989] ECR 341. The protective effect of these rulings was limited by the absence before the 1989 version of any provision invalidating a jurisdiction clause contained in a contract of employment; see Case 25/79: *Sanicentral v Collin* [1979] ECR 3423.

[77]    On the exhaustive character of Section 5, see Case C-462/06: *Glaxosmithkline v Rouard* [2008] ECR I-3965.

of the branch, agency or establishment, deemed to be domiciled in the Member State of the secondary establishment. These provisions echo those on insurance and consumer contracts.

The nature of an individual contract of employment was addressed by the European Court in *Shenavai v Kreischer*,[78] where it emphasised that such contracts create a lasting bond which brings the worker to some extent within the organisational framework of the employer's business, and that they are linked to the place where the activities are pursued, which determines the application of mandatory rules and collective agreements. Thus the concept does not extend to a contract for professional services, such as those of an architect or lawyer, engaged as an independent contractor to carry out a particular task. *A fortiori*, Section 5 does not extend to a commercial contract whereby a company obtains exclusive rights to canvass in its country for advertising in a foreign newspaper.[79]

Accordingly, in *WPP v Benatti*,[80] the English Court of Appeal held that Section 5 did not apply to a self-employed management consultant who for a fee was engaged to devise proposals and strategies to improve the performance of a corporate group. It accepted that for this purpose the objective criteria of an employment contract are the provision of services by one party over a period of time for which remuneration is paid; control and direction over the provision of the services by the counterparty; and integration to some extent of the provider of the services within the organisational framework of the counterparty. But these are not hard-edged criteria which can be mechanistically applied. For example, in the case of a person with a non-executive role, there may be degrees of control and degrees of integration within the organisational framework of the company. Thus the court must carry out an evaluative rather than a tick-box exercise, looking at the terms of the contract aided by evidence about its operation in order to reach an overall view of its character.

In *Samengo-Turner v Marsh & McLennan*,[81] the English Court of Appeal (per Tuckey LJ) held that, for the purposes of Section 5 of the Regulation, an agreement (such as a bonus agreement) which varies or adds to the terms of an earlier contract of employment must be treated as part of the contract of employment, even if on its own it does not contain all the terms usually found in a contract of employment. Moreover, this applies even if the subsequent agreement is concluded not only between the employee and the employer, but also with other companies in the same group; and, in such a case, a claim by one of the other companies against the employee based on the subsequent agreement counts as a claim by an employer for the purposes of Section 5. On the other hand, there is English authority that Section 5 does not extend to a claim by an employer against an employee in tort for conspiracy to interfere unlawfully with a commercial contract between the employer and a supplier.[82]

## Actions Against an Employer

As regards actions against an employer who is domiciled (or secondarily domiciled) in a Member State, Article 19(1) confers jurisdiction on the courts of the State in which the

---

[78]   See Case 266/85, [1987] ECR 239.
[79]   See *Mercury Publicity v Loerke* [1993] ILPr 142 (CA).
[80]   [2007] 2 All ER (Comm) 525 (CA).
[81]   [2007] 2 All ER (Comm) 813 (CA).
[82]   See *Swithenbank Foods Ltd v Bowers* [2002] 2 All ER (Comm) 974 (Judge McGonigal in the High Court).

defendant employer is domiciled (or secondarily domiciled). Article 19(2)(a) confers jurisdiction also on the courts of another Member State for the place where the employee habitually carries out his work or the last place where he did so. If the employee does not or did not habitually carry out his work in any one country, Article 19(2)(b) instead confers jurisdiction on the courts of another Member State for the place where the business which engaged the employee is or was situated. The references to the last place where the employee habitually worked are new.[83] They are apparently aimed at situations where the employment has been terminated prior to the institution of the proceedings.

The concept of the place of habitual work must be understood in the light of the rulings of the European Court under the Brussels Convention. These include *Mulox v Geels*[84] and *Rutten v Cross Medical*,[85] which establish that in cases where the employee carries out his work in more than one country, the concept refers to the place where the employee has established the effective centre of his working activities, at or from which he performs the essential part of his duties towards his employer. Thus, for example, a sales manager will habitually work at the office where he organises his work, even though he makes frequent business trips to other countries. But where, as in *Weber v Universal Ogden Services*,[86] there is no such permanent centre of activities (because, for example, the man worked for the employer as a cook, first on mining vessels or installations in the Dutch continental shelf area,[87] and later on a floating crane in Danish territorial waters), the whole of the duration of the employment relationship must be taken into account. The relevant place will normally be the place where the employee has worked the longest. But, by way of exception, weight will be given to the most recent period of work where the employee, after having worked for a certain time in one place, then takes up his work activities on a permanent basis in a different place.

The situation where an employee is seconded from one employer to another was considered in *Pugliese v Finmeccanica*,[88] which involved an employee who had been recruited by one company to work temporarily for an associated company abroad, and then to return to work for the initial employer in their home country. The plaintiff, an Italian, who had been recruited by Aeritalia, an Italian company, to work initially for Eurofighter in Germany for at least three years, now sought to sue the original Italian employer in Germany. The European Court ruled that, in a dispute between an employee and a first employer, the place where the employee performs his obligations to a second employer can be regarded as the place where he habitually carries out his work when the first employer, with respect to whom the employee's contractual obligations are suspended, has, at the time of the conclusion of the second contract of employment, an interest in the performance of the service by the employee to the second employer in a place decided on by the latter. The existence of such an interest must be determined on a comprehensive basis, taking into consideration all the circumstances

---

83 Article 19(2) otherwise resembles the second limb of Article 5(1) of the Brussels Convention.
84 Case C-125/92, [1993] ECR I-4075.
85 Case C-383/95, [1997] ECR I-57.
86 Case C-37/00, [2002] ECR I-2013.
87 The Court also ruled that work carried out by an employee on fixed or floating installations positioned on or above the part of the continental shelf adjacent to a Member State, in the context of the prospecting and/or exploitation of its natural resources, counts for present purposes as work carried out in the territory of that State.
88 Case C-437/00, [2003] ECR I-3573.

of the case. The relevant factors may include the facts that the conclusion of the second contract was envisaged when the first was being concluded; that the first contract was amended on account of the conclusion of the second contract; that there is an organisational or economic link between the two employers; that there is an agreement between the two employers providing a framework for the co-existence of the two contracts; that the first employer retains management powers in respect of the employee; and that the first employer is able to decide the duration of the employee's work for the second employer.

No court will be competent under Article 19(2) if the employee habitually works or worked in a non-member country. But Article 19(2)(b) enables an employee to sue the employer in the courts of a Member State for the place of the employer's establishment which engaged the employee, if the employee works in several countries without having an effective centre of his working activities, whether or not the countries in which he works are Member States.[89]

By Articles 5(5) and 18(1), the employee can also sue the employer in the courts of a Member State (other than that of the employer's domicile) for the place of the employer's secondary establishment from whose operations the dispute has arisen. Where the employee has no habitual place of work, this seems to overlap with Article 19(2)(b). Under Articles 6(3) and 20(2), the employee can also counterclaim in a court in which he is sued by the employer. The employee can also sue in accordance with a jurisdiction clause under Articles 21(2) and 23, and the employer's submission by appearance will be effective under Articles 21(1) and 24.[90] The normal rules laid down by Articles 27–31 on concurrent actions and interim relief also remain applicable in employment cases.

Section 5 makes no explicit provision or saving for ancillary jurisdiction over a co-defendant as such. Accordingly, the European Court ruled in *Glaxosmithkline v Rouard*[91] that, in view of the exhaustive character of Section 5, an employee who is jointly employed by two employers who are domiciled in different Member States cannot utilise Article 6(1) so as to sue both employers at the domicile of one of them. Thus where, as in that case, an employee is jointly employed by two companies belonging to the same group, one of which is domiciled in France and the other in the United Kingdom, but his place of habitual work is outside Europe, there is no court within the Member States in which he can sue *both* companies for unfair or wrongful dismissal. But in its Report and Green Paper of 21st April 2009,[92] the EC Commission contemplates the possibility of extending Article 6(1) to employment matters.

In addition to the jurisdiction provided for by the Brussels I Regulation, Article 6 of EC Directive 96/71, on the posting of workers in the framework of the provision of services,[93] confers jurisdiction on the courts of the Member State to which a worker is or was posted to entertain claims by the worker to rights (such as the right to minimum rates of pay) conferred by the Directive.

---

[89]  See Gaudemet-Tallon, at para 168.
[90]  See Case C-111/09: *ČPP v Bilas* [2010] All ER (D) 203 (May).
[91]  Case C-462/06, [2008] ECR I-3965.
[92]  COM(2009) 174 final, at section 3.8.2, and COM(2009) 175 final, at question 8.
[93]  [1997] OJ L18/1. See p. 360 below.

**Actions Against an Employee**

Article 20(1) of the Regulation confines jurisdiction over an employee domiciled in a Member State to the courts of the Member State in which the employee is domiciled. Formerly, under Article 5(1) of the Brussels Convention, the employer could also sue the employee at the place of habitual work.[94] In *Samengo-Turner v Marsh & McLennan*,[95] the English Court of Appeal regarded the exclusive character of the jurisdiction of the employee's domicile under Article 20 as justification for the issue of an anti-suit injunction against proceedings brought by the employer in a non-member country.

By way of exception, Article 20(2) permits an employer to counterclaim in the court in which a claim by the employee is pending. Moreover, the employee's submission by appearance will be effective under Articles 21(1) and 24.[96] But Article 21 prevents an employer from suing in reliance on a jurisdiction clause unless it was agreed on after the dispute had arisen.

**Agreements on Jurisdiction**

To ensure the effectiveness of the protective policy, Article 21 invalidates any agreement on jurisdiction in respect of an individual contract of employment, with two exceptions which correspond to the first two made by Articles 13 and 17 for insurance and consumer contracts. The first exception allows an agreement on jurisdiction which is entered into after the dispute has arisen. The second permits an agreement on jurisdiction insofar as it allows the employee to bring proceedings in additional courts.[97]

---

[94]  Under Article 5(1) of the Lugano Convention 1988, in the absence of a place of habitual work in a single country, both parties, not just the employee, may sue in the courts for the place of business through which the employee was engaged. See also Case 32/88: *Six Constructions v Humbert* [1989] ECR 341.

[95]  [2007] 2 All ER (Comm) 813 (CA).

[96]  See Case C-111/09: *ČPP v Bilas* [2010] All ER (D) 203 (May).

[97]  Article 21 of the Regulation echoes Article 17(6) of the Brussels Convention. The Lugano Convention 1988 omits the second exception.

# 6. Exclusive jurisdiction

## OVERRIDING CHARACTER

Article 22 of the Brussels I Regulation provides for exclusive jurisdiction over certain proceedings by reason of their principal subject-matter. The rules laid down by Article 22 are overriding in character. They apply regardless of domicile,[1] appearance,[2] or contrary agreement between the parties to the dispute.[3] A court seised contrary to Article 22 must decline jurisdiction of its own motion,[4] and a judgment given in contravention of Article 22 must be refused recognition and enforcement in the other Member States.[5] Thus, as was recognised by David Donaldson QC in *Choudhary v Bhattar*,[6] the courts of the Member State on which Article 22 confers exclusive jurisdiction are obliged to hear and determine the claim, and cannot decline jurisdiction in favour of a court of a non-member country.

But, as the European Court explained in *Apostolides v Orams*,[7] Article 22 merely designates the Member State whose courts have exclusive international jurisdiction by virtue of subject-matter, and leaves the internal allocation of such jurisdiction between the courts of the designated Member State to the law of that State.

Although the point is not yet definitively settled, it is thought that Article 22 has a reflexive effect, in the sense that it impliedly permits a Member State to apply its provisions analogistically in favour of a non-member country with which a corresponding connection exists.[8]

Article 22 of the Brussels I Regulation[9] provides:

---

[1] See Article 22 itself.

[2] See Article 24.

[3] See Article 23(5).

[4] See Article 25, which provides: 'Where a court of a Member State is seised of a claim which is principally concerned with a matter over which the courts of another Member State have exclusive jurisdiction by virtue of Article 22, it shall declare of its own motion that it has no jurisdiction'. This obligation is binding on an appellate court as well as a court of first instance; see Case 288/82: *Duijnstee v Goderbauer* [1983] ECR 3663.

[5] See Articles 35 and 45; and pp. 233–5 below. Moreover, under EC Regulation 805/2004, creating a European Enforcement Order for Uncontested Claims, [2004] OJ L143/15, the court of origin, before certifying a judgment on an uncontested claim as a European Enforcement Order, must be satisfied that the judgment does not conflict with the rules on exclusive jurisdiction by virtue of subject-matter laid down in Article 22 of the Brussels I Regulation; see pp. 267–71 below.

[6] [2009] EWHC 314 (Ch).

[7] Case C-420/07, [2009] ECR I-3571, at paras 47–52.

[8] See pp. 58–61 above.

[9] Article 22 of the Regulation largely echoes Article 16 of the Brussels Convention. There are minor changes in Article 22(1), (2) and (4). Article 22(4) also consolidates Article VD of the Protocol annexed to the Brussels Convention.

The following courts shall have exclusive jurisdiction, regardless of domicile:

1. in proceedings which have as their object rights in rem in immovable property or tenancies of immovable property, the courts of the Member State in which the property is situated.

However, in proceedings which have as their object tenancies of immovable property concluded for temporary private use for a maximum period of six consecutive months, the courts of the Member State in which the defendant is domiciled shall also have jurisdiction, provided that the tenant is a natural person and that the landlord and the tenant are domiciled in the same Member State;

2. in proceedings which have as their object the validity of the constitution, the nullity or the dissolution of companies or other legal persons or associations of natural or legal persons, or of the validity of the decisions of their organs, the courts of the Member State in which the company, legal person or association has its seat. In order to determine that seat, the court shall apply its rules of private international law;

3. in proceedings which have as their object the validity of entries in public registers, the courts of the Member State in which the register is kept;

4. in proceedings concerned with the registration or validity of patents, trade marks, designs, or other similar rights required to be deposited or registered, the courts of the Member State in which the deposit or registration has been applied for, has taken place or is under the terms of a Community instrument or an international convention deemed to have taken place.

Without prejudice to the jurisdiction of the European Patent Office under the Convention on the Grant of European Patents, signed at Munich on 5 October 1973, the courts of each Member State shall have exclusive jurisdiction, regardless of domicile, in proceedings concerned with the registration or validity of any European patent granted for that State;

5. in proceedings concerned with the enforcement of judgments, the courts of the Member State in which the judgment has been or is to be enforced.

These provisions reflect the view that the matters in question are ones in the regulation of which the State in question has a particularly strong concern. However, the European Court, mindful especially of the fact that Article 22 can impose the jurisdiction of a country in which none of the parties is domiciled, has adopted a restrictive approach towards its interpretation and scope.

## PROPRIETARY RIGHTS IN LAND

Article 22(1) applies to proceedings which have as their principal subject-matter rights in rem in immovable property which is situated in a Member State, and confers exclusive jurisdiction on the courts of the Member State in which the immovable property is situated.[10] It is clear that immovable property means land. But, as the European Court has made clear in *Reichert v Dresdner Bank (No 1)*,[11] *Webb v Webb*,[12] and *Lieber v Goebel*,[13] for Article 22(1) to apply, it is not sufficient that the action is in some way connected with land, or even with ownership of land. The provision is confined to actions which seek to determine the extent, content, ownership or possession of land, or the existence of other rights in rem therein, and to provide the holders of those rights with the protection of the powers which attach to their

---

[10]  Article 22(1) also applies to proceedings which have as their principal subject-matter tenancies of immovable property which is situated in a Member State. On tenancies, see pp. 147–9 below.

[11]  Case 115/88, [1990] ECR I-27.

[12]  Case C-294/92, [1994] ECR I-1717.

[13]  Case C-292/93, [1994] ECR I-2535.

interest. More precisely, the action must be based on a proprietary right, which has effect against the whole world, and not (except in the case of tenancies) on a personal right, which can only be claimed against particular persons.

Accordingly, the European Court has ruled that Article 22(1) does not apply to an action whereby a creditor seeks to have a disposition of land rendered ineffective as against him on the ground that it was made in fraud of his rights by his debtor.[14] Nor to a claim, made after the annulment of a transfer of ownership of a dwelling, for compensation for its prior use.[15] Nor to an action for a declaration that the defendant holds land as trustee for the plaintiff (for example, under a resulting trust arising from purchase in the name of another), and for an order requiring him to execute the documents necessary to vest the legal ownership of the land in the plaintiff.[16] Nor to an action for rescission of a contract for the sale of land and consequential damages.[17] Moreover, as the European Court ruled in *Land Oberösterreich v ČEZ*,[18] Article 22(1) does not apply to actions in respect of a nuisance or other tort affecting land, whether the claim is for damages or for an injunction, since the existence and content of rights in rem (usually rights of ownership) are of only marginal significance in the context of a claim in tort for nuisance affecting or damage to land. The case involved an action, brought in an Austrian court, seeking to prevent a nuisance affecting or likely to affect the plaintiff's Austrian land, caused by ionising radiation emanating from a nuclear power station situated in the Czech Republic.

Similarly, English courts have recognised that Article 22(1) does not extend to a claim by a mortgagee of land against the mortgagor for payment of the mortgage debt.[19] Nor to an action in tort for personal injuries caused by the negligence of an owner or occupier of land; nor even to a claim between a landlord and his tenant for contribution or indemnity in respect of such a liability, if the claim for contribution or indemnity is not based on the terms of the lease.[20]

In view of the rulings of the European Court, it is clear that in general Article 22(1) does not apply to an action based on an equitable interest (such as a beneficial interest under a trust) under English or Irish law, since such an interest is not binding on a purchaser of a legal estate for value without notice.[21] On the other hand, Article 22(1) does apply where the action

---

[14] See Case 115/88: *Reichert v Dresdner Bank (No 1)* [1990] ECR I-27.

[15] See Case C-292/93: *Lieber v Goebel* [1994] ECR I-2535.

[16] See Case C-294/92: *Webb v Webb* [1994] ECR I-1717. See also *Lightning v Lightning Electrical Contractors*, 23rd April 1998 (CA); *Ashurst v Pollard* [2001] Ch 595 (CA), where it was held that Article 22(1) did not apply to an application by the English trustee in bankruptcy of one of the co-owners of Portuguese land against the co-owners, seeking an order for sale of the land; and *Prazic v Prazic* [2006] 2 FLR 1128 (CA), where it was held that Article 22(1) does not apply to proceedings under the Trusts of Land and Appointment of Trustees Act 1996 seeking a declaration establishing the existence of an equitable interest. Cf. *Re Hayward* [1997] Ch 45, where Rattee J held that Article 22(1) and (3) excluded English jurisdiction to entertain an action by an English trustee in bankruptcy of a deceased English owner of Spanish land against a third party who had acquired title to the land through a transaction with the deceased's widow and registration on the Spanish land register, since the plaintiff's claim was to ownership itself of the land and rectification of the land register.

[17] See Case C-518/99: *Gaillard v Chekili* [2001] ECR I-2771.

[18] Case C-343/04, [2006] ECR I-4557.

[19] See *Union de Credit Pour Le Batiment*, 22nd January 1999 (CA).

[20] See *Bell v Exxtor*, 24th February 1993 (CA).

[21] See Case C-294/92: *Webb v Webb* [1994] ECR I-1717; *Lightning v Lightning Electrical Contractors*, 23rd April 1998 (CA); and *Ashurst v Pollard* [2001] Ch 595 (CA).

is based on an equitable interest in land which under the lex situs has become binding on all-comers as a result of registration.[22] More specifically, Article 22(1) applies to an action by a purchaser seeking specific performance of a contract for the sale or other disposition of English land, whether it is brought against the vendor or against a third party, if the estate contract has been duly protected on the register, but not otherwise.[23]

Where a claim based on a proprietary right in land is brought under Article 22(1) in a court of the Member State in which the land is situated against a defendant who is domiciled in another Member State, Article 6(4) enables the same court also to entertain a related contractual claim against the same defendant.

In the case of a dispute as to ownership of land which straddles a frontier between Member States, there is little doubt that Article 22(1) requires severance, so that each part of the estate is subject to the jurisdiction of the courts of the State in which that part is situated.[24] More difficult, however, is the problem of an easement, such as a right of way or a watercourse, claimed for the benefit of a piece of land in one Member State over a nearby piece of land in another Member State. One possible solution would be to regard both States as exclusively competent, and to give priority to the court first seised in accordance with Article 29.[25] But it would probably be better to regard the burden on the servient land as the principal matter, and the benefit to the dominant land as secondary, so that the courts of the State containing the servient land would have exclusive jurisdiction.

What if the dispute concerns ownership of land situated in a non-member country? It is submitted that the proper implication from Article 22 is that, in the case of an equivalent connection with a non-member country, a Member State whose courts are otherwise competent, for example by virtue of the defendant's domicile, is free to authorise or even require them to decline jurisdiction in favour of the non-member country in which the land is situated.[26] Thus, in such a case, the traditional English rule which in general deprives the English courts of jurisdiction to determine title to foreign land will continue to operate.[27]

---

[22]   See *Griggs v Evans* [2004] EWHC 1088 (Prescott QC).

[23]   Cf. the Schlosser Report at paras 169–72, and per Darmon AG in *Webb v Webb* at paras 50–51 and in *Lieber v Goebel* at paras 29–31.

[24]   Cf. Case 158/87: *Scherrens v Maenhout* [1988] ECR 3791, which left open the possibility of a very limited exception in the case of tenancies; and Gaudemet-Tallon, who suggests (at para 88) its extension to rights in rem.

[25]   This solution was favoured by dicta of Poiares Maduro AG in Case C-343/04: *Land Oberösterreich v ČEZ* [2006] ECR I-4557, at paras 81–2. But this point was not considered by the European Court, which rejected his opinion on the question actually involved in the case.

[26]   See Droz, at paras 164–9; Dicey, Morris and Collins, 14th edition (Sweet & Maxwell, 2006), at paras 23-025 to 23-027; *Arkwright v Bryanston* [1990] 2 QB 649 (Potter J); *Konkola Copper Mines v Coromin* [2005] 2 All ER (Comm) 637 (Colman J); *Masri v Consolidated Contractors (No 2)* [2008] 2 All ER (Comm) 1099 (CA), per Lawrence Collins LJ at paras 125–7; *Catalyst Investment Group v Lewinsohn* [2009] EWHC 1964 (Ch) (Barling J); and pp. 58–61 above.

[27]   See *Norris v Chambres* (1861) 3 De GF & J 583; *Deschamps v Miller* [1908] 1 Ch 856; *Re Hawthorne* (1883) 23 ChD 743; and Dicey, Morris and Collins, Rule 114(3). Cf. *Macmillan v Bishopsgate Trust (No 3)* [1995] 1 WLR 978 (Millett J), affirmed on other grounds, [1996] 1 WLR 387 (CA), and *Griggs v Evans* [2004] EWHC 1088 (Prescott QC), where *Norris v Chambres* and *Deschamps v Miller* are explained in terms of choice of law rather than judicial jurisdiction.

# TENANCIES OF LAND

Article 22(1) of the Brussels I Regulation also deals with proceedings principally concerned with a tenancy of land situated in a Member State, and confers exclusive jurisdiction on the courts of the State in which the land is situated. This applies even if the proceedings are based on personal (rather than proprietary) rights, but in other respects the European Court has again adopted a restrictive interpretation, confining the concept of tenancies to agreements which are designed simply or mainly to enable one party to occupy the other's land in return for payment of rent, and are uncomplicated by any substantial additional purposes.

Thus in *Sanders v Van der Putte*,[28] the European Court ruled that Article 22(1) does not extend to an agreement to rent a retail business carried on in immovable property rented from a third person by the lessor, since such an agreement is principally concerned with the operation of a business. Similarly, in *Hacker v Euro-Relais*,[29] it ruled that Article 22(1) does not apply to a contract whereby a travel agent undertakes to procure for a client the use for several weeks of holiday accommodation not owned by the travel agent and to book the travel arrangements. On the other hand, in *Dansommer v Götz*,[30] it ruled that Article 22(1) does apply to a short-term letting of a holiday home, even if the letting is arranged through a travel agent, and the agreement contains ancillary clauses relating to insurance against cancellation and to repayment of the price in the event of insolvency, so long as the agreement does not include the provision of transport.

In *Klein v Rhodos Management*,[31] the European Court ruled that Article 22(1) does not apply to a club membership contract which, in return for a membership fee which represents the major part of the total price, allows members to acquire a right to use on a time-share basis immovable property of a specified type in a specified location and provides for the affiliation of members to a service which enables them to exchange their right of use. Earlier in *Jarrett v Barclays Bank*,[32] the English Court of Appeal had accepted that a time-share agreement, entitling one party to the exclusive occupation of immovable property assumed by the contract to be owned by the other for a specified period in return for a sum of money, constitutes a tenancy within Article 22(1), but had also ruled that Article 22(1) does not apply to a claim by such a tenant, not against the landlord under the time-share agreement, but against a supplier of finance for the acquisition of the tenancy, since such a claim is based not on the tenancy but on the finance agreement.

Article 22(1) makes special provision for a tenancy which is concluded for temporary private use for a maximum period of six consecutive months, where the tenant is an individual and the landlord and the tenant are domiciled in the same Member State (other than the Member State in which the land is situated).[33] In such a case, there is concurrent exclusive

---

[28]  Case 73/77, [1977] ECR 2383.

[29]  Case C-280/90, [1992] ECR I-1111.

[30]  Case C-8/98, [2000] ECR I-393.

[31]  Case C-73/04, [2005] ECR I-8667.

[32]  [1997] 2 All ER 484.

[33]  The corresponding provision in Article 16(1)(b) of the Brussels Convention was narrower, in that it required that the landlord, as well as the tenant, must be an individual.

Under Article 16(1)(b) of the Lugano Convention 1988, only the tenant need be an individual, and it is sufficient as regards domicile that neither party is domiciled in the Contracting State in which the land

jurisdiction, shared by the courts of the Member State in which the land is situated and those of the Member State in which the defendant is domiciled.[34] But where one of the parties is domiciled in the Member State in which the land is situated, the courts of that State retain exclusive jurisdiction under Article 22(1), even where the tenancy is a short-term letting of a holiday home.[35]

Article 22(1) extends to claims based on personal rights (as well as proprietary rights) under a tenancy. As the European Court explained in *Rösler v Rottwinkel*,[36] it extends to any dispute between the landlord and the tenant concerning the existence of the tenancy, the interpretation of its terms, its duration, the giving up of possession to the landlord, the repairing of damage caused by the tenant, or the recovery of rent and of incidental charges payable by the tenant (such as charges for the consumption of water, gas and electricity), and generally to disputes concerning the obligations of the landlord or of the tenant under the terms of the tenancy. Similarly, in *Dansommer v Götz*,[37] the European Court ruled that Article 22(1) applies to a claim by a landlord against his tenant for damage to the premises let, by failing to clean the house properly before his departure and damaging the carpeting and the oven safety mechanism.

The European Court also ruled in *Rösler* that Article 22(1) does not extend to disputes which are only indirectly related to the use of the property let, such as those concerning the loss of holiday enjoyment and travel expenses by a landlord who is also holidaying in another part of the same premises, even where his claim for such losses is based on breach of an express term of the tenancy agreement specifying how the tenant is to use the premises let. It seems probable that this puzzling exception can now be regarded as obsolete in view of the subsequent amendment dealing with certain short-term tenancies and the Court's subsequent decision in *Hacker v Euro-Relais*.[38]

The situation where a single lease relates to land, part of which is situated in one Member State and part in another Member State, was considered by the European Court in *Scherrens v Maenhout*.[39] It held that, as a general rule, in such cases Article 22(1) confers exclusive jurisdiction over the land situated in each Member State on the courts of that State. But, by way of an obiter dictum, it contemplated the possibility of an exception where the lands situated in the two Member States are adjacent to each other, and the land is situated almost entirely in one of the States. In such circumstances, it might be appropriate to regard the land as a single unit, and to treat it as entirely situated in the State containing almost all of it, so as to confer on the courts of that State exclusive jurisdiction over the tenancy.

---

is situated. However, Article IB of the First Protocol to the Lugano Convention 1988 permits a Contracting State to that Convention to make a reservation permitting it not to recognise and enforce under the Convention judgments given in the other Contracting States under Article 16(1)(b) on the basis of the defendant's domicile in respect of a tenancy of land situated in the reserving State. Such reservations have been made by France, Greece and Poland.

Article 22(1) of the Lugano Convention 2007 echoes Article 22(1) of the Brussels I Regulation.

[34]    The exception was created by the 1989 Convention in response to the European Court's refusal in Case 241/83: *Rösler v Rottwinkel* [1985] ECR 99, in the interests of certainty, to recognise an implied exception for short-term lettings or lettings of a holiday home.

[35]    See Case C-8/98: *Dansommer v Götz* [2000] ECR I-393.

[36]    Case 241/83, [1985] ECR 99.

[37]    Case C-8/98, [2000] ECR I-393.

[38]    Case C-280/90, [1992] ECR I-1111.

[39]    Case 158/87, [1988] ECR 3791.

In its Report and Green Paper of 21st April 2009,[40] the EC Commission contemplates the possibility of permitting agreements on jurisdiction in respect of tenancies of business premises, and of introducing some flexibility in relation to tenancies of holiday homes.

## COMPANY LAW

Article 22(2) applies to proceedings which have as their principal subject-matter the validity of the constitution, the nullity or the dissolution of companies or other legal persons or associations of natural or legal persons, or the validity of the decisions of their organs. It confers exclusive jurisdiction on the courts of the Member State in which the company, legal person or association in question has its seat. It also specifies that for this purpose the seat must be determined in accordance with the private international law rules of the forum State.

The explicit requirement to determine the seat in accordance with the lex fori, which was added by the Regulation, is designed to ensure that the harmonised definition of corporate domicile, specified in Article 60 of the Regulation, does not apply for the purpose of Article 22(2). In the United Kingdom, the seat of a company, legal person or association is defined for this purpose by paragraph 10 of Schedule 1 to the Civil Jurisdiction and Judgments Order 2001 (SI 2001/3929).[41] By paragraph 10(2), a company, legal person or association has its seat in the United Kingdom if either: (a) it was incorporated or formed under the law of a part of the United Kingdom; or (b) its central management and control is exercised in the United Kingdom.[42] Similarly, by paragraph 10(3), a company, legal person or association has its seat in a Member State other than the United Kingdom if either: (a) it was incorporated or formed under the law of that State; or (b) its central management and control is exercised in that State. But, by paragraph 10(4), a company, legal person or association does not have its seat in a Member State other than the United Kingdom if either: (a) it has its seat in the United Kingdom by virtue of incorporation or formation under the law of a part of the United Kingdom; or (b) it is shown that the courts of the other Member State in question would not regard it for the purposes of Article 22(2) as having its seat there.

The European Court has construed Article 22(2) restrictively, holding in *Peters v ZNAV*[43] and *Powell Duffryn v Petereit*[44] that it is Articles 2, 5(1) and 23, rather than Article 22(2), which apply to proceedings brought by a company against one of its members or shareholders to recover calls on shares, over-paid dividends, or other sums owing by virtue of the membership relationship and the decisions of the company's organs. A narrow view of the scope of Article 22(2) was again adopted by the European Court in *Hassett v The Medical Defence Union*,[45] where it ruled that Article 22(2) does not apply to an action in which a

---

[40]   COM(2009) 174 final, at section 3.8.2, and COM(2009) 175 final, at question 8.
[41]   This echoes s 43 of the Civil Jurisdiction and Judgments Act 1982, which applied for the purpose of Article 16(2) of the Brussels Convention.
[42]   For the allocation of such jurisdiction between the courts for the three parts of the United Kingdom, see the Civil Jurisdiction and Judgments Act 1982 (as amended), s 43(3)–(5), Schedule 4, rules 4 and 11(b), and Schedule 5, para 1; and the Insolvency Act 1986, ss 117, 220, 221 and 225.
[43]   Case 34/82, [1983] ECR 987.
[44]   Case C-214/89, [1992] ECR I-1745.
[45]   Case C-372/07, [2008] ECR I-7403.

member of a company challenges a decision of the corporate board as infringing the member's rights under the corporate constitution on the ground that, in reaching the decision, the board had failed properly to consider a request to exercise a discretionary power in his favour. The case involved a professional association, established in corporate form, for purposes including the provision of indemnity to its members in cases involving professional negligence on their part. Under the articles of association, any decision concerning a request for an indemnity fell within the absolute discretion of the board. The Court explained that Article 22(2) is confined to disputes in which a party is challenging the validity of a decision of an organ of a company under the company law applicable or under the provisions governing the functioning of its organs, as laid down in its constitution, and that the instant action, challenging the decision of the board to refuse indemnities, was not of that nature.

English case-law has recognised that Article 22(2) does not apply where an issue governed by company law arises incidentally, by way of defence to a claim based on an ordinary contract. Thus in *JP Morgan Chase Bank v Berliner Verkehrsbetriebe*[46] and *Calyon v Wytwornia Sprzetu Komunikacynego PZL Swidnik*,[47] the English High Court held that Article 22(2) does not apply to an action seeking the enforcement of a commercial contract, even if one of the issues in dispute relates to the power of the defendant company to enter into a transaction of the relevant kind, or to the authority of an officer of the defendant company under its corporate constitution to enter into the contract.

On the other hand, in *Grupo Torras v Al-Sabah*,[48] the English Court of Appeal (per Stuart-Smith LJ) took the view that Article 22(2) extends to proceedings principally concerned with the meaning and effect, and not merely the validity, of decisions of corporate organs. He also emphasised that the objective of Article 22(2) is to confer exclusive jurisdiction to decide questions concerning the constitution and internal management of a company on the courts of the Member State in which the company has its seat, since it is generally accepted that the law of the seat determines such matters as the capacity of a company, the composition and powers of its various organs, the formalities and procedures laid down for them, and the extent of an individual member's liability for the company's debts and liabilities. Accordingly, in *Speed Investments Ltd v Formula One Holdings Ltd*,[49] the Court of Appeal applied Article 22(2) to a dispute between shareholders as to the validity of the appointment of certain directors and thus to the composition of the board. Similarly, in *Choudhary v Bhattar*,[50] David Donaldson QC applied Article 22(2) to an action seeking determination of the composition of the board of directors of a company, the composition of its general body of shareholders, and the validity of resolutions adopted by its general meeting; and in *Bezant v Rausing*,[51] Gray J applied Article 22(2) to a claim by a director relating to his removal. Moreover, in *Montani v First Directors Ltd*,[52] Hanna J (in the Irish High Court) accepted jurisdiction under Article 22(2) over a dispute as to ownership of shares in an Irish company.

---

[46]   [2009] EWHC 1627 (Comm) (Teare J).
[47]   [2009] EWHC 1914 (Comm) (Field J).
[48]   [1996] 1 Lloyd's Rep 7 (CA).
[49]   [2005] 1 BCLC 455 (CA).
[50]   [2009] EWHC 314 (Ch).
[51]   [2007] All ER (D) 196 (May).
[52]   [2006] IEHC 92.

It seems clear that Article 22(2) applies to a member's petition for the winding-up of a solvent company, and probable that it extends to a member's petition under s 459 of the (English) Companies Act 1985, based on the allegation that the company's affairs are being conducted in a manner unfairly prejudicial to the member.[53] But difficulties have arisen as to how far it applies to actions brought by a company against its (former) directors or officers. In *Grupo Torras v Al-Sabah*,[54] the English Court of Appeal accepted jurisdiction over an action brought by a Spanish company and its English subsidiary against a large number of its former directors and professional advisers, seeking damages for breach of fiduciary duty and conspiracy to defraud, and restitution of money due under constructive trusts. Stuart-Smith LJ explained that proceedings based on abuse of authority by corporate officers, by way of fraudulent misappropriation of corporate assets for their own benefit, do not fall within Article 22(2). In such circumstances, the officers are not acting as a corporate organ, and the proceedings concern, not the decisions of corporate organs, but the officers' fraud in procuring such decisions to be made; and in the instant case, the existence of any authorisation or ratification by shareholders was not seriously arguable.

On the other hand, he suggested obiter that Article 22(2) would apply to proceedings based on want or excess of authority on the part of corporate officers, whether arising from breach of formal or procedural requirements, or from honest but negligent breach of the general principle that officers of a company must act in good faith in the interests of the company.[55] This dictum seems questionable, especially in view of the restrictive approach which the European Court has almost invariably adopted towards Article 22. It is submitted that proceedings in which a company seeks a pecuniary remedy against its (former) officers for any type of misconduct in the exercise of their powers will not fall within Article 22(2), since the principal subject-matter will be the alleged breach of fiduciary or other duty by the defendants, and any decision of a corporate organ will have only incidental significance.

As regards proceedings concerning the winding-up or reorganisation of an insurance undertaking which is regulated by an EU Member State or an EEA country under EC Directive 2001/17, on the reorganisation and winding-up of insurance undertakings,[56] the Directive confers exclusive jurisdiction on the courts of the regulating State. The Directive applies whether the insurance undertaking is solvent or insolvent; and accordingly, where the insurance undertaking is solvent, the Directive prevails over the Brussels I Regulation in accordance with Article 67 of the Regulation, so that Article 22(2) of the Regulation does not apply.[57] There is also English authority that proceedings concerning a scheme of arrangement in respect of an insurance undertaking, whether it is solvent or insolvent, are outside the scope of all existing Community legislation; neither the Insolvency Regulation, nor the Brussels I Regulation, nor Directive 2001/17 applies to such proceedings.[58] It is, however, difficult to see why the Brussels I Regulation should not apply to proceedings concerning a scheme of arrangement in respect of a solvent company, if the Regulation is not displaced by another Community measure dealing with a specific matter, such as Directive 2001/17.

---

53  Cf. *Re Harrods (Buenos Aires) Ltd* [1992] Ch 72 (CA), [1992] OJ C219/4 (HL).
54  [1996] 1 Lloyd's Rep 7 (CA), affirming [1995] 1 Lloyd's Rep 374 (Mance J).
55  Cf. *Newtherapeutics Ltd v Katz* [1991] Ch 226 (Knox J).
56  [2001] OJ L110/28.
57  See *Re Sovereign Marine and General Insurance Co Ltd* [2007] 1 BCLC 228 (Warren J).
58  See *Re Sovereign Marine and General Insurance Co Ltd* [2007] 1 BCLC 228 (Warren J).

In its Report and Green Paper of 21st April 2009,[59] the EC Commission contemplates the possibility of extending the scope of exclusive jurisdiction in company law under Article 22(2) to additional matters related to the internal organisation and decision-making in a company, and of introducing a uniform definition of the corporate seat for this purpose.

## PUBLIC REGISTERS

Article 22(3) applies to proceedings which have as their object the validity of entries in public registers. It confers exclusive jurisdiction to entertain such proceedings on the courts of the Member State in which the register is kept. This covers, for example, an action seeking rectification of a register of title to land, and thus overlaps with Article 22(1).[60]

## INTELLECTUAL PROPERTY

### National Intellectual Property Rights

Article 22(4) of the Regulation deals with proceedings principally concerned with the registration or validity of patents, trade marks, designs, or other similar rights required to be deposited or registered. It confers exclusive jurisdiction on the courts of the Member State in which the deposit or registration has been applied for, has taken place, or is, under the terms of a Community instrument or an international convention, deemed to have taken place.[61] A typical case for its application is an English petition for the revocation of a patent.[62]

As with other heads of Article 22, the European Court has construed Article 22(4) restrictively. Thus, in *Duijnstee v Goderbauer*,[63] it ruled that Article 22(4) does not apply to a dispute between an employer and an employee relating to their mutual rights in respect of an invention made by the employee, since such issues are governed by the contract of employment and the law governing it, rather than by the law of the country of the patent application or grant.[64] In any event, Article 22(4) does not apply to copyright, since this arises automatically from creation, fixation or publication, without the need for or possibility of any official grant or registration.[65]

---

[59]   COM(2009) 174 final, at section 3.8.2, and COM(2009) 175 final, at question 8.
[60]   See *Re Hayward* [1997] Ch 45 (Rattee J).
[61]   In the United Kingdom, since such rights are granted for the whole country, proceedings within Article 22(4) may be brought in any of its parts at the plaintiff's option. See the Patents Act 1977, s 132; the Trade Marks Act 1994, s 108; the Registered Designs Act 1949, ss 45–7; and the Civil Jurisdiction and Judgments Act 1982, s 17 and Schedule 5, para 2.
[62]   See *Napp Laboratories v Pfizer* [1993] FSR 150; and *Fort Dodge v Akzo* [1998] FSR 222 (CA).
[63]   Case 288/82, [1983] ECR 3663.
[64]   See also the European Patent Convention 2000, Article 60(1), and its annexed Protocol on Jurisdiction and the Recognition of Decisions in respect of the Right to the Grant of a European Patent, especially Articles 4 and 5(2); and the (UK) Patents Act 1977, ss 43(2) and 82.
[65]   See *Pearce v Ove Arup* [2000] Ch 403 (CA), affirming [1997] 3 All ER 31 (Lloyd J); and *Griggs v Evans* [2004] EWHC 1088 (Prescott QC).

Since Article 22(4) is confined to proceedings which are principally concerned with registration or validity, it does not apply to actions for infringement of intellectual property rights (including those derived from an official grant or registration). Infringement actions remain governed by the ordinary provisions of Chapter II, and accordingly the plaintiff will often have a choice of suing in the courts of the defendant's domicile under Article 2 or in the courts of the place of infringement under Article 5(3).[66] Thus, as the Court of Appeal has recognised,[67] the Brussels I Regulation has abrogated the former English rule[68] which deprived the English courts of power to entertain actions for the infringement abroad of foreign intellectual property rights. In particular, Article 2 of the Regulation creates such jurisdiction where the defendant is domiciled in England, and Article 6(1) creates ancillary jurisdiction over co-defendants who are sued in respect of the same infringement but are domiciled in other Member States.[69] Moreover, jurisdiction by virtue of the defendant's domicile extends to an action for the infringement of an intellectual property right existing under the law of a non-member country by acts committed in that country.[70]

But, as regards proceedings for the infringement of parallel patents granted under the European Patent Convention for different Member States, the European Court ruled in *Roche Nederland BV v Primus*[71] that Article 6(1) does not enable the joinder in a single action of claims against different defendants who are domiciled in different Member States in respect of acts committed by each defendant at its own domicile. This is so even where the defendants are companies belonging to the same group, and they acted in an identical or similar manner in accordance with a common policy. In explaining that in such circumstances there was no risk of contradictory decisions being given in infringement proceedings brought in each Member State in which a defendant was domiciled and had acted, the Court emphasised that each of the national patents comprised in a grant under the European Patent Convention is governed by the law of the State for which it is granted. It is clear that Article 6(1) is

---

[66]    See *Re Jurisdiction in Contract and Tort* [1988] ECC 415 (German Supreme Court).

[67]    See *Fort Dodge v Akzo* [1998] FSR 222 (CA); *Pearce v Ove Arup* [2000] Ch 403 (CA), affirming [1997] 3 All ER 31 (Lloyd J); and *Coin Controls v Suzo International* [1997] 3 All ER 45 (Laddie J). See also, on actions for wrongful circumvention of electronic copy-protection, *Sony Computer Entertainment Inc v Ball* [2004] EWHC 1738 (Laddie J).

[68]    See *Potter v Broken Hill* (1906) 3 CLR 479, affirming [1905] VLR 612; *Def Lepp Music v Stuart-Brown* [1986] RPC 273; *James Burrough Distillers v Speymalt Whisky Distributors* [1991] RPC 130; *Tyburn Productions v Conan Doyle* [1991] Ch 75; and *LA Gear v Whelan* [1991] FSR 670.

[69]    See *Fort Dodge v Akzo* [1998] FSR 222 (CA); *Pearce v Ove Arup* [2000] Ch 403 (CA), affirming [1997] 3 All ER 31 (Lloyd J); and *Coin Controls v Suzo International* [1997] 3 All ER 45 (Laddie J). *Pearce* involved an action for infringement of a Dutch copyright. *Fort Dodge* and *Coin Controls* involved foreign patents.

[70]    See *Lucasfilm Ltd v Ainsworth* [2009] FSR 2, where Mann J accepted that the English courts are now competent to entertain an action against an English defendant for infringement of an American copyright by acts committed in the United States, and incidentally to determine questions concerning the subsistence of the copyright. Cf. *Duhan v Radius Television Production Ltd* [2008] 1 IR 506, where Herbert J (in the Irish High Court) ruled that, despite the Brussels I Regulation, the Irish courts lack jurisdiction to entertain an action, even against an Irish defendant, for an infringement of copyright committed in a non-member country, if the existence of the copyright is disputed.

[71]    Case C-539/03, [2006] ECR I-6535. The ruling of the European Court accords with the earlier decision of the English Court of Appeal in *Fort Dodge v Akzo* [1998] FSR 222, overruling on this point *Coin Controls v Suzo International* [1997] 3 All ER 45 (Laddie J).

equally unavailable in otherwise similar circumstances where the parallel patents were not granted by the European Patent Office under the European Patent Convention, but by the various national patent offices of the relevant Member States.[72]

In *GAT v Lamellen*,[73] the European Court ruled that Article 22(4) applies to all proceedings relating to the registration or validity of a patent, whether the issue is raised by way of an action or of a defence or reply, and whether it is raised at the time when the case is brought or at a later stage in the proceedings. The Court accepted that Article 22(4) does not apply to an infringement action in which the validity of the patent allegedly infringed is not disputed. But it insisted that Article 22(4) is applicable where the patent's validity is challenged by way of defence or counterclaim in an infringement action, or in support of an action seeking a declaration of non-infringement. This accords with earlier English case-law,[74] which has also adopted the same approach for other intellectual property rights which arise from an official grant of registration, such as registered trade marks.[75] For Article 22(4) to apply where validity is challenged by way of defence or counterclaim in an infringement action, it seems probable that the challenge must be seriously arguable.

In the Lugano Convention 2007, Article 22(4) is explicitly made applicable 'whether the issue [of registration or validity] is raised by way of an action or as a defence'. This modification is designed to reflect the decision of the European Court in *GAT*. The eventual adoption of a similar amendment to the Brussels I Regulation is contemplated by Annex I to EC Council Decision 2009/430 on the conclusion of the Lugano Convention 2007.[76]

In *Prudential Assurance Co Ltd v Prudential Insurance Co of America*,[77] the Court of Appeal held that the exercise of English jurisdiction over proceedings relating to both infringement and validity of a trade mark registered in the United Kingdom cannot be affected by concurrent proceedings instituted earlier in another Member State in relation to a parallel registration there, and that the determination of the merits of such English proceedings cannot be affected by a judgment given in another Member State in relation to a parallel registration there. This is because the exclusivity arising under Articles 22(4), 25 and 35(1) of the Regulation overrides the normal rules on concurrent proceedings and on the recognition of judgments laid down by Articles 27–30 and 33. This decision has subsequently received support from the European Court's firm recognition in *Roche Nederland BV v Primus*[78] of the separate and territorial character of parallel patents granted for different countries.

---

[72]    In its Report and Green Paper of 21st April 2009, the EC Commission contemplates (without much enthusiasm) the possibility of establishing a specific rule allowing infringement proceedings concerning certain industrial property rights against several defendants to be brought before the courts of the Member State where the defendant co-ordinating the activities or otherwise having the closest connection with the infringement is domiciled. See COM(2009) 174 final, at section 3.4, and COM(2009) 175 final, at question 4.

[73]    Case C-4/03, [2006] ECR I-6509.

[74]    See *Fort Dodge v Akzo* [1998] FSR 222 (CA); agreeing on this point with Laddie J in *Coin Controls v Suzo International* [1997] 3 All ER 45. See also *Sepracor v Hoechst* [1999] FSR 746 (Laddie J).

[75]    See *Prudential Assurance Co Ltd v Prudential Insurance Co of America* [2003] 1 WLR 2295 (CA).

[76]    [2009] OJ L147/1.

[77]    [2003] 1 WLR 2295 (CA).

[78]    Case C-539/03, [2006] ECR I-6535.

As with infringement actions, the ordinary rules on jurisdiction laid down by the Brussels I Regulation, and not Article 22(4), apply to actions based on contractual rights in respect of intellectual property, even where it is sought to enforce a trust arising from a contract against a purchaser with actual notice. Thus the courts of a defendant's domicile have jurisdiction over an action brought by the commissioner of an artistic work against the author and a purchaser from him, seeking to establish that the commission contract gave rise to a trust for the commissioner of the copyrights in the work in all countries, and to compel the purchaser to assign such copyrights to the commissioner.[79]

As regards patents granted in non-member countries, in *Satyam Computer Services Ltd v Upaid Systems Ltd*,[80] Flaux J held that a surviving rule of English law deprives the English courts of jurisdiction to entertain claims which involve the existence or validity of such patents, but that there is no such exclusion in respect of other claims which involve such patents. It seems clear that the compatibility with the Brussels I Regulation of the English exclusionary rule recognised by Flaux J, in cases where the defendant is domiciled in England or there is an English jurisdiction clause, must depend on the reflexive effect of Article 22(4).[81]

### European Patents

The European Patent Convention (which may also be referred to as the Munich Convention) has established a European Patent Office, seated at Munich, and empowered it to grant, on a single application, a bundle of national patents, usually in common form, for such of the Contracting States as are designated in the application. The original version, which may be referred to as the European Patent Convention 1973, was signed at Munich on 5th October 1973 and entered into force on 1st June 1978. It has now been replaced by a revised version, known as the European Patent Convention 2000, which entered into force on 13th December 2007.[82] The Munich Convention is not a European Union measure, but a treaty governed by public international law. Currently, its Contracting States include the twenty-seven EU Member States and the three other Lugano Convention countries. Other Contracting States to the Munich Convention include Croatia, FYR Macedonia and Turkey. As a result of bilateral agreements with the European Patent Organisation, patent applications and grants under the Convention can now be extended to Albania, Bosnia-Herzegovina and Serbia.

In relation to patents granted by the European Patent Office, the second sentence of Article 22(4) of the Brussels I Regulation specifies that, without prejudice to the jurisdiction of the European Patent Office under the Munich Convention, the courts of each Member State shall have exclusive jurisdiction, regardless of domicile, in proceedings concerned with the registration or validity of any European patent granted for that State.[83] Thus each national patent within the bundle granted by the European Patent Office is treated separately for the purpose of the Brussels I Regulation.

---

[79] See *Griggs v Evans* [2004] EWHC 1088 (Prescott QC).

[80] [2008] EWHC 31 (Comm).

[81] On reflexive effect, see pp. 58–61 above.

[82] The European Patent Convention 2000 is implemented in the United Kingdom by the Patents Act 1977, as amended by the Patents Act 2004.

[83] This replaces Article VD of the Protocol annexed to the Brussels Convention.

After the grant of a patent by the European Patent Office, there is a short period in which an opponent may seek revocation of the whole bundle of national patents by means of opposition proceedings brought before the European Patent Office. In addition, an opponent may at any time seek revocation of one of the national patents before a court of the relevant country. Where there are concurrent proceedings in England and before the European Patent Office involving the revocation of a European patent (UK), the English court will usually, in its discretion, allow the English proceedings to continue, despite the existence of concurrent proceedings in the European Patent Office, in view of the substantially greater time which is expected to elapse before the European proceedings are concluded.[84]

On the other hand, proceedings concerning an application for a European patent, instituted after the application has been filed but before a grant has been made, are brought before tribunals within the European Patent Office, and not before national courts, except where the dispute concerns ownership of the invention. As regards proceedings instituted at that stage in which a challenger claims ownership of the invention involved, jurisdiction is allocated between the courts of the Contracting States to the Munich Convention by its annexed Protocol on Jurisdiction and the Recognition of Decisions in respect of the Right to the Grant of a European Patent.[85] The Munich Protocol counts as a specialised convention, so as to prevail over the Brussels I Regulation under Article 71.

The basic rule, laid down by Article 2 of the Munich Protocol, confers jurisdiction on the courts of the Contracting State to the Munich Convention in which the applicant for the European patent has his residence or principal place of business. If the applicant's residence or principal place of business is outside the Contracting States, Article 3 confers jurisdiction on the courts of the Contracting State in which the challenger has his residence or principal place of business. But where the dispute is between an employer and his employee in relation to an invention made by the employee, Article 4 overrides Articles 2 and 3 and instead confers jurisdiction on the courts of the Contracting State in which the employee is mainly employed; or if the State of main employment cannot be determined, on those of the Contracting State in which the employer has his place of business to which the employee is attached. By Article 5, these rules give way to an agreement between the parties, made or confirmed in writing, designating as competent a court or the courts of a Contracting State; but in the case of a dispute between an employer and his employee, only if the agreement is permissible under the law governing the contract of employment. Finally, where otherwise no court of a Contracting State would be competent, Article 6 confers jurisdiction on the German courts. In addition, Article 7 insists that a court seised must of its own motion determine whether it has jurisdiction under these rules.

The Munich Protocol also deals with the problem of concurrent proceedings in different Contracting States based on the same cause of action and between the same parties. Article 8 requires the court subsequently applied to of its own motion to decline jurisdiction in favour of the court first applied to. If the jurisdiction of the first court is being challenged, the subsequent court must stay its proceedings until the first court takes a final decision.

The Munich Protocol also requires, by Articles 9 and 10, that a final decision on ownership given in a Contracting State must be recognised in the other Contracting States. No

---

84    See *Glaxo v Genentech* [2007] All ER (D) 151 (Jun) (Lewison J).
85    The Protocol is implemented in the United Kingdom by ss 82 and 83 of the Patents Act 1977.

special procedure for obtaining recognition may be required, and the decision may not be reviewed, even as regards the jurisdiction of the original court. But recognition may be refused where the applicant for the European patent, not having contested the claim, proves that the initiating document was not notified to him regularly and in sufficient time to enable defence; or where it is proved that the decision is incompatible with another decision given in a Contracting State in proceedings between the same parties which were commenced before those in which the decision in question was given.

The Munich Convention (or European Patent Convention) must be distinguished from the Community Patent Convention (or Luxembourg Convention), which was designed to supplement the Munich Convention by creating a unitary patent for the entire territory of the European Community, to be known as a Community patent. A Community patent would be granted by the European Patent Office to a successful applicant who had so requested, along with patents for non-member countries, such as Switzerland or Turkey, which were parties to the Munich Convention and were designated in the application. The original version of the Community Patent Convention was signed by the EC Member States at Luxembourg on 15th December 1975,[86] and a revised version was signed by them at Luxembourg on 15th December 1989.[87] But in the absence of sufficient ratifications, the Community Patent Convention did not enter into force, and it was eventually abandoned. Instead, on 1st August 2000, the EC Commission made a proposal, based on Article 308 (ex Article 235) of the EC Treaty, for an EC Regulation on the Community Patent.[88] In March 2004, the EC Council failed to reach agreement on the proposal,[89] but discussions have continued, and on 4th December 2009 some measure of agreement was reached by the EU Council.[90]

## Community Trade Marks

In contrast with the failure, despite over thirty years of efforts, to create a Community patent, the European Community has been more successful in creating other Community-wide intellectual property rights. It is now possible to obtain, on application to a European Union office, the grant or registration of a trade mark, a plant variety right, or a design, which provides protection throughout the territory of the Union.

Since 1996 it has been possible to obtain registration of a Community trade mark. The matter was governed initially by EC Regulation 40/94,[91] and is now governed by EC Regulation 207/2009, which will be referred to as 'the new Trade Mark Regulation').[92] A Community trade mark has a unitary character and has effect throughout the European Union. Registration is obtained by application to an EU quasi-institution, the Office for Harmonisation in the Internal Market (Trade Marks and Designs), which is located at Alicante in Spain. In relation to litigation involving a Community trade mark, Title X

---

[86]  See [1976] OJ L17.
[87]  See [1989] OJ L401.
[88]  See [2000] OJ C337E/278.
[89]  See MEMO/04/58, of 12th March 2004.
[90]  See EU Council doc 17229/09, PI 141, COUR 87, of 7th December 2009.
[91]  [1994] OJ L11/1.
[92]  [2009] OJ L78/1. Regulation 207/2009 consolidates the provisions of Regulation 40/94 and various amending regulations.

(Articles 94–108) of the new Trade Mark Regulation derogates in some respects from the Brussels I Regulation, and, in accordance with Article 67 of the Brussels I Regulation, the conflicting provisions of the new Trade Mark Regulation prevail.

Disputes arising in relation to an application for a Community trade mark prior to its registration are determined by the Office, and not by national courts. Decisions made within the Office are appealable to its Board of Appeal, and decisions of the Board of Appeal are subject to judicial review by the EU Court of First Instance.[93] After registration, jurisdiction over disputes concerning a Community trade mark is shared between the Office and the courts of the Member States. By Articles 95 and 96 of the new Trade Mark Regulation, within each Member State the most important proceedings concerning Community trade marks are assigned to a limited number of its courts, designated as Community trade mark courts ('CTM courts'). It is in these courts that actions for actual or threatened infringement of a Community trade mark, including infringements committed between the publication of the application and the registration of the mark, and actions for a declaration of non-infringement, must be brought. Validity may be challenged after registration by means of an application to the Office under Articles 56 and 57, or by way of counterclaim in an infringement action before a CTM court under Articles 96(d) and 100. By Article 100(2), a CTM court must reject a counterclaim for revocation or for a declaration of invalidity if a decision taken by the Office relating to the same subject-matter and cause of action and involving the same parties has already become final.

The allocation of international jurisdiction between the CTM courts of the Member States is governed by Articles 97 and 98 of the new Trade Mark Regulation. By Article 94(2)(a) thereof, these provisions replace those of Articles 2, 4 and 5(3)–(5) of the Brussels I Regulation, on the defendant's domicile, external defendants, the place of a tortious event, and the location of a secondary establishment involved. Instead, Articles 97(1)–(3) and 98(1) of the new Trade Mark Regulation confer general jurisdiction, covering infringements committed or threatened anywhere within the European Union, on the CTM courts of a Member State determined in accordance with the following series of tests. By Article 97(1), jurisdiction is conferred primarily on the CTM courts of the Member State in which the defendant is domiciled. If there are co-defendants, the action may be brought in a Member State in which any of them is domiciled, since Article 94 of the new Trade Mark Regulation maintains the operation of Article 6(1) of the Brussels I Regulation. Secondly, if no defendant is domiciled in any of the Member States, Article 97(1) of the new Trade Mark Regulation confers jurisdiction on the CTM courts of the Member State in which the defendant (or, in view of Article 94(2)(c), one of the defendants) has an establishment. Thirdly, if no defendant is domiciled or has an establishment in any of the Member States, Article 97(2) confers jurisdiction on the CTM courts of the Member State in which the plaintiff (or, presumably, one of the plaintiffs) is domiciled; or if no plaintiff is domiciled in any of the Member States, on the CTM courts of the Member State in which the plaintiff (or, presumably, one of the plaintiffs) has an establishment. Finally, if no party is domiciled or has an establishment in any of the Member States, Article 97(3) confers jurisdiction on the Spanish CTM courts, since the Office has its seat in Spain.

---

[93]   See Articles 58–65 of the new Trade Mark Regulation.

An alternative basis of international jurisdiction over actions for infringement (but not actions for a declaration of non-infringement) is made available by Article 97(5) and 98(2) of the new Trade Mark Regulation. The plaintiff is given the option of suing in the CTM courts of the Member State in which an act of infringement has been committed or threatened, but jurisdiction is limited to acts committed or threatened within the forum State. By Articles 94(2)(b) and 97(4), the international jurisdiction of a CTM court may also be founded on a jurisdiction clause or on the defendant's submission by appearance, in accordance with Articles 23 and 24 of the Brussels I Regulation.

By Article 94 of the new Trade Mark Regulation, concurrent actions in CTM courts of different Member States remain governed by Articles 27–30 of the Brussels I Regulation in cases where validity is not in question. But special provision is made by Article 104 of the new Trade Mark Regulation for cases where the validity of a Community trade mark is already in issue elsewhere. By Article 104(1), a CTM court hearing an action for infringement must, of its own motion if necessary, stay its proceedings where the validity of the Community trade mark is already in issue before another CTM court on account of a counterclaim or where an application for revocation or for a declaration of invalidity has already been filed at the Office. Similarly, by Article 104(2), the Office, when hearing an application for revocation or for a declaration of invalidity must, of its own motion if necessary, stay its proceedings where the validity of the Community trade mark is already in issue on account of a counterclaim before a CTM court. But in both these cases the stay need not be granted if there are special grounds for continuing the hearing. Moreover, where the Office has stayed its proceedings under Article 104(2), the CTM court involved may, at the request of a party, stay its proceedings, and in that event the Office must continue its proceedings. By Article 104(3), where a CTM court stays its proceedings under Article 104, it may order provisional and protective measures for the duration of the stay.

In addition, by Article 100(7) of the new Trade Mark Regulation, in the absence of concurrent proceedings, a CTM court hearing a counterclaim for revocation or for a declaration of invalidity may stay its proceedings, on application by the proprietor of the Community trade mark and after hearing the other parties, and may request the defendant to submit an application for revocation or for a declaration of invalidity to the Office within a specified time limit. Then, if the application to the Office is not made within the time limit, the CTM proceedings continue but the counterclaim is deemed withdrawn. Again, the CTM court may order provisional and protective measures for the duration of its stay.

As regards provisional measures in connection with proceedings relating to the infringement or validity of a Community trade mark, Article 31 of the Brussels I Regulation is excluded by Article 94(2)(a) of the new Trade Mark Regulation. Instead, Article 103(1) of the new Trade Mark Regulation enables application to be made to the courts of a Member State (including but not limited to CTM courts), for such provisional (including protective) measures in respect of a Community trade mark or Community trade mark application as may be available under the law of that State in respect of a national trade mark, even if under the Regulation a CTM court of another Member State has jurisdiction as to the substance of the matter. But, by Article 103(2), only a CTM court whose jurisdiction is based on the domicile or an establishment of a defendant or plaintiff, or on the seat of the Office, or on submission by agreement or appearance, has jurisdiction to grant provisional and protective measures which, subject to any necessary procedure for recognition and enforcement under Chapter III of the Brussels I Regulation, are applicable in the territory of any Member State.

As regards disputes concerning a Community trade mark but not involving infringement or validity, Article 94(1) of the new Trade Mark Regulation makes the Brussels I Regulation fully applicable, subject only to the additional provisions of Article 106 of the new Trade Mark Regulation. By Article 106(1), within the competent Member State, the same courts have jurisdiction as would have jurisdiction by reference to subject-matter and location in the case of actions relating to a national trade mark registered in that State. By Article 106(2), where otherwise no court has jurisdiction, the action may be heard before the Spanish courts, since the Office has its seat in Spain.

Article 109 of the new Trade Mark Regulation addresses the problems arising from simultaneous and successive civil actions, one brought on the basis of a Community trade mark and the other on the basis of a national trade mark. As regards concurrent actions, Article 109(1) applies where actions for infringement, involving the same cause of action and between the same parties, are brought in the courts of different Member States, one seised on the basis of a Community trade mark and the other seised on the basis of a national trade mark. By Article 109(1)(a), where the trade marks concerned are identical and valid for identical goods or services, the court subsequently seised must of its own motion decline jurisdiction in favour of the court first seised. By way of exception, the subsequent court may instead stay its proceedings if the jurisdiction of the first court is contested. By Article 109(1)(b), where the trade marks concerned are identical and valid for similar goods or services, or the trade marks concerned are similar and valid for identical or similar goods or services, the court subsequently seised may stay its proceedings. By Article 109(4), a court which declines jurisdiction or stays proceedings under Article 109(1) may grant provisional, including protective, measures.

As regards successive actions, Article 109(2) requires a court hearing an action for infringement on the basis of a Community trade mark to reject the action if a final judgment on the merits has been given on the same cause of action and between the same parties on the basis of an identical national trade mark valid for identical goods or services. Similarly Article 109(3) requires a court hearing an action for infringement on the basis of a national trade mark to reject the action if a final judgment on the merits has been given on the same cause of action and between the same parties on the basis of an identical Community trade mark valid for identical goods or services. But Article 109(2) and (3) do not apply where the marks in question are merely similar and not identical.[94]

## Community Plant Variety Rights

Another Community-wide intellectual property right, the Community plant variety right, has been created by EC Regulation 2100/94 on Community plant variety rights.[95] Such rights are granted by the EU Plant Variety Office, located at Angers in France.[96] After grant, the invalidation of a Community plant variety right can be sought only by way of proceedings in the Office for cancellation or revocation,[97] but the courts of the Member States have jurisdiction

---

[94]    See *Prudential Assurance Co Ltd v Prudential Insurance Co of America* [2003] 1 WLR 2295 (CA), where the Community trade marks, 'Pru' and 'Prudential', were not identical to the French trade mark, 'Prumerica'.
[95]    [1994] OJ L227/1.
[96]    See [1996] OJ C36/1.
[97]    See Articles 20, 21 and 105 of Regulation 2100/94.

over actions for infringement and over disputes as to ownership.[98] Proceedings in national courts may be stayed to await the outcome of cancellation or revocation proceedings which have been initiated in the Office.[99]

In general, by Article 101(1) of Regulation 2100/94, proceedings in national courts relating to a Community plant variety right were originally subject to the Lugano Convention 1988, rather than the Brussels Convention or the Brussels I Regulation, and are now subject to the Lugano Convention 2007.[100] But, echoing the Trade Mark Regulations, Article 101(2) of Regulation 2100/94 confers general jurisdiction over infringements alleged to have been committed in any of the Member States on the courts of the Member State or other Lugano Convention country in which the defendant is domiciled or, in the absence of such a domicile, has an establishment. If the defendant has neither his domicile nor an establishment in a Member State or other Lugano Convention country, general jurisdiction is conferred on the courts of the Member State in which the plaintiff is domiciled or, in the absence of such a domicile, has an establishment. Finally, if neither party has a domicile or establishment in a Member State or other Lugano Convention country, general jurisdiction is conferred on the French courts, since the Office has its seat in France. By Article 102(3), for these purposes the domicile of a party is now determined in accordance with Articles 59 and 60 of the Lugano Convention 2007. By Article 101(2), an alternative jurisdiction over infringement actions is conferred on the courts of the place of infringement, but limited to infringements committed within the forum State. By Article 101(3), within a competent Member State local jurisdiction is allocated in accordance with the law of the forum State.

Article 102(2) of Regulation 2100/94 now preserves the operation of Articles 5(1), 23 and 24 of the Lugano Convention 2007. The saving for Article 5(1) enables disputes concerning contractual licences under a Community plant variety right to be brought at the place of performance of the contractual obligation on which the claim is based. The savings for Articles 23 and 24 enable effect to be given, as regards actions for infringement or relating to ownership of a Community plant variety right, to an agreement between the parties as to the competent court, and to the defendant's submission by appearance in the proceedings.

## Community Designs

Community-wide rights in both registered and unregistered designs have been created by EC Regulation 6/2002 on Community designs ('the Design Regulation').[101] As with Community trade marks, the registration of a Community design is effected by the Office for Harmonisation in the Internal Market (Trade Marks and Designs), and within each Member State there are courts designated as Community design courts which play a similar role to Community trade mark courts.

As with trade marks, disputes arising in relation to an application for a registered Community design prior to its registration are determined by the Office, and not by national courts, and after registration jurisdiction over disputes concerning a registered Community

---

[98]   See Articles 94–100 of Regulation 2100/94.
[99]   See Article 106(2) of Regulation 2100/94.
[100]  See Article 69(6) of the Lugano Convention 2007.
[101]  [2002] OJ L3/1.

design is shared between the Office and the courts of the Member States. By Articles 80 and 81 of the Design Regulation, within each Member State the most important proceedings concerning Community designs are assigned to a limited number of its courts, designated as Community design courts. It is in these courts that actions for actual or threatened infringement of a Community design, and actions for a declaration of non-infringement, must be brought. A declaration of the invalidity of a registered Community design after registration may be sought by means of an application to the Office under Article 52, or by way of counterclaim in an infringement action before a Community design court under Articles 81(d) and 84–7.

The Design Regulation also provides for the protection of unregistered Community designs. In the case of an unregistered Community design, the Office has no role, and under Article 81(c), the Community design courts deal with applications for a declaration of invalidity even when not made by way of counterclaim in an infringement action.

In relation to litigation involving a Community design, whether registered or unregistered, Title IX (Articles 79–94) of the Design Regulation contains provisions on international jurisdiction, concurrent actions and provisional measures which closely resemble those of Title X of the new Trade Mark Regulation. These provisions in some respects derogate from, and thus prevail over, those of the Brussels I Regulation.[102]

## ENFORCEMENT OF JUDGMENTS

Article 22(5) of the Brussels I Regulation applies to proceedings principally concerned with the enforcement of judgments, and confers exclusive jurisdiction on the courts of the Member State in which the judgment has been or is to be enforced. It might have been supposed that this provision, which is evidently based on a desire to respect the sovereignty of the country of enforcement, would apply both to judgments of the courts of the country of enforcement and to judgments given elsewhere, whether or not within the Member States. However, in *Owens Bank v Bracco*,[103] the European Court ruled that Chapter II (as well as Chapter III) of the Regulation does not apply to proceedings in Member States concerning the recognition and enforcement of judgments given in non-member countries.[104]

In *Reichert v Dresdner Bank (No 2)*,[105] the European Court explained that the essential purpose of Article 22(5) is to enable the courts of the country of execution to apply their own rules in relation to the acts of the enforcing authorities. Thus the provision is confined to disputes arising from measures of execution, especially measures against land or movable property. Accordingly, the Court rejected an absurd argument that Article 22(5) enabled a creditor to bring a 'pauline' action, seeking the setting aside of a fraudulent disposition of

---

[102]    See also Article 95 of the Design Regulation, on parallel actions on the basis of a Community design and a national design right. This differs from Article 109 of the new Trade Mark Regulation in referring to designs 'providing simultaneous protection'.

[103]    Case C-129/92, [1994] ECR I-117.

[104]    For English jurisdiction in such cases, see para 3.1(10) of Practice Direction B supplementing Part 6 of the Civil Procedure Rules, and *Tasarruf Mevduati Sigorta Fonu v Demirel* [2007] 2 All ER 815 (Lawrence Collins J).

[105]    Case C-261/90, [1992] ECR I-2149.

property by his debtor, in the country in which the asset transferred was situated. Such an action no doubt aims to assist the creditor in the ultimate enforcement of his debt, but it is not concerned with a dispute arising from measures taken in execution of a judgment. Earlier, in *AS-Autoteile Service v Mahle*,[106] the European Court had ruled that an action to oppose enforcement, such as that provided for by Article 767 of the German Code of Civil Procedure, falls within Article 22(5), but that Article 22(5) does not enable a party who brings such an action in the courts of the State of enforcement to plead a set-off between the judgment in question and a claim which the courts of that State would otherwise lack jurisdiction to entertain.

In *Kuwait Oil Tanker Co v Qabazard*,[107] the House of Lords ruled that Article 22(5) prevents an English court from enforcing a judgment by garnishing a debt owed by a third person which is situated in another Member State. But in *Masri v Consolidated Contractors (No 2)*,[108] the English Court of Appeal (per Lawrence Collins LJ) held that, after a competent English court has given a judgment in favour of the plaintiff on the merits of a claim, nothing in the Brussels I Regulation prevents the court from making receiving orders and freezing orders, which operate against the judgment debtor personally and have limited effects on third parties, in respect of assets situated abroad, in order to pave the way for enforcement of the English judgment on the merits. This is so regardless of where the defendant is domiciled, and of where the assets in question are located. For the ruling of the European Court in *Van Uden v Deco-Line*[109] establishes that a court which has substantive jurisdiction under Chapter II of the Regulation also has jurisdiction to grant any ancillary orders, and the ruling of the European Court in *Reichert v Dresdner Bank (No 2)*[110] establishes that Article 22(5) is concerned with actual enforcement, and not with steps which may lead to enforcement. Lawrence Collins LJ also accepted that Article 22(5) has reflexive effect, so as to prevent an English court from exercising enforcement jurisdiction in relation to assets located in a non-member country.[111]

---

[106]   Case 220/84, [1985] ECR 2267.
[107]   [2004] 1 AC 300.
[108]   [2008] 2 All ER (Comm) 1099 (CA).
[109]   Case C-391/95, [1998] ECR I-7091.
[110]   Case C-261/90, [1992] ECR I-2149.
[111]   See at paras 125–7.

# 7. Submission

## INTRODUCTION

Section 7 (Articles 23–4) of Chapter II of the Brussels I Regulation provides for jurisdiction based on submission (or prorogation) by the parties involved. Article 23 deals with submission by agreement, and Article 24 with submission by appearance. Articles 23 and 24 derogate from the ordinary rules on jurisdiction laid down by Articles 2–7. But agreements on jurisdiction in respect of insurance, consumer or employment contracts are subject to restrictions imposed by Articles 13–14, 17 and 21, and submission (whether by agreement or appearance) is excluded in respect of matters for which Article 22 imposes exclusive jurisdiction by virtue of subject-matter. Like the other provisions of Chapter II, Articles 23 and 24 give way to conflicting provisions of existing specialised conventions in accordance with Article 71.[1]

As regards submission by agreement, Article 23 of the Brussels I Regulation will eventually be supplemented by a Convention on Choice of Court Agreements, which was adopted at the Hague Conference on Private International Law on 30th June 2005, and which may conveniently be referred to as the Hague Convention 2005. Pursuant to EC Council Decision 2009/397,[2] the Convention was signed on behalf of the European Community on 1st April 2009, but a further Council decision on the acceptance or approval of the Convention will be necessary before the Convention becomes binding on and enters into force for the European Union. When the Convention has entered into force for the Union, the rules on direct jurisdiction specified by Chapter II of the Convention will override the rules specified by Chapter II of the Brussels I Regulation in cases where there is an exclusive choice of court agreement which designates a court or courts of a country which is a Contracting State to the Convention (whether or not it is an EU Member State), and at least one of the parties to which is resident in a country which is a Contracting State to the Convention and is not an EU Member State.[3]

## SUBMISSION BY AGREEMENT

### Introduction

Article 23 of the Brussels I Regulation authorises parties to existing or potential disputes to

---

[1]   See *The Bergen* [1997] 1 Lloyd's Rep 380, where Clarke J held that Article 23 conflicts with and thus gives way to Article 7 of the Convention of 10th May 1952 on the Arrest of Seagoing Ships, which enables jurisdiction to be founded on the arrest of a vessel.

[2]   [2009] OJ L133/1.

[3]   The Hague Convention 2005 is examined at pp. 181–6 below.

enter into agreements designating the court or courts which will be competent to determine such disputes.[4] Such agreements are generally referred to as jurisdiction clauses. Article 23 is a complex provision, which regulates both the formal and essential validity of jurisdiction clauses and their effects. In general, it gives exclusive effect to a valid jurisdiction clause.

Article 23 provides:

(1) If the parties, one or more of whom is domiciled in a Member State, have agreed that a court or the courts of a Member State are to have jurisdiction to settle any disputes which have arisen or which may arise in connection with a particular legal relationship, that court or those courts shall have jurisdiction. Such jurisdiction shall be exclusive unless the parties have agreed otherwise. Such an agreement conferring jurisdiction shall be either:

(a) in writing or evidenced in writing; or
(b) in a form which accords with practices which the parties have established between themselves; or
(c) in international trade or commerce, in a form which accords with a usage of which the parties are or ought to have been aware and which in such trade or commerce is widely known to, and regularly observed by, parties to contracts of the type involved in the particular trade or commerce concerned.

(2) Any communication by electronic means which provides a durable record of the agreement shall be equivalent to 'writing'.
(3) Where such an agreement is concluded by parties, none of whom is domiciled in a Member State, the courts of other Member States shall have no jurisdiction over their disputes unless the court or courts chosen have declined jurisdiction.
(4) The court or courts of a Member State on which a trust instrument has conferred jurisdiction shall have exclusive jurisdiction in any proceedings brought against a settlor, trustee or beneficiary, if relations between these persons or their rights or obligations under the trust are involved.
(5) Agreements or provisions of a trust instrument conferring jurisdiction shall have no legal force if they are contrary to Articles 13, 17 or 21, or if the courts whose jurisdiction they purport to exclude have exclusive jurisdiction by virtue of Article 22.

## Formal Validity

As regards formal validity, Article 23(1) of the Brussels I Regulation makes it sufficient for a jurisdiction clause to satisfy any of four alternative requirements. The agreement may be concluded in writing; or evidenced in writing; or concluded in a form which accords with bilaterally established practices (practices which the parties have established between themselves); or concluded, in international trade or commerce, in a form which accords with a general commercial usage (a usage of which the parties are or ought to have been aware and which, in the relevant branch of international trade or commerce is widely known to, and regularly observed by, parties to contracts of the type involved in the particular trade or commerce concerned).

---

[4]    Articles 23 of the Regulation replaces Article 17 of the Brussels Convention. Article 23(1) provides an amended version of Article 17(1). Article 23(2) contains a new provision on electronic communications. Article 23(3)–(4) corresponds to Article 17(2)–(3). Article 23(5) corresponds to Article 17(4) and (6). The former Article 17(5) is eliminated. Article 17 of the Lugano Convention 1988 differs in substance from the 1989/96 version of the Brussels Convention only in a minor aspect of the last paragraph, dealing with employment contracts; as to this, see p. 142 above.

The first two alternatives (on agreements made or evidenced in writing) date from the original version of the Brussels Convention. The third alternative (on bilaterally established practices) was added by the 1989 Convention. The fourth alternative (on general commercial usages) was introduced by the 1978 Convention and clarified by the 1989 Convention. The only change made by the Regulation to the formal requirements is found in Article 23(2), which specifies that any communication by electronic means which provides a durable record of an agreement on jurisdiction is equivalent to writing.

**Agreements concluded in writing**
As regards the first alternative requirement, relating to an agreement concluded in writing,[5] the European Court ruled in *Estasis Salotti v RÜWA*[6] that it is sufficient to satisfy this requirement that a contract signed by both parties incorporates by express reference another document (such as the standard terms used by one of the parties) which contains a jurisdiction clause; and in *7E Communications v Vertex Antennentechnik*,[7] the English Court of Appeal recognised that the same applies where the contract is concluded by means of a written offer, signed by the offeror, which incorporates by express reference standard terms which include the jurisdiction clause, followed by a written acceptance, signed by the offeree. In *Estasis Salotti*, the European Court also ruled that a chain of express references is acceptable; for example, from the contract itself to an earlier written offer, and thence to a standard form. But it insisted that the reference, or in the case of a chain all the references, must be express, and also that reasonable steps must have been taken by the party relying on the jurisdiction clause to bring it to the knowledge of the other party (for example, by sending him a copy of the document containing it at a suitable time prior to the signature of the contract), unless it can reasonably be assumed that he is already familiar with it (as where the document incorporated contains standard terms recommended by a trade association to which both parties belong).[8]

It is thought that the European Court's ruling in *Estasis Salotti v RÜWA* was misunderstood by the English Court of Appeal in *Credit Suisse Financial Products v SGE*[9] and *7E Communications v Vertex Antennentechnik*,[10] where it held that the requirement of reasonable steps to notify is confined to cases where there is a chain of references. On the other hand, the ruling in *Estasis Salotti* probably justifies the decision of Symons QC in *Lafi v*

---

[5]   For a case where it was alleged that an agreement in writing had been concluded, but the document had subsequently been lost, see *Thomas Cook v Hotel Kaya* [2009] EWHC 720 (QB) (Tugendhat J).
[6]   Case 24/76, [1976] ECR 1831. See also *Standard Steamship Owners' Protection and Indemnity Association (Bermuda) Ltd v GIE Vision Bail* [2004] EWHC 2919 (Cooke J).
[7]   [2007] 2 All ER (Comm) 798 (CA).
[8]   See also *SOFRESA v LNT*, 9th July 1991 (French Court of Cassation), where a delivery note unsuccessfully attempted to incorporate the terms of a subsequently issued bill of lading; and *Stork Colorproofing v Ofmag*, 23rd February 1994 (French Court of Cassation), where failure to communicate the standard form containing the jurisdiction clause rendered a chain of express references ineffective.
See also *Stryker Corp v Sulzer Metco* [2006] IEHC 60, where a buyer had simultaneously sent conflicting offers, one by fax and the other by letter. The fax but not the letter incorporated the seller's standard terms, which included a jurisdiction clause. It is difficult to see any justification for the decision of O'Neill J, allowing the buyer to take advantage of the ambiguity and disregard the jurisdiction clause.
[9]   [1997] ILPr 165.
[10]  [2007] 2 All ER (Comm) 798.

*Meriden*[11] that, where the contract resulted from the acceptance of an order sent by one party to the other, and the sender's standard terms (including a jurisdiction clause) were printed on the back of the order, the objection that there was no reference on the face of the order to the terms printed on the back could not be raised by the party who had itself sent the order with the intention of incorporating its own standard terms as printed on the back.

In any event, general words of incorporation may be construed as not extending to a jurisdiction (or arbitration) clause contained in the document referred to, especially where that document is a related contract between different parties. In particular, general words in a reinsurance contract incorporating the terms of the primary insurance contract,[12] or general words in an excess reinsurance contract incorporating the terms of a primary reinsurance contract,[13] or general words in a bill of lading incorporating the terms of a charterparty,[14] will not be construed as extending to a jurisdiction clause. Somewhat similarly, where in a distribution agreement a clause providing for a mechanical guarantee of the product refers to a standard form, which includes a jurisdiction clause, the reference may be interpreted as incorporating the jurisdiction clause only in relation to claims relating to the mechanical guarantee of the product.[15]

### Agreements evidenced in writing

A series of decisions of the European Court[16] have addressed the situation where there is no agreement in writing, signed by both parties, but one of them has issued to the other a document purporting to confirm the conclusion of an oral contract and specifying its alleged terms, which include a jurisdiction clause, and the recipient has failed to object to the confirmatory document within a reasonable time after receiving it. The Court has laid down a general rule that in such circumstances, for the jurisdiction clause to satisfy the second alternative requirement under Article 23, relating to an agreement evidenced in writing, it must be established that an oral contract was indeed concluded and that it explicitly included the jurisdiction clause itself.[17] The requirement of an agreement evidenced in writing is not satisfied where the oral agreement merely incorporated by reference a document which contained the jurisdiction clause.[18]

But the Court has recognised two exceptional situations in which the issue and receipt without objection of a confirmatory document which includes a jurisdiction clause will satisfy the requirement of an agreement evidenced in writing, despite the fact that the oral agreement did not explicitly refer to jurisdiction. The first is where the oral agreement was

---

[11]  [2000] 2 Lloyd's Rep 51.
[12]  See *AIG Group v The Ethniki* [2000] 2 All ER 566 (CA), affirming [1998] 4 All ER 301 (Colman J); and *AIG v QBE* [2001] 2 Lloyd's Rep 268 (Moore-Bick J).
[13]  See *Dornoch Ltd v Mauritius Union Assurance Co Ltd* [2006] 2 Lloyd's Rep 475 (CA).
[14]  See *Siboti v BP France* [2003] 2 Lloyd's Rep 364 (Gross J).
[15]  See *Nestorway v Ambaflex* [2006] IEHC 235 (Clarke J).
[16]  See Case 25/76: *Segoura v Bonakdarian* [1976] ECR 1851; Case 71/83: *Tilly Russ v Haven* [1984] ECR 2417; Case 221/84: *Berghoefer v ASA* [1985] ECR 2699; Case 313/85: *Iveco Fiat v Van Hool* [1986] ECR 3337; and Case C-106/95: *MSG v Les Gravières Rhénanes* [1997] ECR I-911.
[17]  See Case 71/83: *Tilly Russ v Haven* [1984] ECR 2417, and Case 221/84: *Berghoefer v ASA* [1985] ECR 2699. See also *Bols Distilleries v Superior Yacht Services* [2007] 1 Lloyd's Rep 683 (PC), and *Rolf Barkmann GmbH v Innova House Ltd* [2008] Scot (D) 12/9 (Sheriff Pyle).
[18]  See Case 25/76: *Segoura v Bonakdarian* [1976] ECR 1851.

entered into within the framework of a continuing trading relationship between the parties which was based on a set of standard terms which include the jurisdiction clause.[19] This situation is now likely to be resolved primarily by reference to the third alternative requirement, relating to bilaterally established practices. The second situation is where a written agreement containing the jurisdiction clause has expired but has been tacitly renewed by conduct.[20]

In any event, the decision of the European Court in *MSG v Les Gravières Rhénanes*[21] has established that a confirmatory document which does not satisfy the second alternative requirement, relating to an agreement evidenced in writing, may now be effective under the fourth alternative requirement, relating to general commercial usages.

### Bilaterally established practices

The third alternative (on bilaterally established practices) was added by the 1989 Convention. It refers to an agreement on jurisdiction which is concluded in a form which accords with practices which the parties have established between themselves. The effect is to make explicit and independent a concept which the European Court had previously used in interpreting the requirement of writing in the context of confirmatory documents which were received without objection. The Court had accepted that such a document could evidence in writing an oral agreement which had not explicitly referred to jurisdiction if the oral agreement had been entered into within the framework of a continuing trading relationship between the parties which was based on a set of standard terms which included the jurisdiction clause.[22]

The third alternative requirement, relating to bilaterally established practices, does not in principle require any writing at all. Moreover, the concept of a bilaterally established practice must be interpreted autonomously and applied directly to the facts, without reference to any particular national law.[23] But standard terms previously used by the parties in their mutual dealings will not apply if the negotiations leading to the agreement at issue clearly indicate a contrary intention;[24] and an old practice will not remain operative where there has been a substantial interruption in the business between the parties, and on the resumption new documents are used.[25] To satisfy the requirement, the course of dealing must be such as to have put the counterparty fairly and reasonably on notice that the contract would contain the jurisdiction clause contended for.[26]

---

[19]   See Case 25/76: *Segoura v Bonakdarian* [1976] ECR 1851, and Case 71/83: *Tilly Russ v Haven* [1984] ECR 2417. Cf. *Lejeune v FAIS*, 12th December 1989 (French Court of Cassation).

[20]   See Case 313/85: *Iveco Fiat v Van Hool* [1986] ECR 3337.

[21]   Case C-106/95, [1997] ECR I-911.

[22]   See Case 25/76: *Segoura v Bonakdarian* [1976] ECR 1851, and Case 71/83: *Tilly Russ v Haven* [1984] ECR 2417.

[23]   See *The Kribi* [2001] 1 Lloyd's Rep 76 (Aikens J); and *Knauf v British Gypsum* [2001] 2 All ER (Comm) 332 (David Steel J), reversed on other grounds [2002] 1 WLR 907 (CA).

[24]   See *HDW v CNAN*, 10th January 1990 (French Court of Cassation).

[25]   See *Knauf v British Gypsum* [2001] 2 All ER (Comm) 332 (David Steel J), reversed on other grounds, [2002] 1 WLR 907 (CA). See also, as to a change from one standard form to another, *Thomas Cook v Hotel Kaya* [2009] EWHC 720 (QB) (Tugendhat J).

[26]   See *Calyon v Wytwornia Sprzetu Komunikacynego PZL Swidnik* [2009] EWHC 1914 (Comm) (Field J).

## General commercial usages

The fourth alternative refers to an agreement on jurisdiction concluded, in international trade or commerce, in a form which accords with a usage of which the parties are or ought to have been aware and which in such trade or commerce is widely known to, and regularly observed by, parties to contracts of the type involved in the particular trade or commerce concerned. This provision has received a wide interpretation from the European Court in *MSG v Les Gravières Rhénanes*[27] and *Castelletti v Trumpy*.[28]

In *MSG*, the European Court made clear that the provision is capable of applying to a situation where one of the parties to the contract did not react or remained silent in the face of a commercial letter of confirmation from the other party containing a pre-printed jurisdiction clause, or where one of the parties repeatedly paid without objection invoices issued by the other party containing such a clause. Similarly, in *Castelletti*, the Court indicated that the provision is capable of applying to a situation where a jurisdiction clause is included among the clauses printed on the back of a bill of lading, the front of which has been signed by the parties, but without such signatures constituting an agreement in writing to the clauses printed on the back. In both cases, the Court emphasised that compliance with a relevant usage will establish the existence of an agreement on jurisdiction, as well as its formal validity.

In *MSG* and *Castelletti*, the European Court also recognised that the concept of international trade or commerce has a wide scope. It includes a contract concluded between two companies established in different Member States for the carriage of goods by river; as in *MSG*, which involved a time-charterparty of a vessel by a German company to a French company for carriage of gravel on the Rhine, mainly between French locations. It also includes a contract for the carriage of goods by sea between different States, not necessarily Member States; as in *Castelletti*, which involved a bill of lading contract for the carriage of goods from Argentina to Italy. Similarly, as Cooke J held in *Standard Steamship Owners' Protection and Indemnity Association (Bermuda) Ltd v GIE Vision Bail*,[29] it extends to maritime insurance, including employer's liability insurance in respect of claims by persons employed on board a ship.

In *MSG* and *Castelletti*, the European Court also emphasised that the crucial issue relates to the existence of a usage, and this must be determined, not by reference to the law of a Member State, nor in relation to international trade or commerce in general, but under a Community standard and in relation to the branch of international trade or commerce in which the parties to the contract operate. Such a usage exists where a certain course of conduct is generally and regularly followed by operators in the relevant branch when concluding contracts of a particular type. The relevant branch must be identified in terms of both substance and location; for, as the Court emphasised in *Castelletti*, the course of conduct need not be established in specific countries (such as that of the court seised), nor in all the Member States.[30] Moreover, a specific

---

[27]  Case C-106/95, [1997] ECR I-911.
[28]  Case C-159/97, [1999] ECR I-1597.
[29]  [2004] EWHC 2919 (Comm).
[30]  See also per Tesauro AG in *MSG*, and per Lenz AG in Case C-288/92: *Custom Made v Stawa* [1994] ECR I-2913; and the finding of Aikens J in *The Kribi* [2001] 1 Lloyd's Rep 76, that the jurisdiction clause involved was in a form widely known to and regularly observed by parties to bill of lading contracts of carriage in international liner services, including liner services between Europe and West Africa.

form of publicity (such as may be given by trade associations to their standard forms) cannot be required; and (perhaps surprisingly) it is not fatal that the validity of the jurisdiction clause has been challenged by the bringing of numerous actions before courts other than those designated.

Finally, the European Court has effectively eliminated any separate requirement of actual or presumptive awareness of the usage, by ruling in these cases that awareness will be established whenever, in the branch of trade or commerce in which the parties operate, a particular course of conduct is generally and regularly followed in the conclusion of a particular type of contract, so that it may be regarded as an established usage.

### Corporate constitutions

The effectiveness between a company and its shareholders of a jurisdiction clause contained in the corporate constitution (in English terms, the memorandum and articles of association) was considered by the European Court in *Powell Duffryn v Petereit*,[31] which involved an action by a corporate liquidator against a shareholder claiming payment for shares subscribed for and repayment of dividends wrongly paid. The Court ruled that for the purposes of the Brussels I Regulation, a company's constitution must be regarded as a contract covering both the relations between the shareholders themselves and also their relations with the company. Thus a clause contained in a corporate constitution, and adopted in accordance with the provisions of the applicable national law and of that constitution itself, conferring jurisdiction on a court of a Member State to settle disputes between the company and its shareholders, constitutes an agreement on jurisdiction within the meaning of Article 23.

The Court further ruled that the formal requirements laid down in Article 23 are satisfied in regard to any shareholder if the jurisdiction clause is contained in the corporate constitution, and that constitution is lodged in a place to which the shareholder may have access (such as the registered office of the company) or contained in a public register. It is not clear whether the Court considered that the jurisdiction clause was agreed on in writing, so as to satisfy the first alternative requirement, or in accordance with a general commercial usage, so as to satisfy the fourth alternative. It added that the requirement of Article 23 that a jurisdiction clause must be limited to disputes connected with a particular legal relationship is satisfied if a jurisdiction clause contained in a corporate constitution applies to disputes between the company and its shareholders as such.

### Third parties

In general, an agreement on jurisdiction operates only between the parties thereto, and accordingly a jurisdiction clause contained in a substantive contract only binds the parties to that contract.[32] But the European Court has recognised two exceptions. The first exception applies where a substantive contract (for example, of insurance) is concluded wholly or partly for the benefit of a third party, and it contains a jurisdiction clause which is also designed to

---

[31]   Case C-214/89, [1992] ECR I-1745.

[32]   See *Stadtwerke Essen v Trailigaz* [1988] ECC 291, where the Paris Court of Appeal held that a jurisdiction clause contained in a construction contract was not binding on a sub-contractor; and *Knorr-Bremse v Haldex* [2008] 2 All ER (Comm) 448, where Lewison J held that a jurisdiction clause contained in a written agreement settling a dispute was binding only on the persons named as parties in the written agreement, and not on a subsidiary company owned by one of the named parties.

benefit the third party and which is validly agreed to by the contracting parties in accordance with Article 23. In such a case, the third party may take advantage of the clause, even though he himself has not agreed to it in a manner contemplated by Article 23.[33]

Under the second exception, a jurisdiction clause which was contained in a substantive contract and was validly agreed to by the original contracting parties also operates in favour of and against a third person who, under the national law applicable under the conflict rules of the court seised, has succeeded to the rights and obligations of one of the parties under the contract (such as a subsequent holder of a bill of lading).[34] Under English conflict rules, succession to a bill of lading contract is governed by the proper law of the contract.[35] Probably, as the English courts have ruled, it is sufficient that the third party succeeds to the rights (and not also the obligations) of one of the original parties under the contract. Thus an assignee of a contractual debt will be bound by and entitled under a jurisdiction clause which is contained in the contract from which the debt arises and was agreed between the original parties in accordance with the requirements of Article 23;[36] and as against a carrier under a bill of lading contract, a cargo insurer will be in the same position as its insured.[37]

### No additional requirements

In *Elefanten Schuh v Jacqmain*,[38] the European Court ruled that the formal requirements specified by Article 23 are exhaustive. Thus it is not open to a Member State to require additional formalities, such as that a jurisdiction clause must be expressed in a particular language. This approach was confirmed in *Castelletti v Trumpy*,[39] where the European Court ruled that, in the context of the provision on general commercial usages, the acceptability of the language used (in the instant case, the English language for a bill of lading between an Argentinian shipper and a Danish shipowner in respect of the carriage of goods from Argentina to Italy) depends on whether its use accords with such usages.

---

[33]  See Case 201/82: *Gerling v Treasury Administration* [1983] ECR 2503; and per Léger AG in Case C-159/97: *Castelletti v Trumpy* [1999] ECR I-1597. See also Gaudemet-Tallon, at para 141, agreeing that the principle is not confined to insurance contracts.

[34]  See Case 71/83: *Tilly Russ v Haven* [1984] ECR 2417; Case C-159/97: *Castelletti v Trumpy* [1999] ECR I-1597; and Case C-387/98: *Coreck Maritime v Handelsveem* [2000] ECR I-9337. Cf. *Dresser v Falcongate* [1992] QB 502, where the English Court of Appeal held that a jurisdiction clause contained in a bill of lading could not be binding between a bailor and a sub-bailee, because their mutual relationship was not contractual, but rather a consensual 'bailment on terms'.

[35]  See *The Kribi* [2001] 1 Lloyd's Rep 76 (Aikens J).

It seems that French law does not regard a subsequent holder of a bill of lading, such as a consignee, as succeeding to the rights and obligations of the shipper thereunder. See the decisions of the Court of Cassation in *Meijer v Ethel*, 26th May 1992; *GIE v Plate & Ruys*, 10th January 1995; and *Adriatica v Westfield*, 4th April 1995. See also *SBCN v MB Marine*, 18th October 1994, where the Court of Cassation followed the European Court's ruling in Case C-26/91: *Handte v TMCS* [1992] ECR I-3967, that the relationship between a manufacturer and a sub-purchaser of goods is not contractual for the purposes of the Regulation, and therefore held that a jurisdiction clause contained in a contract of sale between a manufacturer and an initial purchaser is not binding on a sub-purchaser.

[36]  See *Firswood v Petra Bank*, 13th December 1995 (English CA); *Glencore v Metro* [1999] 2 Lloyd's Rep 632 (Moore-Bick J); and *Bank of Tokyo-Mitsubishi v Baskan Gida* [2004] ILPr 26 (Lawrence Collins J), at para 191.

[37]  See *The Kribi* [2001] 1 Lloyd's Rep 76 (Aikens J).

[38]  Case 150/80, [1981] ECR 1671.

[39]  Case C-159/97, [1999] ECR I-1597.

Presumably, however, if a party abusively chose to use a language which he knew the other would not understand, there would be no 'agreement', under an independent Community standard, within the meaning of Article 23.[40] Somewhat similarly, the French Court of Cassation has ruled a jurisdiction clause invalid under Article 23 because it was printed in characters so small as to be unreadable.[41]

### Luxembourg domiciliaries

Until recently, a limited measure of special protection was given to persons domiciled in Luxembourg by Article 63 of the Brussels I Regulation. Where the final place of delivery of goods, or of provision of non-financial services, was in Luxembourg, an agreement on jurisdiction had to be accepted or evidenced in writing satisfying Article 23(1)(a). This exception expired on 1st March 2008, and no corresponding provision is included in the Lugano Convention 2007.

Article 63 of the Brussels I Regulation had replaced Article I(2) of the Protocol annexed to the Brussels Convention, which specified that an agreement conferring jurisdiction, within the meaning of Article 17 of the Convention, was valid with respect to a person domiciled in Luxembourg only if that person had expressly and specifically so agreed. As construed by the European Court in *Porta-Leasing v Prestige*,[42] this required that the provision on jurisdiction should be contained in a clause which was exclusively devoted to jurisdiction, and that the Luxembourg domiciliary should have specifically signed that clause. His signature of the whole contract, which contained the jurisdiction clause, was not sufficient, though it was not necessary for the jurisdiction clause to be contained in a separate document from the contract to which it related. A provision corresponding to Article I(2) of the Protocol annexed to the Brussels Convention is made by Article I(2) of the First Protocol annexed to the Lugano Convention 1988.

### Essential Validity

Even where a jurisdiction clause satisfies the formal requirements specified in Article 23(1), it may lack essential validity because of its excessive scope, or its subject-matter, or because of defective consent.

### Permissible scope

As regards the permissible scope of a jurisdiction clause, Article 23(1) authorises an agreement relating to 'any disputes which have arisen or which may arise in connection with a particular legal relationship'. Thus it is clear that a jurisdiction clause may cover potential as well as existing disputes, and that the disputes need not relate to contractual (as distinct from delictual, proprietary or even familial support) claims.[43]

---

40    See per Lenz AG in Case C-288/92: *Custom Made v Stawa* [1994] ECR I-2913; and Gaudemet-Tallon, at para 124.

41    See *Pavan v Richard*, 27th February 1996.

42    Case 784/79, [1980] ECR 1517.

43    See also *Maimann v Maimann* [2001] EWCA Civ 1132 (CA), which involved a jurisdiction clause relating to a power of attorney.

In *Powell Duffryn v Petereit*,[44] the European Court ruled that the relationship between a company and its shareholders as such is sufficiently particular for this purpose. But in general, by analogy with Articles 6(3) and 28(3), the reference to disputes arising from a particular legal relationship should probably be construed as limiting the permissible scope of a jurisdiction clause to a particular transaction or incident. Accordingly, it will be permissible for a contract to contain a jurisdiction clause referring to 'any dispute arising from or in connection with this contract or anything done in connection with its negotiation, conclusion, performance, non-performance or purported performance, and whether the claim is based on a contractual obligation or otherwise on the law of contract or on the law of tort or restitution'.[45] It will also be permissible for drivers whose vehicles have collided to make an agreement on jurisdiction over 'all claims between us arising from the collision'. But it is less clear whether a long-term exclusive-distribution agreement could validly include a jurisdiction clause extending to disputes relating exclusively to an individual sale contract entered into in pursuance of the umbrella agreement.[46]

**Excluded subject-matter**

As regards subject-matter, an agreement on jurisdiction is invalidated by Article 23(5) if it contravenes the restrictions imposed by Articles 13, 17 or 21 in relation to insurance, consumer or employment contracts,[47] or if the courts whose jurisdiction it purports to exclude have exclusive jurisdiction on account of subject-matter by virtue of Article 22.[48] In the case of insurance, consumer and employment contracts, Articles 13(1), 17(1) and 21(1) ensure that it is only agreements on jurisdiction which were entered into before the dispute arose which may be invalidated. But in the case of exclusive jurisdiction on account of subject-matter under Article 22, the invalidation extends to agreements on jurisdiction which are entered into after the dispute has arisen. It is, however, left to the law of a Member State on which Article 22 confers exclusive jurisdiction to regulate the permissibility of a jurisdiction clause which varies the normal allocation of such jurisdiction between its own courts.[49] It is also permissible for the law of a Member State whose courts are chosen by a jurisdiction clause to respect the reflexive effect of Article 22 by requiring or permitting its courts to decline jurisdiction where the subject-matter of the dispute falls within Article 22 but the connection referred to therein is with a non-member State; for example, a clause choosing an English court for disputes concerning proprietary rights in land situated in New York.[50]

---

[44]  Case C-214/89, [1992] ECR I-1745.

[45]  See *Bank of Scotland v Banque Nationale de Paris* [1996] SLT 103 (Lord Penrose). See also *The Sennar* [1985] 1 WLR 490 (HL); and *ISI v CPAV*, 25th January 1983 (French Court of Cassation).

[46]  Cf. *Gotz v Noge*, 27th February 1996, where the French Court of Cassation ruled that, as a matter of interpretation, a clause contained in one party's standard terms of sale, which had been incorporated by express reference into an exclusive distribution contract, did not apply to the exclusivity obligation itself. See also *Hacker Kuchen v Bosma* [1993] ECC 55, where the Dutch Supreme Court held that a jurisdiction clause contained in individual sale contracts did not apply to disputes relating to the exclusive distribution contract pursuant to which the individual sales were effected.

[47]  See Chapter 5 above.

[48]  See Chapter 6 above.

[49]  For the position in the United Kingdom, see rules 4, 11 and 12(3) of Schedule 4 to the Civil Jurisdiction and Judgments Act 1982, as amended by the Civil Jurisdiction and Judgments Order 2001 (SI 3929/2001).

[50]  See Gaudemet-Tallon, at para 129; and pp. 58–61 above.

In *Sanicentral v Collin*,[51] the European Court made it clear that the Regulation prevents a Member State from imposing additional restrictions relating to the subject-matter in respect of which a jurisdiction clause is permitted. For example, by refusing, before the introduction by the 1989 version of the Brussels Convention of provisions restricting the validity of jurisdiction clauses in relation to employment, to recognise a jurisdiction clause contained in a contract of employment. The Court also ruled in *Sanicentral* that, as regards time, a jurisdiction clause which fulfils the requirements of Article 23 is effective if the action is instituted after the entry into force of the Regulation for the Member State whose court is seised, even if the clause was contained in a contract which was made and broken before that date, and even if the national law previously in force there did not permit jurisdiction clauses in respect of contracts of the relevant type. No doubt the same principle applies negatively, so that a jurisdiction clause contained in a contract of employment made before the entry into force of the Regulation for the forum State is invalidated by Article 23(5) in relation to actions instituted after that date.

**Acceptable choice**

In *Castelletti v Trumpy*,[52] the European Court made clear that Article 23 does not require any objective connection between the parties or the subject-matter of the dispute and the territory of the court chosen. On the contrary Article 23 permits parties to choose a 'neutral' forum. Thus, in that case, it was acceptable to choose an English court by a jurisdiction clause contained in a bill of lading for the carriage of goods by a Danish shipowner from Argentina to Italy. The Court also emphasised that it is not open to a court excluded by the clause to disregard it on the ground that the chosen court would apply different substantive rules in determining the merits of the dispute from those which would have been applied by the court excluded.

It seems clear that Article 23 applies even if, at the date of the agreement on jurisdiction, the relevant relationship was otherwise connected exclusively with a single Member State. A contrary (but, it is thought, always very weak) argument that in such a case the validity of a jurisdiction clause would be governed not by Article 23, but by the law of the otherwise connected State, formerly relied on the reference to 'international jurisdiction' in the Preamble to the Brussels Convention.[53] But now Recital 14 to the Regulation refers broadly to the need to respect the autonomy of the contracting parties. Thus a clause choosing a particular Italian court, contained in a contract of sale of a component between Italian companies, will operate under Article 23 to exclude English jurisdiction under Article 6(2) over a third-party claim between them made in the context of a main action brought by an English purchaser of a machine into which the component had been incorporated.[54] Similarly, Article 23 extends to a clause selecting 'a court of competent jurisdiction in London' for disputes relating to a contract between English parties which has no connection with any other country.[55]

---

[51]    Case 25/79, [1979] ECR 3423.
[52]    Case C-159/97, [1999] ECR I-1597. See also Case 56/79: *Zelger v Salinitri (No 1)* [1980] ECR 89.
[53]    See Gaudemet-Tallon, at paras 113–15.
[54]    See *British Sugar v Babbini* [2005] 1 All ER (Comm) 55 (Judge Seymour QC). See also *Provimi v Aventis* [2003] EWHC 961 (Aikens J).
[55]    See *Snooks v Jani-King* [2006] All ER (D) 325 (Feb) (Silber J).

As the European Court made clear in *Coreck Maritime v Handelsveem*,[56] Article 23 does not require that a jurisdiction clause should designate directly the location of the competent court (as by specifying 'the English High Court' or 'the Paris Commercial Court'). It is sufficient that the clause specifies the competent court or courts by reference to objective factors which are sufficiently precise to permit judicial application, even if they are dependent on the particular circumstances of the case. Thus it was permissible to choose, in a bill of lading contract, the courts of 'the country where the carrier has his principal place of business'. It has even been held by Silber J that a choice of 'a court of competent jurisdiction in London' is effective under Article 23 to prevent the commencement of proceedings in the Swansea District Registry of the English High Court.[57]

### Defective consent

Any agreement, including a jurisdiction clause, may be invalid by reason of lack of consent, owing to such factors as fraud, mistake or improper pressure. Despite the European Court's rulings in *MSG v Les Gravières Rhénanes*[58] and *Castelletti v Trumpy*[59] that compliance with a relevant general commercial usage establishes the existence of an agreement on jurisdiction, as well as its formal validity,[60] it seems clear that it remains possible, even in such cases, for a jurisdiction clause to be rendered invalid by reason of fraud, mistake or improper pressure.

In *Benincasa v Dentalkit*,[61] the European Court ruled that, for reasons of legal certainty, even where a jurisdiction clause is contained in a substantive contract, its validity must be distinguished from that of the substantive contract. Thus the operation of a jurisdiction clause cannot be affected by allegations that the substantive contract containing it is invalid, even for lack of consent, under the national law applicable under the conflict rules of the court seised.[62] Accordingly, in *Ryanair Ltd v Bravofly*,[63] Clarke J held that a defendant is entitled to invoke a jurisdiction clause contained in the alleged contract on which the plaintiff's claim is based, even if the defendant denies the existence or validity of the alleged contract.

But the ruling in *Benincasa* leaves open the situation where it is alleged that there is lack of consent to the jurisdiction clause itself, by reason of fraud, error or pressure relating specifically to that clause.[64] This would be the case where the clause refers to the court for the place where one party's head office is located, and that party misleads the other about such location.

---

56  Case C-387/98, [2000] ECR I-9337.
57  See *Snooks v Jani-King* [2006] All ER (D) 325 (Feb).
58  Case C-106/95, [1997] ECR I-911.
59  Case C-159/97, [1999] ECR I-1597.
60  See also *Deutsche Bank v Asia Pacific Broadband Wireless Communications* [2009] 2 All ER (Comm) 129 (CA), at para 30, where Longmore LJ considered more generally that, if any of the formal requirements specified by Article 17 is satisfied (for example, where the jurisdiction clause is in writing), that will be enough to ensure that the necessary consensus is established in respect of the jurisdiction clause.
61  Case C-269/95, [1997] ECR I-3767.
62  See also, in the context of arbitration clauses, *Westacre Investments v Jugoimport* [1998] 4 All ER 570 (Colman J), affirmed [2000] 1 QB 288 (CA). See also *Morgan v Primacom* [2005] EWHC 508 (Cooke J).
63  [2009] IEHC 41.
64  See *Deutsche Bank v Asia Pacific Broadband Wireless Communications* [2008] 2 Lloyd's Rep 619 (CA); and *Maple Leaf v Rouvroy* [2009] EWHC 257 (Comm) (Andrew Smith J).

In such a case, the analogy of the European Court's ruling in *Tessili v Dunlop*,[65] on the determination of the place of performance of a contractual obligation under Article 5(1), suggests that the issue should be governed by the law applicable under the conflict rules of the court seised.[66]

## Interpretation

In *UBS v HSH Nordbank*,[67] the English Court of Appeal explained that, although in general jurisdiction clauses should be given a wide interpretation, so as to include (for example) claims arising from pre-inception matters such as misrepresentation, a jurisdiction clause must be construed in the light of the transaction as a whole and by reference to the presumed intention of sensible business people. Thus where a transaction involves several related contracts between the same parties, and the various contracts contain inconsistent jurisdiction clauses, a claim that the transaction as a whole was induced by misrepresentation must be regarded as intended to fall with the jurisdiction clause contained in the agreement which is at the commercial centre of the transaction.

The problem of differing jurisdiction clauses contained in various contracts between the same parties was also addressed in *Deutsche Bank v Sebastian Holdings*,[68] where Walker J held that differing jurisdiction clauses contained in earlier contracts did not clash with each other because of their non-exclusive character, and that an exclusive jurisdiction clause contained in later agreements which introduced new and extended arrangements prevailed over the non-exclusive jurisdiction clauses contained in the earlier contracts. But, as Beatson J ruled in *ACP Capital v IFR Capital*,[69] where related contracts between the same parties of different types (such as an advisory agreement and a loan agreement) contain different jurisdiction clauses, claims under each contract will be subject to the jurisdiction clause contained in that contract. In any event, as the Court of Appeal ruled in *AWB Geneva v North America Steamships*,[70] a jurisdiction clause contained in a substantive contract will not normally be applicable to claims based on insolvency law.

## Effects

In general, the effect under Article 23 of a valid agreement on jurisdiction is to confer exclusive jurisdiction on the chosen court or courts. For Article 23(1) specifies that if the parties, one or more of whom is domiciled in a Member State, have agreed that a court or the courts of a Member State are to have jurisdiction to settle any disputes which have arisen or which

---

65    Case 12/76, [1976] ECR 1473; considered at pp. 94–7 above. Jurisdiction clauses are excluded from the scope of the Rome Convention 1980 by Article 1(2)(d), and from the Rome I Regulation by Article 1(2)(e). See p. 292 below.

66    Cf. per Slynn AG in Case 150/80: *Elefanten Schuh v Jacqmain* [1981] ECR 1671, proposing reference to the law of the country whose court is designated by the jurisdiction clause; a view cautiously supported by Gaudemet-Tallon, at para 131.

67    [2009] EWCA Civ 585.

68    [2009] EWHC 2132 (Comm).

69    [2008] EWHC 1627 (Comm).

70    [2007] EWCA Civ 739.

may arise in connection with a particular legal relationship, that court or those courts shall have jurisdiction, and that such jurisdiction shall be exclusive unless the parties have agreed otherwise. Article 23(3) adds that where such an agreement is concluded by parties, none of whom is domiciled in a Member State, the courts of other Member States shall have no jurisdiction over their disputes unless the court or courts chosen have declined jurisdiction.

In *Group Josi v UGIC*,[71] the European Court emphasised that the requirement as to domicile specified by Article 23(1) is satisfied if either the plaintiff or the defendant is domiciled in a Member State, even if the other party is not domiciled in any of the Member States. Although the text of Article 23 is unclear on the point, it is submitted that the normal rule under Article 23(1), giving full effect to a jurisdiction clause, should apply if any of the parties to the agreement on jurisdiction was domiciled in a Member State either at the conclusion of the agreement on jurisdiction, or at the institution of the action in which the agreement is relied on. The limited effect provided for by Article 23(3) should apply only where at neither of those dates was any of the parties to the agreement on jurisdiction domiciled in any of the Member States. Reference to the time of conclusion of the agreement is necessary in order to respect the parties' expectations and achieve legal certainty, while reference to the time of institution of the proceedings accords with the general principles applicable to the existence of jurisdiction adopted by Articles 2–4.[72]

Where a jurisdiction clause has full effect under Article 23(1), because at least one party is domiciled in a Member State, it normally gives rise to exclusive jurisdiction. Thus it has the positive effect of conferring jurisdiction on the chosen court or courts, and the negative effect of excluding the jurisdiction of other courts of the Member States which would otherwise arise from other provisions of the Regulation, such as Articles 2, 5 and 6,[73] or under national law made applicable by Article 4. Moreover, a court whose jurisdiction is excluded by a jurisdiction clause has the same powers as the court chosen by the clause to determine its validity under Article 23,[74] and in England the burden lies on a defendant who relies on a foreign exclusive jurisdiction clause to show a good arguable case for its existence and validity.[75]

There is no doubt that Article 23 has mandatory effect.[76] At one time, the English courts extended their claim to retain a general discretion to decline jurisdiction on grounds of forum non conveniens in favour of a court of a non-member country to cases where there was an English jurisdiction clause, complying with Article 23.[77] But the English courts have now accepted that the European Court's ruling in *Owusu v Jackson*,[78] that the exercise of such a

---

71   Case C-412/98, [2000] ECR I-5925.
72   Cf. Gaudemet-Tallon, at paras 108–09, advocating exclusive reference to the time at which the agreement on jurisdiction was concluded.
73   That Article 23 overrides Article 6(2) on third parties was confirmed by Rix J in *Hough v P & O Containers* [1999] QB 834.
74   See per Léger AG in Case C-159/97: *Castelletti v Trumpy* [1999] ECR I-1597.
75   See *Bank of Tokyo-Mitsubishi v Baskan Gida* [2004] ILPr 26 (Lawrence Collins J), at para 194; and *Hewden Tower Cranes v Wolfkran* [2007] EWHC 857 (TCC) (Jackson J).
76   See *Kitechnology v Unicor* [1995] FSR 765 (CA).
77   See *Eli Lilly v Novo Nordisk* [2000] ILPr 73 (CA); *Mercury Communications v Communication Telesystems International* [1999] 2 All ER (Comm) 33 (Moore-Bick J); and *Sinochem v Mobil* [2000] 1 Lloyd's Rep 670 (Rix J).
78   Case C-281/02, [2005] ECR I-1383.

discretion is incompatible with Article 2 of the Regulation, implies a similar incompatibility with Article 23(1).[79]

The exclusivity provided for by Article 23(1) is explicitly qualified by a proviso: unless the parties have agreed otherwise. This proviso was added by the Regulation, but it reflects a line of decisions by the European Court under the Brussels Convention which emphasised that Article 17 of the Convention was based on the principle of respecting the parties' freedom to choose the competent court or courts.[80] It replaces the former proviso contained in Article 17(5) of the Convention, that if an agreement on jurisdiction was concluded for the benefit of only one of the parties, that party would retain the right to bring proceedings in any other court which had jurisdiction under the Convention.[81]

The new proviso confirms the principles that there is a strong (but not irrebuttable) presumption that parties to an agreement on jurisdiction usually intend exclusive effect, but that where an agreement on jurisdiction indicates clearly that some other effect was intended, the agreement must be respected and given its clearly intended effect.

Thus it remains permissible and effective, as the European Court had accepted in *Meeth v Glacetal*,[82] for parties domiciled in different Member States to agree that actions between them should be brought in the State of the defendant's domicile. The Court added that whether such a clause prevents a defendant, sued at his domicile in accordance with the clause, from invoking in such action a set-off in respect of a related claim depends on the interpretation of the jurisdiction clause. It is perhaps unfortunate that the Court did not explicitly require that an intention by the parties to exclude the raising of a related set-off or counterclaim should be expressed with unmistakable clarity.[83] Conversely, it is permissible and effective for parties to agree that proceedings should be brought at the plaintiff's domicile.[84] Moreover, where a jurisdiction clause indicates clearly that the designated court should have jurisdiction additional to, and not to the exclusion of, that of any court otherwise competent,

---

[79]   See *Equitas v Allstate Insurance* [2009] 1 All ER (Comm) 1137, where Beatson J also emphasised that in such a case very rare and compelling circumstances will be necessary to justify the grant on case-management grounds of a temporary stay until the determination of a proceeding elsewhere. Cf. *Antec International Ltd v Biosafety USA Inc* [2006] All ER (D) 208 (Jan), where Gloster J left open whether the *Owusu* principle extends to cases where English jurisdiction is based on Article 23.

[80]   See Case 23/78, *Meeth v Glacetal* [1978] ECR 2133, and Case 22/85, *Anterist v Crédit Lyonnais* [1986] ECR 1951.

[81]   On Article 17(5) of the Convention, see Case 22/85, *Anterist v Crédit Lyonnais* [1986] ECR 1951, where the European Court ruled that an agreement on jurisdiction could not be regarded as concluded for the benefit of only one of the parties merely because the parties were domiciled in different Contracting States and the agreement chose courts of the State in which that party was domiciled. A common intention to confer an advantage on one of the parties had to be clear from the terms of the jurisdiction clause or the circumstances in which the contract was concluded. See also *Lafi v Meriden* [2000] 2 Lloyd's Rep 51 (Symons QC), where a contract between a Spanish seller and an English buyer contained a clause specifying that 'the seller hereby submits to the non-exclusive jurisdiction of the English courts'.

[82]   Case 23/78, [1978] ECR 2133.

[83]   See also *Glencore Grain v Agros Trading* [1999] 2 Lloyd's Rep 410 (CA), accepting that a claim within the scope of a foreign jurisdiction clause, valid under Article 23, cannot be raised by way of set-off in an English action on an unrelated claim.

[84]   See *Schumacher v Technic-Equipement*, 19th February 1979 (French Court of Cassation).

the agreement must be respected and given its clearly intended non-exclusive effect.[85] But probably an agreement offering a party an unlimited choice of courts in which to sue would not be acceptable.[86]

Where Article 23(3) applies, because no party is domiciled in a Member State, the jurisdiction clause does not necessarily have the positive effect of making the chosen court or courts competent. The chosen courts must determine the existence and exercise of their jurisdiction in accordance with their own law, as provided for by Article 4. Where the English High Court is chosen, it will, in its discretion, accept jurisdiction unless the defendant establishes strong grounds showing that it would be unjust to do so.[87] But the agreement has the immediate negative effect of excluding the jurisdiction of other courts of Member States. This negative effect will cease if the chosen courts decide to decline jurisdiction. No doubt the provision by Article 23(3) for negative effect must be read, like the provision for exclusive effect in Article 23(1), as subject to a contrary intention clearly indicated by the jurisdiction clause.

Article 23 envisages a choice of 'a court or the courts of a Member State'. It is advisable to choose a specific court, such as the English High Court, and thus pre-empt any problem of finding the territorially appropriate court within the chosen State. It is clear that the chosen court need not otherwise have *territorial* competence, but the parties cannot override a Member State's rules allocating competence over categories of subject-matter between different types of court; for instance, by attempting to confer jurisdiction over a commercial contract on a British industrial tribunal.[88] If the parties merely choose the courts in general of a specified Member State, it will be for the law of that State to determine which of its courts shall be competent. It is submitted that in such a case the chosen State is bound to provide at least one competent court, and that if it lacks any applicable rule for selecting that court or courts, all its courts become territorially competent.[89] In any event, in the context of an international maritime contract between foreign parties, the Court of Appeal has construed a clause specifying 'British Courts' as referring to the English High Court.[90]

Since Article 23 is based on the principle of party autonomy, it does not prevent parties who have concluded an agreement on jurisdiction from subsequently concluding a further

---

[85]   See *Kurz v Stella Musical* [1992] Ch 196 (Hoffmann J); *Kitechnology v Unicor* [1995] FSR 765 (CA); *Mercury Communications v Communication Telesystems International* [1999] 2 All ER (Comm) 33 (Moore-Bick J); *Evialis v Siat* [2003] 2 Lloyd's Rep 377 (Andrew Smith J); and *Insured Financial Structures v Elektrocieplownia Tychy* [2003] QB 1260 (CA). In *Evialis*, a clause in an insurance contract providing for service in England on the insurer was construed as creating non-exclusive English jurisdiction over actions against the insurer, and as having no effect on actions brought by the insurer.

[86]   See Gaudemet-Tallon, at para 112.

[87]   See the Civil Procedure Rules 1998 (as amended), rule 6.36, and para 3.1(6) of Practice Direction B thereto; *The Chaparral* [1968] 2 Lloyd's Rep 158; and *Sinochem v Mobil* [2000] 1 Lloyd's Rep 670 (Rix J).

[88]   See the Jenard Report, at p. 38.

[89]   See Gaudemet-Tallon, at para 133. Cf. the Jenard Report, at p. 37. See also, in respect of Scotland, para. 6(5) of Schedule 8 to the Civil Jurisdiction and Judgments Act 1982 (as amended).

[90]   See *The Komninos S* [1991] 1 Lloyd's Rep 370. See also *Snooks v Jani-King* [2006] All ER (D) 325 (Feb), where Silber J held that choice of 'a court of competent jurisdiction in London' is effective under Article 23 to prevent the commencement of proceedings in the Swansea District Registry of the English High Court.

agreement varying or rescinding the earlier agreement.[91] Similarly, as the European Court ruled in *Elefanten Schuh v Jacqmain*[92] and *Spitzley v Sommer Exploitation*,[93] Article 24 (on submission by appearance) prevails over Article 23, so that a court seised of an action or counterclaim in breach of a valid agreement on jurisdiction becomes competent if the defendant thereto enters an appearance without contesting its jurisdiction.

An agreement on jurisdiction which does not satisfy the requirements of Article 23 may have some effect in relation to issues which the Regulation remits to national law, such as the allocation between courts for different areas within a Member State of jurisdiction under Article 2 over defendants domiciled in that State,[94] or the existence of jurisdiction under Article 4 over defendants not domiciled in any Member State.[95]

## Reflexive Effect

Although the wording of Article 23 envisages only agreements which choose a court or the courts of a Member State, it is now clear that Article 23 gives rise to an implied reflexive effect. This derogates from the generally mandatory character of Chapter II of the Regulation, so as to enable a Member State to require or permit its courts to decline jurisdiction in favour of a court of a non-member country which has been chosen by an exclusive jurisdiction clause which would have been valid and effective under Article 23 but for the fact that the chosen court belongs to a non-member country. This approach was effectively endorsed by the European Court in *Coreck Maritime v Handelsveem*,[96] where it explained that Article 23 does not apply to clauses designating a court of a third country, but added that where a court of a Member State is seised in defiance of such a jurisdiction clause, it must assess the validity of the clause according to the law applicable under its own conflict rules. Accordingly, in the context of jurisdiction clauses, the principle of reflexive effect is now accepted and applied by the English courts, so that an otherwise competent English court will, in the exercise of its discretion, decline jurisdiction in favour of a court of a non-member country whose exclusive jurisdiction has been agreed on by the parties, unless the claimant establishes the existence of strong reasons making it unjust to do so.[97]

---

[91]   See *Sinochem v Mobil* [2000] 1 Lloyd's Rep 670 (Rix J).

[92]   Case 150/80, [1981] ECR 1671.

[93]   Case 48/84, [1985] ECR 787.

[94]   See, in England, rule 12 of Schedule 4 to the Civil Jurisdiction and Judgments Act 1982 (as amended).

[95]   See, in England, the Civil Procedure Rules 1998 (as amended), rule 6.36, and para. 3.1(6) of Practice Direction B thereto. Cf. *Assurances Rhone-Mediterranée v COSCO*, 16th January 1996, where the French Court of Cassation refused to allow a Chinese shipowner to invoke a Chinese jurisdiction clause contained in a bill of lading against a holder of the bill, since under French law explicit acceptance was required.

[96]   Case C-387/98, [2000] ECR I-9337, at para 19; citing the Schlosser Report, at para 176.

[97]   See *Berisford v New Hampshire Insurance Co* [1990] 2 QB 631 (Hobhouse J); *Arkwright v Bryanston* [1990] 2 QB 649 (Potter J); *Konkola Copper Mines v Coromin* [2005] 2 All ER (Comm) 637 (Colman J), affirmed [2006] 1 All ER (Comm) 437 (CA); and *Winnetka Trading Corp v Julius Baer* [2008] EWHC 3146 (Ch) (Norris J). See also *The El Amria* [1981] 2 Lloyd's Rep 119 (CA); *Ace Insurance v Zurich Insurance* [2001] 1 Lloyd's Rep 618 (CA); and *Donohue v Armco* [2002] 1 All ER 749 (HL). See also *Europa Carton v Cifal*, 19th December 1978, where the French Court of Cassation gave effect to an agreement between a French company and a German company choosing a Swiss court. For fuller discussion of the principle of reflexive effect, see pp. 58–61 above.

# THE HAGUE CONVENTION 2005

## Introduction

In the late 1990s, work was begun at the Hague Conference on Private International Law with a view to the adoption of a global convention on civil jurisdiction and judgments, with a broad material scope. A Preliminary Draft Convention on Jurisdiction and Foreign Judgments in Civil and Commercial Matters was adopted provisionally by a Special Commission on 30th October 1999,[98] but the Diplomatic Conference held in June 2001 failed to agree on a text.[99] As a result, the project to devise a global convention with wide material scope was abandoned. Instead a much narrower Convention on Choice of Court Agreements was adopted by the Conference on 30th June 2005. It may conveniently be referred to as the Hague Convention 2005.[100] The Convention deals only with exclusive choice of court agreements, and even then excludes consumer and employment cases.

When in force, the Hague Convention 2005 will apply where there is an exclusive choice of court agreement. It will regulate the direct jurisdiction of the courts of the Contracting States in the context of such agreements, and provide for the recognition and enforcement between Contracting States of judgments given pursuant to such agreements.[101] The Convention consists of a Preamble and V Chapters containing 34 Articles, along with an Annex. Chapter I (Articles 1–4) deals with the scope of the Convention and provides some definitions. Chapter II (Articles 5–7) regulates direct judicial jurisdiction. Chapter III (Articles 8–15) provides for the recognition and enforcement of judgments. Chapter IV (Articles 16–26) contains transitional provisions, provides for reservations, and deals with the relationship between the Convention and other international instruments. Chapter V (Articles 27–34) deals with signature, ratification, accession and entry into force, and with the position of Regional Economic Integration Organisations (such as the European Union). The Annex contains a recommended form.

## Adoption by the European Union

On 26th February 2009, the EC Council adopted Decision 2009/397, on the signing on behalf of the European Community of the Hague Convention 2005.[102] The Decision approved the signing on behalf of the European Community of the Hague Convention 2005, and accordingly the Convention was signed on behalf of the European Community on 1st April 2009.[103] A further decision of the EU Council on the acceptance or approval of the Convention by the

---

[98] For its text, see Preliminary Document 11, available at www.hcch.net.

[99] See the Summary of the Outcome of the Discussion in Commission II of the First Part of the Diplomatic Conference, 6th–20th June 2001; available as jdgm2001draft_e.doc at www.hcch.net. This Summary, which contains an interim text prepared by the Permanent Bureau and the co-reporters, reveals the almost complete character of the disagreement.

[100] For its text, see [2009] OJ L133/3.

[101] On recognition and enforcement of judgments under the Convention, see pp. 252–4 below.

[102] For the Decision, see [2009] OJ L133/1.

[103] The Convention has also been signed by the United States of America, and acceded to by Mexico; but it has not yet entered into force.

European Union will be necessary before the Convention becomes binding on the Union as a Regional Economic Integration Organisation in accordance with Article 29 of the Convention.

The signature of the Convention by the European Community was accompanied by a declaration under Article 30(1) of the Convention that the Community exercises competence over all the matters governed by this Convention; and that its Member States will not sign, ratify, accept or approve the Convention, but will be bound by the Convention by virtue of its conclusion by the European Community. For these purposes, the Community comprises all of the Member States except Denmark. By Article 30(2), both the European Union and each of its Member States (other than Denmark) will count as a Contracting State in relation to the Convention.

By Article 26(6)(a) of the Convention, the Convention will not affect the application of the rules of European Union law, whether adopted before or after the Convention, where none of the parties is resident in a Contracting State that is not an EU Member State.[104] By Article 26(6)(b), the Convention will not affect the application of the rules of European Union law in regard to the recognition or enforcement of judgments as between EU Member States.[105]

In view of Articles 3 and 26(6)(a) of the Convention, as regards the direct jurisdiction of the courts of an EU Member State, Chapter II of the Brussels I Regulation will continue to operate, unaffected by the Convention, except where two conditions are fulfilled. First, there must be an exclusive choice of court agreement which designates a court or courts of a country which is a Contracting State to the Convention, whether or not it is also an EU Member State. Secondly, at least one of the parties to the exclusive choice of court agreement must be resident in a country which is a Contracting State to the Convention and which is not also an EU Member State. If both of these conditions are fulfilled, the courts of the EU Member States will have to give priority to the Convention over the Regulation.

Thus, on the assumption that the European Union and the United States have become party to the Convention but Japan has not, the English courts will have to apply Chapter II of the Convention when determining their jurisdiction in the light of an exclusive choice of court agreement which designates an English court, or a French court, or an American court, and to which one of the parties is an American company. But (on the same assumption) the English courts will have to ignore Chapter II of the Convention, and determine their jurisdiction in accordance the Brussels I Regulation (including Article 23 thereof and its implied reflexive effect), where the agreement designates a Japanese court; or where the agreement designates an English court, or a French court, or an American court, but all the parties to the agreement are English, French or Japanese companies.

---

[104]    Similar provision to Article 26(6)(a) is made by Article 26(2) of the Convention in favour of other existing or future treaties, such as the Lugano Conventions 1988 and 2007.

[105]    Similar provision to Article 26(6)(b) is made by Article 26(4) of the Convention in favour of other existing or future treaties between Contracting States, such as the Lugano Conventions 1988 and 2007, except that Article 26(4) insists that the judgment must not be recognised or enforced to a lesser extent than under the Convention. Savings are also made by Article 26(3) in favour of existing treaties with a non-contracting State, and by Article 26(5) in favour of treaties which deal with jurisdiction or the recognition or enforcement of judgments in relation to specific matters.

## The Scope of the Convention

By Article 1(1), the Hague Convention 2005 applies in international cases to exclusive choice of court agreements concluded in civil or commercial matters. By Article 1(2), in relation to direct judicial jurisdiction, a case is international unless the parties are resident in the same Contracting State and the relationship of the parties and all other elements relevant to the dispute, apart from the location of the chosen court, are connected only with that State. By Article 1(3), in relation to recognition and enforcement, a case is international where recognition or enforcement of a foreign judgment is sought. By Article 25(3), a Contracting State with two or more territorial units in which different systems of law apply is not bound to apply the Convention to situations which solely involve such different territorial units.

Article 3(a) defines an exclusive choice of court agreement as an agreement concluded by two or more parties which designates, for the purpose of deciding disputes which have arisen or may arise in connection with a particular legal relationship, the courts of one Contracting State, or one or more specific courts of one Contracting State, to the exclusion of the jurisdiction of any other courts. Article 3(b) adds that a choice of court agreement which designates the courts of one Contracting State, or one or more specific courts of one Contracting State, must be regarded as exclusive unless the parties have expressly provided otherwise. Article 3(c) insists that an exclusive choice of court agreement must be concluded or documented either in writing, or by some other means of communication which renders information accessible so as to be usable for subsequent reference. Article 3(d) adds that an exclusive choice of court agreement which forms part of a contract must be treated as an agreement independent of the other terms of the contract, and that the validity of the exclusive choice of court agreement cannot be contested solely on the ground that the substantive contract is not valid.

Article 4(1) defines a judgment as any decision on the merits given by a court, whatever it may be called, including a decree or order. The concept extends to a determination of costs or expenses by the court (including an officer of the court), provided that the determination relates to a decision on the merits which may be recognised or enforced under the Convention. But an interim measure of protection does not count as a judgment.

Article 4(2) specifies that, for the purposes of the Convention, an entity or person other than a natural person must be considered to be resident in each of the following States: the State where it has its statutory seat; the State under whose law it was incorporated or formed; the State where it has its central administration; and the State where it has its principal place of business. No definition is offered of the residence of an individual, but Article 26 requires that the Convention should be interpreted so far as possible to be compatible with other treaties in force for Contracting States, whether concluded before or after the Convention. It therefore seems likely that within the European Union the references by the Convention to the residence of an individual will be treated as equivalent to his domicile, determined in accordance with the Brussels I Regulation, the Lugano Convention 1988 and the Lugano Convention 2007.

A wide range of matters are excluded from the scope of the Hague Convention 2005 by Article 2. By Article 2(1), the Convention does not apply to exclusive choice of court agreements to which an individual acting primarily for personal, family or household purposes (a consumer) is a party; nor to exclusive choice of court agreements relating to contracts of employment (including collective agreements).

Article 2(2) provides a long list of matters which are excluded from the scope of the Convention. Some of these excluded matters resemble matters which are excluded from the Brussels I Regulation. Thus Article 2(2)(a)–(e) refer to the status and legal capacity of natural persons; maintenance obligations; other family law matters (including matrimonial property regimes and other rights or obligations arising out of marriage or similar relationships); wills and succession; and insolvency, composition and analogous matters. Other matters excluded by Article 2(2) of the Convention resemble matters in respect of which the Brussels I Regulation provides for exclusive jurisdiction on account of subject-matter. Thus Article 2(2)(l)–(p) refers to rights in rem in immovable property, and tenancies of immovable property; the validity, nullity, or dissolution of legal persons, and the validity of decisions of their organs; the validity of intellectual property rights other than copyright (author's rights and neighbouring rights); infringement of intellectual property rights other than copyright (author's rights and neighbouring rights), except where infringement proceedings are brought for breach of a contract between the parties relating to such rights, or could have been brought for breach of such a contract; and the validity of entries in public registers. Yet other exclusions by Article 2(2) of the Convention relate to certain matters to which the ordinary rules specified by the Brussels I Regulation apply. Thus Article 2(2)(f)–(k) refers to the carriage of passengers and goods; marine pollution, limitation of liability for maritime claims, general average, and emergency towage and salvage; anti-trust (competition) matters; liability for nuclear damage; claims for personal injury brought by or on behalf of individuals; and tort claims for damage to tangible property which do not arise from a contractual relationship. By Article 2(3), proceedings are not excluded from the scope of the Convention where a matter referred to in Article 2(2) arises merely as a preliminary question or by way of defence, and not as an object of the proceedings.

By Article 2(4), the Convention does not apply to arbitration and related proceedings. By Article 2(5)–(6), proceedings are not excluded from the scope of the Convention by the mere fact that a State, including a government, a governmental agency or any person acting for a State, is a party thereto; but nothing in the Convention affects privileges and immunities of States or of international organisations, in respect of themselves and of their property.

By Article 17(1), proceedings under a contract of insurance or reinsurance are not excluded from the scope of the Convention on the ground that the contract of insurance or reinsurance relates to a matter to which the Convention does not apply. By Article 17(2)(a), recognition and enforcement of a judgment in respect of liability under the terms of a contract of insurance or reinsurance may not be limited or refused on the ground that the liability under that contract includes liability to indemnify the insured or reinsured in respect of a matter to which the Convention does not apply.

By Article 31, the Convention will enter into force on the first day of the month following the expiration of three months after the deposit of the second instrument of ratification, acceptance, approval or accession; and for each State or Regional Economic Integration Organisation subsequently ratifying, accepting, approving or acceding to it, on the first day of the month following the expiration of three months after the deposit of its instrument of ratification, acceptance, approval or accession. By Article 16(1), the Convention will apply to exclusive choice of court agreements concluded after its entry into force for the State of the chosen court. By Article 16(2), it will not apply to proceedings instituted before its entry into force for the State of the court seised.

Article 23 requires that, in the interpretation of the Convention, regard must be had to its international character and to the need to promote uniformity in its application.

## Reservations and Extensions

Article 19 of the Convention enables a State to make a reservation declaring that its courts may refuse to determine disputes to which an exclusive choice of court agreement applies if, except for the location of the chosen court, there is no connection between that State and the parties or the dispute.

Article 21(1) of the Convention enables a State to make a reservation declaring that it will not apply the Convention to a specific matter, where it has a strong interest in making the exclusion, but the exclusion should be no broader than necessary, and the specific matter excluded must be clearly and precisely defined. By Article 21(2), where such a reservation has been made, the Convention will not apply with regard to the specified matter in the Contracting State which made the reservation. Moreover, the Convention will not apply with regard to the specified matter in other Contracting States, where an exclusive choice of court agreement designates a court or courts of the State which made the reservation.

Conversely, Article 22 provides for the reciprocal extension of the Convention to judgments given pursuant to a non-exclusive choice of court agreement. Article 22(1) enables a Contracting State to declare that its courts will recognise and enforce judgments given by courts of other Contracting States designated in a choice of court agreement concluded by two or more parties which meets the requirements of Article 3(c) of writing or accessibility, and which designates, for the purpose of deciding disputes which have arisen or may arise in connection with a particular legal relationship, a court or courts of one or more Contracting States (a non-exclusive choice of court agreement). By Article 22(2), where recognition or enforcement of a judgment given in a Contracting State which has made such a declaration is sought in another Contracting State which has also made such a declaration, the judgment must be recognised and enforced under this Convention, if three conditions are met. The court of origin must have been designated in a non-exclusive choice of court agreement; no judgment must exist which was given by any other court before which proceedings could be brought in accordance with the non-exclusive choice of court agreement, and no proceeding must be pending between the same parties in any other such court on the same cause of action; and the court of origin must have been the court first seised. It seems that the European Union does not intend to make a declaration extending the Convention to non-exclusive choice of court agreements under Article 22.

## Direct Jurisdiction

Article 5 of the Convention deals with the positive effect of an exclusive choice of court agreement in the State chosen. By Article 5(1), the court or courts of a Contracting State designated in an exclusive choice of court agreement have jurisdiction to decide a dispute to which the agreement applies, unless the agreement is null and void under the law of that State. By Article 5(2), such a court cannot decline to exercise jurisdiction on the ground that the dispute should be decided in a court of another State. Article 5(3) makes savings in favour of rules on jurisdiction related to subject matter or to the value of the claim; and for rules on the internal allocation of jurisdiction among the courts of a Contracting State. It insists, however, that where under such rules the chosen court has discretion as to whether to transfer a case, due consideration should be given to the choice of the parties.

Article 6 deals with the negative effect of an exclusive choice of court agreement in other

Contracting States. It requires a court of a Contracting State other than that of the chosen court to suspend or dismiss proceedings to which an exclusive choice of court agreement applies. This obligation is subject to five exceptions. The first exception applies where the agreement is null and void under the law of the State of the chosen court. The second applies where a party lacked the capacity to conclude the agreement under the law of the State of the court seised. The third applies where giving effect to the agreement would lead to a manifest injustice or would be manifestly contrary to the public policy of the State of the court seised. The fourth applies where, for exceptional reasons beyond the control of the parties, the agreement cannot reasonably be performed. The final exception applies where the chosen court has decided not to hear the case.

Article 7 specifies that interim measures of protection are not governed by the Convention. The Convention neither requires nor precludes the grant, refusal or termination of interim measures of protection by a court of a Contracting State, and does not affect whether or not a party may request or a court should grant, refuse or terminate such measures.

**Recognition and Enforcement**

Chapter III (Articles 8–15) of the Convention applies where a judgment has been given by a court of a Contracting State designated in an exclusive choice of court agreement, and deals with the recognition and enforcement of the judgment in other Contracting States. These provisions are examined in Chapter 10 below.[106]

## SUBMISSION BY APPEARANCE

Article 24 of the Brussels I Regulation confers jurisdiction over a defendant, additional to that derived from other provisions of Chapter II, on a court of a Member State before which he enters an appearance without contesting its jurisdiction, unless another court has exclusive jurisdiction by virtue of subject-matter under Article 22.[107]

In *Group Josi v UGIC*,[108] the European Court indicated obiter that the defendant's domicile (as well as the plaintiff's domicile) is wholly irrelevant to the operation of Article 24. In view of this dictum, as well the analogy of Article 23 and the history of the negotiations, it is clear that Article 24 derogates from Article 4 and applies even where the defendant is not domiciled in any Member State, as well as where he is domiciled in another Member State.[109] It follows that the *Owusu* principle,[110] that the jurisdictional bases specified by the Regulation

---

[106]   See pp. 252–4 below.

[107]   Article 24 of the Regulation replaces Article 18 of the Brussels Convention.

[108]   Case C-412/98, at paras 44–5: 'Admittedly, under Article 18 of the Convention, the voluntary appearance of the defendant establishes the jurisdiction of a court of a Contracting State before which the plaintiff has brought proceedings, without the place of the defendant's domicile being relevant. However, although the court seised must be that of a Contracting State, that provision does not further require that the plaintiff be domiciled in such a State.'

[109]   See also Droz, at paras 221 and 230–32; and per Darmon AG in Case C-318/93: *Brenner v Dean Witter Reynolds* [1994] ECR I-4275, at para 15. Cf. Gaudemet-Tallon, at para 144.

[110]   See Case C-281/02: *Owusu v Jackson* [2005] ECR I-1383.

are mandatory and override any judicial discretion to decline jurisdiction in favour of a supposedly more appropriate court of a non-member country, applies where jurisdiction arises under Article 24 from the defendant's appearance, even if the defendant is domiciled in a non-member country.[111]

The dictum in *Group Josi* suggests that Article 24 also derogates from Article 2, so as to override the law of the Member State in which the defendant is domiciled on the allocation of jurisdiction between the courts for its territories or districts. In the United Kingdom, corresponding provision for local defendants is in any event made by rule 13 of Schedule 4 to the Civil Jurisdiction and Judgments Act 1982 (as amended). But Article 24 does not override rules of the law of the forum State on the allocation of jurisdiction between its courts in terms of subject-matter. Thus, for example, appearance before an English industrial tribunal could not enable it to entertain a claim relating to a commercial contract.

In view of the explicit exclusion from Article 24 of cases where another court has exclusive jurisdiction by virtue of subject-matter under Article 22, it is probable that, where the subject-matter falls within Article 22, the effect of the defendant's appearance before a territorially inappropriate court of the exclusively competent Member State is not governed by Article 24, but is remitted by Article 22 to the law of the forum State. This appears to be assumed in the United Kingdom by rules 11 and 13 of Schedule 4 to the Civil Jurisdiction and Judgments Act 1982 (as amended). Article 24 is also subject to the reflexive effect of Article 22 in favour of external countries.[112] On the other hand, appearance founds jurisdiction under Article 24 even where the parties had previously concluded an agreement designating some other court as exclusively competent in accordance with Article 23.[113]

For an appearance to create jurisdiction under Article 24 of the Brussels I Regulation, the appearance must not be 'entered to contest the jurisdiction'. In the Brussels Convention, Article 18 excluded an appearance 'entered solely to contest the jurisdiction'. But the change in wording is not significant, for in a series of decisions[114] the European Court had already ruled that a defendant may, without submitting to the jurisdiction, simultaneously raise defences as to both jurisdiction and merits, provided that his challenge to the jurisdiction is made no later than the submissions which under the procedural law of the court seised are regarded as the first defence addressed to the court, and it is clear that the change in wording is designed to confirm these rulings. Moreover, the right to raise simultaneously defences as to jurisdiction and merits applies even if the defendant also counterclaims and joins a third party.[115]

In England, the procedure for disputing the court's jurisdiction is regulated by rule 11 of the Civil Procedure Rules 1998 (as amended), under which a defendant must make any application to challenge jurisdiction within fourteen days after filing an acknowledgment of service. If there is no challenge within that period, the defendant is treated as having accepted

---

[111] This point appears to have been overlooked in *Global Multimedia International Ltd v Ara Media Services* [2007] 1 All ER (Comm) 1160 (Morritt C).

[112] See Gaudemet-Tallon, at para 145.

[113] See Case 150/80: *Elefanten Schuh v Jacqmain* [1981] ECR 1671.

[114] See Case 150/80: *Elefanten Schuh v Jacqmain* [1981] ECR 1671; Case 27/81: *Rohr v Ossberger* [1981] ECR 2431; Case 25/81: *CHW v GJH* [1982] ECR 1189; and Case 201/82: *Gerling v Treasury Administration* [1983] ECR 2503.

[115] See *Rank Film Distributors v Lanterna* [1992] ILPr 58 (Saville J); and Gaudemet-Tallon, at para 148.

the court's jurisdiction,[116] unless the court exercises its power under rule 3.1(2)(a) of the Civil Procedure Rules to extend the time for a challenge to the jurisdiction, a power which remains available after the fourteen day period has expired.[117] In any event, there will be submission by appearance where the defendant has taken a step in the proceedings which unequivocally indicates his acceptance of the court's jurisdiction; for example, where, without clearly and expressly indicating that he reserves his right to challenge the jurisdiction, he seeks an extension of time for filing his defence, or advances a defence on the merits, or threatens to seek the striking out of the claim on grounds relating to the merits,[118] or makes an application for discovery of documents relevant to the merits.[119]

In Ireland, it has been emphasised that a defendant who enters an unqualified appearance only accepts the jurisdiction of the court to entertain the case which has been formulated against him by the plaintiff at that stage, and not some wider case which the plaintiff may subsequently try to advance.[120] But in England submission by appearance is treated as extending to subsequent amendments to the claims which in substance relate to the same subject-matter as the original action.[121] Moreover, there will be submission by appearance if the defendant, after unsuccessfully contesting the jurisdiction up to the court of last resort, then proceeds to file a defence on the merits.[122]

In *Mietz v Intership Yachting Sneek*,[123] the European Court effectively ruled that Article 24 does not apply to an appearance entered in a proceeding for the grant of provisional or protective measures. In order to prevent the circumvention of the rules on substantive jurisdiction laid down by Chapter II of the Regulation by the grant of excessive provisional or protective measures in erroneous reliance on Article 31,[124] it ruled that Article 24 does not apply where the defendant appears before a court dealing with interim measures in the context of fast procedures intended to grant provisional or protective measures in case of urgency and which do not prejudice the examination of the substance. Such an appearance cannot by itself confer on that court, under Article 24, unlimited jurisdiction to order any provisional or protective measure which the court might consider appropriate if it had jurisdiction under the Regulation as to the substance of the matter.

---

116   See *Maple Leaf v Rouvroy* [2009] EWHC 257 (Comm) (Andrew Smith J).
117   See *Sawyer v Atari Interactive Inc* [2005] EWHC 2351 (Collins J); and *Global Multimedia International Ltd v Ara Media Services* [2007] 1 All ER (Comm) 1160 (Morritt C).
118   See *Global Multimedia International Ltd v Ara Media Services* [2007] 1 All ER (Comm) 1160 (Morritt C). See also *Re Anderson Owen Ltd* [2009] EWHC 2837 (Ch) (Norris J).
119   See *Caltex v Metro* [1999] 2 Lloyd's Rep 724 (Rix J).
120   See *Murray v Times Newspapers* [1997] 3 IR 97 (Irish Supreme Court).
121   See *Maple Leaf v Rouvroy* [2009] EWHC 257 (Comm) (Andrew Smith J).
122   See *Marc Rich v Impianti (No 2)* [1992] 1 Lloyd's Rep 624 (CA).
123   Case C-99/96, [1999] ECR I-2277, at para 52.
124   On Article 31, see Chapter 9 below.

# 8. Concurrent proceedings

## INTRODUCTION

Chapter II of the Brussels I Regulation frequently gives a plaintiff a choice of Member States in which to sue. Hence, in order to reduce the risk of irreconcilable judgments being given by courts of different Member States, and also to increase co-ordination in the exercise of judicial functions within the European Union so as to promote litigational economy and avoid waste, Section 9 (Articles 27–30) of Chapter II regulates the problem of proceedings simultaneously pending in courts of different Member States in respect of similar or related disputes. Recital 15 explains that in the interests of the harmonious administration of justice it is necessary to minimise the possibility of concurrent proceedings and to ensure that irreconcilable judgments will not be given in two Member States. Thus there must be a clear and effective mechanism for resolving cases of lis pendens and related actions.

Section 9 is based primarily on a simple test of chronological priority, under which the court subsequently seised is required or invited to defer to the court first seised, rather than on a judicial evaluation of the relative appropriateness or convenience of the two fora. In the case of similar actions, Article 27 imposes on the court subsequently seised a mandatory obligation to decline jurisdiction in favour of the court first seised. In the case of dissimilar but related actions, Article 28 gives the second court a discretion to stay its proceedings, or in certain circumstances to decline jurisdiction altogether, in favour of the first court. But in no case do these provisions authorise the first court to give way to the second court.[1]

Similar actions are governed by Article 27 of the Regulation,[2] which provides:

> (1) Where proceedings involving the same cause of action and between the same parties are brought in the courts of different Member States, any court other than the court first seised shall of its own motion stay its proceedings until such time as the jurisdiction of the court first seised is established. (2) Where the jurisdiction of the court first seised is established, any court other than the court first seised shall decline jurisdiction in favour of that court.

Related actions are governed by Article 28 of the Regulation,[3] which provides:

> (1) Where related actions are pending in the courts of different Member States, any court other than the court first seised may stay its proceedings.

---

[1]    See *Cronos Containers v Palatin* [2003] 2 Lloyd's Rep 489. But where Article 4 remits the jurisdiction of the first court to its own law, because the defendant is not domiciled in any Member State, such remission includes any power conferred by the relevant national law to decline jurisdiction on grounds such as forum non conveniens; see pp. 66–7 above.

[2]    Article 27 echoes Article 21 of the 1989/96 version of the Brussels Convention.

[3]    Article 28 follows Article 22 of the Brussels Convention, with minor amendments.

(2) Where these actions are pending at first instance, any court other than the court first seised may also, on the application of one of the parties, decline jurisdiction if the court first seised has jurisdiction over the actions in question and its law permits the consolidation thereof.
(3) For the purposes of this Article, actions are deemed to be related where they are so closely connected that it is expedient to hear and determine them together to avoid the risk of irreconcilable judgments resulting from separate proceedings.

Conflicts of exclusive jurisdiction are dealt with by Article 29 of the Regulation,[4] which provides: 'Where actions come within the exclusive jurisdiction of several courts, any court other than the court first seised shall decline jurisdiction in favour of that court'.

Article 30 of the Regulation contains a new provision, dealing with the time at which a court becomes seised. It provides:

For the purposes of this Section, a court shall be deemed to be seised:

(1) at the time when the document instituting the proceedings or an equivalent document is lodged with the court, provided that the plaintiff has not subsequently failed to take the steps he was required to take to have service effected on the defendant, or
(2) if the document has to be served before being lodged with the court, at the time when it is received by the authority responsible for service, provided that the plaintiff has not subsequently failed to take the steps he was required to take to have the document lodged with the court.

In this connection, Recital 15 explains that there must be a clear and effective mechanism for obviating problems flowing from national differences as to the determination of the time when a case is regarded as pending, and that for the purposes of the Regulation that time should be defined autonomously.

Section 9 is concerned with actions which are simultaneously pending in courts of different Member States. Thus if both actions are instituted in the same Member State, the problem is impliedly remitted to the law of the Member State in question. In the United Kingdom, analogous provisions have not been adopted for concurrent actions in courts of its different parts. Instead, s 49 of the Civil Jurisdiction and Judgments Act 1982 leaves the matter to be dealt with under the more general principle of forum non conveniens.

The Regulation also ignores the problem of simultaneous actions, one in a Member State and the other in a non-member country, and the English and Irish courts have taken the view that Section 9 does not have reflexive effect. Thus a court on which the Regulation confers jurisdiction, for example on the basis of the defendant's domicile, cannot decline jurisdiction in favour of a court of a non-member country in which similar or related proceedings have already been instituted.[5] In any event, as the European Court ruled in *Owens Bank v Bracco*,[6] Section 9 does not apply to proceedings in Member States concerning the recognition and enforcement of judgments given in external countries.

According to English case-law, for Section 9 to apply, both actions must fall within the material scope of the Regulation as defined by Article 1. Thus Section 9 does not apply if one

---

⁴   Article 29 echoes Article 23 of the Brussels Convention.
⁵   See *Goshawk Dedicated Ltd v Life Receivables Ireland Ltd* [2008] ILPr 50 (Clarke J); *Catalyst Investment Group v Lewinsohn* [2009] EWHC 1964 (Ch) (Barling J); and pp. 58–61 above.
⁶   Case C-129/92, [1994] ECR I-117.

of the proceedings falls within the bankruptcy exclusion under Article 1(2)(b),[7] or within the arbitration exclusion under Article 1(2)(d).[8] It may plausibly be suggested, however, that there is no good reason why Article 28 (on related actions) should not apply so as to enable the staying of a second action which is principally concerned with an excluded matter so as to await a decision in a first action, falling within the Regulation, in which an excluded matter is incidentally involved.[9] There is also English authority that Section 9 does not apply where the first proceeding is confined to an investigative measure, designed to preserve evidence or establish facts relevant to liability to be determined in separate, subsequent, substantive proceedings;[10] or where the first proceedings are merely for protective relief, and the second proceedings are for determination of the merits of the dispute.[11]

The European Court made clear in *Overseas Union Insurance v New Hampshire Insurance*[12] that Section 9 applies regardless of the domicile of the parties to the actions, and thus applies even if the defendant in either or both of the actions is not domiciled in any of the Member States. Moreover, as the European Court ruled in *The Maciej Rataj*,[13] Section 9 remains applicable in cases where the existence of jurisdiction is governed by a specialised convention within the scope of Article 71 (such as the Brussels Convention of 1952 on the Arrest of Seagoing Ships), but the specialised convention contains no provision dealing with concurrent actions. Similarly, as Simon J held in *Sony v RH Freight Services*,[14] where a specialised convention (such as the Geneva Convention of 1956 on carriage by road) contains a provision dealing with similar actions, but contains no provision dealing with related actions, Article 28 of the Brussels I Regulation remains applicable to related actions.

## SIMILAR ACTIONS

### The Mechanism

In the case of concurrent proceedings in respect of similar disputes, Article 27 imposes mandatory obligations on the court subsequently seised, which must be performed of the court's own motion if necessary. No exception is available on such grounds as that the court subsequently seised considers that proceedings in the country of the court first seised are excessively slow.[15]

The mechanism established by Article 27 requires the court subsequently seised ('the second court') to stay its own proceedings until the jurisdiction of the court first seised

---

7    See per Mance J held in *Grupo Torras v Al-Sabah* [1995] 1 Lloyd's Rep 374.
8    See *The Hari Bhum* [2005] 1 Lloyd's Rep 67 (CA).
9    See Gaudemet-Tallon, at para 298, arguing that Article 28 would apply where a German petition for divorce was followed by a French application for maintenance.
10   See *Miles Platts v Townroe* [2003] 1 All ER (Comm) 561 (CA).
11   See *Rank Film Distributors v Lanterna* [1992] ILPr 58 (Saville J); *Fox v Taher* [1997] ILPr 441 (CA); and *Boss Group v Boss France* [1997] 1 WLR 351 (CA).
12   Case C-351/89, [1991] ECR I-3317.
13   Case C-406/92, [1994] ECR I-5439.
14   [2007] All ER (D) 310 (Feb).
15   See Case C-116/02: *Gasser v MISAT* [2003] ECR I-14693.

('the first court') is established. Once the jurisdiction of the first court has been established, the second court must decline jurisdiction in favour of the first court. It is for the first court to determine its own jurisdiction. As the European Court emphasised in *Overseas Union Insurance v New Hampshire Insurance*[16] and *Gasser v MISAT*,[17] Article 27 does not permit the second court, even where the jurisdiction of the first court is contested, itself to examine the jurisdiction of the first court.[18]

If the first court eventually decides that it is incompetent, the second court will lift its stay and permit its action to proceed. The first court's jurisdiction is probably not established while an appeal against its decision accepting jurisdiction is pending.[19] Conversely, Article 27(1) remains applicable after a decision by the court first seised that it has no jurisdiction, while an appeal is pending against that decision.[20] But there is no provision enabling a court, on holding that it lacks jurisdiction, to order that the action be transferred to a competent court of another Member State.[21] Thus it may be advisable, where the defendant disputes the jurisdiction of the court first seised, for the plaintiff to bring a second action elsewhere before the relevant limitation period expires.

Article 27 does not apply where the proceedings in the first court have proceeded to judgment, or have been discontinued, between the time when the proceedings were brought in the second court, and the time when the second court determines whether it should decline jurisdiction. Article 27 applies where there are concurrent proceedings at the time when the second court makes its determination.[22]

**The Same Cause of Action**

Article 27 applies to similar actions, which it defines as 'proceedings involving the same cause of action and between the same parties'. In other language versions (such as the French), a triple identity is required: the same object, the same cause, and the same parties. In contrast, Article 28 applies to related (but dissimilar) actions, which are defined by Article 28(3) as other actions which 'are so closely connected that it is expedient to hear and determine them together to avoid the risk of irreconcilable judgments resulting from separate proceedings'.

It is clear that the similar actions to which Article 27 applies are a narrower category than the related actions to which Article 28 applies or would, but for Article 27, apply. However, the European Court, invoking the need to prevent irreconcilable judgments being given by courts of different Member States, has construed Article 27 widely. In *Gubisch v Palumbo*[23]

---

[16]   Case C-351/89, [1991] ECR I-3317.
[17]   Case C-116/02, [2003] ECR I-14693.
[18]   See also *Bank of Tokyo-Mitsubishi v Baskan Gida* [2004] ILPr 26 (Lawrence Collins J); and *Morgan v Primacom* [2005] EWHC 508 (Cooke J). For exceptions, see pp. 198–9 below.
[19]   See *William Grant v Marie-Brizard* [1996] SCLR 987 (Scottish Outer House). Cf. Gaudemet-Tallon, at para 290, regarding the point as doubtful.
[20]   See *Moore v Moore* [2007] EWCA Civ 361 (CA), at para 103.
[21]   Cf. 28 US Code, s 1404(a), which in the United States enables one federal district court to order that an action before it be transferred to a sister court for another district.
[22]   See *Tavoulareas v Tsavliris (No 2)* [2006] 1 All ER (Comm) 130 (Andrew Smith J).
[23]   Case 144/86, [1987] ECR 4861.

and *The Maciej Rataj*,[24] it established that Article 27 applies where inconsistent claims are made between the same parties in respect of the same contract or other factual situation, even if the position of the parties in the actions is reversed (the plaintiff in the first action being defendant in the second action, and the defendant in the first action being plaintiff in the second action), and accordingly different relief is sought.[25] On the other hand, as the European Court ruled in *Gantner v Basch*,[26] account must be taken only of the claims of the respective plaintiffs, to the exclusion of the submissions (such as a claim to set-off) by a defendant.

Thus in *Gubisch v Palumbo*,[27] the European Court ruled that Article 27 applies where one party to a contract brings an action before a court of one Member State for the rescission or discharge of the contract whilst an action by the other party to enforce the same contract is pending before a court of another Member State. It explained that both actions were based on the same contractual relationship, one being aimed at giving effect to the contract, and the other at depriving it of any effect. Thus the question whether the contract was binding lay at the heart of both actions. The subsequent action for rescission or discharge of the contract could be regarded as simply a defence against the first action, brought in the form of independent proceedings before a court of another Member State. While the two actions must have the same subject-matter, this does not mean that the two claims must be entirely identical.

Similarly in *The Maciej Rataj*,[28] which involved damage to cargo carried under bill of lading contracts, the European Court ruled that Article 27 applied to an action seeking to have the defendant shipowner held liable for causing loss and ordered to pay damages, and an earlier action brought by the shipowner seeking a declaration that he was not liable for that loss. It explained that the actions had the same cause, being based on the same facts and the same legal rule, and the same object, since the issue of liability was central to both actions and the reversal in the position of the parties (as plaintiff and defendant) was immaterial.

On the other hand, in *Maersk Olie & Gas v de Haan & de Boer*,[29] the European Court ruled that an application to a court of a Member State by a shipowner for the establishment of a liability limitation fund, in which the potential victim of the damage (for example, to an oil-rig) is indicated, and an action for damages brought before a court of another Member State by that victim against the shipowner, are not similar actions within Article 27 of the Regulation, but are related actions within Article 28.[30] It emphasised that the victim's claim is based on tort, while the shipowner's claim is based on its right of limitation. In its Report and Green Paper of 21st April 2009,[31] the EC Commission contemplates the possibility of providing for the consolidation of proceedings aimed at setting up a liability fund with individual liability proceedings.

---

24   Case C-406/92, [1994] ECR I-5439.
25   See also *Bank of Tokyo-Mitsubishi v Baskan Gida* [2004] ILPr 26 (Lawrence Collins J).
26   Case C-111/01, [2003] ECR I-4207.
27   Case 144/86, [1987] ECR 4861.
28   Case C-406/92, [1994] ECR I-5439.
29   Case C-39/02, [2004] ECR I-9657.
30   Cf. *The Happy Fellow* [1998] 1 Lloyd's Rep 13, where the English Court of Appeal had taken the view that in such cases Article 27 probably applied.
31   COM(2009) 174 final, at section 3.8.2, and COM(2009) 175 final, at question 8.

These rulings probably justify the decision of Lord Gill (in the Scottish Outer House) in *William Grant v Marie-Brizard*[32] that claims between the same parties for the same amount are within Article 27, even if in one court the claim is based on contract and in the other court it is based on tort, and that Article 27 applies even where in the first court the relevant claim was raised as a counterclaim by the court of its own motion. It is less clear whether Sheen J was correct to hold in *The Linda*[33] that admiralty cross-claims between the same parties and arising from the same collision fall within Article 27. In any event, it seems clear that Cooke J was correct in ruling in *Morgan v Primacom*[34] that Article 27 does not apply, even where the dispute is between the same parties and relates to the same contract, if the first action is concerned exclusively with one obligation under the contract, and the second is concerned with other obligations under the contract; for example, in the case of a loan, where the first action is brought by the debtor and seeks only the invalidation of the contractual provision concerning the interest payable, while the second action is brought by the creditor and seeks enforcement of contractual provisions preventing the debtor from selling assets without the creditor's consent and requiring the debtor to provide financial information to the creditor.

In *Underwriting Members of Lloyd's Syndicate 980 v Sinco*,[35] Beatson J held that a subsequent English claim for damages for breach of an English jurisdiction clause does not involve the same cause of action as an earlier proceeding on the merits brought earlier in a court of another Member State in breach of the jurisdiction clause. This decision seems to ignore the mutual trust between the courts of the Member States, which has been emphasised in recent decisions of the European Court.

**The Same Parties**

The operation of Article 27 in relation to multi-party litigation was considered by the European Court in *The Maciej Rataj*.[36] It ruled that, where some but not all of the parties to the second action are the same as the parties to the first action, Article 27 requires the second court seised to decline jurisdiction only to the extent to which the parties to the second proceedings are also parties to the first action. It does not prevent the second proceedings from continuing between the other parties. The consequent undesirable fragmentation of proceedings may in some cases be mitigated by Article 28, on related actions. The Court also ruled that an action in rem against a ship[37] must be treated for the purpose of Article 27 as an action against the shipowner or other person interested in the ship against whom the plaintiff would wish to proceed in personam if he entered an appearance.[38]

The concept of a party was considered by the European Court in *Drouot Assurances v Consolidated Metallurgical Industries*.[39] It accepted that the requirement under Article 27

---

32    [1996] SCLR 987.
33    [1988] 1 Lloyd's Rep 175.
34    [2005] EWHC 508 (Comm).
35    [2009] 1 All ER (Comm) 272.
36    Case C-406/92, [1994] ECR I-5439.
37    See pp. 113–15 above.
38    See similarly *The Deichland* [1990] QB 361 (CA), on Articles 2 and 3 of the Regulation; and *Republic of India v India Steamship Co Ltd (No 2)* [1998] AC 878, on s 34 of the Civil Jurisdiction and Judgments Act 1982 (concerning merger of a cause of action in a judgment for the plaintiff).
39    Case C-351/96, [1998] ECR I-3075.

that the parties to both actions must be the same does not eliminate all possibility of identification by virtue of privity (for example, between an insurer and its insured). But it emphasised that such identification is possible only when, with regard to the subject-matter of both actions, the interests of the persons in question are identical and indissociable (or indivisible). Thus a shipowner and its hull insurer could not be regarded as the same party in the context of claims relating to contribution to general average. Similarly, in *Sony v RH Freight Services*,[40] Simon J held that there cannot be identification of a cargo-owner and its loss insurer in respect of a claim against a carrier, where there is a potential claim for damages greater than the sum insured.[41]

The question of identification of two entities as the same party was subsequently considered by the English Court of Appeal in *Kolden v Rodette*.[42] Lawrence LJ concluded that, in relation to a contractual claim, there is sufficient privity of interest between an assignor and an assignee of the claim. For in such a case there is such a degree of identity between the interests of the assignor and the assignee that a judgment given against one of them would have the force of res judicata as against the other, and it is immaterial that an assignment passes only the benefit and not the burden of a contract, and that the assignor remains liable to the other party to the contract for the non-performance of its outstanding contractual obligations. Moreover, the question of identification must be determined by reference to the claims, and to the defences. Similarly, there is sufficient identity of interest between a company in solvent liquidation and its liquidator, as regards a claim by a creditor of the company.[43]

In *Glencore v Shell*,[44] Rix J held that Article 27 does not apply where the first proceeding is an ordinary action in contract for the price of goods, and the second is an interpleader proceeding initiated by the person liable for the price, seeking determination as to which of various claimants (including the plaintiff in the first action) has the best right to the price. For the interpleader application is based on the existence of other adverse claims, it invokes a special procedure for relief, and it requires determination of the relative titles of the adverse claimants. It therefore involves a different cause of action from the first proceeding. In contrast, in *Glencore v Metro*,[45] Moore-Bick J reached the opposite conclusion in a similar multi-party situation, but where in the second country the person liable for the price did not interplead but joined the plaintiff in the first country as a third party in proceedings brought by other claimants.

---

[40]    [2007] All ER (D) 310 (Feb).
[41]    See also *Mecklermedia v DC Congress* [1998] Ch 40, where Jacob J refused to treat a licensor of intellectual property and his licensee as the same party for the purposes of Article 27; and *Turner v Grovit* [1999] 1 WLR 794 (CA), involving sister companies in the same group.
[42]    [2008] 3 All ER 612 (CA).
[43]    See *Re Cover Europe Ltd* [2002] BPIR 931 (Kosmin QC).
[44]    [1999] 2 Lloyd's Rep 692. See also *Cool Carriers v HSBC Bank* [2001] 2 Lloyd's Rep 22 (Tomlinson J), on jurisdiction to entertain interpleader proceedings against claimants domiciled in external countries.
[45]    [1999] 2 Lloyd's Rep 632.

**The Time of Seisin**

The time at which a court is seised of an action for the purpose of Articles 27–9 of the Brussels I Regulation is now governed by Article 30. By Article 30(1), a court is regarded as seised at the time when the document instituting the proceedings or an equivalent document is lodged with the court, provided that the plaintiff has not subsequently failed to take the steps he was required to take to have service effected on the defendant. By Article 30(2), if the document has to be served before being lodged with the court, the court is regarded as seised at the time when the document is received by the authority responsible for service, provided that the plaintiff has not subsequently failed to take the steps he was required to take to have the document lodged with the court. Recital 15 explains that there must be a clear and effective mechanism for resolving cases of lis pendens and related actions and for obviating problems flowing from national differences as to the determination of the time when a case is regarded as pending; and that for the purposes of the Regulation that time should be defined autonomously.

In substance, Article 30 imposes a rule in favour of the date of the issue of the instituting document, rather than the date of its service. In *WPP v Benatti*,[46] the English Court of Appeal ruled that the provisos to Article 30 only require that the claimant should not have subsequently failed to take the steps which he was required to take. They do not require actual service, and it is immaterial that the document was served irregularly, by reason of the absence of a translation, under the EC Regulations on service between Member States.[47]

Under Article 30, in the case of multiple defendants, one must focus separately on each pair of opposing parties;[48] and in the case of third-party proceedings, the relevant date will be that of the issue of the document originating the claim against the third party. Moreover, in *Underwriting Members of Lloyd's Syndicate 980 v Sinco*,[49] Beatson J held that for the purpose of Article 30, an additional claim for a different breach of the same contract, made by amendment in an already pending action, must be treated as a separate action, of which the court must be regarded as seised at the date of the amendment.

Formerly, the date of seisin under Articles 21–3 of the Brussels Convention was determined in accordance with the ruling of the European Court in *Zelger v Salinitri (No 2)*.[50] The court first seised was the one before which the requirements for proceedings to become definitively pending were first fulfilled, such requirements being determined in respect of each court in accordance with the law of the Contracting State to which that court belonged. The general trend under the laws of the Contracting States was for an action to be regarded as becoming definitely pending, not at the issue of the originating document, but at its service on the defendant. This solution was adopted for English actions by the Court of Appeal,[51]

---

46   [2007] 2 All ER (Comm) 525 (CA).
47   The EC Regulations on service are examined at pp. 62–6 above.
48   See *WPP v Benatti* [2007] 2 All ER (Comm) 525 (CA).
49   [2009] 1 All ER (Comm) 272.
50   Case 129/83, [1984] ECR 2397.
51   See *Dresser v Falcongate* [1992] QB 502, and *Neste Chemicals v DK Line* [1994] 3 All ER 180. In the case of English third-party proceedings, the relevant date was that of service on the third party; see *Glencore v Metro* [1999] 2 Lloyd's Rep 632 (Moore-Bick J). See also *Molins v GD* [2000] 2 Lloyd's Rep 234 (CA), holding that an Italian court was not seised before service of its writ in a manner

which also recognised that, in the case of multiple defendants, one had to focus separately on each pair of opposing parties,[52] and that the concept of definitive pendency excluded any possibility of relation-back (as by considering, after service of the originating document, that the action had been pending since its issue).[53] Similarly, an English court was not seised of an admiralty action in rem against a ship (not already in the custody of the court) until service or arrest, whichever occurred earlier.[54]

The transitional operation of Article 30 of the Regulation was considered by Andrew Smith J in *Tavoulareas v Tsavliris*.[55] He ruled that Article 30 now applies to the determination of the time of seisin of both courts, whenever the action brought before the court which is considering the question of concurrent actions was instituted after the commencement date of the Regulation for its State, even if the action in a court of another Member State was instituted at an earlier date.

The adoption of a uniform rule on the time of seisin, replacing the former reference to the law of the country in which an action is brought, is unquestionably welcome. But the merits of the reference by Article 30 to the date of the issue, rather than the service, of the originating document seem very questionable. For, in the most common situation, the parties are in reversed positions in the two courts. Thus the danger of a party commencing proceedings in ignorance that the other party has already commenced proceedings elsewhere which will have priority has been greatly increased, and a massive and undeserved advantage has been conferred on a party who speedily issues an originating document and then delays service until the last moment permissible under the law of the country in which he desires to litigate.

In its Report and Green Paper of 21st April 2009,[56] the EC Commission favoured the clarification of Article 30(2) by specifying that the authority responsible for service is the first authority receiving the documents to be served. It also considered that, in the light of the importance of the date and time of receipt, the authorities responsible for service and the courts, as appropriate, should note when exactly they receive the documents for purposes of service, or when exactly the document instituting proceedings is lodged with the court.

---

compatible with Article IV of the 1968 Protocol; and *Tavoulareas v Tsavliris* [2004] EWCA Civ 48 (CA), holding that (normally at least) a Greek court was not seised until service in accordance with EC Regulation 1348/2000, where applicable. Cf. *Phillips v Symes* [2008] UKHL 1, where a minority of the House of Lords (Lady Hale and Lord Mance) would have overruled *Dresser v Falcongate* and adopted a rule that the English court was seised at the issue of the claim form.

[52]   See *Grupo Torras v Al-Sabah* [1996] 1 Lloyd's Rep 7 (CA); *Fox v Taher* [1997] ILPr 441 (CA), and *Glencore v Metro* [1999] 2 Lloyd's Rep 632 (Moore-Bick J).

[53]   See *Grupo Torras v Al-Sabah* [1996] 1 Lloyd's Rep 7 (CA). Cf. *Phillips v Symes* [2008] UKHL 1, where the House of Lords, in the exercise of discretion under the Civil Procedure Rules, upheld the effectiveness of a defective service of an English claim form, and thereby achieved priority for the English action under Article 21 of the Lugano Convention 1988; and *Olafsson v Gissurarson (No 2)* [2008] 1 All ER (Comm) 1106 (CA).

[54]   See *The Freccia del Nord* [1989] 1 Lloyd's Rep 388 (Sheen J); and *The Turquoise Bleu* [1996] 1 ILRM 406 (Irish High Court).

[55]   [2006] 1 All ER (Comm) 109.

[56]   COM(2009) 174 final, at section 3.5, and COM(2009) 175 final, at question 5.

## Relation with other Provisions

In *Overseas Union Insurance v New Hampshire Insurance*[57] and *Gasser v MISAT*,[58] the European Court emphasised that under Article 27 it is for the first court to determine its own jurisdiction; and that even where the jurisdiction of the first court is contested, Article 27 does not permit the second court itself to examine the jurisdiction of the first court. The Court explained that the second court is never in a better position than the first court to determine whether the first court has jurisdiction. Such jurisdiction is determined directly by the rules of the Regulation, which are common to both courts and may be interpreted and applied with the same authority by each of them.

In these cases, the European Court admitted by way of an obiter dictum the possibility of an exception where the question is whether the second court has exclusive jurisdiction by virtue of subject-matter (such as proprietary rights in land) under Article 22. Such an exception seems justifiable in view of the provisions of Articles 35 and 45 whereby a judgment given in breach of Article 22 must be refused recognition and enforcement under Chapter III in the other Member States. This exception was accepted and applied by the English Court of Appeal in *Speed Investments Ltd v Formula One Holdings Ltd*[59] in the context of corporate matters governed by Article 22(2).

Another exception was recognised by the European Court in *Von Horn v Cinnamond*[60] in relation to the transitional situation where the first action was brought before, and the second after, the entry into force of the Community legislation between the two Member States involved.[61] The first action had been brought in Portugal before, and the second in England after, the entry into force of the Accession Convention 1989 between Portugal and the United Kingdom. In view of the absence of explicit provisions addressing the transitional operation of Article 27, the Court took account of the transitional provisions on recognition and enforcement.[62] It effectively ruled that in such a case the second court must apply Article 27 if the first court had assumed jurisdiction on the basis of a rule which accorded with the provisions of Chapter II of the Regulation, or with those of a convention which was in force between the two States concerned when the first proceedings were instituted, and must do so provisionally if the first court had not yet ruled on whether it had jurisdiction. On the other hand, the second court must not apply Article 27 if the first court had assumed jurisdiction on the basis of a rule which did not accord with the provisions of Chapter II, nor with those of a convention which was in force between those two States when the first proceedings were instituted.

But, apart from cases of exclusive jurisdiction by subject-matter under Article 22, and of the transitional situation addressed in *Von Horn*, the decisions in *Overseas Union* and *Gasser* have established that Article 27 creates an invariable rule that the second court cannot itself

---

[57]  Case C-351/89, [1991] ECR I-3317.
[58]  Case C-116/02, [2003] ECR I-14693.
[59]  [2005] 1 BCLC 455 (CA).
[60]  Case C-163/95, [1997] ECR I-5451.
[61]  In any event, Article 27 does not apply where both actions were instituted before the relevant commencement date; see *Davy International v Voest Alpine* [1999] 1 All ER 103 (CA).
[62]  On these, see pp. 236–7 below.

examine the jurisdiction of the first court.[63] In particular, as the Court ruled in *Gasser*, the second court must initially stay its proceedings and eventually decline jurisdiction under Article 27, even if the first court's jurisdiction is contested on the ground that there is an agreement between the parties choosing the second court in accordance with Article 23. Thus the European Court has definitively rejected the extraordinary interpretation adopted by the English Court of Appeal (per Steyn LJ) in *Continental Bank v Aeakos*,[64] that Article 27 was inapplicable where the second court considered itself exclusively competent under Article 23.

To the present writer, the ruling in *Gasser* is entirely welcome. The need for the mechanism established by Article 27 with a view to resolving conflicts of jurisdiction is as great in cases where there is an alleged agreement on jurisdiction as in any other. There is no reason to presume that the alleged agreement exists or is valid, or that the court allegedly designated by the agreement is intended by the Regulation to have a predominant role in determining the existence and validity of the alleged agreement. Such existence and validity must be determined in accordance with the requirements of Article 23 and the decisions of the European Court on its interpretation, and the court allegedly chosen by the agreement is in no better position than any other court of a Member State to do so. However, in its Report and Green Paper of 21st April 2009,[65] the EC Commission contemplates that some amendment may be desirable with a view to strengthening the effect of jurisdiction clauses in the face of pending proceedings.

**Concurrent Exclusive Jurisdiction**

Article 29 of the Regulation supplements Article 27 by specifying that where actions come within the exclusive jurisdiction of several courts, a court subsequently seised must decline jurisdiction in favour of the court first seised. Article 29 envisages situations in which the same claim is subject to the concurrent exclusive jurisdiction of courts of two or more Member States on account of its subject-matter under Article 22. The solution adopted is to give mandatory priority to the court first seised. There is a clear implication that the judgment of the first court must be recognised in the other Member States, including a Member State which had concurrent exclusive jurisdiction over the claim.[66]

It is clear that the situation envisaged by Article 29 may arise in relation to tenancies of land under Article 22(1), which in certain cases explicitly confers concurrent exclusive jurisdiction on the situs and the domicile.[67] It may also arise under Article 22(2), which confers exclusive jurisdiction over certain matters of company law on the courts of the Member State in which the company involved has its seat, since a company may be seated both in the country in which

---

[63]    Even before *Gasser*, it had been accepted by Andrew Smith J in *Evialis v Siat* [2003] 2 Lloyd's Rep 377 that there is no exception to Article 27 for disputes concerning insurance contracts.

[64]    [1994] 1 WLR 588 (CA). See also *Kloeckner v Gatoil* [1990] 1 Lloyd's Rep 177 (Hirst J); *IP Metal v Ruote (No 2)* [1994] 2 Lloyd's Rep 560 (CA); *Toepfer v Molino Boschi* [1996] 1 Lloyd's Rep 510 (Mance J); *Toepfer v Cargill* [1997] 2 Lloyd's Rep 98 (Colman J) and [1998] 1 Lloyd's Rep 379 (CA); *Bank of Scotland v Banque Nationale de Paris* [1996] SLT 103 (Lord Penrose); *Glencore v Metro* [1999] 2 Lloyd's Rep 632 (Moore-Bick J); and *The Kribi* [2001] 1 Lloyd's Rep 76 (Aikens J).

[65]    COM(2009) 174 final, at section 3.3, and COM(2009) 175 final, at question 3.

[66]    See Gaudemet-Tallon, at para. 93 For an exception under the Lugano Convention 1988, see Article IB of its First Protocol; and pp. 147–8 above.

[67]    See pp. 147–9 above.

it was incorporated and has its registered office, and also in another country in which its central management and control is actually exercised.[68] Another case which may fall within Article 29, on a possible interpretation of Article 22(1), is where the dispute concerns an easement benefiting land in one Member State and burdening land in another Member State.[69]

## Possible Reform

In its Report and Green Paper of 21st April 2009,[70] the EC Commission contemplates that the operation of Article 27 might be improved by strengthening of the communication and interaction between the courts seised in parallel proceedings, and/or by the exclusion of the application of Article 27 in the case of negative declaratory relief.

## RELATED ACTIONS

### Scope

Article 28 deals with related but dissimilar actions. Related actions are defined by Article 28(3) as ones which are so closely connected that it is expedient to hear and determine them together to avoid the risk of irreconcilable judgments resulting from separate proceedings. But it is clear that Article 28 does not apply to similar actions to which Article 27 applies. It is also clear that actions may be related even though they are not between the same parties.

The concept of related actions was considered by the European Court in *The Maciej Rataj*[71] in the context of actions brought in different Member States against the same shipowner by owners of different parts of a bulk cargo, shipped under separate but identical contracts between the relevant cargo-owner and the shipowner, seeking damages for contamination alleged to have occurred during the voyage. In holding that this situation fell within Article 28, the Court distinguished the concept of irreconcilability used in Article 28(3) from that used in Article 34(3) (on denial of recognition to judgments).[72] It adopted a broad interpretation of Article 28, as covering all cases where separate trial and judgment would involve a risk of conflicting decisions, even if the judgments could be separately enforced and their legal consequences would not be mutually exclusive.

This broad approach was subsequently qualified slightly by the European Court in *Roche Nederland BV v Primus*,[73] where it ruled that, for actions to be related, there must be a risk of contradictory decisions. For decisions to be regarded as contradictory, it is not sufficient that there is a divergence in the outcome of the dispute. The divergence must also arise in the context of the same situation of law and fact. Thus, in view of the territorial character of intellectual property rights, no sufficient divergence arises where there are claims for infringement of parallel patents, granted for several Member States, against several defendants, domiciled

---

68   See pp. 149–52 above.
69   See p. 146 above.
70   COM(2009) 174 final, at section 3.5, and COM(2009) 175 final, at question 5.
71   Case C-406/92, [1994] ECR I-5439.
72   See also *Grupo Torras v Al-Sabah*, [1995] 1 Lloyd's Rep 374 (Mance J).
73   Case C-539/03, [2006] ECR I-6535.

in different Member States, and each defendant is sued for an infringement committed in the State of its domicile. On the other hand, in *Freeport v Arnoldsson*,[74] the European Court ruled that claims may be related even if they have different legal bases; for example, where claims in respect of the same loss are made by the same plaintiff against different defendants, and the claim against one defendant is contractual, while the claim against the other defendant is based on tort.[75]

In view of *The Maciej Rataj*,[76] a broad view of the scope of Article 28 was adopted by the House of Lords (per Lord Saville) in *Sarrio v Kuwait Investment Authority*,[77] where it rejected the view of the Court of Appeal (per Evans LJ) that, for Article 28 to apply, there had to be a risk of conflicting judgments on primary issues relating to facts necessary to establish a cause of action. The House emphasised that a broad common-sense approach must be applied to the question of whether actions are related. This involves bearing in mind the objective of Article 28, applying the simple wide test set out in Article 28, and refraining from an over-sophisticated analysis of the matter. Accordingly, the House declined jurisdiction under Article 28 over an English action in tort seeking damages for negligent mis-statements by the defendant which had induced the plaintiff to enter into a contract with the defendant's subsidiary, in favour of an earlier Spanish action seeking to hold the defendant liable on the same contract by piercing the corporate veil. Similarly, in *D v P*,[78] Connell J held that a wife's claim against her husband for maintenance for herself was related to her claim for maintenance for their children. Again, in *Prazic v Prazic*,[79] the Court of Appeal held that an English application by a wife under the Trusts of Land and Appointment of Trustees Act 1996, seeking a declaration establishing her entitlement to an equitable interest in property owned by the husband, was related to her claim for ancillary relief in French divorce proceedings. However, in *Popely v Popely*,[80] Finlay Geoghegan J adopted a rather restrictive approach to Article 28, in holding that claims between the same parties, who had been informal business partners, were not related because they involved ownership of different items of property.

In *Research in Motion UK Ltd v Visto Corp*,[81] the English Court of Appeal emphasised that, in contrast to Article 27, which requires comparison of the claims made in the two proceedings, Article 28 also involves consideration of the defences. Moreover, Article 28 requires an assessment of the degree of connection, and then a value judgment as to the expediency of hearing the two actions together (assuming that they could be so heard) in order to avoid the risk of inconsistent judgments. Article 28 does not say that any possibility of inconsistent judgments means that they are inevitably related. Rather Article 28 leaves it open to a court to acknowledge a connection, or a risk of inconsistent judgments, but to say that the

---

[74]  Case C-98/06, [2007] ECR I-8319.

[75]  The Court overruled its earlier dictum to the contrary, adopted in Case C-51/97: *Réunion Européenne v Spliethoff's Bevrachtingskantoor* [1998] ECR I-6511, at para 50. See also pp. 116–19 above.

[76]  Case C-406/92, [1994] ECR I-5439.

[77]  [1999] AC 32 (HL), reversing [1997] 1 Lloyd's Rep 113 (CA), and substantially restoring [1996] 1 Lloyd's Rep 650 (Mance J). See also *Bank of Tokyo-Mitsubishi v Baskan Gida* [2004] ILPr 26 (Lawrence Collins J).

[78]  [1998] 2 FLR 25.

[79]  [2006] 2 FLR 1128 (CA).

[80]  [2006] 4 IR 356.

[81]  [2008] 2 All ER (Comm) 560 (CA).

connection is not sufficiently close, or the risk is not sufficiently great, to make the actions related for the purposes of the Article. Ultimately, the Court of Appeal concluded that English proceedings for a declaration about an English patent and a particular product were not related to Italian proceedings for declarations concerning other patents and other products.

## Mechanism

The solution to the problem of related actions adopted by Article 28 is to confer discretionary powers on the second court. It is authorised by Article 28(1) to stay its own proceedings, so as to enable it to have the benefit of the first court's judgment before it reaches its own decision.[82] It is also authorised by Article 28(2) to decline jurisdiction altogether, in order to enable the whole matter to be determined by the first court. A third choice remains available, in that the second court may, after due consideration, refuse both to stay its proceedings and to decline jurisdiction in favour of the first court. The second court will then proceed to determine its action, without waiting for the first court to determine the first action. In that event, there may be a rush to judgment, since the first judgment on the merits, given by either of the courts, will qualify for recognition by the other court under Chapter III of the Regulation. For Chapter III makes no exception to the obligation to grant recognition and enforcement to judgments given in other Member States on account of the pendency of related proceedings in a court of the State addressed.[83] As the English Court of Appeal recognised in *WPP v Benatti*,[84] the first court has no power to interfere with the discretion conferred by Article 22 on the second court.

Under the Regulation, the power of the second court to decline jurisdiction under Article 28(2) is limited to situations where both actions are pending at first instance, but its power merely to stay its proceedings under Article 28(1) is not subject to this restriction. Formerly, Article 22 of the Brussels Convention subjected both powers to this condition. In *Bank of Scotland v Banque Nationale de Paris*,[85] Lord Penrose found the reasons for this restriction to be unclear, and in *SNPAA v Boa*[86] the French Court of Cassation ruled that the requirement of pendency at first instance is designed only to prevent a party being deprived of a level of jurisdiction. It therefore upheld a decision by a French appellate court to decline jurisdiction in favour of Dutch proceedings which were still pending at first instance. In any event, Article 37 of the Regulation deals with the situation where in the first country an appeal is pending against a first instance judgment, by permitting a court of a Member State in which recognition is sought of a judgment given in another Member State to stay its proceedings if an ordinary appeal against the judgment has been lodged.[87]

---

[82]    Cf. *Reichhold v Goldman Sachs* [2000] 1 WLR 173 (CA), staying temporarily an English action to await determination of a subsequently commenced related arbitral proceeding between different parties.

[83]    See Droz, at para 518; and *Brasserie du Pecheur v Kreissparkasse Main-Spessart*, 14th May 1996 (French Court of Cassation).

[84]    [2007] 2 All ER (Comm) 525 (CA).

[85]    [1996] SLT 103.

[86]    27th October 1992.

[87]    See pp. 264–6 below.

The power of the second court under Article 28(2) to decline jurisdiction in favour of the first court is made subject to further conditions: there must be an application by one of the parties for such an order; the first court must have jurisdiction to entertain both actions; and the law of the Member State to which the first court belongs must permit consolidation of the actions.[88] The jurisdiction of the first court to entertain both actions must exist independently of Article 28. For, as the European Court ruled in *Elefanten Schuh v Jacqmain*,[89] Article 28 does not confer jurisdiction on a court to entertain an action in respect of which it is otherwise incompetent. In particular, it does not make good the deficiencies of Article 6, which in some, but by no means all, cases empowers a court to entertain an action on the ground that it is related to another action of which the court is already seised. Moreover, it seems clear that if the second court has exclusive jurisdiction over the dispute before it by virtue of subject-matter under Article 22, it has power to stay its proceedings under Article 28(1) but not to decline jurisdiction under Article 28(2).[90]

As regards the exercise of discretion under Article 28, English courts have recognised that the second court must not treat the legal system of one Member State as superior or inferior to that of another, and that a stay should not be refused on the ground that it would deprive one of the parties of a procedural advantage which is available under the law of the second court; for example, in respect of the possibility of obtaining summary judgment without trial, or of a wider discovery of documents.[91]

Some useful guidelines as to the operation of Article 28 were offered by Mance J in *Grupo Torras v Al-Sabah*.[92] He explained that the definition of related actions laid down by Article 28(3) allows a broad consideration of closeness of connection, expediency and the risk of irreconcilable judgments, and in addition Article 28(1) provides for a discretion. Satisfaction of the criteria for related actions set out in Article 28(3) is by itself likely to create a prima facie case for a stay, but considerations of forum conveniens enter into the question whether a stay should actually be granted under the discretion provided by Article 28(1). Thus the second court may consider matters such as the extent of the relatedness, the stage reached in each set of proceedings, and the proximity of each court to the subject-matter of the case. The discretion under Article 28(1) involves a reassessment of the significance of the relatedness in the light of any considerations not explicitly embraced by Article 28(3). But an important factor in relation to the discretion under Article 28(1) is that there is no possibility that the court first seised may decline jurisdiction on grounds of forum non conveniens, even where the second court may regard itself as the appropriate forum.[93] Thus any decision to refuse a

---

[88]     Article 28(2) of the Regulation makes it clear that it is the law of the country of the first court, rather than that of the second court, which must permit consolidation. The less clear wording of Article 22(2) of the Brussels Convention was interpreted to the same effect in *Sarrio v Kuwait Investment Authority* [1999] AC 32 (HL).

[89]     Case 150/80, [1981] ECR 1671.

[90]     Cf. Gaudemet-Tallon, at para 302, arguing that Article 28 would not apply at all in such a case.

[91]     See *Virgin Aviation v CAD Aviation* [1991] ILPr 79 (Ognall J); and *Sarrio v Kuwait Investment Authority* [1996] 1 Lloyd's Rep 650 (Mance J), ultimately restored, without reference to this point, [1999] AC 32 (HL).

[92]     [1995] 1 Lloyd's Rep 374.

[93]     This must be qualified in one respect. If the first court's jurisdiction is based on Article 4 because the defendant is not domiciled in a Member State, it may have power under its own law to decline jurisdiction on grounds of forum non conveniens. Such a scenario is most likely where the two courts are British and Irish.

stay under the discretion in Article 28 has the unpalatable implication that there is bound to be concurrent litigation, unless the litigation before the first court is voluntarily abandoned. This is a powerful consideration which must inevitably make for caution before concluding that there are other factors which overall justify a refusal of the stay towards which satisfaction of Article 28(3) will by itself already point.[94] On the other hand, as Rimer J recognised in *Trustor v Barclays Bank*,[95] the second court may exercise its discretion against staying its proceedings if there is likely to be substantial delay in the determination of the first proceedings, especially if a complicated network of related litigation makes at least some risk of irreconcilable judgments almost inevitable.

In *Morgan v Primacom*,[96] Cooke J held that the ruling of the European Court in *Gasser v MISAT*,[97] that Article 27 does not permit the second court to examine the jurisdiction of the first court, even where the jurisdiction of the first court is contested by reference to a jurisdiction clause in favour of the second court having effect under Article 23, does not extend to Article 28. Accordingly, applying the discretion conferred by Article 28, the English court will normally refuse to stay or decline jurisdiction where related proceedings fall within the scope of a valid English jurisdiction clause. But the contrary view was adopted in *J v P*,[98] where Sumner J held that even under Article 28 the second court must defer to the first court on questions of jurisdiction, including as to the existence of an agreement on jurisdiction under Article 23.

### Possible Reform

In its Report and Green Paper of 21st April 2009,[99] the EC Commission contemplates the possibility of introducing into Article 28 uniform rules permitting the consolidation of actions by and/or against several parties. It also envisages that the risk of negative conflicts of jurisdiction could be addressed by a co-operation and communication mechanism between the courts involved, and by an obligation on the part of the court which declined jurisdiction to re-open the case if the court first seised declines jurisdiction.

## ANTI-SUIT INJUNCTIONS

### The Traditional English Law

The English courts have traditionally claimed a discretionary power to restrain a party by injunction from commencing or continuing to prosecute proceedings in a foreign court. In the absence of a jurisdiction or arbitration agreement, the power has been exercised cautiously. Thus in *SNIA v Lee Kui Jak*,[100] the Privy Council emphasised that an anti-suit injunction

---

[94]    See also *Bank of Tokyo-Mitsubishi v Baskan Gida* [2004] ILPr 26 (Lawrence Collins J), at para 228.

[95]    [2000] WL 1675230, *The Times* of 22nd November 2000 (Rimer J).

[96]    [2005] EWHC 508 (Comm).

[97]    Case C-116/02, [2003] ECR I-14693.

[98]    [2007] EWHC 704 (Fam).

[99]    COM(2009) 174 final, at section 3.5, and COM(2009) 175 final, at question 5.

[100]   [1987] AC 871.

should not be granted unless the English court is satisfied that the continuance of the foreign proceedings would be oppressive. It explained that this normally requires not only that the English court should consider itself the natural forum for the determination of the dispute, but also that the continuance of the foreign proceedings would cause injustice to the defendant there (as by substantially prejudicing his position in connection with a related claim against a third person), and that the prevention of the foreign proceedings would not unjustly deprive the plaintiff there of a legitimate advantage. Moreover, owing to the absence of any sufficient English interest, an English court will usually refuse to grant an anti-suit injunction designed to prevent an English party from suing in one foreign court, where the appropriate forum is another foreign court.[101]

A different approach has been adopted, however, where a foreign action is brought in breach of an agreement for English exclusive jurisdiction or arbitration. In such circumstances, the English courts have readily granted an anti-suit injunction unless the party suing abroad has established strong reasons why it should not be held to its contract.[102]

## The Impact of the Brussels I Regulation

The rulings of the European Court in *Gasser v MISAT*,[103] *Turner v Grovit*,[104] and *Allianz v West Tankers*[105] have now unequivocally established that the Brussels I Regulation precludes the grant of an injunction whereby a court of a Member State prohibits a party to proceedings pending before it from commencing or continuing legal proceedings before a court of another Member State in respect of a matter within the scope of the Regulation.

Prior to these rulings, there had been some indications of acceptance by the English courts that, at least in the absence of an English jurisdiction or arbitration clause, it would be contrary to the Regulation for an English court to grant an anti-suit injunction against proceedings in another Member State in respect of such a matter.[106] But no such inhibitions had been recognised in the presence of an English jurisdiction or arbitration clause.[107]

---

[101]  See *Airbus Industrie v Patel* [1999] 1 AC 119 (HL), reversing [1997] 2 Lloyd's Rep 8 (CA). See also *Amoco (UK) Exploration Co v British American Offshore Ltd* [1999] 2 Lloyd's Rep 772 (Langley J), on service abroad under the Civil Procedure Rules 1998.

[102]  See *Continental Bank v Aeakos* [1994] 1 WLR 588 (CA); *The Angelic Grace* [1995] 1 Lloyd's Rep 87 (CA); *Ultisol v Bouygues* [1996] 2 Lloyd's Rep 140 (Clarke J); *Donohue v Armco* [2002] 1 All ER 749 (HL); and *The Kribi* [2001] 1 Lloyd's Rep 76 (Aikens J). See also *Credit Suisse v MLC* [1999] 1 Lloyd's Rep 767 (Rix J); and *Shell v Coral Oil* [1999] 1 Lloyd's Rep 72 (Moore-Bick J). Cf. *Toepfer v Cargill* [1997] 2 Lloyd's Rep 98 (Colman J); and *Mediterranean Shipping Co v Atlantic Container Line* [1999] CLY 4441 (CA).

[103]  Case C-116/02, [2003] ECR I-14693.

[104]  Case C-159/02, [2004] ECR I-3565.

[105]  Case C-185/07, [2009] ECR I-663.

[106]  See *Airbus Industrie v Patel* [1997] 2 Lloyd's Rep 8 (CA), reversed on other grounds, [1999] 1 AC 119 (HL); and the excellent decision of Donaldson QC in *Turner v Grovit* [1999] 1 All ER (Comm) 445, reversed by the Court of Appeal (per Laws LJ), [1999] 1 WLR 794, but eventually referred by the House of Lords to the European Court, [2002] 1 WLR 107, and determined as Case C-159/02, [2004] ECR I-3565.

[107]  See especially *Continental Bank v Aeakos* [1994] 1 WLR 588 (CA); and *The Angelic Grace* [1995] 1 Lloyd's Rep 87 (CA).

Eventually, in *Turner v Grovit*,[108] the Court of Appeal (per Laws LJ) reasserted a broad power of the English courts to issue anti-suit injunctions against proceedings in other Member States on grounds of oppression or abuse, even where there was no jurisdiction or arbitration agreement involved, and especially where there were earlier English proceedings which had priority under Article 27 of the Regulation. The willingness of the Court of Appeal to 'shoot it out' in this context had also emerged from dicta in *Phillip Alexander Securities v Bamberger*[109] that a judgment obtained in knowing breach of an English anti-suit injunction would normally be refused recognition or enforcement on grounds of public policy, even (it seems) where the anti-suit injunction had been granted on an erroneous understanding of the situation.[110]

Insofar as the assertion of an English power to issue anti-suit injunctions in respect of proceedings in courts of other Member States falling within the scope of the Brussels I Regulation was based on the presence of an English jurisdiction clause, the assertion relied on the argument that Article 23 of the Regulation (on jurisdiction clauses) prevails over Article 27 (on similar actions). But that argument was rejected by the European Court in the clearest terms in *Gasser v MISAT*,[111] where it ruled that the court subsequently seised cannot itself examine the jurisdiction of the first court, but must initially stay its proceedings and eventually decline jurisdiction under Article 27, even if the first court's jurisdiction is contested on the ground that there is an agreement between the parties choosing the second court in accordance with Article 23.

Insofar as the assertion of the power was based on an arbitration agreement, it relied on the argument that the subject-matter of the English proceedings for an anti-suit injunction was the issue whether the determination of the substantive dispute between the parties should be by the foreign court or by arbitration, and that the English proceedings seeking the anti-suit injunction were therefore excluded from the scope of the Brussels I Regulation by Article 1(2)(d). But that argument was difficult to reconcile with the European Court's ruling in *Van Uden v Deco-Line*[112] that a valid arbitration agreement has the effect of excluding the substantive jurisdiction of all courts under Articles 2 and 5-24 of the Regulation.[113]

Eventually, in *Turner v Grovit*,[114] the European Court rejected, emphatically and in unqualified terms, the admissibility of anti-suit injunctions in the context of the Brussels I Regulation. The Court concluded that the Regulation precludes the grant of an injunction whereby a court of a Member State prohibits a party to proceedings pending before it from commencing or continuing legal proceedings before a court of another Member State; and this is so even where that party is acting in bad faith with a view to frustrating existing

---

108    [1999] 1 WLR 794 (CA).
109    [1997] ILPr 73 (CA). See also *The Hari Bhum* [2004] 1 Lloyd's Rep 206 (Moore-Bick J).
110    Cf. *Motorola Credit Corp v Uzan* [2004] 1 WLR 113, where the Court of Appeal, in refusing to uphold worldwide freezing orders in support of substantive proceedings in New York against defendants who were resident in Turkey and had no substantial assets in England, took into account the existence of Turkish anti-suit injunctions.
111    Case C-116/02, [2003] ECR I-14693.
112    Case C-391/95, [1998] ECR I-7091.
113    See further the analysis at pp. 35–42 above.
114    Case C-159/02, [2004] ECR I-3565. The case was referred by the House of Lords, [2002] 1 WLR 107.

proceedings. In *Allianz v West Tankers*,[115] the European Court further ruled that it is incompatible with the Regulation for a court of a Member State to make an order to restrain a person from commencing or continuing proceedings before the courts of another Member State on the ground that such proceedings would be contrary to an arbitration agreement.

In *Turner v Grovit*,[116] the European Court explained that the Regulation is necessarily based on the trust which the Member States accord to one another's legal systems and judicial institutions. It is inherent in that principle of mutual trust that, within the scope of the Regulation, the rules on jurisdiction that it lays down, which are common to all the courts of the Member States, may be interpreted and applied with the same authority by each of them. Similarly, otherwise than in a small number of exceptional cases listed in Article 35(1), which are limited to the stage of recognition or enforcement and relate only to certain rules of special or exclusive jurisdiction not relevant in the instant case, the Regulation does not permit the jurisdiction of a court to be reviewed by a court in another Member State. A prohibition imposed by a court, backed by a penalty, restraining a party from commencing or continuing proceedings before a foreign court, undermines the latter court's jurisdiction to determine the dispute. Any injunction prohibiting a claimant from bringing such an action must be seen as constituting interference with the jurisdiction of the foreign court which, as such, is incompatible with the system of the Regulation.

The European Court further explained that, insofar as the conduct for which the defendant is criticised consists in recourse to the jurisdiction of a court of another Member State, the judgment made as to the abusive nature of that conduct implies an assessment of the appropriateness of bringing proceedings before a court of another Member State. Such an assessment runs counter to the principle of mutual trust which underpins the Regulation and prohibits a court, except in special circumstances not applicable in the instant case, from reviewing the jurisdiction of the court of another Member State.[117] Moreover, it is not permissible for the application of national procedural rules to impair the effectiveness of the Regulation, and that result would follow from the grant of an anti-suit injunction which has the effect of limiting the application of the rules on jurisdiction laid down by the Regulation. Further, recourse to such measures renders ineffective the specific mechanisms provided for by the Regulation for cases of concurrent actions. It is also liable to give rise to situations involving conflicts for which the Regulation contains no rules. For the possibility cannot be excluded that, even if an injunction had been issued in one Member State, a decision might nevertheless be given by a court of another Member State; or that the courts of two Member States which allowed such measures might issue contradictory injunctions.

In *Allianz v West Tankers*,[118] the European Court ruled that it is incompatible with the Brussels I Regulation for a court of a Member State to make an order to restrain a person from

---

[115]   Case C-185/07, [2009] ECR I-663.

[116]   Case C-159/02, [2004] ECR I-3565.

[117]   See also *Tavoulareas v Tsavliris* [2006] 1 All ER (Comm) 109, where Andrew Smith J relied on the reasoning in *Turner v Grovit* in refusing, when setting aside an English default judgment, to impose a condition requiring the defendant to pay the sum claimed into court, since the ground on which the condition was requested by the plaintiff involved criticism of the defendant's conduct in relation to concurrent proceedings in Greece.

[118]   Case C-185/07, [2009] ECR I-663. The ruling was given on a reference from the House of Lords, [2007] UKHL 4. See also pp. 35–42 above.

commencing or continuing proceedings before the courts of another Member State on the ground that such proceedings would be contrary to an arbitration agreement. It accepted that the proceedings giving rise to the anti-suit injunction were outside the scope of the Regulation, since their subject-matter and the rights which they served to protect were covered by the exclusion for arbitration. Nonetheless, it explained that such proceedings had consequences which undermined the effectiveness of the Regulation, by preventing the attainment of the objectives of unification of the rules of conflict of jurisdiction in civil and commercial matters and the free movement of decisions in those matters, in particular by preventing a court of another Member State from exercising the jurisdiction conferred on it by the Regulation.

In *Masri v Consolidated Contractors (No 3)*,[119] the English Court of Appeal (per Lawrence Collins LJ) confirmed that nothing in the Brussels I Regulation or the Lugano Convention 1988 prevents an English court from granting an anti-suit injunction against the commencement or continuance of proceedings in a country which is neither an EC Member State nor a Lugano Convention country, even if the defendant is domiciled in an EC Member State or a Lugano Convention country.[120] Moreover, where the English court has been properly seised of, or has given judgment on, a substantive claim on the merits, its substantive jurisdiction carries with it the ancillary and incidental power to grant an anti-suit injunction in respect of proceedings outside the European Union and the Lugano Convention countries. Moreover, an interim anti-suit injunction counts as a provisional measure, within Article 31 of the Brussels I Regulation.

## The Merits

To the present writer, the rulings of the European Court in *Turner v Grovit*[121] and *Allianz v West Tankers*[122] are entirely welcome. The undesirability of anti-suit injunctions in any circumstances becomes clear when one takes account of the likely reaction from the foreign court whose proceedings are affected. In an American decision, *James v Grand Trunk Western Railroad*,[123] the Illinois Supreme Court granted a counter-injunction against enforcement of a Michigan anti-suit injunction against an Illinios action in respect of a railway accident which had occurred in Michigan. Bristow J said: 'This court need not, and will not, countenance having its right to try cases, of which it has proper jurisdiction, determined by the courts of other States, through their injunctive process. We are not only free to disregard such out-of-State injunctions, and to adjudicate the merits of the pending action, but we can protect our jurisdiction from such usurpation by the issuance of a counter-injunction restraining the enforcement of the out-of-State injunction.'

Greater wisdom was shown more recently by the California Supreme Court in *Advanced Bionics v Medtronic*,[124] which involved a non-competition clause in an employment contract,

---

119   [2008] 2 All ER (Comm) 1146 (CA).
120   See also *SCOR v Eras International (No 2)* [1995] 2 All ER 278 (Potter J); and *Ultisol v Bouygues* [1996] 2 Lloyd's Rep 140 (Clarke J).
121   Case C-159/02, [2004] ECR I-3565.
122   Case C-185/07, [2009] ECR I-663.
123   152 NE2d 858 (1958).
124   59 P3d 231 (California, 2002).

and conflicting anti-suit injunctions obtained by the first and second employers in the first and second employment States, Minnesota and California, enjoining the other employer from proceeding with litigation in the other State. The California Supreme Court eventually gave way and lifted its anti-suit injunction on grounds of comity and judicial restraint.[125] Disappointingly, the traditionally accepted view that the US Constitution does not prevent a court of one State of the Union from issuing an injunction barring a party from maintaining litigation in a sister State, but does not compel any deference outside the rendering State, has recently been endorsed by a cautious dictum of Ginsburg J in the United States Supreme Court in *Baker v General Motors*.[126]

In the context of international commerce, the anti-suit injunction threatens to lead ultimately to situations in which the operations of major multinational companies are brought to a halt through the sequestration of the assets, and the imprisonment of the senior executives, of each company involved – in the case of one of the parties, in the country in which an anti-suit injunction has been issued, and in the case of the other party, in the country in which a counter-injunction has been issued. While the merits of international capitalism may be questioned, there is little to be said for arbitrary obstruction arising from judicial chauvinism.

---

[125]  See also the remarks of Wilson J in *S v S* [1997] 1 WLR 1200, in the context of a dispute concerning financial relief on divorce: 'I cannot ignore the fact that, subject to appeal, the court in New York has unequivocally sought to arrogate to itself all financial issues between the parties. I pay regard thereto not by reason of comity, important though that principle may sometimes remain, but for practical reasons. If I were to refuse the stay and the wife were to proceed here through divorce to ventilate financial claims, the husband would, I consider, not find it difficult to persuade the court in New York to make orders designed to curb or obstruct what it would regard as the wife's wrongful activities in the English court and to reverse the effect of any award that she might thereby secure. The wife does, after all, have substantial assets there. I should hesitate before condemning the parties to conflict of that order.'

[126]  522 US 222 (1998). The actual ruling was that a court of an American State lacks jurisdiction to control courts elsewhere by precluding them, in actions brought by strangers to the instant litigation, from determining for themselves what witnesses are competent to testify and what evidence is relevant and admissible in their search for the truth; for example, by means of an injunction forbidding a party to the instant proceedings from giving evidence in other proceedings, even if subpoenaed by the court seised of the other proceedings.

# 9. Provisional measures and taking evidence

## INTRODUCTION

In this chapter, we shall focus on Article 31 of the Brussels I Regulation, which enables a court of a Member State which lacks substantive jurisdiction to order provisional measures in support of substantive proceedings in another Member State. We shall also examine EC Regulation 1206/2001, under which a court of a Member State may request a court of another Member State to take evidence for use by the requesting court.

## PROVISIONAL MEASURES

### Article 31 of the Brussels I Regulation

Article 31 of the Brussels I Regulation[1] enables application to be made to the courts of a Member State for such provisional, including protective, measures as may be available under the law of that State, even if, under the Regulation, the courts of another Member State have jurisdiction as to the substance of the matter.

This provision confers an additional jurisdiction, limited to provisional measures. In any event, as the European Court made clear in *Van Uden v Deco-Line*[2] and *Mietz v Intership Yachting Sneek*,[3] a court which has substantive jurisdiction under Articles 2 and 5–24 also has jurisdiction to order any provisional or protective measures which may prove necessary. In *Morgan v Primacom*,[4] Cooke J held that this applies even where the court has stayed its substantive proceedings under Article 27(1), while awaiting a decision on jurisdiction from a previously seised court of another Member State; but not where the court has declined jurisdiction under Article 27(2) in favour of the court first seised.

The power to order provisional measures conferred by Article 31 is not limited to cases where the defendant is domiciled in another Member State. It applies in any situation where the court from which provisional relief is requested lacks jurisdiction to determine the merits of the dispute by reason of any provision of Chapter II; for example, because another Member State has exclusive jurisdiction under Articles 22 or 23. It is, however, applicable only where the substantive dispute, in respect of which the provisional measure is sought, falls within the material scope of the Regulation as defined by Article 1.[5] Nonetheless, it applies where the

---

[1]   Article 31 echoes Article 24 of the Brussels Convention.
[2]   Case C-391/95, [1998] ECR I-7091, at paras 19–22.
[3]   Case C-99/96, [1999] ECR I-2277, at paras 40–41.
[4]   [2005] EWHC 508.
[5]   See Case 143/78: *De Cavel v De Cavel (No 1)* [1979] ECR 1055; Case 120/79: *De Cavel v De Cavel (No 2)* [1980] ECR 731; and Case 25/81: *CHW v GJH* [1982] ECR 1189.

substantive proceedings are to be conducted before arbitrators, for provisional measures are not in principle ancillary to arbitration proceedings, but are ordered in parallel to such proceedings and are intended as measures of support; thus they concern not arbitration as such but the protection of the substantive rights.[6] Moreover, it is immaterial whether the substantive action has already been commenced or is to be commenced subsequently.[7]

The principle which underlies Article 31 is that the courts of each Member State should be willing to assist the courts of another Member State by providing such interim relief as would be available if its own courts were seised of the substantive proceedings.[8] Thus Article 31 permits the making of an order (such as a French 'saisie conservatoire' or an English *Mareva* injunction) freezing assets which belong to the defendant and are located in the territory of the granting court, so as to prevent their disappearance before the merits of the plaintiff's claim have been determined by a court of another Member State, and thus to ensure their availability to meet an eventual judgment for the plaintiff on the merits which will be given in another Member State if his claim succeeds. Similarly, Article 31 enables an English court to grant a temporary injunction against an alleged breach of contract, in aid of a contemplated substantive action in another Member State, to operate until the hearing of an interim application by the court having substantive jurisdiction.[9]

On the other hand, the European Court has emphasised in *Reichert v Dresdner Bank (No 2)*[10] and *St Paul Dairy Industries v Unibel Exser*[11] that Article 31 is intended to avoid losses to the parties resulting from the long delays inherent in international proceedings, and is confined to measures which are intended to preserve a factual or legal situation so as to safeguard rights whose recognition is sought elsewhere from the court having jurisdiction as to the substance of the matter. Thus, as the Court ruled in *Reichert*, Article 31 does not extend to an application by a creditor, whereby he seeks to obtain the revocation in regard to him of a transfer of property effected by his debtor in fraud of his rights, since its purpose is to vary the legal situation of the debtor's assets and of the transferee by ordering revocation of the disposition. Nor, as the European Court ruled in *St Paul*, does Article 31 extend to an application for a measure ordering the hearing of a witness before substantive proceedings are initiated, for the purpose of enabling the applicant to decide whether to bring a case, to determine whether it would be well founded, and to assess the relevance of evidence which might be adduced.

In *Denilauler v Couchet Frères*,[12] the European Court established that a provisional order which is made without the defendant having been summoned to appear and is intended to be enforced without prior service on him is not enforceable in other Member States under Chapter III of the Regulation. Subsequently, in *Van Uden v Deco-Line*[13] and *Mietz v Intership*

---

6     See Case C-391/95: *Van Uden v Deco-Line* [1998] ECR I-7091, at paras 33–4.
7     See Case C-391/95: *Van Uden v Deco-Line* [1998] ECR I-7091, at para 34.
8     See per Millett LJ in *Credit Suisse v Cuoghi* [1998] QB 818 (CA).
9     See *Nike v Rosicky* [2007] EWHC 1967 (Ch), where Patten J enforced a sponsorship agreement by granting a temporary injunction preventing a footballer who was domiciled and employed in England from wearing boots bearing a rival manufacturer's trade mark. The substantive dispute was subject to an exclusive jurisdiction agreement in favour of the Dutch courts.
10     Case C-261/90, [1992] ECR I-2149.
11     Case C-104/03, [2005] ECR I-3481.
12     Case 125/79, [1980] ECR 1553. See pp. 224–6 below.
13     Case C-391/95, [1998] ECR I-7091.

*Yachting Sneek*,[14] the European Court effectively ruled that the jurisdiction conferred by Article 31 is confined to measures which are designed to be enforceable in the State in which they are granted. It ruled that the granting of provisional measures under Article 31 is conditional on the existence of a real connecting link between the subject-matter of the measures sought and the territory of the forum State.[15] Moreover, the interim payment of a contractual consideration does not constitute a provisional measure within Article 31 unless, firstly, repayment to the defendant of the sum awarded is guaranteed if the plaintiff is unsuccessful as regards the substance of his claim, and, secondly, the measure sought relates only to specific assets of the defendant located or to be located within the territory of the forum State.[16] But it seems that there is no requirement in Article 31 that there should be an emergency situation.[17]

In *Sandisk v Philips Electronics*,[18] which involved an application for an interlocutory injunction requiring the defendant to give a specified notice to the plaintiff before commencing proceedings to enforce patents, in refusing the application, Pumfrey J explained that the nature of the connection required by *Van Uden* between the subject-matter of the provisional or protective measures sought and the forum territory may be purely physical, by way of the presence of assets in the forum territory, or may arise from control, in that the addressee is present in the forum territory and immediately susceptible to such coercive measures to secure compliance as may be necessary.

In *Mietz v Intership Yachting Sneek*,[19] the European Court went further and created an additional exception to the general rule under Chapter III of the Regulation which prevents review of the jurisdiction of the court of origin by the court addressed, in order to prevent the abuse of Article 31 from undermining the scheme of Chapter II.[20] It emphasised the importance of ensuring that enforcement under Chapter III in another Member State of provisional or protective measures allegedly founded on the jurisdiction laid down in Article 31, but which go beyond the limits of that jurisdiction, does not result in circumvention of the rules on substantive jurisdiction set out in Chapter II. For the jurisdiction recognised by Article 31 constitutes, within the context of the Regulation, a special regime. Thus enforcement under Chapter III must be refused where: (i) the judgment was delivered at the end of proceedings which were not, by their very nature, proceedings as to substance, but summary proceedings for the granting of interim measures; (ii) the measure ordered (such as an unconditional interim payment) is not a provisional or protective measure permissible under Article 31; and (iii) the original court had either expressly indicated in its judgment that it had based its jurisdiction on Article 31, or had been silent as to the basis of its jurisdiction.

---

[14]    Case C-99/96, [1999] ECR I-2277.
[15]    See *Van Uden*, at paras 37–40.
[16]    See *Van Uden*, at paras 41–7, and *Mietz*, at paras 42–3. See also *Wermuth v Wermuth* [2003] 1 WLR 942 (CA), holding that an order in divorce proceedings for maintenance pending suit is not a provisional measure permissible under Article 31 of the Regulation. See also *Channel Tunnel Group v Balfour Beatty* [1993] AC 334, where the House of Lords refused to grant an interlocutory order requiring the continued performance of a construction contract, since such an order would largely pre-empt the substantive decision of the agreed arbitrators.
[17]    See *Krupp v Schlumberger*, 10th March 1992 (French Court of Cassation). Cf. Gaudemet-Tallon, at paras 267–71.
[18]    [2007] EWHC 332 (Ch).
[19]    Case C-99/96, [1999] ECR I-2277.
[20]    See also *Comet Group v Unika Computer* [2004] ILPr 1.

In its Report and Green Paper of 21st April 2009,[21] the EC Commission suggested that a new approach to provisional measures could be adopted, under which the courts of the Member State which have substantive jurisdiction would be empowered to discharge, modify or adapt a provisional measure granted by a court of another Member State under Article 31. The requirement of a connection between the measure and the territory of the court granting it could then be abandoned. The role of the court seised of a request under Article 31 would be to assist the proceedings on the merits by 'lending remedies', particularly when effective protection was not available in all the Member States, without interfering with the jurisdiction of the court having substantive jurisdiction. When such assistance was no longer needed, the court having substantive jurisdiction would be able to set aside the foreign measure.

Less radically, the Commission also suggested that it might be appropriate to specify that ex parte measures can be recognised and enforced under the Regulation if the defendant has the opportunity to contest the measure subsequently; and that the guarantee of repayment of an interim payment, required under Article 31, need not consist of a provisional payment or a bank guarantee.

## English Freezing Orders

Under s 25 of the Civil Jurisdiction and Judgments Act 1982, as extended by the Civil Jurisdiction and Judgments Act 1982 (Interim Relief) Order 1997 (SI 1997/302),[22] the English High Court has power to grant interim relief in aid of any substantive proceedings in a foreign court. It is immaterial whether or not the foreign proceedings have already been commenced; whether the foreign court is a court of another part of the United Kingdom, or of another EU Member State or Lugano Convention country, or of some other country; and whether or not the subject-matter of the foreign proceedings falls within the scope of the Brussels I Regulation or the Lugano Conventions.[23] But the foreign proceedings must be substantive proceedings, for the determination of the merits of a claim, or for the enforcement of an existing judgment on the merits, and must not themselves be proceedings solely for interim relief in support of other proceedings pending or to be brought in a third country or in arbitration.[24] Under ss 2 and 44 of the Arbitration Act 1996, the English court has a similar power to grant interim relief in support of English or foreign arbitration proceedings. But

---

21    COM(2009) 174 final, at section 3.6, and COM(2009) 175 final, at question 6.

22    The Order entered into force on 1st April 1997. Minor amendments to s 25 were made by the Civil Jurisdiction and Judgments Order 2001 (SI 2001/3929), Schedule 2, Part IV, para 10). These provisions also apply to the Northern Irish High Court. On the grant of interim relief in Scotland, see s 27 of the 1982 Act (as amended by SI 2001/3929, Schedule 2, Part IV, para 11). On its grant in Ireland, see the (Irish) European Communities (Civil and Commercial Judgments) Regulations 2002, reg 10.

For service abroad of an English application for interim relief in support of foreign proceedings, see para 3.1(5) of Practice Direction B supplementing Part 6 of the Civil Procedure Rules 1998 (as amended). It seems that an application for interim relief under s 25 exposes the applicant to an English counterclaim on the merits in respect of related issues; see *Balkanbank v Taher* [1995] 1 WLR 1067 (CA).

23    See *Credit Suisse v Cuoghi* [1998] QB 818 (CA); and *Seidel v Dominion Petroleum Administrative Services Ltd* [2008] All ER (D) 107 (Mar) (Norris J).

24    See *ETI Euro Telecom International NV v Republic of Bolivia* [2009] 2 All ER (Comm) 37 (CA); and *Kensington International Ltd v Republic of Congo* [2008] 1 WLR 1144 (CA).

neither the power under the 1982 Act nor the power under the 1996 Act extends to an arbitration under the Washington Convention of 18th March 1965 on the Settlement of Investment Disputes between States and Nationals of Other States.[25]

As Lord Bingham CJ explained in *Credit Suisse v Cuoghi*,[26] in exercising its power under s 25 of the 1982 Act to grant interim relief in aid of substantive proceedings in a foreign court, the English court will recognise its subordinate role and take care to avoid obstructing or hampering the management of the case by the court seised of the substantive proceedings or creating a risk of conflicting, inconsistent or overlapping orders in other courts. Thus it may weigh against the grant of English relief that the primary court could have granted such relief and has not done so, particularly if the primary court has been asked to grant such relief and declined. On the other hand, it will weigh in favour of granting such relief that a defendant is domiciled, resident or present in England, and so is liable to effective enforcement of a personal order.

It has been established since 1988 that in appropriate circumstances, and subject to the Brussels I Regulation, an English court may grant a freezing order in respect of assets situated abroad. An order relating to foreign assets should, however, specify that it is not to affect third parties in relation to acts abroad except: (i) as regards persons who are resident in England, have been given written notice at their English residence, and are able to prevent acts abroad which assist in the infringement of the order; or (ii) to the extent that its recognition or enforceability has been established by a decision of the relevant foreign court.[27]

Before the 1997 Order, the English courts had been very reluctant to grant an order freezing foreign assets in support of a foreign substantive action.[28] The position changed after the 1997 Order as a result of the ruling by the Court of Appeal in *Credit Suisse v Cuoghi*[29] that a worldwide freezing order in support of foreign substantive proceedings, rather than one limited to English assets, will be appropriate if: (i) it would have been appropriate if the English court had been seised of the substantive proceedings; (ii) the defendant is domiciled or resident in England; and (iii) there is no danger that its grant would obstruct the management of the case by the court seised of the substantive proceedings or give rise to confusion in third countries. But it is now clear that, insofar as it depends on Article 31 of the Brussels I Regulation, the power of the English courts to grant a freezing order in support of substantive proceedings elsewhere is limited by the rulings of the European Court in *Van Uden* and *Mietz* to orders designed to be enforced against assets or persons in England. This limitation applies where the subject-matter of the dispute falls within the material scope of the Regulation as defined by Article 1, and Chapter II of the Regulation deprives the English court of substantive jurisdiction in favour of a court of another Member State.

---

[25]   See *ETI Euro Telecom International NV v Republic of Bolivia* [2009] 2 All ER (Comm) 37 (CA).

[26]   [1998] QB 818 (CA).

[27]   See *Babanaft International v Bassatne* [1990] Ch 13 (CA); *Republic of Haiti v Duvalier* [1990] QB 202 (CA); and *Derby v Weldon* [1990] Ch 65 (CA). For guidelines relating to applications to the English court for permission to enforce a worldwide freezing order abroad, see *Dadourian Group International Inc v Simms* [2006] 3 All ER 48 (CA).

[28]   See *Rosseel v Oriental Commercial* [1990] 3 All ER 545 (CA); *The Xing Su Hai* [1995] 2 Lloyd's Rep 15 (Rix J); and *Bautrading v Nordling* [1997] 3 All ER 718 (CA).

[29]   [1998] QB 818 (CA).

The circumstances in which the English courts will grant a worldwide freezing order in support of foreign substantive proceedings were further considered by the Court of Appeal in *Motorola Credit Corp v Uzan*,[30] where worldwide injunctions were sought in England in support of proceedings in New York in which massive international commercial fraud was alleged against defendants, most of whom were resident in Turkey, and anti-suit injunctions had been issued by Turkish courts. Potter LJ explained that there are five particular considerations which the court should bear in mind, when considering the question whether it is inexpedient to make an order. Firstly, whether the making of the order will interfere with the management of the case in the primary court; for example, where the order is inconsistent with an order in the primary court or overlaps with it. Secondly, whether it is the policy in the primary jurisdiction not itself to make worldwide orders. Thirdly, whether there is a danger that the orders made will give rise to disharmony or confusion and/or risk of conflicting inconsistent or overlapping orders in other jurisdictions, in particular the courts of the State where the person enjoined resides or where the assets affected are located. If so, then respect for the territorial jurisdiction of that State should discourage the English court from using its unusually wide powers against a foreign defendant. Fourthly, whether at the time when the order is sought there is likely to be a potential conflict as to jurisdiction rendering it inappropriate and inexpedient to make a worldwide order. Fifthly, whether, in a case where jurisdiction is resisted and disobedience to be expected, the court will be making an order which it cannot enforce. In the result, the Court of Appeal upheld worldwide injunctions against one defendant who was resident and had substantial assets in England, and against another defendant who was resident in Turkey but had substantial assets in England, but refused injunctions against defendants who were resident in Turkey and had no assets in England.

In *Masri v Consolidated Contractors (No 2)*,[31] the English Court of Appeal (per Lawrence Collins LJ) held that, after a competent English court has given a judgment in favour of the plaintiff on the merits of a claim, nothing in the Brussels I Regulation prevents the court from making receiving orders and freezing orders, which operate against the judgment debtor personally and have limited effects on third parties, in respect of assets situated abroad, in order to pave the way for enforcement of the English judgment on the merits. This is so regardless of where the defendant is domiciled, and of where the assets in question are located. For the ruling of the European Court in *Van Uden v Deco-Line*[32] establishes that a court which has substantive jurisdiction under Chapter II of the Regulation also has jurisdiction to grant any ancillary orders, and the ruling of the European Court in *Reichert v Dresdner Bank (No 2)*[33] establishes that Article 22(5) is concerned with actual enforcement, and not with steps which may lead to enforcement.[34]

---

[30]    [2004] 1 WLR 113.
[31]    [2008] 2 All ER (Comm) 1099 (CA). See also *Masri v Consolidated Contractors* [2008] EWCA Civ 1367 (CA), and *Masri v Consolidated Contractors* [2009] EWCA Civ 36 (CA).
[32]    Case C-391/95, [1998] ECR I-7091.
[33]    Case C-261/90, [1992] ECR I-2149.
[34]    See also *Franses v Al Assad* [2007] All ER (D) 415 (Oct), where Henderson J granted a freezing order in respect of Spanish assets of a French debtor under an English judgment, but with a proviso that the English freezing order would lapse once the Spanish protective measures sought by the creditor were in place, as well as a requirement of an undertaking by the creditor to continue to apply diligently for the Spanish protective measures.

In *Masri v Consolidated Contractors (No 3)*,[35] the English Court of Appeal (per Lawrence Collins LJ) confirmed that nothing in the Brussels I Regulation or the Lugano Convention 1988 prevents an English court from granting an anti-suit injunction against the commencement or continuance of proceedings in a country which is neither an EU Member State nor a Lugano Convention country, even if the defendant is domiciled in an EU Member State or a Lugano Convention country. Moreover, where the English court has been properly seised of, or has given judgment on, a substantive claim on the merits, its substantive jurisdiction carries with it the ancillary and incidental power to grant an anti-suit injunction in respect of proceedings outside the European Union and the Lugano Convention countries. Moreover, an interim anti-suit injunction counts as a provisional measure, within Article 31 of the Brussels I Regulation.

In *Banco Nacional de Comercio Exterior SNC v Empresa de Telecomunicaciones de Cuba SA*,[36] the Court of Appeal (per Tuckey LJ) emphasised that, as regards the taking of protective measures in the context of enforcement under Chapter III of the Brussels I Regulation of a judgment given in another Member State, the English court will usually confine its intervention to the grant of a domestic (rather than a worldwide) freezing order, especially if the defendant is not resident in England.

Where an English or Northern Irish court declines jurisdiction over an admiralty action in rem in favour of arbitration or a foreign court, it will normally retain the property arrested or require the provision of equivalent security for the satisfaction of the eventual award or judgment in the same way as if the merits were to be determined in the English action in rem.[37]

## Other Restrictions under European Law

The grant of interim relief is also affected by Article 18(1) of the Treaty on the Functioning of the European Union,[38] which prohibits, within the scope of application of the European Treaties, discrimination on grounds of nationality. The European Court has ruled that, in view of the simplification in the reciprocal enforcement of judgments between Member States which has been achieved by the Brussels I Regulation, Article 18(1) of the Treaty prevents a court of a Member State, seised of an action on the merits, from treating parties from other Member States less favourably than local parties, as regards the granting of protective measures against a defendant's local assets.[39] It has also held that the same applies to the requiring of security for costs from a plaintiff.[40] Security for costs may be required of an

---

[35]   [2008] 2 All ER (Comm) 1146 (CA).

[36]   [2007] 2 All ER (Comm) 1093 (CA).

[37]   See s 26 of the Civil Jurisdiction and Judgments Act 1982, and *The Bazias 3* [1993] QB 673 (CA). For arrest in Scotland under s 27, see *Clipper Shipping v SO Investment* [1989] ECC 216 (Outer House).

[38]   This replaces Article 12(1) of the EC Treaty (as amended).

[39]   See Case C-398/92: *Mund & Fester v Hatrex* [1994] ECR I-467.

[40]   See Case C-43/95: *Data Delecta v MSL Dynamics* [1996] ECR I-4661; and Case C-323/95: *Hayes v Kronenberger* [1997] ECR I-1711. See also *Fitzgerald v Williams* [1996] 2 All ER 171 (CA); the Civil Procedure Rules 1998 (as amended), rule 25.13(2)(a); and *Pitt v Bolger* [1996] 2 ILRM 68 (Keane J). Cf. *Greenwich Ltd v National Westminster Bank* [1999] 2 Lloyd's Rep 308 (Blackburne J), refusing this benefit to a company incorporated and resident in the Isle of Man.

insolvent foreign plaintiff in the same way as against an insolvent local plaintiff,[41] but in England rule 25.13(2)(c) of the Civil Procedure Rules 1998 (as amended) now limits the power to require a party to give security for costs by reason of its suspected insolvency to corporate parties.

In *Nasser v United Bank of Kuwait*,[42] the Court of Appeal ruled that, in view of the Human Rights Act 1998, an individual resident outside the European Union and the other Lugano Convention countries should be required to provide security for costs only where there are objectively justified grounds relating to obstacles to or the burden of enforcement in the context of the particular foreign claimant or country concerned. Thus in the case of an American claimant, any order should be related to the probable extra burden (in terms of costs and delay) of taking enforcement steps in the United States against the claimant, as compared with enforcement steps in the United Kingdom or another EU Member State or Lugano Convention country.

## TAKING EVIDENCE

EC Regulation 1206/2001 on Co-operation between the Courts of the Member States in the Taking of Evidence in Civil or Commercial Matters[43] provides for a procedure whereby a court of a Member State may request a court of another Member State to take evidence. The Regulation entered into force on 1st January 2004 for the fourteen then Member States other than Denmark; on 1st May 2004 for the ten then acceding Member States;[44] and on 1st January 2007 for Bulgaria and Romania.[45]

By Article 1(1), Regulation 1206/2001 applies in civil or commercial matters, but Article 1(2) insists that the evidence requested must be intended for use in judicial proceedings, commenced or contemplated. By Article 21(1), in relations between the Member States, the Regulation prevails over other provisions contained in bilateral or multilateral agreements or arrangements concluded by the Member States, and in particular over the Hague Convention of 1st March 1954 on Civil Procedure and the Hague Convention of 18th March 1970 on the Taking of Evidence Abroad in Civil or Commercial Matters. But Article 21(2) permits Member States to maintain or conclude agreements or arrangements between two or more of them to further facilitate the taking of evidence, provided that they are compatible with the Regulation. By Article 21(3), the EC Commission must be notified of such agreements or arrangements.

---

[41] See *Chequepoint v McClelland* [1997] QB 51 (CA).

[42] [2002] 1 WLR 1868. See also *Prince Radu of Hohenzollern v Houston* [2006] All ER (D) 96 (Mar) (Eady J).

[43] For its text, see [2001] OJ L174/1. Along with Regulation 1206/2001, the EC Council adopted Decision 2001/470, establishing a European judicial network in civil and commercial matters; [2001] OJ L174/25.

[44] See the Athens Act of Accession 2003, Article 2.

[45] See the Luxembourg Act of Accession 2005, Articles 2 and 56; [2005] OJ L157.

**The Request**

By Article 2 of Regulation 1206/2001, the request to take evidence is transmitted by the court before which the proceedings are commenced or contemplated directly to the court of another Member State which has been designated as competent for the performance of the taking of evidence. By Article 4, the request must specify (inter alia) the nature and subject-matter of the case and a brief statement of the facts; a description of the taking of evidence to be performed; where the request is for the examination of a person, the name and address of the person to be examined, and the questions to be put to him or a statement of the facts about which he is to be examined; and where the request is for any other form of taking of evidence, the documents or other objects to be inspected.

In *Tedesco v Tomasoni Fittings*,[46] Kokott AG concluded that the Regulation extends to a request for a description of goods in accordance with Articles 128 and 130 of the Italian Industrial Property Code, which involves a description of an object allegedly infringing a patent, and includes the search, documentation and removal of relevant commercial documents and the seizure of samples. She explained that requests under the Regulation are not limited to the hearing of witnesses. The taking of evidence may also include documents or other objects which may be visually examined or inspected by experts. The taking of evidence consists of the sensory perception and appraisal of an item capable of constituting evidence. The testimony of a witness is heard, documents are read, and other objects are examined. Judicial co-operation under the Regulation extends to all those acts. But the evidence must be described with a sufficient degree of precision that the link to the proceedings commenced or contemplated is evident, and the judicial co-operation is limited to the items which are themselves capable of constituting proof, and does not extend to circumstances which are linked only indirectly to the judicial proceedings.

By Article 7, the requested court must send an acknowledgement of receipt to the requesting court. By Article 8, if a request cannot be executed because it does not contain all of the necessary information, the requested court must inform the requesting court thereof without delay, and must request it to send the missing information, which should be indicated as precisely as possible.

**Performance of the Request**

By Article 10(1) of Regulation 1206/2001, the requested court must execute the request without delay and, at the latest, within ninety days of receipt of the request. By Article 10(2), the requested court must execute the request in accordance with the law of the State requested. By Article 10(3)–(4), if the requesting court has called for the request to be executed in accordance with a special procedure provided for by the law of the requesting State, or has asked the requested court to use communications technology at the performance of the taking of evidence (such as video-conference and tele-conference), the requested court must comply with such a requirement unless the procedure or use is incompatible with the law of the State requested or it gives rise to major practical difficulties.

---

[46]  Case C-175/06, [2007] ECR I-7929. The reference was withdrawn after Kokott AG had given her opinion.

As regards refusal under Article 10(3) of the performance of a request in accordance with a procedure provided for by the law of the requesting State where that procedure is incompatible with the law of the requested State or gives rise to major practical difficulties, in *Tedesco v Tomasoni Fittings*[47] Kokott AG explained that the proviso does not come into play simply because the requested measure under the foreign law does not correspond exactly with domestic law and national practice. Rather, the requested court must make all possible efforts, as far as the available means permit, to put into practice the measure governed by the law of the requesting State. If it proves impossible due to conflicting provisions of domestic law or major practical difficulties to carry out the request precisely as envisaged by the foreign law, the request may not simply be returned unexecuted in its entirety. Rather, the requested court must perform the measure sought in a modified manner so as to comply with domestic law requirements. Where even that approach is impossible, there remains the possibility of applying an analogous procedure in accordance with domestic law.

Articles 11 and 12 make provision for the presence, at the performance of the taking of evidence by the requested court, of the parties or their representatives, and of representatives of the requesting court (such as judges or experts). By Article 13, in executing a request, the requested court must where necessary apply the appropriate coercive measures in accordance with the law of the State requested which applies to the execution of similar requests made by its national authorities or a party concerned.

By Article 15, if the requested court is not in a position to execute the request within ninety days of receipt, it must inform the requesting court thereof, giving the grounds for the delay as well as the estimated time expected to be needed to execute the request. By Article 16, after execution of the request, the requested court must send without delay to the requesting court the documents establishing the execution of the request and, where appropriate, return the documents received from the requesting court, accompanied by a confirmation of execution.

## Refusal

Article 14 deals with the grounds on which the requested court may refuse to execute a request. By Article 14(1), a request for the hearing of a person must not be executed when the person concerned justifiably claims the right to refuse to give evidence, or to be prohibited from giving evidence, under the law of the State requested, or under the law of the requesting State.

By Article 14(2), the execution of a request may be refused in the following cases: (a) if the request does not fall within the scope of the Regulation as specified by Article 1; or (b) if, under the law of the Member State of the requested court, the execution of the request does not fall within the functions of the judiciary; or (c) if the requesting court has failed to comply within thirty days with a request of the requested court to complete the request under Article 8. By Article 14(3), execution may not be refused by the requested court solely on the ground that under the law of the State requested a court of the State requested has exclusive jurisdiction over the subject matter of the action, or that the law of the State requested would not admit the right of action on it. By Article 14(4), if execution of the request is refused under Article 14(2), the requested court must notify the requesting court thereof within sixty days of receipt of the request by the requested court.

---

[47]    Case C-175/06, [2007] ECR I-7929.

As regards refusal under Article 14(2)(b), in *Tedesco v Tomasoni Fittings*[48] Kokott AG explained that a distinction must be drawn between ordering a measure for evidence to be taken and the performance thereof. Execution of a request to obtain evidence cannot be refused simply on the basis that performance of certain forms of taking evidence does not fall within the scope of judicial activities. The decisive factor is that courts are entitled to order the requested measures. Moreover, refusal to perform cannot be justified by the lack of judicial power in a situation where a measure for the preservation of evidence is not performed by the court itself but by an independent institution of the justice system, such as a supervising solicitor who is engaged by the court and acts as its officer.

### Taking Evidence Directly

Regulation 1206/2001 also provides for a procedure whereby a court of a Member State requests permission to take evidence directly in another Member State. By Article 17(1), where a court requests to take evidence directly in another Member State, it must submit a request to the central body or competent authority designated under Article 3 in that State. By Article 17(2), direct taking of evidence may only take place if it can be performed on a voluntary basis without the need for coercive measures; and where the direct taking of evidence implies that a person is to be heard, the requesting court must inform that person that the performance will take place on a voluntary basis. By Article 17(3), the taking of evidence must be performed by a member of the judicial personnel or by some other person (such as an expert) designated in accordance with the law of the requesting State.

By Article 17(4), the central body or the competent authority of the requested State must, within thirty days of receiving the request, inform the requesting court whether the request is accepted and, if necessary, under what conditions according to the law of the State requested such performance is to be carried out. In particular, the central body or the competent authority may assign a court of the State requested to take part in the performance of the taking of evidence in order to ensure the proper application of Article 17 and the conditions that have been set out. By Article 17(6), subject to the conditions laid down in accordance with Article 17(4), the requesting court must execute the request in accordance with the law of the requesting State.

By Article 17(5), the central body or the competent authority may refuse direct taking of evidence only if the request does not fall within the scope of the Regulation as specified by Article 1; or if the request does not contain all of the information necessary under Article 4; or if the direct taking of evidence requested is contrary to fundamental principles of law in the State requested.

In *Masri v Consolidated Contractors*,[49] the House of Lords ruled that rule 71.2 of the (English) Civil Procedure Rules 1998, which enables a judgment creditor to obtain an order requiring an officer of a corporate judgment debtor to attend court to provide information about the judgment debtor's means, or about any other matter about which information is needed to enforce a judgment or order, does not enable an order for examination to be made

---

48    Case C-175/06, [2007] ECR I-7929.
49    [2009] UKHL 43, reversing [2008] EWCA Civ 876.

against an officer who is resident abroad. The House thus avoided the need to consider whether, in the case of an officer resident in another Member State, such an order would conflict with or undermine the effectiveness of Regulation 1206/2001. The Court of Appeal had ruled that such an order would not conflict with or undermine the effectiveness of the Regulation.

# 10.  Recognition and enforcement of judgments

## INTRODUCTION

### Scope

As between the twenty-seven EU Member States (including Denmark),[1] Chapter III (Articles 32–56) of the Brussels I Regulation regulates the recognition and enforcement in each Member State of judgments given by the courts of the other Member States. As Recital 10 emphasises, Chapter III applies even if the judgment debtor is domiciled in a non-member country. By way of supplementation, Chapter IV (Articles 57–8) provides for the enforcement in a Member State of 'authentic instruments' drawn up or registered, and settlements approved by courts, in other Member States.

Provision similar to that made by the Regulation is made by Titles III and IV of the Lugano Convention 1988, which at present apply to recognition and enforcement between (on the one hand) the pre-2004 EC Member States, Poland and Norway, and (on the other hand) Switzerland and Iceland, as well as between Switzerland and Iceland themselves; and by Titles III and IV of the Lugano Convention 2007, which at present apply to recognition and enforcement between (on the one hand) the EU Member States and (on the other hand) Norway.[2]

As regards subject-matter, Chapter III of the Brussels I Regulation is confined to judgments which are principally concerned with matters which fall within the scope of the Regulation as defined by Article 1,[3] and the court addressed is not bound by the original court's decision on this point.[4] Chapter III also gives way to specialised conventions in accordance with Article 71.[5]

As regards time, Chapter III of the Brussels I Regulation is limited by Article 66 to judgments given after the entry into force of the Regulation for both the Member State of origin and the Member State addressed.[6] By Article 66(1) and (2)(a), Chapter III has full operation

---

[1]   The extension of the Brussels I Regulation to Denmark, in the face of Article 69 of the EC Treaty, was effected by means of an Agreement between the European Community and Denmark, [2005] OJ L299/62, which was approved by the EC Council in its Decisions 2005/790 and 2006/325, [2005] OJ L299/61 and [2006] OJ L120/22.

[2]   See Article 54B(1) and (2)(c) of the Lugano Convention 1988; and Articles 64(1) and (2)(c) and 69(6) of the Lugano Convention 2007.

[3]   See pp. 26–43 above.

[4]   See Gaudemet-Tallon, at para 319.

[5]   See pp. 44–6 above.

[6]   If the judgment was given before that date, the Brussels Convention, the Lugano Convention 1988, and the earlier bilateral conventions listed in Article 69 of the Regulation, continue to apply. See Articles 69 and 70(2) of the Regulation, and *T v L* [2008] IESC 48 (Irish Supreme Court).

where the judgment was given after the entry into force of the Regulation for both of the States involved, and the original proceedings were instituted after the entry into force of either the Regulation itself, or the Brussels Convention, or the Lugano Convention 1988, for both of those States.

Where the judgment was given after the entry into force of the Regulation for both of the States involved, but at the institution of the original proceedings neither the Regulation itself, nor the Brussels Convention, nor the Lugano Convention 1988 had entered into force for both of the States, Chapter III of the Regulation applies, but it operates subject to a transitional provision for jurisdictional review, laid down by Article 66(2)(b). This makes recognition and enforcement subject to a further requirement, that the jurisdiction of the original court should have been founded upon rules which accorded with those provided for either in Chapter II of the Regulation, or in a convention concluded between the Member State of origin and the Member State addressed which was in force when the proceedings were instituted.[7]

Chapter IV of the Regulation applies only to documents formally drawn up or registered as authentic instruments, and settlements approved by a court, after its entry into force in both the State of origin and the State addressed.[8]

As Articles 32, 33 and 38 make clear, Chapter III of the Regulation deals only with the recognition and enforcement in each Member State of judgments given in the other Member States. Thus it does not apply to the recognition or enforcement in one part of a Member State of judgments given in other parts of the same State; for example, the recognition and enforcement in England of Scottish or Northern Irish judgments. Nor does it apply to the recognition or enforcement in a Member State of judgments given in non-member countries.[9] Further, as the European Court ruled in *Owens Bank v Bracco*,[10] it does not apply to the recognition or enforcement in a Member State of a judgment given in another Member State, if that judgment is principally concerned with the recognition or enforcement of a judgment given in a non-member country.

Moreover, a declaration of enforceability obtained under Chapter III of the Regulation in one Member State in respect of a judgment given in another Member State does not constitute a judgment which can be recognised or enforced under Chapter III in a third Member State. Rather, one should seek in the third Member State recognition or enforcement of the original judgment on the merits.[11]

In view both of the definition of a judgment given by Article 32, and of the exclusion of arbitration from the scope of the Regulation by Article 1(2)(d), Chapter III applies neither to

---

[7] On this requirement of jurisdictional review, see pp. 236–7 below. For similar provisions, see Article 54(2) of the Brussels Convention; Article 34(3) of the 1978 Convention; Article 12(2) of the 1982 Convention; Article 29(2) of the 1989 Convention; Article 13(2) of the 1996 Convention; Article 54(2) of the Lugano Convention 1988; and Article 63(2)(b) of the Lugano Convention 2007.

[8] See Article 66(1).

[9] Cf. Gaudemet-Tallon, at para 341, suggesting (unconvincingly) that the reflex effect of the provisions on jurisdiction over insurance and consumer contracts and exclusive jurisdiction by subject-matter prevents recognition of external judgments inconsistent with these provisions. In its Report and Green Paper of 21st April 2009, the EC Commission envisages the possibility of an amendment designed to introduce common rules on the recognition and enforcement of judgments given in external countries; see COM(2009) 174 final, at section 3.2, and COM(2009) 175 final, at question 2.

[10] Case C-129/92, [1994] ECR I-117.

[11] See Gaudemet-Tallon, at para 320.

the recognition and enforcement of arbitral awards themselves, nor to the recognition and enforcement of judgments which are principally concerned with arbitral awards (such as a judgment authorising enforcement of, or varying, or setting aside, an arbitral award).[12]

## Judgments

As the European Court explained in *Solo Kleinmotoren v Boch*,[13] references in the Brussels I Regulation to a 'judgment' are to a decision emanating from a judicial body of a Member State, deciding on its own authority on the issues between the parties. Thus the concept excludes a court settlement, falling within Chapter IV of the Regulation, even if it was reached in a court of a Member State and brings legal proceedings to an end, since such settlements are essentially contractual in that their terms depend primarily on the parties' intention. But, as the Court of Appeal recognised in *Landhurst Leasing v Marcq*,[14] the concept extends to a judgment which is entered by consent, as where a party agrees to a judgment being entered by conceding the issues.

Article 32 of the Regulation defines a 'judgment' as one given by a court or tribunal of a Member State, and adds that it is immaterial what the judgment may be called (such as a decree, order, decision, or writ of execution), and that a determination of costs or expenses by a court officer is included. Thus, as was recognised by the European Court in *Maersk Olie & Gas v de Haan & de Boer*,[15] the concept includes an admiralty judgment ordering the establishment of a limitation fund. In addition, Article 62 of the Regulation, taken with Article 2(2)(c) of the Agreement between the European Community and Denmark,[16] extends the concept of a court so as to include, as regards summary proceedings in Sweden concerning orders to pay and assistance, the Swedish enforcement service, and in matters relating to maintenance, the Danish administrative authorities.[17]

There is no requirement, even for enforcement, that the judgment should award a sum of money. Chapter III provides for enforcement (as well as recognition), so long as the judgment is enforceable in the original country, whether it is for the payment of money or for other relief (such as the specific performance of a contract).[18] If the enforceability of the judgment in the original country is disputed, the court addressed may adjourn its proceedings to enable an attempt at enforcement to be made in the original country.[19]

---

[12]    See *ABCI v Banque Franco-Tunisienne* [1996] 1 Lloyd's Rep 485 (Waller J), affirmed on other issues [1997] 1 Lloyd's Rep 531 (CA); and *ED & F Man Sugar Ltd v Lendoudis* [2008] 1 All ER 952 (Christopher Clarke J).

[13]    Case C-414/92, [1994] ECR I-2237.

[14]    [1998] ILPr 822.

[15]    Case C-39/02, [2004] ECR I-9657.

[16]    See note 1 above.

[17]    Article 62 (taken with the Agreement with Denmark) echoes Article VA of the Protocol annexed to the Brussels Convention. In contrast, Article VA of the First Protocol annexed to the Lugano Convention 1988 refers to decisions on maintenance made by Danish, Icelandic and Norwegian administrative authorities, and to decisions of the Finnish ulosotonhaltija/overexekutor. In the Lugano Convention 2007, Article 62 specifies that for its purposes the expression 'court' includes any authorities designated by a State bound by the Convention as having jurisdiction in the matters falling within the scope of the Convention.

[18]    See Article 38; the Schlosser Report, at p. 132; and *EMI v Watterbach* [1992] 1 QB 115.

[19]    See *Von Mitchke-Collande v Kramer* [2005] EWHC 977 (Burton J).

Nor is there any requirement that the judgment should in any sense be final in the original country.[20] On the contrary, Chapter III applies even if the judgment is subject to any form of appeal or review there, whether in a higher court or in the court which gave the judgment. Provision is, however, made by Articles 37 and 46 to enable a court addressed to stay its proceedings or require the applicant for enforcement to give security where an ordinary appeal is pending or admissible in the original country.[21] Thus judgments on preliminary issues and interlocutory judgments or orders, as well as judgments given at the conclusion of a trial, have to be recognised and enforced under Chapter III.[22] However, as the Schlosser Report explains, interlocutory decisions which are not intended to govern the legal relationships of the parties, but to arrange the further conduct of the proceedings, such as orders for the taking of evidence, are not within the scope of Chapter III.[23]

A further exception relates to ex parte orders. In *Denilauler v Couchet Frères*,[24] the European Court ruled that judgments authorising provisional or protective measures, which are delivered without the defendant having been summoned to appear, and which are intended to be enforced without prior service, do not fall within the scope of Chapter III. This is because Articles 34(2) and 53(2) cannot be applied to such judgments without distorting their substance and scope; because the whole of the Regulation is designed to ensure that the procedural rights of the defence are observed; and because such judgments require particular judicial care, and the courts of the State where the assets to be frozen are located are best able to evaluate the relevant circumstances and impose suitable conditions. The case involved a French *saisie conservatoire*, designed to freeze a bank account in Germany, but the ruling clearly covers an English freezing order, in the normal case where it is obtained ex parte. Similarly, in *EMI v Watterbach*,[25] Hobhouse J refused to enforce a German injunction against infringement of copyright, granted under a procedure whereby it took effect immediately on its issue, without service, and would remain in force until the court, on the defendant's application, set it aside. On the other hand, Chapter III does apply to an English freezing order obtained by means of a summons inter partes;[26] or to an English freezing order which was initially made ex parte, but has subsequently been continued after the defendant has been notified of and given an opportunity to contest the order.[27]

In *Mærsk Olie & Gas v de Haan & de Boer*,[28] the European Court ruled that Chapter III applied to a provisional judgment of a Dutch court ordering the establishment of an admiralty limitation fund. It explained that Chapter III is not limited to decisions which terminate a dispute in whole or in part, but extends to provisional or interlocutory decisions. Moreover,

---

[20]    See Case C-183/90: *Van Dalfsen v Van Loon* [1991] ECR I-4743; the Jenard Report at p. 43; and the Schlosser Report, at p. 126.

[21]    See pp. 264–6 below.

[22]    See *The Heidberg* [1994] 2 Lloyd's Rep 287 (Diamond QC in QBD); and *The Tjaskemolen (No 2)* [1997] 2 Lloyd's Rep 476 (Clarke J).

[23]    See the Schlosser Report, at pp. 126–7.

[24]    Case 125/79, [1980] ECR 1553. See also Case C-474/93: *Hengst v Campese* [1995] ECR I-2113.

[25]    [1992] 1 QB 115.

[26]    See per Browne-Wilkinson V-C in *Derby v Weldon*, *The Times* of 15th November 1988, affirmed and extended on other grounds, [1990] Ch 65 (CA).

[27]    See *Normaco v Lundman* [1999] ILPr 381 (Carnwath J).

[28]    Case C-39/02, [2004] ECR I-9657.

it extends to decisions taken at the conclusion of an initial phase of the proceedings in which both parties were not heard, provided that the order could have been the subject of submissions by both parties before the issue of its recognition or enforcement under the Regulation came to be addressed. In the instant case, the Dutch order had no legal effect prior to being notified to claimants, who could then assert their rights before the court which had made the order by challenging both the right of the debtor to benefit from a limitation of liability and the amount of that limitation, and who could also lodge an appeal against that order challenging the jurisdiction of the court which had adopted it.

In *Gambazzi v DaimlerChrysler*,[29] the European Court explained that, for judgments to fall within the scope of the Regulation, it is sufficient that they are judicial decisions which, before their recognition and enforcement are sought in another Member State, have been, or have been capable of being, in the State of origin and under various procedures, the subject of an inquiry in adversary proceedings. Thus judgments by default fall within the scope of the Regulation. The case involved the enforcement in Italy of an English judgment which had been given without hearing the defendant, who had entered appearance but had been excluded from the proceedings by reason of his failure to comply with disclosure orders. The English decisions took the form of a judgment and an order given in default of appearance in civil proceedings which, as a rule, adhere to the adversarial principle. Thus the fact that the court entered judgment as if the defendant, who had entered appearance, was in default, could not prevent the categorisation of those decisions as judgments, but could be taken into consideration with regard to their compatibility with the public policy of the State in which enforcement was sought.

## Recognition and Enforcement

Chapter III of the Brussels I Regulation provides for both the recognition and the enforcement of judgments. It both defines the substantive conditions for granting, and specifies the procedure for obtaining, recognition or enforcement.

Recognition of a judgment implies that the judgment is treated as conclusive of the matters which it determined. Enforcement of a judgment implies that the judgment ordered something to be done (such as the payment of a sum of money or the actual performance of a contract) or not to be done (as in the case of an injunction prohibiting the commission of an act which would constitute a breach of contract or a tort), and that steps of an official nature are taken with a view to ensuring that the order is complied with. Under Chapter III, the same substantive conditions apply to both recognition and enforcement, except that for enforcement there is an additional requirement that the judgment should be enforceable in the original country.[30]

In *Hoffmann v Krieg*,[31] the European Court accepted that a judgment which is recognised

---

[29]    Case C 394/07, [2009] ECR I-2563.

[30]    See Articles 34–6, 38 and 45. The substantive conditions for recognition and enforcement under Chapter III are considered at pp. 229–52 below. As regards enforceability in the original country, see pp. 229–31 below.

[31]    Case 145/86, [1988] ECR 645. See similarly Case C-420/07: *Apostolides v Orams*, [2009] ECR I-3571, at para 66; the Jenard Report, at p. 43; *Re the Enforcement of a Swiss Maintenance Agreement* [1988] ECC 181 at 187 (German Supreme Court); and 28 US Code s 1738. Cf. the Schlosser Report, at pp. 127–8; and *Hart v American Airlines* 304 NYS2d 810 (1969).

under Chapter III must in principle have the same effects in the State addressed as it has in the State in which it was given. This principle, that recognition involves giving the recognised judgment the same conclusive effects as it has in the original country under its law (rather than such effects as would be given under the law of the State addressed to a similar judgment given by its own courts, or would be given by the law of the State addressed to foreign judgments which are recognised otherwise than under the Regulation) seems inherent in the very concept of recognition. Thus the State addressed must follow the law of the original country in determining what claims or issues were determined and are foreclosed by the judgment, and what persons are bound by it (for example, by virtue of privity with the actual parties).[32]

The procedure for obtaining enforcement is elaborated in detail by Articles 38-56. It involves an ex parte application for a declaration of enforceability to a court of the State addressed, on which an immediate decision must be given. The decision on the initial application is subject to an appeal inter partes, and the decision on the appeal to a single further appeal on a point of law. The unified procedure leads to the making of a declaration of enforceability, and once this is obtained the actual measures of enforcement are governed mainly by the law of the State addressed. An ex parte declaration of enforceability enables the applicant to take protective measures against the respondent's property, but definitive enforcement is delayed until the appeal inter partes has become time-barred or has been disposed of. There are also provisions as to legal aid, and on the documentary evidence to be produced by the applicant.[33]

As regards mere recognition (without enforcement), Article 33(1) and (3) provides that no special procedure is required, and that recognition may be sought incidentally in any proceedings in which it is relevant. Alternatively, by Article 33(2), an interested party may use the enforcement procedure laid down in Articles 38–56 to apply for a decision establishing recognition. But this procedure is not made available to a party who seeks a decision establishing non-recognition.

As regards merger of the original cause of action, the European Court ruled in *De Wolf v Cox*[34] that the enforcement procedure specified in Articles 38–56 is exclusive. Thus a plaintiff who has obtained in one Member State a judgment which is enforceable in another Member State under Chapter III cannot bring an ordinary action in the latter State against the same defendant in respect of the same cause of action.[35]

## Authentic Instruments and Court Settlements

Chapter III of the Brussels I Regulation is supplemented by Chapter IV (Articles 57–58), which provides for the enforcement in a Member State, by means of the procedure specified

---

[32]  See also *The Tjaskemolen (No 2)* [1997] 2 Lloyd's Rep 476, where Clarke J looked to Dutch law as showing that a Dutch order releasing a vessel from arrest was not designed to prevent its re-arrest elsewhere; and *Barrett v Universal-Island Records Ltd* [2006] EMLR 21, where, in the context of the recognition in England of a New York judgment dismissing an action, Lewison J held that an English court should not give a foreign judgment greater preclusive effect in England than it would have in its home country.

[33]  Procedure under Chapter III is examined more fully in Chapter 11 below.

[34]  Case 42/76, [1976] ECR 1759.

[35]  See also the (UK) Civil Jurisdiction and Judgments Act 1982, s 34.

in Chapter III, of 'authentic instruments' drawn up or registered, and settlements (of litigation) approved by courts, in other Member States.[36] The instrument or settlement must be enforceable (without a confirmatory judgment) in the State of origin. Enforcement must be refused, at the appellate stage in the proceedings for a declaration of enforceability in the State addressed, if enforcement of the instrument or settlement is manifestly contrary to public policy in that State. But there are no other substantive requirements for enforcement.

Authentic instruments are familiar in the Continental countries. Such an instrument is one which is drawn up by a public officer, such as a notary, signed by the parties in his presence, and witnessed by him, thus establishing an especially formal and probative record of the transaction, and enabling a party in whose favour an obligation evidenced by the instrument is undertaken to proceed directly to measures of execution on the basis of the instrument, as if it were a judgment, without bringing an action before a court. Thus Article 57 applies mainly to notarial instruments which evidence an immediate obligation to pay a definite sum of money, and which usually contain a statement of direct enforceability.[37] In *Unibank v Christensen*,[38] which involved a Danish 'gaeldsbrev', the European Court ruled that an acknowledgement of indebtedness which is enforceable under the law of the State of origin, but whose authenticity has not been established by a public authority or other authority empowered for that purpose by that State, does not constitute an authentic instrument within the meaning of Article 57. Authentic instruments are unknown in English internal law, but in Scotland an instrument establishing a clearly defined contractual obligation can be entered in a public register, and an extract from the register will then be enforceable by execution in the same way as a judgment, and will fall within Article 57.[39] By Article 57(2), arrangements relating to maintenance obligations, concluded with administrative authorities or authenticated by them, are treated as authentic instruments within Article 57.[40]

The nature of a court settlement, within Article 58, and its difference from a judgment, within Chapter III, was explained by the European Court in *Solo Kleinmotoren v Boch*.[41] Court settlements are essentially contractual, in that their terms depend primarily on the parties' intention, even though they are reached in a court of a Member State and bring legal proceedings to an end. They are distinct from judgments, which emanate from a judicial body of a Member State, deciding on its own authority on the issues between the parties.

Authentic instruments and court settlements differ from judgments in that they lack the conclusive effect of res judicata and, being contractual in nature, can be rendered invalid by such factors as mistake, misrepresentation, incapacity or prohibited purpose. Chapter IV recognises the lack of conclusiveness by providing only for enforcement, and not mere recog-

---

[36]   In the United Kingdom, see also the Civil Jurisdiction and Judgments (Authentic Instruments and Court Settlements) Order 2001 (SI 2001/3928).

[37]   See Droz, at paras 606–16; and Gaudemet-Tallon, at para 417. See also *Bautrading v Nordling* [1997] 3 All ER 718 (CA), which involved a 'schuldanerkenntnis' under German law.

[38]   Case C-260/97, [1999] ECR I-3715.

[39]   See the Schlosser Report, at p. 136.

[40]   Article 57(2) is derived from Article VE of the Protocol annexed to the Brussels Convention, which was added by the Accession Convention 1996. There is no similar provision in the Lugano Convention 1988, but a corresponding provision is made by Article 57(2) of the Lugano Convention 2007.

[41]   Case C-414/92, [1994] ECR I-2237. See also *Re the Enforcement of a Swiss Maintenance Agreement* [1988] ECC 181 (German Supreme Court).

nition. It seems that, if the respondent puts forward a serious argument that the instrument or settlement is invalid, the court addressed of enforcement proceedings under Chapter IV should stay its proceedings, and perhaps meanwhile permit provisional enforcement, or permit enforcement conditionally on the applicant providing security, so as to enable the respondent to bring an action for the annulment of the instrument or settlement in a court competent under Chapter II of the Regulation.[42]

**Other EU Measures**

On 21st April 2004, the Parliament and Council adopted EC Regulation 805/2004, creating a European Enforcement Order for Uncontested Claims, which may conveniently be referred to as the Uncontested Claims Regulation.[43] This Regulation applies from 21st October 2005 in the twenty-four then existing Member States other than Denmark, and from 1st January 2007 in Bulgaria and Romania.[44]

Subject to certain safeguards in respect of procedure, this dismal and unprincipled measure enables the court of origin to certify a judgment on an uncontested claim as a European Enforcement Order. Subject only to very narrow exceptions, the judgment will then be recognised and enforceable in other Member States without the need to obtain a declaration of enforceability there and without any possibility of opposing its recognition. The exceptions relate to irreconcilability with an earlier judgment; respect for existing conventions between a Member State and an external country; and challenges to the judgment or the certificate pending in the country of origin. The new procedure extends to authentic instruments and court settlements in respect of uncontested claims. But an applicant for recognition or enforcement always retains the option of proceeding in accordance with the Brussels I Regulation. Provision for a judgment to be recognised and enforceable in other Member States without the need to obtain a declaration of enforceability there is also made by the Payment Order Regulation,[45] and the Small Claims Regulation.[46]

These regulations are examined in Chapter 11 below.

## SUBSTANTIVE REQUIREMENTS

The basic principle, laid down by Articles 33 and 38 of the Brussels I Regulation, is that a judgment to which Chapter III applies must be recognised and enforced in the other Member States. The principle is reinforced by Articles 36 and 45(2), which emphasise that in no circumstances may the court addressed review the substance (the merits) of the judgment; and by Article 35(3), which in most cases prevents the court addressed from reviewing the jurisdiction of the original court. A very limited range of exceptions, in which recognition and enforcement must be refused, are specified by Articles 34–5 and 45(1). The specified

---

[42]  See Droz, at paras 618–24 and 628.
[43]  For its text, see [2004] OJ L143/15.
[44]  See the Luxembourg Act of Accession 2005, Articles 2 and 56; [2005] OJ L157.
[45]  EC Regulation 1896/2006, creating a European Order for Payment Procedure, [2006] OJ L399/1.
[46]  EC Regulation 861/2007, establishing a European Small Claims Procedure, [2007] OJ L199/1.

exceptions are exhaustive,[47] but in these cases the Regulation insists that recognition and enforcement be denied, regardless of the traditional law of the State addressed.[48]

The exceptions under Articles 34–5 and 45(1) relate to judgments whose recognition is incompatible with the public policy of the State addressed; default judgments where the defendant was not served with the originating document in sufficient time and in such a way as to enable him to arrange for his defence; judgments which are irreconcilable with other judgments; and, in a very limited range of situations, judgments given in proceedings over which the original court lacked jurisdiction.[49]

The judgment need not be final. If in the original country an ordinary appeal is pending or admissible, the court addressed has a discretion under Articles 37 and 46 to stay its own proceedings pending the disposal of the appeal in the original country.[50] But, by Articles 38 and 53–5, for a judgment to be enforceable (as distinct from merely recognisable) under Chapter III, it must be enforceable in the original country, and the applicant for enforcement has the burden of establishing such enforceability. This requirement was narrowly construed by the European Court in *Coursier v Fortis Bank*,[51] which involved the enforcement in Luxembourg of a French judgment for the repayment of a loan which had become unenforceable in France as a result of bankruptcy proceedings in respect of the debtor there. The Court ruled, rather surprisingly, that it is enough that the judgment is, in formal terms, enforceable in character, as where it bears a formal order for enforcement, even if it can no longer be enforced in the original country because of some subsequent development, such as payment of the debt or the debtor's bankruptcy.[52] But, as Tugendhat J held in *La Caisse Regional Du Credit Agricole Nord De France v Ashdown*,[53] a judgment which simply establishes the validity and amount of a claim provable in insolvency proceedings is not enforceable abroad under Chapter III.

A narrow approach to the requirement of enforceability in the original country was again adopted in *Apostolides v Orams*,[54] where the European Court ruled that the fact that a judgment given by the courts of a Member State, concerning land situated in an area of that State over which its Government does not exercise effective control, cannot as a practical matter be enforced where the land is situated, does not mean that such a judgment is unenforceable for the purposes of Article 38(1) of the Regulation. The case involved the enforcement in England of a Cypriot judgment in favour of the original owner, a Greek Cypriot, of land situated in northern Cyprus against an English purchaser of the land from a vendor who derived title from the Turkish Cypriot authority there. The judgment ordered both delivery of the land and payment of damages to the original owner.

---

[47]   See *Guittienne v SNCI*, 6th March 1996 (French Court of Cassation).
[48]   See Gaudemet-Tallon, at paras 381–3.
[49]   These exceptions are examined at pp. 233–52 below.
[50]   See pp. 264–6 below.
[51]   Case C-267/97, [1999] ECR I-2543.
[52]   At that time, before the entry into force of EC Regulation 1346/2000 on Insolvency Proceedings, [2000] OJ L160/1, the effects of an insolvency judgment had to be determined by the court of the State addressed in accordance with its own rules of private international law.
[53]   [2007] All ER (D) 277 (Mar).
[54]   Case C-420/07, [2009] ECR I-3571.

In some Continental countries, a court which grants an injunction also fixes a periodic penalty payment in the event of non-compliance, but the court has power to reduce the amount of the penalty subsequently. To deal with this form of procedure, Article 49 provides that a judgment which orders a periodic payment by way of penalty is to be enforceable in the other Member States only if the amount of the payment has been finally determined by the courts of the original country. Despite a contrary suggestion in the Schlosser Report,[55] it seems clear that Article 49 does not prevent an English court from enforcing a French injunction, to which the French court has coupled a periodic penalty payment, by measures which ignore the penalty payment, such as committal or sequestration. In its Report and Green Paper of 21st April 2009,[56] the EC Commission contemplates the possibility of facilitating the recovery of penalties.

## No Review of the Merits

Articles 36 and 45(2) of the Brussels I Regulation specify that under no circumstances may a judgment be reviewed as to its substance by a court in which recognition or enforcement is sought. Thus it is not open to the court addressed to consider whether the original court made some error in determining the underlying dispute. It is immaterial whether the alleged error is of fact or of law; whether it relates to the law of the State of origin, or that of the State addressed, or that of any other country; and whether it is of substantive law or conflict law.[57]

In *Krombach v Bamberski*,[58] the European Court confirmed that Articles 36 and 45(2) prevent the court addressed from refusing recognition solely on the ground that there is a discrepancy between the legal rule applied by the court of the State of origin and that which would have been applied by the court of the State addressed if it had been seised of the dispute, and also from reviewing the accuracy of the findings of law or fact made by the court of the State of origin. Similarly, in *Renault v Maxicar*,[59] it ruled that recognition cannot be refused on the ground that the original judgment involved an error of European Union law, for example as to the legitimacy under Articles 34–6 or 102 of the Treaty on the Functioning of the European Union of a design right in spare parts.

The prohibition of substantive review does not prevent the court addressed from holding that the Regulation is not applicable because the subject-matter of the judgment falls outside the scope of the Regulation as defined by Article 1.[60] But the Regulation omits any provision equivalent to Article 27(4) of the Brussels Convention, which prevented recognition and enforcement where the judgment involved the decision of a preliminary question of individual status or capacity, matrimonial property or succession, in a manner inconsistent with the

---

[55]  At p. 132.

[56]  COM(2009) 174 final, at section 3.8.3, and COM(2009) 175 final, at question 8.

[57]  This accords with the traditional English law. See *Godard v Gray* (1870) LR 6 QB 139; *Henderson v Henderson* (1844) 115 ER 111; *Ellis v McHenry* (1871) LR 6 CP 228; the Administration of Justice Act 1920, ss 9(2)–(3); and the Foreign Judgments (Reciprocal Enforcement) Act 1933, ss 2(1)–(2) and 4(1).

[58]  Case C-7/98, [2000] ECR I-1935.

[59]  Case C-38/98, [2000] ECR I-2973.

[60]  See Gaudemet-Tallon, at paras 319 and 333.

conflict law of the State addressed. Accordingly, such situations will now have to be evaluated under the public-policy proviso contained in Article 34(1).

It is clear that the prohibition on substantive review by Articles 36 and 45(2) limits the scope of the public-policy proviso contained in Article 34(1). In *Krombach v Bamberski*,[61] the European Court explained that recourse to public policy can be envisaged only where recognition or enforcement of the judgment would be at variance to an unacceptable degree with the legal order of the State addressed inasmuch as it infringes a fundamental principle. The infringement would have to constitute a manifest breach of a rule of law regarded as essential in the legal order of the State addressed, or of a right recognised as fundamental within that legal order.

Under the traditional English law, the rule against reviewing the merits of a foreign judgment is subject to a major exception where the judgment is alleged to have been obtained by fraud. The English court is obliged to review the merits of the underlying dispute in order to ascertain the existence of fraud, even where the party alleging fraud relies on evidence which he placed or could have placed before the foreign court.[62] There is an exception where the claim that the foreign judgment had been obtained by fraud has been litigated and rejected in a second, separate action in the foreign country, and the second judgment is not itself impeachable in England on any ground.[63] An English decision refusing to recognise or enforce an external judgment on grounds of fraud has no effect outside England.[64]

Since the Brussels I Regulation makes no specific provision for judgments obtained by fraud, it has been recognised, in the light of the Schlosser Report,[65] by Phillips J in *Interdesco v Nullifire*,[66] and by the Court of Appeal in *SISRO v Ampersand Software*,[67] that the application to European judgments of the traditional English exception for fraud would contravene the Regulation. Normally the remedy for fraud must be sought in the original country. It is only acceptable for the court addressed to invoke the public-policy proviso specified by Article 34(1) against recognition on account of fraud in the rare situation where there is cogent newly discovered evidence, such as would enable the re-opening of a judgment obtained in the country addressed, but the law of the original country denies any possibility of proceedings to re-open the judgment. A similar approach, requiring cogent evidence, not available at the time of the arbitration proceedings, has been adopted where the enforcement of a foreign arbitration award under the New York Convention is opposed on the ground that the award was obtained by fraud.[68]

The Brussels I Regulation does not cope well with judgments which are variable by reason of subsequent changes of circumstance, as is typically the case for orders for periodical

---

61    Case C-7/98, [2000] ECR I-1935.
62    See *Abouloff v Oppenheimer* (1882) 10 QBD 295; *Vadala v Lawes* (1890) 25 QBD 310; the Administration of Justice Act 1920, s 9(2)(d); the Foreign Judgments (Reciprocal Enforcement) Act 1933, s 4(1)(a)(iv); *Syal v Heyward* [1948] 2 KB 443; *Jet Holdings v Patel* [1990] 1 QB 335; and *Owens Bank v Bracco* [1992] 2 AC 443. Cf. Case C-183/90: *Van Dalfsen v Van Loon* [1991] ECR I-4743.
63    See *House of Spring Gardens v Waite* [1991] 1 QB 241 (CA).
64    See *Clarke v Fennoscandia Ltd* [2007] UKHL 56.
65    At p. 128. See also Gaudemet-Tallon, at para 354.
66    [1992] 1 Lloyd's Rep 180.
67    [1994] ILPr 55.
68    See *Westacre Investments v Jugoimport-SDRP* [2000] 1 QB 288 (CA), affirming [1998] 4 All ER 570 (Colman J).

payments by way of maintenance under family law. According to the Schlosser Report,[69] power to vary a maintenance order belongs neither to the court which originally made the order, as such, nor to a court in which enforcement of a foreign order is sought under Chapter III of the Regulation. For the purpose of jurisdiction, an application for variation must be treated as a separate proceeding, and the necessary connecting-factor under Chapter II must exist at the institution of the application for variation. Presumably, however, the obligation of recognition imposed by Chapter III requires a court which is competent to vary a foreign order to determine the merits of the application in accordance with the law of the country in which the original order was made. Thus a court of one Member State will not be able to modify a maintenance order made in another Member State by remitting arrears if the order is unmodifiable as regards arrears under the law of the country of origin.[70]

## No Review of Jurisdiction (with Minor Exceptions)

### The general rule
Articles 35(3) and 45(1) of the Brussels I Regulation explicitly preclude the court addressed from reviewing the jurisdiction of the original court, save in certain specified cases. Thus the general rule under the Regulation is that it is for the original court to determine whether it has jurisdiction in accordance with Chapter II, and its decision upholding its jurisdiction is binding on the courts of the other Member States when recognition or enforcement is sought under Chapter III. Similarly, a judgment must be recognised and enforced under the Regulation despite the fact that the original court, in breach of Article 27, failed to decline jurisdiction in favour of a similar action commenced earlier in another Member State (such as the State addressed).[71]

In excluding jurisdictional review, the Regulation departs from the usual international practice. The exclusion is apparently based on the close relationship between the Member States and their strong mutual confidence in each other's courts. It contrasts with the traditional English law, under which a foreign judgment is denied recognition and enforcement unless the original court was competent under the very restrictive English rules on indirect jurisdiction, which require that the party against whom the judgment is invoked should either have been resident in the original country or have submitted by express agreement or by appearance to the jurisdiction of the original court. It is not enough under the traditional English law that some or all of the acts and events which gave rise to the cause of action occurred in the original country, and that an equivalent connection with England would have conferred direct jurisdiction on the English courts.[72] In excluding jurisdictional review, the

---

[69] At paras 98–108.

[70] See to similar effect *Heron v Heron*, 703 NE2d 712 (1998), decided under the full-faith-and-credit clause in the US Constitution.

[71] See *The Heidberg* [1994] 2 Lloyd's Rep 287 (Diamond QC); *Tavoulareas v Tsavliris (No 2)* [2006] EWHC 414 (Comm) (Tomlinson J), affirmed [2007] 2 All ER (Comm) 356 (CA); and *Brasserie du Pecheur v Kreissparkasse Main-Spessart*, French Court of Cassation, 14th May 1996.

[72] See *Schibsby v Westenholz* (1870) LR 6 QB 155; *Singh v Rajah of Faridkote* [1894] AC 670; *Emanuel v Symon* [1908] 1 KB 302; *Turnbull v Walker* (1892) 67 LT 767; *Re Trepca Mines* [1960] 1 WLR 1273; *Sidmetal v Titan* [1966] 1 QB 828; *Adams v Cape Industries* [1990] Ch 433; *Lucasfilm v Ainsworth* [2009] FSR 2 (Mann J); the Administration of Justice Act 1920, s 9(2)(a) and (b); the Foreign

Regulation also goes beyond the requirements of recognition and enforcement imposed by federal law in the United States in respect of judgments of a court of a sister State[73] or even of a federal court for another district.[74]

Thus a defendant who is sued in a court which he considers to lack jurisdiction should, in his own interests, appear in the original court for the purpose of contesting its jurisdiction. It is true that in cases where another Member State has exclusive jurisdiction by subject-matter under Article 22, or where the defendant is domiciled in another Member State and does not appear, the original court is required by Articles 25 and 26(1) to consider its jurisdiction of its own motion. But it is not unlikely that, if the defendant fails to appear and place his evidence and arguments before the court, it will reach an erroneous decision in favour of its competence. That decision will usually not be open to review when recognition or enforcement is sought in another Member State.

There are three exceptions, where the Brussels I Regulation requires the court addressed to review the international jurisdiction of the original court, and to refuse recognition and enforcement if the original court lacked jurisdiction under Chapter II of the Regulation.

### The exception for insurance, consumer contracts, and exclusive jurisdiction by subject-matter

The first exception, laid down by Article 35(1) of the Regulation, is where the dispute falls within the scope of Articles 8–14, 15–17 or 22, which deal respectively with insurance, consumer contracts, and exclusive jurisdiction by subject-matter, and the original court assumed jurisdiction contrary to those provisions. The rationale is to prevent the policies of protecting policy-holders and consumers, and respecting the interests of the State of exclusive jurisdiction, from being undermined. Perhaps surprisingly, the Regulation fails to extend this exception to cases where the original court assumed jurisdiction contrary to Articles 18–21, on employment contracts.

The significance of this exception is greatly reduced by the supplementary rule, laid down by Article 35(2), that for this purpose the court addressed is bound by the findings of fact on which the original court based its jurisdiction. Nonetheless the Court of Appeal has ruled in *Prudential Assurance Co Ltd v Prudential Insurance Co of America*[75] that an important effect of Article 35(1), taken with Article 22(4), is to prevent a decision given in one Member State on the validity of a local patent or trade mark from giving rise to an estoppel binding in proceedings concerning the validity, or the validity and infringement, or possibly the infringement alone, of another patent or trade mark granted or registered in another Member State.

In *Apostolides v Orams*,[76] the European Court ruled that Article 35(1) of the Brussels I Regulation does not authorise the court of a Member State to refuse recognition or enforce-

---

Judgments (Reciprocal Enforcement) Act 1933, ss 4(1)(a)(ii), 4(2)(a), and 11(2); and the Civil Jurisdiction and Judgments Act 1982, ss 32 and 33.

[73] See, for example, *Milliken v Meyer* 311 US 457 (1940), *McGee v International Life Insurance Co* 355 US 220 (1957), and *Hanson v Denckla* 357 US 235 (1958). Cf. *Baldwin v Iowa State Traveling Men's Assoc* 283 US 522 (1931), and *Durfee v Duke* 375 US 106 (1963). See also, as to inter-provincial recognition and enforcement in Canada, *Morguard v De Savoye* (1990) 76 DLR4th 256.

[74] See Karnezis, *Registration in Federal District Court of Judgment of Another Federal Court under 28 USCA § 1963*, 194 ALR Fed 531 (updated since 2004).

[75] [2003] 1 WLR 2295 (CA).

[76] Case C-420/07, [2009] ECR I-3571.

ment of a judgment given by the courts of another Member State concerning land situated in an area of the latter State over which its government does not exercise effective control. The Court explained that Article 22 merely designates the competent Member State, and leaves to the law of that State the internal allocation of jurisdiction between its courts. Moreover, the prohibition of jurisdictional review by Article 35(3) prevents review of the internal jurisdiction of a court of the Member State which has exclusive jurisdiction under Article 22.

**The exception for existing agreements with external countries**
The second exception, laid down by Articles 35(1) and 72 of the Regulation, is designed to offer some protection to persons domiciled or habitually resident outside the Member States from judgments given on excessive jurisdictional bases under Article 4. This is achieved by preserving the operation of undertakings which before the entry into force of the Regulation had been given by a Member State to an external country in accordance with Article 59 of the Brussels Convention.

Article 59 of the Brussels Convention had authorised a Contracting State to conclude with an external country a convention on the recognition and enforcement of judgments, and in such a convention to undertake an obligation towards the external country not to recognise in certain cases judgments given in other Contracting States against defendants domiciled or habitually resident in the external country. The relevant cases were ones where Article 4 applied, and the judgment could only be founded on a ground of jurisdiction specified in Article 3(2). Two such conventions were concluded by the United Kingdom, the Ottawa Convention with Canada[77] and the Canberra Agreement with Australia.[78]

Where such a convention is in operation, the courts of the Member State which has given the undertaking must in certain circumstances refuse to recognize and enforce a judgment given in another Member State against a defendant who was domiciled or habitually resident in the relevant external country. The relevant time for ascertaining the defendant's domicile is obviously that of the institution of the original action. For this purpose, an individual is treated in the United Kingdom as domiciled in Canada or Australia if he is resident there and the nature and circumstances of his residence indicate that he has a substantial connection therewith.[79] A corporation or association is domiciled in Canada if it is incorporated or formed under a law in force in Canada and has a registered office there, or if its central management and control is exercised in Canada.[80] Whether a company or other legal person or association is domiciled in Australia is now determined in accordance with Article 60 of the Brussels I Regulation. Probably under the Ottawa Convention it is enough for the defendant to be domiciled or habitually resident anywhere in Canada, including Quebec, even

---

[77]   The Ottawa Convention of 24th April 1984, providing for the Reciprocal Recognition and Enforcement of Judgments in Civil and Commercial Matters, which entered into force on 1st January 1987. See also the Reciprocal Enforcement of Foreign Judgments (Canada) Order 1987 (SI 1987/468), as amended, most recently by SI 1995/2708.
[78]   The Canberra Agreement of 23rd August 1990, providing for the Reciprocal Recognition and Enforcement of Judgments in Civil and Commercial Matters, which entered into force on 1st September 1994. See also the Reciprocal Enforcement of Foreign Judgments (Australia) Order 1994 (SI 1994/1901).
[79]   See Article IX(2) of the Ottawa Convention, para 9(7) of Schedule 1 to the Civil Jurisdiction and Judgments Order 2001 (SI 2001/3929), and s 41(7) of the 1982 Act.
[80]   See Article IX(2) of the Ottawa Convention, and s 42(6) of the 1982 Act.

though the provisions of that Convention on reciprocal recognition and enforcement of judgments have not yet been extended to Quebec.

The circumstances justifying refusal of recognition under Article 72 of the Brussels I Regulation are that, in view of the findings of fact on which the original court based its jurisdiction, which are binding on the court addressed under Article 35(2), jurisdiction to entertain the original action was governed by Article 4, and under the law of the State of origin[81] jurisdiction could only be founded on a excessive ground. The grounds which are regarded as excessive are those specified in Article 3(2) and Annex I, such as the defendant's nationality or presence, or the plaintiff's nationality, domicile or residence, or the presence or seizure of property. But, in view of Article 59(2) of the Brussels Convention, the presence or seizure of property situated in the State of origin is not regarded as an excessive ground if the action was based on a claim to or involving that property, or to a debt secured on that property.

No further undertakings as envisaged in Article 72 of the Brussels I Regulation can now be entered into by a Member State, for as a result of the Regulation the matter has entered into the exclusive competence of the Community. As regards future agreements, paragraph 1 of the First Joint Statement of the Council and Commission, on the adoption of the Regulation, declares that they will pay particular attention to the possibility of engaging in negotiations with a view to the conclusion of international agreements which would mitigate the consequences of Chapter III of the Regulation for persons domiciled in third States, in respect of judgments founded on certain national grounds of jurisdiction.

Article 59 of the Lugano Convention 1988 echoes Article 59 of the Brussels Convention. In the Lugano Convention 2007, Article 68 echoes Article 72 of the Brussels I Regulation in preserving the operation of existing undertakings given by a Contracting State to an external country, and also contains a further provision that the Convention does not prevent Contracting Parties from entering into further such undertakings.

**The transitional exception**
The third exceptional case in which jurisdictional review is required under the Brussels I Regulation arises from Article 66(2)(b), which applies to the transitional situation where the judgment was given after the entry into force of the Brussels I Regulation for both the Member State of origin and the Member State addressed, but in proceedings which were instituted at a time when neither the Brussels I Regulation, nor the Brussels Convention, nor the Lugano Convention 1988 had entered into force in both States.

By Article 66, Chapter III of the Brussels I Regulation does not apply at all if the judgment was given before the entry into force of the Regulation for both of the States involved. The recognition and enforcement of such judgments will remain governed by the Brussels Convention or the Lugano Convention 1988, if otherwise applicable.[82] Conversely, Chapter III has full operation if the judgment was given after that date, and the original proceedings were instituted after the entry into force of either the Regulation itself, or the Brussels Convention, or the Lugano Convention 1988, for both of those States.

In the transitional situation where the judgment was given after the entry into force of the Brussels I Regulation for both the Member State of origin and the Member State

---

81   See the Jenard Report, at p. 61.
82   See *T v L* [2008] IESC 48 (Irish Supreme Court), especially per Fennelly J at para 74.

addressed,[83] but in proceedings which were instituted at a time when neither the Brussels I Regulation, nor the Brussels Convention, nor the Lugano Convention 1988 had entered into force in both States, Chapter III applies, but subject to the proviso that jurisdiction was founded upon rules which accorded with those provided for either in Chapter II of the Regulation,[84] or in a convention between the State of origin and the State addressed which was in force when the original action was instituted.[85] It seems clear that, in reviewing jurisdiction by reference to Chapter II, one must treat as Member States those in respect of which the Regulation was already in force or entered into force on the date when it entered into force between the State of origin and the State addressed. The other conventions referred to are the bilateral conventions which are listed in Article 69 and accordingly replaced by the Brussels I Regulation, and the conventions on particular matters referred to in Article 71 and accordingly given priority over the Brussels I Regulation.

Since the Brussels I Regulation was not in fact in force in both States at the institution of the original action, the original court will not have applied Chapter II, or at any rate will not have treated the State addressed as a Member State. Thus the special provision for jurisdictional review is necessary to prevent recognition and enforcement of judgments founded on excessive bases of jurisdiction against defendants domiciled in the State addressed, and for the same reason there is no provision that in the transitional case the court addressed must accept the findings of fact relevant to jurisdiction made by the original court.

However, the European Court seems willing to minimise the effect of the proviso for jurisdictional review in transitional cases. In *Von Horn v Cinnamond*,[86] it indicated that, insofar as the jurisdiction of the original court envisaged by the transitional provisions derives from the reference by Article 4 to the law of the State of origin, the court addressed should restrict itself to ascertaining whether the conditions for the application of Article 4 are satisfied, such as that the defendant is not domiciled in a Member State. The court addressed should not also assess the jurisdiction of the original court in the light of the law of the State of origin. More generally, it seems from rulings of the European Court on similar provisions of the Brussels IIA Regulation that, for the necessary accordance to be established, it is sufficient either that the original court had explicitly assumed jurisdiction on a basis similar to one provided for by the Regulation or a relevant convention,[87] or that the court addressed finds that a jurisdictional base accepted by the Regulation or a relevant convention had in fact existed.[88]

### The exception relating to provisional measures

A further case of jurisdictional review, relating to infringement of Article 31 of the Regulation, on provisional measures, has emerged from the European Court's decision in

---

[83]  This includes the situation where an appellate judgment is given after the relevant commencement date, affirming a first-instance judgment given before that date; see *Lacoste v Keely Group* [1999] 1 ILRM 510 (O'Sullivan J).

[84]  See, for example, *ITL France v Medtrafina*, 16th April 1996 (French Court of Cassation); and *CCO v Medtrafina*, 11th March 1997 (French Court of Cassation).

[85]  See also the 1968 Convention, Article 54(2); the 1978 Convention, Article 34(3); the 1982 Convention, Article 12(2); the 1989 Convention, Article 29(2); the 1996 Convention, Article 13(2); the Lugano Convention 1988, Article 54(2); and the Lugano Convention 2007, Article 63(2).

[86]  Case C-163/95, [1997] ECR I-5451.

[87]  See Case C-435/06: *C* [2007] ECR I-10141.

[88]  See Case C-168/08: *Hadadi v Mesko* [2009] ECR I-6871.

*Mietz v Intership Yachting Sneek.*[89] The Court emphasised the importance of ensuring that enforcement under Chapter III in another Member State of provisional or protective measures allegedly founded on the jurisdiction laid down in Article 31, but which go beyond the limits of that jurisdiction, does not result in circumvention of the rules on jurisdiction as to the substance set out in Chapter II. For the jurisdiction recognised by Article 31 constitutes, within the context of the Regulation, a special regime. Thus enforcement under Chapter III must be refused where: (i) the judgment was delivered at the end of proceedings which were not, by their very nature, proceedings as to substance, but summary proceedings for the granting of interim measures; (ii) the measure ordered (such as an unconditional interim payment) is not a provisional or protective measure within the meaning of Article 31; and (iii) the original court had either expressly indicated in its judgment that it had based its jurisdiction on Article 31, or had been silent as to the basis of its jurisdiction.

**Further exceptions under the Lugano Conventions**
The Lugano Convention 1988 permits jurisdictional review in three additional cases. Firstly, by Articles 28(2) and 54B(3), recognition or enforcement may be refused where the respondent is domiciled in a Contracting State to the Lugano Convention which is not an EU Member State, and the jurisdiction of the original court was based on a ground which is contrary to Title II of the Lugano Convention, unless the judgment may otherwise be recognised or enforced under any rule of law in the State addressed. For this purpose, by Article 28(3), the court addressed is bound by the findings of fact on which the original court based its jurisdiction. Since the wording of these provisions is permissive, judicial discretion is not excluded.[90] In the Lugano Convention 2007, this first additional ground for refusal is retained unchanged by Articles 35(1)–(2) and 64(3).

Secondly, by Articles 28(2) and 57(4) of the Lugano Convention 1988, recognition or enforcement may be refused where the original court assumed jurisdiction in pursuance of a specialised convention to which the State addressed is not a party, and the respondent is domiciled in the State addressed, unless the judgment may otherwise be recognised or enforced under any rule of law in the State addressed. Again, by Article 28(3), the court addressed is bound by the findings of fact on which the original court based its jurisdiction; and, since the wording of these provisions is permissive, judicial discretion is not excluded.[91] In the Lugano Convention 2007, this second additional ground for refusal is retained by Articles 35(1)–(2) and 67(4), and extended to cases where the State addressed is an EU Member State, and the specialised convention is one which would have to be concluded by the European Union, and the respondent is domiciled in any of its Member States.

Thirdly, by Article IB of the Protocol annexed to the Lugano Convention 1988, a Contracting State may make a reservation against its recognition and enforcement of judgments given in the other Contracting States under Article 16(1)(b) on the basis of the defendant's domicile in respect of tenancies of immovable property situated in the reserving State.[92] This third additional ground for refusal is not retained in the Lugano Convention 2007.

---

[89]   Case C-99/96, [1999] ECR I-2277. See also *Comet Group v Unika Computer* [2004] ILPr 1.
[90]   See Gaudemet-Tallon, at para 451.
[91]   See Gaudemet-Tallon, at para 451.
[92]   On tenancies, see pp. 147–9 above.

## Public Policy

By Articles 34(1) and 45(1) of the Brussels I Regulation, a judgment is not to be recognized or enforced under Chapter III if its recognition is manifestly contrary to public policy in the State addressed. A similar proviso for the English public policy exists in the traditional English law on recognition and enforcement of foreign judgments.[93]

The European Court has consistently emphasised that the public-policy proviso in Article 34(1) should operate only in exceptional cases,[94] and that the limits of the concept are a matter for interpretation of the Regulation, to be determined by the European Court.[95]

Article 35(3) of the Regulation specifically forbids the use of public policy to extend jurisdictional review, and in *Krombach v Bamberski*,[96] the European Court ruled that this applies even where the original court wrongly founded its jurisdiction over a defendant domiciled in the State addressed on a rule which takes account of nationality. Moreover, in *Hoffmann v Krieg*[97] and *Hendrikman v Magenta Druck & Verlag*,[98] the European Court ruled that recourse to the public-policy proviso is precluded when the issue is dealt with by a specific provision such as Article 34(2), on notification of the defendant, or Article 34(3), on irreconcilability with a local judgment.

In *Krombach v Bamberski*,[99] the European Court explained that, in view of the prohibition on reviewing the substance of the judgment, imposed by Articles 36 and 45(2), the court addressed cannot refuse recognition solely on the ground that there is a discrepancy between the legal rule applied by the court of the State of origin and that which would have been applied by the court of the State addressed if it had been seised of the dispute. Similarly, the court of the State addressed cannot review the accuracy of the findings of law or fact made by the court of the State of origin. Recourse to public policy can be envisaged only where recognition or enforcement of the judgment would be at variance to an unacceptable degree with the legal order of the State addressed inasmuch as it infringes a fundamental principle. The infringement would have to constitute a manifest breach of a rule of law regarded as essential in the legal order of the State addressed, or of a right recognised as fundamental within that legal order. Accordingly, the European Court ruled in *Renault v Maxicar*[100] that public policy cannot be invoked on the ground that the original judgment involved an error

---

93   See, for example, *Re Macartney* [1921] 1 Ch 522, on the common law; the Administration of Justice Act 1920, ss 9(1) and (2)(f); and the Foreign Judgments (Reciprocal Enforcement) Act 1933, s 4(1)(a)(v).

94   See Case 145/86: *Hoffmann v Krieg* [1988] ECR 645; Case C-78/95: *Hendrikman v Magenta Druck & Verlag* [1996] ECR I-4943; Case C-7/98: *Krombach v Bamberski* [2000] ECR I-1935; and Case C-420/07: *Apostolides v Orams* [2009] ECR I-3571.

95   See Case C-7/98: *Krombach v Bamberski* [2000] ECR I-1935; and Case C-420/07: *Apostolides v Orams* [2009] ECR I-3571.

96   Case C-7/98, [2000] ECR I-1935.

97   Case 145/86, [1988] ECR 645.

98   Case C-78/95, [1996] ECR I-4943.

99   Case C-7/98, [2000] ECR I-1935.

100   Case C-38/98: *Renault v Maxicar* [2000] ECR I-2973. Cf. Case C-126/97: *Eco Swiss China Time v Benetton* [1999] ECR I-3055, which dealt with the relevance of Article 101 of the Treaty on the Functioning of the European Union in the context of judicial proceedings for the annulment of a local arbitration award.

of Community law, for example as to the legitimacy under Articles 34–6 or 102 of the Treaty on the Functioning of the European Union of a design right in spare parts. Similarly, in *Apostolides v Orams*,[101] the European Court ruled that public policy cannot be invoked on the ground that the judgment concerned land situated in an area of the State of origin over which its government did not exercise effective control, and thus could not, as a practical matter, be enforced where the land was situated. Somewhat similarly, the European Court of Human Rights has accepted that a court requested to enforce a foreign judgment need only carry out a limited review of the compatibility of the judgment with the European Convention on Human Rights.[102]

The Brussels I Regulation omits any provision corresponding to Article 27(4) of the Brussels Convention, which prevented recognition and enforcement where the original court, in order to arrive at its judgment, had decided a preliminary question concerning individual status or capacity, matrimonial property, or succession on death, in a way which conflicted with a private international law rule of the State addressed, unless the same result would have been reached by the application of the private international law rules of that State. The matters in question are, of course, ones to which, when they form the principal subject-matter of proceedings, the Regulation is wholly inapplicable under Article 1(2)(a).[103] Article 27(4) could have applied, for example, where the judgment had upheld a defence of minority to a claim for damages for breach of contract, by applying the law of the defendant's nationality or domicile, when the court addressed would have rejected the defence, by applying the law governing the contract. It could also have applied where the judgment had awarded maintenance ancillarily in divorce proceedings, and the divorce was for some reason denied recognition in the State addressed.[104] It seems that under the Regulation the problems formerly addressed by Article 27(4) may now be dealt with under the public-policy proviso, as they are in traditional English law,[105] provided that recognition can be regarded as involving a clear breach of a principle regarded as fundamental in the State addressed.

It seems possible to identify five categories of situation in which public policy may legitimately be invoked under Article 34(1) of the Regulation.[106]

### Procedural unfairness

The first type of situation in which public policy may legitimately be invoked under Article 34(1) of the Regulation is where, despite proper notification of the institution of the original action satisfying Article 34(2), a party was in some other way denied a reasonable opportu-

---

[101]   Case C-420/07, [2009] ECR I-3571.

[102]   See *Lindberg v Sweden*, 15th January 2004.

[103]   See pp. 29–32 above.

[104]   See *T v L* [2008] IESC 48, where the Irish Supreme Court (per Fennelly J) refused under Article 27(4) of the Convention to recognise a Dutch maintenance order, made ancillarily to a Dutch divorce decree, because the divorce was not recognised in Ireland.

[105]   See *Gray v Formosa* [1963] P 259, and *Lepre v Lepre* [1965] P 52.

[106]   A sixth possible situation, which had emerged from the decision of the English Court of Appeal in *Phillip Alexander Securities v Bamberger* [1997] ILPr 73, involved a judgment obtained in knowing breach of an anti-suit injunction which had been issued in the State addressed. But this possibility must be regarded as obsolete in view of the European Court's ruling in Case C-159/02: *Turner v Grovit* [2004] ECR I-3565 that the Brussels I Regulation in all circumstances precludes the grant of an anti-suit injunction against proceedings in a court of another Member State.

nity to present his case, or was otherwise prejudiced by the use by the original court (perhaps in breach of its own law) of a procedure which is considered seriously unfair by the standards of the State addressed. A similar ground for refusal of recognition exists in traditional English law,[107] and denial of recognition on this basis reflects the principle specified by Article 6(1) of the European Convention on Human Rights, that in the determination of his civil rights and obligations, everyone is entitled to a fair and public hearing by an independent and impartial tribunal.

This type of ground was accepted by the European Court in *Krombach v Bamberski*,[108] where a French court, hearing a prosecution for manslaughter and an ancillary civil claim by relatives of the victim, had ordered the accused to appear in person; and on his failure to do so, had refused to hear his defence counsel. The European Court ruled that a court of a Member State is entitled to hold that a refusal to hear the defence of an accused person who is not present at the hearing constitutes a manifest breach of a fundamental right, and therefore to deny recognition under Article 34(1), despite the fact that Article 61 was inapplicable because of the intentional character of the offence.[109] Similarly, in *Maronier v Larmer*,[110] the English Court of Appeal refused on grounds of public policy to enforce a Dutch judgment given in proceedings which had been reactivated after twelve years without the defendant's knowledge, and without his becoming aware of the reactivation until after the time for appealing against the judgment had expired. On similar grounds, the French Court of Cassation has refused to enforce an English order for costs against a claimant whose action had been dismissed after he had failed to comply with an order to give security for costs.[111] Unacceptable denial of a hearing could also occur where the plaintiff in the original action, after agreeing to allow extra time for filing a defence, had proceeded to obtain a default judgment in breach of the agreement.[112]

In *Gambazzi v DaimlerChrysler*,[113] the European Court ruled that under Article 34(1) the court addressed may take into account, with regard to public policy, the fact that the court of origin had ruled on the applicant's claims without hearing the defendant, who had entered an appearance before it but had been excluded from the proceedings by order on the ground that he had not complied with obligations imposed by an order for disclosure made earlier in the same proceedings. But it insisted that recognition may be refused only if, following a comprehensive assessment of the proceedings and in the light of all the circumstances, it appears to the court addressed that the exclusion measure constituted a manifest and disproportionate infringement of the defendant's right to be heard. The European Court explained that for this purpose the court addressed must take into account the circumstances in which the earlier

---

[107] See *Jacobson v Frachon*, (1927) 44 TLR 103, and *Adams v Cape Industries* [1990] Ch 433.

[108] Case C-7/98, [2000] ECR I-1935.

[109] On Article 61, see p. 249 below.

[110] [2003] QB 620 (CA). See also *Citibank v Rafidian Bank* [2003] ILPr 49.

[111] See *Pordea v Times Newspapers*, 16th March 1999; cited in *Nasser v United Bank of Kuwait* [2002] 1 WLR 1868, at para 43. The French Court of Cassation has also refused to recognise a judgment which it regarded as insufficiently reasoned, unless the implied reasoning was shown by other documents produced; see *Polypetrol v SGR*, 9th October 1991, and Gaudemet-Tallon, at para 353.

[112] See *Levin v Gladstein* 55 SE 371 (1906); and *Restatement, Second, Conflict of Laws* (1971), § 115.

[113] Case C 394/07, [2009] ECR I-2563. The case involved the enforcement in Italy of an English judgment.

orders were adopted. It must examine whether and to what extent the defendant had the opportunity to be heard as to the subject-matter and scope of a disclosure order before it was made, and what legal remedies were available to the defendant, after the disclosure order was made, in order to request its amendment or revocation. The court addressed must identify the legal remedies which were available to the defendant and verify that they offered him the possibility of being heard, in compliance with the adversarial principle and the full exercise of the rights of defence. Following completion of such verification, it is for the court addressed to carry out a balancing exercise in order to assess whether, in the light of the objective of the efficient administration of justice pursued by the original court, the exclusion of the defendant from the proceedings amounted to a manifest and disproportionate infringement of his right to be heard.

The seriously unfair procedure followed by the original court was one of the grounds on which the English Court of Appeal refused, in *Adams v Cape Industries*,[114] to enforce at common law a judgment of an American federal court, given against a defaulting defendant in a personal-injury action brought by numerous plaintiffs. The American court, in unexpected breach of its own procedural law, had assessed damages without receiving evidence of the particular injuries sustained by the individual plaintiffs. It had instead fixed an average amount for all the plaintiffs, and left it to their counsel to distribute the total award so arrived at between them. An argument that the defendant should have applied to the American court to have the judgment set aside on the ground of this procedural irregularity, an application which would have succeeded if made timeously, rather than raising the objection in England when enforcement here was sought, was rejected on the ground that the defendant had not been aware of the method of assessment used until enforcement in England was threatened. Slade LJ conceded, however, that if a foreign law were to provide for the plaintiff to serve a notice specifying a sum claimed as damages, and then for a default judgment to be entered for that sum without proof or judicial assessment, such a procedure would usually be considered unobjectionable, provided that, after due allowance had been made for differences between the foreign law and English law in levels of award and in substantive law, the amount of the actual award was not irrational.

Slade LJ also took the view that, even if the only procedural impropriety related to the assessment of damages, the judgment creditor could not invoke the foreign judgment for the purpose merely of establishing liability, so as to obtain an English judgment under which damages would be assessed by the English court, even though he considered that such a result would 'get closer to substantial justice' than total dismissal of the claim. Why such limited recognition should be impossible at common law is far from clear, and it is submitted that such severance is permissible under the Brussels I Regulation, since Article 48 specifies that where a foreign judgment has been given in respect of several matters and the declaration of enforceability cannot be given for all of them, the court addressed shall give it for one or more of them, and that an applicant may request a declaration of enforceability limited to parts of a judgment.

### Non-procedural factors
The second type of situation in which public policy may legitimately be invoked is where the

---

[114]   [1990] Ch 433.

court addressed considers that recognition of the judgment would be unconscionable because of the outrageous character of the substantive rule applied by the original court. Examples might be where the judgment has upheld and enforced a contract to pay a fee to an assassin for carrying out an assassination, or to a lobbyist for obtaining a public contract by bribing officials.[115] At one time, an English court considered that a maintenance order against the father of a non-marital child, lasting beyond the child's minority, fell into this category,[116] but a more tolerant approach to such an order may be expected today.[117]

On the other hand, in view of the (UK) Protection of Trading Interests Act 1980, an English court would probably invoke public policy against the enforcement under the Brussels I Regulation of a judgment awarding multiple damages, at least as regards the multiple element of the amount awarded. Section 5 of the 1980 Act prevents the enforcement under traditional English law of a foreign judgment for multiple damages. Even the unmultiplied element of the damages awarded, representing the actual loss found by the foreign court to have been sustained, is rendered unenforceable in England. Section 6 goes further by enabling in certain circumstances a person who has satisfied, or suffered enforcement abroad of, a foreign judgment for multiple damages, to sue in England for recoupment of the multiple element paid or enforced. Section 7 provides for the reciprocal enforcement of foreign recoupment judgments. However, a restrictive approach to the interpretation of the 1980 Act is now adopted. Thus severance is possible where the sum awarded by the judgment comprises an identifiable sum awarded as multiple damages in respect of one claim, and another identifiable sum awarded as ordinary damages in respect of another claim.[118] Moreover, enforcement is possible of a compensatory sum, awarded by the judgment as a separate head, even though the judgment also contains another head awarding a multiple of the sum.[119]

In contrast, there appears to be no English policy against the enforcement of foreign judgments awarding exemplary or aggravated damages, for example where the defendant has perversely refused to meet a clearly justified claim, if no multiplication is involved,[120] unless perhaps the amount awarded is entirely irrational.[121] However, there is a serious likelihood that courts of other Member States will invoke public policy in order to avoid enforcing English judgments awarding damages for libel, since such awards may be viewed as grossly

---

[115] See *Westacre Investments v Jugoimport-SDRP* [1999] 3 All ER 864 (CA), which involved an arbitration award. Enforcement of the award was authorised on the grounds that the allegation of bribery had been made before and rejected by the arbitrators, and cogent subsequently discovered evidence was not now offered.

[116] See *Re Macartney* [1921] 1 Ch 522.

[117] For a tolerant approach to foreign rules under the Brussels Convention, see *Copraf v Savict*, 11th March 1997, where the French Court of Cassation rejected an argument that an Italian judgment allowing both interest and currency indexation contravened French public policy. See also *Reisdorff*, 12th July 1994 (French Court of Cassation), enforcing a German order for maintenance of a child, dating back to the child's birth, despite the fact that paternity was established and the maintenance order made much later; and Gaudemet-Tallon, at para. 352.

[118] See *Lewis v Eliades* [2004] 1 All ER (Comm) 545 (CA), affirming [2003] 1 All ER (Comm) 850.

[119] See *Lucasfilm Ltd v Ainsworth* [2009] FSR 2 (Mann J).

[120] See *General Textiles v Sun & Sand Agencies* [1978] 1 QB 279.

[121] See *Adams v Cape Industries* [1990] Ch 433.

excessive in amount, and as impairing the right to freedom of expression conferred by Article 10 of the European Convention on Human Rights.[122]

The third type of situation in which public policy may legitimately be invoked is where recognition of the judgment would be contrary to the political interests of the State addressed in the conduct of its economic or foreign policies. Examples might be where the judgment upholds and enforces a contract whose conclusion was prohibited by the exchange-control legislation of the State addressed,[123] or a contract which amounts to a conspiracy to commit acts which are criminally prohibited in the country where they are intended to be performed, such as a contract to smuggle goods into a country which prohibits the import of goods of that nature.[124]

The fourth type of case is where cogent evidence has been discovered since the judgment was given, but there is no way of having the matter re-opened in the original country.[125]

The fifth type of case is where there are irreconcilable judgments given by courts of different countries, and there is no other applicable provision dictating which of them should prevail. This situation is less likely to occur under the Brussels I Regulation than previously under the Brussels Convention in view of the wider scope of Article 34(4) of the Regulation.[126]

## Inadequate Notice of the Original Action

By Articles 34(2) and 45(1) of the Brussels I Regulation,[127] recognition and enforcement of a judgment must be refused where it was given in default of appearance, and the defendant was not served with the document which instituted the proceedings or with an equivalent document in sufficient time and in such a way as to enable him to arrange for his defence, unless the defendant failed to commence proceedings to challenge the judgment when it was possible for him to do so.

These provisions depart substantially from Articles 27(2) and 34(2) of the Brussels Convention, by which a judgment was not to be recognised or enforced if it was given in default of appearance, and the defendant was not duly served with the document which instituted the original proceedings or with an equivalent document in sufficient time to enable him to arrange for his defence.[128] Under the Regulation, the manner as well as the time of service is subjected exclusively to a Community standard, but the defendant is expected to challenge

---

[122] See Vick and MacPherson, 'Anglicising Defamation Law in the European Union' (1996) 36 Virginia Journal of International Law 933, at pp. 995–7.

[123] Cf. *Boissevain v Weil* [1950] AC 327.

[124] Cf. *Foster v Driscoll* [1929] 1 KB 470, and *Regazzoni v Sethia* [1958] AC 301.

[125] See *Interdesco v Nullifire* [1992] 1 Lloyd's Rep 180, and *SISRO v Ampersand Software* [1994] ILPr 55 (CA); and p. 232 above.

[126] See pp. 249–52 below.

[127] For a corresponding exception to recognition and enforcement under the traditional English law on foreign judgments, see *Jacobson v Frachon* (1927) 138 LT 386; the Administration of Justice Act 1920, s 9(2)(c); and the Foreign Judgments (Reciprocal Enforcement) Act 1933, s 4(1)(a)(iii). See also, on the American constitutional requirement of due process, *Mullane v Central Hanover Bank & Trust Co* 339 US 306 (1950), and *Dobkin v Chapman* 236 NE2d 451 (1968).

[128] See also Article 46(2) of the Brussels Convention, which required an applicant for recognition or enforcement of a default judgment to produce a document which established that the party in default had been served with the document instituting the proceedings or with an equivalent document.

the judgment in the State of origin where possible. The provision on challenge in the original country overrules the decision of the European Court in *Minalmet v Brandeis*,[129] and may be viewed as undesirably weakening a useful deterrent to inadequate service.

As under the Brussels Convention, judgments authorising provisional or protective measures, which are delivered without the defendant having been summoned to appear, and which are intended to be enforced without prior service, do not fall within the scope of Chapter III of the Regulation.[130]

**Cumulative protection**

The protection conferred by Articles 34(2) and 45(1) of the Brussels I Regulation at the stage of recognition or enforcement is in addition to that conferred in the original action by Article 26(2)–(4) of the Brussels I Regulation, in conjunction with Article 19 of EC Regulation 1393/2007 on the Service in the Member States of Judicial and Extrajudicial Documents in Civil or Commercial Matters,[131] and with Article 15 of the Hague Convention of 15th November 1965 on the Service Abroad of Judicial and Extrajudicial Documents in Civil or Commercial Matters.[132] Under Article 26, where the defendant is domiciled or resident in another EC Member State or another Contracting State to the Hague Convention, the original court is required to stay its proceedings so long as it is not shown that the defendant has been able to receive the document instituting the proceedings or an equivalent document in sufficient time to enable him to arrange for his defence, or that all necessary steps have been taken to that end.

The cumulative nature of the protection conferred on the defendant in the State of origin and in the State addressed was emphasised by the European Court in its rulings under the Brussels Convention. Thus in *Pendy Plastic Products v Pluspunkt*,[133] it ruled that the court addressed may refuse to grant recognition and enforcement of a judgment, even though the court of the State of origin had regarded it as proved that the defendant, who failed to enter an appearance, had had an opportunity to receive service of the document instituting the proceedings in sufficient time to enable him to make arrangements for his defence. Similarly, in *Klomps v Michel*,[134] it ruled that even if the court of origin had held in separate adversary proceedings that service had been duly effected, the court addressed was still required to examine whether service was effected in sufficient time to enable the defendant to arrange for his defence. But the availability of relief in the State addressed is now restricted by the new proviso to Article 34(2), which insists that the defendant should challenge the judgment in the State of origin, when it is possible for him to do so.

In any event, as the European Court confirmed in *Klomps v Michel*[135] and *Debaecker v Bouwman*,[136] Article 34(2) has a wider scope than Article 26, in that the protection of Article 34(2) extends to every defendant, regardless of his domicile.

---

[129]  Case C-123/91, [1992] ECR I-5661.

[130]  See Case 125/79, *Denilauler v Couchet Frères* [1980] ECR 1553; and pp. 225–6 above.

[131]  [2007] OJ L324/79. Except in relation to Denmark, Regulation 1393/2007 has replaced Regulation 1348/2000, [2000] OJ L160/37. See pp. 62–6 above.

[132]  See pp. 67–8 above.

[133]  Case 228/81, [1982] ECR 2723.

[134]  Case 166/80, [1981] ECR 1593. See also *Coverbat v Jackson*, 31st January 1997 (CA).

[135]  Case 166/80, [1981] ECR 1593.

[136]  Case 49/84, [1985] ECR 1779.

**Default judgments**

For recognition to be denied under Article 34(2), the judgment must have been given in default of appearance. In *Sonntag v Waidmann*,[137] the European Court ruled that a defendant is deemed to have appeared where, in connection with a claim for compensation joined to criminal proceedings, he answered at the trial through counsel of his own choice to the criminal charges, but did not express a view on the civil claim, on which oral argument was also submitted in the presence of his counsel. On the other hand, as the European Court ruled in *Hendrikman v Magenta Druck & Verlag*,[138] Article 34(2) applies where the defendant was not validly represented in the original proceedings, even though the judgment was not in formal terms given in default of appearance, because someone purporting to represent the defendant, but in fact acting without his authority, appeared before the original court.

In *Tavoulareas v Tsavliris (No 2)*,[139] Tomlinson J held that a judgment counted as a default judgment where the only participation by the defendant had been to join in a request for an agreed adjournment, while at the same time protesting that the court lacked jurisdiction, and the judgment was expressed by the court rendering it to be given in default of appearance. In affirming this decision, the Court of Appeal explained that appearance occurs only where the defendant either lodges with the court a formal document of defence (whether as to the merits or as to jurisdiction), or is present at a hearing before the court.

Under the Brussels Convention, the European Court had ruled in *Klomps v Michel*[140] that Article 27(2) of the Convention remained applicable to a judgment which was originally given in default of appearance, even if the defendant subsequently lodged an objection against the judgment, but a court of the State of origin held the objection inadmissible as out of time. Similarly, in *Maersk Olie & Gas v de Haan & de Boer*,[141] it had ruled that Article 27(2) remained applicable despite the fact that the defendant had unsuccessfully appealed against the judgment on the sole ground that the original court lacked jurisdiction. But the availability of relief in the State addressed is now restricted by the new proviso to Article 34(2), which insists that the defendant should challenge the judgment in the State of origin, when it is possible for him to do so.

**The instituting document**

As the European Court ruled, in the context of German and Italian summary proceedings, in *Klomps v Michel*[142] and *Hengst v Campese*,[143] the instituting document referred to in Article 34(2) is the document or documents whose service enables the plaintiff, under the law of the State of origin, to obtain, in default of appropriate action taken by the defendant, a decision capable of being recognised or enforced under the Regulation. Similarly, in *Maersk Olie & Gas v de Haan & de Boer*,[144] which involved Dutch proceedings for the establishment of an admiralty limitation fund, under which a provisional order determining the maximum amount

---

[137]   Case C-172/91, [1993] ECR I-1963.
[138]   Case C-78/95, [1996] ECR I-4943.
[139]   [2006] EWHC 414 (Comm) (Tomlinson J); affirmed [2007] 2 All ER (Comm) 356 (CA).
[140]   Case 166/80, [1981] ECR 1593.
[141]   Case C-39/02, [2004] ECR I-9657.
[142]   Case 166/80, [1981] ECR 1593.
[143]   Case C-474/93, [1995] ECR I-2113.
[144]   Case C-39/02, [2004] ECR I-9657.

of liability is initially adopted by the court at the conclusion of a unilateral procedure, and this is then followed by reasoned submissions by both parties, the European Court ruled that the provisional order must be treated as a document equivalent to a document instituting proceedings under Article 34(2) of the Regulation.

### Sufficiency of service

Under Article 34(2) of the Brussels I Regulation, the manner as well as the time of service is subjected exclusively to a Community standard, referring to sufficiency for the purpose of enabling the defendant to arrange for his defence. Thus in *ASML v Semiconductor Industry Services*,[145] the European Court recognised that under the Regulation a mere formal irregularity in service, which does not adversely affect the rights of defence, is not sufficient to prevent recognition and enforcement.[146]

In contrast, Article 27(2) of the Brussels Convention required due service, which the European Court construed as referring to service in accordance with the law of the State of origin and the conventions binding on that State, so that recognition would have to be refused where (for example) the service was irregular under the law and conventions of the State of origin because the documents served were not accompanied by a translation, even if the notification was sufficient to enable the defendant to arrange for his defence, unless under the law and conventions of the State of origin the irregularity had been cured by subsequent acts.[147] Moreover, in *Scania v Rockinger*,[148] the European Court ruled that, under Article 27(2) of the Brussels Convention and Article IV(1) of its Protocol, where an international convention on service was applicable between the State of origin and the State addressed, the question whether the document instituting the proceedings was duly served had to be determined in the light of the provisions of the convention on service. This was without prejudice to the use of direct transmission between public officers where the State addressed had not officially objected, in accordance with Article IV(2) of the Protocol.

Under Article 27(2) of the Brussels Convention, the European Court supplemented the requirement of due service by construing the requirement of sufficient time to enable defence as requiring the use of a method of service which satisfied a Community standard. This required the use, so far as practicable, of a method which was likely to be effective in bringing the matter to the defendant's attention. Otherwise the time for arranging defence would not begin.[149] Application of the Community standard involved consideration of all the circumstances, including ones arising after formal service (for example, on a public official) had been effected, and in particular it was relevant both that the defendant had by absconding prevented

---

145 Case C-283/05, [2006] ECR I-12041, especially at paras 20 and 43–7.
146 Cf. *Tavoulareas v Tsavliris* (No 2) [2007] 2 All ER (Comm) 356, where the English Court of Appeal insisted that Article 34(2) of the Brussels I Regulation requires formal service in a manner which complies with EC Regulations 1348/2000 and 1393/2007, where applicable.
147 See Case 166/80: *Klomps v Michel* [1981] ECR 1593; and Case C-305/88: *Lancray v Peters* [1990] ECR I-2725. See also *Noirhomme v Walklate* [1992] 1 Lloyd's Rep 427; and *Selco v Mercier* [1996] SLT 1247. Cf. Case C-474/93: *Hengst v Campese* [1995] ECR I-2113.
148 Case C-522/03, [2005] ECR I-8639.
149 See Case 166/80: *Klomps v Michel* [1981] ECR 1593; and Case 49/84: *Debaecker v Bouwman* [1985] ECR 1779. See also *TSN v Jurgens* [2001] WL 606474 (Jack J), affirmed [2002] 1 WLR 2459 (CA).

the formal service from reaching him, and that after the formal service the plaintiff had become aware of the defendant's new address.[150] No doubt a similar approach will be applied to the explicit requirement by Article 34(2) of the Regulation of service 'in sufficient time and in such a way as to enable [the defendant] to arrange for his defence'.

As regards the period for arranging defence, account may be taken only of the time available for taking steps to prevent the issue of a default judgment which is enforceable under the Regulation, and not of any further period after the entry of a default judgment in which application could be made to have the matter re-opened.[151] But the relevant period for determining sufficiency is the period during which a notice of appearance will in fact prevent the issue of a judgment by default. Thus where under the law of the original country a valid notice of appearance entered at any time prior to the issue of a default judgment would have prevented its issue, the relevant period ends at the actual issue of the default judgment, rather than at the earliest date on which a default judgment could have been entered.[152] A period of five or nine weeks for entering an appearance will normally be considered sufficient.[153] In any event, the proviso added at the end of Article 34(2) of the Regulation now prevents a defendant from invoking this objection to recognition and enforcement if he failed to commence proceedings to challenge the judgment in the original country when it was possible for him to do so.

### The proviso on possible challenge

Article 34(2) of the Brussels I Regulation has added a proviso which prevents a defendant from opposing recognition and enforcement of a default judgment on the ground of insufficiency of service, where he failed to commence proceedings to challenge the judgment in the original country when it was possible for him to do so.

In *ASML v Semiconductor Industry Services*,[154] the European Court construed the proviso as meaning that it is possible for a defendant to bring proceedings to challenge a default judgment against him only if he was in fact acquainted with the contents of the judgment, and that this requires the judgment to have been served on him in sufficient time and in such a way as to enable him to arrange for his defence before the courts of the State of origin. The Court explained that the requirement is not of due service of a default judgment in compliance with all applicable formalities, but of service of the judgment in sufficient time and in such a way as to enable the defendant to arrange for his defence. Thus a mere formal irregularity, which does not adversely affect the rights of defence, is not sufficient to prevent the application of the proviso.

The new insistence that the defendant should, where possible, challenge the judgment in the State of origin has been strengthened by the ruling of the European Court in *Apostolides v Orams*[155] that the recognition or enforcement of a default judgment cannot be refused under Article 34(2) where the defendant was able to and did in fact commence proceedings in the State of origin to challenge the default judgment, and those proceedings enabled him to argue

---

[150]   See Case 49/84: *Debaecker v Bouwman* [1985] ECR 1779.

[151]   See Case 166/80: *Klomps v Michel* [1981] ECR 1593.

[152]   See *TSN v Jurgens* [2002] 1 WLR 2459 (CA).

[153]   See *TSN v Jurgens* [2002] 1 WLR 2459 (CA); and *Lacoste v Keely Group* [1999] 1 ILRM 510 (O'Sullivan J).

[154]   Case C-283/05, [2006] ECR I-12041.

[155]   Case C-420/07, [2009] ECR I-3571.

that he had not been served with the instituting or equivalent document in sufficient time and in such a way as to enable him to arrange for his defence. This is so even if his application in the State of origin was rejected on the ground that he had failed to show any arguable defence on the merits.[156]

## The Lugano Conventions

Article 27(2) the Lugano Convention 1988 echoes Article 27(2) of the Brussels Convention, and Article 34(2) of the Lugano Convention 2007 echoes Article 34(2) of the Brussels I Regulation. But Article III(1) of the First Protocol to the Lugano Convention 2007 enables Switzerland to make a reservation whereby it will not apply the proviso specified in Article 34(2) on challenge in the original country. If Switzerland makes such a reservation, the proviso on challenge will also be inapplicable by the other Contracting Parties in respect of judgments rendered by the Swiss courts.

## Civil Proceedings Ancillary to a Criminal Prosecution

A further provision designed to protect the defendant's procedural rights is contained in Article 61 of the Brussels I Regulation.[157] This applies, without prejudice to more favourable provisions of national laws, where a person domiciled in a Member State is prosecuted in a criminal court of another Member State of which he is not a national for an offence which was not intentionally committed. In such a case, he may be defended by persons qualified to do so, even if he does not appear in person. But the court seised may order appearance in person. Then, in the case of failure to appear, a civil judgment given without his having had the opportunity to arrange for his defence need not be recognized or enforced in the other Member States.

In *Rinkau*,[158] the European Court ruled that this provision extends to any offence whose definition does not require the existence of intent by the accused to commit the punishable act or omission, but that it is confined to criminal proceedings in which the accused's civil liability, arising from the elements of the offence for which he is being prosecuted, is in question, or on which such liability might subsequently be based.

In the case of a prosecution for an intentional offence, the public-policy proviso specified by Article 34(1) enables recognition of an ancillary civil judgment to be refused where the defendant did not appear in person and the court therefore refused to hear his representative.[159]

## Irreconcilable Judgments

Articles 34(3) and (4) and 45(1) of the Brussels I Regulation deal with the problem of irreconcilable judgments. By Articles 34(3) and 45(1), a judgment given in one Member State must not be recognised or enforced in another Member State if it is irreconcilable with a judgment

---

[156]  Cf. *Tavoulareas v Tsavliris (No 2)* [2006] EWHC 414 (Comm) (Tomlinson J); affirmed without addressing the effect of actual challenge, [2007] 2 All ER (Comm) 356 (CA).

[157]  Article 61 echoes Article II of the Protocol annexed to the Brussels Convention.

[158]  Case 157/80, [1981] ECR 1391.

[159]  See Case C-7/98: *Krombach v Bamberski* [2000] ECR I-1935; and pp. 240–42 above.

given in a dispute between the same parties in the State addressed. By Articles 34(4) and 45(1), a judgment given in one Member State must not be recognised or enforced in another Member State if it is irreconcilable with an earlier judgment given in a third Member State or in a non-member country involving the same cause of action and between the same parties, provided that the earlier judgment fulfils the conditions necessary for its recognition in the Member State addressed.[160]

As the European Court explained in *Hoffmann v Krieg*,[161] judgments are irreconcilable with each other for the purpose of Article 34 where they entail mutually exclusive legal consequences.[162] It proceeded to rule, rather surprisingly, that there was irreconcilability between a German maintenance order and a subsequent Dutch divorce, as regards the period following the divorce, on the questionable assumption that the maintenance order necessarily presupposed the continued existence of a matrimonial relationship. The ruling has been followed, loyally rather than enthusiastically, by English courts in the context of Irish maintenance orders followed by English divorces.[163] Similarly, the Irish Supreme Court has refused under Article 34(3) to recognise a Dutch maintenance order, made ancillarily to a Dutch divorce decree, as being irreconcilable with an Irish decision refusing to recognise the divorce.[164]

In *Italian Leather v WECO Polstermöbel*,[165] the European Court ruled that Article 34(3) extends to provisional measures (such as an interlocutory injunction prohibiting the infringement of a trade mark). Moreover, a foreign judgment granting such an interlocutory injunction is irreconcilable with a local judgment between the same parties refusing to grant such an injunction, even if the conflicting effects of the two judgments are due to differences in the procedural requirements for the grant of such relief laid down by the laws of the two countries. Further, Article 34(3) has a mandatory character, so that once the court addressed finds that the relevant irreconcilability exists, it is bound to refuse to recognise the foreign judgment.

Where the irreconcilability is between a local judgment and a judgment given in another Member State, Article 34(3) gives priority to the local judgment, regardless of the order in which the judgments were given.[166] It is, however, confined to judgments between the same parties, though there is no requirement that they should be in respect of the same cause of

---

[160]    Article 34(4) of the Regulation is wider than its predecessor, Article 27(5) of the Brussels Convention, which dealt with irreconcilability with an earlier judgment given in an external country, but not with an earlier judgment given in another Member State.
[161]    Case 145/86, [1988] ECR 645.
[162]    Cf. Case C-406/92: *The Maciej Rataj* [1994] ECR I-5439, where the Court gave a wider scope to Article 28 on related actions, as applying where separate trial and judgment would involve the risk of conflicting decisions, even if they would not have mutually exclusive legal consequences.
[163]    See *Macaulay v Macaulay* [1991] 1 WLR 179; and *Ex parte Emmett* [1993] 2 FLR 663. Cf. *Bragg v Bragg* [1925] P 20; *Wood v Wood* [1957] P 254; *Qureshi v Qureshi* [1972] Fam 173; and *Newmarch v Newmarch* [1978] Fam 79.
[164]    See *T v L* [2008] IESC 48, affirming *DT v FL* [2007] ILPr 56 (McKechnie J).
[165]    Case C-80/00, [2002] ECR I-4995.
[166]    See Case 145/86: *Hoffmann v Krieg* [1988] ECR 645; and Gaudemet-Tallon, at para 373. The position is similar under traditional English law; see *Vervaeke v Smith* [1983] 1 AC 145, *Man v Haryanto* [1991] 1 Lloyd's Rep 429 (CA), the Administration of Justice Act 1920, s 9(1), and the Foreign Judgments (Reciprocal Enforcement) Act 1933, s 4(1)(a)(v) and (b).

action. Presumably the reference in Article 34(3) to the same parties should be construed in the same way as in Article 27, on concurrent similar actions. Thus an admiralty judgment in rem against a ship will be treated as equivalent to a personal judgment against the shipowner, and where some but not all the parties were common to both actions, Article 34(3) will apply to the judgments insofar as they affect the common parties.[167] The local judgment need not be final,[168] but it must be an actual judgment, and not merely a court settlement falling within Chapter IV of the Regulation,[169] nor merely a pending action, in favour of which the foreign court should have declined jurisdiction under Article 27.[170]

Where the irreconcilability is between judgments given in two different Member States other than the State addressed, or between a judgment given in another Member State and a judgment given in an external country, Article 34(4) gives priority to the earlier judgment.[171] But its operation is confined to cases where the judgments involve the same cause of action and are between the same parties, and where the earlier judgment fulfils the conditions necessary for its recognition in the State addressed. In the United Kingdom, in relation to an external judgment, the last condition means simply that the judgment must comply with the substantive requirements for recognition at common law or under s 8 of the Foreign Judgments (Reciprocal Enforcement) Act 1933, and does not require that its recognition should have been established by proceedings in the United Kingdom.[172] No doubt the reference in Article 34(4) to the same parties must have the same meaning as in Article 34(3), and the reference to the same cause of action must be construed widely, in accordance with the European Court's rulings on Article 27.[173] But in any event Article 34(4) fails to resolve the problem of conflicting issue estoppels arising from judgments dealing with different causes of action.

Probably Article 34(4) extends to the situation where, from the viewpoint of the State addressed, there is concurrent exclusive jurisdiction of another Member State under Article 22 and of a non-member country under its reflexive effect. For example, where an English court is faced with conflicting Dutch and New York judgments in a dispute concerning corporate matters falling within Article 22(2) in respect of a company which is incorporated and has its registered office in the Netherlands but has its actual headquarters in New York.[174]

The provisions of Article 34(3) and (4) do not cover all possible situations involving irreconcilable judgments. Uncovered situations may arise where the judgments give rise to

---

[167]  See Case C-406/92: *The Maciej Rataj* [1994] ECR I-5439; and pp. 194–5 above.

[168]  See Gaudemet-Tallon, at para 371.

[169]  See Case C-414/92: *Solo Kleinmotoren v Boch* [1994] ECR I-2237. See also *Virani v Joubert Laurencin*, 11th February 1997 (French Court of Cassation), and *Landhurst Leasing v Marcq* [1998] ILPr 822 (CA).

[170]  See *Brasserie du Pecheur v Kreissparkasse Main-Spessart*, 14th May 1996 (French Court of Cassation); and Gaudemet-Tallon, at para 369.

[171]  For a similar preference for the earlier judgment in traditional English law, see *Showlag v Mansour* [1995] 1 AC 431 (PC), and the Foreign Judgments (Reciprocal Enforcement) Act 1993, s 4(1)(b). Cf. the preference given to the later judgment under the full faith and credit clause of the US Constitution, as construed in *Treinies v Sunshine Mining Co* 308 US 66 (1939).

[172]  See the Schlosser Report, at para 205; and Gaudemet-Tallon, at para 378.

[173]  See Gaudemet-Tallon, at para 377. On Article 27, see Case 144/86: *Gubisch v Palumbo* [1987] ECR 4861; Case C-406/92: *The Maciej Rataj* [1994] ECR I-5439; and pp. 192–5 above.

[174]  See Gaudemet-Tallon, at para 93.

conflicting estoppels even though they were not given between the same parties or, as regards Article 34(4), in respect of the same cause of action. Since it is logically impossible simultaneously to give full effect to two judgments which are irreconcilable with each other, to the extent that, even after a broad and purposive interpretation of Articles 34(3) and (4), no solution is provided, the solution to the logical impasse will have to be found in the reference to the public policy of the State addressed made by Article 34(1).

## THE HAGUE CONVENTION 2005

On 26th February 2009, the EC Council adopted Decision 2009/397, on the signing on behalf of the European Community of the Hague Convention of 30th June 2005 on Choice of Court Agreements.[175] The Decision approved the signing on behalf of the European Community of the Hague Convention 2005, and accordingly the Convention was signed on behalf of the European Community on 1st April 2009.[176] A further decision of the EU Council on the acceptance or approval of the Convention by the European Union will be necessary before the Convention becomes binding on the Union as a Regional Economic Integration Organisation in accordance with Article 29 of the Convention.

The Hague Convention 2005 deals with cases in which there is an exclusive choice of court agreement. Chapter II (Articles 5–7) of the Convention regulates the direct jurisdiction of the courts of the Contracting States in the context of such agreements,[177] and Chapter III (Articles 8–15) provides for the recognition and enforcement between Contracting States of judgments given pursuant to such agreements. By Article 26(6)(b), the Convention will not affect the application of the rules of European Union law in regard to the recognition or enforcement of judgments as between EU Member States. Somewhat similarly, by Article 26(4), the Hague Convention will not affect the application of other existing or future treaties between Contracting States, such as the Lugano Conventions 1988 and 2007, for the purposes of obtaining recognition or enforcement of judgments, except that the judgment must not be recognised or enforced to a lesser extent than under the Hague Convention. Thus, once the Convention has entered into force for the European Union, the main impact of its Chapter III within the Union will be in respect of the recognition and enforcement of judgments given in non-European Contracting States (such as judgments given in the United States of America).[178]

By Article 8(1) of the Hague Convention 2005, a judgment given by a court of a Contracting State designated in an exclusive choice of court agreement must be recognised

---

[175]   For the Decision, see [2009] OJ L133/1. This section should be read in conjunction with the discussion of the Convention in Chapter 7, at pp. 181–6 above.

[176]   The Convention has also been signed by the United States of America, and acceded to by Mexico; but it has not yet entered into force.

[177]   On the provisions on direct jurisdiction, see pp. 181–6 above.

[178]   See also Article 20 of the Convention, which enables a Contracting State to make a reservation enabling its courts to refuse to recognise or enforce a judgment given by a court of another Contracting State, if the parties were resident in the requested State, and the relationship of the parties and all other elements relevant to the dispute, other than the location of the chosen court, were connected only with the requested State.

and enforced in other Contracting States in accordance with Chapter III of the Convention, and recognition or enforcement may be refused only on the grounds specified in the Convention. By Article 8(3), a judgment must be recognised only if it has effect in the State of origin, and must be enforced only if it is enforceable in the State of origin. By Article 8(4), recognition or enforcement may be postponed or refused if the judgment is the subject of review in the State of origin or if the time-limit for seeking ordinary review has not expired; but a refusal does not prevent a subsequent application for recognition or enforcement of the judgment.

Article 8(5) of the Convention extends Chapter III to judgments given by a court of a Contracting State pursuant to a transfer of the case from the chosen court in the same Contracting State under Article 5(3). But where the chosen court had discretion as to whether to transfer the case to another court, recognition or enforcement of the judgment may be refused against a party who objected to the transfer in a timely manner in the State of origin. Article 12 extends Chapter III to judicial settlements which have been approved by a court of a Contracting State designated in an exclusive choice of court agreement, or which have been concluded before such a court in the course of proceedings, and which are enforceable in the same manner as a judgment in the State of origin.

By Article 8(2), except as regards such review as is necessary for the application of the provisions of the Chapter, there must be no review of the merits of the judgment given by the court of origin. Moreover, the court addressed will be bound by the findings of fact on which the court of origin based its jurisdiction, unless the judgment was given by default.

Various grounds on which recognition or enforcement may be refused are specified by Articles 9–11. The first case, specified by Article 9(a), is where the choice of court agreement was null and void under the law of the State of the chosen court, unless the chosen court has determined that the agreement is valid. The second, specified by Article 9(b), is where a party lacked the capacity to conclude the choice of court agreement under the law of the requested State.

The third case, specified by Article 9(c)(i), is where the document which instituted the proceedings or an equivalent document, including the essential elements of the claim, was not notified to the defendant in sufficient time and in such a way as to enable him to arrange for his defence. This ground is excluded where the defendant entered an appearance and presented his case without contesting notification in the court of origin, provided that the law of the State of origin permitted notification to be contested. The fourth case, specified by Article 9(1)(c)(ii), is where the instituting or equivalent document was notified to the defendant in the requested State in a manner which is incompatible with fundamental principles of the requested State concerning service of documents. The fifth case, specified by Article 9(d), is where the judgment was obtained by fraud in connection with a matter of procedure.

The sixth case, specified by Article 9(e), is where recognition or enforcement would be manifestly incompatible with the public policy of the requested State, and this includes situations where the specific proceedings leading to the judgment were incompatible with fundamental principles of procedural fairness of that State. The seventh case, specified by Article 11(1), is where, and to the extent that, the judgment awards damages, including exemplary or punitive damages, which do not compensate a party for actual loss or harm suffered. But, in this context, Article 11(2) insists that the court addressed must take into account whether and to what extent the damages awarded by the court of origin serve to cover costs and expenses relating to the proceedings. Moreover, Article 17(2)(b) adds that recognition and enforcement of a judgment in respect of liability under the terms of a contract of insurance or reinsurance may not be limited or refused on the ground that the liability under that contract includes liability to indemnify the insured or reinsured in respect of an award of damages to which Article 11 might apply.

The eighth case, specified by Article 9(f), is where the judgment is inconsistent with a judgment given in the requested State in a dispute between the same parties. The ninth case, specified by Article 9(g), is where the judgment is inconsistent with an earlier judgment given in another State between the same parties on the same cause of action, provided that the earlier judgment fulfils the conditions necessary for its recognition in the requested State.

Further cases are specified by Article 10, which deals with situations where a matter which is excluded from the scope of the Convention by Articles 2(2) or 21 arose as a preliminary question.[179] By Article 10(1), the ruling on the excluded question must not be recognised or enforced under the Convention. By Article 10(2) and (4), recognition or enforcement of a judgment may be refused where, and to the extent that, the judgment was based on a ruling on the excluded matter. But Article 10(3) restricts the scope of Article 10(2), in the case of judgment based on a ruling on the validity of an intellectual property right other than copyright (comprising author's rights and neighbouring rights), to cases where that ruling is inconsistent with a judgment or a decision of a competent authority on that matter given in the State under the law of which the intellectual property right arose, or where proceedings concerning the validity of the intellectual property right are pending in that State.

Some provisions relating to procedure are made by Articles 13–15 of the Convention. Article 13 deals with documents to be produced by a party seeking recognition or enforcement. Article 14 subjects the procedure for recognition, declaration of enforceability or registration for enforcement, and the enforcement of the judgment, to the law of the requested State, unless the Convention provides otherwise. It also requires the court addressed to act expeditiously. Article 15 requires recognition or enforcement to be granted in respect of a severable part of a judgment, where recognition or enforcement of that part is applied for, or where only part of the judgment is capable of being recognised or enforced under the Convention.

---

[179]   On these exclusions, see pp. 183–5 above.

# 11. Enforcement procedure

## INTRODUCTION

The normal procedure for obtaining enforcement in an EU Member State of a civil judgment given by a court of another Member State is specified by Chapter III of the Brussels I Regulation. The procedure involves an ex parte application to a court of the Member State addressed for a declaration of enforceability, followed by an inter partes appeal, and a further appeal on a point of law. The actual measures of enforcement are in general governed by the law of the State addressed.

In some exceptional cases, certain other EC regulations apply. These are the Uncontested Claims Regulation,[1] the Payment Order Regulation,[2] and the Small Claims Regulation.[3] These regulations dispense with the need for a declaration of enforceability, and endeavour to make a judgment within their scope enforceable in the other Member States with only minimal exceptions. The abolition by these Regulations of the requirement of a declaration of enforceability, issued by a court of the State addressed, reflected a political mandate agreed on by the European Council at Tampere in 1999 and at the Hague in 2004.

In its Report on the Application of the Brussels I Regulation, issued in April 2009,[4] the EC Commission referred to a study which it had commissioned on the practical application of the Regulation. As regards the existing enforcement procedure under the Regulation, the study showed that, when the application is complete, first instance proceedings before the courts in the Member States tend to last, on average, from seven days to four months. When, however, the application is incomplete, proceedings last longer. Applications are often incomplete and judicial authorities ask for additional information, in particular translations. Most applications for a declaration of enforceability are successful (between 90% and 100%). Only between 1% and 5% of the decisions are appealed. Appeal proceedings may last between one month and three years, depending on the different procedural cultures in the Member States and the workload of the courts, but challenges to the declaration of enforceability are rarely successful.

In the Report and the accompanying Green Paper,[5] the EC Commission emphasised its view that the main objective of the revision of the Brussels I Regulation should be the abolition of the exequatur procedure in all matters covered by the Regulation. It explained that, in an internal market without frontiers, it is difficult to justify subjecting citizens and businesses

---

[1]    Regulation 805/2004, creating a European Enforcement Order for Uncontested Claims, [2004] OJ L143/15. See pp. 267–75 below.

[2]    EC Regulation 1896/2006, creating a European order for payment procedure, [2006] OJ L399/1. See pp. 275–80 below.

[3]    EC Regulation 861/2007, establishing a European Small Claims Procedure, [2007] OJ L199/1. See pp. 280–84 below.

[4]    COM(2009) 174 final, at para 3.1.

[5]    COM(2009) 175 final, in connection with question 1.

to the burden of such a procedure in terms of costs and time when asserting their rights abroad. If applications for declarations of enforceability are almost always successful and recognition and enforcement of foreign judgments is very rarely refused, aiming for the objective of abolishing the exequatur procedure in all civil and commercial matters should be realistic.

It is submitted that this viewpoint is wholly misconceived. From a claimant's viewpoint, the existing procedure for the obtaining of a declaration of enforceability under the Brussels I Regulation appears to be working well. At a practical level, it seems likely that the abandonment of that procedure in favour of enforcement without a specific procedure in the State addressed is likely to increase, rather than reduce, the costs and delays incurred. Moreover, since most cases of transnational enforcement involve the enforcement at the defendant's domicile of a judgment given elsewhere, the effect of the change envisaged will usually be to reduce from an already low level the protection which a defendant can obtain from the courts of his own country. It must be borne in mind that the proceedings in the court of origin may have been unsatisfactory in various ways. They may even have been totally abusive, as where the claim was brought in a country with which the defendant had no connection whatever, the proceedings were concealed from him until enforcement in his own country was sought, and every allegation which was made by the claimant in the court of origin (whether the allegation is relevant to the substantive claim, or to the jurisdiction of the court of origin, or to service on the defendant) was false in fact and its falsity was known to the claimant. It is therefore submitted that the abolition of the need for a declaration of enforceability, which has been effected in limited cases by the Uncontested Claims Regulation, the Payment Order Regulation, and the Small Claims Regulation, should be reversed, rather than extended.

Thus the proper direction of reform should be to strengthen the powers of the court addressed to review the procedure in, and the jurisdiction of, the court of origin. Such a strengthening of the rights of the defendant would also make the European system more closely resemble that of the United States, where enforcement between courts of sister States, and even between sister federal district courts sitting in different States, is subject to a procedure before a court of the State addressed in which the defendant can challenge both the jurisdiction of the court of origin, and the fairness of the procedure used, on the basis of standards derived from the federal constitution.[6] In contrast, the European system appears to be driven increasingly by a principle of co-operation between public institutions, regardless of the legitimate interests of the private persons involved.

## THE BRUSSELS I REGULATION

**Introduction**

The procedure for obtaining in a Member State, under Chapter III of the Brussels I

---

[6]   See *Milliken v Meyer* 311 US 457 (1940); *McGee v International Life Insurance Co* 355 US 220 (1957); *Hanson v Denckla* 357 US 235 (1958); and Karnezis, *Registration in Federal District Court of Judgment of Another Federal Court under 28 USCA § 1963*, 194 ALR Fed 531 (updated since 2004).

Regulation, a declaration of enforceability in respect of a judgment given in another Member State, is defined by Articles 38–56. The European Court has ruled that this procedure ('the Chapter III procedure') is exclusive.[7] But its exclusivity has been relaxed by Article 47(1) of the Regulation, which permits the grant of provisional, including protective, measures in accordance with the law of the State addressed in support of a judgment which is recognisable but in respect of which a declaration of enforceability has not been made.

In the United Kingdom, the procedure leads to an order that the judgment be registered for enforcement, and a separate application is necessary in each part of the United Kingdom (England and Wales; Scotland; Northern Ireland; and Gibraltar).[8] A decision given in one part of the United Kingdom authorising or refusing registration has no binding effect in the other parts of the United Kingdom.[9]

Once the declaration of enforceability (or registration for enforcement) has been obtained, the actual measures of execution (such as seizure and sale of the judgment debtor's chattels, or garnishment of his bank account) are governed by the law of the State addressed.[10] Partial enforceability may be ordered; for example where the judgment deals with several claims, one of which is outside the scope of the Regulation as defined by Article 1.[11]

By Article 33(2), the Chapter III procedure may also be used to obtain a decision establishing recognition of a judgment. In any event, by Article 33(3), recognition may be invoked incidentally whenever relevant. The Chapter III procedure cannot, however, be used to obtain a declaration of non-recognition, though the law of the State addressed may make an ordinary action available for this purpose.[12] The Chapter III procedure is also available, under Chapter IV, for the enforcement of an authentic instrument or court settlement.[13] It has also been made available by Article 25 of the Insolvency Regulation in respect of certain judgments connected with an insolvency proceeding.[14]

There are three possible stages to the Chapter III procedure: an initial ex parte application, a normal appeal inter partes, and a single further appeal on a point of law.

## The Initial Application

The initial application under the Chapter III procedure may be made by any interested party;[15] in other words, by anyone on whom rights are conferred by the judgment under the law of the original country.[16]

---

7 See Case 42/76: *De Wolf v Cox* [1976] ECR 1759.
8 See Article 38(2) and Annexes II and III of the Regulation. For supplementary British legislation, see the Civil Jurisdiction and Judgments Order 2001 (SI 2001/3929), Schedule 1, paras 2–6, and the Civil Procedure Rules 1998 (as amended), Part 74, Section I.
9 See the Schlosser Report, at p. 132. See also *Clarke v Fennoscandia Ltd* [2007] UKHL 56.
10 See Case 148/84: *Deutsche Genossenschaftsbank v Brasserie du Pecheur* [1985] ECR 1981, and Case 119/84: *Capelloni v Pelkmans* [1985] ECR 3147.
11 See Article 48; and Case C-220/95: *Van den Boogaard v Laumen* [1997] ECR I-1147.
12 See Gaudemet-Tallon, at para 385.
13 See pp. 227–9 above.
14 See pp. 522–3 below.
15 See Articles 33(2) and 38(1).
16 See the Jenard Report, at p. 49; and Gaudemet-Tallon, at para 387.

The type of court to which the application must be made is designated by Article 39(1) and Annex II of the Regulation (as substituted by Annex II of Regulation 280/2009).[17] In most Member States, the designated court is one which normally sits at first instance, though in Italy it is one which normally sits at intermediate appeal. In England, except in the case of a maintenance order, the initial application is made to the High Court, Queen's Bench Division, where it will normally be determined by a master.[18] In the case of a maintenance order, the application is transmitted via the Lord Chancellor to an English magistrates' court, where it is determined by the prescribed officer of the court.[19]

By Article 39(2), the jurisdiction of local courts is determined by reference to the place of domicile of the respondent (the party against whom enforcement is sought) at the date of the application,[20] or to the place of enforcement (in other words, a place where the respondent has assets).[21] This gives the applicant a choice of venue, between the respondent's domicile and the place of enforcement.[22] Presumably, if the respondent is not domiciled in the State addressed, and he has no assets there or mere recognition is sought, the applicant will have an unlimited choice of venue.[23] But Article 39(2) is concerned only with the determination of venue between co-ordinate courts of the same State; for example, whether one who seeks to enforce a German judgment in France should apply to the district court for Paris, Bordeaux or Marseilles. Thus it has no application in the United Kingdom unless the judgment is a maintenance order, since Article 38(2) and Annex II effectively provide that the four parts of the United Kingdom must be treated as separate States for the purpose of enforcement of judgments given in the other Member States.

By Article 40, in general the procedure for making the application is governed by the law of the State addressed,[24] and usually the applicant must give an address for service within the

---

[17]   [2009] OJ L93/13. Article 39(1) also enables a Member State to require the initial application to be submitted to an administrative authority.

[18]   See Annex II of the Regulation; and the Civil Procedure Rules 1998, rule 2.4. Similarly, the application is made in Northern Ireland to the High Court; in Scotland to the Court of Session; and in Gibraltar to the Supreme Court. In Ireland, the application is made to the High Court, where it is determined by the Master; see the European Communities (Civil and Commercial Judgments) Regulations 2002, reg 4.

[19]   See Annex II of the Regulation; and the Civil Jurisdiction and Judgments Order 2001, Schedule 1, para 3(1)–(2). Similarly, the application is transmitted in Northern Ireland and Gibraltar to a magistrates' court, and in Scotland to a sheriff court. In the other Member States (with the exception of Cyprus and Malta), an application for enforcement of a maintenance order is made to the same court as in the case of any other judgment. But in Ireland, although the application for enforcement of a maintenance order is made to and determined by the High Court, the actual measures of enforcement will usually be taken by a District Court; see the European Communities (Civil and Commercial Judgments) Regulations 2002, regs 3–6.

[20]   See per La Pergola AG in Case C-260/97: *Unibank v Christensen* [1999] ECR I-3715.

[21]   See the Jenard Report, at p. 49.

[22]   Cf. Article 32(2) of the Brussels Convention, which gave priority to the respondent's domicile.

[23]   See Gaudemet-Tallon, at para 386.

[24]   See Article 40(1). By the Civil Procedure Rules 1998 (as amended), rule 74.4(6), where the judgment is not in English, an application to the English court must be supported by a translation of the judgment; and where interest is recoverable on the judgment under the law of the State of origin, the application must be supported by written evidence stating either the amount of interest which has accrued up to the date of the application, or stating the rate of interest, the date from which it is recoverable, and the date on which it ceases to accrue.

area of the court addressed.[25] In *Carron v Germany*,[26] the European Court ruled that the address for service must be given in accordance with the law of the State addressed, and if that law is silent as to the time at which the address must be given, it must be given no later than the date on which the decision authorising enforcement is served on the respondent. Moreover, the consequences of failure to furnish an address for service are in general governed by the law of the State addressed, but the sanction provided must neither cast doubt on the validity of the declaration of enforceability nor in any way prejudice the respondent's rights. By Article 51, no security of any kind may be required of an applicant for enforcement on the ground that he is a foreign national or is not domiciled or resident in the State addressed.

Articles 40(3) and 53–6 of the Regulation specify the documents which must be attached to the application.[27] The Regulation has simplified these requirements and reduced the burden on the applicant by providing for the issue by the court of origin of a certificate in a standardised form containing the relevant information.[28] By Article 53(1), a party seeking recognition or applying for a declaration of enforceability must produce an authentic copy of the judgment.[29] By Articles 53(2) and 54, a party applying for a declaration of enforceability must also produce a certificate issued by a court of the State of origin using the standard form in Annex V of the Regulation.[30] This will, inter alia, give information as to the date of service of the document instituting the proceedings where the judgment was given in default of appearance, the names of parties to whom legal aid was granted, and the persons against whom the judgment is enforceable in the State of origin. There is no longer a requirement that the judgment itself should have been served.[31]

By Article 55(1), if the certificate is not produced, the court addressed may specify a time for its production or accept an equivalent document or, if it considers that it has sufficient information before it, dispense with its production. By Article 55(2), if the court addressed so

---

[25]     See Article 40(2). But in Germany he must instead appoint a representative ad litem; and in the United Kingdom, in the case of a maintenance order, the clerk of the magistrates' or sheriff court addressed will act as the applicant's representative ad litem unless he otherwise requests; see the Jenard Report at p. 50, and the Schlosser Report at p. 134. In its Report and Green Paper of 21st April 2009, the EC Commission contemplates the possibility of removing the requirement to designate an address for service of process or to appoint a representative ad litem; see COM(2009) 174 final, at section 3.8.3, and COM(2009) 175 final, at question 8.

[26]     Case 198/85, [1986] ECR 2437.

[27]     See also (in the United Kingdom) the Civil Jurisdiction and Judgments Order 2001, Schedule 1, para 8; and the Civil Procedure Rules 1998 (as amended), rules 74.4(6), 74.12 and 74.13.

[28]     For the position under the Brussels Convention, see its Articles 33(3) and 46–9.

[29]     In its Report and Green Paper of 21st April 2009, the EC Commission contemplates the possibility of establishing a uniform standard form, available in all official Community languages, and containing an extract of the judgment. See COM(2009) 174 final, at section 3.8.3, and COM(2009) 175 final, at question 8.

[30]     The form specified in Annex V is also used for court settlements. Annex VI defines another form of certificate for use with authentic instruments. See Articles 57(4) and 58.

[31]     See Article 42(2) of the Regulation. Cf. Article 47(1) of the Brussels Convention, and Case C-275/94: *Van der Linden v Berufsgenossenschaft der Feinmechanik und Elektrotechnik* [1996] ECR I-1393. See also *Guittienne v SNCI*, 6th March 1996, where the French Court of Cassation ruled that irregularities in the service of the original judgment, required by Article 47(1) of the Brussels Convention, could not justify refusal of recognition or enforcement.

requires, a translation of the documents must be produced; the translation must be certified by a person qualified to do so in one of the Member States.[32] By Article 56, no legalisation or other similar formality may be required in respect of a judgment, certificate or translation, or of a document appointing a representative ad litem.

As regards legal aid, Article 50(1) of the Regulation applies in favour of an applicant for enforcement who in the State of origin had benefited from complete or partial legal aid or exemption from costs or expenses. It entitles him to benefit in the enforcement procedure from the most favourable legal aid or the most extensive exemption from costs or expenses provided for by the law of the State addressed. Article 50(2), which was added by the Agreement with Denmark, extends such benefits to an applicant who requests the enforcement of a decision given by an administrative authority in Denmark in respect of maintenance, if he presents a statement from the Danish Ministry of Justice to the effect that he fulfils the financial requirements to qualify for the grant of complete or partial legal aid or exemption from costs or expenses.[33] Article 50 of the Regulation goes beyond Article 44 of the Brussels Convention[34] in covering not only the initial application but also the ordinary and further appeals; though not the actual measures of execution.

Article 41 of the Regulation insists that the judgment should be declared enforceable immediately on completion of the formalities specified in Article 53 (which deals with the documents to be produced in support of the application), without any review under Articles 34 and 35 (which specify the substantive requirements relating to public policy, service, irreconcilability, and jurisdictional review). It also insists that the party against whom enforcement is sought shall not at this stage of the proceedings (the determination of the initial application) be entitled to make any submissions on the application. In this connection, Recital 17 explains that, by virtue of the principle of mutual trust, the procedure for making enforceable in one Member State a judgment given in another must be efficient and rapid. To that end, the declaration that a judgment is enforceable should be issued virtually automatically after purely formal checks of the documents supplied, without there being any possibility for the court to raise of its own motion any of the grounds for non-enforcement provided for by the Regulation.

Article 41 of the Regulation goes beyond Article 34(1) of the Brussels Convention, which merely required that the court initially applied to should give its decision without delay; and added that the party against whom enforcement was sought should not at this stage be entitled to make any submissions on the application. But the object remains the same: to give the applicant the advantage of surprise, and to ensure that the judgment becomes provisionally enforceable against the respondent's assets under Article 47 before he has an opportunity to dispose of them or remove them to another country.[35] Probably Article 41 does not prevent the court initially applied to from rejecting the application of its own motion if it appears from the documents produced by the applicant that the judgment does not fall within the material scope of the Regulation as defined by Article 1. In any event, the initial application will almost always succeed in obtaining a declaration of enforceability.

---

[32]   By the Civil Procedure Rules 1998 (as amended), rule 74.4(6), where the judgment is not in English, an application to the English court must be supported by a translation of the judgment.
[33]   In the Lugano Convention 2007, Article 50(2) extends also to decisions of Icelandic and Norwegian administrative authorities in respect of maintenance.
[34]   See the Jenard Report, at p. 54.
[35]   See the Jenard Report, at p. 50; and Case 119/84: *Capelloni v Pelkmans* [1985] ECR 3147.

By Article 42(1) of the Regulation, the decision on the initial application must forthwith be brought to the notice of the applicant in accordance with the procedure laid down by the law of the State addressed. By Article 42(2), the declaration of enforceability must be served on the respondent (the party against whom enforcement is sought),[36] accompanied by the judgment, if not already served on him. Then Article 43(1) enables the decision on the initial application to be appealed against by either party.

## Provisional Enforcement Pending Appeal

By Article 47(2)–(3) of the Regulation,[37] a declaration of enforceability carries with it the power to proceed to protective measures, but during the time specified by Article 43(5) for lodging an appeal against the declaration of enforceability, and until any such appeal has been determined, no measures of enforcement may be taken other than protective measures against the property of the party against whom enforcement is sought.[38]

In *Capelloni v Pelkmans*,[39] the European Court explained that while, as regards such protective measures, the Regulation leaves questions not specifically dealt with to the procedural law of the court addressed, such national procedural rules must be compatible with the principles laid down by Article 47. Consequently, Article 47 overrides various national requirements: ones whereby a party who has obtained a declaration of enforceability cannot proceed directly with protective measures against the respondent's property, but must obtain a further order from the court addressed specifically authorising him to do so; ones whereby provisional measures are limited to a shorter period than the time for lodging and determining an appeal under Article 43; and ones whereby a party who has taken protective measures must obtain a confirmatory judgment in respect of the measures taken. However, the Regulation does not prevent the respondent from complaining, in accordance with national procedures, of irregularities or abuses which he alleges to have occurred in the course of the execution of the protective measures.

Probably, in England, Article 47 entitles a judgment creditor to obtain, as a protective measure, a freezing order or an order for payment into court, without showing urgency or a risk that assets will be dissipated or removed.[40] In *Banco Nacional de Comercio Exterior SNC v Empresa de Telecomunicaciones de Cuba SA*,[41] the Court of Appeal (per Tuckey LJ) emphasised that, as regards the taking of protective measures in the context of enforcement under Chapter III of the Brussels I Regulation of a judgment given in another Member State, the English court will usually confine its intervention to the grant of a domestic (rather than a worldwide) freezing order, especially if the defendant is not resident in England. It also concluded that the English practice, whereby a freezing order will normally be granted only

---

[36]  See also *Barnaby v Mullen* [1997] 2 ILRM 341 (Irish Supreme Court).

[37]  Article 47(2)–(3) echoes Article 39 of the Brussels Convention.

[38]  See also, in the United Kingdom, the Civil Jurisdiction and Judgments Order 2001, Schedule 1, paras 2(3) and 3(4).

[39]  Case 119/84, [1985] ECR 3147.

[40]  See the Jenard Report at p. 52, the Schlosser Report at pp. 134–5, and the (UK) Civil Jurisdiction and Judgments Order 2001, Schedule 1, para. 3. See also the (Irish) European Communities (Civil and Commercial Judgments) Regulations 2002, reg 10(3) and (4).

[41]  [2007] 2 All ER (Comm) 1093 (CA).

if the applicant gives an undertaking to provide compensation for losses caused by the order to third parties if the court subsequently so orders, is compatible with Article 47(2) of the Brussels I Regulation. In Ireland, it has been held that protective measures include an order setting aside a conveyance of property made by the defendant in order to prevent enforcement of the judgment.[42] The power to take protective measures is, of course, limited to the period of appeal.[43]

Article 47(1) of the Regulation adds a saving (not found in the Brussels Convention) that, when a judgment must be recognised in accordance with the Regulation, nothing prevents the applicant from availing himself of provisional, including protective, measures in accordance with the law of the Member State requested, without a declaration of enforceability under Article 41 being required.[44] In *Banco Nacional de Comercio Exterior SNC v Empresa de Telecomunicaciones de Cuba SA*,[45] Tuckey LJ explained that all parts of Article 47 are directed at enforcement of a foreign judgment. Article 47(1) deals with the position before a declaration of enforceability has been made. It merely establishes that if the applicant is able to show that he has a judgment which must be recognised, he is not prevented from availing himself of protective measures before the formalities which lead to the making of a declaration of enforceability have been completed. Such measures might well be necessary as soon as judgment has been given in another Member State, or at least before the formalities required for the making of a declaration of enforceability, which include translation, have been completed. Each of the provisions of Article 47 deals with the time at which things can or cannot be done. Thus Article 47(1) deals with the time before the making of a declaration of enforceability; Article 47(2) with the time after the making of a declaration of enforceability; and Article 47(3) with the time after the making of a declaration of enforceability where there is an appeal pending.

## The Normal Appeal

By Article 43(1) and (3), the decision on the initial application under the Chapter III procedure may be appealed against by either party, and the appeal is dealt with in accordance with the rules governing procedure in contradictory matters. Thus the appeal is inter partes, and it is at this stage that full consideration is given to whether the judgment falls within the scope of Chapter III and whether there is any ground for refusing recognition or enforcement under Articles 34–6, 38 and 45. In general, it is for the party who opposes recognition or enforcement to establish the existence of a ground for its refusal.[46] By Article 45(1), the appellate court should give its decision without delay.

The court to which the appeal lies is specified by Article 43(3) and Annex III of the Regulation (as substituted by Annex III of Regulation 280/2009).[47] In England, except in the case of a maintenance order, the appeal lies to the High Court, where it will be determined by

---

[42]    See *Barnaby v Mullen* [1996] 2 ILRM 24 (Kinlen J); reversed on other grounds, [1997] 2 ILRM 341 (Irish Supreme Court).

[43]    See *Rayner v Cafenorte* [1999] 2 Lloyd's Rep 750 (CA).

[44]    See also the Civil Procedure Rules 1998 (as amended), rule 74.9(3).

[45]    [2007] 2 All ER (Comm) 1093 (CA).

[46]    See the Jenard Report, at p. 43; and Gaudemet-Tallon, at paras 397–8.

[47]    [2009] OJ L93/13.

a judge of the Queen's Bench Division.[48] Similarly, in Scotland, Northern Ireland, and Gibraltar, except in the case of a maintenance order, the appeal is to the same court (the Court of Session, the High Court, or the Supreme Court) as determined the initial application. In the case of a maintenance order, the appeal lies to the English, Northern Irish or Gibraltar magistrates' court, or Scottish sheriff court, which dealt with the initial application.

In the other Member States (with the exception of Cyprus and Malta), no distinction is made between maintenance orders and other judgments. In some countries[49] the same court deals with both the initial application and the appeal. In most countries,[50] the appeal is determined by a higher court than the court which dealt with the application. In Belgium and the Netherlands, a respondent's appeal against a declaration of enforceability lies to the court which made the declaration, but an applicant's appeal against a refusal to make a declaration of enforceability lies to a higher court. Conversely, in France, a respondent's appeal against a declaration of enforceability lies to a higher court, but an applicant's appeal against a refusal to make a declaration of enforceability is determined within the court which rejected the application.

By Article 43(5), an appeal against a declaration of enforceability must be lodged within one month of service of the declaration. But if the party against whom enforcement is sought is domiciled in a Member State other than the State addressed, the time for appealing is two months and runs from the date of service on the appellant, either in person or at his residence.[51] No extension of time may be granted on account of distance.[52] In *Verdoliva v Van der Hoeven*,[53] the European Court ruled that Article 43(5) requires due service of the declaration of enforceability, in accordance with the procedural rules of the Member State addressed. Thus in cases of failure of service, or defective service, of the declaration of enforceability, the mere fact that the party against whom enforcement is sought has notice of the declaration of enforceability is not sufficient to cause time to run for the purposes of the time-limit fixed in Article 43(5).

By Article 43(4), in the case of an appeal by the applicant for enforcement against a refusal of a declaration of enforceability, if the respondent (the party against whom enforcement is sought) fails to appear before the appellate court, Article 26(2)–(4), on staying proceedings

---

[48]    Permission to appeal is not required; see the Civil Procedure Rules 1998 (as amended), rule 74.8(2).

[49]    Ireland, Italy, Sweden, Cyprus, Slovenia, and Lithuania. Also Iceland under the Lugano Conventions.

[50]    Germany, Luxembourg, Denmark, Greece, Spain, Portugal, Austria, Finland, Malta, Poland, Hungary, the Czech Republic, Slovakia, Latvia, Estonia, Bulgaria, and Romania. Also Switzerland and Norway under the Lugano Conventions.

[51]    In England, rule 74.8(4)(a) of the Civil Procedure Rules 1998 (as amended) purports to require service of the notice of appeal within one month, or where service is to be effected on a party not domiciled in England two months, of service of the registration order.

[52]    In England, rule 74.8(3) of the Civil Procedure Rules 1998 (as amended) purports to enable a judgment debtor not domiciled in a Member State to make within two months of service of the registration order an application to extend the time for appealing against the order, and then to authorise the court to extend the period for filing an appellant's notice against the order on grounds other than distance. But in *TSN v Jurgens* [2001] WL 606474, Jack J considered that under Article 43(5) no extension is possible, even for reasons other than distance.

[53]    Case C-3/05, [2006] ECR I-1579.

until proper steps have been taken to notify the defendant in sufficient time to enable him to arrange for his defence, apply even where the respondent is not domiciled within the Member States.[54] This applies even where the initial application was rejected solely because the documents required by Article 53 were not produced at the proper time.[55]

In *Deutsche Genossenschaftsbank v Brasserie du Pecheur*,[56] the European Court construed Article 43 as preventing any appeal *against a declaration of enforceability* by an interested third party, such as another creditor of the judgment debtor, but accepted that interested third parties may take proceedings to challenge *measures of execution* in accordance with the law of the State addressed. This approach was confirmed by the European Court in *Draka NK Cables v Omnipol*,[57] where it ruled that a creditor of a judgment debtor cannot lodge an appeal against a decision on a request for a declaration of enforceability if he has not formally appeared as a party in the proceedings in which another creditor of the debtor applied for the declaration of enforceability.

In *Hoffmann v Krieg*,[58] the European Court ruled that, in general, where a respondent fails to raise by way of an appeal under Article 43 an objection which could have been so raised, he cannot subsequently raise that objection at the stage of actual execution. But it admitted an exception where this would have the result of compelling the court addressed to disregard a local judgment on a matter excluded from the scope of the Regulation, such as a decree of divorce.

By Article 46(1) and (2) of the Regulation, the court with which an appeal under Article 43 is lodged may, on the application of the party against whom enforcement is sought, stay its proceedings if an ordinary appeal (or, in the case of a British or Irish judgment, any form of appeal) has been lodged against the judgment in the State of origin, or if the time for such an appeal has not yet expired.[59] In the latter case, it may also specify the time within which such an appeal is to be lodged. Article 46 of the Regulation applies whether the appeal against the decision on the initial application is brought by the applicant for enforcement or by the respondent to the application. Formerly Article 38 of the Brussels Convention, which conferred corresponding powers, applied only in an appeal by the respondent to the application for enforcement.

Somewhat similarly, Article 37 of the Regulation enables a court of a Member State in which recognition is sought of a judgment given in another Member State to stay its proceedings if an ordinary appeal against the judgment has been lodged (or in the case of a British or Irish judgment, if enforcement is suspended in the State of origin by reason of an appeal). Probably Article 37 applies to incidental recognition only, and Article 46 applies where the Chapter III procedure is used with a view to obtaining a decision establishing recognition.[60]

---

54    In England, rule 74.8(4)(b) of the Civil Procedure Rules 1998 (as amended) requires the notice of appeal to be served within one month of the decision on the application for registration.
55    See Case 178/83: *Firma P v Firma K* [1984] ECR 3033.
56    Case 148/84, [1985] ECR 1981.
57    Case C-167/08, [2009] ECR I-3477.
58    Case 145/86, [1988] ECR 645.
59    See, for example, *Von Mitchke-Collande v Kramer* [2005] EWHC 977 (Burton J), which also establishes that if the enforceability of the judgment in the original country is disputed, the court hearing the ordinary appeal in the State addressed may adjourn its proceedings to enable an attempt at enforcement to be made in the original country.
60    Contra: Gaudemet-Tallon, at para 394.

Although Article 37 expressly refers only to an appeal which has actually been lodged, it should probably be construed, by analogy with Article 46, as permitting a stay where the time for appeal has not yet expired and a party intends to appeal.[61]

In *Industrial Diamond Supplies v Riva*,[62] the European Court ruled that any appeal, including one to the national court of last resort (in the instant case, the Italian Court of Cassation), which may result in the annulment or amendment of the judgment and whose lodging is confined to a defined period commencing by virtue of the judgment, constitutes an ordinary appeal for the purpose of Articles 37 and 46. Thus an application to the court which gave the judgment (for example, an application to set aside a default judgment and proceed with trial of the merits) counts as an ordinary appeal if there is a time-limit, running from the judgment, for such applications.[63] But, as Phillips J held in *Interdesco v Nullifire*,[64] a French application known as a *recours en revision*, to set aside a judgment on the ground that it was procured by fraud, is not an 'ordinary appeal', since such an application may be filed at any time after the judgment, so long as it is filed within two months of the applicant's becoming aware of the facts relied on.

Article 46(3) of the Regulation confers on the court hearing an appeal under Article 43 a further power, to make enforcement conditional on the provision of such security as it determines. In *Brennero v Wendel*,[65] the European Court ruled that this power can only be exercised in a judgment which finally disposes of the appeal, and not by way of an interim order in the course of the appellate proceedings. It also indicated that this power can be exercised even where there is no appeal in the original country, in order to protect a party in case his further appeal in the country addressed succeeds.

In *Van Dalfsen v Van Loon*,[66] the European Court emphasised that Article 45(2), which prohibits substantive review, prevents the court addressed, in exercising its powers under Article 46, from assessing the chances of success of the appeal in the State of origin, though it may take into consideration submissions which the respondent was unable to put before the original court.[67] In view of this, it may be advisable for the party resisting enforcement, instead of seeking a stay of proceedings or an order for security under Article 46 in the court addressed, to apply for a stay of execution in the original country pending his appeal there. Such a stay, if granted, will also prevent enforcement in the State addressed.

As regards the staying of an appeal in the State addressed by reason of a pending appeal in the State of origin, in *Banco Nacional de Comercio Exterior SNC v Empresa de Telecomunicaciones de Cuba SA*,[68] Tomlinson J emphasised that a principle in favour of the general enforceability of judgments without awaiting the outcome of an appeal is inherent in the permissive nature of the powers conferred by Articles 37 and 46 and was confirmed by

---

[61]   See the Jenard Report, at pp. 46–7.

[62]   Case 43/77, [1977] ECR 2175.

[63]   See the Schlosser Report, at pp. 129–30.

[64]   [1992] 1 Lloyd's Rep 180. Accord: Gaudemet-Tallon, at para 402.

[65]   Case 258/83, [1984] ECR 3971.

[66]   Case C-183/90, [1991] ECR I-4743.

[67]   For criticism, see Gaudemet-Tallon, at para 402. See also per Léger AG in Case C-432/93: *SISRO v Ampersand* [1995] ECR I-2269.

[68]   [2007] EWHC 2322 (Comm). See also *DHL GBS v Fallimento Finmatica* [2009] EWHC 291 (Comm) (Tomlinson J).

the ruling of the European Court in *Van Dalfsen v Van Loon*,[69] which also established that an assessment by the court addressed of the chances of success of an ordinary appeal lodged or to be lodged in the State of origin amounts to a review of the foreign judgment as to its substance, which is prohibited by Articles 36 and 45(2). Thus any stay of the appeal in the State addressed will have to be based on the prejudice likely to accrue in the event of a successful appeal in the State of origin after unconditional enforcement of the judgment, and in this context an English court, as the court addressed, will respect a reasoned decision of the court of origin refusing to suspend enforcement because there is no likelihood of any such prejudice.

## The Further Appeal

From the decision given on the normal appeal, Article 44 and Annex IV provide for a single further appeal on a point of law. This may be brought by the applicant for enforcement or by the respondent to the application, but not by an interested third party.[70] By Article 45(1), the court hearing the further appeal should give its decision without delay. If the normal appeal resulted in the making or affirming of a declaration of enforceability, the judgment remains enforceable despite the lodging of the further appeal.[71]

In the United Kingdom, the court to which the further appeal lies is specified by the Civil Jurisdiction and Judgments Order 2001, Schedule 1, paragraph 4. Except in the case of a maintenance order, the further appeal in England and Northern Ireland lies to the Court of Appeal, no leave being required, or alternatively, under the 'leapfrog' procedure, to the Supreme Court of the United Kingdom.[72] In the case of a maintenance order, the further appeal in England is by way of case stated to the High Court; and in Northern Ireland it lies to the Court of Appeal. In Scotland, in the case of both 'ordinary' judgments and maintenance orders, the further appeal lies to the Inner House of the Court of Session.

Under the Brussels Convention, the European Court ruled in a series of cases[73] that the further appeal lay only against a judgment which disposed entirely of the normal appeal and decided whether the original judgment merited recognition or enforcement in the State addressed. No appeal lay against any decision made by the court dealing with the normal appeal under Article 38 of the Convention (the predecessor of Article 46 of the Regulation) granting, refusing to grant, or lifting a stay of proceedings, or requiring or refusing to require security, even if that decision was contained in the same judgment as disposed of the normal appeal. Moreover, the court dealing with a further appeal had no power to impose or reimpose a stay of proceedings. But now Article 46(1) of the Regulation refers specifically to a court with which an appeal is lodged under Article 43 or Article 44, and thus ensures that a court dealing with a further appeal has the same powers as a court dealing with a normal appeal to stay proceedings, or to make enforcement conditional on the provision of security.

---

69    Case C-183/90, [1991] ECR I-4743.
70    See Case C-172/91: *Sonntag v Waidmann* [1993] ECR I-1963.
71    See Case 258/83: *Brennero v Wendel* [1984] ECR 3971; and Gaudemet-Tallon, at para 404.
72    See *Landhurst Leasing v Marcq* [1997] CLY 626 (CA); and Part 3 of the Constitutional Reform Act 2005, under which the judicial role of the House of Lords has been transferred to the newly created Supreme Court of the United Kingdom.
73    See Case 258/83: *Brennero v Wendel* [1984] ECR 3971; Case C-183/90: *Van Dalfsen v Van Loon* [1991] ECR I-4743; and Case C-432/93: *SISRO v Ampersand* [1995] ECR I-2269.

**Measures of Execution**

Once a declaration of enforceability has been obtained, the actual measures of execution (such as seizure and sale of the judgment debtor's chattels, or garnishment of his bank account) are governed by the law of the State addressed.[74] This is subject to Article 47, which restricts execution to provisional measures against the respondent's property, until the time for lodging the normal appeal against the declaration of enforceability has expired and any such appeal has been disposed of.[75]

In the United Kingdom, under Schedule 1 to the Civil Jurisdiction and Judgments Order 2001, a judgment (other than a maintenance order) which is registered under the Brussels I Regulation is enforceable in the same way as a judgment given by the registering court.[76] In the case of a money judgment, the judgment debt bears interest in accordance with particulars of the law of the State of origin, registered along with the judgment;[77] and the reasonable costs of obtaining registration are also recoverable.[78] Where the judgment awards a sum of money which is expressed in a foreign currency, it is registered without converting the sum into sterling, though such conversion will usually be necessary for the purpose of execution and will then take place at the rate prevailing on the date of the application for the relevant measure of execution.[79]

A maintenance order which is registered in England under the Brussels I Regulation is enforceable in the same way as an English magistrates' court maintenance order, within the meaning of s 150(1) of the Magistrates' Courts Act 1980, made by the registering court.[80] But sums (including arrears) which are payable in the United Kingdom under a maintenance order by virtue of the registration must be paid in sterling, and conversion takes place at the exchange rate prevailing on the date of registration.[81]

## UNCONTESTED CLAIMS

On 21st April 2004, the EC Parliament and Council adopted Regulation 805/2004 creating a European Enforcement Order for Uncontested Claims, which may conveniently be referred to as the Uncontested Claims Regulation.[82] The Regulation applies in and between all the EU

---

[74]   See Case 148/84: *Deutsche Genossenschaftsbank v Brasserie du Pecheur* [1985] ECR 1981, and Case 119/84: *Capelloni v Pelkmans* [1985] ECR 3147.

[75]   See pp. 261–2 above.

[76]   See para 2(2) of Schedule 1. Thus events such as payment, which have occurred after the registered judgment was given by the original court, may be taken into account in the context of the English measures of execution, in the same way as in the case of an English judgment; see per Schiemann LJ in *Landhurst Leasing v Marcq* [1998] ILPr 822.

[77]   See para 5(1) of Schedule 1.

[78]   See para 2(1) of Schedule 1.

[79]   See *Miliangos v Frank* [1976] AC 443.

[80]   See para 3 of Schedule 1.

[81]   See para 6 of Schedule 1.

[82]   For its text, see [2004] OJ L143/15. It gives effect to the Council programme of 30th November 2000 of further measures for the implementation of the principle of mutual recognition of decisions in civil and commercial matters, [2001] OJ C12/1, which envisaged in the first stage measures dealing with (inter alia) uncontested claims.

Member States except Denmark.[83] It entered into force on 21st January 2004, but applies from 21st October 2005.[84]

The purpose of the Uncontested Claims Regulation, as specified by Article 1, is to create a European Enforcement Order for uncontested claims, so as to permit, by laying down minimum standards, the free circulation of judgments, court settlements and authentic instruments throughout the Member States, without any intermediate proceedings needing to be brought in the Member State of enforcement prior to recognition and enforcement. Thus Chapter II of the Uncontested Claims Regulation enables a court of a Member State which has given a judgment on an uncontested claim to issue a certificate, certifying the judgment as a European Enforcement Order, provided that the minimum procedural standards laid down by Chapter III have been satisfied. The certificate then renders the judgment enforceable in the other Member States, without the need for a declaration of enforceability to be obtained from a court of the State addressed, as would have been required under the Brussels I Regulation. Under Chapter IV, enforcement procedures, including measures of actual execution, remain governed by the law of the State addressed, which must treat a certified judgment in the same way as a local judgment. With minimal exceptions, any challenge to the judgment or the certificate must be made in the State of origin.

Recital 9 asserts that the procedure now provided should offer significant advantages as compared with the procedure involving a declaration of enforceability provided for in the Brussels I Regulation, in that there is no need for approval by the judiciary in a second Member State with the delays and expenses that this entails. The extent to which delay and expense will really be reduced will eventually become apparent. But it seems well arguable that any such reduction is being purchased at a wholly disproportionate price, by way of the elimination of the well-established and widely accepted traditional protection of the defendant's right to a hearing by means of review on this point by the courts of the country of enforcement. Mutual trust does not justify a systematic refusal to rectify mistakes of a kind which are notoriously frequent even in well-ordered systems. It is therefore suggested that the Uncontested Claims Regulation is a wholly regrettable development.

By Article 27, the Uncontested Claims Regulation does not affect the possibility of seeking recognition and enforcement in accordance with the Brussels I Regulation of a judgment, a court settlement or an authentic instrument on an uncontested claim. By Article 22, the Uncontested Claims Regulation does not affect agreements by which Member States undertook, prior to the entry into force of the Brussels I Regulation, pursuant to Article 59 of the Brussels Convention, not to recognise certain judgments given, in particular in other Contracting States to the Brussels Convention, against defendants domiciled or habitually resident in a non-member country.[85]

**Scope**

In general, the Uncontested Claims Regulation has the same material scope as the Brussels I

---

[83]    See Recitals 24 and 25, and Article 2(3). For its operation in England, see also rules 74.27 to 74.33 of the Civil Procedure Rules 1998 (as amended).

[84]    See Article 33.

[85]    On such undertakings, see pp. 235–6 above.

Regulation. For Article 2(1)–(2) of the Uncontested Claims Regulation echoes Article 1 of the Brussels I Regulation, as well as specifying that the Uncontested Claims Regulation does not extend to the liability of the State for acts and omissions in the exercise of State authority. But, by Article 3, the Uncontested Claims Regulation is limited to uncontested claims. It applies only to judgments, court settlements and authentic instruments on uncontested claims, and to decisions delivered following challenges to judgments, court settlements or authentic instruments certified as European Enforcement Orders.

An uncontested claim is defined by Articles 3(1) and 4(2). The claim must be for payment of a specific sum of money which has fallen due, or for which the due date is indicated in the judgment, court settlement or authentic instrument. It must also be uncontested, in the sense that one of the following four conditions is satisfied: (a) the debtor has expressly agreed to the claim, by admission or by means of a settlement which has been approved by or concluded before a court in the course of proceedings; or (b) the debtor has never objected to the claim, in compliance with the relevant procedural requirements under the law of the Member State of origin, in the course of the court proceedings;[86] or (c) the debtor has not appeared or been represented at a court hearing regarding that claim, after having initially objected to the claim in the course of the court proceedings, provided that such conduct amounts to a tacit admission of the claim or of the facts alleged by the creditor under the law of the Member State of origin; or (d) the debtor has expressly agreed to the claim in an authentic instrument. In this connection, Recital 5 explains that the concept of uncontested claims should cover all situations in which a creditor, given the verified absence of any dispute by the debtor as to the nature or extent of a pecuniary claim, has obtained either a court decision against the debtor, or an enforceable document which requires the debtor's express consent, being a court settlement or an authentic instrument.

Article 4(1) and (7) of the Uncontested Claims Regulation defines a 'judgment' in the same way as Articles 32 and 62 of the Brussels I Regulation. Article 4(3)(a) defines an 'authentic instrument' as a document which has been formally drawn up or registered as an authentic instrument, and the authenticity of which relates both to its signature and its content and has been established by a public authority or other authority empowered for that purpose by the Member State in which it originates. Article 4(3)(b) extends the concept of an authentic instrument so as to include an arrangement relating to maintenance obligations which has been concluded with administrative authorities or authenticated by them.

By Article 26, the Uncontested Claims Regulation applies only to judgments given, to court settlements approved or concluded, and to documents formally drawn up or registered as authentic instruments, after the entry into force of the Regulation. Read literally, this refers to 21st January 2004, on which the Regulation (retrospectively) entered into force under Article 33(1). Read sanely, it refers to 21st October 2005, from which the Regulation applies under Article 33(2).

---

[86] Recital 6 explains that the absence of objections from the debtor can take the shape of default of appearance at a court hearing, or of failure to comply with an invitation by the court to give written notice of an intention to defend the case.

## Certification

Chapter II (Articles 5–11) of the Uncontested Claims Regulation provides for a judgment on an uncontested claim to be certified by the court of origin as a European Enforcement Order. The certificate granted in the State of origin replaces the declaration of enforceability which would have to be obtained in the State of enforcement under the Brussels I Regulation. Thus Article 5 of the Uncontested Claims Regulation specifies that a judgment which has been certified as a European Enforcement Order in the Member State of origin must be recognised and enforced in the other Member States without the need for a declaration of enforceability and without any possibility of opposing its recognition. By Article 9, the certificate follows the standard form contained in Annex I of the Regulation, and uses the same language as the judgment.[87]

By Articles 3(1), 4(6) and 6(1), the certificate is issued upon an application at any time to the court of origin; that is, the court or tribunal seised of the proceedings at the time of fulfilment of the conditions which render the claim uncontested (the debtor's agreement to the claim, by admission or court settlement; his failure to object to the claim; or his subsequent non-appearance).[88] By Article 7, where a judgment on an uncontested claim includes an enforceable decision on the amount of costs related to the court proceedings (including interest rates), the certificate also covers the costs, unless the debtor has specifically objected to his obligation to bear such costs in the course of the court proceedings, in accordance with the law of the Member State of origin.

Article 6(1) specifies the conditions to which the issue of the certificate by the court of origin is made subject.[89] Firstly, Article 6(1)(a) requires that the judgment must be enforceable in the Member State of origin, and Article 11 restricts the effect of the certificate to the extent of the enforceability of the judgment.[90]

Secondly, certain jurisdictional rules must have been respected. By Article 6(1)(b), the judgment must not conflict with the rules on jurisdiction laid down in sections 3 and 6 of Chapter II of the Brussels I Regulation (which deal with insurance contracts, and with exclusive jurisdiction by subject-matter). Further, by Article 6(1)(d), where the claim relates to a contract concluded by a person (the consumer) for a purpose which can be regarded as being outside his trade or profession, and the debtor is the consumer, and the claim is uncontested by reason of the debtor's failure to object or subsequent non-appearance, the certificate must be issued only where the judgment was given in the Member State of the debtor's domicile within the meaning of the Brussels I Regulation.

---

[87]   By Article 6(3), where a decision has been delivered following a challenge to a certified judgment, a replacement certificate is, upon application at any time, to be issued, using the standard form in Annex V, if the decision on the challenge is enforceable in the Member State of origin.

[88]   On applications to English courts for the issue of certificates in respect of English judgments, see also rule 74.28 of the Civil Procedure Rules 1998 (as amended).

[89]   By Article 8, if only parts of the judgment meet the requirements of the Regulation, a partial certificate should be issued for those parts.

[90]   In addition, by Article 6(2), where a judgment certified as a European Enforcement Order has ceased to be enforceable or its enforceability has been suspended or limited, a certificate indicating the lack or limitation of enforceability is, upon application at any time to the court of origin, to be issued, using the standard form in Annex IV. On applications to English courts under Article 6(2), see also rule 74.29 of the Civil Procedure Rules 1998 (as amended).

Thirdly, where the judgment is uncontested by virtue of the debtor's failure to object or subsequent non-appearance, Article 6(1)(c) of the Uncontested Claims Regulation requires that the court proceedings in the Member State of origin should have met the requirements set out in Chapter III of the Regulation, which lays down minimum standards for uncontested claims procedures.

By Article 10(1), upon application to the court of origin, the certificate may be rectified or withdrawn. The certificate is to be rectified where, due to a material error, there is a discrepancy between the judgment and the certificate. The certificate is to be withdrawn where it was clearly wrongly granted, having regard to the requirements of the Regulation. By Article 10(2) and (3), the law of the Member State of origin applies to the rectification or withdrawal of the certificate, and the application may be made using the standard form in Annex VI of the Regulation.[91] By Article 10(4), no other appeal lies against the issuing of the certificate. By Article 21(2), under no circumstances may the judgment or its certification as a European Enforcement Order be reviewed as to their substance in the Member State of enforcement.

## The Minimum Procedural Standards

Chapter III (Articles 12–19) of the Uncontested Claims Regulation defines minimum standards for uncontested claims procedures. As Recital 19 explains, the Regulation does not imply an obligation for the Member States to adapt their national legislation to the minimum procedural standards, but provides an incentive to do so by making available a more efficient and rapid enforceability of judgments in other Member States only if the minimum standards are met. By Articles 3(1), 6(1)(c) and 12, the court of origin must not issue a certificate in respect of a judgment unless the court proceedings in the State of origin met these requirements. They apply where the claim is uncontested by virtue of the debtor's non-objection or subsequent non-appearance, but not where the claim is uncontested by virtue of the debtor's express agreement. By Articles 6(3) and 12(2), they also apply to the issuing of a certificate or a replacement certificate in respect of a decision following a challenge to a judgment where, at the time of that decision, the claim is uncontested by virtue of the debtor's non-objection or subsequent non-appearance.

The minimum standards specified by Articles 13–15 relate to the methods and proof of service of the instituting or an equivalent document and of any summons to a hearing.[92] Article 13 provides for service with proof of receipt by the debtor. Article 13(1) permits: (i) personal service attested by an acknowledgement of receipt, including the date of receipt, which is signed by the debtor; (ii) personal service attested by a document signed by the competent person who effected the service, stating that the debtor has received the document or refused to receive it without any legal justification, and the date of the service; (iii) postal service attested by an acknowledgement of receipt, including the date of receipt, which is signed and returned by the debtor; and (iv) service by electronic means such as fax or e-mail,

---

[91]    On applications to English courts under Article 10, see also rule 74.30 of the Civil Procedure Rules 1998 (as amended).

[92]    By Article 28, the Uncontested Claims Regulation does not affect the application of EC Regulation 1393/2007 on the Service in the Member States of Judicial and Extrajudicial Documents in Civil or Commercial Matters, [2007] OJ L324/79, which has replaced EC Regulation 1348/2000, [2000] OJ L160/37.

attested by an acknowledgement of receipt, including the date of receipt, which is signed and returned by the debtor. In the case of a summons to a court hearing, Article 13(2) also permits service which is effected orally at a previous court hearing on the same claim, and stated in the minutes of that hearing. According to Recital 14, the methods of service listed in Article 13 are characterised by full certainty that the document served has reached its addressee.

Article 14 provides for service without proof of receipt by the debtor. It permits (i) personal service at the debtor's personal address on persons who are living in the same household as the debtor or are employed there; (ii) where the debtor is self-employed or is a legal person, personal service at the debtor's business premises on persons who are employed by the debtor; (iii) deposit of the document in the debtor's mailbox; (iv) deposit of the document at a post office or with competent public authorities and the placing in the debtor's mailbox of written notification of that deposit, provided that the written notification clearly states the character of the document as a court document or the legal effect of the notification as effecting service and setting in motion the running of time for the purposes of time limits; (v) postal service, where the debtor has his address in the State of origin; and (vi) service by electronic means, attested by an automatic confirmation of delivery, if the debtor has expressly accepted this method of service in advance. But Article 14(2) insists in all these cases that the debtor's address must be known with certainty. Moreover, in the case of service at the debtor's personal address or business premises, and deposit or placing in his mailbox, but not of postal service to the debtor's address in the State of origin, Article 14(3)(a) insists that the service must be attested by a document signed by the competent person who effected the service, indicating the method of service used, and the date of service, and where the document has been served on a person other than the debtor, the name of that person and his relation to the debtor. In the case of service at the debtor's personal address or business premises on a person living or employed there, Article 14(3)(b) accepts, as an alternative, attestation by an acknowledgement of receipt by the person served. According to Recital 14, the methods of service listed in Article 14 are characterised by a very high degree of likelihood that the document served has reached its addressee.

Article 15 offers a further possibility: service in accordance with Article 13 or 14 on a representative of the debtor. According to Recital 16, this applies both to situations in which a debtor (such as a legal person) cannot represent himself in court and a person to represent him is determined by law, and to situations where the debtor has authorised another person (in particular a lawyer) to represent him in the specific court proceedings at issue.

The minimum standards specified by Articles 16 and 17 relate to the provision of information to the debtor about the claim or the procedural steps necessary to contest the claim. By Article 16, the instituting or equivalent document must have contained the following particulars: (i) the names and the addresses of the parties; (ii) the amount of the claim; (iii) if interest on the claim is sought, the interest rate and the period for which interest is sought, unless statutory interest is automatically added to the principal under the law of the State of origin; and (iv) a statement of the reason for the claim. By Article 17, the following must have been clearly stated, in or together with the instituting or equivalent document or a summons to a court hearing: (i) the procedural requirements for contesting the claim, including the time-limit for contesting the claim in writing or the time for the court hearing; (ii) the name and the address of the institution to which to respond or before which to appear; (iii) whether it is mandatory to be represented by a lawyer; and (iv) the consequences of an absence of objection or default of appearance (in particular, where applicable, the possibility that a judgment may be given or enforced against the debtor, and the liability for costs related to the court proceedings).

Article 18 provides in two cases for the cure of non-compliance with the minimum standards for service and information laid down by Articles 13–17. The first case, specified by Article 18(1), is based on the debtor's failure in certain circumstances to challenge the judgment in the original country after its entry and service. Thus non-compliance with the procedural requirements of Articles 13–17 is cured, and a judgment may be certified as a European Enforcement Order, if: (a) the judgment has been served on the debtor in compliance with Articles 13 or 14; and (b) it was possible for the debtor to challenge the judgment by means of a full review, and the debtor has been duly informed, in or together with the judgment, about the procedural requirements for such a challenge (including the name and address of the institution with which it must be lodged; and, where applicable, the time-limit for so doing); and (c) the debtor has failed to challenge the judgment in compliance with the relevant procedural requirements. The second case, specified by Article 18(2), is confined to non-compliance with the requirements of Article 13 or Article 14 as to service. Such non-compliance is cured if it is proved by the conduct of the debtor in the court proceedings that he has personally received the document to be served in sufficient time to arrange for his defence.

Article 19 provides for minimum standards in respect of the debtor's right to apply for a review of the judgment. Firstly, by Article 19(1)(a), a judgment cannot be certified as a European Enforcement Order unless the debtor is entitled, under the law of the Member State of origin, to apply for a review of the judgment where the instituting or equivalent document, or a summons to a court hearing, was served by a method provided for in Article 14, and service was not effected in sufficient time to enable him to arrange for his defence, without any fault on his part, and the debtor acts promptly in applying for the review. Secondly, by Article 19(1)(b), a judgment cannot be certified unless the debtor is entitled, under the law of the Member State of origin, to apply for a review of the judgment where he was prevented from objecting to the claim by reason of force majeure, or due to extraordinary circumstances without any fault on his part, and he acts promptly in applying for the review. Article 19(2) makes it clear that Member States remain free to grant access to a review of a judgment under more generous conditions.

## Enforcement

Chapter IV (Articles 20–23) of the Uncontested Claims Regulation deals with the enforcement of certified judgments. By Article 20(1), enforcement procedures are, in general, governed by the law of the Member State of enforcement, and a judgment certified as a European Enforcement Order must be enforced under the same conditions as a judgment given in the Member State of enforcement. Despite the insistence of the Regulation on eliminating the need for a declaration of enforceability to be obtained in the State addressed, Recital 8 indicates that it is open to the United Kingdom to apply to certified judgments from other Member States registration procedures similar to those applicable under the Civil Jurisdiction and Judgments Act 1982 to the enforcement in one part of the United Kingdom of judgments given in other parts of the United Kingdom; but the United Kingdom has failed to make use of this invitation.

By Article 20(2), the creditor must provide the competent enforcement authorities of the

Member State of enforcement with an authentic copy of the judgment and of the European Enforcement Order certificate, and in some cases a translation of the certificate into an official language of the Member State of enforcement.[93] By Article 20(3), no security, bond or deposit may be required of a party who in one Member State applies for enforcement of a judgment certified as a European Enforcement Order in another Member State on the ground that he is a foreign national or that he is not domiciled or resident in the Member State of enforcement.

By Article 21(2), under no circumstances may a certified judgment or its certification as a European Enforcement Order be reviewed as to substance in the Member State of enforcement. The sole grounds for refusal of enforcement of a certified judgment in the State addressed are specified by Articles 21(1) and 22. By Article 21(1), upon application by the debtor, enforcement must be refused by the competent court in the Member State of enforcement in certain cases where the certified judgment is irreconcilable with an earlier judgment. The earlier judgment may have been given in a Member State or in an external country, but it must have involved the same cause of action and the same parties. The earlier judgment must also either have been given in the Member State of enforcement, or it must fulfil the conditions necessary for its recognition there. Finally, the irreconcilability must not have been raised as an objection in the court proceedings in the Member State of origin, nor must it have been capable of being so raised.[94]

By Article 22, the Uncontested Claims Regulation does not affect agreements by which Member States undertook, prior to the entry into force of the Brussels I Regulation, pursuant to Article 59 of the Brussels Convention, not to recognise certain judgments given, in particular in other Contracting States to the Brussels Convention, against defendants domiciled or habitually resident in a non-member country.[95] Although no procedure is specified, it seems clear that this impliedly entitles the debtor to apply to a court of the State addressed for an order preventing enforcement of a certified judgment which falls within the scope of an undertaking referred to in Article 22.

Article 23 provides for a stay or limitation of enforcement to be imposed in the State of enforcement in certain circumstances. It applies where in the State of origin the debtor has challenged a certified judgment, including by way of an application for review under Article 19 (on grounds relating to his inability to arrange for his defence), or has applied for the rectification or withdrawal of the certificate in accordance with Article 10 (on grounds relating to errors in the certificate, or in the decision to grant the certificate). In such circumstances, the competent court or authority in the Member State of enforcement may, upon application by the debtor: (a) limit the enforcement proceedings to protective measures; or (b) make enforcement conditional on the provision of such security as it determines; or (c) under exceptional circumstances, stay the enforcement proceedings.[96]

---

[93] On applications for enforcement in England, see also rule 74.31 of the Civil Procedure Rules 1998 (as amended).

[94] On applications to English courts under Article 21(1), see also rule 74.32 of the Civil Procedure Rules 1998 (as amended).

[95] On such undertakings, see pp. 235–6 above.

[96] On applications to English courts under Article 23, see also rule 74.33 of the Civil Procedure Rules 1998 (as amended).

**Court Settlements and Authentic Instruments**

Chapter V (Articles 24–5) deals with court settlements and authentic instruments. Article 24 provides for the enforcement of a settlement of an uncontested claim which has been approved by or concluded before a court in the course of proceedings, and which is enforceable in the Member State in which it was approved or concluded. By Article 24(1), such a settlement is, upon application to the court which approved it or before which it was concluded, to be certified as a European Enforcement Order using the standard form in Annex II. By Article 24(2), a certified settlement is to be enforced in the other Member States without the need for a declaration of enforceability and without any possibility of opposing its enforceability. By Article 24(3), in general the provisions of Chapters II and IV, on certification and enforcement, apply as appropriate.

Article 25 provides for the enforcement of an authentic instrument concerning an uncontested claim which was drawn up or registered and is enforceable in a Member State. By Article 25(1), such an instrument is, upon application to the authority designated by the Member State of origin (in which it was drawn up or registered), to be certified as a European Enforcement Order, using the standard form in Annex III. By Article 25(2), a certified instrument is to be enforced in the other Member States without the need for a declaration of enforceability and without any possibility of opposing its enforceability. By Article 25(3), in general the provisions of Chapters II and IV, on certification and enforcement, apply as appropriate.

## THE EUROPEAN PAYMENT ORDER

Further provision in relation to uncontested claims has been made by EC Regulation 1896/2006, creating a European Order for Payment Procedure,[97] which may conveniently be referred to as the Payment Order Regulation. This Regulation became applicable on 12th December 2008[98] in all the Member States other than Denmark.[99] It creates a unified procedure for the collection of pecuniary claims for a specific amount in cross-border cases. The procedure involves an ex parte application to a court of a Member State for a European payment order.[100] After the order has been made by the court, it is served on the defendant. If he lodges a statement of opposition, the case proceeds as an ordinary civil proceeding. If he fails to lodge a statement of opposition, the court declares the order for payment enforceable, and it then becomes enforceable throughout the Member States, without the need for a declaration of enforceability in the State of enforcement.

---

[97]   [2006] OJ L399/1.
[98]   See Article 33.
[99]   See Recitals 31 and 32, and Article 2(3).
[100]   By Article 5(3), 'court' includes an authority of a Member State with relevant competence. By Article 26, all procedural issues not specifically dealt with in the Regulation are remitted to national law. As regards courts and procedure in England, see Article 2 of the High Court and County Courts Jurisdiction Order 1991 (as amended); and rules 78.1 to 78.11 of the Civil Procedure Rules 1998 (as amended).

**Purpose and Scope**

Article 1(1) of the Payment Order Regulation explains that its purpose is: (a) to simplify, speed up, and reduce the costs of litigation in cross-border cases concerning uncontested pecuniary claims by creating a European order for payment procedure; and (b) to permit the free circulation of European orders for payment throughout the Member States by laying down minimum standards, compliance with which renders unnecessary any intermediate proceedings in the Member State of enforcement prior to recognition and enforcement. More fundamentally, Recital 6 explains that the swift and efficient recovery of outstanding debts over which no legal controversy exists is of paramount importance for economic operators in the European Union, as late payments constitute a major reason for insolvency threatening the survival of businesses, particularly small and medium-sized enterprises, and resulting in numerous job losses. By Article 4, the European order for payment procedure is established for the collection of pecuniary claims for a specific amount which have fallen due at the time when the application for a European order for payment is submitted.

Article 1(2) makes clear that the procedure made available by the Regulation is not exclusive or mandatory for claimants. It specifies that the Regulation does not prevent a claimant from pursuing a claim within its scope by making use of another procedure available under the law of a Member State or under European Union law.

As regards material scope, Article 2 of the Payment Order Regulation largely echoes the Brussels I Regulation. By Article 2(1), the Payment Order Regulation applies to civil and commercial matters, whatever the nature of the court or tribunal, but does not extend to revenue, customs or administrative matters, nor to the liability of the State for acts and omissions in the exercise of State authority. By Article 2(2), the Regulation does not apply to matrimonial property, succession, insolvency proceedings, and social security. A further exclusion, by Article 2(2)(d), is of claims arising from non-contractual obligations, unless either (i) they have been the subject of an agreement between the parties or there has been an admission of debt, or (ii) they relate to liquidated debts arising from joint ownership of property.

The Regulation is limited by Article 2(1) to cross-border cases. A cross-border case is defined by Article 3(1) as one in which at least one of the parties is domiciled or habitually resident in a Member State other than the forum State. By Article 3(2), domicile is to be determined in accordance with Articles 59 and 60 of the Brussels I Regulation. By Article 3(3), the relevant moment for determining whether there is a cross-border case is the time when the application for a European order for payment is submitted in accordance with the Regulation.

**Jurisdiction**

By Article 6(1) of the Payment Order Regulation, jurisdiction under the Regulation is determined in accordance with the relevant rules of European Union law, in particular the Brussels I Regulation. But where the claim relates to a contract concluded by a person, the consumer, for a purpose which can be regarded as being outside his trade or profession, and the defendant is the consumer, Article 6(2) confines jurisdiction to the courts of the Member State in which the defendant is domiciled, within the meaning of Article 59 of the Brussels I Regulation.

## The Application

The contents of an application for a European order for payment are regulated by Article 7 of the Payment Order Regulation. By Article 7(1), the application must be made using standard form A as set out in Annex I. By Article 7(2), the application must specify the parties; the court applied to; the amount of the claim; particulars relating to interest claimed; the cause of the action, including a description of the circumstances invoked as the basis of the claim; a description of evidence supporting the claim; the grounds for jurisdiction; and the cross-border nature of the case. Recital 13 indicates that in the application the claimant should be obliged to provide information which is sufficient to clearly identify and support the claim, in order to place the defendant in a position to make a well-informed choice either to oppose the claim or to leave it uncontested. By Article 7(3), the application must contain a declaration by the claimant that the information provided is true to the best of his knowledge and belief.

By Article 8, the court seised of an application for a European order for payment must examine, as soon as possible and on the basis of the application form, whether the requirements set out in Articles 2–4 and 6–7 (which relate to subject-matter, cross-border character, specific amount, jurisdiction, and contents of the application) are met, and whether the claim appears to be founded. Recital 16 explains that the court should examine the application, including the issue of jurisdiction and the description of evidence, on the basis of the information provided in the application form; and that this allows the court to examine prima facie the merits of the claim, and inter alia to exclude clearly unfounded claims or inadmissible applications.

By Article 11(1), the court must reject the application if (a) the requirements set out in Articles 2–4 and 6–7 are not met, or (b) the claim is clearly unfounded.[101] The claimant will be informed of the grounds for the rejection by means of standard form D as set out in Annex IV. By Article 11(2), there is no right of appeal against the rejection of the application; but Recital 17 indicates that this does not preclude a possible review of the decision rejecting the application at the same level of jurisdiction in accordance with national law. By Article 11(3), the rejection of the application does not prevent the claimant from pursuing the claim by means of a new application for a European order for payment or of any other procedure available under the law of a Member State.

By Article 12(1)–(2), if the requirements referred to in Article 8 are met, the court must issue, as soon as possible and normally within thirty days of the lodging of the application, a European order for payment using standard form E as set out in Annex V, together with a copy of the application form. By Article 12(3), in the order for payment the defendant will be advised of his options: (a) to pay the amount indicated in the order to the claimant; or (b) to oppose the order by lodging with the court of origin a statement of opposition, to be sent within thirty days of service of the order on him. By Article 12(4), in the order the defendant will also be informed that: (a) the order was issued solely on the basis of the information which was provided by the claimant and was not verified by the court; (b) the order will become enforceable unless a statement of opposition has been lodged with the court in accordance with Article 16; and (c) where a statement of opposition is lodged, the proceedings will

---

[101] See also Articles 9 and 10, on completion, rectification and modification of the application.

continue before the competent courts of the Member State of origin in accordance with the rules of ordinary civil procedure unless the claimant has explicitly requested that the proceedings be terminated in that event.

By Article 12(5), the court must ensure that the order is served on the defendant in accordance with the law of the State in which the service is to be effected by a method which meets the minimum standards laid down in Articles 13–15, which resemble those specified by Articles 13–15 of the Uncontested Claims Regulation.[102] By Article 27, the Regulation does not affect the application of EC Regulation 1393/2007 on the Service in the Member States of Judicial and Extrajudicial Documents in Civil or Commercial Matters, which has replaced EC Regulation 1348/2000.[103]

By Article 16(1), the defendant may lodge a statement of opposition to the European order for payment with the court of origin using standard form F as set out in Annex VI. The form must be supplied to him together with the order. By Article 16(2), the statement of opposition must be sent within thirty days of service of the order on the defendant. By Article 16(3), the defendant must indicate in the statement of opposition that he contests the claim, but he does not have to specify the reasons for this. Recital 23 indicates that, although the defendant may submit his statement of opposition using the standard form set out in the Regulation, the courts should take into account any other written form of opposition if it is expressed in a clear manner.

By Article 17(1), if a statement of opposition is entered within the time-limit laid down in Article 16(2), the proceedings will continue before the competent courts of the Member State of origin in accordance with the rules of ordinary civil procedure, unless the claimant has explicitly requested that the proceedings be terminated in that event. By Article 17(3), the claimant must be informed whether the defendant has lodged a statement of opposition and of any transfer to ordinary civil proceedings.

## Enforcement

By Article 18(1), if within the time-limit laid down in Article 16(2), taking into account an appropriate period of time to allow a statement to arrive, no statement of opposition has been lodged with the court of origin, the court of origin must without delay declare the European order for payment enforceable, using standard form G as set out in Annex VII. The court must verify the date of service. By Article 18(3), the court must send the enforceable European order for payment to the claimant.

By Article 19, a European order for payment which has become enforceable in the Member State of origin must be recognised and enforced in the other Member States without the need for a declaration of enforceability and without any possibility of opposing its recognition. This is subject to the exceptions, relating to irreconcilability with an earlier judgment, to payment, and to review in the State of origin, which are specified by Articles 22 and 23. By Article 21(1), enforcement procedures are governed by the law of the Member State of enforcement, and a European order for payment which has become enforceable must be enforced under the same conditions as an enforceable decision issued in the Member State of

---

[102]    See pp. 271–2 above.
[103]    See pp. 62–6 above.

enforcement. By Article 21(2), for enforcement in another Member State, the claimant must provide the competent enforcement authorities of the Member State of enforcement with a copy of the European order for payment, as declared enforceable by the court of origin, which satisfies the conditions necessary to establish its authenticity; and in some cases with a translation of the order. By Article 22(3), under no circumstances may a European order for payment be reviewed as to its substance in the Member State of enforcement.[104]

Article 22(1) provides for the refusal of enforcement, upon application by the defendant, by the competent court in the Member State of enforcement, in certain cases where the European order for payment is irreconcilable with an earlier decision or order. It is immaterial whether the earlier decision or order was given in an EC Member State or in an external country, but it must have involved the same cause of action and the same parties. The earlier decision or order must also fulfil the conditions necessary for its recognition in the Member State of enforcement, and the irreconcilability must not have been capable of being raised as an objection in the court proceedings in the Member State of origin.

By Article 22(2), enforcement must also, upon application, be refused if and to the extent that the defendant has paid to the claimant the amount awarded in the European order for payment.

### Review in the State of Origin

Article 20 provides for review of the European order for payment before a competent court in the Member State of origin, upon an application made by the defendant after the expiry of the time limit laid down in Article 16(2), in three exceptional cases.[105]

The first case, specified by Article 20(1)(a), is where the order for payment was served by one of the methods provided for in Article 14 (on service without proof of receipt by the defendant), and service was not effected in sufficient time to enable him to arrange for his defence, without any fault on his part, and the defendant acts promptly in applying for the review. The second case, specified by Article 20(1)(b), is where the defendant was prevented from objecting to the claim by reason of force majeure or due to extraordinary circumstances without any fault on his part, and he acts promptly in applying for the review. The third case, specified by Article 20(2), is where the order for payment was clearly wrongly issued, having regard to the requirements laid down in the Regulation, or due to other exceptional circumstances.

Recital 25 explains that review in exceptional cases should not mean that the defendant is given a second opportunity to oppose the claim. During the review procedure, the merits of the claim should not be evaluated beyond the grounds resulting from the exceptional circumstances invoked by the defendant. But the relevant exceptional circumstances could include a situation where the European order for payment was based on false information provided in the application form.

By Article 20(3), if the court rejects the defendant's application on the basis that none of the grounds for review referred to in Article 20(1)–(2) apply, the European order for payment

---

[104] As to enforcement in England, see rules 78.9 to 78.11 of the Civil Procedure Rules 1998 (as amended).

[105] As to review in England, see also rule 78.8 of the Civil Procedure Rules 1998 (as amended).

remains in force. If the court decides that the review is justified for one of the reasons laid down in Article 20(1)–(2), the European order for payment becomes null and void.

Article 23 applies in the Member State of enforcement where the defendant has applied for a review under Article 20 in the State of origin. In this situation, the competent court in the Member State of enforcement may, upon application by the defendant: (a) limit the enforcement proceedings to protective measures; or (b) make enforcement conditional on the provision of such security as it determines; or (c) under exceptional circumstances, stay the enforcement proceedings.

## THE SMALL CLAIMS PROCEDURE

EC Regulation 861/2007, establishing a European Small Claims Procedure,[106] may conveniently be referred to as the Small Claims Regulation. It became applicable on 1st January 2009 in all of the Member States except Denmark.[107] As Article 1 explains, the Regulation establishes a European procedure for small claims intended to simplify and speed up litigation concerning small claims in cross-border cases, and to reduce costs. The procedure is available to litigants as an alternative to the procedures existing under the laws of the Member States.[108] The Regulation also eliminates the intermediate proceedings necessary to enable recognition and enforcement in other Member States of judgments given in a Member State under the European small claims procedure.

A small claim is defined by Article 2(1) of the Regulation as a claim whose value does not exceed 2,000 at the time when the claim form is received by the competent court, excluding all interest, expenses and disbursements. It seems that the claim must be monetary in nature, though it need not be for a specific sum (such as the price of goods or services supplied), but could be for damages to be assessed by the court.

Article 2(1) also confines the scope of the Regulation to civil and commercial matters, to the exclusion of revenue, customs or administrative matters, and of the liability of the State for acts and omissions in the exercise of State authority (acta jure imperii). Article 2(2) also excludes individual status or capacity; matrimonial property; maintenance obligations; succession; insolvency proceedings; social security; arbitration; employment law; tenancies of immovable property, with the exception of actions on monetary claims; and violations of privacy and of rights relating to personality, including defamation. Article 2(1) also confines the Regulation to cross-border cases, and Article 3 adopts a definition of these which is similar to that specified by Article 3 of the Payment Order Regulation.

### The European Small Claims Procedure

The European small claims procedure is established by Chapter II (Articles 4–19) of the Small Claims Regulation.[109] By Article 4(1), the claimant commences the procedure by fill-

---

[106]    [2007] OJ L199/1.

[107]    See Recitals 37 and 38 and Articles 2(3) and 29.

[108]    See also Recital 8, which refers to the procedure as an optional tool, additional to the possibilities existing under the laws of the Member States, which remain unaffected.

[109]    On languages and translations, see Article 6 and Recitals 18 and 19. By Article 19, procedural

ing in standard claim Form A, as set out in Annex I, and lodging it with the competent court or tribunal. In England, such applications must be commenced in a county court.[110] The claim form must include a description of evidence supporting the claim and be accompanied, where appropriate, by any relevant supporting documents.[111] By Article 4(3), where a claim is outside the scope of the Regulation, the court informs the claimant to that effect; and unless the claimant withdraws the claim, the court proceeds with it in accordance with the relevant procedural law applicable in the forum State. By Article 4(4), where the court considers the information provided by the claimant to be inadequate or insufficiently clear or if the claim form is not filled in properly, the court will usually give the claimant the opportunity to complete or rectify the claim form or to supply supplementary information or documents or to withdraw the claim, and will use standard Form B, as set out in Annex II, for this purpose. Where the claim appears to be clearly unfounded or the application inadmissible, or where the claimant fails to complete or rectify the claim form within the time specified, the application will be dismissed. Recital 13 indicates that the concepts of 'clearly unfounded' in the context of the dismissal of a claim and of 'inadmissible' in the context of the dismissal of an application should be determined in accordance with national law.

By Article 5(1), the European small claims procedure is normally a written procedure. The court will hold an oral hearing if it considers this to be necessary or if a party so requests, but such a request may be refused if the court considers that, with regard to the circumstances of the case, an oral hearing is obviously not necessary for the fair conduct of the proceedings.

By Article 5(2), after receiving a properly filled in claim form, the court will fill in Part I of the standard answer Form C, as set out in Annex III. Then a copy of the claim form, and, where applicable, of the supporting documents, together with the answer form, will be served on the defendant in accordance with Article 13. These documents should be dispatched within fourteen days of receiving the properly filled in claim form. By Article 5(3), the defendant should submit his response within thirty days of service of the claim form and answer form, by filling in Part II of standard answer Form C, accompanied where appropriate by any relevant supporting documents, and returning it to the court, or in any other appropriate way not using the answer form. By Article 5(4), within fourteen days of receipt of the response from the defendant, the court should dispatch a copy of the response, together with any relevant supporting documents, to the claimant. By Article 5(5), if in his response the defendant claims that the value of a non-monetary claim exceeds the 2,000 limit, the court should decide, within thirty days of dispatching the response to the claimant, whether the claim is within the scope of the Regulation.

Article 5(6) and (7) deals with counterclaims. Recitals 16 and 17 explain that the concept of a counterclaim should be interpreted in the same way as in Article 6(3) of the Brussels I Regulation, as arising from the same contract or facts as those on which the original claim was based; and that a right of set-off invoked by the defendant does not constitute a counterclaim for the purpose of the Small Claims Regulation. By Article 5(6), any counterclaim should be submitted using standard Form A, and such a counterclaim, along

---

issues not dealt with by Regulation are governed by the law of the forum State. As to procedure in England, see rules 78.1 and 78.12-78.22 of the Civil Procedure Rules 1998 (as amended).

[110]    See Article 6B of the High Court and County Courts Jurisdiction Order 1991 (as amended).

[111]    See also Recital 12, which indicates that the claimant may, where appropriate, submit further evidence during the procedure.

with any relevant supporting documents, must be served on the claimant in accordance with Article 13. These documents should be dispatched within fourteen days of receipt. The claimant has thirty days from service to respond to any counterclaim. By Article 5(7), if the counterclaim exceeds the 2,000 limit, the claim and counterclaim cannot proceed under the European small claims procedure, but will be dealt with in accordance with the relevant procedural law applicable in the forum State. Otherwise a counterclaim is dealt with in a similar way to other claims.

By Article 7(1), the court must deal with a case within thirty days of receipt of the response from the defendant (or where there is a counterclaim, the response of the original claimant), by either giving a judgment, or by demanding further details concerning the claim from the parties within a specified period not exceeding thirty days, or by taking evidence in accordance with Article 9, or by summoning the parties to an oral hearing to be held within thirty days of the summons. By Article 7(2), the court must give judgment either within thirty days of any oral hearing or after having received all information necessary for giving the judgment; and the judgment must be served on the parties in accordance with Article 13. By Article 7(3), if the court or tribunal has not received an answer from the relevant party within the thirty-day period for his initial response to a claim or counterclaim, it must give a judgment on the claim or counterclaim.

By Article 8, the court may hold an oral hearing through video-conference or other communication technology if the technical means are available. By Article 9(1), the court determines the means of taking evidence and the extent of the evidence necessary for its judgment under the rules applicable to the admissibility of evidence. It may admit the taking of evidence through written statements of witnesses, experts or parties. It may also admit the taking of evidence through video-conference or other communication technology if the technical means are available. By Article 9(2), the court may take expert evidence or oral testimony only if it is necessary for giving the judgment; and in making its decision as to this, the court must take costs into account. By Article 9(3), the court must use the simplest and least burdensome method of taking evidence.

By Article 10, representation by a lawyer or other legal professional is not mandatory. By Article 11, the Member States must ensure that the parties can receive practical assistance in filling in the forms. By Article 12(1), the court must not require the parties to make any legal assessment of the claim. By Article 12(2), if necessary, the court must inform the parties about procedural questions.[112] By Article 12(3), whenever appropriate, the court or tribunal must seek to reach a settlement between the parties.

By Article 13(1), documents must be served by postal service attested by an acknowledgement of receipt, including the date of receipt. By Article 13(2), if such service is not possible, service may be effected by any of the methods provided for in Articles 13 or 14 of the Uncontested Claims Regulation.

By Article 14(1), where the court sets a time-limit, the party concerned must be informed of the consequences of not complying with it. By Article 14(2), the court may extend the time-limits for a party to supplement a claim form, or to respond to a claim or counterclaim, in exceptional circumstances, if necessary in order to safeguard the rights of the parties. By Article 14(3), if in exceptional circumstances it is not possible for the court to respect the

---

[112]   See also Recitals 21 and 22.

time-limits for serving a claim or counterclaim, or for dealing with a case, it must do so as soon as possible. Recital 23 adds that the court should act as soon as possible even when the Regulation does not prescribe any time-limit for a specific phase of the procedure.

By Article 15(1), the judgment is enforceable notwithstanding any possible appeal, and the provision of a security cannot be required. By Article 16 and Recital 29, the unsuccessful party must bear the costs of the proceedings, except to the extent that they were unnecessarily incurred or are disproportionate to the value of the claim.

By Article 17, the possibility of an appeal against a judgment given under the European Small Claims Procedure is remitted to the law of the forum State, along with the time-limit for such an appeal.[113] But Article 18 imposes minimum standards for the review of a judgment at the instance of a defendant who was unable to arrange for his defence. This right to review resembles that specified by Article 19 of the Uncontested Claims Regulation.

## Recognition and Enforcement

The recognition and enforcement in other Member States of a judgment given under the European small claims procedure is governed by Chapter III (Articles 20–23) of the Small Claims Regulation.[114] By Recital 33, Chapter III extends to the determination of costs made by court officers in connection with a judgment given pursuant to the procedure specified in the Regulation.

By Article 20(1), a judgment given in a Member State under the European small claims procedure must be recognised and enforced in another Member State, without the need for a declaration of enforceability and without any possibility of opposing its recognition. By Article 20(2), at the request of one of the parties, the court of origin must issue a certificate concerning such a judgment, using standard Form D, as set out in Annex IV. By Article 21(1), enforcement procedures are in general governed by the law of the State of enforcement, but the judgment must be enforced under the same conditions as a judgment given in the Member State of enforcement. By Article 21(2), the party seeking enforcement must produce a copy of the judgment which satisfies the conditions necessary to establish its authenticity, and a copy of the certificate issued by the court of origin. In some cases, he must also produce a translation of the certificate.[115]

By Article 22(2), under no circumstances may a judgment given under the European small claims procedure be reviewed as to its substance in the Member State of enforcement. An exception is made by Article 22(1), which enables enforcement to be refused in certain cases where the judgment is irreconcilable with an earlier judgment. The exception resembles those specified by Article 21(1) of the Uncontested Claims Regulation, and by Article 22(1) of the Payment Order Regulation.[116]

A further exception is made by Article 23 of the Small Claims Regulation, which applies where in the State of origin a party has challenged a judgment given under the European small claims procedure (by way of an appeal which is available under its law) or where such

---

[113]   See also Recital 26.
[114]   On enforcement in England, see also rules 78.20–78.22 of the Civil Procedure Rules 1998 (as amended).
[115]   See also rule 78.20 of the Civil Procedure Rules 1998 (as amended).
[116]   See also rule 78.21 of the Civil Procedure Rules 1998 (as amended).

a challenge is still possible, or where a party has made an application for review under Article 18. In such circumstances, the competent court of the Member State of enforcement may, upon application by the party against whom enforcement is sought: (a) limit the enforcement proceedings to protective measures; or (b) make enforcement conditional on the provision of such security as it determines; or (c) under exceptional circumstances, stay the enforcement proceedings.[117] By Article 15(2), these powers are also available to the enforcing court where the judgment is to be enforced in the Member State of origin.

---

[117]    See also rule 78.22 of the Civil Procedure Rules 1998 (as amended).

PART III


Choice of Law in Respect of Obligations

# 12.  Contracts

## INTRODUCTION

### The Rome I Regulation

In litigation relating to contracts, choice of the applicable substantive law is now regulated by EC Regulation 593/2008 on the Law Applicable to Contractual Obligations, which is usually referred to as the Rome I Regulation.[1] The Regulation was adopted by the Parliament and Council on 17th June 2008. By Articles 28 and 29, the Regulation entered into application on 17th December 2009 and applies to contracts concluded after that date.[2] In view of the decision of the United Kingdom to opt in to the application of the Regulation after its adoption, the Regulation applies to all the EU Member States except Denmark.[3]

By Article 24(1), the Regulation replaces the EC Convention, opened for signature at Rome on 19th June 1980, on the Law Applicable to Contractual Obligations, which may conveniently be referred to as the Rome Convention 1980.[4] The Convention had entered into force in all twenty-seven Member States.[5] By Article 17, the Convention does not apply to contracts concluded before its commencement date for the forum State.[6] The Convention

---

[1]  For its text, see [2008] OJ L177/6.

[2]  Article 27(1) requires the Commission, by 17th June 2013, to submit a report on the application of the Regulation, accompanied (if appropriate) by proposals for its amendment.

[3]  See Recitals 45 and 46, and Article 1(4); and EC Commission Decision 2009/26, [2009] OJ L10/22, giving effect to the request from the United Kingdom to accept the Rome I Regulation, and specifying that the Regulation will apply in the United Kingdom from 17th December 2009, the same date as for the other Member States.

[4]  For the text of the Rome Convention 1980, as amended by the Accession Conventions of 1984, 1992, 1996 and 2005, see [2005] OJ C334/1. The Convention was not based directly on Article 220 of the EEC Treaty, but arose from a decision of the Member States to attempt further harmonisation in the sphere of private international law. By Article 24(2) of the Regulation, insofar as the Regulation replaces the provisions of the Convention, any reference to the Convention must be understood as a reference to the Regulation.

[5]  See the Accession Conventions of 1984, 1992, 1996 and 2005; the Luxembourg Act of Accession 2005, Article 3(3)–(4) and Annex 1, para 1, [2005] OJ L157; and EC Council Decision 2007/856, [2007] OJ L347/1. In the United Kingdom, the Convention was given the force of law by the Contracts (Applicable Law) Act 1990.

[6]  The commencement dates were: for the United Kingdom, France, Germany, Italy, Belgium, Luxembourg, Denmark, and Greece – 1st April 1991; for the Netherlands – 1st September 1991; for Ireland – 1st January 1992; for Spain – 1st September 1993; for Portugal – 1st September 1994; for Sweden – 1st October 1998; for Austria – 1st December 1998: for Finland – 1st April 1999; for Latvia and Slovenia – 1st May 2006; for Hungary – 1st June 2006; for the Czech Republic – 1st July 2006; for Slovakia – 1st August 2006; for Estonia – 1st October 2006; for Cyprus – 1st November 2006; for Lithuania – 1st December 2006; for Malta – 1st January 2007; for Poland – 1st August 2007; and for Bulgaria and Romania – 15th January 2008.

remains applicable to contracts concluded before 17th December 2009. It also remains fully applicable in Denmark, and in the French overseas territories.[7]

The process which led to the adoption of the Rome I Regulation by the EC Parliament and Council commenced with the issue by the EC Commission on 14th January 2003 of a Green Paper on the conversion of the Rome Convention into a Community instrument and its modernisation.[8] Eventually, on 15th December 2005, the Commission presented a Proposal for a Regulation on the Law Applicable to Contractual Obligations.[9] On 29th November 2007, the Parliament adopted a resolution on first reading, amending the Proposal and approving the Proposal as amended.[10] The Parliamentary amendments were subsequently accepted by the Council, and ultimately the Regulation was adopted accordingly.

Although the Commission Proposal of 15th December 2005 envisaged substantial changes to the rules established by the Rome Convention 1980, these changes were largely eliminated by the amendments adopted by the Parliament and accepted by the Council. Thus the Regulation as adopted closely resembles the Convention. Since the Regulation is a measure operating under the Treaty on the Functioning of the European Union, Article 267 of the Treaty enables the European Court to give preliminary rulings on its interpretation at the request of national courts, whether the national court is a court of first instance, of intermediate appeal, or of last resort.[11]

As regards the Rome Convention 1980, it was not until August 2004 that the European Court gained power to give preliminary rulings on its interpretation, as a result of the entry into force of the Brussels Protocols, signed on 19th December 1988.[12] These Protocols enable a preliminary ruling to be requested, at its discretion, by an appellate court of a Contracting State which has ratified the First Protocol.[13] Even in the case of a court of last resort, the making of a reference is discretionary. So far only one ruling has been given by the European Court on the interpretation of the Rome Convention 1980, but a substantial case-law on the Convention has developed at national level (especially in the United Kingdom). Guidance on the interpretation of the Rome Convention may also be drawn from the Giuliano and Lagarde Report.[14] In view of the substantial similarity between the Convention and the Regulation, the case-law on the Convention, and the Giuliano and Lagarde Report, may be of assistance in the interpretation of the Regulation.

---

[7]    See Article 24(1) of the Regulation, and Article 355 of the Treaty on the Functioning of the European Union.

[8]    See COM(2002) 654 final.

[9]    See COM(2005) 650 final.

[10]   See JUSTCIV 320, 3rd December 2007.

[11]   The restriction to courts of last resort of the power to request a ruling on the interpretation of measures relating to civil judicial co–operation, formerly imposed by Article 68 of the EC Treaty, has been eliminated by the Treaty of Lisbon. In view of the character of the Regulation as a European Union instrument, and the interpretative role of the European Court, the Regulation omits as unnecessary any provision corresponding to Article 18 of the Convention, which specifies that, in its interpretation and application, regard should be had to the international character of its rules and to the desirability of achieving uniformity in their interpretation and application.

[12]   For the text of the Protocols, see [1998] OJ C27/47 and 52.

[13]   Such references cannot yet be made by Irish courts, since Ireland has not ratified the First Protocol.

[14]   For its text, see [1980] OJ C282. On the use of the Report by United Kingdom courts, see s 3(3)(a) of the 1990 Act.

The choice-of-law rules laid down by the Rome I Regulation (or the Rome Convention 1980) are binding on the courts of the Member States for which the Regulation (or the Convention) has entered into force. But they are not necessarily applicable in arbitration proceedings, even if the arbitral tribunal has its seat in such a State. Thus, by s 46 of the (English) Arbitration Act 1996, an arbitral tribunal seated in England must decide the dispute: (a) in accordance with the internal law chosen by the parties as applicable to the substance of the dispute, or (b) if the parties so agree, in accordance with such other considerations as are agreed by them or determined by the tribunal. If or to the extent that there is no such choice or agreement, the tribunal applies the law determined by the conflict rules which it considers applicable.[15]

The Rome I Regulation applies regardless of reciprocity, since Article 2 provides that any law specified by the Regulation must be applied whether or not it is the law of a Member State.[16] Thus the Rome I Regulation almost entirely avoids the discriminatory character of the Brussels I Regulation.[17] More generally, Article 1(1) of the Rome I Regulation specifies that the Regulation applies, in situations involving a conflict of laws, to contractual obligations in civil and commercial matters.[18] It is also clear from Article 3(3)[19] that the Regulation applies even where the only foreign element arises from a choice of law agreed to by the parties, and the situation is otherwise exclusively connected with a single country; as where a contract concluded in England between English residents and requiring all performances to take place in England contains a clause choosing French law as governing the contract.

Article 22(1) of the Regulation adds that where a State (such as the United Kingdom) comprises several territories, each of which has its own rules of law in respect of contractual obligations, each territory (such as England and Wales; Scotland; or Northern Ireland) counts as a country for the purposes of identifying the law applicable under the Regulation.[20] While Article 22(2) of the Regulation permits such a State not to apply the Regulation to conflicts solely between the laws of its own territories, the United Kingdom will no doubt continue to reject this invitation to pointless complication.[21]

## Material Scope

Article 1(1) of the Rome I Regulation specifies that the Regulation applies, in situations involving a conflict of laws, to contractual obligations in civil and commercial matters, and

---

[15] Similarly, in France, the parties may choose to instruct an arbitrator not to apply any particular law; see Mayer and Heuzé, *Droit International Privé*, 9th edition (Montchrestien, 2007), at paras 702 and 704.

[16] This echoes Article 2 of the Rome Convention 1980.

[17] There is a minor exception in respect of insurance. See Articles 1(2)(j) and 7 of the Rome I Regulation, and Article 1(3) of the Rome Convention 1980.

[18] Similarly, Article 1(1) of the Rome Convention 1980 specifies that the rules of the Convention apply to contractual obligations in any situation involving a choice between the laws of different countries.

[19] This echoes Article 3(3) of the Rome Convention 1980.

[20] This echoes Article 19(1) of the Convention.

[21] A similar invitation offered by Article 19(2) of the Convention was rejected by s 2(3) of the Contracts (Applicable Law) Act 1990.

adds that it does not apply, in particular, to revenue, customs or administrative matters.[22] The Regulation does not attempt to define contractual obligations, except by means of the exclusions specified in Article 1(2). But Recital 7 indicates that the substantive scope and the provisions of the Regulation should be consistent with the Brussels I Regulation and the Rome II Regulation.

Thus it seems clear that the concept of a contract, for the purpose of the Rome I Regulation, must be given an independent meaning, defined by European Union law in the light of the purposes of the Regulation and of the general trend which emerges from the laws of the Member States, viewed as a whole, rather than as being remitted to the law of the country whose court is seised. Moreover, the concept should be understood as having essentially the same meaning as in Article 5(1) of the Brussels I Regulation, so as to refer to obligations freely assumed by one party towards another.[23] In any event, the concept should not be restricted by technical rules of the internal lex fori, such as the English rule requiring consideration, which are designed to regulate the validity, rather than define the nature, of a contract.[24] On the other hand, it seems clear that, since the Regulation does not attempt to regulate proprietary issues, the effect of a contract for the sale or other disposition of property on ownership of the property, even as between the parties to the contract, remains subject to any forum conflict rule which gives ultimate control to the law of the country in which the property is situated.[25]

The material scope of the Rome I Regulation is, however, restricted to some extent by Article 1(2), which excludes certain transactions, terms and issues from the ambit of the Regulation, thus remitting them (in the absence of other EU legislation) to the traditional conflict rules of the court seised.

### Excluded transactions

A group of exclusions, specified by Article 1(2)(a)–(c) of the Rome I Regulation,[26] seem designed to cover all contracts which fall within the sphere of family law.[27] Article 1(2)(a) refers to questions involving the status or legal capacity of natural persons. Article 1(2)(b) refers to obligations arising out of family relationships and relationships deemed by the law applicable to such relationships to have comparable effects, including maintenance obligations. Article 1(2)(c) refers to obligations arising out of matrimonial property regimes, property regimes of relationships deemed by the law applicable to such relationships to have comparable effects to marriage, and wills and succession.[28] Recital 8 explains that family

---

22    In the Rome Convention 1980, Article 1(1) specified, less elaborately, that the rules of the Convention applied to contractual obligations in any situation involving a choice between the laws of different countries.

23    See pp. 80–82 above.

24    See *Re Bonacina* [1912] 2 Ch 394 (CA).

25    See *Hardwick Game Farm v SAPPA* [1966] 1 WLR 287, per Diplock LJ at 330; and *Glencore v Metro* [2001] 1 Lloyd's Rep 284 (Moore-Bick J).

26    These exclusions resemble those specified by Article 1(2)(a) and (b) of the Rome Convention 1980, but the references to relationships having comparable effects are new.

27    See the Giuliano and Lagarde Report, at p. 10. Thus the Rome I Regulation avoids the perverse distinction between maintenance and matrimonial property made by the Brussels I Regulation; see pp. 29–32 above.

28    See *Halpern v Halpern* [2007] 2 All ER (Comm) 330 (CA), holding that a compromise of an

relationships cover parentage, marriage, affinity and collateral relatives, and that the references to relationships having comparable effects to marriage and other family relationships should be interpreted in accordance with the law of the forum State.

Article 1(2)(d) of the Regulation excludes from its scope obligations arising under bills of exchange, cheques and promissory notes, and under other negotiable instruments, to the extent that the obligations under such other negotiable instruments arise out of their negotiable character.[29] Recital 9 adds that this extends to bills of lading, to the extent that the obligations under the bill of lading arise out of its negotiable character. This exclusion reflects the special character of negotiable instruments. Such a document is designed to crystallise a definite obligation in precise terms, with a view to ease of transfer, and the normal choice-of-law rules adopted by the Regulation, which would permit the taking into account of connections not apparent on the face of the instrument, would clearly be unsuitable. Such instruments are, moreover, subject to special conflict rules both in the United Kingdom[30] and in Continental countries.[31] Though the content of these special rules appears far from ideal, very little litigation seems to arise from them.[32]

The exclusion, by Article 1(2)(h) of the Regulation,[33] of the constitution of trusts and the relationship between settlors, trustees and beneficiaries seems designed merely to remove any possible misunderstanding by Continental courts that trusts form part of the law of contract, rather than the law of property or associations.

With regard to insurance, a very limited exclusion is made by Article 1(2)(j) of the Regulation, in respect of insurance contracts arising out of operations carried out by organisations other than undertakings referred to in Article 2 of EC Directive 2002/83 concerning life assurance,[34] the object of which is to provide benefits for employed or self-employed persons belonging to an undertaking or group of undertakings, or to a trade or group of trades, in the event of death or survival or of discontinuance or curtailment of activity, or of sickness related to work or accidents at work. Thus the exclusion is confined to insurance contracts whereby an insurer who is not established within the European Union provides death, unemployment or sickness benefits in connection with particular employers or trades. Apart from this, insurance contracts are within the scope of the Regulation, and in many cases are regulated specifically by Article 7.[35] In contrast, under the Rome Convention 1980, an important exclusion was made by Article 1(3) and (4) in respect of contracts of insurance (other than reinsurance) covering risks situated within the European Community. Instead, the matter was

---

arbitration dealing with a dispute as to whether assets outside an estate should be brought into account in order that one party should gain his fair share does not fall within the exclusion from the Regulation of contracts relating to wills and succession.

[29]   This echoes Article 1(2)(c) of the Rome Convention 1980.

[30]   See the Bills of Exchange Act 1882, s 72.

[31]   See the Geneva Conventions of 7th June 1930 and 19th March 1931, for the Settlement of Certain Conflicts of Laws in connection with (respectively) Bills of Exchange or Cheques. See also Mayer and Heuzé, at para 691.

[32]   Cf. *European Capital Trade Finance Ltd v Antenna Hungaria*, 23rd February 1996 (CA), where the instrument counted as a promissory note under the English, but not the Geneva, definition.

[33]   This echoes Article 1(2)(g) of the Rome Convention 1980.

[34]   [2002] OJ L345/1; as last amended by Directive 2008/19, [2008] OJ L76/44.

[35]   On insurance, see pp. 360–68 below.

regulated by EC Directive 88/357[36] in the case of non-life insurance, and by EC Directive 2002/83[37] in the case of life insurance.

### Excluded terms

Whatever the type of contract, Article 1(2)(e) of the Rome I Regulation[38] excludes the validity and interpretation of arbitration or jurisdiction clauses from its scope.[39] The apparent rationale is that such questions are to a large extent dealt with by Article 23 of the Brussels I Regulation, or by Articles II and V of the New York Convention of 1958 on the Recognition and Enforcement of Foreign Arbitral Awards. Even so, there seems little reason for excluding the Rome I Regulation from questions not dealt with by the other measures; for example, the effect of fraud or mistake on the validity of a jurisdiction clause. Thus when the Regulation is reviewed, it might be useful to substitute for the exclusion contained in Article 1(2)(e) a provision that the Rome I Regulation is not to prejudice the operation of the New York Convention 1958 in relation to arbitration agreements, nor that of EC Regulation 44/2001 in relation to agreements on the choice of a court or courts. In any event, the exclusion does not extend to the substantive contract which contains an arbitration or jurisdiction clause. Nor does it prevent such a clause from being taken into account in determining the proper law of the substantive contract under Articles 3 and 4 of the Regulation.[40]

### Excluded issues

Other exclusions relate to particular issues, rather than types of transaction or clause. Article 1(2)(a) of the Regulation refers to questions involving the status or legal capacity of individuals, subject to a saving for the rule in favour of capacity specified by Article 13.[41]

Article 1(2)(f) of the Regulation refers to questions governed by company law, such as the creation (by registration or otherwise), legal capacity, internal organisation or winding-up of companies and other bodies (corporate or unincorporated), and the personal liability of officers and members as such for the obligations of a company or body.[42] This exclusion extends to any liability of a director which arises by virtue of his office, with the result that in England such liabilities are governed by the law of the place of incorporation.[43] Article 1(2)(g) of the Regulation[44] refers to the question whether an agent is able to bind a principal, or an organ to bind a company or other body (corporate or unincorporated), to a third party.[45]

---

36   [1988] OJ L172.
37   [2002] OJ L345.
38   This echoes Article 1(2)(d) of the Rome Convention 1980.
39   See *Akai v People's Insurance* [1998] 1 Lloyd's Rep 90 (Thomas J); *OT Africa Line v Magic Sportswear Corp* [2005] 2 Lloyd's Rep 170 (CA); and *Tamil Nadu Electricity Board v St-CMS Electric Company* [2007] EWHC 1713 (Comm) (Cooke J). See also *Soc Château Tour Saint Christophe v Aström*, decided by the French Court of Cassation on 16th February 1999, invalidating under French law a clause requiring arbitration in Sweden, contained in a contract of employment to be performed in France.
40   See the Giuliano and Lagarde Report at p. 12; and pp. 306–7 below.
41   These provisions echo Articles 1(2)(a) and 11 of the Rome Convention 1980. See pp. 328–9 below.
42   This echoes Article 1(2)(e) of the Convention.
43   See *Base Metal Trading Ltd v Shamurin* [2005] 1 All ER (Comm) 17 (CA).
44   This echoes Article 1(2)(f) of the Convention.
45   See pp. 329–31 below.

In the Regulation, a new exclusion specified by Article 1(2)(i) refers to obligations arising out of dealings prior to the conclusion of a contract. Recital 10 explains that these are covered by Article 12 of the Rome II Regulation.[46]

Article 1(3) of the Regulation refers to evidence and procedure.[47] This is explicitly made subject to Article 18 (on the burden of proof, presumptions, and modes of proof), and must be read restrictively in the light of Article 12 (which subjects various issues, such as the assessment of damages, to the law which governs the contract).[48] One effect of the exclusion is that the Regulation does not affect rules as to the burden of pleading and proving the content of the applicable foreign law; such as the English rule that the possible applicability of foreign law must be ignored unless a party invokes a foreign rule by appropriate pleading and proof.

These exclusions reflect the conception that, even where there is a contract involved, the issues in question should not be regarded as contractual for choice-of-law purposes. But an issue which is excluded from the scope of the Regulation may nonetheless be subjected by the conflict rules of the forum Member State to the law which governs a contract, and such a reference must now be understood as a reference to the proper law of the contract, ascertained in accordance with the Regulation.[49]

## Relationship with Other EU Measures

The relationship of the Rome I Regulation with other European Union legislation is addressed by Article 23. This specifies that, with the exception of Article 7 (on insurance), the Regulation is not to prejudice the application of provisions of European Union law which, in relation to particular matters, lay down conflict rules relating to contractual obligations.[50] Recital 40 explains that a situation where conflict rules are dispersed among several instruments and where there are differences between those rules should be avoided, but that the Regulation should not exclude the possibility of inclusion of conflict rules relating to contractual obligations in provisions of European Union law with regard to particular matters.

Accordingly, the Rome I Regulation gives way to the explicit provisions on choice of law contained in Directive 93/13, on unfair terms in consumer contracts;[51] Directives 94/47, 97/7, 1999/44 and 2002/65, dealing with various other substantive aspects of consumer protection;[52] and Directive 96/71, on the posting of workers in the framework of the provision of services.[53] In contrast, the exception made by Article 23 of the Rome I Regulation for Article 7 thereof,

---

[46] See pp. 333–5 and Chapter 15 below.

[47] This echoes 1(2)(h) of the Convention.

[48] These provisions echo Article 10 and 14 of the Convention. See pp. 331–2 below.

[49] See *Marubeni v Mongolian Government (No 1)* [2002] 2 All ER (Comm) 873 (Aikens J).

[50] Similarly, Article 20 of the Rome Convention 1980 specified that the Convention did not affect the application of provisions which, in relation to particular matters, laid down choice-of-law rules relating to contractual obligations, and which were or would be contained in acts of EC institutions, or in national laws harmonised in implementation of such acts.

[51] [1993] OJ L95/29. See pp. 354–5 below.

[52] See [1994] OJ L280/83; [1997] OJ L144/19; [1999] OJ L171/12; and [2002] OJ L271/16; and pp. 354–5 below.

[53] [1997] OJ L18/1. See also per Bot AG in Case C-346/06: *Rüffert v Land Niedersachsen* [2008] ECR I-1989, at para 12; and p. 360 below.

which deals with insurance, ensures that the Rome I Regulation (unlike the Rome Convention 1980) replaces the choice-of-law provisions contained in Directive 88/357,[54] on non-life insurance, and Directive 2002/83,[55] on life insurance.

Moreover, an EU measure which explicitly lays down only a harmonised mandatory rule of substantive law may impliedly create a choice-of-law rule determining its scope, so as to override the Rome II Regulation. Thus, in *Ingmar v Eaton Leonard*,[56] the European Court ruled that Articles 17 and 18 of Directive 86/653, on self-employed commercial agents,[57] which guarantee certain rights to commercial agents after termination of agency contracts, are applicable where the commercial agent carried on his activity in a Member State, even if the principal is established in a non-member country and a clause of the contract stipulates that the contract is to be governed by the law of that country.

Recital 40 to the Rome I Regulation also declares that the Regulation should not prejudice the application of other instruments laying down provisions designed to contribute to the proper functioning of the internal market, insofar as they cannot be applied in conjunction with the law designated by the rules of the Regulation. It explains that the application of provisions of the applicable law designated by the rules of the Regulation should not restrict the free movement of goods and services as regulated by Community instruments, such as Directive 2000/31 on Electronic Commerce.[58] But in view of Recital 23 and Articles 1(4) and 3(3) of Directive 2000/31, it is difficult to see how that Directive can have any relevance to questions of private international law. Similarly, in view of Recital 90 and Articles 3(2) and 17(15) of Directive 2006/123 on services in the internal market,[59] it is difficult to see how that Directive can have any relevance to questions of private international law.[60]

### Relationship with Other International Conventions

In the Rome I Regulation, Articles 25 and 26 address the relationship of the Regulation with existing international conventions. By Article 25(1), the Regulation is not to prejudice the application of international conventions to which one or more Member States are parties at the time when the Regulation is adopted and which lay down conflict rules relating to contractual obligations. But, by Article 25(2), as between Member States, the Regulation takes precedence over conventions concluded exclusively between two or more of them, insofar as such conventions concern matters governed by the Regulation.

In addition, Article 26(1) requires Member States to notify the Commission by 17th June 2009 of the conventions referred to in Article 25(1). After that date, Member States are to notify the Commission of all denunciations of such conventions. By Article 26(2), the Commission is to publish in the Official Journal of the European Union, within six months of

---

[54]   [1988] OJ L172. See pp. 360–68 below.
[55]   [2002] OJ L345. See pp. 360–68 below.
[56]   Case C-381/98, [2000] ECR I-9305.
[57]   [1986] OJ L382/17.
[58]   [2000] OJ L178/1.
[59]   [2006] OJ L376/36.
[60]   See, further, pp. 374–5 below.

receipt of the relevant notifications, a list of the said conventions, and the said denunciations. Recital 41 explains that this is designed to improve accessibility.

In contrast, subject to procedural safeguards, the Rome Convention gave way to other international conventions, even where a Member State subsequently became a party to the other convention.[61] Under the Regulation, the saving by Article 25 is limited to conventions to which a Member State is already a party at its adoption. As regards future conventions, Recital 42 merely envisages that the Commission will make a proposal to the European Parliament and the Council concerning the procedures and conditions according to which Member States would be entitled to negotiate and conclude, on their own behalf, agreements with third countries in individual and exceptional cases, concerning sectoral matters, and containing provisions on the law applicable to contractual obligations. This has led to the adoption of EC Regulation 662/2009.[62]

Existing multilateral conventions which deal principally with choice of law in the contractual sphere include the Hague Convention of 15th June 1955 on the Law Applicable to International Sales of Goods; and the Hague Convention of 14th March 1978 on the Law Applicable to Agency. The 1955 Convention is now in force between France, Italy, Denmark, Sweden, Finland, Norway, Switzerland, and Niger (but not the United Kingdom); and the 1978 Convention is now in force between France, the Netherlands, Portugal, and Argentina (but not the United Kingdom).[63] Since, in both cases, the parties include external countries, the saving specified by Article 25(1) of the Regulation is operative, and not the exception specified by Article 25(2).

Other international conventions harmonise substantive rules on particular types of contract, and specify the transnational scope of the substantive rules in question, so as to override the normal choice-of-law rules. Sometimes poor drafting of such provisions on territorial scope has caused problems. Thus the (British) Carriage by Sea Act 1924, implementing the Hague Rules on bills of lading, merely made the Rules applicable to shipments from the United Kingdom, with the result that they could be avoided, as regards English courts, by choosing English law to govern a shipment from another Contracting State.[64] But now the (British) Carriage by Sea Act 1971, implementing the Hague-Visby Rules, has made them applicable to shipments from either the United Kingdom or another Contracting State, with the result that in the case of such a shipment they override a choice of a foreign proper law.[65]

Also noteworthy is Article VIII(2)(b) of the International Monetary Fund Agreement signed at Bretton Woods in 1944, by which exchange contracts which involve the currency of an IMF Member State and which contravene exchange control regulations of that State, maintained or imposed consistently with the IMF Agreement, are rendered unenforceable in other Member States.[66] Since the breakdown of the system of fixed parities in the early

---

[61] See Articles 21, 23 and 24.

[62] [2009] OJ L200/25. See pp. 296–7 below.

[63] After joining the Hague Conference, the European Community has concluded that it should not adopt the 1978 Convention; see JUSTCIV 235, 6th November 2008.

[64] See *Vita Food Products v Unus Shipping* [1939] AC 277, overruling *The Torni* [1932] P 78.

[65] See *The Hollandia* [1983] 1 AC 565. Cf. *Vimar Seguros Y Reaseguros v M/V Sky Reefer* 515 US 528 (1995).

[66] This provision is implemented in the United Kingdom by the Bretton Woods Agreements Act 1945 and the Bretton Woods Agreements Order 1946 (SR&O 1946/36).

1970s, Article VIII(2)(b) has been construed narrowly. Thus a contract counts as an exchange contract only when it provides for the exchange of one currency for another, and not (for example) for the sale of goods, or insofar as it is a monetary transaction in disguise.[67]

## The Regulation on External Agreements relating to Obligations

EC Regulation 662/2009, establishing a procedure for the negotiation and conclusion of agreements between Member States and third countries on particular matters concerning the law applicable to contractual and non-contractual obligations, was adopted by the Parliament and Council on 13th July 2009.[68] It will remain in force at least until August 2020.[69]

As Article 1(1) explains, Regulation 662/2009 establishes a procedure by which, under certain conditions, the EC Commission may authorise a Member State to amend an existing agreement with a non-member country, or to negotiate and conclude a new agreement with a non-member country. By Article 1(2), the Regulation applies to agreements concerning particular matters falling, entirely or partly, within the scope of the Rome I Regulation and the Rome II Regulation. By Recital 9 and Articles 1(3) and 4(2), Regulation 662/2009 does not apply where the European Union has already concluded an agreement with the non-member country concerned on the same subject-matter (in the sense that the agreements regulate in substance the same specific legal issues); nor where a relevant negotiating mandate with a view to concluding a European Union agreement with the non-member country concerned is specifically envisaged within the next 24 months.[70]

By Article 2(1)(a), Regulation 662/2009 applies primarily to bilateral agreements between a Member State and a non-member country. By Article 2(1)(b), it also extends to a regional agreement between a limited number of Member States and of non-member countries which are neighbours of Member States, which is intended to address local situations and which is not open for accession to other States.[71]

Several conditions are imposed by Articles 4 and 8 of the Regulation before an authorisation may be granted by the Commission to the Member State, initially to open formal negotiations, and eventually to conclude a negotiated agreement. By Article 4(2)(a), at the initial stage the Member State concerned must have provided information showing that it has a specific interest in concluding the agreement due to economic, geographic, cultural, historical, social or political ties between the Member State and the non-member country concerned. By Article 4(2)(b), at both stages it must appear, on the basis of the information provided by the Member State, that the envisaged agreement would not render European Union law ineffective and would not undermine the proper functioning of the system established by

---

[67]     See *Wilson Smithett & Cope v Terruzzi* [1976] QB 683, and *United City Merchants v Royal Bank of Canada* [1983] 1 AC 168.

[68]     See [2009] OJ L200/25.

[69]     See Articles 13 and 14.

[70]     Such a mandate may emerge from consultations between the Commission and the Member States following the notification by a Member State seeking authorisation under the Regulation. See Recital 12 and Article 11.

[71]     See also Recital 10, which refers to certain regional agreements between a few Member States and a few non-member countries, for example two or three, intended to address local situations and not open for accession to other States.

European Union law. By Article 4(2)(c), at both stages the envisaged agreement must not undermine the object and purpose of the Union's external relations policy as decided by the Union.

By Article 5(1) of the Regulation, the Commission decision authorising a Member State to open formal negotiations on an agreement may be accompanied by negotiating guidelines and a request for the inclusion of particular clauses in the envisaged agreement. In any event, by Article 5(2), the agreement must contain a clause providing for either the denunciation or the direct replacement of the agreement, in the event of the conclusion of a subsequent agreement by the European Union, or the European Union and its Member States, with the same non-member country on the same subject-matter. By Article 7, the Commission may participate as an observer in the negotiations between the Member State and the non-member country. In any event, the Commission must be kept informed of the progress and results throughout the different stages of the negotiations.

By Article 8(1) of the Regulation, before signing a negotiated agreement, the Member State concerned must notify the outcome of the negotiations to the Commission and transmit to it the text of the agreement. By Article 8(2) and (3), if the negotiated agreement fulfils the conditions and requirements referred to in Articles 4(2)(b) and (c) and 5(2), the Commission gives a decision authorising the Member State to conclude the agreement.

**Factual Complexities**

Contracts connected with more than one country may conveniently be referred to as transnational contracts.[72] Determination of the law which governs the substantive rights and obligations of the parties under such contracts is one of the most important issues in private international law. Such contracts constitute the channel for international trade. They give rise to a substantial quantity of litigation. They also present factual patterns of almost infinite complexity and variation. It seems appropriate to identify some of the possible factual complexities.

Typically, the parties to a transnational contract reside or carry on business in different countries from each other. A party may have places of business in several countries, and more than one of these establishments may be involved in the formation or performance of the contract. The contract may have been negotiated by communications between the respective places of business of the parties, and the determination of its place of conclusion may involve the application of rules which differ as between the connected laws to facts which may be in dispute.

The place of performance of a transnational contract is not necessarily the same for all the obligations under the contract. Even if a principal or characteristic obligation is identifiable, its place of performance may not have been specified in the contract, and the implied or default location may differ according to the various connected laws. A contract may also give one of the parties a choice of places at which to perform or require performance.

A transnational contract may contain an express clause specifying the law by which the parties intended that the contract should be governed. It may contain a jurisdiction or arbitration clause, specifying the forum by which disputes connected with the contract were

---

[72]   See per Lord Diplock in *Amin Rasheed v Kuwait Insurance Co* [1984] 1 AC 50.

intended to be determined. It may be expressed in a standard form which had been drafted in contemplation of the law of its country of origin. The chosen law, the specified forum, or the origin of the standard form used, may be that of, or located in, a country otherwise lacking any apparent connection with the contract.

On the substantive issues, one connected law, but not another, may contain rules rendering the contract, or one or more of its terms, invalid, or may even prohibit performance under criminal penalty. One of the connected laws may suffer from insufficient development, and thus offer no ascertainable solution to many of the issues which may arise in relation to contracts of the relevant kind.

### Outline of the Rome I Regulation

The main principle adopted by the Rome I Regulation is that most issues relating to a contract are governed by a single law, which the Regulation refers to as the law governing or applicable to the contract, but which may more conveniently be referred to by the traditional English term, the proper law of the contract. In general, the proper law is determined in accordance with the rules laid down by Articles 3 and 4 of the Regulation. These refer, primarily, to a choice of law expressly agreed on by the parties to the contract; secondarily, to a choice of law impliedly, but clearly, agreed on by the parties; and finally, in default of any such choice, in most cases to the law of the residence of the characteristic performer. These rules on the proper law are designed to respect and support the expectations of the contracting parties, in accordance with the primary objective of contract law; to promote certainty, predictability, commercial convenience, and uniformity of results, regardless of forum; and thus to facilitate the conduct and promote the growth of international trade and commerce.[73]

Savings for public policy or overriding interests are made by Articles 9 and 21 of the Regulation. The extent to which the proper law is applicable to or to some extent displaced in relation to particular issues is clarified by Articles 10–13 and 18. For certain particular types of contract (contracts of carriage, consumer contracts, insurance contracts, and employment contracts), special rules, often designed to protect the weaker party, are laid down by Articles 5–8. Rules dealing with the voluntary assignment of claims, subrogation, recourse between debtors, and set-off, are provided by Articles 14–17.

Renvoi is excluded by Article 20 of the Rome I Regulation, which specifies that the application of the law of any country specified by the Regulation means the application of the rules of law in force in that country, other than its rules of private international law.[74] This echoes Article 15 of the Rome Convention 1980, and accords with the traditional English law.[75] But (unlike the Convention) Articles 7(3) and 20 of the Regulation make an exception, admitting renvoi in the case of insurance of mass risks located within the European Union.[76] However,

---

[73]   On choice-influencing considerations, see the American Law Institute's Restatement, Second, Conflict of Laws, § 6. See also Mayer and Heuzé, at para 695.

[74]   This is so even where the conflict rule of the law which governs the contract refers to another law because it characterises the issue as non-contractual; see *Mobil North Sea* [1997] Rev Crit DIP 702 (French Court of Cassation), and Mayer and Heuzé, at para 706.

[75]   See *Re United Railways of Havana* [1960] Ch 52 (CA), and *Amin Rasheed v Kuwait Insurance Co* [1984] 1 AC 50 (HL). Cf. *American Motorists Ins Co v ARTRA Group* 659 A2d 1295 (Md, 1995).

[76]   The exception echoes Article 7 of Directive 88/357, and Article 32 of Directive 2002/83. See pp. 360–68 below.

the exclusion of renvoi does not in itself prevent respect for self-limiting rules, whereby a proper law confines the application of certain of its substantive rules to contracts entirely domestic to, or connected in some particular way with, its territory. This is exemplified in the context of exemption clauses by the Dutch rule applied in *Sayers v International Drilling*,[77] and the British rules laid down by ss 26 and 27(1) of the Unfair Contract Terms Act 1977. But self-limiting rules may be incompatible with Articles 5(2)–(3), 6, 7(3) and 8 of the Rome I Regulation, which are designed to protect passengers, consumers, employees, and insurance policy-holders.

## THE PROPER LAW – EXPRESS CHOICE

Under the Rome I Regulation (as under the Rome Convention 1980, as well as the traditional English law),[78] the proper law of a contract is determined primarily by reference to any express agreement on the point concluded by the parties to the contract. Only in the absence of any, or any valid, express choice is reference made, secondarily, to an implied choice of the parties, the residence of the characteristic performer, or the closest connection. Thus Article 3(1) of the Regulation specifies that a contract is governed by the law chosen by the parties, and that the choice may be made expressly by the terms of the contract.[79] Recital 11 explains that the parties' freedom to choose the applicable law should be one of the corner-stones of the system of conflict rules in matters of contractual obligations. Since no require-ment of writing or other formality is required for an express choice of law, an oral agreement on the applicable law, concluded in the negotiations leading to the conclusion of a substan-tive contract in writing, will be effective.[80]

Usually any express choice of law is made by a clause contained in the contract as concluded, but Article 3(2) of the Regulation[81] permits an express choice to be agreed on after the conclusion of the contract (so as to replace the proper law resulting from a previous express or implied choice or from the absence of choice).[82] It specifies, however, that such a subsequent choice cannot prejudice the formal validity of the contract, nor adversely affect the rights of third parties (such as guarantors or beneficiaries). Probably a subsequent choice will normally have retroactive effect, unless a contrary intention is indicated.[83] It also seems

---

[77]   [1971] 3 All ER 163 (CA).

[78]   See *R v International Trustee* [1937] AC 500; *Vita Food Products v Unus Shipping* [1939] AC 277; *Co Tunisienne de Navigation v Co d'Armement Maritime* [1971] AC 572; and *Amin Rasheed v Kuwait Insurance Co* [1984] 1 AC 50.

[79]   In full, Article 3(1) of the Regulation provides: 'A contract shall be governed by the law chosen by the parties. The choice shall be made expressly or clearly demonstrated by the terms of the contract or the circumstances of the case. By their choice the parties can select the law applicable to the whole or to part only of the contract.'

[80]   See *Oakley v Ultra Vehicle Design Ltd* [2005] EWHC 872 (Lloyd LJ).

[81]   This echoes Article 3(2) of the Convention.

[82]   In principle Article 3(2) also permits a subsequent implied choice of law, but such a choice seems likely to be very rare. In *Soc Hick Hargreaves v Soc CAC Degremont*, 30th May 2000, the French Court of Cassation held that an implied agreement to change the proper law could not be inferred from a failure to invoke the chosen law in earlier summary proceedings for an expert inquiry.

[83]   See Mayer and Heuzé, at para 716.

consistent with the policy of the Regulation to accept an express choice agreed on before the contract, so that, for example, a long-term distribution agreement could effectively provide that particular contracts of sale subsequently concluded between the same parties pursuant to the agreement should be governed by a specified law, unless the particular contract should otherwise provide.

A very minor restriction on the effect of an express choice is imposed by Article 3(3) of the Regulation, which specifies that where all other elements relevant to the situation at the time of the choice are located in a country other than the country whose law has been chosen, the choice of the parties shall not prejudice the application of provisions of the law of that other country which cannot be derogated from by agreement. Recital 15 explains that this rule should apply whether or not the choice of law was accompanied by a choice of court or tribunal, and that no substantial change is intended as compared with Article 3(3) of the Rome Convention. Thus where parties resident in France negotiate and contract in France for performance exclusively in France, but include a clause providing for English jurisdiction and English law, the English court will have to give effect to all the mandatory rules contained in French internal law; but, subject to that, the choice of English law will be effective. It is noteworthy that Article 3(3) applies however minimal the policy underlying the relevant mandatory rule may be; as in the case of the English doctrine of consideration. But it may be doubted whether a case caught by Article 3(3) will arise more often than a solar eclipse visible in London.

Article 3(4) of the Regulation extends the principle underlying Article 3(3) to mandatory provisions of Community law.[84] By Article 3(4), where all other elements relevant to the situation at the time of the choice are located in one or more Member States, the parties' choice of a law other than the law of a Member State shall not prejudice the application of provisions of Community law, where appropriate as implemented in the Member State of the forum, which cannot be derogated from by agreement.

The narrow scope of Article 3(3) was confirmed by the decision of Cooke J in *Caterpillar Financial Services v SNC Passion*,[85] which involved a contract of loan between an American lender and a French borrower, whereby finance was provided for the construction of a vessel in Singapore, and which contained a clause choosing English law as the proper law. In holding that Article 3(3) did not make French mandatory rules applicable to this contract, he emphasised that Article 3(1) gives parties freedom to choose the law applicable to the agreement which they are making. Article 3(3) provides an exception to this in cases where the agreement is entirely domestic in content, so that the choice of a foreign law is designed to circumvent the mandatory rules of the country which alone is concerned with the transaction. If, however, there are other elements, apart from the choice of law and jurisdiction clause, which are relevant to the situation at the time of concluding the agreement and which are connected with other countries, the agreement is not a domestic agreement of concern only to one country, and Article 3(3) does not apply. Moreover, Article 3(3) refers to elements which are relevant to the *situation*, which is a wider concept than elements which are relevant to the *contract*, and a much wider concept than elements which are relevant to the mandatory rules of the law of any one country.

---

[84]   In the Rome Convention 1980, there was no explicit provision which corresponds to Article 3(4) of the Regulation.
[85]   [2004] 2 Lloyd's Rep 99.

The very limited scope of the exception specified by Article 3(3) reinforces the clear intention evinced by Article 3(1) that in all other cases an express choice of law should be effective. Thus the Regulation requires an express choice to be respected even if the chosen law has no other connection with the contract,[86] and even if the choice was made for the purpose of avoiding mandatory rules contained in the law of the country which is most closely connected with the contract, and which would in the absence of express or implied choice have been the proper law under Article 4. The rationale for the freedom to choose an unconnected law is commercial convenience.[87] The substantive rules contained in the chosen law may be well developed and familiar to the parties, while those of all the connected laws may be obscure or a matter for speculation. Parties may find it convenient to use the same law for associated transactions (such as a chain of sales of the same goods), and the connection with the other transactions may not be immediately apparent from the contract. Moreover, it would have been senseless to introduce the French doctrine of evasion of law in a context where the primary choice-of-law rule is based on intention, and the test of closest connection has only a supplementary role, to provide a default solution where no intention is apparent.[88] Thus the rule laid down by s 27(2)(a) of the (British) Unfair Contract Terms Act 1977, whereby the controls imposed by the Act on the validity of exemption clauses remain applicable despite a contractual term choosing a foreign law, where the term was imposed wholly or mainly for the purpose of enabling the party imposing it to evade the operation of the Act, seems incompatible with the Regulation. On the other hand, an expressly chosen law will apply even where its effect is to invalidate the contract.[89]

It is clear that under the Rome I Regulation (as under the Rome Convention 1980) the proper law, whether chosen by the parties or determined by reference to the characteristic performance or the closest connection, must be the law of a country, in the sense of a territory having its own legal rules on contracts.[90] Thus it cannot be the general principles of law

---

[86] For a similar approach under traditional English law, see *Vita Food Products v Unus Shipping* [1939] AC 277, where the Privy Council (on appeal from Nova Scotia) upheld an express choice of English law in a bill-of-lading contract for the carriage of herrings from Newfoundland to New York in a Nova Scotian ship. See also *Akai v People's Insurance* [1998] 1 Lloyd's Rep 90 (Thomas J); and Mayer and Heuzé, at para 705.

[87] See *OT Africa Line v Magic Sportswear Corp* [2005] 2 Lloyd's Rep 170 (CA), where an express choice of English law was contained in a bill of lading issued by the Ontario office of an English shipowner to a Delaware shipper in respect of a voyage from New York to Liberia.

[88] Cf Mayer and Heuzé, at paras 700 and 705, who accept with regret that the Regulation excludes the French doctrine of evasion, and thus that it does not enable a court to disregard a choice of an unconnected law made for the purpose of evading a mandatory rule which is common to all the connected laws.

[89] See *Fraser v Buckle* [1996] 1 IR 1, where the Irish Supreme Court gave effect to an express choice of English law in a contract between English heir-locators and an Irish resident, under which the heir-locators pursued the client's claim to an inheritance in New Jersey in return for a share in the proceeds. But the contract was void for champerty under English, Irish and New Jersey laws. See also *The Evia Luck* [1992] 2 AC 152; *Duarte v Black & Decker* [2008] 1 All ER (Comm) 401 (Field J); and Mayer and Heuzé, at para 709.

[90] See Articles 1(1), 2, 4 and 22 of the Regulation; Articles 1(1), 2, 4 and 19 of the Convention; *Shamil Bank of Bahrain v Beximco Pharmaceuticals* [2004] 2 Lloyd's Rep 1 (CA); *Halpern v Halpern* [2007] 2 All ER (Comm) 330 (CA); Dicey, Morris and Collins, *The Conflict of Laws*, 14th edition (Sweet & Maxwell, 2006), at para 32-081; Mayer and Heuzé, *Droit International Privé*, 9th edition

recognised by civilised nations, or the Unidroit Principles of International Commercial Contracts 2004,[91] or European Union law,[92] or public international law, or Islamic law (as a generic religious law, independent of its adoption and interpretation in any particular territory).[93]

In the EC Commission's Proposal of 15th December 2005,[94] Article 3(2) would have enabled the parties to choose as the applicable law the principles and rules of the substantive law of contract recognised internationally or in the Community. But this provision was deleted from the Regulation as adopted. Instead Recital 12 to the Regulation merely declares that the Regulation does not preclude parties from incorporating by reference into their contract a non-State body of law or an international convention. But it is clear that such an incorporation would merely introduce into the contract terms whose validity and effect would be governed by the proper law, which would still be that of a territorial unit. Recital 13 adds that, if the Community were to adopt, in an appropriate legal instrument, rules of substantive contract law, including standard terms and conditions, a provision of the instrument could enable parties to choose to apply those rules.

It must be borne in mind, however, that the conflict rules laid down by the Rome I Regulation are not necessarily applicable in arbitration proceedings, for it is open to the law of the country in which an arbitration is seated to enable the parties to empower the arbitrator to decide disputes in accordance with non-legal considerations. Such a power is indeed accorded by s 46 of the (English) Arbitration Act 1996, which requires an arbitral tribunal seated in England to decide a dispute in accordance with the internal law chosen by the parties as applicable to the substance of the dispute; or if the parties so agree, in accordance with such other considerations as are agreed by them or determined by the tribunal; or if there is no such choice or agreement, in accordance with the law determined by the conflict rules which the tribunal considers applicable.[95] Thus an English court will stay proceedings brought in breach of an arbitration clause, even though some set of principles other than the law of a particular country has been chosen as the applicable law to govern the disputes, and will enforce an award made by arbitrators applying any considerations agreed between the parties.[96] Similarly, in France, the parties may choose to instruct an arbitrator not to apply any particular law.[97]

---

(Montchrestien, 2007), at paras 701–03; and the decision of the French Court of Cassation in *Messageries Maritimes* [1950] Rev Crit DIP 609.

[91]   See www.unidroit.org/english/principles/contracts/main.htm (last visited on 22nd July 2008).

[92]   See Articles 272 and 340(1) of the Treaty on the Functioning of the European Union, whereby a contract between the European Union and a private person is governed by the national law which constitutes its proper law, even when the dispute comes before the European Court pursuant to a jurisdiction clause.

[93]   See *Shamil Bank of Bahrain v Beximco Pharmaceuticals* [2004] 2 Lloyd's Rep 1 (CA); *Halpern v Halpern* [2007] 2 All ER (Comm) 330 (CA); and *Musawi v RE International (UK) Ltd* [2008] 1 All ER (Comm) 607 (David Richards J).

[94]   See COM(2005) 650 final.

[95]   See also, on the enforcement of foreign arbitral awards under the New York Convention (1958), *Deutsche Schachtbau- und Tiefbohrgesellschaft v Ras Al Khaimah National Oil Co* [1990] AC 295.

[96]   See *Halpern v Halpern* [2007] 2 All ER (Comm) 330 (CA), at paras 37–8; and *Musawi v RE International (UK) Ltd* [2008] 1 All ER (Comm) 607, where David Richards J enforced an English award which, as required by the arbitration agreement, had determined the dispute in accordance with Shia Sharia law.

[97]   See Mayer and Heuzé, at paras 702 and 704.

It also seems clear that under the Rome I Regulation parties are limited, in choosing the proper law, to the laws of countries which exist at the time of the choice. On the other hand, they cannot limit their choice to the content of a law as it exists at the time of contracting or on some other specified date, but must accept subsequent changes in its substantive rules which the chosen law makes applicable to existing contracts, except insofar as such retroactive effects may infringe a stringent public policy of the forum.[98] Thus parties cannot validly choose ancient Roman law, as disclosed in Justinian's Digest. Nor can they effectively choose French law as it stands at the date of contracting. Probably, in the last-mentioned case, the reference to the date will be disregarded, and the clause will then operate as a normal choice of French law.[99]

Moreover, since Article 3 of the Regulation refers to a choice *by the parties*, it seems probable that the parties cannot confer on one of them a unilateral power subsequently to designate the proper law (whether directly or indirectly, for example by fixing the location of a relevant factor, such as the seat of an arbitration proceeding).[100] On the other hand, there seems no reason why parties should not be able to subject the identity of the proper law to the resolution of a contingency over which none of the parties has control.[101] Thus, for example, a contract of loan could validly specify that it is governed by Swiss law, but that if Swiss law should be altered so as to impose restrictions on the chargeable rate of interest, then German law should apply instead.

Perhaps the greatest practical problem in connection with express choice concerns clauses whose meaning is less than clear. Like any contractual term, a choice-of-law clause may be void for uncertainty. This result will arise if the forum finds itself unable to ascribe to the clause any definite meaning identifying a particular law as the proper law. In such a case, the clause will probably have the effect under the Regulation of eliminating the possibility of an implied choice, and making operative the tests of the characteristic performer's residence and the closest connection under Article 4. It is now clear from the decision of the English Court of Appeal in *Centrax v Citibank*[102] that under the Regulation the forum applies the principles of contractual interpretation contained in its own internal law in determining the meaning (or lack of any discernible meaning) of an ambiguous choice-of-law clause.

---

[98]  See *R v International Trustee* [1937] AC 500, where the House of Lords gave effect to American legislation adopted in 1933, invalidating gold clauses contained in contracts concluded in 1917; Dicey, Morris and Collins, 14th edition, at para 32-082; and Mayer and Heuzé, at para 708.

[99]  See also Mayer and Heuzé, at para 708, who accept that this would normally be the result, but envisage that in exceptional circumstances a stabilisation provision could prevent the clause from operating as a valid choice of the proper law.

[100]  Similarly, a unilateral option was not permissible under the traditional English law. See *The Armar* [1981] 1 WLR 207 (CA); *The Iran Vojdan* [1984] 2 Lloyd's Rep 380 (Bingham J); *The Stolt Marmaro* [1985] 2 Lloyd's Rep 428 (CA); *The Star Texas* [1993] 2 Lloyd's Rep 445 (CA); *Sonatrach Petroleum Corp v Ferrell International Ltd* [2002] 1 All ER (Comm) 627 (Colman J); *Lexington Insurance v AGF Insurance* [2009] UKHL 40 (HL); and Dicey, Morris and Collins, at para 32-086. Cf. *Du Pont de Nemours v Agnew* [1987] 2 Lloyd's Rep 585 (CA); *King v Brandywine Reinsurance Co* [2004] Lloyd's Rep. IR 554 (Colman J), reversed [2005] 1 Lloyd's Rep 655 (CA); and Dicey, Morris and Collins, at para 32-087.

[101]  See *The Mariannina* [1983] 1 Lloyd's Rep 12 (CA); *CGU International Insurance v Szabo* [2002] 1 All ER (Comm) 83 (Toulson J); and Dicey, Morris and Collins, at para 32-087.

[102]  [1999] 1 All ER (Comm) 557 (CA).

The problem of ambiguity and possible uncertainty is illustrated by the decision of the House of Lords under the traditional English law in *Co Tunisienne de Navigation v Co d'Armement Maritime*,[103] which involved a tonnage contract between a French carrier and a Tunisian shipper for the carriage of a quantity of oil between two Tunisian ports by several voyages over a period of months in ships owned, controlled or chartered by the carrier. The contract was expressed on a standard form designed for a voyage charterparty, and contained a clause choosing the law of the flag of the vessel carrying the goods. In the House of Lords, the majority (which included Lord Diplock), relying on a finding that the parties contemplated that the carrier would, at least primarily, use its own ships, which all flew the French flag, managed to construe the choice-of-law clause as referring to the law of the flag of the vessels owned by the carrier, and thus to French law. The minority (which included Lord Wilberforce) felt unable to interpret or rewrite the clause in this way, and concluded that it was void for uncertainty.

The last phrase of Article 3(1) of the Regulation specifies that by their choice the parties can select the law applicable to the whole or to part only of the contract.[104] Thus, perhaps regrettably, the Regulation permits the parties to choose different proper laws for different parts of a contract.[105] But it seems proper to require that the parts should be logically severable because they relate to distinct transactions. Thus where a contract provides both for a sale of goods and the supply of technical assistance, severance will be possible between the sale and the assistance. On the other hand, severance by reference to issues or terms (for example, as between the validity and effect of exclusion clauses, and all other issues relating to the contract) should not be permitted.[106] In any event, there must be a single law which governs issues such as frustration which affect the contract as a whole.[107]

This approach to severance by party choice accords with that adopted by the European Court in *Intercontainer Interfrigo v Balkenende Oosthuizen*[108] to severance in the absence of party choice under Article 4 of the Rome Convention 1980. Severance in the absence of party choice is no longer possible under Article 4 of the Rome I Regulation, but in the context of Article 4 of the Rome Convention 1980 the European Court ruled that a part of a contract may be governed by a law other than that applied to the rest of the contract only where the object of that part is independent in relation to the purpose of the rest of the contract. Even then, each part of a contract must be made subject to one single law; and, in particular, the rules relating to the prescription of a right must fall under the same legal system as that applied to the corresponding obligation.

That severance is usually inadvisable is apparent from the decision of the English Court of Appeal in *Centrax v Citibank*,[109] which involved a contract for electronic payment services.

---

103   [1971] AC 572.

104   This echoes the last phrase of Article 3(1) of the Convention.

105   Such scission of the proper law must be distinguished from the incorporation by express reference of the terms of an enactment from one country into a contract governed by the law of another country, so as to remain unaffected by the subsequent repeal or amendment of the enactment in its country of origin. As to this practice, see Dicey, Morris and Collins, at paras 32-088 to 32-090.

106   See Mayer and Heuzé, at para 710.

107   See *Centrax v Citibank* [1999] 1 All ER (Comm) 557 (CA); and Dicey, Morris and Collins, at paras 32-050 to 32-053.

108   Case C-133/08, [2010] All ER (EC) 1.

109   [1999] 1 All ER (Comm) 557 (CA). See also *The Amazonia*, [1990] 1 Lloyd's Rep 236 (CA).

The clause read: 'This Agreement and all documents, agreements and instruments related to this Agreement shall be governed by and interpreted according to the laws of the State of New York, United States of America, provided that any action or dispute between the parties regarding any Payment Instrument shall be governed by and interpreted according to the laws of the country or state in which the Drawee of such Payment Instrument is located'. The customer sued the bank, complaining that the bank had wrongfully debited the customer's account in respect of cheques forged by an employee of the customer. The bank was based in New York, but the cheques were drawn on its London branch, and the customer sought to invoke the (English) Unfair Contract Terms Act 1977, so as to invalidate terms of the contract on which the bank was relying in defence. The Court of Appeal applied English principles of construction to the choice-of-law clause, and by a majority concluded that where, as in the present action, the dispute raised the interpretation or effect of the contract and went beyond the validity and effect of the payment instrument, the law of New York was to be applied.

Moreover, as the English Court of Appeal recognised in *Shamil Bank of Bahrain v Beximco Pharmaceuticals*,[110] it is not open to parties to designate two different laws as simultaneously governing the whole contract. Thus where a financing agreement specified that 'subject to the principles of Glorious Sharia'a, this agreement shall be governed by and construed in accordance with the laws of England,' the reference to Islamic law was construed as merely decorative and therefore ignored. Similarly in *Halpern v Halpern*,[111] the Court of Appeal ruled that an express choice of a religious law would not render the contract unenforceable, but would be ignored for the purposes of identifying the proper law. It also indicated that severance of the proper law in respect of part of a contract is possible only with regard to the interpretation of the severed part, and that matters such as mistake or repudiation, which affect the contract as a whole, are governed by the proper law of the contract as a whole.

By Article 3(5) of the Regulation,[112] the existence and validity of the consent of the parties to a choice-of-law clause must be determined in accordance with the same provisions, contained in Articles 10, 11 and 13, as apply to their consent to other contractual terms. This applies to such issues as offer and acceptance; misrepresentation or undue pressure;[113] formal validity; and individual capacity.

## THE PROPER LAW – IMPLIED CHOICE

In the absence of an express choice, Article 3 of the Rome I Regulation directs the court to consider next whether an implied choice of law by the parties can be discovered. It is sufficient under Article 3(1) that the parties' choice, though not expressed in the contract, is 'clearly demonstrated by the terms of the contract or the circumstances of the case'. This wording differs slightly from Article 3(1) of the Rome Convention 1980, which required the

---

[110]  [2004] 2 Lloyd's Rep 1 (CA).
[111]  [2007] 2 All ER (Comm) 330 (CA).
[112]  This echoes Article 3(4) of the Convention.
[113]  On economic pressure, such as the blacking of a vessel in the context of a labour dispute, see *The Rickmers Tianjin* AD 2007 No 2, decided by the Swedish Labour Court, and discussed by Carolina Saf, (2007) 9 Swiss Yearbook of Private International Law 481.

choice to be 'demonstrated with reasonable certainty by the terms of the contract or the circumstances of the case'.[114] It is possible that the verbal alteration may be designed to inhibit slightly the discovery of an implied choice.

The Regulation (like the Convention) agrees with the traditional English law in its post-war phase[115] in adopting a fairly restrictive approach to the discovery of an implied choice. Some factor which supplies a clear indication in favour of a particular law, as being evidently much more suitable to achieve the purposes of the parties in entering into the contract, is necessary. Otherwise the court should accept that no choice, express or implied, has been made by the parties, and should proceed to apply the default rules laid down by Article 4.[116]

The factors which may amount to a clear indication, warranting the recognition of an implied choice, cannot be definitively listed, but it is in principle unlikely that a sufficiently strong indication will have escaped attention up to the present date. English case-law prior to the Convention indicates that the clearest possible indication arises where, as matters stand at the time of contracting, one connected law upholds the validity of the contract and all its terms, while another connected law would have total or partial invalidating effect.[117] In such circumstances, a choice of the validating law is necessary to give effect to the contract as concluded. A similar situation arises where one connected law is familiar with the relevant type of contract, and contains well-established detailed rules for interpreting and supplementing its express terms, while the content of another connected law in relation to such contracts, as matters stand at the time of contracting, is a matter for the broadest speculation.[118] In such circumstances, a choice of the adequately developed law is necessary to give sufficient certainty to the contract. Although these factors of validation or adequate supplementary content have not been considered by English courts since the entry into force of the Rome Convention, there is no reason to suppose that the Convention or the Regulation has altered the position in these respects.

Another factor which usually amounts to a clear indication of an implied choice of law by the parties is the inclusion in the contract of a jurisdiction clause, specifying the court which will be competent to hear disputes relating to the contract. Recital 12 of the Regulation recognises cautiously that an agreement between the parties to confer on one or more courts or tribunals of a Member State exclusive jurisdiction to determine disputes under the contract should be one of the factors to be taken into account in determining whether a choice of law has been clearly demonstrated.[119] The English case-law accepts, much more emphatically,

---

[114]    In the French text, both the Regulation and the Convention require a choice which results 'de façon certaine des dispositions du contrat ou des circonstances de la cause'.

[115]    See especially *Bonython v Australia* [1951] AC 201; *Re United Railways of Havana* [1961] AC 1007; and *Amin Rasheed v Kuwait Insurance Co* [1984] 1 AC 50.

[116]    Cf. *Zebrarise Ltd v de Nieffe* [2005] 1 Lloyd's Rep 154, where Judge Havelock-Allan QC inferred under common law principles a choice of English law in respect of a loan agreed on in Switzerland by an English solicitor resident in Belgium to an English resident in connection with a purchase of Irish land.

[117]    See *Peninsular Line v Shand* (1865) 16 ER 103; *Re Missouri Steamship Co* (1889) 42 ChD 321; *Hamlyn v Talisker Distillery* [1894] AC 202; *Spurrier v La Cloche* [1902] AC 445; *Sayers v International Drilling* [1971] 3 All ER 163; *Coast Lines v Hudig & Veder* [1972] 2 QB 34; and *Co Tunisienne de Navigation v Co d'Armement Maritime* [1971] AC 572, per Lord Wilberforce at 598.

[118]    See *Amin Rasheed v Kuwait Insurance Co* [1984] 1 AC 50.

[119]    It may be considered disappointing that this is the only provision in the Regulation which offers any explicit guidance as to the factors from which an implied choice may properly be discovered.

that a jurisdiction clause normally implies a choice of the substantive law of the country whose court is chosen.[120] The same applies to an arbitration clause if the arbitral tribunal designated is one which, as is generally known, will usually apply a particular substantive law.[121] The rationale is that dispute resolution is simplified if the chosen forum applies the law with which it is most familiar, and (where relevant) that a choice of a neutral forum (in a country where neither party is resident) is designed also to render applicable a neutral law. But a jurisdiction or arbitration clause will be outweighed by the factor of validity, where the law of the chosen forum would invalidate a contract which would be valid under another connected law.[122]

In some circumstances, the use of a standard form not containing a forum clause may be an important indication in favour of an implied choice of the law of the country of origin of the form, at least if one of the parties is resident in that country and the other contracts through a broker there.[123] Thus there may be an implied choice of English law in a reinsurance contract, where the contract is made between an English insurer and a Swiss reinsurer, it covers part of the risk, it is concluded in the context of a London market placement involving English reinsurers, and it uses English forms incorporating London market wording resonant of English law.[124]

Another factor capable of amounting to a clear indication of an implied choice may arise from the connection between several related contracts. Where, as a matter of commercial reality, related contracts need to be governed by the same law if their purpose is to be achieved, an implied choice to that effect may be discovered. This is most obviously the case with regard to a guarantee in the strictest sense, involving an intention that the guarantor should

---

[120] See *The Komninos S* [1991] 1 Lloyd's Rep 370, decided under the traditional English law; and *Marubeni v Mongolian Government* [2002] 2 All ER (Comm) 873 (Aikens J), decided under the Rome Convention 1980. See also *King v Brandywine Reinsurance Co* [2005] 1 Lloyd's Rep 655 (CA).

[121] See *Co Tunisienne de Navigation v Co d'Armement Maritime* [1971] AC 572, decided under the traditional English law; and *Egon Oldendorff v Libera Corp* [1995] 2 Lloyd's Rep 64 (Mance J) and [1996] 1 Lloyd's Rep 380 (Clarke J), confirming that the Convention had not altered the position. See also *King v Brandywine Reinsurance Co* [2005] 1 Lloyd's Rep 655 (CA). But no implication as to the proper law can be drawn from a clause under which the place of arbitration is to be chosen by one of the parties; see *The Star Texas* [1993] 2 Lloyd's Rep 445 (CA).

[122] See *Co Tunisienne de Navigation v Co d'Armement Maritime* [1971] AC 572, per Lord Wilberforce at 598.

[123] See *Tiernan v Magen Insurance* [2000] ILPr 517 (Longmore J), *Tonicstar v American Home Assurance* [2004] EWHC 1234 (Morison J), *Munchener Ruckverischerungs Gesellschaft v Commonwealth Insurance Co* [2004] EWHC 914 (Comm) (Morison J), and *Tryg Baltica v Boston Compania De Seguros* [2004] EWHC 1186 (Cooke J), in all of which the implied choice accorded with the result of applying the presumption in favour of the reinsurer's residence under Article 4(2). See also *Miller v Whitworth* [1970] AC 583; and *Wasa International Insurance v Lexington Insurance* [2008] 1 All ER (Comm) 286 (Simon J), affirmed sub nom. *Lexington Insurance v AGF Insurance* [2009] UKHL 40 (HL).

[124] See *Gard Marine v Tunnicliffe* [2009] EWHC 2388 (Comm) (Hamblen J). See also *Travelers Casualty v Sun Life* [2006] All ER (D) 26 (Nov), where Christopher Clarke J held that Ontario law was applicable (by implied choice or closest connection) to an insurance in favour of an Ontario insured and its subsidiaries, which had been negotiated between an Ontario broker and a New York office of the leading insurer, the wording of which had been reviewed by the insured's lawyers in Ontario and New York, and under which 40% of the risk was subscribed by Ontario insurers, although the leading insurer was English and 60% of the risk was subscribed by English insurers.

assume a secondary obligation identical to the primary obligation of the main debtor. Thus the guarantee obligation will be governed by the law which governs the obligation guaranteed.[125] Somewhat similarly, all obligations arising from a letter of credit (between the beneficiary and the issuing bank; between the beneficiary and the correspondent bank; and between the two banks) will normally be governed by a single law, that of the country in which is situated the banking establishment at which the documents are to be presented and through which the letter is payable.[126] On the same basis, a counter-undertaking given by one bank will be governed by the law which governs the performance bond given by another bank at the former's request.[127] Similarly, the need for a single law to govern a group insurance policy, under which worldwide cover is provided to a parent company and its subsidiaries, may indicate an implied choice of the law of the country in which both the insurer and the leading policy-holder were resident and the contract was negotiated and concluded.[128] Again a commission agreement relating to the sale of a vessel which is in course of construction may be impliedly subjected to the law which had been expressly chosen to govern the shipbuilding contract between the same parties.[129] Moreover, weight may be sometimes attached to the fact that a contract is one of a group of similar contracts between one party (for example, as employer or principal) and numerous others (for example, as employees or agents), with the result that all such contracts may be governed by the law of the residence of the party common to all the similar contracts.[130]

The relation between connected contracts must not, however, be given a weight beyond the needs of the commercial situation. Thus a letter of credit or a performance bond will not be affected by the law governing the underlying supply contract.[131] Similarly, in the case of reinsurance, although the risk covered will usually be the same as that covered by the primary insurance contract, the law governing the reinsurance contract will not be influenced by that chosen in or otherwise governing the primary insurance contract.[132]

---

[125]    See *Bank of Scotland v Butcher* [1998] EWCA Civ 1306, holding that a guarantee by an English and a Scottish director of a Scottish company of the company's liabilities to a Scottish bank was governed by Scottish law. See also *Broken Hill Pty v Xenakis* [1982] 2 Lloyd's Rep 304.

[126]    See *Bank of Baroda v Vysya Bank* [1994] 2 Lloyd's Rep 87 (Mance J); *Attock Cement v Romanian Bank for Foreign Trade* [1989] 1 WLR 1147 (CA); *BCCHK v Sonali Bank* [1995] 1 Lloyd's Rep 22 (Cresswell J); *Chailease Finance Corp v Credit Agrocole Indosuez* [2000] 1 Lloyd's Rep 348 (CA); and *Marconi Communications v Pan Indonesia Bank* [2005] EWCA Civ 422 (CA), affirming [2004] 1 Lloyd's Rep 594 (David Steel J). Although this case-law relies on Article 4(5) to achieve the necessary unity, it may be thought that the use of implied choice under Article 3 would be more appropriate.

[127]    See *Wahda Bank v Arab Bank* [1996] 1 Lloyd's Rep 470 (CA).

[128]    See *American Motorists Insurance v Cellstar* [2003] ILPr 22 (CA).

[129]    See *Lurssen v Halle* [2009] EWHC 2607 (Comm) (Simon J).

[130]    See *Sayers v International Drilling* [1971] 3 All ER 163 (CA), and *Mercury Publicity v Loerke* [1993] ILPr 142 (CA).

[131]    See cases cited in notes 126 and 127 above. See also *Raiffeisen Zentralbank v National Bank of Greece* [1999] 1 Lloyd's Rep 408 (Tuckey J), where an agreement between banks for the further financing of a shipbuilding project was regarded an autonomous agreement, independent of the surrounding transactions.

[132]    See *Gan Insurance v Tai Ping Insurance* [1999] Lloyd's Rep 472 (CA). See similarly *Dornoch Ltd v Mauritius Union Assurance Co Ltd* [2006] 2 Lloyd's Rep 475 (CA), dealing with associated reinsurance contracts.

In any event, as the Court of Appeal recognised in *Samcrete v Land Rover*,[133] a choice otherwise implied may be negated by the negotiations leading to the contract, as where a guarantor deletes from the form proffered by the other party a clause expressly choosing the same law as governs the main contract under which the obligation guaranteed arises.

## THE PROPER LAW – CLOSEST CONNECTION

In the absence of any valid express or implied choice by the parties, the proper law of a contract is in most cases determined in accordance with the default rules laid down by Articles 4 and 5 of the Rome I Regulation.

Article 4 of the Regulation provides:

1. To the extent that the law applicable to the contract has not been chosen in accordance with Article 3 and without prejudice to Articles 5 to 8, the law governing the contract shall be determined as follows:

(a) a contract for the sale of goods shall be governed by the law of the country where the seller has his habitual residence;
(b) a contract for the provision of services shall be governed by the law of the country where the service provider has his habitual residence;
(c) a contract relating to a right in rem in immovable property or to a tenancy of immovable property shall be governed by the law of the country where the property is situated;
(d) notwithstanding point (c), a tenancy of immovable property concluded for temporary private use for a period of no more than six consecutive months shall be governed by the law of the country where the landlord has his habitual residence, provided that the tenant is a natural person and has his habitual residence in the same country;
(e) a franchise contract shall be governed by the law of the country where the franchisee has his habitual residence;
(f) a distribution contract shall be governed by the law of the country where the distributor has his habitual residence;
(g) a contract for the sale of goods by auction shall be governed by the law of the country where the auction takes place, if such a place can be determined;
(h) a contract concluded within a multilateral system which brings together or facilitates the bringing together of multiple third-party buying and selling interests in financial instruments, as defined by Article 4(1), point (17) of Directive 2004/39/EC, in accordance with non-discretionary rules and governed by a single law, shall be governed by that law.

2. Where the contract is not covered by paragraph 1 or where the elements of the contract would be covered by more than one of points (a) to (h) of paragraph 1, the contract shall be governed by the law of the country where the party required to effect the characteristic performance of the contract has his habitual residence.
3. Where it is clear from all the circumstances of the case that the contract is manifestly more closely connected with a country other than that indicated in paragraphs 1 or 2, the law of that other country shall apply.
4. Where the law applicable cannot be determined pursuant to paragraphs 1 or 2, the contract shall be governed by the law of the country with which it is most closely connected.

---

[133]   [2001] EWCA Civ 2019.

Article 5 of the Regulation deals with contracts of carriage. As regards contracts for the carriage of goods,[134] Article 5(1) and (3) provides:

1. To the extent that the law applicable to a contract for the carriage of goods has not been chosen in accordance with Article 3, the law applicable shall be the law of the country of habitual residence of the carrier, provided that the place of receipt or the place of delivery or the habitual residence of the consignor is also situated in that country. If those requirements are not met, the law of the country where the place of delivery as agreed by the parties is situated shall apply.

3. Where it is clear from all the circumstances of the case that the contract, in the absence of a choice of law, is manifestly more closely connected with a country other than that indicated in paragraphs 1 or 2, the law of that other country shall apply.

These provisions replace Article 4 of the Rome Convention 1980, which provides:

1. To the extent that the law applicable to the contract has not been chosen in accordance with Article 3, the contract shall be governed by the law of the country with which it is most closely connected. Nevertheless, a severable part of the contract which has a closer connection with another country may by way of exception be governed by the law of that other country.

2. Subject to the provisions of paragraph 5 of this Article, it shall be presumed that the contract is most closely connected with the country where the party who is to effect the performance which is characteristic of the contract has, at the time of conclusion of the contract, his habitual residence, or, in the case of a body corporate or unincorporate, its central administration. However, if the contract is entered into in the course of that party's trade or profession, that country shall be the country in which the principal place of business is situated or, where under the terms of the contract the performance is to be effected through a place of business other than the principal place of business, the country in which that other place of business is situated.

3. Notwithstanding the provisions of paragraph 2 of this Article, to the extent that the subject matter of the contract is a right in immovable property or a right to use immovable property it shall be presumed that the contract is most closely connected with the country where the immovable property is situated.

4. A contract for the carriage of goods shall not be subject to the presumption in paragraph 2. In such a contract if the country in which, at the time the contract is concluded, the carrier has his principal place of business is also the country in which the place of loading or the place of discharge or the principal place of business of the consignor is situated, it shall be presumed that the contract is most closely connected with that country. In applying this paragraph single voyage charter-parties and other contracts the main purpose of which is the carriage of goods shall be treated as contracts for the carriage of goods.

5. Paragraph 2 shall not apply if the characteristic performance cannot be determined, and the presumptions in paragraphs 2, 3 and 4 shall be disregarded if it appears from the circumstances as a whole that the contract is more closely connected with another country.

It is evident that in this respect the provisions of the Regulation have been drafted much more elaborately than those of the Convention. But the differences are essentially in matters of detail. Both the Regulation and the Convention provide in substance for a rebuttable presumption, in most cases in favour of the residence of the characteristic performer, which may be displaced by establishing clearly a closer connection with another country.

---

[134]   Article 5(2) deals with contracts for the carriage of passengers. See pp. 355–6 below.

## The Main Presumption

The main effect of Article 4 of the Rome I Regulation is to provide in most cases[135] for a rebuttable presumption in favour of the law of the characteristic performer's residence, which may be displaced by establishing clearly a closer connection with another country. Thus Article 4(2) refers to the law of the country where the party required to effect the characteristic performance of the contract has his habitual residence, and the function of Article 4(1)(a)–(b) and (e)–(f) is to indicate the party who counts as the characteristic performer in the case of certain types of contract.[136]

A similar presumption existed under Article 4 of the Rome Convention 1980.[137] The Convention did not attempt to define the concept of characteristic performance, but it was clear from the Giuliano and Lagarde Report[138] that it was the supply of goods or services, rather than the receipt of or payment for them, which constituted the characteristic performance referred to by Article 4(2) of the Convention. Thus the presumption amounted to a preference for the law of the seller or other supplier's country.[139]

---

[135]  The presumption in favour of the law of the characteristic performer's residence does not apply to: certain contracts involving land, for which Article 4(1)(c) provides a presumption in favour of the lex situs; auction sales, for which Article 4(1)(g) provides a presumption in favour of the location of the auction; contracts concluded within a market in financial instruments, for which Article 4(1)(h) provides a presumption in favour of the law which governs the relevant market; contracts of carriage of goods, for which Article 5(1) provides a more limited presumption in favour of the carrier's residence; contracts for the carriage of passengers, for which Article 5(2) provides a limited presumption in favour of the passenger's residence; certain consumer contracts, which are governed by Article 6; insurance contracts covering mass risks, for which Article 7(3) provides a presumption in favour of the location of the risk; and contracts of employment, which are governed by Article 8.

[136]  Recital 19 explains that where there has been no choice of law, the applicable law should be determined in accordance with the rule specified for the particular type of contract. Where the contract cannot be categorised as being one of the specified types or where its elements fall within more than one of the specified types, it should be governed by the law of the country where the party required to effect the characteristic performance of the contract has his habitual residence. In the case of a contract consisting of a bundle of rights and obligations capable of being categorised as falling within more than one of the specified types of contract, the characteristic performance of the contract should be determined having regard to its centre of gravity.

[137]  In *Samcrete v Land Rover* [2001] EWCA Civ 2019, Potter LJ explained that, while the structure of Article 4 of the Convention might have suggested a three-stage exercise by the court in approaching the problem of determining the applicable law in the absence of choice, in reality Article 4(1) merely introduced the concept of closest connection before indicating the process of reasoning to be applied in determining it. Accordingly, the application of Article 4 involved essentially a two-stage process: first, under Article 4(2), to identify the characteristic performance of the contract and the country of the party who is to effect it, and then to ascertain what factors, if any, might lead the court to disregard the presumption under Article 4(5). Moreover, in the latter respect, the burden of proof lay on the party who asserted that the presumption in Article 4(2) should be disregarded.

[138]  At p. 20.

[139]  The presumption in favour of the characteristic performer's residence substantially accords with the trend in the traditional English law of preferring the law of the common residence of the parties to that of the principal place of performance. See *Jacobs Marcus v Credit Lyonnais* (1884) 12 QBD 589; and *Zivnostenska Bank v Frankman* [1950] AC 57. On the other hand, where the parties resided in different countries, the traditional English law tended to prefer the place of principal performance, rather than the residence of the principal or characteristic performer. See *R v International Trustee* [1937] AC 500; *Re United Railways of Havana* [1961] AC 1007; and *Power Curber v National Bank*

The rationale for Article 4 of the Regulation, as laconically explained by Recital 16, is that, to contribute to the general objective of the Regulation, legal certainty in the European judicial area, the conflict rules should be highly foreseeable; but the courts should retain a degree of discretion to determine the law that is most closely connected to the situation. A fuller explanation may be that a narrow doctrine of implied choice, as provided by Article 3, takes care of situations where one of the connected laws is clearly more suitable for use in interpreting and supplementing the terms of the contract. Thus Article 4 deals with cases where there is usually no strong reason of justice or convenience for applying any given law rather than another.[140] In such cases, there is merit in the certainty and predictability which can arise from a strong presumption in favour of the law of the supplier's residence.

Indeed, it may be wondered why the Regulation does not more vigorously pursue its aim of certainty and foreseeability, by eliminating the possibility of displacement in favour of the law of a clearly more closely connected country, and converting the presumption in favour of the characteristic performer's residence into a firm rule (subject of course to an express or implied choice by the parties under Article 3). Such a strengthening was indeed proposed by the EC Commission in its Proposal of 15th December 2005,[141] but was rejected by the Parliament and Council, and thus removed from the Regulation as adopted.

The Regulation endeavours to restrict the displacement of the presumption by insisting in Article 4(3) that it must be 'clear from all the circumstances of the case that the contract is manifestly more closely connected with a country other than' that of the characteristic performer's residence. Unfortunately, it fails to indicate any perspective by reference to which the importance of the various connections (such as the residences of parties, and the places of negotiation and performance) can be evaluated. In the present writer's opinion, there can be no principled basis for such an evaluation, other than in terms of the relative suitability of the various connected laws to fulfil the apparent intention of the parties in concluding the contract. But if from that perspective a clearly preferable solution is identifiable, an implied choice of the relevant law should be recognised under Article 3.

### Identifying the characteristic performer

In the Regulation, the concept of characteristic performance is clarified by Article 4(1)(a)–(b) and (e)–(f). These sub-paragraphs identify the characteristic performer as: (a) the seller, in the case of a contract for the sale of goods;[142] (b) the service provider, in the case of a contract for the provision of services;[143] (e) the franchisee, in the case of a franchise contract; and (f)

---

*of Kuwait* [1981] 1 WLR 1233. One clear advantage possessed by the reference to the characteristic performer's residence is that it avoids difficulties arising from the uncertain or multiple character which may be possessed by the place of performance. See *Bonython v Australia* [1951] AC 201.

[140]   The protection of weaker parties is not a concern of Article 4, but of other provisions, such as Articles 5(2), 6, 7(3) and 8.

[141]   See COM(2005) 650 final.

[142]   But Article 4(1)(g) makes an exception in the case of a contract for the sale of goods by auction. Then the presumption is in favour of the law of the country where the auction takes place, if such a place can be determined.

[143]   Recital 17 to the Rome I Regulation indicates that for the purpose of Article 4 the concepts of sale of goods and provision of services should be interpreted in the same way as under Article 5 of the Brussels I Regulation, except that for the present purpose these concepts exclude franchise and distribution contracts, since they are the subject of specific rules.

the distributor, in the case of a distribution contract.[144] Similarly, Article 7(2) identifies the characteristic performer as the insurer, in the case of an insurance contract covering a large risk. In the case of an option to purchase, it is the seller who counts as the characteristic performer.[145]

The reference by Article 4(1)(b) of the Regulation to the service provider's residence confirms a line of English decisions under the Convention which have referred a contract for a bank account to the law of the country in which the branch at which the account is kept is situated, since the characteristic performance, repayment of the sum deposited, is to be effected through that branch;[146] a contract whereby an insurance broker is instructed to arrange insurance to the law of the country in which the broker carries on business;[147] a contract under which an architect is to design a building to the law of the architect's residence;[148] a contract to provide new ongoing multimedia video content for a specified period to the law of the provider's residence;[149] and a reinsurance contract to the law of the rein-

---

[144]    Article 4(1)(f) of the Regulation overrules the decision of the English Court of Appeal in *Print Concept v GEW* [2001] ECC 36 that in the case of a distribution agreement, it was the manufacturer's obligation to supply the goods, rather than the distributor's obligation to promote them, which constituted the characteristic performance under the Convention, so that Article 4(2) pointed to the law of the manufacturer's residence.

The Regulation as adopted does not contain any specific provision identifying the characteristic performer in the case of a contract relating to intellectual or industrial property rights. Article 4(1)(f) of the Commission's Proposal of 15th December 2005 indicated that in such a case the transferor or assignor of the rights would be the characteristic performer. In Case C-533/07: *Falco and Rabitsch v Weller-Lindhorst* [2009] ECR I-3327, Trstenjak AG opined (at paras 67–9) that a contract for the licensing of an intellectual property right (such as a copyright) does not count as a contract for the provision of services within Article 4(1)(b) of the Rome I Regulation; but the European Court confined its attention to the Brussels I Regulation.

[145]    See *Standard Bank v Agrinvest* [2007] EWHC 2595 (Comm) (Teare J).

[146]    See *Sierra Leone Telecommunications v Barclays Bank* [1998] 2 All ER 821 (Cresswell J); and *Walsh v National Irish Bank* [2007] IEHC 325 (McKechnie J). See also *Raiffeisen Zentralbank v National Bank of Greece* [1999] 1 Lloyd's Rep 408 (Tuckey J), which involved an agreement between banks whereby, in order to enable one bank to provide additional finance for a shipbuilding project, the other bank undertook to divert to the bank providing the additional finance the stage payments which it was already bound to make to the building purchaser. It was held that the obligation to divert the payments constituted the characteristic obligation, so that Article 4(2) of the Convention pointed to the law of the residence of the bank which undertook to divert.

[147]    See *HIB v Guardian Insurance* [1997] 1 Lloyd's Rep 412 (Longmore J). See also *Albon v Naza Motor Trading* [2007] 2 All ER 719, where Lightman J held that the agent was the characteristic performer of contracts of agency in respect of the sale or acquisition of cars; and *Sharab v Prince Al-Waleed Bin Takak Bin Abdul-Aziz Al-Saud* [2008] All ER (D) 16 (Aug), where, in the context of a contract of agency in respect of the sale of an aircraft, Powell QC held that, in the case of an agency contract, the characteristic performance is that of the agent.

The Regulation as adopted contains no specific provision on contracts of agency. Cf. Article 7(1) of the Commission's Proposal of 15th December 2005, which specified that, in the absence of a choice under Article 3, a contract between principal and agent would be governed by the law of the country in which the agent had his habitual residence, unless the agent exercised or was to exercise his main activity in the country in which the principal had his habitual residence, in which case the law of that country applied.

[148]    See *Latchin v General Mediterranean Holidays* [2002] CLC 330 (Andrew Smith J).

[149]    See *Pablo Star Ltd v Emirates Integrated Telecommunications Co* [2009] EWCA Civ 1044.

surer's residence.[150] On the other hand, Article 4(1)(b) of the Regulation appears to overrule some English decisions under the Convention which have ruled that, in the case of a unilateral contract for services (such as a promise to pay a fee and/or expenses if certain services are rendered, without a reciprocal promise to provide the services), it is the party who promises to pay, and not the service provider, who counts as the characteristic performer.[151]

Another English ruling under the Convention which appears to remain applicable under the Regulation is that, in the case of a contract whereby money is invested in a company, whether by the issue of shares or by way of loan, the characteristic performance is the issue of the shares or the repayment of the loan.[152] As to loans in general, it has been held in England that it is the borrower who counts as the characteristic performer,[153] but in Scotland that it is the lender who counts as the characteristic performer.[154] A further possibility is to look to the residence of the lender where it is a bank or similar institution, on the basis that lending then counts as a financial service, but to the residence of the borrower in other cases, on the ground that repayment of the principal money is then the characteristic performance. It is greatly to be regretted that the Regulation fails explicitly to resolve this conundrum.

Unlike the Convention,[155] the Regulation does not provide for severance between parts of a contract in the absence of an express or implied choice by the parties. Instead, by Article 4(2) of the Regulation, where the elements of the contract would be covered by more than one of the sub-paragraphs of Article 4(1), the contract is governed by the law of the characteristic performer's habitual residence. Recital 19 explains that, in the case of a contract consisting of a bundle of rights and obligations capable of being categorised as falling within more than one of the specified types of contract, the characteristic performance of the contract should be determined having regard to its centre of gravity. Thus where, for example, the contract provides for the sale of goods by A to B for a price in cash, and also for the provision of services by B to A for a monetary consideration, one must (if possible) identify the characteristic performer by reference to the centre of gravity of the contract. This may not be an easy task.

---

[150]   See *Gan Insurance v Tai Ping Insurance* [1999] Lloyd's Rep 472 (CA); and *Tonicstar v American Home Assurance* [2004] EWHC 1234 (Morison J).

[151]   See *Ark Therapeutics v True North Capital* [2006] 1 All ER (Comm) 138 (Nigel Teare QC); and *Armstrong International v Deutsche Bank Securities* [2003] All ER (D) 195 (Jul) (Judge Reid QC).

[152]   See *Mirchandani v Somaia* [2001] WL 239782 (Morritt V-C). But see Article 4(1)(h) of the Regulation, on contracts concluded within a multilateral market in financial securities.

[153]   See *Tavoulareas v Tsavliris* [2006] 1 All ER (Comm) 109 (Andrew Smith J).

[154]   See *Atlantic Telecom GmbH* [2004] SLT 1031 (Lord Brodie in the Outer House of the Court of Session).

[155]   See the last sentence of Article 4(1) of the Convention, which specified that a severable part of a contract which had a closer connection with another country could by way of exception be governed by the law of that other country. In Case C-133/08: *Intercontainer Interfrigo v Balkenende Oosthuizen* [2010] All ER (EC) 1, the European Court ruled that, under Article 4 of the Convention, a part of a contract could be governed by a law other than that applied to the rest of the contract only where the object of that part was independent in relation to the purpose of the rest of the contract. Even then, each part of a contract had to be made subject to one single law; and, in particular, the rules relating to the prescription of a right had to fall under the same legal system as that applied to the corresponding obligation. See also *Bank of Scotland v Butcher* [1998] EWCA Civ 1306 (CA); and *CGU International Insurance v Szabo* [2002] Lloyd's Rep IR 196 (Toulson J).

### Identifying the relevant residence

Article 4 of the Rome I Regulation refers throughout to the 'habitual residence' of the characteristic performer. The concept of habitual residence is defined by Article 19, which provides:

> 1. For the purposes of this Regulation, the habitual residence of companies and other bodies, corporate or unincorporated, shall be the place of central administration.
> The habitual residence of a natural person acting in the course of his business activity shall be his principal place of business.
> 2. Where the contract is concluded in the course of the operations of a branch, agency or any other establishment, or if, under the contract, performance is the responsibility of such a branch, agency or establishment, the place where the branch, agency or any other establishment is located shall be treated as the place of habitual residence.
> 3. For the purposes of determining the habitual residence, the relevant point in time shall be the time of the conclusion of the contract.

Recital 39 explains that, for the sake of legal certainty, there should be a clear definition of habitual residence, in particular for companies and other bodies, corporate or unincorporated. Unlike Article 60(1) of the Brussels I Regulation, which establishes three criteria, the conflict rule should proceed on the basis of a single criterion; otherwise the parties would be unable to foresee the law applicable to their situation.

It will be noticed that no definition is offered of the habitual residence of an individual who is not acting in the course of his own business.[156] As regards companies, the primary reference by Article 19(1) of the Rome I Regulation to the place of central administration contrasts with the Rome Convention 1980, where Article 4(2) referred to the principal place of business, in the usual case where the contract was entered into in the course of the company's trade or profession, and also with the Commission's Proposal of 15th December 2005, where Article 18(1) referred to a company's principal establishment. Thus the Regulation as adopted appears to connect a company with the place where the board of directors (or equivalent managerial organ) usually meets, rather than the place from which its most important and numerous trading transactions with third parties are negotiated.[157] This change seems quite extraordinary.

No doubt the reference in Article 19(2) of the Rome I Regulation to a branch, agency or other establishment must be construed as equivalent to a secondary establishment under Article 5(5) of the Brussels I Regulation,[158] and as not including a merely electronic presence in the form of a web-server.[159] Article 19(2) of the Rome I Regulation follows Article 4(2) of the Rome Convention 1980 in referring to the location of the secondary establishment in cases where, under the contract, performance is the responsibility of the establishment. To satisfy this proviso, the contract must expressly or impliedly require that the performance should be effected through the establishment. It is not enough that the parties expected the contract to be performed through the establishment, if there was no contractual requirement

---

[156] As to this, see pp. 430–33 below.
[157] See pp. 72–4 above.
[158] See pp. 109–10 above.
[159] See Directive 2000/31 on Electronic Commerce, [2000] OJ L178/1, Recital 19 and Article 2(c).

to that effect.[160] But Article 19(2) of the Regulation departs from Article 4(2) of the Convention in offering an alternative condition, so as to refer to the location of the secondary establishment in cases where the contract is concluded in the course of the operations of the establishment. The new condition appears far more sensible, since it is on the establishment which negotiates the contract that the other party's attention will normally be focused. One wonders, however, what solution is envisaged where, for example, the company (possibly a bank) has its central administration in New York, but it has a branch in London by which the contract was concluded, and another branch in Paris from which performance of the contract is required. The safest solution is probably to revert to the place of central administration in cases where several branches are relevantly involved.

Article 19(3) of the Rome I Regulation specifies that, for the purposes of determining the habitual residence, the relevant point in time is that of the conclusion of the contract. This echoes Article 4(2) of the Rome Convention 1980, and accords with the traditional English rule that connections which come into existence after the conclusion of the contract are irrelevant except in support of a (rarely successful) argument that there was a subsequent implied agreement to vary the proper law.[161] It also indicates that a puzzling suggestion in the Giuliano and Lagarde Report[162] that, in determining the country of the closest connection, account may be taken of factors which supervened after the conclusion of the contract, should be regarded as ill-considered and erroneous.[163]

Article 4(4) of the Regulation, echoing Article 4(5) of the Convention, recognises that there are cases where the characteristic performance cannot be determined, and thus there is no applicable presumption. In such cases, Article 4(4) of the Regulation subjects the contract to the law of the country with which it is most closely connected. Recital 21 adds that, in order to determine the country of closest connection, account should be taken, inter alia, of whether the contract in question has a very close relationship with another contract or contracts.

Article 4(4) of the Regulation clearly applies to a contract to exchange guns for butter, or hotel accommodation for advertising; or, as Mann J held in *Apple Corps v Apple Computer*,[164] an agreement for the worldwide division of the use of a trade mark in terms of fields of use (computers and sound recordings). It probably also applies to a contract for the sale and lease-back of equipment.[165] Other cases in which the characteristic performance may be unclear are contracts between authors and publishers, and contracts for corporate acquisitions.[166]

---

[160]    See *Ennstone Building Products v Stanger* [2002] 1 WLR 3059 (CA). See also *Iran Continental Shelf Oil Co v IRI International Corp* [2002] EWCA Civ 1024 (CA). Cf. *Soc Ammerlaan Agro Projecten v Soc Les Serres de Cosquerou*, decided by the French Court of Cassation on 2nd March 1999.

[161]    See *Co Tunisienne de Navigation v Co d'Armement Maritime* [1971] AC 572. Cf. the suggestion of Simon J in *Lurssen v Halle* [2009] EWHC 2607 (Comm) that it is legitimate to consider the terms of a later contract between the parties as part of the circumstances of the case in discovering an implied choice under Article 3(1).

[162]    At p. 20.

[163]    See *Marconi Communications v Pan Indonesia Bank* [2005] EWCA Civ 422 (CA).

[164]    [2004] ILPr 34.

[165]    See Young, [1991] LMCLQ 314 at 322–3.

[166]    See Juenger, (1997) 45 AJCL 195.

**Rebutting the presumption**

Article 4(3) of the Rome I Regulation specifies that where it is clear from all the circumstances of the case that the contract is manifestly more closely connected with a country other than that indicated in Article 4(1) or (2), the law of that other country shall apply. Recital 20 describes this as an escape clause, and adds that for this purpose account should be taken, inter alia, of whether the contract in question has a very close relationship with another contract or contracts.[167]

The wording of Article 4(3) of the Regulation differs from that of Article 4(5) of the Rome Convention 1980, which merely provided for the presumptions to be disregarded if it appeared from the circumstances as a whole that the contract was more closely connected with another country. In contrast, the Regulation requires the closer connection to be clear and manifest. Thus a more restrictive approach to the escape clause is envisaged.

Perhaps the most problematic issue in determining the proper law under the Rome Convention 1980 concerned the strength of the presumption laid down by Article 4(2) in favour of the law of the characteristic performer's residence. In *Intercontainer Interfrigo v Balkenende Oosthuizen*,[168] the European Court ruled that under Article 4(5) of the Convention the presumption is rebutted where it is clear from the circumstances as a whole that the contract is more closely connected with another country. The Court rejected the alternative view, favoured by Bot AG, that under the Convention the presumption should be adhered to unless the presumptive country had little real connection with the contract, or the presumption lacked any genuine connecting value.

Some clarification of the position under the Convention had also emerged from English and Scottish decisions. Firstly, the reference in Article 4(5) of the Convention to a closer connection had to be understood in terms of geographical location only, rather than party intention. Thus the relevant factors were the residences of the parties and the places of performance of the various obligations under the contract.[169] Secondly, the presumption in Article 4(2) of the Convention could be most easily rebutted in cases where the place of performance differed from the place of business of the party whose performance was characteristic of the contract.[170] Thirdly, after some confusion, a consensus had emerged that for the presumption in favour of the characteristic performer's residence to be displaced, it had to be *clearly* shown that the contract had a closer connection with some other country.[171] But, despite such

---

[167]    In contrast, the Commission's Proposal of 15th December 2005 would have converted the presumptions into firm rules. The test of closest connection would have been eliminated, except in cases where no presumption was applicable.

[168]    Case C-133/08, [2010] All ER (EC) 1.

[169]    See per Hobhouse LJ in *Credit Lyonnais v New Hampshire Insurance Co* [1997] 2 Lloyd's Rep 1 (CA), and per Potter LJ in *Samcrete v Land Rover* [2001] EWCA Civ 2019 (CA).

[170]    See per Mance J in *Bank of Baroda v Vysya Bank* [1994] 2 Lloyd's Rep 87, and per Potter LJ in *Samcrete v Land Rover* [2001] EWCA Civ 2019 (CA). Cf. *Caledonia Subsea v Microperi* [2003] SC 70 (Inner House).

[171]    See *Definitely Maybe v Marek Lieberberg* [2001] 1 WLR 1745 (Morison J); *Samcrete v Land Rover* [2001] EWCA Civ 2019 (CA); *Ennstone Building Products v Stanger* [2002] 1 WLR 3059 (CA); *Iran Continental Shelf Oil Co v IRI International Corp* [2002] EWCA Civ 1024 (CA); *Caledonia Subsea v Microperi* [2003] SC 70 (Inner House), affirming [2001] SCLR 634 (Lord Hamilton); *Waldwiese Stiftung v Lewis* [2004] EWHC 2589 (Ch) (Mann J); *Ophthalmic Innovations International (UK) Ltd v Ophthalmic Innovations International Inc* [2004] EWHC 2948 (Lawrence Collins J);

clarification, some uncertainty remained as to what combination of factors would clearly establish a closer connection.

Since it was obvious that the place of the characteristic performance could differ from the residence of the characteristic performer, and evident that Article 4(2) of the Convention deliberately preferred the residence to the place of performance, some further factor was necessary to displace the presumption. As regards a contract for the sale of goods, in *Grant v Brizard*,[172] Lord Hamilton held that the fact that the contract was concluded in the context of a long-term agreement for the exclusive distribution of such goods in the buyer's country was not enough to displace the presumption in favour of the law of the seller's country. On the other hand, in *Ferguson Shipbuilders v Voith Hydro*,[173] Lord Penrose found it sufficient that the sale was of a component, to be delivered and then incorporated into a larger machine in the buyer's country. In that case, a German company had manufactured in Germany and delivered in Scotland propeller systems for incorporation in ships under construction by a Scottish shipbuilding company in Scotland.

In the context of services, preference was ultimately accorded to the place of performance in *Definitely Maybe v Marek Lieberberg*,[174] where an English company had contracted to provide a band to perform at concerts in Germany organised by a German company. In concluding that overall the contract had a closer connection with Germany than with England, Morison J emphasised that Germany was the place of performance by both parties, where the band were to perform and the organiser was to make arrangements and provide facilities for the performance (such as marketing, promotion, security and equipment). Preference was also given to the place of performance in *Albon v Naza Motor Trading*,[175] where Lightman J held that South African law applied to a contract of agency between an English agent and a Malaysian principal in respect of the acquisition of cars in South Africa and their export to Malaysia.

On the other hand, the presumption was ultimately adhered to in *Caledonia Subsea v Micoperi*,[176] which involved a contract for diving services to be provided by a Scottish company to an Italian company in connection with the 'post trenching' of a pipeline in Egyptian waters. The place of the characteristic performance was substantially, but not exclusively, in Egypt, where the actual diving operations took place, but preparatory and supervisory activities took place elsewhere, including in Scotland. Lord Hamilton, whose decision was subsequently affirmed by the Inner House, explained that the effecting of the characteristic performance was significantly related to the country where the performer had its principal place of business, and the multinational character of the operations tended to favour the certainty of the presumptive country, not least where the alternative was the country of neither contracting party. The presumption was also adhered to in *Latchin v General*

---

*Marconi Communications v Pan Indonesia Bank* [2005] EWCA Civ 422 (CA); *Sharab v Prince Al-Waleed Bin Takak Bin Abdul-Aziz Al-Saud* [2008] All ER (D) 16 (Aug) (Powell QC); and Dicey, Morris and Collins (2006), at para 32-125. Cf. *Credit Lyonnais v New Hampshire Insurance Co* [1997] 2 Lloyd's Rep 1 (CA).

[172]   19th January 1998.
[173]   [2000] SLT 229.
[174]   [2001] 1 WLR 1745.
[175]   [2007] 2 All ER 719.
[176]   [2003] SC 70 (Inner House), affirming [2001] SCLR 634 (Lord Hamilton).

*Mediterranean Holidays*,[177] where the contract was negotiated in England between parties resident in England, although it was for the design of a building to be erected in Morocco; and in *Ennstone Building Products v Stanger*,[178] where the contract was between English companies for advice on a problem concerning a building in Scotland, and the advice was to be received in England.

The place of performance might be preferred where, as in *Kenburn Waste Management v Bergmann*,[179] the characteristic obligation was a negative obligation to achieve a result in a given country. Thus the Court of Appeal (affirming Pumfrey J) applied Article 4(5) of the Convention so as to hold that an agreement by the German owner of a European patent not to make threats of infringement actions against the English customers of an English manufacturer of competing products was governed by English law. As Pumfrey J had noted, the contract had no objective connection with the patentee's German residence as such at all.

In *Samcrete v Land Rover*,[180] an Egyptian parent company had guaranteed the liability of its subsidiary to pay for products supplied by an English company under a distribution contract expressly governed by English law, but the negotiations leading to the guarantee negated any implied choice of the law governing it. The Court of Appeal accepted that, for the purpose of Article 4(2) of the Convention, the characteristic obligation in the case of a guarantee was the guarantor's obligation to pay as promised. But ultimately they found that a closer connection with England was clearly demonstrated, so that English law applied under Article 4(5) of the Convention. England was not only the residence of the supplier/payee, but also the place of payment and the place of delivery of the products supplied.

## The Minor Presumptions

There are four types of contract in respect of which Articles 4 and 5 of the Rome I Regulation exclude the presumption in favour of the characteristic performer's residence and substitute a different presumption. These are certain contracts relating to land; sales of goods by auction; contracts concluded within a multilateral market in financial instruments; and contracts for the carriage of goods. In all these cases, the special presumption made applicable by Articles 4(1) and 5(1) remains subject to the usual escape clause, specified by Articles 4(3) and 5(3), in favour of the law of a country which is clearly and manifestly more closely connected.

### Contracts relating to land

Article 4(1)(c) of the Rome I Regulation applies to contracts relating to a proprietary right in land, or to a tenancy of land, and creates a presumption in favour of the law of the country where the land is situated. An exception is provided by Article 4(1)(d), in the case of a tenancy of land which is concluded for temporary private use for a period of no more than six consecutive months between parties who are habitually resident in the same country. In that case, the presumption is in favour of the landlord's habitual residence.

---

[177]  [2002] CLC 330 (Andrew Smith J).
[178]  [2002] 1 WLR 3059 (CA).
[179]  [2002] ILPr 33 (CA), affirming [2002] FSR 44.
[180]  [2001] EWCA Civ 2019. See also *Commercial Marine Piling Ltd v Pierse Contracting Ltd* [2009] EWHC 2241 (TCC) (Ramsey J).

Article 4(1)(c) of the Regulation resembles Article 4(3) of the Rome Convention 1980, but Article 4(1)(d) is new. In traditional English law, there was a similar preference for the lex situs in the case of a contract for the transfer or creation of an interest in land if the parties were resident in different countries.[181] But if the parties resided in the same country, traditional English law tended to give preference to the law of the common residence rather than the lex situs.[182] It is unclear how far it may now be proper to invoke the escape clause so as to subject a contract relating to land to the law of the common residence.[183]

### Sales of goods by auction

Article 4(1)(g) of the Regulation applies to contracts for the sale of goods by auction.[184] It introduces a presumption in favour of the law of the country where the auction takes place, if such a place can be determined. No doubt the saving is designed to take account of the difficulty of identifying the location of an auction which takes place on the Internet. Where the saving applies, the normal presumption under Article 4(1)(a) in favour of the seller's residence becomes applicable.

### Contracts concluded within a multilateral market in financial instruments

Article 4(1)(h) of the Rome I Regulation applies to contracts which are concluded within a multilateral system which brings together or facilitates the bringing together of multiple third-party buying and selling interests in financial instruments, as defined by Article 4(1)(17) of EC Directive 2004/39 on Markets in Financial Instruments,[185] in accordance with non-discretionary rules and governed by a single law. It provides a presumption in favour of the law which governs the relevant multilateral system. Recital 18 to the Regulation indicates that multilateral systems include regulated markets and multilateral trading facilities as referred to in Article 4 of Directive 2004/39, and that a multilateral system need not involve a central counterparty.

Financial instruments are elaborately but widely defined by Article 4(1)(17) and Annex I, Section C, of Directive 2004/39 as the following: (1) transferable securities; (2) money-market instruments; (3) units in collective investment undertakings; (4) options, futures, swaps, forward rate agreements and any other derivative contracts relating to securities, currencies, interest rates or yields, or other derivatives instruments, financial indices or financial measures which may be settled physically or in cash; (5) options, futures, swaps, forward rate agreements and any other derivative contracts relating to commodities that must be settled in cash or may be settled in cash at the option of one of the parties (otherwise than by reason of a default or other termination event); (6) options, futures, swaps, and any other

---

181    See *Mount Albert BC v Australasian Life Insurance Soc* [1938] AC 224.
182    See *Re Courtney* [1835–42] All ER Rep 415; *British South Africa Co v De Beers Consolidated Mines* [1910] 2 Ch 502 (reversed on other grounds, [1912] AC 52); *Mercantile Investment Co v River Plate Co* [1892] 2 Ch 303; *Re Smith* [1916] 2 Ch 206; and *Re Anchor Line* [1937] 1 Ch 483.
183    In Case C-133/08: *Intercontainer Interfrigo v Balkenende Oosthuizen* [2010] All ER (EC) 1, Bot AG (at para 78) favoured the rebuttal of the presumption under the Convention in favour of the lex situs, in the case of a seasonal rental of land between parties resident in the same other Member State. But the European Court did not address this point.
184    There was no provision in the Convention corresponding to Article 4(1)(g).
185    [2004] OJ L145/1. The Directive was last amended by Directive 2008/10, [2008] OJ L76/33.

derivative contract relating to commodities that can be physically settled provided that they are traded on a regulated market and/or a multilateral trading facility; (7) options, futures, swaps, forwards and any other derivative contracts relating to commodities, that can be physically settled not otherwise mentioned in paragraph (6) and not being for commercial purposes, which have the characteristics of other derivative financial instruments, having regard to whether, inter alia, they are cleared and settled through recognised clearing houses or are subject to regular margin calls; (8) derivative instruments for the transfer of credit risk; (9) financial contracts for differences; and (10) options, futures, swaps, forward rate agreements and any other derivative contracts relating to climatic variables, freight rates, emission allowances or inflation rates or other official economic statistics that must be settled in cash or may be settled in cash at the option of one of the parties (otherwise than by reason of a default or other termination event), as well as any other derivative contracts relating to assets, rights, obligations, indices and measures not otherwise mentioned in Section C, which have the characteristics of other derivative financial instruments, having regard to whether, inter alia, they are traded on a regulated market or a multilateral trading facility, are cleared and settled through recognised clearing houses or are subject to regular margin calls.

Article 4(1)(14) of Directive 2004/39 defines a regulated market as a multilateral system operated and/or managed by a market operator, which brings together or facilitates the bringing together of multiple third-party buying and selling interests in financial instruments – in the system and in accordance with its non-discretionary rules – in a way that results in a contract, in respect of the financial instruments admitted to trading under its rules and/or systems, and which is authorised and functions regularly and in accordance with the provisions of Title III of the Directive. Article 4(1)(15) of the Directive defines a multilateral trading facility as a multilateral system, operated by an investment firm or a market operator, which brings together multiple third-party buying and selling interests in financial instruments – in the system and in accordance with non-discretionary rules – in a way that results in a contract in accordance with the provisions of Title II of the Directive.

## Contracts for the carriage of goods

As regards contracts for the carriage of goods, Article 5(1) of the Regulation provides for a presumption in favour of the law of the habitual residence of the carrier, provided that either the place of receipt, or the place of delivery, or the habitual residence of the consignor, is also situated in that country. If those requirements are not met, there is a presumption in favour of the law of the country where the place of delivery as agreed by the parties is situated. It seems clear that delivery refers to the discharge of the goods at the end of the voyage. By Article 5(3), the presumption is displaced where it is clear from all the circumstances of the case that the contract, in the absence of a choice of law, is manifestly more closely connected with a country other than that indicated in Article 5(1), and the law of that other country then applies.

Recital 22 explains that single-voyage charterparties and other contracts whose main purpose is the carriage of goods should be treated as contracts for the carriage of goods; that 'consignor' refers to any person who enters into a contract of carriage with the carrier; and that 'the carrier' refers to the party to the contract who undertakes to carry the goods, whether or not he performs the carriage himself.

The first limb of Article 5(1) of the Regulation, referring to the carrier's habitual residence, supported by an additional factor, accords with Article 4(4) of the Rome Convention

1980, except that the Convention referred to the principal place of business (rather than the habitual residence) of the carrier and the consignor. The second limb, referring to the place of delivery, is new. Under the Convention, no presumption was then applicable, but simply a direct reference to the closest connection.[186]

In *Intercontainer Interfrigo v Balkenende Oosthuizen*,[187] which involved a contract for the hire of railway wagons by a Belgian company to a Dutch company for use in transporting goods between Amsterdam and Frankfurt, the European Court ruled that Article 5(1) of the Regulation applies to a charterparty, other than a single-voyage charterparty, only when the main purpose of the contract is not merely to make available a means of transport, but the actual carriage of goods. It explained that, in order to ascertain that purpose, it is necessary to take into consideration the objective of the contractual relationship and, consequently, all the obligations of the party who effects the performance which is characteristic of the contract. In a charterparty, the owner, who effects such a performance, undertakes as a matter of course to make a means of transport available to the charterer. However, it is conceivable that the owner's obligations relate not merely to making available the means of transport but also to the actual carriage of goods, and the contract then falls within the scope of Article 5(1) of the Regulation since its main purpose is the carriage of goods. One may conclude from this ruling that Article 5(1) applies to a normal time charter of a ship, under which the shipowner retains control of the ship, employs the crew, and itself carries out the carriage of goods, but not a bareboat charter, under which the shipowner provides the ship to the charterer, who employs the crew and carries out the carriage of goods.

In the context of the escape device provided by Article 5(3) in favour of a clearly and manifestly closer connection, the flag or registration of the vessel involved in a contract for carriage by sea does not appear to be of much importance.[188]

## PARTICULAR ISSUES

The Rome I Regulation takes pains to make clear that most issues relating to a contract are usually governed by its proper law. Thus Articles 10–12 and 18 of the Regulation provide for the application of the proper law to questions of formation; essential validity; formal validity; interpretation; performance; remedies; discharge; time-limitation; the consequences of nullity; presumptions and the burden of proof; and modes of proof.[189]

---

[186]     See per Bot AG in Case C-133/08: *Intercontainer Interfrigo v Balkenende Oosthuizen* [2010] All ER (EC) 1. He also considered that, in the case of a contract between a Belgian carrier and a Dutch client for the carriage of goods by rail from the Netherlands to Germany, the closest connection was with the Netherlands, as the residence of the client and the place of loading.

[187]     Case C-133/08, [2010] All ER (EC) 1.

[188]     In contrast, the traditional English guideline of last resort for a contract for the carriage of goods by sea, between parties resident in different countries, referred to the law of the flag of the vessel involved. See *Lloyd v Guibert* (1865) LR 1 QB 115; *The Assunzione* [1954] P 150; and *Coast Lines v Hudig & Veder* [1972] 2 QB 34.

[189]     Articles 10–12 and 18 of the Regulation largely accord with Articles 8–10 and 14 of the Rome Convention 1980.

On the other hand, the Regulation also makes provision in certain circumstances for the application of a law other than the proper law to questions of formation;[190] essential validity;[191] formal validity;[192] remedies;[193] the manner of performance;[194] individual capacity;[195] and modes of proof.[196] Moreover, as well as making a classic saving for the exclusion of foreign law which conflicts with the forum's stringent public policy,[197] it permits respect to be accorded to overriding interests asserted by the lex fori or by the law of the place of performance.[198]

**Interpretation, Performance and Discharge**

By Article 12(1)(a), (b) and (d) of the Rome I Regulation,[199] interpretation, performance, and discharge (the various ways of extinguishing obligations) are expressly included among the issues governed by the proper law. Article 18(1) adds that the proper law applies to the extent that, in matters of contractual obligations, it contains rules which raise presumptions of law or determine the burden of proof.[200]

Interpretation includes the resolution of ambiguities in an express term of a contract; for example, where a contract specifies the money of account (in which a debt is measured) by means of a name (such as dollars) which is capable of referring to the currencies of several countries,[201] or as regards the scope of the risk insured by an insurance contract.[202] It also includes supplementation by means of rules which resolve issues on which the express terms of the contract are silent; for example, as to the respective obligations of the parties to a contract of sale in relation to the obtaining of any necessary export licence.[203] Moreover, where two agreements are governed by the same proper law, it is for that law to determine, as a matter of interpretation, whether they should be treated as a single agreement.[204]

As regards performance, Article 12(2) of the Regulation[205] adds a minor exception that, in relation to the manner of performance and the steps to be taken in the event of defective performance, regard must be had to the law of the country in which performance takes place. This seems to reflect Lord Wright's remark in *Mount Albert BC v Australasian Assurance*

---

[190]  See Article 10(2), which echoes Article 8(2) of the Convention.
[191]  See Articles 3(3)–(4) and 9. Article 9 departs significantly from Article 7 of the Convention.
[192]  See Article 11, which offers additional bases for validation, as compared with Article 9 of the Convention.
[193]  See Article 12(1)(c), which accords with Article 10(1)(c) of the Convention.
[194]  See Article 12(2), which echoes Article 10(2) of the Convention.
[195]  See Article 13, which echoes Article 11 of the Convention.
[196]  See Article 18(2), which echoes Article 14(2) of the Convention.
[197]  See Article 21, which echoes Article 16 of the Convention.
[198]  See Article 9, which departs significantly from Article 7 of the Convention.
[199]  These provisions echo Article 10(1)(a), (b) and (d) of the Rome Convention 1980.
[200]  This substantially echoes Article 14(1) of the Convention. See also *Re Cohn* [1945] Ch 5; and *The Rosso* [1982] 3 All ER 841 (CA).
[201]  See *Bonython v Australia* [1951] AC 201.
[202]  See *CGU International Insurance v Astrazeneca Insurance* [2005] EWHC 2755 (Comm) (Cresswell J).
[203]  See *Pound v Hardy* [1956] AC 588.
[204]  See *Carnoustie v ITWF* [2002] 2 All ER (Comm) 657 (Siberry QC).
[205]  This echoes Article 10(2) of the Convention.

*Soc*[206] that the law of the place of performance may regulate the minor details of performance, but not so as to affect the substance of the obligation. Article 12(2) no doubt applies to such issues as the scope of normal business hours, within which delivery should be effected under a contract of sale;[207] and probably to whether, where a contractual debt is expressed in a currency other than that of the place of payment, the debtor has the option (in the absence of an express agreement to the contrary) of paying by means of local currency of equivalent value, instead of paying in the currency of account itself.[208] It also ensures that a sea-carrier is able to comply with a requirement under the law of the country of discharge that a bill of lading should after presentation be returned to the customs agent, marked if necessary to show that delivery has been made.[209]

Discharge includes the extinction or reduction of obligations by supervening legislation (for example, abrogating gold-value clauses; reducing the rate of interest payable; or imposing a moratorium on payments);[210] and their frustration as a result of supervening factual difficulties in their performance.[211] But in England, it has long been recognised that a stringent public policy may displace a foreign proper law if it insists on a performance which has been prohibited at the place of performance under criminal penalty,[212] and this situation is now specifically addressed by Article 9(3) of the Regulation.[213] In England the forum's stringent public policy may also be invoked to displace foreign rules as to the effect on existing contracts of the outbreak of a war involving the United Kingdom.[214]

### Essential Validity and Formation

Article 10(1) of the Rome I Regulation[215] provides that the existence and validity of a contract, or of any term of a contract, must be determined by the putative proper law of the contract (the law which would govern the contract under the Regulation if the contract or term were valid). This applies both to questions of essential validity and to questions of formation.

As regards essential validity, Article 10(1) applies the putative proper law to questions concerning the essential validity of the contract as a whole, such as the need for consideration,[216] or the effect of infringement of exchange restrictions.[217] It also makes the putative proper law applicable to questions concerning the validity of a particular term, such as an

---

[206] [1938] AC 224.
[207] See Dicey, Morris and Collins, at para 32-199.
[208] See Dicey, Morris and Collins, at para 32-200.
[209] See *East West Corp v DKBS 1912* [2002] 2 Lloyd's Rep 182 (Thomas J); affirmed on other points, [2003] 2 All ER 700 (CA).
[210] See *R v International Trustee* [1937] AC 500; *Mount Albert BC v Australasian Assurance Soc* [1938] AC 224; *National Bank of Greece and Athens v Metliss* [1958] AC 509; and *Adams v National Bank of Greece and Athens* [1961] AC 255.
[211] See *Jacobs v Crédit Lyonnais* (1884) 12 QBD 589.
[212] See pp. 339–41 below.
[213] See pp. 343–5 below.
[214] See *Ertel Bieber v Rio Tinto* [1918] AC 260.
[215] This echoes Article 8(1) of the Rome Convention 1980.
[216] See *Re Bonacina* [1912] 2 Ch 394 (CA).
[217] See *Kahler v Midland Bank* [1950] AC 24; and *Zivnostenska Bank v Frankman* [1950] AC 57.

exemption clause,[218] a clause restrictive of competition,[219] a clause preventing challenge of an intellectual property right,[220] a clause fixing an interest rate,[221] or a gold-value clause.[222] But it is in relation to essential validity that the exceptions in respect of overriding interests and public policy, under Articles 9 and 21 of the Regulation, have most importance.[223]

Article 10(1) extends to formation, so that in general the putative proper law determines such issues as the existence of a sufficient offer and acceptance or other formative acts.[224] Thus it determines whether a contract has been validly formed if the letter of acceptance is lost in the post;[225] or if an offer, expressed to remain open for a specified time, is purportedly accepted during that time despite an intervening attempted revocation; or if an offeror remains silent in the face of a purported acceptance which attempts to vary the terms of the original offer. Similarly, the putative proper law normally determines whether a contract has validly incorporated another document by reference, and whether an incomplete agreement has been subsequently completed by a further agreement.[226] The putative proper law also determines whether a person has become a party to an existing contract between others; for example as the holder of a bill of lading.[227]

Under Article 10(1), the putative proper law normally determines whether a party's consent is invalidated by mistake, non-fraudulent misrepresentation, non-disclosure of material facts,[228] or improper economic pressure.[229] But in England a stringent public policy under Article 21 will usually be invoked against a foreign rule which denies relief against fraud or non-economic pressure.[230]

---

[218] See *Peninsular Line v Shand* (1865) 16 ER 103; *Re Missouri Steamship Co* (1889) 42 ChD 321; *Vita Food Products v Unus Shipping* [1939] AC 277; *Sayers v International Drilling* [1971] 3 All ER 163; and *Coast Lines v Hudig & Veder* [1972] 2 QB 34.

[219] See *Apple Corps v Apple Computer* [1992] FSR 431; and *South African Breweries Ltd v King* [1900] 1 Ch 273. Cf. *Rousillon v Rousillon* (1880) 14 ChD 351, on respect for mandatory rules of the lex fori.

[220] See *Apple Corps v Apple Computer* [1992] FSR 431.

[221] See *Mount Albert BC v Australasian Life Ins Soc* [1938] AC 224.

[222] See *R v International Trustee* [1937] AC 500.

[223] On these provisions, see pp. 338–45 below.

[224] See *Albeko v Kamborian Shoe Machine Co* (1961) 111 LJ 519; *The Parouth* [1982] 2 Lloyd's Rep 351 (CA); *Union Transport v Continental Lines* [1992] 1 WLR 15 (HL); and *The Lake Avery* [1997] 1 Lloyd's Rep 540 (Clarke J).

[225] See *Albeko v Kamborian Shoe Machine Co* (1961) 111 LJ 519.

[226] See *Egon Oldendorff v Libera Corp* [1995] 2 Lloyd's Rep 64 (Mance J). See also *The Atlantic Emperor (No 1)* [1989] 1 Lloyd's Rep 548 (CA). But it is for the lex fori (and not for a putative proper law) to determine which (if either) of two possible jurisdiction or arbitration clauses, indicative of different countries, has been incorporated into a contract; see *The Heidberg* [1994] 2 Lloyd's Rep 287 (Judge Diamond QC), and *Dornoch Ltd v Mauritius Union Assurance Co Ltd* [2006] 2 Lloyd's Rep 475 (CA).

[227] See *The Ythan* [2006] 1 All ER 367 (Aikens J).

[228] See *Mackender v Feldia* [1967] 2 QB 590.

[229] See *Trendtex v Credit Suisse* [1982] AC 679; and *The Evia Luck* [1992] 2 AC 152. See also Kidner, (1994) 23 ILJ 109 at 124–6. See also *The Rickmers Tianjin* AD 2007 No 2, decided by the Swedish Labour Court, and discussed by Carolina Saf, (2007) 9 Swiss Yearbook of Private International Law 481.

[230] See *Kaufman v Gerson* [1904] 1 KB 591; *Mackender v Feldia* [1967] 2 QB 590; and *Royal Boskalis v Mountain* [1999] QB 674 (CA).

As regards formation, an exception is made by Article 10(2) of the Regulation,[231] which enables a party to rely upon the law of his habitual residence to establish that he did not consent, if it appears from the circumstances that it would not be reasonable to determine the effect of his conduct in accordance with the putative proper law. This would probably apply where an English resident ignored an offer (or counter-offer) received from abroad and governed by a foreign law under which silence was treated as consent. It is clear that for this purpose a person's habitual residence must be ascertained in accordance with Article 19 of the Regulation.[232]

But in general Article 10(2) will be applied with caution. Thus in *Egon Oldendorff v Libera Corp*,[233] Mance J explained that, in evaluating such a defence, the court should adopt a dispassionate, internationally minded approach, and that the onus is on the party invoking the exception to bring himself within its provisions. He ultimately rejected the defendant's argument for the application of Japanese law under Article 10(2) on the ground that it required a London arbitration clause to be ignored, contrary to ordinary commercial expectations, and despite every indication that the defendant had actually considered and accepted the clause, and that it was precisely the sort of clause which would be expected in an international charter agreement. A similar approach was adopted by Morison J in *Horn Linie v Panamericana Formas E Impresos*,[234] in relation to a party's consent to a choice-of-law clause. In upholding an English law and English jurisdiction clause contained in a bill of lading issued by a German shipowner in respect of a carriage from Germany to Colombia, he explained that the mere fact that by agreeing to an English jurisdiction and English law clause the cargo-owner had offended Colombian public policy was not of itself a good reason for holding that its consent to the clause was not truly given, or that it would be unfair or unreasonable to hold the cargo-owner to its bargain.

Article 10 of the Regulation is extended by Article 3(5),[235] so as to cover the existence and essential validity of the parties' consent to a choice-of-law clause. Thus it will usually be for the law designated in a choice-of-law clause to determine whether that clause itself was agreed to by means of sufficient acts of offer and acceptance, and whether a party's consent to the clause was invalidated by factors such as misrepresentation. While logical objections can be made to such a 'boot-strap' approach, it is thought that the solution adopted is sufficiently intelligible, and that the proviso in Article 10(2) should be adequate to protect the legitimate expectations of a party who denies having agreed to a choice-of-law clause invoked by the other party.

A further problem arises in the case of negotiations involving a 'battle of forms', each containing a different choice-of-law clause. In this situation, the proper course, in the view of the present writer, is first to determine whether there is a contract on the terms of the first-issued form, taking into account its choice-of-law clause in accordance with Articles 3(5) and

---

[231]   This echoes Article 8(2) of the Convention.

[232]   On Article 19, see pp. 315–16 above. Under the Convention, it was less than clear how the habitual residence of a company should be determined for the purpose of Article 8(2).

[233]   [1995] 2 Lloyd's Rep 64. See also *Welex v Rosa Maritime* [2002] 2 Lloyd's Rep 701 (David Steel J), affirmed on other points [2003] 2 Lloyd's Rep 509 (CA); and *Morin v Bonhams & Brooks* [2003] 2 All ER (Comm) 36 (Hirst QC), affirmed on other points [2004] 1 Lloyd's Rep 702 (CA).

[234]   [2006] EWHC 373 (Comm).

[235]   This echoes Article 3(4) of the Convention.

10; and then whether there is (also) a contract on the terms of the second-issued form, taking similar account of its choice-of-law clause. If one concludes thereby that there are two mutually inconsistent contracts, the later-formed contract supersedes the earlier to the extent of the inconsistency.[236]

## Formal Validity

As regards formalities, Article 11 of the Rome I Regulation lays down a rule of alternative reference, reflecting a policy of validation, designed to facilitate the conclusion of transactions.[237] Probably if a contract is invalid under all the laws referred to by Article 11, but with different effects, the law which has the least invalidating effect applies.[238] Article 11(1) deals with the situation where a contract is concluded between persons who, or whose agents, are in the same country at the time of its conclusion. In this situation, the contract is formally valid if it satisfies either the formal requirements of its proper law, or those of the law of the country where it is concluded.[239]

Article 11(2) deals with the situation where a contract is concluded between persons who, or whose agents, are in different countries at the time of its conclusion. In this situation, the contract is formally valid if it satisfies either the formal requirements of its proper law, or those of the law of a country where one of the parties or agents is present at the time of conclusion, or those of the law of a country where one of the parties is habitually resident at that time. Thus in this situation, on the assumption that there are only two parties to the contract, there are up to five different laws, compliance with any of whose formal requirements is sufficient: the proper law of the contract; the law of the country in which a party or his agent is present and acting; the law of the country in which the other party or his agent is present and acting; the law of the habitual residence of one party; and the law of the habitual residence of the other party.[240]

Article 11(3) deals with the formal validity of a unilateral act intended to have legal effect relating to an existing or contemplated contract. Such an act is formally valid if it satisfies either the formal requirements of the actual or putative proper law of the existing or contemplated contract, or those of the law of the country where the unilateral act is done, or those of the law of the country where the person by whom it is done is habitually resident at that time.[241]

In addition, Article 18(2) of the Regulation[242] enables a contract (or a unilateral act intended to have legal effect) to be proved by any mode of proof which is recognised either

---

[236]    Cf. Dicey, Morris and Collins, at para 32-165.

[237]    Article 11 replaces Article 9 of the Rome Convention 1980, and adopts a solution even more favourable to formal validity.

[238]    See the Giuliano and Lagarde Report, at p. 30.

[239]    This accords with Article 9(1) and (3) of the Convention.

[240]    This solution is more favourable to validity than that provided by Article 9(2) and (3) of the Convention, which referred to the proper law and to the law of a country in which each party or agent is present and acting, but not to habitual residence.

[241]    This solution is more favourable to validity than that provided by Article 9(4) of the Convention, which referred to the proper law and to the law of the country in which the act was done, but not to habitual residence.

[242]    This echoes Article 14(2) of the Convention.

by the law of the forum, or by any law which is applicable to its formal validity under Article 11 and under which the contract (or unilateral act) is formally valid, provided that such mode of proof can be administered by the forum. This effectively overrides the traditional English approach to the Statute of Frauds 1677, which was extended by means of procedural characterisation to contracts made abroad and governed by foreign law.[243]

By way of exception, Article 11(5) of the Regulation[244] subjects a contract whose subject-matter is a right in rem in immovable property or a tenancy of immovable property to the formal requirements of the law of the country where the property is situated, if by that law those requirements are imposed irrespective of the country where the contract is concluded and of its proper law, and those requirements cannot be derogated from by agreement. The requirements referred to probably include those imposed by s 2 of the (English) Law of Property (Miscellaneous Provisions) Act 1989, under which a contract for the sale or other disposition of an interest in land can only be made in writing.

## Capacity

The capacity of both individuals and companies to contract is excluded from the scope of the Rome I Regulation by Article 1(2)(a) and (f),[245] and thus continues to be governed by the conflict rules of the forum country. But an exception specified by Article 13 insists that, in the case of a contract concluded between persons who are in the same country, an individual who would have capacity under the law of that country may invoke his incapacity resulting from the law of another country only if the other party to the contract was aware of the incapacity at the time of the conclusion of the contract, or was not aware of it as a result of negligence.[246] Article 13 reflects an exception invented by French case-law in 1861[247] to the French rule referring capacity to the law of the nationality of the person in question.[248]

Thus, subject to the exception specified by Article 13 of the Regulation, the English courts continue to determine a person's capacity to contract in accordance with traditional English conflict rules. These include a special rule for marriage settlements, referring each party's

---

[243]　　See *Leroux v Brown* (1852) 12 CB 801. Cf. *The Rosso* [1982] 3 All ER 841 (CA).

[244]　　This substantially accords with Article 9(6) of the Convention.

[245]　　Article 1(2)(a) refers to questions involving the status or legal capacity of natural persons, and Article 1(2)(f) to questions governed by the law of companies and other bodies, corporate or unincorporated, such as the legal capacity of companies and other bodies, corporate or unincorporated. These provisions echo Article 1(2)(a) and (e) of the Rome Convention 1980.

[246]　　This echoes Article 11 of the Convention.

[247]　　See *De Lizardi v Chaise* Sirey 61.1.305 (1861), a decision of the Chambre des Requêtes of the Court of Cassation.

[248]　　An analogous provision is made by Article 19 of the Hague Convention of 19th October 1996 on Jurisdiction, Applicable Law, Recognition, Enforcement and Co-operation in Respect of Parental Responsibility and Measures for the Protection of Children, in respect of a transaction entered into between persons present in the same State, being a third party and another person who would be entitled to act as a child's legal representative under the law of the State where the transaction was concluded. Article 19 insists that the validity of such a transaction cannot be contested, and the third party cannot be held liable, on the sole ground that the other person was not entitled to act as the child's legal representative under the law designated by Chapter III of the Hague Convention 1996, unless the third party knew or should have known that the parental responsibility was governed by that law. On the Hague Convention 1996, see Chapter 17 below.

capacity to the law of his or her domicile;[249] and a special rule for contracts for the disposition of land, referring capacity to the lex situs.[250] As regards the capacity of an individual (as distinct from a company) to enter into other contracts, English law probably follows a rule of alternative reference, designed to favour validity, under which it is sufficient that an individual has capacity either under the proper law of the contract, or under his personal law.

Thus it is probably sufficient under the English rule that an individual has capacity under the proper law of the contract, now ascertained in accordance with the Rome I Regulation,[251] and with full respect given to an express choice of law by the parties.[252] This approach reflects a desire to respect the expectations of the undoubtedly capable party, and to facilitate international trade, in which incapacitating rules are viewed as a tiresome nuisance, which it is permissible to avoid by the choice of a validating law. It is probably alternatively sufficient under the English rule, where an individual lacks capacity under the proper law, that he has capacity by the law of his domicile.[253] Here the rationale is that incapacities are presumably imposed in order to protect immature, weak-minded or otherwise inadequate persons, and that only the personal law can have an interest in imposing protection sufficient to justify burdening international commerce. But in the case of a company, it seems that the English rule insists that capacity should exist both under the proper law of the contract, and under the law of the country of incorporation.[254]

## Representation

By Article 1(2)(g), the Rome I Regulation does not apply to 'the question whether an agent is able to bind a principal, or an organ to bind a company or other body corporate or unincorporated, in relation to a third party'.[255] Thus such questions of representation are left to the conflict rules of the forum country.

---

[249]   See *Re Cooke's Trusts* (1887) 56 LT 737; *Cooper v Cooper* (1888) 13 AppCas 88; and *Viditz v O'Hagan* [1900] 2 Ch 87.

[250]   See *Bank of Africa v Cohen* [1909] 2 Ch 129.

[251]   See Young, [1991] LMCLQ 314 at 318; and *Marubeni v Mongolian Government (No 1)* [2002] 2 All ER (Comm) 873 (Aikens J).

[252]   See *Male v Roberts* (1800) 3 Esp 163; *McFeetridge v Stewarts & Lloyds* [1913] SC 773; *Charron v Montreal Trust* (1958) 15 DLR(2d) 240; and *Bodley Head v Flegon* [1972] 1 WLR 680. Cf. Dicey, Morris and Collins, Rule 209(1), referring to the law most closely connected, rather than the proper law as normally ascertained.

[253]   Cf. Dicey, Morris and Collins, Rule 209(1), which refers to the person's domicile and residence.

[254]   See Dicey, Morris and Collins, Rule 162(1); *Carse v Coppen* [1951] SLT 145, holding in accordance with Scottish internal law (as it then stood) that a Scottish company could not create a floating charge over its English assets; *Kutchera v Buckingham International Holdings Ltd* [1988] IR 61; and *Continental Enterprises Ltd v Shandong Zhucheng Foreign Trade Group Co* [2005] EWHC 92 (Comm), where David Steel J held that a contract governed by English law was invalid because the buyer, a Chinese company, lacked capacity under its corporate constitution and Chinese law to engage in foreign trade. See also *Haugesund Kommune v Depfa ACS Bank* [2010] EWCA Civ 579, where the Court of Appeal invalidated a contract of loan, governed by English law, between a Norwegian local authority and an Irish subsidiary of a German bank, on the ground that the local authority lacked power under Norwegian law to obtain loans for speculative purposes. It proceeded to disregard a further Norwegian rule, validating a contract despite incapacity where the other party had acted in good faith, on the ground that the consequences of incapacity to contract are governed by the putative proper law of the contract in question.

[255]   This echoes Article 1(2)(f) of the Rome Convention 1980. The EC Commission's Proposal of

**The scope of the exclusion**

It is clear that this exclusion has no bearing on the mutual rights and obligations of the principal and the agent. The Regulation *does* apply to a contract between a principal and an agent, as is clear from the decision of Longmore J in *HIB v Guardian Insurance*[256] that, in accordance with Article 4, a contract whereby an insurance broker is instructed to arrange insurance will normally be governed by the law of the country in which the broker carries on business.

On the other hand, the exclusion applies in disputes between the principal and the third party, where the agent's authority affects the validity of the main contract. It also applies in disputes between the agent and the third party, for example where the third party sues the agent for breach of a warranty of authority. In both cases, the exclusion covers questions of actual authority, ostensible authority, ratification, and the intervention of an undisclosed principal. Article 1(2)(g) does not extend to questions as to whether a company itself lacks power to enter into a contract, but such questions are excluded from the scope of the Regulation by Article 1(2)(f), as questions of legal capacity governed by company law.

**Actual authority**

As regards actual authority, it seems clear that, since the existence of actual authority depends on the terms and interpretation of the agreement between the principal and the agent, it should be determined in accordance with the proper law of the contract between them.[257] Similarly, in the case of a corporate organ, actual authority depends on the corporate constitution and (under English conflict rules) the law of the country in which the company was incorporated.

**Other authority**

As regards authority other than actual authority, the current trend in English law is to refer to the putative proper law of the main contract (the contract concluded between the agent and the third party), as determined under the Rome I Regulation.[258] This applies to ostensible (or

---

15th December 2005 would have confined the exclusion to corporate organs, as distinct from ordinary agents. It would also (by its Article 7) have laid down particular conflict rules for contracts of agency, for the relationship between the principal and the third party, and for the relationship between the agent and the third party. But these rules were deleted from the Regulation as adopted.

256    [1997] 1 Lloyd's Rep 412. See also the decision of the French Court of Cassation in *Bismuth v Association L'Avenir Sportif de La Marsa* [2001] Journal du Droit International 97, applying French law under Article 4 to a claim for commission by a French agent who had acted for a Tunisian football club in the transfer of a player between a French club and the Tunisian club. See also *Chatenay v Brazilian Submarine Telegraph Co* [1891] 1 QB 79 (CA); *Edinburgh Assurance Co v Burns*, 479 FSupp 138 (CD Cal, 1979), affirmed 669 F2d 1259 (C9, 1981); the American Law Institute's Restatement, Second, Conflict of Laws, § 291; and the Hague Convention of 14th March 1978 on the Law Applicable to Agency, Articles 5 and 6.

257    See *Ruby v Commercial Union* (1933) 150 LT 38 (CA); *Marubeni v Mongolian Government (No 1)* [2002] 2 All ER (Comm) 873 (Aikens J); *Marubeni v Mongolian Government (No 2)* [2004] 2 Lloyd's Rep 198 (Cresswell J), affirmed [2005] 1 WLR 2497 (CA); *SEB Trygg v Manches* [2005] 2 Lloyd's Rep 129 (Gloster J), affirmed [2006] 1 WLR 2276 (CA); Dicey, Morris and Collins, at para 33-434; and *Edinburgh Assurance Co v Burns* 479 FSupp 138 (CD Cal, 1979), affirmed 669 F2d 1259 (C9, 1981). Cf. *Sinfra v Sinfra* [1939] 2 All ER 675 (Lewis J).

258    See *Marubeni v Mongolian Government (No 1)* [2002] 2 All ER (Comm) 873 (Aikens J); *Marubeni v Mongolian Government (No 2)* [2004] 2 Lloyd's Rep 198 (Cresswell J), affirmed [2005] 1

apparent) authority and usual authority,[259] to ratification,[260] and to the possibility and effect of the intervention of an undisclosed principal.[261] In contrast, Articles 11 and 15 of the Hague Convention of 14th March 1978 on the Law Applicable to Agency refer such issues to the law of the country in which the agent had his business establishment at the time of his acts, or in some cases to the law of the country in which the agent acted.[262]

With regard to ostensible or usual authority, it is submitted that neither of these approaches is satisfactory. Since the question of ostensible or usual authority arises where actual authority is lacking, and its main effect is to render the principal liable on a contract which he had not actually authorised, the appropriate conflict rule should utilise a connection of the principal, such as his habitual residence, determined in accordance with Article 19 of the Rome I Regulation.

On the other hand, with regard to ratification and to the intervention of an undisclosed principal, the English approach seems justifiable. For such situations involve a choice by the principal to claim rights and incur liabilities under a contract already concluded between the agent and the third party, and there seems no reason why a principal who makes such a choice should not have to take the main contract, including its proper law, as he finds it.

## Procedure

Article 1(3) of the Rome I Regulation[263] excludes evidence and procedure from the scope of the Regulation, thus leaving them to be governed by the lex fori in accordance with traditional

---

WLR 2497 (CA); *SEB Trygg v Manches* [2005] 2 Lloyd's Rep 129 (Gloster J), affirmed [2006] 1 WLR 2276 (CA); and Dicey, Morris and Collins, Rule 228.

[259] See *Marubeni v Mongolian Government (No 1)* [2002] 2 All ER (Comm) 873 (Aikens J); *Marubeni v Mongolian Government (No 2)* [2004] 2 Lloyd's Rep 198 (Cresswell J), affirmed [2005] 1 WLR 2497 (CA); *SEB Trygg v Manches* [2005] 2 Lloyd's Rep 129 (Gloster J), affirmed [2006] 1 WLR 2276 (CA); and *Calyon v Wytwornia Sprzetu Komunikacynego PZL Swidnik* [2009] EWHC 1914 (Comm) (Field J).

[260] See *Presentaciones Musicales v Secunda* [1994] Ch 271 (CA); *Merrill Lynch v Municipality of Piraeus* [1997] CLC 1214 (Cresswell J); *Marubeni v Mongolian Government (No 1)* [2002] 2 All ER (Comm) 873 (Aikens J); *Marubeni v Mongolian Government (No 2)* [2004] 2 Lloyd's Rep 198 (Cresswell J), affirmed [2005] 1 WLR 2497 (CA); and *SEB Trygg v Manches* [2005] 2 Lloyd's Rep 129 (Gloster J), affirmed [2006] 1 WLR 2276 (CA). See also *Edinburgh Assurance Co v Burns* 479 FSupp 138 (CD Cal, 1979), affirmed 669 F2d 1259 (C9, 1981).

[261] See *Maspons v Mildred* (1882) 9 QBD 530 (CA); affirmed (1883) 8 AppCas 874.

[262] See also the American Law Institute's Restatement, Second, Conflict of Laws, § 292(2), referring to the law of the country where the agent dealt with the third person, provided at least that the principal had authorised the agent to act on his behalf in that state or had led the third person reasonably to believe that the agent had such authority; *Stockmen's Livestock Exchange v Thompson* 520 NW2d 255 (South Dakota, 1994); and *Nucor v Aceros* 28 F3d 572 (C7 for Indiana, 1994).

For the purposes of the relationship between the principal or the agent and a third party, Article 7(2)–(4) of the EC Commission's Proposal of 15th December 2005 would have subjected all types of authority to the law of the country in which the agent had his habitual residence when he acted. But the applicable law would instead have been that of the country in which the agent acted, if either the principal or the third party had his habitual residence in that country, or the agent acted at an exchange or auction. Moreover, where the law applicable to the relationship between the principal and the third party had been designated in writing by the principal or the agent and expressly accepted by the third party, the law so designated would have been applicable to questions of the agent's authority.

[263] This echoes Article 1(2)(h) of the Rome Convention 1980.

rules. The exclusion is explicitly made subject to Article 18(1),[264] which makes applicable rules of the proper law which raise presumptions of law or determine the burden of proof; and to Article 18(2),[265] which enables a contract or other act intended to have legal effect to be proved by any mode of proof which is recognised either by the law of the forum, or by any law which is made applicable to its formal validity by Article 11 and under which it is formally valid, provided that such mode of proof can be administered by the forum.[266]

### Remedies

By Article 12(1)(c) of the Rome I Regulation, the proper law governs, within the limits of the powers conferred on the court by its procedural law, the consequences of a total or partial breach of obligations, including the assessment of damages insofar as it is governed by rules of law.[267] This cautious formulation ensures that English courts will not be required to follow a foreign proper law to the length of making available non-monetary remedies, such as orders for specific performance, in circumstances where English law would limit the plaintiff to monetary remedies; for example, because specific performance would necessitate continuing judicial supervision.[268]

On the other hand, the Regulation encourages the application of the proper law to the greatest extent practicable in connection with the assessment of damages. Not only to questions of remoteness of damage, admissible heads of damage, and mitigation of loss, but even to mere quantification, insofar as the proper law supplies a rule sufficiently definite that a court elsewhere can apply it with reasonable accuracy. This substantially accords with the approach which was recently adopted for tort cases under the Private International Law (Miscellaneous Provisions) Act 1995 by the English Court of Appeal in *Harding v Wealands*,[269] but was eventually rejected in that context by the House of Lords.[270]

Moreover, as the Court of Appeal ruled in *Lesotho Highlands Development Authority v Impregilo*,[271] the proper law must be applied in determining the currency in which a monetary judgment should be given, and also whether the claimant is entitled to interest on unpaid sums, whether by virtue of a contractual term or of a rule of law. They also ruled that, if the rate of interest is not fixed by a contractual term, it must be determined in accordance with the lex fori, but this seems questionable.

---

[264]   This substantially echoes Article 14(1) of the Convention.
[265]   This echoes Article 14(2) of the Convention.
[266]   On formal validity, see pp. 327–8 above.
[267]   This substantially echoes Article 10(1)(c) of the Rome Convention 1980. The Regulation is slightly more elaborate, in referring to the consequences of a total or partial breach of obligations, instead of merely to the consequences of breach.
[268]   See Dicey, Morris and Collins, at para 32-203.
[269]   [2005] 1 All ER 415 (CA). See also *D'Almeida v Becker* [1953] 2 QB 329.
[270]   See *Harding v Wealands* [2007] 2 AC 1. On the assessment of damages under the Rome II Regulation, see pp. 406–8 below.
[271]   [2003] 2 Lloyd's Rep 497 (CA), affirming [2003] 1 All ER (Comm) 22 (Morison J). The decision of the Court of Appeal was reversed on other grounds (relating to the limits of judicial supervision of an arbitral award) by the House of Lords, [2006] 1 AC 221.

## Time Limitation

By Article 12(1)(d), the Rome I Regulation specifies that the proper law governs prescription and limitation of actions.[272] In England, this substantive characterisation of time-limits for bringing actions was anticipated by the Foreign Limitation Periods Act 1984, which largely implemented Law Commission Report No 114 (1982) on the Classification of Limitation in Private International Law. Previously English law had resolutely insisted on treating time-limits for bringing actions as a matter of procedure, governed by the lex fori.[273]

Section 2 of the 1984 Act makes an exception where the application of a foreign rule on time limitation would conflict with English public policy, and declares that such a conflict exists where the application of the foreign rule would cause undue hardship to one of the parties.[274] It also requires any foreign rule under which time does not run while a party is absent from a given country to be disregarded.[275] In addition, s 1(3) insists in all cases on the English rule that it is the issue of the claim form, rather than (for example) its service, which constitutes the commencement of English proceedings for limitation purposes.[276]

As regards undue hardship, English courts have disregarded a foreign one-year period for personal injury actions, where the claimant had been long hospitalised and had been led by the defendant to believe that her claim would be met by its insurers;[277] or a limitation period contained in a law which the parties did not realise was the proper law of the relevant contract.[278] But a foreign one-year period for an industrial disease claim, running from the date at which the plaintiff obtained knowledge of the injury, and within which the plaintiff was in fact able to obtain relevant legal advice, has been respected.[279]

## The Consequences of Nullity

Article 12(1)(e) of the Rome I Regulation subjects to the proper law the consequences of nullity of the contract. This reflects the idea that coherence requires that the law which imposes invalidity, usually the proper law, should be allowed also to determine its consequences; for example, as regards the restoration of or payment for benefits received. Similar considerations underlie the provision in s 1 of the (English) Law Reform (Frustrated

---

[272]   This echoes Article 10(1)(d) of the Rome Convention 1980.

[273]   See also Stone, [1985] 4 LMCLQ 497; *Sun Oil v Wortman* 486 US 717 (1988); and the American Law Institute's Restatement, Second, Conflict of Laws, § 142, as revised in 1988.

[274]   But s 2 of the 1984 Act does not enable an otherwise applicable *English* limitation rule to be disregarded by reference to public policy or undue hardship; see *Chagos Islanders v Attorney General* [2003] EWHC 2222 (Ouseley J), affirmed on other grounds [2004] EWCA Civ 997.

[275]   See also *George v Douglas Aircraft* 332 F2d 73 (1964).

[276]   See also s 4(3), which preserves English discretion to grant or refuse equitable relief, such as specific performance or an injunction, by reference to English conceptions of acquiescence or unreasonable delay, even where the substantive dispute is governed by foreign law. Such relief must be refused if a definite limitation period is applicable to such relief under the foreign law and has expired; but otherwise the foreign law is merely to be taken into account in the exercise of the English discretion.

[277]   See *Jones v Trollope Colls*, 'The Times' of 26th January 1990 (CA).

[278]   See *The Komninos S* [1991] 1 Lloyd's Rep 370 (CA).

[279]   See *Durham v T & N*, 1st May 1996 (CA). See also *Arab Monetary Fund v Hashim* [1996] 1 Lloyd's Rep 589 (CA).

Contracts) Act 1943 making the Act, which deals with the consequences of frustration, applicable to contracts governed by English law.

Article 12(1)(e) of the Regulation echoes Article 10(1)(e) of the Rome Convention 1980, but under the Convention reservations excluding the application of Article 10(1)(e) were permitted by Article 22, and such reservations were made by the United Kingdom[280] and by Italy. The British reservation was probably illusory, since the decision of the House of Lords in *The Evia Luck*[281] indicated the rule laid down by Article 10(1)(e) accorded with traditional English law. In that case, the House applied English law as the expressly chosen proper law of a contract entered into under economic pressure between foreigners abroad, to establish not only the illegitimacy of the economic pressure and the resulting invalidity of the contract, but also the existence of a consequential restitutionary right to recover back money paid under the contract. In any event, no such reservation is possible under the Regulation.

A complication arises from the fact that Article 1(2)(i) of the Rome I Regulation excludes from the scope of the Regulation obligations arising out of dealings prior to the conclusion of a contract, and Recital 10 explains that such obligations are covered by Article 12 of the Rome II Regulation. Thus there is some uncertainty as to whether it is Article 12(1)(e) of the Rome I Regulation, or Article 12 of the Rome II Regulation, which applies to a restitutionary or tortious claim which arises from the invalidity of a contract on account of acts or omissions which occurred during the negotiations which led to the conclusion of the contract. For example, where there is a claim for rescission or annulment of a contract on account of misrepresentation or non-disclosure, and a consequential claim for the restoration of benefits transferred between the parties in pursuance of the contract. But the question of which provision applies to the consequential claim seems to have no real importance, since Article 12(1) of the Rome II Regulation subjects a non-contractual obligation arising out of dealings prior to the conclusion of a contract, regardless of whether the contract was actually concluded or not, to the law which applies to the contract, or which would have been applicable to the contract if it had been entered into. Thus the actual or putative proper law of the contract will apply to the consequential restitutionary claim, whether reference is made to Article 12(1)(e) of the Rome I Regulation, or to Article 12(1) of the Rome II Regulation.[282] Moreover, Article 12(1) of the Rome II Regulation ensures that the actual or putative proper law of the contract applies to a tortious claim which arises from the misrepresentation or non-disclosure, independently of annulment or rescission of the contract.

Another complication arises in relation to a restitutionary claim which arises from the

---

280   See the Contracts (Applicable Law) Act 1990, s 2(2).

281   [1992] 2 AC 152. See also Kidner, (1994) 23 ILJ 109 at 124–6. Cf. *Baring Brothers v Cunninghame DC* [1996] WL 1093491, an interest-swap case, where Lord Penrose (in the Outer House of the Court of Session) favoured application to a restitutionary claim of the law of country with which the critical events have their closest connection, rather than the law expressly chosen as governing the invalid contract.

282   It is only where the actual or putative proper law of the contract cannot be determined, for example because the negotiations broke down owing to disagreement about the inclusion of a choice-of-law clause, that Article 12(2) of the Rome II Regulation subjects a non-contractual obligation arising out of dealings prior to the conclusion of a contract to a law determined by reference to common habitual residence, place of injury, and closest connection, in a manner similar to the determination of the law applicable to an ordinary tort under Article 4 of that Regulation.

invalidity of a contract for reasons other than pre-contractual dealings. For example, a claim for the restoration of benefits transferred between the parties in pursuance of a contract which is invalid on account of incapacity or of an illegal purpose. In this case, the uncertainty is as to whether the consequential restitutionary claim is governed by the actual or putative proper law of the contract in accordance with Article 12(1)(e) of the Rome I Regulation, or is subject to Article 10 of the Rome II Regulation as a non-contractual obligation arising out of unjust enrichment. If it is Article 10 of the Rome II Regulation which applies in such cases, Article 10(1) will normally subject the restitutionary claim to the law which governs the contract, but Article 10(4) will make available an exception in favour of the law of another country which is manifestly more closely connected with the restitutionary obligation.

More generally, although the rule subjecting the consequences of invalidity to the law which governs the contract may be seen as promoting coherence and avoiding unnecessary complication, this is not so in the exceptional cases where the invalidity arises from a law which is not the proper law of the contact, but which nonetheless is applicable to the relevant issue under the Rome I Regulation. For example, where a party's consent to the contract is negated by reference to the law of his residence under Article 10(2); or a consumer contract is invalidated by reference to a mandatory requirement of the law of the consumer's residence under Article 6(2). To take proper account of such exceptional cases, it is suggested that the consequences of invalidity should have been subjected to the law which in the particular situation gives rise to the invalidity under the Regulation, rather than to the proper law of the contract as such.

**Voluntary Assignment and Contractual Subrogation**

Article 14 of the Rome I Regulation deals with the voluntary assignment of and contractual subrogation to a contractual right. By Article 14(1), the relationship between assignor and assignee under a voluntary assignment or contractual subrogation of a claim against another person (the debtor) is governed by the law which applies to the contract between the assignor and assignee under the Regulation. By Article 14(2), the law governing the assigned or subrogated claim determines its assignability, the relationship between the assignee and the debtor, the conditions under which the assignment or subrogation can be invoked against the debtor, and whether the debtor's obligations have been discharged. Article 14(3) adds that for this purpose the concept of assignment includes outright transfers of claims, transfers of claims by way of security, and pledges or other security rights over claims.

Article 14 largely accords with Article 12 of the Rome Convention 1980. Although the Convention did not explicitly refer to contractual subrogation, its inclusion was probably implied. Article 14(1) of the Regulation refers to the relationship between assignor and assignee, instead of to the mutual obligations of assignor and assignee. Recital 38 explains that the new formulation is designed to make it clear that Article 14(1) extends to the proprietary aspects of an assignment, as between assignor and assignee, in legal orders where such aspects are treated separately from the obligational aspects; but adds that it should not cover preliminary questions, but should be strictly limited to aspects which are directly relevant to the voluntary assignment or contractual subrogation in question. Article 14(3) is new, but it probably serves only to make explicit what was implied in the Convention.

Article 14 of the Regulation applies to a voluntary assignment of or a contractual subrogation to a particular contractual right, or of the benefit of a particular contractual obligation, such as an insurer's obligation to indemnify the insured.[283] It does not extend to an assignment of some other type of asset, such as shares in a company,[284] nor to a general transfer of assets, such as may occur on insolvency, marriage or death. An assignment is voluntary if it is effected by an intentional act of the owner, as distinct from a compulsory legal process (such as the enforcement of a judgment). Similarly, a subrogation is contractual if it is intentionally provided for by a transaction between the parties thereto, rather than arising from a legal rule (for example, the rule under which an insurer who has paid a claim by its insured is entitled to pursue in the name of its insured claims for the same loss against third parties).

Article 14(1) establishes a rule subjecting the relationship between the assignor and the assignee to the proper law of the assignment, determined as if the assignment were a contract between them.[285] Article 14(2) establishes a rule subjecting the relationship between the assignee and the debtor, and also the effect of the assignment on the relationship between the assignor and the debtor, to the proper law of the original contract from which the claim assigned arose. For to subject the effect of the assignment on the relationship between the assignor and the debtor to a different law from that governing the relationship between the assignee and the debtor could produce the perverse result that, as a result of the assignment, the debtor incurred double liability, or was released from the claim altogether. It may be thought regrettable that Article 14 did not simply subject the validity and effect of the assignment, as between all the parties (the assignor, the assignee and the debtor), to the proper law of the contract from which the claim assigned arose.

In *The Mount I*,[286] which involved a voluntary assignment of the benefit of an insurer's obligation to indemnify its insured, Mance LJ explained that Article 14(1) regulates the position of the assignor and assignee as between themselves. Under Article 14(2), the contract giving rise to the obligation governs not merely its assignability, but also the relationship between the assignee and the debtor and the conditions under which the assignment can be invoked as against the debtor, as well as any question whether the debtor's obligations have been discharged. On its face, Article 14(2) treats as matters within its scope, and expressly provides for, issues both as to whether the debtor owes monies to and must pay the assignee (their relationship) and under what conditions, for example as regards the giving of notice. Thus, in that case, the validity of the assignment between the assignor, the assignee and the debtor was governed by English law, as the law expressly chosen in both the insurance contract and the assignment, rather than by French law, that of the debtor's residence. This applied in particular to the necessity for and mode of notice to the debtor.

It will be apparent that Article 14 contains no provision designed to regulate questions of priority between a voluntary assignee and a third party who claims under an involuntary assignment (such as a judgment creditor, who seeks to garnish the claim to satisfy a judgment against the assignor). However, Article 27(2) requires the Commission to submit, by 17th

---

[283]    See *The Mount I* [2001] 1 Lloyd's Rep 597 (CA). See also *Le Feuvre v Sullivan* (1855) 14 ER 389.

[284]    See *Macmillan v Bishopsgate Investment Trust (No 3)* [1996] 1 WLR 387 (CA).

[285]    As regards the validity between the assignor and the assignee of an assignment by way of gift, under Articles 14(1) and 4(2) there is a strong presumption in favour of the law of the habitual residence of the assignor. See *Waldwiese Stiftung v Lewis* [2004] EWHC 2589 (Ch) (Mann J).

[286]    [2001] 1 Lloyd's Rep 597 (CA).

June 2010, a report on the question of the effectiveness of an assignment or subrogation of a claim against third parties, and the priority of the assigned or subrogated claim over a right of another person. The report should be accompanied, if appropriate, by a proposal to amend the Regulation, and an assessment of the impact of the provisions to be introduced.

### Legal Subrogation

Article 15 of the Rome I Regulation deals with legal subrogation to a contractual claim.[287] Such subrogation arises from a legal rule, such as a rule under which an insurer who has paid a claim by its insured is entitled to pursue in the name of its insured claims for the same loss against third parties, rather than from an agreement between the parties to the subrogation.[288]

Article 15 of the Regulation specifies that where a person (the creditor) has a contractual claim against another (the debtor), and a third person has a duty to satisfy the creditor, or has in fact satisfied the creditor in discharge of that duty, the law which governs the third person's duty to satisfy the creditor is to determine whether and to what extent the third person is entitled to exercise against the debtor the rights which the creditor had against the debtor under the law governing their relationship. Thus, for example, where cargo is damaged in the course of carriage, whether and to what extent the cargo-insurer has a right of subrogation, by operation of law, to the insured cargo-owner's claim for the damage against the carrier, based on a breach of the contract of carriage between the cargo-owner and the carrier, is subjected to the proper law of the insurance contract. But the subrogation cannot confer on the cargo-insurer rights against the carrier greater than those possessed by the cargo-owner under the proper law of the contract of carriage.

### Recourse between Debtors

Article 16 of the Rome I Regulation deals with recourse between several debtors who are liable for the same claim.[289] It applies where a creditor has a claim against several debtors who are liable for the same claim, and one of the debtors (the payer) has already satisfied the claim in whole or in part. It then subjects the payer's right to claim recourse from the other debtors to the law which governs the payer's obligation towards the creditor. But it insists that the other debtors may rely on the defences they had against the creditor to the extent allowed by the law governing their obligations towards the creditor.

It seems clear that, for Article 16 to apply, the claim by the creditor against all the debtors must be a contractual claim.[290] It seems likely that the creditor's claim will usually arise from a single contract to which the creditor and all the debtors are parties, or at least from a group

---

[287]    Very similar provision in respect of subrogation to a tortious or restitutionary claim is made by Article 19 of the Rome II Regulation. See p. 409 below.

[288]    Article 15 substantially accords with Article 13(1) of the Rome Convention 1980. The Regulation makes explicit that Article 15 is confined to legal subrogation, contractual subrogation being treated in the same way as voluntary assignment under Article 14. But a similar result was probably implied by Articles 12 and 13(1) of the Convention.

[289]    Article 16 substantially accords with Article 13(2) of the Rome Convention 1980.

[290]    Where the creditor's claim is tortious or restitutionary in character, Article 20 of the Rome II Regulation subjects the payer's right to claim recourse from the other debtors to the law which governs

of related contracts between the creditor and one or more of the debtors which are governed by the same law. It also seems probable that Article 16 will give way to a contrary agreement between the debtors, if such an agreement is valid under its proper law. Certainly the broad effect of Article 16 will usually be to subject a claim for recourse between contractual debtors to the law governing the contract or contracts from which the debt arises.

### Set-off

Article 17 of the Rome I Regulation deals with set-off. It specifies that, where the right to set-off is not agreed by the parties, set-off is governed by the law applicable to the claim against which the right to set-off is asserted.

There was no provision on set-off in the Rome Convention, but the principle in favour of the law which governs the claim against which the right to set-off is asserted is admitted by Article 6 of the Insolvency Regulation.[291] It is unclear whether, for Article 17 of the Rome I Regulation to apply, both claims must be contractual in nature, or whether it is sufficient that the claim against which the set-off is asserted is contractual in character.

## PUBLIC POLICY AND OVERRIDING INTERESTS

The Rome I Regulation derogates from its main rule, referring most contractual issues to the proper law, by making important exceptions in favour of the public policy or overriding interests of the forum country. Article 21 of the Regulation contains a traditional saving permitting the forum country to insist on respect for its own stringent public policy. It specifies that the application of a provision of the law of any country specified by the Regulation may be refused if such application is manifestly incompatible with the public policy (ordre public) of the forum.[292]

This traditional saving is supplemented by Article 9(2) of the Rome I Regulation, which enables the forum country to assert and give effect to overriding interests in the application of its own mandatory rules. It specifies that nothing in the Regulation restricts the application of the overriding mandatory provisions of the law of the forum. This substantially accords with Article 7(2) of the Rome Convention 1980, which specified that nothing in the Convention restricted the application of the rules of the law of the forum in a situation where they were mandatory irrespective of the law otherwise applicable to the contract. But Article 9(1) of the Regulation has introduced a definition of overriding mandatory provisions, as referring to provisions, the respect for which is regarded as crucial by a country for safeguarding its public interests, such as its political, social or economic organisation, to such an extent that they are applicable to any situation falling within their scope, irrespective of the law otherwise applicable to the contract under this Regulation. This appears to narrow the

---

the payer's obligation towards the creditor. But Article 20 contains no explicit saving enabling the other debtors to rely on the defences they had against the creditor to the extent allowed by the law governing their obligations towards the creditor.

[291] EC Regulation 1346/2000 on Insolvency Proceedings, [2000] OJ L160/1. See pp. 532–3 below.

[292] Article 21 echoes Article 16 of the Rome Convention 1980.

scope of the forum's power to assert and give effect to an overriding interest, by requiring that the substantive rule of the law of the forum which is involved must be one which is regarded as crucial for safeguarding the public interests of the forum country.[293]

In addition, Article 9(3) of the Regulation permits respect to be given to overriding mandatory provisions which are contained in the law of the place of performance, and which render performance unlawful. This replaces a wider provision made by Article 7(1) of the Convention, which permitted respect to be given in certain circumstances to overriding interests asserted by a third country (a country which was neither that of the forum nor that of the proper law). But reservations excluding the application of Article 7(1) were authorised by Article 22(1)(a), and such reservations were made by the United Kingdom,[294] Ireland, Germany, Luxembourg, Portugal, Latvia and Slovenia. No reservation excluding Article 9(3) of the Regulation is permitted.

## Public Policy of the Forum Country

The public policy proviso under Article 21 of the Regulation refers primarily to the rare cases where the relevant foreign rule (as applied to the particular facts) departs so radically from the concepts of fundamental justice accepted in the forum country that its application would be intolerably offensive to the judicial conscience there, even when all the connecting-factors (except as to the forum seised) are with the country of the rule.[295] Such a situation arises in an English court where the foreign proper law would uphold the validity of a contract which was entered into under what English law regards as illegitimate non-economic pressure.[296] Article 21 also prevents the enforcement in any EU Member State of a contract which infringes the competition rules laid down by Article 101 of the Treaty on the Functioning of the European Union.[297] Another effect of Article 21 in England is to preserve the traditional rule which insists on the invariable application of the English substantive rules as to the effect on existing contracts of the outbreak of a war to which the United Kingdom is a party.[298]

It was reasonably clear under the Rome Convention 1980 that Article 16 (which corresponds to Article 21 of the Rome I Regulation) enabled the continued operation in England of the traditional English rules which are designed to prevent the English courts from encouraging or requiring parties to perform acts abroad whose performance would contravene the criminal law of the country where the performance would take place. In the Regulation, specific provision in this matter is now made by Article 9(3), but there seems no compelling

---

[293] See also Recital 37, which explains that considerations of public interest justify giving the courts of the Member States the possibility, in exceptional circumstances, of applying exceptions based on public policy and overriding mandatory provisions; and notes that the concept of 'overriding mandatory provisions' should be distinguished from the expression 'provisions which cannot be derogated from by agreement' and should be construed more restrictively.

[294] See s 2(2) of the Contracts (Applicable Law) Act 1990.

[295] See per Simon P in *Cheni v Cheni* [1965] P 85.

[296] See *Kaufman v Gerson* [1904] 1 KB 591 (CA), which involved a threat to prosecute the promisor's husband for embezzlement; and *Royal Boskalis v Mountain* [1999] QB 674 (CA), which involved a threat by the Iraqi government to detain the contractor's equipment and personnel in Iraq as the first Gulf war became imminent.

[297] See Case C-126/97: *Eco Swiss China Time v Benetton International* [1999] ECR I-3055.

[298] See *Ertel Bieber v Rio Tinto* [1918] AC 260.

reason why Article 21 should not also be used for this purpose. At all events, there is no reason to doubt that under the Regulation the English courts will continue to adhere to their traditional rules in this matter.

The first of these English rules applies where the parties' actual common intention at the time of contracting was that the contract should be performed by means of an act done in defiance of a known criminal prohibition imposed by the law of the country where the act was intended to be performed. In such circumstances, the entire contract will be regarded as illegal and unenforceable in England, even if the unlawful intention is concealed by the documentation and revealed only by oral testimony, and even if the contract is governed by a foreign proper law which takes a different view of its validity.[299] An analogous result will be reached where the guilty intention to perform in defiance of a known prohibition was possessed by one, but not the other, of the parties. The guilty party will then be unable to enforce the contract at all, but (unless performance would inevitably require breach of the prohibition in the country where it was imposed, in which case a variation on the second rule would apply) the innocent party will be able to do so.[300]

The second English rule relating to criminal prohibitions applies where there was no such guilty intention but, unknown to the parties, there in fact existed at the time of contracting, or there came into force between the time of contracting and the time for performance, in a country where the contract necessarily required an act of performance to be done, a criminal prohibition against the doing of that act. In such a case, if the contract is governed by English law, and the illegality is supervening, then at least the obligation whose performance is prohibited will be pro tanto frustrated and discharged. Such a situation arose in *Ralli v Naviera*,[301] which involved a charterparty governed by English law for a voyage from India to Spain. The contract provided for payment of freight in Spain on arrival, but during the voyage a Spanish decree came into force prohibiting payment or receipt of freight at a rate exceeding a statutory limit, which was lower than the agreed rate. The Court of Appeal held that, under English law as the proper law, the supervening Spanish decree had the effect of frustrating the obligation to pay the contractual freight insofar as it exceeded the statutory limit. Probably a similar result would have followed if the prohibition had existed at the time of contracting, but had not come to the knowledge of the parties until after the voyage had commenced. If, however, the prohibition had become known to the parties before any substantial performance (such as the commencement of the loading) had been carried out, it would seem proper to regard the entire contract as frustrated.

But if the proper law were that of a third country, it is probable that in cases of unintentional illegality the English courts would respect a rule of the foreign proper law which substi-

---

[299]   See *Foster v Driscoll* [1929] 1 KB 470 (CA), which involved a conspiracy to ship whisky into the United States during the 'prohibition' era; *Regazzoni v Sethia* [1958] AC 301 (HL), where a contract expressed in the documents as a sale CIF Genoa was in fact intended to be performed by exporting the goods from India in breach of an Indian prohibition on exports destined ultimately for South Africa; and *Royal Boskalis v Mountain* [1999] QB 674 (CA), which involved a contract governed by Iraqi law and intended to be performed by acts to be carried out in the Netherlands and Switzerland in breach of Dutch and Swiss prohibitions imposed in implementation of United Nations' financial sanctions against Iraq in consequence of its invasion of Kuwait. See also *Ispahani v Bank Melli Iran* [1998] Lloyd's Rep Bank 133 (CA).

[300]   See *Royal Boskalis v Mountain* [1999] QB 674 (CA).

[301]   [1920] 2 KB 287.

tuted for the prohibited obligation a similar obligation to be performed in a different country where its performance was not prohibited. An example would be the *Ralli* situation, with the variation that the proper law was German, and German law substituted an obligation to pay the excess freight in Hamburg or London. On the other hand, if a foreign proper law were to insist on maintaining the obligation to perform in the original country, in defiance of the prohibition there, that would produce a situation contrary to stringent English public policy, and English conflict law would insist on discharging the obligation as if the contract were governed by English internal law.[302]

For the second rule (on unintentional illegality) to apply, the prohibited act must be an act of performance; that is, an act which the contract necessarily requires to be done by way of its performance. It is not enough that the prohibited act is merely a preparatory step which a party may need to take in order to reach a position from which he can carry out the contractually required performance.[303] Thus a promise governed by English law to pay money in London will not normally be affected by the parties' awareness that the payer's assets are all located in Ruritania, and that the remission of funds from Ruritania to enable the payment to be made is prohibited by Ruritanian law unless the consent of the Ruritanian central bank is obtained. Unless it is clearly shown that the parties intended that if necessary the funds should be 'smuggled out' without such consent, there will be a valid contract, under which the payer effectively gives an absolute warranty that he will succeed in obtaining the necessary consent.

### Overriding Interests of the Forum Country

Article 9(2) of the Rome I Regulation specifies that nothing in the Regulation restricts the application of the overriding mandatory provisions of the law of the forum. Overriding mandatory provisions are defined by Article 9(1) of the Regulation as provisions, the respect for which is regarded as crucial by a country for safeguarding its public interests, such as its political, social or economic organisation, to such an extent that they are applicable to any situation falling within their scope, irrespective of the law otherwise applicable to the contract under the Regulation.[304] Recital 37 indicates that Article 9(2) should only be applied in exceptional circumstances, and that the concept of overriding mandatory provisions is narrower than that of provisions which cannot be derogated from by agreement, as referred to in Article 3(3)–(4).[305] Thus, for Article 9(2) to apply, the relevant substantive rule contained in the law of the forum must not only be one which, at least in a situation purely internal to the forum country, cannot be excluded by a contractual term designed to do so, and which invalidates such a term. The relevant substantive rule must also be one whose opera-

---

[302] See F.A. Mann (1937) 18 BYIL 97.

[303] See *Kleinwort v Ungarische Baumwolle* [1939] 2 KB 678 (CA); *Bodley Head v Flegon* [1972] 1 WLR 680; *Toprak v Finagrain* [1979] 2 Lloyd's Rep 98; *Libyan Arab Foreign Bank v Bankers Trust* [1988] 1 Lloyd's Rep 259; *Libyan Arab Foreign Bank v Manufacturers Hanover Trust (No 2)* [1989] 1 Lloyd's Rep 608; and *Tamil Nadu Electricity Board v St-CMS Electric Co* [2007] EWHC 1713 (Comm) (Cooke J). See also *Mount Albert BC v Australasian Assurance Soc* [1938] AC 224; *Society of Lloyd's v Fraser* [1999] Lloyd's Rep IR 156 (CA); and *Society of Lloyd's v White* [2002] ILPr 10 (Cresswell J).

[304] These provisions replace Article 7(2) of the Rome Convention 1980. For an interesting discussion of Article 7(2), and of relevant German case-law, see Knofel, *Mandatory Rules and Choice of Law: A Comparative Approach to Article 7(2) of the Rome Convention* [1999] JBL 239.

[305] On Article 3(3)–(4), see p. 300 above.

tion is regarded by the forum country as so crucial for the safeguarding of its public interests that the forum's conflict rules require its application in any situation falling within its scope, even though the contract is governed by a foreign proper law. The effect is to go beyond the traditional concept of the forum's stringent public policy, so as to confer on the lex fori a further, but limited, power to define and effectuate its own overriding interests in invalidating contracts governed by foreign law.

As is confirmed by the reference in Article 9(1) to a country's interests, Article 9(2) utilises the concept of interest analysis, which was isolated in the United States by Brainerd Currie[306] and has become a major choice-influencing factor in American case-law in recent decades.[307] The concept is essentially that a country may be said to have an interest in the application to a transnational situation of a substantive rule contained in its internal law, if a policy or purpose which the substantive rule is designed to promote or achieve would be furthered to a substantial extent by the application of the substantive rule in the determination of the case in question, in view of the factual connections between the parties, acts and events involved in the case and the country in question.

Where the lex fori contains an invalidating substantive rule, Article 9(2) authorises the forum country (by legislation or judicial decision) to define its interests in the application of its substantive rule; to weigh them against other choice-influencing considerations, such as the general policies favouring party expectations, the convenient conduct of international trade, legal certainty, and uniformity of result (regardless of forum), which underlie the proper law doctrine; and ultimately to determine the circumstances (if any) in which the forum country's invalidating interest will be given overriding effect in its courts. But the forum country is expected to proceed with caution before concluding that its interest is of sufficient importance to justify derogation from the operation of the proper law, and the assertion of an overriding interest by the forum country under Article 9(2) should rarely occur.

Despite the reference in Article 9(1) to a country's public interests, and to its political, social or economic organisation, there is no reason to doubt that Article 9(2) can be applied to mandatory rules of the lex fori which are designed to protect weaker parties, such as small businesses when transacting with large or medium-sized businesses. Indeed, there are overriding mandatory rules of European Union law which have this purpose. Thus in *Ingmar v Eaton Leonard*,[308] the European Court ruled that Articles 17 and 18 of EC Directive 86/653,[309] which guarantee certain rights to commercial agents after the termination of agency contracts, must be applied where the commercial agent carried on his activity in a Member State, even if the principal is established in a non-member country and a clause of

---

[306]   See his *Selected Essays on the Conflict of Laws* (Duke University Press, 1963).

[307]   See Restatement, Second, Conflict of Laws (1971), §§ 6, 187 and 188. As regards contracts, § 187 makes an exception to the application of the law of the country chosen by the parties, where application of the chosen law would be contrary to a fundamental policy of a country which has a materially greater interest than the chosen country in the determination of the particular issue, and whose law would be applicable in the absence of choice. According to Symeonides, in his Twenty-Second Annual Survey of Choice of Law in the American Courts, (2009) 56 American Journal of Comparative Law 269, twenty-three of the American States now follow the approach advocated by the Second Restatement in respect of choice of law in respect of contracts.

[308]   Case C-381/98, [2000] ECR I-9305. Cf. *Allium v Alfin*, decided by the French Court of Cassation on 28th November 2000.

[309]   [1986] OJ L382/17.

the contract stipulates that the contract is to be governed by the law of that country. In traditional English law (before the Rome Convention 1980), overriding effect was sometimes given to mandatory rules of the lex fori designed to protect a consumer habitually resident and acting in the forum country,[310] or an employee working in the forum country. But it is probable that the protection of consumers and employees should now be effected under the specific provisions of the Regulation designed for that purpose, to the exclusion of Article 9(2).[311]

Article 9(2) also authorises the assertion of overriding interests in the application of rules which serve more general purposes. Thus, as illustrated by traditional English case-law (before the Rome Convention), a forum rule against champerty (invalidating a contract by which a person who has no legitimate interest in a dispute agrees to finance litigation in return for a share of the proceeds) may be insisted on whenever the litigation to be financed is to take place in a court of the forum country.[312] A forum rule against unreasonable restraint of trade may be applied whenever the contract prejudices trade which would take place in the forum country;[313] and a forum provision against tie-in clauses in patent licences may be applied to any licence under a forum patent.[314] Forum exchange control legislation may be applied to borrowings anywhere by a forum national or resident;[315] and forum legislation restricting credit in the interests of currency stability may be applied to all contracts concluded in the forum country.[316]

It seems unlikely that Article 9(2) can preserve the operation in the United Kingdom of s 27(2)(a) of the Unfair Contract Terms Act 1977, which specifies in effect that the controls imposed by the Act on the validity of exemption clauses are applicable if the proper law is foreign by express or implied choice, but the country of closest connection is a part of the United Kingdom, and an express or implied choice of a foreign law was imposed wholly or mainly for the purpose of evading the 1977 Act. For Article 7(2) seems designed to enable the forum country to assert overriding interests on the basis of objective connections, rather than of nebulous concepts such as evasive purpose; and it is difficult to see how a sufficiently strong interest can exist in situations where the non-application of the invalidating rule would have been regarded as entirely tolerable in the absence of an evasive intent.

**Overriding Interests of a Third Country**

Article 9(3) of the Rome I Regulation specifies that effect may be given to the overriding mandatory provisions of the law of the country where the obligations arising out of the

---

[310] See *English v Donnelly* [1958] SC 494.
[311] See Chapter 13 below.
[312] See *Grell v Levy* (1864) 143 ER 1052, and *Re Trepca Mines* [1963] Ch 199.
[313] See *Rousillon v Rousillon* (1880) 14 ChD 351. See also *Duarte v Black & Decker* [2008] 1 All ER (Comm) 401, where Field J held that the public policy proviso, now specified by Article 21 of the Regulation, would ensure the operation of the English rules on restraint of trade to invalidate restrictive covenants contained in a contract of employment in respect of an employee who was and would be working in England, despite any choice of a foreign law under which the covenants would be enforceable.
[314] See *Chiron v Murex* [1993] FSR 567 (CA).
[315] See *Boissevain v Weil* [1950] AC 327.
[316] See *Kay's Leasing v Fletcher* (1964) 116 CLR 124.

contract have to be or have been performed, in so far as those overriding mandatory provisions render the performance of the contract unlawful. It adds that, in considering whether to give effect to those provisions, regard must be had to their nature and purpose and to the consequences of their application or non-application.

This provision appears to address the situation where a contract which is governed by the law of a country other than the forum country imposes obligations which are valid under its proper law but whose performance would involve the infringement of a criminal prohibition imposed by the law of the place of intended or agreed performance. In England, the solutions traditionally adopted in this context were preserved under the Rome Convention 1980 by the saving in favour of the forum's public policy specified by Article 16 of the Convention.[317] There is no reason to doubt that under the Regulation the English courts remain free to retain the solutions traditionally adopted, and it seems probable that this power can now be ascribed both to Article 9(3) and to the saving in favour of the forum's public policy now specified by Article 21 of the Regulation.

Article 9(3) of the Regulation replaces a much wider provision specified by Article 7(1) of the Convention. Article 7(1) provided that: 'When applying under this Convention the law of a country, effect may be given to the mandatory rules of the law of another country with which the situation has a close connection, if and in so far as, under the law of the latter country, those rules must be applied whatever the law applicable to the contract. In considering whether to give effect to these mandatory rules, regard shall be had to their nature and purpose and to the consequences of their application or non-application.' But reservations excluding the application of Article 7(1) were authorised by Article 22(1)(a), and such reservations were made by the United Kingdom,[318] Ireland, Germany, Luxembourg, Portugal, Latvia and Slovenia.

In the absence of a reservation, Article 7(1) of the Convention entrusted a discretionary power to the court seised, applicable where a foreign law had asserted an interest in having one of its mandatory rules applied in certain circumstances to contracts which were governed by other laws. The forum was directed to have regard to the nature and purpose of the mandatory substantive rule, and to the consequences of its application or non-application. Thus the forum was invited to evaluate the legitimacy of the asserted interest, and to weigh it against the considerations (such as unfair disappointment of the expectations of the party against whom the invalidating rule would operate) which favoured adherence to the proper law.

Accordingly, it might have been expected that (in the absence of a reservation) the operation of Article 7(1) of the Convention would largely have depended on whether or not the lex fori would have asserted an overriding interest in the application of a substantially similar mandatory rule in a substantially converse situation. If so, Article 7(1) would usually have led to respect for the corresponding foreign interest. An example would be a champertous agreement, governed by American law, for the financing of litigation to take place in New Zealand; on the assumptions that American law has no objection to champerty, while New Zealand law, like English internal law, objects to such an arrangement as increasing the risk of deception of courts by false evidence. If not, the forum would usually have adhered to the proper law. Thus the effect of Article 7(1) could have been seen as an advancement in international

---

[317]    See pp. 339–41 above.
[318]    See s 2(2) of the Contract (Applicable Law) Act 1990.

legal co-operation and harmony. Accordingly, the present writer dissented from the consensus among commentators in the United Kingdom approving the British reservation excluding Article 7(1).

The effect of the reservation in the United Kingdom was illustrated by *Akai v People's Insurance*,[319] where Thomas J upheld in accordance with the expressly chosen English law a commercial insurance contract between an Australian policy-holder and a Singapore insurer, and disregarded the invalidation of certain terms by protective Australian legislation, which had been held applicable by the Australian High Court. Similarly, in *Shell v Coral Oil*,[320] which involved a contract for exclusive distribution of oil products in the Lebanon, Moore-Bick J gave effect to an express choice of English law, so as to deprive the distributor of the protection of mandatory rules of Lebanese law.[321]

---

[319]   [1998] 1 Lloyd's Rep 90.
[320]   [1999] 1 Lloyd's Rep 72.
[321]   See also *OT Africa Line v Magic Sportswear* [2005] 2 Lloyd's Rep 170, where the Court of Appeal upheld in accordance with the expressly chosen English law an English jurisdiction clause contained in a bill of lading in respect of goods shipped in New York for carriage to Liberia, despite the invalidity of the clause under the law of Canada, where the bill of lading was issued by a Canadian agent of the English shipowner, and where freight was payable.

# 13.  Protected contracts

## INTRODUCTION

With a view to protecting weaker parties, special choice-of-law rules are laid down for certain types of contract by Articles 5–8 of the Rome I Regulation.[1] Article 5(2)–(3) applies to contracts for the carriage of passengers;[2] Article 6 applies to certain consumer contracts;[3] Article 7 deals with insurance contracts;[4] and Article 8 applies to individual employment contracts.[5] These provisions will be examined in this chapter.

## CONSUMER CONTRACTS

### Scope

Article 6 of the Rome I Regulation lays down special conflict rules for certain consumer contracts which satisfy an elaborate definition containing both substantive and territorial elements. The definition in many respects resembles that used in Article 15 of the Brussels I Regulation.[6] It departs substantially from that used in Article 5 of the Rome Convention, which accorded in many respects with that used in Article 13 of the Brussels Convention.[7] The contracts which fall within the scope of Article 6 of the Rome I Regulation may conveniently be referred to as protected consumer contracts.

As regards substantive elements, Article 6(1) refers to 'a contract concluded by a natural person for a purpose which can be regarded as being outside his trade or profession (the consumer) with another person acting in the exercise of his trade or profession (the professional)'. This contrasts with the reference in Article 5(1) of the Rome Convention 1980 to 'a contract the object of which is the supply of goods or services to a person ('the consumer')

---

[1]   Recital 23 explains that, as regards contracts concluded with parties regarded as being weaker, those parties should be protected by conflict-of-law rules that are more favourable to their interests than the general rules.

[2]   There was no specific provision in the Rome Convention 1980 on contracts for the carriage of passengers.

[3]   This replaces Article 5 of the Rome Convention 1980. There are important changes to the definition of a protected consumer contract.

[4]   This replaces provisions of EC Directives 88/357 and 2002/83.

[5]   This replaces Article 6 of the Rome Convention 1980.

[6]   See pp. 131–7 above.

[7]   The European Court had indicated in Case 96/00: *Gabriel* [2002] ECR I-6367 that concepts used in Article 5 of the Rome Convention 1980 and Article 13 of the Brussels Convention would be given the same interpretation in both provisions.

for a purpose which can be regarded as being outside his trade or profession, or a contract for the provision of credit for that object'. The new definition explicitly requires that the consumer must be an individual, rather than a corporate entity. The new definition also makes explicit the requirement, which was implied in the old definition,[8] that the supplier must be, or at least appear to the consumer to be, acting in the course of his trade or profession. Under both definitions, the purchaser must not be acting for business purposes; or, where he is acting partly for business purposes and partly for non-business purposes, his business purpose must be of negligible importance in relation to the transaction; and in any event he must not have so conducted himself as to create the impression in the supplier that he was acting for business purposes.[9]

Unlike the old definition, the new definition makes no reference to the supply of goods or services. Thus a sale of land is no longer excluded by the primary definition. But Article 6(4)(c) of the Regulation provides a specific exclusion for a contract relating to a right in rem in immovable property or a tenancy of immovable property, other than a contract relating to the right to use immovable properties on a timeshare basis within the meaning of EC Directive 94/47. Thus contracts for the sale or letting of land, other than on a timeshare basis, do not count as protected consumer contracts, within the scope of Article 6.[10]

Further exclusions from the scope of Article 6 of the Regulation are made by Article 6(4)(a), which refers to a contract for the supply of services, where the services are to be supplied to the consumer exclusively in a country other than that of his habitual residence; and by Article 6(4)(b), which refers to a contract of carriage, other than a contract relating to package travel within the meaning of EC Directive 90/314. These exclusions substantially accord with those previously made by Article 5(4) and (5) of the Rome Convention 1980.

It is also clear that Article 6 does not apply to insurance contracts in respect of mass risks located within the European Union, since the opening phrase of Article 6(1) gives priority to Article 7. This is confirmed by Recital 32, which also explains that, owing to the particular nature of insurance contracts, the specific provisions of Article 7 should ensure an adequate level of protection of policy-holders. But it seems probable that Article 6 does apply to insurance contracts in respect of mass risks located outside the European Union.[11]

**Financial services**

Since, unlike the old definition under the Rome Convention 1980, the new definition of consumer contracts under the Rome I Regulation makes no reference to the supply of goods or services, a sale of financial instruments or securities is no longer excluded by the primary definition. But as regards financial instruments, transferable securities, and units in collective investment undertakings, complicated exclusions from Article 6 of the Regulation are provided by Article 6(1)(d)–(e).

The first exclusion, by Article 6(1)(d), refers to rights and obligations which constitute a financial instrument, and rights and obligations constituting the terms and conditions governing the issuance or offer to the public and public take-over bids of transferable securities, and

---

[8]  See the Giuliano and Lagarde Report, at p. 23; EC Directive 93/13, Article 2(c); and Case 96/00: *Gabriel* [2002] ECR I-6367.

[9]  See Case C-464/01: *Gruber v Bay Wa* [2005] ECR I-439.

[10]  See also Recital 27.

[11]  See p. 367 below.

the subscription and redemption of units in collective investment undertakings insofar as these activities do not constitute provision of a financial service. The second exclusion, by Article 6(1)(e), along with Article 4(1)(h), refers to a contract concluded within a multilateral system which brings together or facilitates the bringing together of multiple third-party buying and selling interests in financial instruments, as defined by Article 4(1)(17) of EC Directive 2004/39,[12] in accordance with non-discretionary rules and governed by a single law. These exclusions are further explained by Recitals 18, 26 and 28–31.

Recital 30 to the Rome I Regulation explains that, for the purposes of the Regulation, financial instruments and transferable securities are the instruments referred to in Article 4 of EC Directive 2004/39. Financial instruments are elaborately but widely defined by Article 4(1)(17) and Annex I, Section C, of Directive 2004/39 as the following: (1) transferable securities; (2) money-market instruments; (3) units in collective investment undertakings; (4) options, futures, swaps, forward rate agreements and any other derivative contracts relating to securities, currencies, interest rates or yields, or other derivatives instruments, financial indices or financial measures which may be settled physically or in cash; (5) options, futures, swaps, forward rate agreements and any other derivative contracts relating to commodities that must be settled in cash or may be settled in cash at the option of one of the parties (otherwise than by reason of a default or other termination event); (6) options, futures, swaps, and any other derivative contract relating to commodities that can be physically settled provided that they are traded on a regulated market and/or a multilateral trading facility; (7) options, futures, swaps, forwards and any other derivative contracts relating to commodities, that can be physically settled not otherwise mentioned in paragraph (6) and not being for commercial purposes, which have the characteristics of other derivative financial instruments, having regard to whether, inter alia, they are cleared and settled through recognised clearing houses or are subject to regular margin calls; (8) derivative instruments for the transfer of credit risk; (9) financial contracts for differences; and (10) options, futures, swaps, forward rate agreements and any other derivative contracts relating to climatic variables, freight rates, emission allowances or inflation rates or other official economic statistics that must be settled in cash or may be settled in cash at the option of one of the parties (otherwise than by reason of a default or other termination event), as well as any other derivative contracts relating to assets, rights, obligations, indices and measures not otherwise mentioned in Section C, which have the characteristics of other derivative financial instruments, having regard to whether, inter alia, they are traded on a regulated market or a multilateral trading facility, are cleared and settled through recognised clearing houses or are subject to regular margin calls. In addition, Article 4(1)(18) of Directive 2004/39 defines 'transferable securities' as those classes of securities which are negotiable on the capital market, with the exception of instruments of payment, and as including (a) shares in companies and other securities equivalent to shares in companies, partnerships or other entities, and depositary receipts in respect of shares; (b) bonds or other forms of securitised debt, including depositary receipts in respect of such securities; and (c) any other securities giving the right to acquire or sell any such transferable securities or giving rise to a cash settlement determined by reference to transferable securities, currencies, interest rates or yields, commodities or other indices or measures.

---

[12]    [2004] OJ L145/1. The Directive was last amended by Directive 2008/10, [2008] OJ L76/33.

Recital 28 to the Rome I Regulation explains that it is important to ensure that rights and obligations which constitute a financial instrument are not covered by the general rule applicable to consumer contracts, as that could lead to different laws being applicable to each of the instruments issued, therefore changing their nature and preventing their fungible trading and offering. Likewise, whenever such instruments are issued or offered, the contractual relationship established between the issuer or offeror and the consumer should not necessarily be subject to the mandatory application of the law of the consumer's habitual residence, as there is a need to ensure uniformity in the terms and conditions of an issuance or offer. The same rationale should apply with regard to the multilateral systems covered by Article 4(1)(h), in respect of which it should be ensured that the law of the consumer's habitual residence will not interfere with the rules applicable to contracts concluded within those systems or with the operator of such systems.

Recital 29 to the Rome I Regulation adds that, for the purposes of the Regulation, references to rights and obligations constituting the terms and conditions governing the issuance, offers to the public or public take-over bids of transferable securities, and references to the subscription and redemption of units in collective investment undertakings should include the terms governing, inter alia, the allocation of securities or units, rights in the event of over-subscription, withdrawal rights and similar matters in the context of the offer, as well as the matters referred to in Articles 10, 11, 12 and 13 of the Regulation, thus ensuring that all relevant contractual aspects of an offer binding the issuer or the offeror to the consumer are governed by a single law.

On the other hand, Recital 26 to the Rome I Regulation explains that, for the purposes of the Regulation, financial services such as investment services and activities and ancillary services provided by a professional to a consumer, as referred to in sections A and B of Annex I to EC Directive 2004/39, and contracts for the sale of units in collective investment undertakings, whether or not covered by EC Directive 85/611,[13] should be subject to Article 6 of the Regulation. Consequently, when a reference is made to terms and conditions governing the issuance or offer to the public of transferable securities or to the subscription and redemption of units in collective investment undertakings, the reference should include all aspects binding the issuer or offeror to the consumer, but should not include those aspects involving the provision of financial services.

Section A of Annex I to EC Directive 2004/39 lists the following as investment services and activities: (1) reception and transmission of orders in relation to one or more financial instruments; (2) execution of orders on behalf of clients; (3) dealing on own account; (4) portfolio management; (5) investment advice; (6) underwriting of financial instruments and/or placing of financial instruments on a firm commitment basis; (7) placing of financial instruments without a firm commitment basis; and (8) operation of Multilateral Trading Facilities. Section B of the Annex lists the following as ancillary services: (1) safekeeping and administration of financial instruments for the account of clients, including custodianship and related services such as cash/collateral management; (2) granting credits or loans to an investor to allow him to carry out a transaction in one or more financial instruments, where the firm granting the credit or loan is involved in the transaction; (3) advice to undertakings

---

[13]  [1985] OJ L375/3. This Directive was last amended by EC Directive 2008/18, [2008] OJ L76/42.

on capital structure, industrial strategy and related matters and advice and services relating to mergers and the purchase of undertakings; (4) foreign exchange services where these are connected to the provision of investment services; (5) investment research and financial analysis or other forms of general recommendation relating to transactions in financial instruments; (6) services related to underwriting; and (7) investment services and activities as well as ancillary services of the type included under Section A or B of Annex 1 related to the underlying of the derivatives included under paragraphs 5, 6, 7 and 10 of Section C, where these are connected to the provision of investment or ancillary services.

Recital 18 to the Rome I Regulation explains that multilateral systems should be those in which trading is conducted, such as regulated markets and multilateral trading facilities as referred to in Article 4 of EC Directive 2004/39, regardless of whether or not they rely on a central counterparty. Article 4(1)(14) of the Directive defines a regulated market as a multilateral system operated and/or managed by a market operator, which brings together or facilitates the bringing together of multiple third-party buying and selling interests in financial instruments – in the system and in accordance with its non-discretionary rules – in a way that results in a contract, in respect of the financial instruments admitted to trading under its rules and/or systems, and which is authorised and functions regularly and in accordance with the provisions of Title III of the Directive. Article 4(1)(15) of the Directive defines a multilateral trading facility as a multilateral system, operated by an investment firm or a market operator, which brings together multiple third-party buying and selling interests in financial instruments – in the system and in accordance with non-discretionary rules – in a way that results in a contract in accordance with the provisions of Title II of the Directive.

Recital 31 adds that nothing in the Rome I Regulation should prejudice the operation of a formal arrangement designated as a system under Article 2(a) of EC Directive 98/26 on settlement finality in payment and securities settlement systems.[14]

The complexity and opaqueness of these provisions, designed to determine whether a contract concluded for investment purposes may be treated as a consumer contract, may be regarded as offering a perfect example of how not to proceed.

### The territorial requirement

Like the Rome Convention 1980, the Rome I Regulation insists on imposing a territorial requirement for the application of the consumer-protective provisions, designed to ensure that the consumer is guaranteed the protection offered by the law of his country of habitual residence only in cases where the contract or the supplier has a sufficient connection with that country. But the Rome I Regulation has redefined the necessary territorial connection so as to accord with that used in the Brussels I Regulation. The Rome Convention 1980 had utilised a territorial requirement similar to that used by the Brussels Convention.

In the Rome I Regulation, the territorial requirement is specified by Article 6(1), which insists that the professional must either (a) pursue his commercial or professional activities in the country where the consumer has his habitual residence; or (b) by any means, direct such activities to that country or to several countries including that country; and also (in either case) that the contract must fall within the scope of such activities. Recital 25 explains that consumers should be protected by such rules of the country of their habitual residence as

---

14    [1998] OJ L166/45.

cannot be derogated from by agreement, provided that the consumer contract has been concluded as a result of the professional pursuing his commercial or professional activities in that particular country; and that the same protection should be guaranteed if the professional, while not pursuing his commercial or professional activities in the country where the consumer has his habitual residence, directs his activities by any means to that country or to several countries including that country, and the contract is concluded as a result of such activities.

In this connection, Recital 24 further explains that the conflict rule should make it possible to cut the cost of settling disputes concerning what are commonly relatively small claims and to take account of the development of distance-selling techniques. It adds that consistency with the Brussels I Regulation requires both that there be a reference to the concept of directed activity as a condition for applying the consumer protection rule, and that the concept be interpreted harmoniously in the Brussels I Regulation and the Rome I Regulation. The Recital also refers to a joint declaration by the Council and the Commission on Article 15 of the Brussels I Regulation, which states that for Article 15(1)(c) of the Brussels I Regulation to be applicable, it is not sufficient for an undertaking to target its activities at the Member State of the consumer's residence, or at a number of Member States including that Member State; a contract must also be concluded within the framework of its activities. The declaration also states that the mere fact that an Internet site is accessible is not sufficient for Article 15 to be applicable, although a factor will be that this Internet site solicits the conclusion of distance contracts and that a contract has actually been concluded at a distance, by whatever means; and that, in this respect, the language or currency which a website uses does not constitute a relevant factor.

The new requirement of the supplier's activities in or directed to the consumer's country replaces the three alternative requirements formerly specified by Article 5(2) of the Rome Convention 1980. The first alternative was that the conclusion of the contract was preceded by a specific invitation addressed to the consumer in the country of his habitual residence or by advertising there, and that he had taken in that country all the steps necessary on his part for the conclusion of the contract. The second was that the supplier or his agent had received the consumer's order in that country. The third was that the contract was for the sale of goods and the consumer had travelled from that country to another country and given his order there, his journey having been arranged by the seller for the purpose of inducing the consumer to buy.

As regards the first alternative under the Rome Convention 1980, the European Court had indicated in *Gabriel*[15] that the concepts of advertising and specific invitation had a wide scope. It explained that they covered all forms of advertising carried out in the consumer's country, whether disseminated generally by the press, radio, television, cinema or any other medium, or addressed directly, for example by means of catalogues sent specifically to that State. They also covered commercial offers made to the consumer in person, in particular by an agent or door-to-door salesman. Further, the reference to the steps necessary for the conclusion of the contract extended to any document written or other step taken by the consumer in his country which expressed his wish to take up the invitation made by the supplier.

---

[15]    Case 96/00, [2002] ECR I-6367.

As regards advertising, it is thought that the advertising did not need to have been aimed specifically at the consumer's country.[16] It should have been sufficient for this purpose that the advertisement had come to the attention of the consumer in his country through normal commercial channels there, that it had induced him to enter into the negotiations which led to the conclusion of the contract, and that nothing done by the consumer had caused the supplier reasonably to suppose that such was not the case. In any event, it seemed necessary that the advertisement should have been a factor actually inducing the consumer to enter into the contract. As regards the second alternative, the reference to an agent of the supplier included anyone acting on his behalf, including staff manning a stand at a short-term exhibition.[17]

It was reasonably clear that the requirements of Article 5 of the Rome Convention 1980 would normally have been satisfied in the case of consumer contracts which were concluded by electronic means. For, in the ordinary case of a consumer ordering goods or services electronically from a website maintained by the supplier, the webpage amounted both to a specific invitation to anyone who downloaded it in the country where he did so, and also to advertising in that country, and the consumer was usually in the country of his habitual residence when he downloaded the page and filled in and uploaded the order form.[18] The risk of unfair surprise to the trader was largely eliminated if it was recognised that the Convention had to be construed as respecting the principles of predictability[19] and good faith.[20] Accordingly, a consumer who misled the supplier as to the location of the consumer's habitual residence, as by entering on the electronic order form an address (perhaps of a relative or friend) in a different country, would have been estopped from relying on his actual habitual residence so as to satisfy the definition if the trader would have rejected the order (probably by setting his software in advance to do so) if he had known the consumer's true habitual residence.

It seems probable that the new territorial requirement will have a very similar effect to its predecessor. A minor difference is that the new requirement will usually be satisfied where the consumer contracts online from an Internet café while on a visit to a country other than his habitual residence. But the principle of good faith will remain applicable, despite the fact that (unlike the Commission's original proposal of 15th December 2005)[21] the Rome I Regulation as adopted does not contain a specific provision excluding protection if the professional did not know where the consumer had his habitual residence and this ignorance was not attributable to his negligence.

Perhaps the most disappointing feature of the Rome I Regulation is its failure to offer any protection to the 'mobile' consumer, who contracts abroad in circumstances where it would be unreasonable to subject the supplier to the law of the consumer's residence. For example,

---

16    Cf. the confused discussion in the Giuliano and Lagarde Report, at p. 24, which referred to catalogues aimed specifically at the consumer's country, but added that an advertisement appearing in special editions of an American publication intended for European countries would suffice.
17    See the Giuliano and Lagarde Report, at p. 24.
18    Cf. the Giuliano and Lagarde Report, at p. 24.
19    See (on the Brussels Convention) Case C-26/91: *Handte v TMCS* [1992] ECR I-3967; and Case C-51/97: *Réunion Européenne v Spliethoff's Bevrachtingskantoor* [1998] ECR I-6511.
20    See (on the Brussels Convention) Case 25/76: *Segoura v Bonakdarian* [1976] ECR 1851; and Case C-464/01: *Gruber v Bay Wa* [2005] ECR I-439.
21    See COM(2005) 650 final.

where an English visitor to France purchases goods at a shop in Paris. Under the Regulation (as under the Convention), the contract is governed by Articles 3 and 4 in the same way as a commercial contract. This is emphasised by Article 6(3) of the Regulation, which specifies that if the territorial requirement is not fulfilled, the law applicable to a contract between a consumer and a professional must be determined pursuant to Articles 3 and 4. Such a result is deeply unsatisfying. It means that the English visitor, buying at a shop in Paris, is vulnerable to an express choice of the law of Haiti. Admittedly, Article 3(4) would ensure that he would still benefit from the substantive rules of consumer protection laid down by the various EU Directives.[22] But, beyond that, he could be deprived of protection which exists under both English and French laws. It is submitted that a far superior solution would have been to give the mobile consumer, despite any choice of law by the parties, the benefit of the mandatory rules for the protection of consumers as weaker parties which are contained in the law of the *supplier's* habitual residence.

Article 27(1) of the Rome I Regulation requires the EC Commission, by 17th June 2013, to submit a report on the application of the Regulation, accompanied if appropriate by proposals for its amendment. The report must include an evaluation on the application of Article 6, in particular as regards the coherence of Community law in the field of consumer protection. It may be hoped that the report will pay particular attention to the position of the mobile consumer.

**The Protective Regime**

In the case of a protected consumer contract (within the scope of Article 6 of the Rome I Regulation), Articles 6(1)-(2) and 11(4) of the Regulation provide three special choice-of-law rules. These rules substantially accord with those formerly specified by Articles 5(2)-(3) and 9(5) of the Rome Convention 1980.

Firstly, by Article 6(1) of the Regulation, in the absence of an express or implied choice of law by the parties in accordance with Article 3, the law of the consumer's habitual residence becomes the proper law. The tests of the closest connection and the characteristic performer's residence, laid down for other cases by Article 4, are wholly excluded in the case of protected consumer contracts.

Secondly, by Article 6(2) of the Regulation, if there is an express or implied choice of law by the parties in accordance with Article 3, the choice remains effective to designate the proper law, but the proper law operates subject to provisions of the law of the consumer's habitual residence which are designed to protect consumers as weaker parties, and which cannot be derogated from by agreement. The effect is to give the consumer the cumulative benefit of the protective rules of the chosen law and those of the law of his habitual residence. On any given point, the protective rule which is more favourable to the consumer prevails. Moreover, in contrast with Article 9(2),[23] there is no need for the law of the consumer's habitual residence to have asserted an overriding interest in the application of its protective rule. Thirdly, by Article 11(4), the formal validity of a protected consumer contract is governed exclusively by the law of the consumer's habitual residence.[24]

---

22 See pp. 354–5 below.
23 See pp. 341–3 above.
24 See also *English v Donnelly* [1958] SC 494.

In view of the particular and detailed provisions of Article 6 of the Regulation, which seem designed to deal exhaustively with the protection of consumers as weaker parties, it is thought that Article 9(2) cannot be invoked for the purpose of consumer protection.[25] Admittedly, the unavailability of Article 9 for purposes of consumer protection means that a 'mobile' consumer (who contracts while visiting the supplier's country) can be deprived of all protection (other than protection under the EU Directives on substantive consumer law),[26] by a clause choosing the law of a non-member country. It is indeed disappointing that the Regulation has failed to include a provision dealing specifically with consumer contracts which are not sufficiently connected with the country of the consumer's habitual residence to justify the application of its law. In such cases, the consumer should have been given the protection of the mandatory rules of the supplier's country, despite a choice by the parties of some other law. But the use of Article 9(2) to give a consumer the protection of the lex fori would seem to undermine the scheme carefully, if not always wisely, established by Article 6. On the other hand, there is no reason why Article 9(2) should not be invoked for the purpose of applying to a consumer contract mandatory rules whose aim is to protect the supplier (as by imposing a penal rate of interest where payment is delayed) or the general public interest (as by insisting on a minimum deposit, with a view to restricting credit in the interests of currency stability).

It seems probable that Article 6 of the Regulation has the effect of overriding self-limiting rules, such as those specified in the United Kingdom by ss 26 and 27(1) of the Unfair Contract Terms Act 1977, which prevent the controls on exemption clauses imposed by the 1977 Act from operating in the case of an international supply contract (as defined by s 26), or in cases where the proper law of the contract is the law of a part of the United Kingdom by choice of the parties but the closest connection is with a country outside the United Kingdom. For Article 6 is designed to establish a definitive solution to the protection of a consumer as a weaker party, overriding any national legislation dealing with choice of law or with the transnational operation of protective rules; and the continued operation of ss 26 or 27(1) in relation to a protected consumer contract could have the effect of denying the application of British mandatory rules designed to protect weaker parties in a manner inconsistent with the objectives of Article 6, and thus of undermining the effectiveness of the Regulation.[27]

## The Directives on Substantive Consumer Law

The harmonisation at European Union level of various aspects of substantive law in respect of consumer contracts has been achieved by a series of Directives. These also contain provisions affecting choice of law. The operation of the Directives is not affected by the Rome I Regulation, since Article 23 specifies that the Regulation does not prejudice the application of provisions of European Union law which, in relation to particular matters, lay down conflict rules relating to contractual obligations.

---

[25]   See the decision of the German Supreme Court in *Grand Canaries* [1997] NJW 1697. Cf. the Giuliano & Lagarde Report, at p. 28; and Knofel, *Mandatory Rules and Choice of Law: A Comparative Approach to Article 7(2) of the Rome Convention* [1999] JBL 239. See also *Moquin v Deutsche Bank* (2000) Revue Critique de Droit International Privé 29 (French Court of Cassation).

[26]   See pp. 354–5 below.

[27]   Cf. Case 365/88: *Hagen v Zeehaghe* [1990] ECR I-1845.

Directive 93/13, on unfair terms in consumer contracts,[28] renders unfair terms used in a contract concluded with a consumer by a seller or supplier not binding on the consumer, but the contract continues to bind the parties upon the rest of its terms, if it is capable of continuing in existence without the unfair terms. The Directive contains a choice-of-law provision in Article 6(2), which requires Member States to ensure that a consumer does not lose the protection granted by the Directive through a choice of the law of a country outside the European Economic Area as the proper law, if the contract has a close connection with the territory of the Member States. This seems designed to cover cases where the territorial connections referred to in Article 6 of the Regulation are not located in a single Member State. For example, where an English consumer purchases goods for cash in a Paris shop, and there is an express choice of Swiss law. The European Court has confirmed that Article 6(2) of the Directive has a wider scope than Article 6 of the Rome I Regulation.[29]

Provisions corresponding to Article 6(2) of Directive 93/13 are contained in Article 12(2) of Directive 97/7,[30] on the protection of consumers in respect of distance contracts; in Article 7(2) of Directive 1999/44,[31] on certain aspects of the sale of consumer goods and associated guarantees; and in Article 12(2) of Directive 2002/65,[32] on the distance marketing of consumer financial services. But Article 9 of Directive 94/47,[33] on the protection of purchasers in respect of certain aspects of contracts relating to the purchase of the right to use immovable properties on a timeshare basis, requires Member States to ensure that, whatever the law applicable may be, the purchaser is not deprived of the protection afforded by the Directive, if the immovable property concerned is situated within the territory of a Member State.

## CARRIAGE OF PASSENGERS

Articles 5(2) and (3) of the Rome I Regulation apply to contracts for the carriage of passengers. These provisions are new. Under the Rome Convention 1980, contracts for the carriage of passengers were treated as ordinary contracts, governed by Articles 3 and 4.

In the case of a contract for the carriage of passengers, Article 5(2) of the Regulation permits the parties to choose the proper law in accordance with Article 3, but restricts the range of laws which are available to be chosen. The parties may choose the law of one of the following countries: the passenger's habitual residence; the carrier's habitual residence; the carrier's place of central administration; the place of departure; and the place of destination.

In the absence of such a choice, Article 5(2) provides a presumption in favour of the law of the passenger's habitual residence, provided that either the place of departure or the place of destination is situated in that country. Otherwise there is a presumption in favour of the law of the carrier's habitual residence. But Article 5(3) provides for rebuttal of these presumptions where it is clear from all the circumstances of the case that the contract is

---

28 [1993] OJ L95/29.
29 See Case C-70/03: *Commission v Spain* [2004] ECR I-7999.
30 [1997] OJ L144/19.
31 [1999] OJ L171/12.
32 [2002] OJ L271/16.
33 [1994] OJ L280/83.

manifestly more closely connected with a country other than the country indicated by the presumptions. In that case, the law of the manifestly more closely connected country applies.

Recital 32 explains that, owing to the particular nature of contracts of carriage, specific provisions should ensure an adequate level of protection of passengers. Thus Article 6, on protected consumer contracts, should not apply to such contracts.

## EMPLOYMENT CONTRACTS

### Scope

With a view to protecting employees as weaker parties, Article 8 of the Rome I Regulation[34] makes special provision for individual contracts of employment. No explicit definition of such contracts is offered, but it is clear that (in contrast to protected consumer contracts) the concept of an individual contract of employment must be understood solely in substantive (rather than territorial) terms.

It is thought that the concept of an individual contract of employment must be given an autonomous Community meaning, similar to that adopted by the European Court for the purpose of the Brussels I Regulation. Thus the contract must create a lasting bond which brings the worker to some extent within the organisational framework of the employer's business, so that the concept does not extend to a contract for professional services, such as those of an architect or lawyer, engaged as an independent contractor to carry out a particular task.[35] For the purpose of Article 8 of the Rome I Regulation, an ancillary agreement between an employer and an employee, such as an agreement relating to the participation of the employee in an incentive scheme and to his not working for a competitor after leaving the employment, is treated as part of the contract of employment.[36]

### The Protective Regime

Article 8(2)–(4) of the Rome I Regulation[37] determines the proper law of an employment contract in the absence of a choice of law made by the parties in accordance with Article 3. The primary rule, laid down by Article 8(2), is that the proper law is that of the country in or from which the employee habitually carries out his work in performance of the contract; and the country of habitual work remains unchanged even if the employee is temporarily employed in another country. Recital 36 adds that work carried out in another country should be regarded as temporary if the employee is expected to resume working in the country of origin after carrying out his tasks abroad. But if there is no ascertainable country of habitual work, Article 8(3) refers instead to the law of the country in which the place of business

---

[34] This substantially echoes Article 6 of the Rome Convention 1980.

[35] See Case 266/85: *Shenavai v Kreischer* [1987] ECR 239.

[36] See *Duarte v Black & Decker* [2008] 1 All ER (Comm) 401 (Field J). See also *Samengo-Turner v Marsh & McLennan* [2007] 2 All ER (Comm) 813 (CA), on Section 5 of the Brussels I Regulation.

[37] These echo Article 6(2) of the Rome Convention 1980.

through which the employee was engaged is situated.[38] Ultimately, both of these rules are reduced to rebuttable presumptions by Article 8(4), which operates where it appears from the circumstances as a whole that the contract is more closely connected with a country other than that indicated in Article 8(2) or (3), and subjects the contract to the law of that other country.

The reference in Article 8(2) to the country *in which or, failing that, from which* the employee habitually carries out his work in performance of the contract is evidently designed to adopt the approach followed by European Court under the Brussels Convention and the Brussels I Regulation. In *Mulox v Geels*[39] and *Rutten v Cross Medical*,[40] the Court ruled that in cases where the employee carries out his work in more than one country, reference must be made to the place where the employee has established the effective centre of his working activities, at or from which he performs the essential part of his duties towards his employer. For example, a sales manager will be regarded as habitually working at the office where he organises his work, even though he makes frequent business trips to other countries. But where, as in *Weber v Universal Ogden Services*,[41] there is no such permanent centre of activities (for example because the man worked for the employer as a cook, first on mining vessels or installations in the Dutch continental shelf area, and later on a floating crane in Danish territorial waters), the whole of the duration of the employment relationship must be taken into account. The relevant place will normally be the place where the employee has worked the longest; but, by way of exception, weight will be given to the most recent period of work where the employee, after having worked for a certain time in one place, then takes up his work activities on a permanent basis in a different place.

Recital 36 to the Rome I Regulation also indicates that the conclusion of a new contract of employment with the original employer or an employer belonging to the same group of companies as the original employer should not preclude the employee from being regarded as carrying out his work in another country temporarily. This too reflects the approach followed by European Court under the Brussels Convention and the Brussels I Regulation. In *Pugliese v Finmeccanica*,[42] which involved an Italian employee who had been recruited by Aeritalia, an Italian company, to work initially for Eurofighter in Germany for at least three years, the European Court ruled that, in a dispute between an employee and a first employer, the place where the employee performs his obligations to a second employer can be regarded as the place where he habitually carries out his work, when the first employer, with respect to whom the employee's contractual obligations are suspended, has, at the time of the conclusion of the second contract of employment, an interest in the performance of the service by the employee to the second employer in a place decided on by the latter. The existence of such an interest must be determined on a comprehensive basis, taking into consideration all the circumstances of the case. The relevant factors may include the facts that the conclusion of the second contract was envisaged when the first was being concluded; that the first contract

---

[38] See *Booth v Phillips* [2004] 1 WLR 3292 (Teare QC), applying Article 8(3) in the case of a man employed as chief engineer on a sea-going vessel. The reference in Article 8(3) of the Rome I Regulation to a place of business no doubt has a similar meaning to the reference to an establishment in Article 5(5) of the Brussels I Regulation; as to which, see pp. 109–10 above.

[39] Case C-125/92, [1993] ECR I-4075.

[40] Case C-383/95, [1997] ECR I-57.

[41] Case C-37/00, [2002] ECR I-2013.

[42] Case C-437/00, [2003] ECR I-3573.

was amended on account of the conclusion of the second contract; that there is an organisational or economic link between the two employers; that there is an agreement between the two employers providing a framework for the co-existence of the two contracts; that the first employer retains management powers in respect of the employee; and that the first employer is able to decide the duration of the employee's work for the second employer.

The rationale for the final reference by Article 8(4) of the Rome I Regulation to the closest connection is less than clear. Possibly the purpose is concealed discrimination, the intention being that where the employee habitually works in an EU country, the presumption in favour of the place of habitual work will prevail. But that where an employee who is habitually resident in an EU country is recruited to work outside the European Union for an employer who is resident in an EU country, the presumption will be rebutted and the law of the EU country to which both parties belong, or, where they belong to different EU countries, that of the EU country to which the employer belongs, will apply.[43] In any event, for the applicable presumption to be rebutted, a closer connection elsewhere must be clearly demonstrated, and rebuttal is very unlikely if the place of habitual work and the location of the engaging establishment are in the same country.[44]

By Article 8(1) of the Regulation,[45] an express or implied choice of law by the parties in accordance with Article 3 is effective in determining the proper law of an employment contract, but such a choice operates subject to the rules for the protection of the employee as a weaker party which are contained in the law which in the absence of choice would have been applicable under Article 8(2)–(4), and which under that law cannot be derogated from by agreement.[46] As in the case of the similar provision applicable to consumer contracts,[47] the Regulation gives overriding effect to such mandatory rules, regardless of whether or not the law containing them has asserted an overriding interest in their application. But it seems clear that the mandatory rules referred to by Article 8(1) are confined to ones whose purpose is to protect employees as weaker parties.[48] The reference does not extend to mandatory rules which are designed to protect employers (for example, by ensuring that they have a right to dismiss, or make deductions from pay, in certain circumstances); nor to ones which pursue a general public interest (for example, by prohibiting, or subjecting to a licensing scheme, the carrying out of certain economic activities thought likely to endanger the environment). Moreover, as Field J explained in *Duarte v Black & Decker*,[49] the reference is confined to specific provisions whose overriding purpose is to protect employees, and does not extend to rules contained in the general law of contract, such as the English rules which invalidate covenants in restraint of trade.

---

[43]   For an analogous decision, see *Nunez v Hunter Fan Co* 920 FSupp 716 (SD Texas, 1996).

[44]   See *Base Metal Trading Ltd v Shamurin* [2004] 1 All ER (Comm) 159 (Tomlinson J); affirmed [2005] 1 All ER (Comm) 17 (CA).

[45]   This substantially echoes Article 6(1) of the Rome Convention 1980.

[46]   See *Gasalho v Tap Air Portugal*, 17th October 2000 (French Court of Cassation).

[47]   See pp. 353–4 above.

[48]   See also Recital 35, which explains that employees should not be deprived of the protection afforded to them by provisions which cannot be derogated from by agreement, or which can only be derogated from to their benefit.

[49]   [2008] 1 All ER (Comm) 401.

In view of the specific and apparently exhaustive character of Article 8, it is thought that Article 9(2), on overriding mandatory provisions of the lex fori, cannot be used for the purpose of providing further protection to an employee as a weaker party.[50] On the other hand, in view of the failure of Article 11 (on formal validity) to make special provision for contracts of employment, it is permissible to utilise Article 9(2) for the purpose of applying mandatory formal requirements (especially those imposed by the law of the country in which the employee habitually works) to such contracts.[51] It also seems permissible to invoke Article 9(2) for the purpose of applying to an employment contract mandatory rules designed to protect the employer, or to serve a general public interest.

The Giuliano and Lagarde Report indicates[52] that the mandatory rules envisaged by Article 8 are not confined to provisions relating to the contract of employment itself, but extend to provisions concerning industrial health and safety; and that Article 8 extends to void contracts and de facto employment relationships. Despite this, in *Base Metal Trading Ltd v Shamurin*,[53] the English Court of Appeal firmly rejected the argument that Article 8 extends to claims in tort between an employer and an employee arising from things done in the performance of the contract of employment. It was accepted, however, that in such circumstances the fact that under Article 8 the contract of employment is governed by the law of a given country is an important connection with that country for the purpose of determining the country with which the tort has the most significant connection, and whose law may thus be applicable to the tort, by displacement of the general rule in favour of the law of the country in which the events constituting the tort occurred, under the exception specified by s 12 of the (UK) Private International Law (Miscellaneous Provisions) Act 1995.[54] No doubt the same approach will be adopted by the English courts in the context of Article 4(3) of the Rome II Regulation, which has now replaced s 12 of the 1995 Act.[55]

In any event, it seems clear that, in view of its purpose, Article 8 extends to claims for unfair dismissal or in respect of unlawful discrimination in relation to employment, despite the statutory character of such rights, and that it overrides any self-limiting territorial rule contained in legislation which creates such claims, such as a restriction to cases where the employee's work is performed in the country in question. Thus the Regulation requires that the country whose law governs, or whose mandatory rules for the protection of employees have overriding effect in respect of, a contract of employment under Article 8 should admit any claim for unfair dismissal, or in respect of unlawful discrimination in relation to employment, which it would (apart from the Regulation) have admitted if the case had been connected exclusively with its own territory. Unfortunately, this obvious point has not yet been accepted in England.[56]

---

[50] A dictum to the contrary was expressed by Bot AG in Case C-346/06: *Rüffert v Land Niedersachsen* [2008] ECR I-1989, at para 11, but the issue was not considered by the European Court.

[51] See the Giuliano and Lagarde Report, at p. 32.

[52] At pp. 25–6.

[53] [2005] 1 All ER (Comm) 17 (CA); affirming [2004] 1 All ER (Comm) 159 (Tomlinson J). See also [2002] CLC 322 (Moore-Bick J).

[54] See also *Johnson v Coventry Churchill* [1992] 3 All ER 14 (Kay QC); and *Glencore v Metro* [2001] 1 Lloyd's Rep 284 (Moore-Bick J).

[55] On choice of law in tort under the Rome II Regulation, see Chapter 14 below.

[56] On unfair dismissal, see *Lawson v Serco* [2006] 1 All ER 823 (HL), and *Bleuse v MBT*

**The Directive on the Posting of Workers**

An important exception to the rules laid down by Article 8 of the Rome I Regulation is made by EC Directive 96/71, on the posting of workers in the framework of the provision of services.[57] By virtue of Recital 34 and Article 23 of the Regulation, since the Directive lays down conflict rules relating to a particular matter, it prevails over the Regulation.

The Directive applies where an undertaking, in the framework of the transnational provision of services, posts a worker for a limited period to a Member State other than the State in which he normally works.[58] Three kinds of posting are covered. The first is where the undertaking posts workers to the territory of a Member State on its own account and under its own direction, under a contract concluded between the undertaking and a service recipient operating in the receiving State. This applies, for example, where an undertaking established in Poland posts Polish workers, for its account and under its direction, to Germany, in the framework of a construction sub-contract concluded between the Polish undertaking and the main construction contractor, which operates in Germany.[59] The second is where the undertaking posts workers to an establishment or an undertaking owned by the same group in the receiving State. The third is where the undertaking is a temporary employment undertaking or placement agency, and it hires out a worker to a user undertaking established or operating in the receiving State. In any event, there must be an employment relationship between the undertaking making the posting and the worker during the period of posting.[60]

Where it applies, the Directive requires the Member States to ensure that, regardless of the law otherwise applicable to the employment relationship, a posting undertaking guarantees to workers posted to their territory the minimum terms and conditions of employment relating to certain matters (such as minimum rates of pay) which are mandatorily applicable in the Member State where the work is carried out.[61] Thus, insofar as the Directive applies, the worker receives the benefit of protective rules contained in the law of the country where he temporarily, but not habitually, works.

## INSURANCE CONTRACTS

**The Rome Convention and the Insurance Directives**

Prior to the entry into force of the Rome I Regulation, insurance contracts were to a large extent excluded from the scope of the Rome Convention 1980. By Article 1(3) and (4), the Convention excluded from its scope contracts of insurance (other than reinsurance) covering risks situated within the European Community. Instead, choice of law in respect of such

---

*Transport* [2008] IRLR 264 (Elias J in the EAT). On discrimination, see s 1 of the Equal Pay Act 1970 (as amended); ss 6 and 10 of the Sex Discrimination Act 1975 (as amended); ss 4 and 8 of the Race Relations Act 1976 (as amended); ss 4(6) and 68 of the Disability Discrimination Act 1995; and *Williams v University of Nottingham* [2007] IRLR 660 (Wilkie J in the EAT).

57   [1997] OJ L18/1.
58   See Articles 1(1) and 2(1).
59   See Case C-346/06: *Rüffert v Land Niedersachsen* [2008] ECR I-1989.
60   See Article 1(3). See also Recital 4.
61   See Article 3.

contracts was regulated by Article 7 of EC Directive 88/357 (as amended by Article 27 of Directive 92/49)[62] in the case of non-life insurance, and by Article 32 of EC Directive 2002/83[63] in the case of life insurance. The Directives had been transposed in the United Kingdom by the Financial Services and Markets Act 2000 (Law Applicable to Contracts of Insurance) Regulations 2001 (SI 2001/2635), made under the Financial Services and Markets Act 2000.[64]

In contrast, if the risk was not located within the Community, under the definitions of location specified by the Directives, or if the contract was of reinsurance, the choice-of-law rules laid down by the Rome Convention 1980 *did* apply. The parties were then free to choose the governing law, expressly or by implication, in accordance with Article 3 of the Convention, and in default of choice the law of the country of an establishment of the insurer involved in the transaction would normally apply under Article 4.[65] But, since insurance is a financial service, it seems probable that in some cases an insurance contract covering a non-European risk counted as a protected consumer contract, within Article 5 of the Convention.[66] In that event, in default of an express or implied choice by the parties, Article 5 subjected the contract to the law of the policy-holder's habitual residence; and a choice of law by the parties operated subject to the mandatory rules for the protection of weaker parties contained in the law of the policy-holder's habitual residence. Moreover, where the Convention applied, the operation of the proper law could be displaced by mandatory rules or public policy, under Articles 3(3), 7 or 16 of the Convention.

**The Scope of the Rome I Regulation**

In contrast to the Rome Convention 1980, the Rome I Regulation excludes from its scope a very limited category of insurance contracts. The exclusion, specified by Article 1(2)(j), is

---

62    [1988] OJ L172 and [1992] OJ L228.

63    [2002] OJ L345. This had replaced Article 4 of EC Directive 90/619, [1990] OJ L330.

64    For the transposition of the Directives in Ireland, see the European Communities (Non-Life Insurance) Regulations 1976 (SI 115/1976); the European Communities (Non-Life Insurance) (Amendment) (No 2) Regulations 1991 (SI 142/1991); the European Communities (Non-Life Insurance) (Amendment) Regulations 1992 (SI 244/1992); the European Communities (Non-Life Insurance) Framework Regulations 1994 (SI 359/1994); and the European Communities (Life Assurance) Framework Regulations 1994 (SI 360/1994).

65    See *Amin Rasheed v Kuwait Insurance Co* [1984] 1 AC 50; *CGU International Insurance v Szabo* [2002] Lloyd's Rep IR 196 (Toulson J); *American Motorists Insurance v Cellstar* [2003] ILPr 22 (CA); *Sun Alliance v Asuransri Dayin Mitra v Pelumin* [2006] EWHC 812 (Comm) (Langley J); *Dornoch v Mauritius Union Assurance* [2006] 2 Lloyd's Rep 475 (CA); and *Lexington Insurance v AGF Insurance* [2009] UKHL 40 (HL), affirming *Wasa International Insurance v Lexington Insurance* [2008] 1 All ER (Comm) 286 (Simon J).

   Cf. *Travelers Casualty v Sun Life* [2006] All ER (D) 26 (Nov), where Christopher Clarke J held that Ontario law was applicable (by implied choice or closest connection) to an insurance in favour of an Ontario insured and its subsidiaries, which had been negotiated between an Ontario broker and a New York office of the leading insurer, and under which 40% of the risk was subscribed by Ontario insurers, although the leading insurer was English and 60% of the risk was subscribed by English insurers.

66    The only serious argument against the application of Article 5 of the Rome Convention 1980 to some insurance contracts would rely on the analogy of the Brussels Convention and the Brussels I Regulation, for the purposes of which it seems clear that an insurance contract can never count as a protected consumer contract.

confined to insurance contracts which arise out of operations carried out by organisations which are not established within the European Union, and of which the object is to provide benefits for employed or self-employed persons belonging to an undertaking or group of undertakings, or to a trade or group of trades, in the event of death or survival, or of discontinuance or curtailment of activity, or of sickness related to work or accidents at work. Since such activities and contracts are (for some mysterious reason) also excluded from EC Directive 2002/83 on life insurance by Article 3(3) thereof, it seems that the law governing such contracts must be determined in accordance with the conflict rules of the forum.

Subject to this minor exclusion, the Rome I Regulation applies to all types of insurance contract. The Regulation applies both to life insurance, and to non-life insurance, and also to reinsurance. It applies both to large risks and to mass risks. It applies regardless of whether or not the insurer or the policy-holder is resident or established, or the risk is located, within the European Union. As Article 23 makes clear, it replaces the choice-of-law provisions contained in the Directives. But the change is more of form than substance, since Article 7 of the Regulation to a large extent echoes Article 7 of EC Directive 88/357 (as amended) and Article 32 of EC Directive 2002/83.[67]

One consequence of the extension of the Rome I Regulation so as to apply to almost all insurance contracts is that the possibility of displacement of the proper law by mandatory rules or public policy is now governed by Articles 3(3)–(4), 9 and 21 of the Regulation, rather than by corresponding provisions of the Directives.

## The Effect of the Rome I Regulation

In the Rome I Regulation, Article 7(2) lays down specific rules for determining the proper law of an insurance contract covering a large risk, whether the risk is situated within the European Union or elsewhere. As regards an insurance contract covering a mass risk, specific rules for determining the proper law are laid down by Article 7(3), but these are limited to cases where the risk is situated within the European Union.

In addition, Article 7(4) provides further rules which apply to insurance contracts covering risks for which a Member State imposes an obligation to take out insurance. It seems clear from Article 7(1) that Article 7(4) is limited to contracts which fall within the scope of Article 7(2) or Article 7(3), and thus that Article 7(4) does not extend to insurance contracts covering a mass risk which is situated outside the European Union. Article 7(1) also specifies that Article 7 does not apply to reinsurance contracts.

In cases not dealt with by Article 7, the Regulation treats an insurance or reinsurance contract in the same way as an non-insurance contract. Thus in general such contracts are subject to the ordinary rules for determining the proper law, laid down by Articles 3 and 4 of the Regulation, which refer primarily to an express or implied choice by the parties, and secondarily (in the absence of such a choice) to a residence of the characteristic performer or to a manifestly closer connection. Accordingly, since Article 7(1) excludes reinsurance

---

[67]   It is perhaps because of the very limited character of the substantive changes made by the Regulation in relation to insurance contracts that Article 27 singles out such contracts as a matter to be specifically addressed in the report on the application of the Regulation, to be submitted by the EC Commission by 17th June 2013.

contracts from the scope of Article 7, party choice is available in the case of any reinsurance contract, regardless of whether it covers a large risk or a mass risk, and of where the risk is situated. Moreover, in default of choice, a reinsurance contract will usually be governed by the law of a country in which is located an establishment of the reinsurer which is involved in the transaction.

Since Article 7(1) makes Article 7 inapplicable to an insurance contract covering a mass risk which is situated outside the European Union, in general such a contract is subject to the ordinary rules for determining the proper law, laid down by Articles 3 and 4. These rules are certainly applicable where, in obtaining the insurance, the policy-holder was acting in the course of a business. But the position is much less clear where the policy-holder was not acting in the course of a business. For in such cases it is arguable that Article 6, on consumer contracts, may be applicable. If so, the effect would be that, in certain cases, in default of an express or implied choice by the parties, Article 6 would subject the contract to the law of the policy-holder's habitual residence; and in such cases a choice of law by the parties would operate subject to the mandatory rules for the protection of weaker parties contained in the law of the policy-holder's habitual residence.

At first sight, it may seem that Recital 32 prevents Article 6 from ever applying to an insurance contract. The Recital specifies that, owing to the particular nature of insurance contracts, specific provisions should ensure an adequate level of protection of policy-holders; and that therefore Article 6 should not apply in the context of those particular contracts. But such a blanket exclusion is not reflected in the operative text, since (so far as is relevant) Article 6 merely begins by specifying that it operates without prejudice to Article 7, and Article 7 excludes from its scope insurance contracts covering a mass risk which is situated outside the European Union. Thus if one ignores the Recital, one would undoubtedly conclude that, in the case of an insurance contract covering a mass risk situated outside the European Union, Article 6 would apply if its requirements were otherwise satisfied. So it may be argued that a mere recital cannot prevail against the clear wording of the operative text, especially as Recital 32 is not entirely unambiguous, since it might be read as excluding Article 6 only where Article 7 provides adequate protection for policy-holders. Moreover, it may be suggested that no sensible purpose would be served by the exclusion of Article 6 in the relevant scenario, and that such an exclusion would depart without explanation from the solution which would probably have been reached under the Rome Convention 1980. No doubt a realist would explain the ambiguity as probably designed to reflect a failure to resolve a disagreement between delegations. In any event, it may be thought that the resulting uncertainty constitutes a major defect of the Regulation.

## Large Risks and Mass Risks

Article 7(2) of the Regulation adopts the distinction between large risks and mass risks drawn by Article 5(d) and the Annex of Directive 73/239 on non-life insurance,[68] as amended by Article 5 of Directive 88/357[69] and Article 2 of Directive 90/618.[70] In using the distinction

---

[68]   [1973] OJ L228.
[69]   [1988] OJ L172.
[70]   [1990] OJ L330.

for the purpose of choice of law, the Regulation echoes an amendment to Article 7(1)(f) of Directive 88/357 made by Article 27 of Directive 92/49.[71] The main effect of the elaborate definition is that business risks are usually regarded as large, except where the policy-holder is regarded as a small business.

Under the definition of large risks provided by Directive 73/239 as amended, many transport risks are regarded as large risks, regardless of the policy-holder's business character or size. This applies to damage to or loss of ships, aircraft, or railway rolling stock; damage to or loss of goods in transit or baggage, irrespective of the form of transport; and liability arising out of the use of ships or aircraft, including carrier's liability.

Risks relating to credit or suretyship are regarded as large risks if the policy-holder is engaged in and the risks relate to a business activity, whether the business is large, medium-sized or small. A wide variety of risks are regarded as large risks if the policy-holder is engaged in and the risks relate to a large or medium-sized business activity. As regards size, two of the following three conditions must be fulfilled in respect of the policy-holder or the group to which it belongs: (1) that the balance-sheet total exceeds 6.2 million; (2) that the net turnover exceeds 12.8 million; (3) that the average number of employees during the financial year exceeds 250. The risks in this category include damage to or loss of most types of property (including motor vehicles) by various causes (including fire, storm and theft); financial losses of various kinds; and various liabilities, including ones arising out of the use of motor vehicles.

The only kinds of non-life risk which can never be regarded as large are accident and sickness benefits (including benefits for industrial injury or occupational disease, or for injury to passengers), and legal expenses. But life risks can never be regarded as large. Risks other than large risks are regarded as mass risks.

## The Law Governing Large Risks

Article 7(2) of the Rome I Regulation specifies the rules for determining the proper law of an insurance contract covering a large risk. By Article 7(1), these rules apply regardless of whether the risk covered is situated within the European Union, but they do not apply to reinsurance contracts.

The primary rule specified by Article 7(2) of the Regulation subjects an insurance contract covering a large risk to the law expressly or impliedly chosen by the parties in accordance with Article 3. This accords with the solution formerly adopted for insurance of risks situated outside the European Community by Article 3 of the Rome Convention, and for insurance of large risks situated within the European Community by Article 7(1)(f) of Directive 88/357 (as amended).

In the absence of a choice by the parties, Article 7(2) of the Regulation provides for an insurance contract covering a large risk a rebuttable presumption in favour of the law of the country where the insurer has his habitual residence. But this presumption will be rebutted where it is clear from all the circumstances of the case that the contract is manifestly more closely connected with another country, and the law of that other country will then apply. These default rules closely resemble those formerly adopted for insurance of risks situated

---

[71]   [1992] OJ L228.

outside the European Community by Article 4 of the Rome Convention. They differ, however, from those formerly adopted for insurance of risks situated within the European Community by Article 7(1)(h) of Directive 88/357, where the rebuttable presumption was in favour of the law of the Member State in which the risk was situated (usually a residence or establishment of the policy-holder).

Where an insurance contract covers a large risk for which a Member State imposes an obligation to take out insurance, the additional rules specified by Article 7(4) apply.[72]

Although Article 7(2) of the Regulation does not apply to reinsurance contracts, they are subject to similar rules under Articles 3 and 4 of the Regulation. Thus, subject to the exceptions which relate to compulsory insurance, in substance the normal regime provided by the Regulation for 'ordinary' or non-insurance contracts extends to all insurance contracts covering large risks, wherever the risk is located, and also to reinsurance contracts.

## The Law Governing Mass Risks

Article 7(3) of the Rome I Regulation specifies the rules for determining the proper law of an insurance contract covering a mass risk. By Article 7(1), these rules are confined to cases where the risk covered is situated within the European Union, and they do not apply to reinsurance contracts. Under the Regulation, an insurance contract covering a mass risk which is situated outside the European Union is subject to the same rules as an ordinary non-insurance contract, or perhaps in some cases as a protected consumer contract.

Recital 33 explains that where an insurance contract covering a mass risk covers more than one risk, at least one of which is situated in a Member State and at least one of which is situated in a non-member country, the special rules on insurance contracts in the Regulation should apply only to the risk or risks situated in the relevant Member State or Member States. Thus in such a case one must split the contract for choice-of-law purposes into at least two contracts, one covering the European risks and the other the non-European risks. Such an approach had been strenuously resisted (admittedly in the context of large risks) by the English courts in the period before the adoption of the Regulation.[73]

By Article 7(6), the Regulation adopts the rules laid down by Article 2(d) of Directive 88/357 and Article 1(1)(g) of Directive 2002/83 as to where a risk is situated. The general rule is that, where the policy-holder is an individual, the risk is located in the country where he has his habitual residence; or, where the policy-holder is a legal person, the risk is located in the country where its establishment to which the contract relates is situated. For this purpose, where one member of a corporate group takes out an insurance policy covering other companies in the group, another company in the group for whose activities insurance cover is obtained counts as an establishment of the policy-holder who obtains the insurance cover.[74] But there are three exceptions. In the case of insurance of buildings, or of buildings and their

---

[72]  See pp. 367–8 below.

[73]  See *American Motorists Insurance v Cellstar* [2002] 2 Lloyd's Rep 216 (David Steel J) and [2003] ILPr 22 (CA); *Travelers Casualty v Sun Life* [2004] Lloyd's Rep IR 846 (Jonathan Hirst QC); *CGU International Insurance v Astrazeneca Insurance* [2005] EWHC 2755 (Comm) (Cresswell J); and *Travelers Casualty v Sun Life* [2006] All ER (D) 26 (Nov) (Christopher Clarke J).

[74]  See Case C-191/99: *Kvaerner v Staatssecretaris van Financiën* [2001] ECR I-4447; and *American Motorists Insurance v Cellstar* [2003] ILPr 22 (CA).

contents under the same policy, the risk is located in the country where the property is situated. In the case of insurance of vehicles of any type, the risk is located in the country of registration.[75] In the case of policies of a duration of four months or less covering travel or holiday risks, the risk is located in the country where the policy-holder took out the policy.

In the case of an insurance contract covering risks situated within the European Union, Article 7(3) of the Rome I Regulation allows the parties a limited freedom to make an express or implied choice of the proper law in accordance with Article 3. By Article 7(3)(i), the law chosen must be one of the following: (a) the law of a Member State where the risk is situated at the time of conclusion of the contract; (b) the law of the country where the policy-holder has his habitual residence;[76] (c) in the case of life assurance, the law of the Member State of which the policy-holder is a national; (d) for insurance contracts covering risks limited to events occurring in a single Member State other than the Member State where the risk is situated, the law of the Member State in which the events are to occur; and (e) where the policy-holder pursues a business activity, and the insurance contract covers two or more risks which relate to such activities and are situated in different Member States, the law of any of those Member States, or the law of the country of habitual residence of the policy-holder.[77]

In certain cases, Article 7(3)(ii) of the Regulation extends the range of choice by reference to the conflict rules of a Member State whose internal law may be chosen under Article 7(3)(i). It enables parties to choose another law where this is permissible under the conflict rules of the Member State in which the risk is situated, or in which the policy-holder has his habitual residence, or in which is located one of the risks relating to a business activity of the policy-holder.[78] This extension of choice constitutes an exception to the exclusion of renvoi by Article 20 of the Regulation.

Article 7(3)(iii) of the Regulation provides a default rule, applicable to an insurance contract covering a mass risk situated within the European Union, where no valid express or implied choice of law has been made by the parties. The contract is then governed by the law of the Member State in which the risk is situated at the time of conclusion of the contract. This is a firm rule, without any exception in favour of a manifestly closer connection.[79] By

---

[75]    See also Article 4 of Directive 2005/14, [2005] OJ L149/14, which applies where a vehicle is dispatched from one Member State to another, and treats the risk as situated in the Member State of destination, immediately upon acceptance of delivery by the purchaser for a period of thirty days, even though the vehicle has not formally been registered in the Member State of destination.

[76]    See *American Motorists Insurance v Cellstar* [2003] ILPr 22 (CA).

[77]    Article 7(3)(i) of the Regulation broadly follows Article 7(1)(a)–(c) and (e) of Directive 88/357 and Article 32 of Directive 2002/83. But the Regulation refers to a corporate policy-holder's habitual residence, determined in accordance with Article 19, rather than its central administration as such.

[78]    Article 7(3)(ii) of the Regulation broadly follows Article 7(1)(a) and (d) of Directive 88/357 and Article 32 of Directive 2002/83. See also *American Motorists Insurance v Cellstar* [2003] ILPr 22 (CA), and *Evialis v Siat* [2003] 2 Lloyd's Rep 377 (Andrew Smith J).

[79]    This contrasts with Article 7(1)(h) of Directive 88/357, under which if no valid choice had been made by the parties, the contract was governed by the law of the country, from amongst those from which choice was permissible, with which it was most closely connected, and the contract was rebuttably presumed to be most closely connected with the Member State in which the risk was situated. See *Credit Lyonnais v New Hampshire Insurance* [1997] 2 Lloyd's Rep 1, where the English Court of Appeal adhered to the presumption, and applied English law, that of the corporate policy-holder's secondary establishment to which the contract related, rather than French law, that of the policy-holder's central administration.

Article 7(5), for this purpose, where the contract covers risks situated in more than one Member State, the contract must be treated as constituting several contracts, each relating to only one Member State.[80]

Where an insurance contract covers a risk for which a Member State imposes an obligation to take out insurance, the additional rules specified by Article 7(4) apply.

Article 7(1) of the Rome I Regulation prevents Article 7 from applying to insurance contracts covering mass risks situated outside the European Union. Thus, under the Regulation, an insurance contract which covers a mass risk situated outside the European Union, and which is not a protected consumer contract within Article 6, is subject to the same choice-of-law rules as an 'ordinary' or non-insurance contract. Accordingly, the contract is governed by the law expressly or impliedly chosen by the parties in accordance with Article 3; and in the absence of such a choice there is a rebuttable presumption in favour of the law of a residence of the insurer, in accordance with Article 4. The result is that no protection is offered to a policy-holder which is a small business where the risk is located outside Europe.

It is unclear whether the same applies where the policy-holder is a consumer, or whether in this case the policy-holder can take advantage of Article 6 of the Regulation if its requirements are otherwise satisfied. The opening phrase of Article 6(1) specifies that Article 6 operates without prejudice to Article 7, and thus indicates that it is only where Article 7 applies that Article 6 is displaced. Accordingly, since Article 7 applies to insurance of mass risks only where the risk is located within the European Union, Article 6 remains applicable where a mass risk is located outside the European Union, and the policy-holder is an individual not acting in the course of a business, and the other conditions for the application of Article 6 are fulfilled. On the other hand, Recital 32 specifies that, owing to the particular nature of insurance contracts, specific provisions should ensure an adequate level of protection of policy-holders; and that therefore Article 6 should not apply in the context of those particular contracts.

It is submitted that the ambiguity or contradiction should be resolved in favour of the availability of Article 6, both on the technical ground that the main text of the Regulation should prevail over a mere recital, especially where the recital itself is not entirely unambiguous, and on the substantial ground that in case of doubt the Regulation should be construed so as to minimise, rather than maximise, the discrimination made between policy-holders according to the location of the risk. Moreover the availability of Article 6 in this situation would accord with the solution which would probably have been reached under the Rome Convention 1980.

## Compulsory Insurance

Article 7(4) of the Regulation specifies some additional rules which apply to insurance contracts covering risks for which a Member State imposes an obligation to take out insurance. It seems clear from Article 7(1) that Article 7(4) is limited to contracts which fall within the scope of Article 7(2) or Article 7(3), and thus that Article 7(4) does not extend to insurance

---

[80] This contrasts with Article 7(1)(h) of Directive 88/357, under which a severable part of the contract which had a closer connection with another country, amongst those from which choice was permissible, could by way of exception be governed by the law of that other country.

contracts covering a mass risk which is situated outside the European Union. Article 7(1) also specifies that Article 7 does not apply to reinsurance contracts.

Article 7(4)(a) of the Regulation specifies, in its first limb, that an insurance contract will not satisfy the obligation to take out insurance unless it complies with the specific provisions relating to that insurance laid down by the Member State which imposes the obligation. This echoes Article 8(2) of Directive 88/357, and may be regarded as uncontroversial.

Article 7(4)(a) of the Regulation proceeds to add, in its second limb, that where the law of the Member State in which the risk is situated and the law of the Member State imposing the obligation to take out insurance contradict each other, the latter will prevail. This echoes Article 8(3) of Directive 88/357, but its effect is far from clear. One possible interpretation is that any difference between the relevant laws should be regarded as a contradiction, with the result that the law of the Member State imposing the obligation to take out insurance is exclusively applicable in all cases of compulsory insurance to which Article 7(4) applies. But this approach would render the option conferred on the forum State by Article 7(4)(b) illusory. Another possible interpretation is that the two limbs of Article 7(4)(a) should be read together, so as to yield a single rule that an insurance contract will not satisfy an obligation to take out insurance unless it complies with the relevant requirements specified by the law of the Member State which imposes the obligation, and that for this purpose the law of the State in which the risk is situated is immaterial. But this approach may read too much into the juxtaposition of the two limbs, especially as they are derived from distinct paragraphs of the Directive. No wholly convincing interpretation is apparent.

By Article 7(4)(b) of the Regulation, by way of derogation from Article 7(2) and (3), a Member State may lay down that the insurance contract shall be governed by the law of the Member State which imposes the obligation to take out insurance. This echoes the permission formerly offered by Article 8(4)(c) of Directive 88/357,[81] which had not been utilised by the United Kingdom, but had been utilised by Ireland.[82]

By Article 7(5) of the Regulation, for these purposes, where the contract covers risks situated in more than one Member State, the contract must be treated as constituting several contracts, each relating to only one Member State.

---

[81]    In addition, Article 7(2)(ii) of Directive 88/357 formerly permitted a Member State to stipulate in its law that the mandatory rules of the law of the Member State imposing the obligation to take out insurance could be applied if and insofar as, under that law, those rules had to be applied whatever the law applicable to the contract, but no corresponding provision is made by the Regulation.

[82]    See Article 26(1)(c) of the (Irish) European Communities (Non-Life Insurance) Framework Regulations 1994 (SI 359/1994).

# 14.  Torts

## INTRODUCTION

### The Rome II Regulation

In litigation relating to torts or restitutionary obligations, choice of the applicable substantive law is now regulated by EC Regulation 864/2007 on the Law Applicable to Non-contractual Obligations, which is usually referred to as the Rome II Regulation.[1] The Regulation was adopted by the EC Parliament and Council on 11th July 2007.[2] By Articles 31 and 32, the Regulation became applicable on 11th January 2009, and it applies to events giving rise to damage which occur after that date. Since the United Kingdom and Ireland elected to participate in the adoption and application of the Regulation, it applies in all the Member States except Denmark.[3] Thus, in the United Kingdom, the choice-of-law rules specified by the Regulation have replaced those laid down by Part III of the Private International Law (Miscellaneous Provisions) Act 1995.

The Rome II Regulation lays down choice-of-law rules for torts and restitutionary obligations. It is designed to complement the EU measures (the Rome Convention 1980, and its successor, the Rome I Regulation) on the law applicable to contractual obligations.[4] The general purposes underlying the harmonisation of choice-of-law rules effected by the Rome II Regulation are disclosed by various recitals. In substance, these relate to the achievement of certainty, predictability and uniformity of result, regardless of forum; the achievement of justice in individual cases; and the achievement of a reasonable balance between the interests of the parties involved.

Thus Recital 6 explains that the proper functioning of the internal market creates a need, in order to improve the predictability of the outcome of litigation, certainty as to the law

---

[1]  For its text, see [2007] OJ L199/40.

[2]  The legislative procedure leading to the adoption of the Regulation was initiated by a proposal presented by the EC Commission on 22nd July 2003; see COM(2003) 427 final. A resolution on first reading was adopted by the European Parliament on 6th July 2005; see JUSTCIV 132, 13th July 2005. An amended proposal was presented by the Commission on 21st February 2006; see COM(2006) 83 final. Common Position 22/2006 was adopted by the Council on 25th September 2006; see [2006] OJ C289E/68. A resolution on second reading was adopted by the European Parliament on 18th January 2007; see JUSTCIV 7, 24th January 2007. An agreement between the Council and the Parliament, settling all outstanding issues, was reached in conciliation committee on 15th May 2007; see Council press release 9713/07 (Presse 111), 16th May 2007, and Commission press release IP/07/679, 16th May 2007. The text so agreed on was approved by the Council on 28th June 2007, and by the Parliament on 10th July 2007; see Council doc 11313/07 of 28th June 2007, and Parliamentary doc P6_TA-PROV(2007)0317, A6-0257/2007.

[3]  See Recitals 39–40 and Article 1(4) of the Regulation.

[4]  On these, see Chapters 12 and 13 above.

applicable and the free movement of judgments, for the conflict rules in the Member States to designate the same national law, irrespective of the country of the court in which an action is brought. Recital 13 adds that uniform rules applied irrespective of the law they designate may avert the risk of distortions of competition between Community litigants. Recital 14 emphasises that the requirement of legal certainty and the need to do justice in individual cases are essential elements of an area of justice, and asserts that the Regulation provides for the connecting factors which are the most appropriate to achieve these objectives. By providing for a general rule and also for specific rules and, in certain provisions, for an escape clause, it creates a flexible framework and enables the court seised to treat individual cases in an appropriate manner. Recital 16 explains that uniform rules should enhance the foreseeability of court decisions and ensure a reasonable balance between the interests of the person claimed to be liable and the person who has sustained damage. Recital 19 adds that specific rules should be laid down for special torts where the general rule does not allow a reasonable balance to be struck between the interests at stake.

The Rome II Regulation contains 32 Articles arranged in VII Chapters. Chapter I (Articles 1–3) deals with the scope of the Regulation and provides some definitions. Chapter II (Articles 4–9) specifies the choice-of-law rules which apply to torts. Chapter III (Articles 10–13) specifies the choice-of-law rules which apply to restitutionary obligations. Chapter IV (Article 14) enables the parties involved to choose the applicable law by agreement. Chapters V and VI (Articles 15–22 and 23–8) lay down some further rules which apply both to torts and to restitutionary obligations. These deal with such matters as the range of issues which are governed by the applicable law, the meaning of habitual residence, and the exceptional intervention of the forum's public policy. Chapter VII (Articles 29–32) deals with such matters as the commencement date.

## Material Scope

By Article 1(1), the Rome II Regulation applies, in situations involving a conflict of laws, to non-contractual obligations in civil and commercial matters. It does not apply, in particular, to revenue, customs or administrative matters, nor to the liability of the State for acts and omissions in the exercise of State authority ('acta iure imperii'). Recital 9 explains that claims arising out of 'acta iure imperii' include claims against officials who act on behalf of the State, and liability for acts of public authorities, including liability of publicly appointed office-holders.

Recital 7 recognises that the substantive scope and the provisions of the Regulation should be consistent with the Brussels I Regulation[5] and the instruments dealing with the law applicable to contractual obligations (the Rome Convention 1980 and, now, the Rome I Regulation).[6] Recital 8 adds that the Regulation applies irrespective of the nature of the court or tribunal seised. Recital 11 explains that, since the concept of a non-contractual obligation varies from one Member State to another, for the purposes of the Regulation 'non-contractual obligation' should be understood as an autonomous concept.

---

[5]    On the Brussels I Regulation, see Chapters 2–11 above.

[6]    On these, see Chapters 12 and 13 above. Similarly, Recital 7 to the Rome I Regulation notes that the substantive scope and the provisions of that Regulation should be consistent with the Brussels I Regulation and the Rome II Regulation.

In view of these provisions and recitals, and of the decisions of the European Court on the scope of the Brussels Convention and the Brussels I Regulation,[7] it may be concluded that the Rome II Regulation is confined to claims which are governed by private law, and does not apply to disputes between a private person and a public authority which arise out of acts done by the public authority in the exercise of its powers as such, or which involve a relationship entailing the exercise by the State of powers going beyond those existing under the rules applicable to relations between private persons.

The Regulation deals with two classes of non-contractual obligation: torts, which are dealt with by Chapter II (Articles 4–9); and restitutionary obligations, which are dealt with by Chapter III (Articles 10–13). Further rules, applicable to both torts and restitutionary obligations, are laid down by Chapters IV–VI (Articles 14–28). The present chapter of this work will examine choice of law in respect of torts, and the following chapter will consider restitutionary obligations.

The Rome II Regulation does not explicitly provide a substantive definition of a tort. Indications are offered by Recital 11, which declares that, since the concept of a non-contractual obligation varies from one Member State to another, for the purposes of the Regulation 'non-contractual obligation' should be understood as an autonomous concept. It also explains that the conflict rules set out in the Regulation extend to non-contractual obligations arising out of strict liability. Recital 12 adds that the law applicable should also govern the question of the capacity to incur liability in tort. Despite the limited character of these indications, it seems clear that the concept of a tort refers to an act which is wrongful, other than by reason of its being a breach of contract or trust, and which therefore gives rise to liability to pay compensation for loss arising therefrom. In contrast, a restitutionary obligation does not require a wrongful act, but arises from a situation involving unjust enrichment, unauthorised agency, or pre-contractual dealings.

Article 2 contains some definitions, designed to ensure that the Regulation extends to threatened torts, and that references to damage extend to a corresponding result in the case of restitutionary claims. Thus Article 2(1) specifies that, for the purposes of the Regulation, damage covers any consequence arising out of tort, unjust enrichment, negotiorum gestio or culpa in contrahendo. By Article 2(2), the Regulation extends to non-contractual obligations which are likely to arise. By Article 2(3), any reference in the Regulation to an event giving rise to damage includes events giving rise to damage which are likely to occur, and any reference to damage includes damage which is likely to occur.

Various matters are excluded from the scope of the Regulation by Article 1(2) and (3). Many of these exclusions resemble ones made by the Rome Convention 1980 and the Rome I Regulation.[8] Thus there are exclusions from the Rome II Regulation by Article 1(2)(a) in respect of obligations arising out of family relationships, and relationships deemed by the law applicable to such relationships to have comparable effects, including maintenance obligations;

---

[7]    See Case 29/76: *LTU v Eurocontrol* [1976] ECR 1541; Case 814/79: *Netherlands v Rüffer* [1980] ECR 3807; Case C-172/91: *Sonntag v Waidmann* [1993] ECR I-1963; Case C-167/00: *VKI v Henkel* [2002] ECR I-8111; Case C-271/00: *Gemeente Steenbergen v Baten* [2002] ECR I-10489; Case C-266/01: *Tiard* [2003] ECR I-4867; Case C-433/01: *Freistaat Bayern v Blijdenstein* [2004] ECR I-981; Case C-265/02: *Frahuil v Assitalia* [2004] ECR I-1543; and Case C-292/05: *Lechouritou v Germany* [2007] ECR I-1519.

[8]    See pp. 290–93 above.

and by Article 1(2)(b) in respect of obligations arising out of matrimonial property regimes, property regimes of relationships deemed by the law applicable to such relationships to have comparable effects to marriage, and wills and succession. In this connection, Recital 10 explains that family relationships refer to parentage, marriage, affinity and collateral relatives; and that the reference to relationships having comparable effects to marriage and other family relationships should be interpreted in accordance with the law of the forum.[9] The rationale for these exclusions appears to be the absence of harmonised choice-of-law rules in the Community as regards family law.[10]

But the Rome II Regulation contains no exclusion, corresponding to Article 1(2)(a) of the Rome I Regulation, in respect of questions involving the capacity of individuals. In contrast, Recital 12 to the Rome II Regulation explains that the law applicable to a tort should also govern the question of capacity to incur liability in tort. Moreover, it seems clear the family exclusions do not apply to situations where the claim arises from the ordinary law of tort, but a defence is raised by reference to an immunity which arises from a family relationship. For example, where the claim is for personal injury arising from a road accident, but it is brought by one spouse against the other, or by a child against his parent, and the defendant invokes a rule which eliminates liability in tort by reason of the familial relationship.

Another exclusion from the Rome II Regulation relates to negotiable instruments. Article 1(2)(c) refers to obligations arising under bills of exchange, cheques and promissory notes, and other negotiable instruments to the extent that the obligations under such other negotiable instruments arise out of their negotiable character.[11]

A further exclusion relates to obligations governed by company law. Article 1(2)(d) refers to obligations arising out of the law of companies and other bodies corporate or unincorporated, regarding matters such as the creation (by registration or otherwise), legal capacity, internal organisation, or winding-up of companies and other bodies corporate or unincorporated, the personal liability of officers and members as such for the obligations of the company or body, and the personal liability of auditors to a company or to its members in the statutory audits of accounting documents.[12] This exclusion reflects the view that such matters should be referred to the law governing the company or entity.[13] As regards auditors, since the reference is to their liability to the company audited or to its members, the exclusion appears not to cover a claim against an auditor by a potential purchaser of a company.[14] But it seems that the reference in Article 1(2)(d) to the legal capacity of companies and other bodies overrides the indication by Recital 12 that the law applicable to a tort should also govern the question of capacity to incur liability in tort.

---

[9]   These provisions accord with Article 1(2)(b) and (c) and Recital 8 of the Rome I Regulation.
[10]   See the Explanatory Memorandum accompanying the EC Commission Proposal of 22nd July 2003, COM(2003) 427 final, at p. 8.
[11]   This accords with Article 1(2)(d) of the Rome I Regulation.
[12]   Except for the addition of the reference to auditors, this accords with Article 1(2)(f) of the Rome I Regulation.
[13]   See the Explanatory Memorandum accompanying the EC Commission Proposal of 22nd July 2003, COM(2003) 427 final, at p. 9.
[14]   See the Draft Report by Diana Wallis MEP, rapporteur, to the EP Committee on Legal Affairs, 2003/0168(COD), 11th November 2004.

Another exclusion from the Rome II Regulation relates to trusts. Article 1(2)(e) refers to obligations arising out of the relations between the settlors, trustees and beneficiaries of a trust created voluntarily. In contrast, Article 1(2)(h) of the Rome I Regulation refers to the constitution of trusts and the relationship between settlors, trustees and beneficiaries, thus extending to trusts which arise by operation of law. The limitation of the exclusion in the Rome II Regulation to trusts which were created voluntarily seems designed to ensure greater consistency with the 1985 Hague Convention on recognition of trusts, and to avoid difficulty or confusion arising from the employment of the trust in common-law countries as a device for dealing with situations such as unjust enrichment.[15]

A further exclusion, specified by Article 1(2)(f), is for obligations arising out of nuclear damage. This reflects the international scheme of nuclear liability established by various treaties.[16] Another exclusion, specified by Article 1(3), applies (subject to certain exceptions) to evidence and procedure.[17]

A more surprising (and, indeed, controversial) exclusion, specified by Article 1(2)(g), refers to obligations arising out of violations of privacy and rights relating to personality, including defamation. Although this provision is clearly motivated by sensitivity relating to freedom of speech, the exclusion is not confined to claims against the media. In this connection, Article 30(2) requires the EU Commission to submit, by the end of 2008, a study on the situation in the field of the law applicable to non-contractual obligations arising out of violations of privacy and rights relating to personality, taking into account rules relating to freedom of the press and freedom of expression in the media, and conflict issues related to EC Directive 95/46 on Data Protection. This review clause emerged from the Conciliation Committee, as a compromise between the Council's insistence on excluding these matters from the Regulation, and the Parliament's desire to include and specifically regulate them.

For the time being, however, in the United Kingdom, defamation claims (for libel or slander) remain subject to the common law rules which in general require double actionability under the lex fori and the lex loci delicti, since neither the Private International Law (Miscellaneous Provisions) Act 1995,[18] nor the Rome II Regulation, extends to such claims. Moreover, the Rome II Regulation does not apply to a claim for breach of confidence or invasion of privacy by way of publication of personal information, even though, in *Douglas v Hello! Ltd*,[19] the English Court of Appeal characterised such a claim not as a tort claim, but as a restitutionary claim for unjust enrichment, and therefore applied a common-law conflict rule in favour of the law of the country where the publication took place and the enrichment occurred. However, the Rome II Regulation appears to be applicable to claims for slander of

---

[15] See the Draft Report by Diana Wallis MEP, rapporteur, to the EP Committee on Legal Affairs, 2003/0168(COD), 11th November 2004.

[16] See the Explanatory Memorandum accompanying the EC Commission Proposal of 22nd July 2003, COM(2003) 427 final, at p. 9, referring to Paris Convention of 29th July 1960, the Additional Convention of Brussels of 31st January 1963, the Vienna Convention of 21st May 1963, the Convention on Supplementary Compensation of 12th September 1997, and the Protocol of 21st September 1988.

[17] Article 1(3) makes a saving for Articles 21 and 22, which deal with the formal validity of unilateral acts, the burden of proof, and modes of proof. These provisions resemble Articles 1(3) and 18 of the Rome I Regulation.

[18] See s 13 of the 1995 Act.

[19] [2006] QB 125.

title, slander of goods, or other malicious falsehood, since these relate to property or commercial reputation, rather than privacy or personality.

## Territorial Scope

By Article 3, any law specified by the Rome II Regulation must be applied, whether or not it is the law of a Member State. This accords with Article 2 of the Rome I Regulation, and avoids the entirely perverse complexity which would arise from any attempt to distinguish between intra-Union and extra-Union disputes.

As regards States with more than one legal system, Article 25(1) of the Rome II Regulation specifies that where a State comprises several territorial units, each of which has its own rules of law in respect of non-contractual obligations, each territorial unit must be considered as a country for the purposes of identifying the law applicable under the Regulation. Article 25(2) adds that a Member State within which different territorial units have their own rules of law in respect of non-contractual obligations is not required to apply the Regulation to conflicts solely between the laws of such units. These provisions accord with Article 22 of the Rome I Regulation. No doubt, as in the case of the Rome Convention, the United Kingdom will decline to utilise the invitation to introduce pointless complexity and confusion by excluding the operation of the Regulations in cases connected only with its own territories.

Unlike the initial Proposal presented by the EC Commission in 2003,[20] the Rome II Regulation as adopted contains no specific provision as to the notional location of installations on the continental shelf,[21] ships on the high seas,[22] and aircraft in the airspace.

## Relationship with Other Community Legislation

Article 27 specifies that the Regulation is not to prejudice the application of provisions of European Union law which, in relation to particular matters, lay down conflict rules relating to non-contractual obligations. In this connection, Recital 35 emphasises that a situation where conflict rules are dispersed among several instruments, and where there are differences between those rules, should be avoided, but adds that the Regulation does not exclude the possibility of inclusion of conflict rules relating to non-contractual obligations in provisions of European Union law with regard to particular matters.

Recital 35 also declares that the Regulation should not prejudice the application of other instruments laying down provisions designed to contribute to the proper functioning of the internal market, insofar as they cannot be applied in conjunction with the law designated by the rules of the Regulation; and that the application of provisions of the applicable law designated by the rules of the Regulation should not restrict the free movement of goods and

---

[20]    COM(2003) 427 final.
[21]    See Case C-37/00: *Weber v Universal Ogden Services* [2002] ECR I-2013, treating installations on the continental shelf as part of the adjacent State for the purpose of jurisdiction over an employment dispute under the Brussels I Regulation.
[22]    See Case C-18/02: *DFDS Torline v SEKO* [2004] ECR I-1417, on the relevance of the nationality or flag of a ship for the purpose of jurisdiction under Article 5(3) of the Brussels I Regulation.

services as regulated by European Union instruments, such as Directive 2000/31 on Electronic Commerce.[23]

It is worth noting that this almost platitudinous declaration is the only remaining trace of Article 23(2) of the initial proposal made by the EC Commission in 2003,[24] which specified that the Regulation was not to prejudice the application of EU instruments which, in relation to particular matters and in areas co-ordinated by such instruments, subjected the supply of services or goods to the laws of the Member State where the service-provider was established and, in the area co-ordinated, allowed restrictions on freedom to provide services or goods originating in another Member State only in limited circumstances. This was concerned with the principles of mutual recognition and home-country control, utilised by EU measures relating to the internal market, and was designed to reassure the e-commerce lobby, who had campaigned in favour of the absurd proposition that measures such as Directive 2000/31 on Electronic Commerce in some way affected judicial jurisdiction and choice of law in relation to claims under private law.[25]

In reality, it is clear that the relevant principles of internal market law have no bearing on questions of private international law, and this is explicitly recognised both by Directive 2000/31 on Electronic Commerce,[26] and by Directive 2006/123, on Services in the Internal Market.[27] Thus the declaration in Recital 35 to the Rome II Regulation must be understood as merely recognising that, where an internal market measure precludes a Member State from applying a regulatory requirement contained in its internal law to a supplier from another Member State, the fact that the Rome II Regulation subjects a tort or restitutionary claim to the law of the first-mentioned State does not override the preclusion arising from the internal market measure.

### Relationship with Existing International Conventions

Article 28(1) provides that the Rome II Regulation is not to prejudice the application of international conventions to which one or more Member States are parties at the time when the Regulation is adopted, and which lay down conflict rules relating to non-contractual obligations. But, by Article 28(2), as between Member States, the Regulation takes precedence over conventions concluded exclusively between two or more of them, insofar as such conventions concern matters governed by the Regulation.[28] By Article 29(1), the Member States had to notify the Commission by 11th July 2008 of the conventions referred to in Article 28(1); and thereafter they must notify the Commission of all denunciations of such conventions. By Article 29(2), the Commission must publish in the Official Journal of the European Union,

---

23    [2000] OJ L178/1.

24    COM(2003) 427 final.

25    See Stone, 'Internet Consumer Contracts and European Private International Law' (2000) 9 Information & Communications Technology Law 5; and Stone, 'The Treatment of Electronic Contracts and Torts in Private International Law under European Community Legislation' (2002) 11 Information & Communications Technology Law 121.

26    See Directive 2000/31, [2000] OJ L178/1, Articles 1(4) and 3(3), the Annex, and Recitals 23 and 55–6.

27    See Directive 2006/123, [2006] OJ L376/36, Articles 3(2) and 17(15) and Recital 90.

28    Article 28 accords with Article 25 of the Rome I Regulation.

within six months of receipt, a list of the notified conventions, and the notified denunciations.[29]

Relevant conventions include the Hague Convention of 4th May 1971 on the Law Applicable to Traffic Accidents, and the Hague Convention of 2nd October 1973 on the Law Applicable to Products Liability. The parties to the Hague Convention 1971 include the following EU Member States: France, Belgium, the Netherlands, Luxembourg, Spain, Austria, Poland, the Czech Republic, Slovakia, Slovenia, Latvia and Lithuania; but not the United Kingdom. Other parties to that Convention are Switzerland, Bosnia-Herzegovina, Croatia, Macedonia, Serbia, Montenegro and Belarus. The parties to the Hague Convention 1973 include the following EU Member States: France, the Netherlands, Luxembourg, Spain, Finland and Slovenia; but not the United Kingdom. Other parties to that Convention are Norway, Croatia, Macedonia, Serbia and Montenegro. Since neither of the Hague Conventions is in force between EU Member States only, the effect of Article 28 is that, in the Member States which are already party to them, and in the absence of denunciation, the Hague Conventions will prevail over the Regulation. But Article 30(1) requires that the report on the application of the Regulation, which must be submitted by the Commission by 20th August 2011, and is to be accompanied if necessary by proposals for its adaptation, must include a study on the effects of Article 28 with respect to the Hague Convention 1971 on Traffic Accidents.

Recital 37 to the Rome II Regulation envisaged that the EC Commission would make a proposal to the European Parliament and the Council concerning the procedures and conditions according to which Member States would be entitled to negotiate and conclude on their own behalf agreements with third countries in individual and exceptional cases, concerning sectoral matters, containing provisions on the law applicable to non-contractual obligations. Accordingly, EC Regulation 662/2009, establishing a procedure for the negotiation and conclusion of agreements between Member States and third countries on particular matters concerning the law applicable to contractual and non-contractual obligations, was adopted by the Parliament and Council on 13th July 2009.[30] Regulation 662/2009 is examined in Chapter 12 above.[31]


## THE MAIN RULES

### Introduction

The main rules on the law applicable to a tort claim are laid down by Article 4 of the Rome II Regulation. These rules apply to most types of tort. Exceptional rules applicable to certain particular torts (product liability; unfair competition; restriction of competition; infringement of intellectual property; environmental damage; and industrial action) are specified by Articles 5–9 of the Regulation.

---

[29]   See also Recital 36, which explains that such publication is designed to make the rules more accessible. Article 29 resembles Article 26 of the Rome I Regulation.
[30]   See [2009] OJ L200/25.
[31]   See pp. 296–7 above.

Article 4 of the Regulation specifies:

1. Unless otherwise provided for in this Regulation, the law applicable to a non-contractual obligation arising out of a tort/delict shall be the law of the country in which the damage occurs irrespective of the country in which the event giving rise to the damage occurred and irrespective of the country or countries in which the indirect consequences of that event occur.

2. However, where the person claimed to be liable and the person sustaining damage both have their habitual residence in the same country at the time when the damage occurs, the law of that country shall apply.

3. Where it is clear from all the circumstances of the case that the tort/delict is manifestly more closely connected with a country other than that indicated in paragraphs 1 or 2, the law of that other country shall apply. A manifestly closer connection with another country might be based in particular on a pre-existing relationship between the parties, such as a contract, that is closely connected with the tort/delict in question.

Despite its triple structure, in substance Article 4 lays down a single general rule, containing two limbs, and a single exception thereto. Thus the combined effect of Article 4(1) and (2) is to establish a general rule whose operation depends on the existence or otherwise of an habitual residence common to the parties. If both parties were habitually resident in the same country, the tort is governed by the law of that country. If no such common habitual residence existed, the tort is governed by the law of the place of injury.[32] Then Article 4(3) provides an exception, described by Recital 18 as an escape clause, in favour of the law of another country which has a manifestly closer connection with the tort.[33] The general rule laid down by Article 4(1) and (2) is definite in content, and probably rather firm in effect. In contrast, the exception specified by Article 4(3) is vague or flexible in content, but probably rather limited in scope.[34]

Article 4 envisages that a single law will govern the various issues which may arise in the context of a tort claim between a given plaintiff and a given defendant.[35] This approach is

---

[32]  Cf. Recital 18, which explains that the general rule in the Regulation should be the lex loci damni provided for in Article 4(1), and that Article 4(2) should be seen as an exception to this general principle, creating a special connection where the parties have their habitual residence in the same country.

[33]  Recital 18 explains that Article 4(3) should be understood as an escape clause from Article 4(1) and (2), where it is clear from all the circumstances of the case that the tort is manifestly more closely connected with another country.

[34]  A rather different approach to the main rules was proposed in the resolution on first reading adopted by the European Parliament on 6th July 2005; see JUSTCIV 132, 13th July 2005. There the main rules consisted of a general rule referring simply to the law of the country in which the damage occurs or is likely to occur, along with an exception in favour of the law of another country with which it is clear from all the circumstances of the case that the tort is manifestly more closely connected. A common habitual residence of the parties was merely a factor included in those mentioned as relevant to the establishment of a manifestly closer connection.

[35]  This contrasts with the approach proposed in the resolution on first reading adopted by the European Parliament on 6th July 2005; see JUSTCIV 132, 13th July 2005. This insisted that, in resolving the question of the applicable law, the court seised should, where necessary, subject each specific issue of the dispute to separate analysis. The Parliamentary approach resembles s 12 of the (United Kingdom) Private International Law (Miscellaneous Provisions) Act 1995, which enables a particular issue to be subjected to the law of the country with which that issue has the most significant connection.

reinforced by Article 15, which subjects a long (but non-definitive) list of broad issues to the law which is applicable under Article 4. Accordingly, the law which is applicable by virtue of Article 4 may conveniently be referred to as the proper law of the tort. On the other hand, Article 4 also envisages that different laws may apply as between different pairs of party, even though the claims arise out of the same incident.

The rules laid down by Article 4 are neutral as between the parties and as regards the content and purposes of the conflicting laws. They seem to require the application of the substantive rules contained in a law whose identity is determined solely by reference to connecting-factors. No account is taken of whether the substantive rules so chosen favour the plaintiff or the defendant; of whether their purpose is deterrence or compensation; or of whether the country whose law is chosen, or any other country, may be regarded as having a substantial interest in the application of its substantive rules (in preference to the different substantive rules of another connected country) in the circumstances of the case. These choice-of-law rules are country-selecting, rather than rule-selecting, in character.

To this content-neutrality a rather minor qualification is made by Article 17, which specifies that, in assessing the conduct of the person claimed to be liable, account must be taken, as a matter of fact and insofar as is appropriate, of the rules of safety and conduct which were in force at the place and time of the event giving rise to the liability.[36] Recital 34 indicates that this refers to all regulations having any relation to safety and conduct, in operation in the country in which the harmful act was committed, such as road safety rules in the case of an accident. As an obvious example of the operation of Article 17, one may envisage a claim between persons habitually resident in England, arising from a road accident in France. Although, under Article 4, liability will be governed by English law, as that of the common habitual residence, in determining whether a driver has acted with reasonable care, as his duty under English law requires, one must take account of the French rule of the road which specifies that normally the correct course is to keep to the right, rather than (as in England) to the left, side of the road.[37]

The reference made by Article 4 is always to the internal law of the relevant country. Renvoi is excluded by Article 24, which declares that the application of the law of any country specified by the Regulation means the application of the rules of law in force in that country other than its rules of private international law.[38]

---

[36]   Article 17 accords with both the traditional English law, and the Hague Convention of 4th May 1971 on Traffic Accidents, and the Hague Convention of 2nd October 1973 on Products Liability. See *The Halley* (1868) LR 2 PC 193; *Kuwait Airways v Iraqi Airways (Nos 4 and 5)* [2002] 2 AC 883; Article 7 of the Hague Convention 1971; and Article 9 of the Hague Convention 1973.

[37]   See also *Ellis v Parto* 918 P2d 540 (Washington, 1996), applying the law of the place of the accident to 'rules governing vehicle turnarounds', despite a common residence elsewhere. See also *Douglas v Hello! Ltd* [2006] QB 125, where, in the context of a claim for breach of confidence or invasion of privacy by way of publication of personal information, which was governed by English law as that of the place of publication, the English Court of Appeal accepted that the law of the place where the events to which the information related took place (New York) could be relevant to whether there was a reasonable expectation that the events would remain private.

[38]   This accords with traditional English law. See s 9(5) of the Private International Law (Miscellaneous Provisions) Act 1995.

### The Law of the Common Habitual Residence

Article 4(2) of the Rome II Regulation ensures that the law of the country in which both parties were habitually resident will normally prevail over the law of the country in which the events constituting the tort occurred. But it will remain possible, under Article 4(3), for the law of the country in which the events constituting the tort occurred, or even that of a third country, to prevail over the law of the common residence, on the basis that it is the country with which the tort has a manifestly closer connection.

Ancillary rules on the habitual residence of companies and other bodies, and of self-employed individuals, are laid down by Article 23.[39] As regards a company or other body, corporate or unincorporated, Article 23(1) specifies that its place of central administration must be treated as its habitual residence; but that where the event giving rise to the damage occurs, or the damage arises, in the course of operation of a branch, agency or other establishment, the location of that establishment must be treated as its habitual residence. Probably, the place of central administration of a company is the place at which its principal managerial organ (in English terms, its board of directors) usually meets, rather than the office from which its main trading activities are conducted.[40] As regards an individual acting in the course of business activity on his own account,[41] Article 23(2) specifies that his principal place of business must be treated as his habitual residence. Unfortunately, the Regulation offers no definition of habitual residence for an individual who is not, or not relevantly, engaged in a business activity on his own account.

The preference given by Article 4 to the common habitual residence over the place of the events constituting the tort reflects a general international trend in recent decades. Thus, as regards the measure of damages to be awarded in respect of road accidents, both at common law and under the Private International Law (Miscellaneous Provisions) Act 1995, the English courts have usually awarded higher damages in accordance with the law of the common residence than would have been available under the law of the place of the accident.[42] In the United States, ever since *Babcock v Jackson*,[43] the plaintiff has usually been given the benefit of the law of the common residence where it favours him in respect of a wide variety of issues.[44] After

---

[39]  Somewhat similar provision in relation to contracts is made by Article 19 of the Rome I Regulation.

[40]  See *The Rewia* [1991] 2 Lloyd's Rep 325 (CA); and *King v Crown Energy* [2003] ILPr 28.

[41]  The Explanatory Memorandum accompanying the EC Commission Proposal of 22nd July 2003 refers to individuals exercising a liberal profession or business activity in a self-employed capacity; see COM(2003) 427 final, at p. 27.

[42]  See *Boys v Chaplin* [1971] AC 356, decided under an interest-based exception to the double actionability rule at common law; *Edmunds v Simmonds* [2001] 1 WLR 1003, decided under the exception to the law of the place of injury in favour of a substantially more significant connection, specified by s 12 of the 1995 Act; and *Harding v Wealands* [2006] UKHL 32, decided on the basis of procedural characterisation. See also *Johnson v Coventry Churchill* [1992] 3 All ER 14, applying the law of the common residence of the employer and the employee so as to avoid the employer's social-security-related immunity existing under the law of the place where the construction accident occurred.

[43]  191 NE2d 279 (1963).

[44]  As regards duties to guest passengers, see *Babcock v Jackson* 191 NE2d 279 (New York, 1963); *Tooker v Lopes* 249 NE2d 394 (New York, 1969); *Clark v Clark* 222 A2d 205 (New Hampshire, 1966); *Wilcox v Wilcox* 133 NW2d 408 (Wisconsin, 1965); and *Wessling v Paris* 417 SW2d 259 (Kentucky, 1967). On a 'slip and fall accident', see *Esser v McIntire* 661 NE2d 1138 (Illinois, 1996).

earlier rulings to the contrary,[45] the current trend in American courts is also to apply that law where it favours the defendant,[46] though there are some recent decisions which give the plaintiff the benefit of the law of the place of the accident.[47] Enactments closely resembling Article 4(2) of the Rome II Regulation have been adopted in Germany,[48] Switzerland[49] and Quebec.[50] Moreover, results similar to those envisaged by Article 4(2) may often be reached under the Hague Convention 1971 on Traffic Accidents, and in Turkey under Article 34(3) of Act 5718 of 27th November 2007 on Private International Law and International Civil Procedure.

---

As regards inter-spousal claims, see *Haumschild v Continental Casualty* 95 NW2d 814 (Wisconsin, 1959); *Thompson v Thompson* 193 A2d 439 (New Hampshire, 1963); and *Brown v Church of the Holy Name of Jesus* 252 A2d 176 (Rhode Island, 1969). As regards the measure of damages, see *Reich v Purcell* 432 P2d 727 (California, 1967). As regards a vehicle owner's liability for the negligence of a hirer-driver, see *Levy v Daniels* 143 A 163 (Connecticut, 1928); *Farber v Smolack* 229 NE2d 36 (New York, 1975); *Sexton v Ryder* 320 NW2d 843 (Michigan, 1982); and *Veasley v CRST International* 553 NW2d 896 (Iowa, 1996). As regards a tavern-keeper's liability for injuries caused by its customers, see *Schmidt v Driscoll Hotel* 82 NW2d 365 (Minnesota, 1957); and *Rong Yao Zhou v Jennifer Mall Restaurant* 534 A2d 1268 (District of Columbia, 1987). As regards contributory negligence, see *Sabell v Pacific Intermountain Express Co* 536 P2d 1160 (Colorado, 1975); *Wallis v Mrs Smith's Pie Co* 550 SW2d 453 (Arkansas, 1977); and *Noble v Moore* [2002] WL 172665 (Connecticut, 2002). As regards exemplary damages, see *Bryant v Silverman* 703 P2d 1190 (Arizona, 1985).

[45] On duties to guest passengers, see *Milkovitch v Saari* 203 NW2d 408 (Minnesota, 1973); *Conklin v Horner* 157 NW2d 579 (Wisconsin, 1968); *Arnett v Thompson* 433 SW2d 109 (Kentucky, 1968); *Gagne v Berry* 290 A2d 624 (New Hampshire, 1972); *Heath v Zellmer* 151 NW2d 664 (Wisconsin, 1967); and *Zelinger v State Sand & Gravel Co* 156 NW2d 466 (Wisconsin, 1968). On intra-familial claims, see *Arnett v Thompson* 433 SW2d 109 (Kentucky, 1968); *Taylor v Bullock* 279 A2d 585 (New Hampshire, 1971); *Gordon v Gordon* 387 A2d 339 (New Hampshire, 1978); and *Zelinger v State Sand & Gravel Co* 156 NW2d 466 (Wisconsin, 1968).

[46] On duties to guest passengers, see dicta in *Neumeier v Kuehner* 286 NE2d 454 (1972); and *Heinze v Heinze* 742 NW2d 465 (Nebraska, 2007). On immunity between co-employees, see *Hunker v Royal Indemnity Co* 204 NW2d 897 (Wisconsin, 1973). On charitable immunity, see *Schultz v Boy Scouts of America* 480 NE2d 679 (New York, 1985); and *Gilbert v Seton Hall University* 332 F3d 105 (New York, 2003). On the measure of damages, see *Collins v Trius* 663 A2d 570 (Maine, 1995); and *Greenwell v Davis* 180 SW3d 287 (Texas, 2005). On the exclusion of tort liability for road accidents in favour of a no-fault insurance scheme providing limited amounts of compensation, see *Myers v Langlois* 721 A2d 129 (Vermont, 1998); and *Lessard v Clarke* 736 A2d 1226 (New Hampshire, 1999). As regards exclusion of tort liability in favour of workmen's compensation, see *Jaiquay v Vasquez* 948 A2d 955 (Connecticut, 2008). As regards a vehicle owner's liability for the negligence of a hirer-driver, see *Oyola v Burgos* 864 A2d 624 (Rhode Island, 2005). As regards product liability and contributory negligence, see *General Motors Corp v Eighth Judicial District* 134 P3d 111 (Nevada, 2006). As regards product liability and time limitation, see *Ganey v Kawasaki Motors* 461 SW3d 872 (Arkansas, 2006). See also Symeonides, (2000) 48 AJCL 143.

[47] As regards a vehicle owner's liability for the negligence of a hirer-driver, see *Fu v Fu* 733 A2d 1133 (New Jersey, 1999). On employer's liability, see *Rigdon v Pittsburgh Tank & Tower Co* 682 So2d 1303 (Louisiana, 1996). As regards a restriction on the maximum amount of damages awardable, and also contributory negligence, see *Erie Insurance Exchange v Heffernan* 925 A2d 636 (Maryland, 2007). On charitable immunity, see *PV v Camp Jaycee* 962 A2d 453 (New Jersey, 2008).

[48] See the EGBGB (as amended in 1999), Article 40(2).

[49] See the Federal Statute on Private International Law 1987, Article 133.

[50] See the Civil Code 1991, Article 3126. See also the Louisiana Civil Code, Article 3544(1), which applies the law of the country in which both parties were domiciled at the time of the injury to issues pertaining to loss distribution and financial protection.

In contrast, France had retained a rigid rule in favour of the law of the place of injury, even where the parties were both habitually resident in the same other country, except where the Hague Conventions on Traffic Accidents or Products Liability applied.[51] Moreover, a rigid rule in favour of the law of the country in which the tort occurred has recently been adopted in both Canada[52] and Australia.[53] In the United States, a rigid rule in favour of the law of the place of injury has been retained by ten of the States.[54]

The merit of a systematic preference for the law of the common residence over that of the place where the tort occurred, as adopted by Article 4(2) of the Rome II Regulation, is open to doubt. Certainly there are some situations in which it seems clear that the law of the common residence should prevail. In particular, in the case of most issues relating to a road accident, it seems desirable to apply the law of the common residence where it requires higher standards of conduct, or provides higher levels of compensation, than the law of the place of the accident. For the law of the common residence has a substantial interest in protecting its resident plaintiff, both in respect of his physical safety and his financial position, and (at least in the usual case where the defendant's residence coincides with the place of registration of his vehicle) its application can hardly defeat the legitimate expectations of its resident defendant and his insurer. Even so, it is suggested that, in order to avoid injustice to the liability insurer, a person involved in a road accident as a driver, a driver's employer or a vehicle-owner should be treated for this purpose as habitually resident in the country where his vehicle is registered.[55] Moreover, the law of the place of the accident lacks any substantial conflicting interest, since its rules on road accidents are not intended to encourage dangerous or risk-taking activity, but to protect the financial position of resident defendants and their insurers.

Thus it seems proper to apply the law of the common residence to a road accident, where its rules are more favourable to the plaintiff than those of the place of injury, in relation to

---

51    See Mayer, *Droit International Privé*, 5th edition (Montchrestien 1994), pp. 443–51.

52    See *Tolofson v Jensen* (1994) 120 DLR4th 289 (Supreme Court of Canada). The rule in favour of the place where the tort occurred is absolutely rigid in inter-provincial cases; see *Bezan v Vander Hooft* [2004] ABCA 44 (Alberta CA). But in international cases there is a very limited exception which occasionally permits application of the law of the common residence. See *Hanlan v Sernesky* (1998) 38 OR(3d) 479 (Ontario CA), affirming (1997) 35 OR(3d) 603; *Wong v Wei* (1999) 87 ACWS(3d) 465 (British Columbia); *Wong v Lee* (2002) 58 OR(3d) 398 (Ontario CA); and *Roy v North American Leisure Group* (2004) 246 DLR(4th) 306 (Ontario CA).

53    See *Pfeiffer v Rogerson* (2000) 203 CLR 503 (High Court of Australia), and *Renault v Zhang* (2002) 187 ALR 1 (High Court of Australia). The rule in favour of the place where the tort occurred is absolutely rigid in inter-provincial cases. But in international cases it may be possible to treat certain questions of assessment of damages as procedural, and it is certainly possible to escape to the law of the common residence by means of renvoi (as in *Neilson v Overseas Projects Corp of Victoria Ltd* [2006] 3 LRC 494 (High Court of Australia)).

54    See Symeonides, in his Annual Survey of American Choice-of-Law Cases, (1996) 44 AJCL 181, (1997) 45 AJCL 447, (1998) 46 AJCL 233, (1999) 47 AJCL 327, (2000) 48 AJCL 143, (2001) 49 AJCL 1, (2002) 50 AJCL 1, (2003) 51 AJCL 1, (2004) 52 AJCL 9, (2005) 53 AJCL 559, (2006) 54 AJCL 697, (2008) 56 AJCL 243, and (2009) 57 AJCL 269.

55    This problem seems most likely to arise in Europe in cases where a tourist hires a car in the country which he is visiting (as happened in *Edmunds v Simmonds* [2001] 1 WLR 1003), or where a person changes his habitual residence but his car remains registered in the country from which he moved (as appears to have happened in *Harding v Wealands* [2006] UKHL 32).

such issues as the duty and standard of care owed by a driver to a gratuitous passenger; the possibility of liability between members of a family; the possible immunity from liability of a charitable body; the admissible heads of damage, and other questions affecting the measure of damages; the period within which proceedings must be commenced; and the existence of vicarious liability (including that of a vehicle-owner for the negligence of a driver to whom he has hired the vehicle; and that of a tavern-keeper for the negligent driving of a customer who has left the tavern). The same approach seems justified in respect of other kinds of accident giving rise to physical injuries, except perhaps where it is apparent that the lower standards of conduct or compensation accepted by the law of the place of the accident are designed to encourage risk-taking activity.

It is submitted, however, that preference for the law of the common residence is not justified in converse situations where, in respect of the same issues arising in relation to a road or similar accident, the law of the common residence accepts *lower* standards of conduct, or provides *lower* levels of compensation, than the law of the place of the accident. Certainly the law of the common residence has an interest in protecting its resident defendant (and his insurer) from possibly excessive financial burdens. But the law of the place of the accident has a substantial conflicting interest in maintaining the deterrent effect of its rules in respect of all conduct within its borders, and also in protecting the financial security of persons who are physically injured within its borders, even if they reside elsewhere. Since each country has a substantial interest in the application of its own substantive rules, it is submitted that the law of the place of the accident should apply, as it would have done between parties not having a common residence.

Displacement of the law of the place of the accident in cases where that country has a substantial interest in applying its rules seems to the present writer to involve an unjustifiable disregard for the territorial sovereignty of that country, and for the normal expectations of most private persons (who tend to envisage the application of law on a territorial basis), without any sufficient countervailing advantage. Where substantial interests of different legal orders conflict, judicial weighing to determine the greater interest cannot be done on a principled basis, and in practice is likely to lead to preference for the law of the forum. The desirable solution to such conflicting interests is therefore to adhere to the law of the place of the accident. Thus, in accident cases involving the issues presently under discussion, the preferable solution is not, as under Article 4(2) of the Regulation, to prefer the law of the common residence regardless of its content, but to apply either the law of the common residence or that of the place of injury, whichever is more favourable to the plaintiff. Unfortunately, it seems clear that the Regulation intends that the law of the common residence should be applied in accident cases even when it favours the defendant, and that the exception provided by Article 4(3) cannot properly be used to substitute a rule for accident cases which gives the plaintiff the benefit of either the law of the common residence or the law of the place of the accident, whichever is more favourable to him.

The operation of Article 4(2) in cases of intentional physical interference with person or property also seems open to criticism. It is submitted that it would have been better to have adhered to the law of the place where the tort occurred, despite a common residence elsewhere, for all issues arising in respect of torts (such as battery; false imprisonment; and trespass to land or chattels) which involve deliberate interference with the plaintiff's person or tangible property. The case is perhaps clearest where the intentional interference involves the purported exercise of police powers, a situation which admittedly is excluded from the scope of the Rome II Regulation by Article 1 as a public rather than a civil matter. Thus if, for example, an arrest takes place in France, respect for French sovereignty, as well as the need for certainty, requires that the grounds which justify arrest, the manner in which an arrest should be effected, the amount of force which may properly be used in effecting an arrest, and the remedies open to a person unlawfully arrested, should be referred to French law; even if, for example, the person arrested is an Englishman and the person who makes the arrest is an English policeman who has been summoned through Interpol or Europol to assist the French police.[56] But even where no public authority is involved, the interest of any country in regulating the deliberate use of force within its borders is so strong that it should only be overridden by a stringent public policy against scandalous or unconscionable rules. Thus, for example, Spanish law should govern all aspects of a tort claim between English football supporters arising from a fight in a bar near the Real Madrid ground before or after a match which the parties were visiting Spain in order to attend. Unfortunately, it seems clear that the Regulation intends that the law of the common residence should be applied even in cases of intentional interference, and that the exception provided by Article 4(3) cannot properly be used to confine Article 4(2) to accident cases.

On the other hand, in one respect, Article 4(2) is too narrowly written, since it does not extend to cases where the parties are habitually resident in different countries, but (so far as relevant) the laws of those countries are identical to each other and different from that of the country where the tort occurred. Where it would be appropriate to apply, in preference to the law of the country where the tort occurred, that of the country in which both parties were habitually resident, it will be equally appropriate to apply the law common to the different countries in each of which one of the parties was habitually resident. For example, if English and Irish laws both admit the award of damages for pain and suffering in personal injury cases, but Maltese law does not, such an award should be possible in favour of an Irish plaintiff against an English defendant in respect of injuries arising from a road accident in Malta.[57] Despite the narrow wording of Article 4(2) in this respect, it seems probable that the exception in favour of a manifestly closer connection, provided for by Article 4(3), will usually be invoked to achieve this result.[58]

It has been noted that Article 4 envisages that different laws may apply as between different pairs of party even though the claims arise out of the same incident. Thus, for example, a plaintiff who has a common residence with the defendant will see his claim governed by the law of the common residence under Article 4(2), while another plaintiff who suffers similar injuries as a result of the same conduct but who is resident in the country where the events

---

[56]   See *District of Columbia v Coleman* 667 A2d 811 (District of Columbia, 1995), applying the law of the place of the incident in favour of a foreign police officer in respect of the permissible degree of force.

[57]   See *Reich v Purcell* 432 P2d 727 (California, 1967); *Pfau v Trent Aluminium Co* 263 A2d 129 (New Jersey, 1970); *Chila v Owens* 348 FSupp 1207 (New York, 1972); and *Gross v McDonald* 354 FSupp 378 (Pennsylvania, 1973).

[58]   The possibility of equivalent laws was recognised in the resolution on first reading adopted by the European Parliament on 6th July 2005; see JUSTCIV 132, 13th July 2005. This referred to 'the fact that the person(s) claimed to be liable and the person(s) sustaining loss or damage have their habitual residence in the same country or that the relevant laws of the country of habitual residence of the person(s) claimed to be liable and of the country of habitual residence of the person(s) sustaining loss or damage are substantially identical'.

occurred will see his claim subjected to the law of the place of injury under Article 4(1). There is no doubt that this can lead to strange results, perhaps amounting to arbitrary discrimination. The facts of an American case, *Tooker v Lopes*,[59] provide a useful illustration. Two gratuitous passengers in the same car were injured in Michigan as a result of the ordinarily, but not grossly, negligent driving by their driver, who was habitually resident in New York, where the car was registered. Under New York law, a driver was liable to his gratuitous passenger for ordinary negligence; but, under Michigan law, a driver was not liable to his gratuitous passenger in the absence of gross negligence. The driver and one of the passengers were habitually resident in New York, but the other passenger was habitually resident in Michigan. Under the Rome II Regulation, as indeed under New York conflict rules,[60] the New York passenger's claim succeeds and the Michigan passenger's claim fails. To the present writer, it is hard to accept this result. Thus it is suggested that the exception under Article 4(3) should be invoked so as to apply the law of the place of the tort to all the claims in multi-party situations where the application of the law of the common residence between some of the parties would produce an unjustifiable discrimination between parties who were otherwise involved in the same way in the same incident.

### The Law of the Place of Direct Injury

Under the general rule laid down by the Rome II Regulation, in the absence of a common habitual residence, the law applicable to a tort is that of the place of direct injury. Article 4(1) makes applicable 'the law of the country in which the damage occurs irrespective of the country in which the event giving rise to the damage occurred and irrespective of the country or countries in which the indirect consequences of that event occur'. Recital 17 adds that in cases of personal injury or damage to property, the country in which the damage occurs is the country where the injury was sustained or the property was damaged respectively. Thus, where the various events constituting the tort have occurred in more than one country, the reference is to the country in which the plaintiff incurred his direct or initial injury; and not to that of the country in which the defendant's wrongful conduct occurred, nor to that of the country in which the plaintiff suffered further loss, consequential on his initial injury.

It is clear that the decisions of the European Court, distinguishing between the direct injury and consequential loss for the purpose of jurisdiction under Article 5(3) of the Brussels I Regulation, will also be relevant to the application of Article 4(1) of the Rome II Regulation. Thus where a bank is sued for wrongful cancellation of credit in connection with a building project, the direct injury arises in the country where the project is suspended and the plaintiff's subsidiary is rendered insolvent, and only consequential loss is incurred at the plaintiff's residence in another country.[61] Similarly, where a person is wrongfully arrested and his tangible property is wrongfully seized, the direct injury arises in the country where the arrest and the seizure take place, and only consequential financial loss is incurred at his residence in another country.[62] Again, where a consignee of goods which have been damaged in the

---

[59]    249 NE2d 394 (New York, 1969).
[60]    See *Tooker v Lopes* 249 NE2d 394 (New York, 1969), and *Neumeier v Kuehner* 286 NE2d 454 (New York, 1972).
[61]    See Case 220/88: *Dumez v Hessische Landesbank* [1990] ECR I-49.
[62]    See Case C-364/93: *Marinari v Lloyd's Bank* [1995] ECR I-2719.

course of a transport operation comprising carriage by sea and then by land sues the maritime carrier, the direct injury arises at the place where the maritime carrier had to deliver the goods, and not at the consignee's residence, where it received the goods at the conclusion of the transport operation and discovered the damage to them.[63] Similarly, in the case of a claim against a financial advisor for a loss sustained as a result of a speculative investment, the direct injury arises in the country where the loss of the plaintiff's assets is incurred, and not in another country where the plaintiff is resident and his assets are concentrated and in which he suffers consequential financial loss.[64] But where direct injury is sustained in several countries, the laws of all these countries will have to be applied on a distributive basis, each law applying to the injury sustained in its territory.[65]

As regards the tort of inducing a breach of contract, it seems that the country of the direct injury under Article 4(1) is the country in which the breach induced occurred and the plaintiff suffered direct financial loss (for example, by failing to receive a benefit contracted for), even if the defendant's act of inducement took place elsewhere.[66] As regards liability for false statements made by the defendant and relied on by the plaintiff, it seems that the country of the direct injury is the country in or from which goods were delivered or money was paid as a result of the plaintiff's reliance on the statement; rather than the country where the statement was issued by the defendant, or the country where the plaintiff received the statement and acted in reliance on it by taking decisions or giving instructions leading to the delivery or payment elsewhere.[67]

The preference under Article 4(1) for the place of direct injury over the place of the defendant's conduct accords with the solution adopted in the United Kingdom by s 11 of the Private International Law (Miscellaneous Provisions) Act 1995 for cases of physical injury to person or property. It also accords with the traditional laws of France and the Netherlands, and with the current laws of Switzerland[68] and Turkey.[69] It further accords with the approach adopted in the United States in the minority of States which still adhere rigidly to the law of the place where the tort occurred.[70] On the other hand, in Germany, Article 40(1) of the Introductory Law to the Civil Code (as amended in 1999) gave the plaintiff an option between

---

[63]   See Case C-51/97: *Réunion Européenne v Spliethoff's Bevrachtingskantoor* [1998] ECR I-6511.

[64]   Case C-168/02: *Kronhofer v Maier* [2004] ECR I-6009.

[65]   See the Explanatory Memorandum, note 16 above, at p. 11. See also Case C-68/93: *Shevill v Presse Alliance* [1995] ECR I-415.

[66]   See *Metall und Rohstoff v Donaldson Lufkin & Jenrette* [1990] QB 391 (CA).

[67]   See *Domicrest v Swiss Bank Corp* [1999] QB 548 (Rix J); *Dunhill v Diffusion Internationale de Maroquinerie de Prestige* [2002] ILPr 13 (Rokison QC); *Raiffeisen Zentralbank v National Bank of Greece* [1999] 1 Lloyd's Rep 408 (Tuckey J); *ABCI v Banque Franco-Tunisienne* [2003] 2 Lloyd's Rep 146 (CA); *Bank of Tokyo-Mitsubishi v Baskan Gida* [2004] ILPr 26 (Lawrence Collins J); *London Helicopters v Heliportugal* [2006] 1 All ER (Comm) 595 (Simon J); and *Crucial Music Corporation v Klondyke Management* [2008] 1 All ER (Comm) 642 (Livesey QC).

[68]   See the Explanatory Memorandum, note 16 above, at p. 11.

[69]   See Article 34(1) and (2) of Act 5718 of 27th November 2007 on Private International Law and International Civil Procedure.

[70]   See *Alabama Great Southern Railroad Co v Carroll* 11 So 803 (Alabama, 1892); and *Laboratory Corp of America v Hood* 911 A2d 841 (Maryland, 2006). Cf. *Fanning v Dianon Systems* [2006] WL 2385210 (Colorado, 2006).

the law of the place of the defendant's conduct and the law of the place of injury. The plaintiff was also given an option in Italy and Poland.[71]

The rationale of Article 4(1) is addressed by Recital 16, which explains that the rule strikes a fair balance between the interests of the person claimed to be liable and the person sustaining the damage, and also reflects the modern approach to civil liability and the development of systems of strict liability.[72] It is submitted that a rule subjecting a tort to the law of the place of the direct injury is indeed preferable to a rule in favour of the law of the place of the defendant's conduct, and is also preferable to a rule making applicable whichever of those two laws is more favourable to the plaintiff, for the following reasons. A rule in favour of the law of the place of the direct injury promotes certainty. The place of injury is easily determined, at least in cases of physical injury. The rule will rarely defeat any legitimate expectation of the defendant; and a plaintiff who is injured in his own country has little ground for complaint if he is denied the benefit of more favourable rules laid down in the country where the defendant resided and acted.

### The Law of the Manifestly Closer Connection

By way of exception to the general rule laid down by Article 4(1)–(2) of the Rome II Regulation in favour of the law of the common residence or the place of injury, Article 4(3) gives preference to a manifestly closer connection. The first sentence of Article 4(3) specifies: 'Where it is clear from all the circumstances of the case that the tort/delict is manifestly more closely connected with a country other than that indicated in paragraphs 1 or 2, the law of that other country shall apply'. Its second sentence adds: 'A manifestly closer connection with another country might be based in particular on a pre-existing relationship between the parties, such as a contract, that is closely connected with the tort/delict in question'. Recital 18 describes Article 4(3) as an escape clause from Article 4(1) and (2), applicable where it is clear from all the circumstances of the case that the tort is manifestly more closely connected with another country.[73]

Little guidance is given by the Regulation as to the scope of the exception, or to the meaning of the concept of a manifestly closer connection, other than by reference to a pre-existing relationship between the parties, as mentioned in the second sentence of the provision. In its

---

[71]    See the Explanatory Memorandum, note 16 above, at p. 11.

[72]    See also the Explanatory Memorandum, note 16 above, at pp. 11–12. This declared that the Commission's objectives in confirming the lex loci delicti rule were to guarantee certainty in the law, and to strike a reasonable balance between the parties. It noted that in most cases the place of direct injury coincides with the plaintiff's country of residence. It added that a rule giving the plaintiff the option of choosing the law most favourable to him would go beyond the plaintiff's legitimate expectations and would reintroduce uncertainty in the law. Moreover, the solution adopted reflects the modern approach to civil liability, which is no longer oriented towards punishing for fault-based conduct. The compensatory function is now dominant, as can be seen from the proliferation of no-fault strict liability schemes.

[73]    See also the Explanatory Memorandum, note 16 above, at p. 12, which explains that Article 4(3) aims to bring a degree of flexibility, enabling the court to adapt the rigid rule to an individual case so as to apply the law which reflects the centre of gravity of the situation. It adds that, since the provision generates a degree of unforeseeability as to the applicable law, it must remain exceptional; and that its truly exceptional character is emphasised by the requirement of a 'manifestly' closer connection.

vagueness as to its central concept, Article 4(3) resembles the traditional English rule laid down by s 12 of the Private International Law (Miscellaneous Provisions) Act 1995, which provides for displacement of the law of the country in which the events constituting the tort occurred, and which is therefore applicable under the general rule laid down by s 11.[74] The displacement under s 12 is in favour of the law of another country with which the tort has a more significant connection, and which is therefore in all the circumstances substantially more appropriate for determining the relevant issue. Section 12 requires a comparison of the significance of the various connecting factors with the two countries, and specifies that the relevant factors include ones relating to the parties, to any of the events which constitute the tort, or to any of the circumstances or consequences of those events. But no guidelines are offered to assist in evaluating the significance of a connection or group of connections, in itself or in comparison with that of another connection or group, or in otherwise evaluating the substantial appropriateness of a solution. This extraordinary vagueness reflects the Law Commissions' earlier Consultation Paper,[75] which had considered and specifically rejected every known principle by which relative significance could be ascribed to various connections. The resulting English case-law has adopted a restrictive approach to s 12, so that its ultimate effect is essentially to make applicable in accident cases the law of the habitual residence of both parties at the time of the accident where that law is more favourable to the plaintiff than that of the country in which the accident occurred.[76]

The essentially meaningless formulas adopted by Article 4(3) of the Rome II Regulation and s 12 of the 1995 Act may be contrasted with the serious attempt at definition or at least guidance adopted in the United States by the American Law Institute's Restatement, Second, Conflict of Laws (1971), §§ 6 and 145.[77] This adopts a rule subjecting the rights and liabilities of the parties with respect to an issue in tort to the internal law of the country which, with respect to that issue, has the most significant relationship to the occurrence and the parties. It specifies that relevant contacts include: (a) the place where the injury occurred; (b) the place where the conduct causing the injury occurred; (c) the domicile, residence, nationality, place of incorporation and place of business of the parties; and (d) the place where the relationship, if any, between the parties is centred. It also attempts to give meaning to the concept of significance, by requiring that the significance of the contacts should be evaluated with respect to

---

[74]   In Turkey, an escape device similar to Article 4(3) of the Rome II Regulation, and to s 12 of the 1995 Act, is provided for by Article 34(3) of Act 5718 of 27th November 2007 on Private International Law and International Civil Procedure.

[75]   Working Paper 87, Consultative Memorandum 62 (1984).

[76]   See *Edmunds v Simmonds* [2001] 1 WLR 1003; and *Roerig v Valiant Trawlers* [2002] 1 All ER 961 (CA). See also *Harding v Wealands* [2006] UKHL 32, using procedural characterisation to achieve a similar result.

[77]   In the United States, the largest group of States now follow either the 'most significant relationship' approach advocated by Restatement Second, or a similar approach involving 'significant contacts'. Symeonides, in his Annual Survey of American Choice-of-Law Cases, (1996) 44 AJCL 181, (1997) 45 AJCL 447, (1998) 46 AJCL 233, (1999) 47 AJCL 327, (2000) 48 AJCL 143, (2001) 49 AJCL 1, (2002) 50 AJCL 1, (2003) 51 AJCL 1, (2004) 52 AJCL 9, (2005) 53 AJCL 559, (2006) 54 AJCL 697, (2008) 56 AJCL 243 and (2009) 57 AJCL 269, lists twenty-seven States (or equivalent) in this category. See also *Huynh v Chase Manhattan Bank* 465 F3d 992 (C9, 2006), applying Restatement Second to time-limitation in actions brought in federal courts under federal-question jurisdiction. A similar approach has been adopted in Ireland; see *Grehan v Medical Inc* [1988] ECC 6, and *McKenna v Best Travel*, 17th December 1996 (Lavan J).

the particular issue, and in the light of the following factors: (a) the needs of the inter-state and international systems; (b) the relevant policies of the forum; (c) the relevant policies of other interested countries, and the relative interests of those countries in the determination of the particular issue; (d) the protection of justified expectations; (e) the basic policies underlying the particular field of law; (f) certainty, predictability and uniformity of result; and (g) ease in the determination and application of the law to be applied.[78]

It is very obscure how far the exception provided by Article 4(3) of the Rome II Regulation can be utilised where there is no pre-existing relationship between the parties, as referred to in the second sentence. The wording suggests that such application is in principle possible, albeit in rare circumstances. Perhaps the clearest case for such application is where the parties reside in different countries whose laws are in relevant respects identical to each other but different from the law of the place of injury. In that situation, the application under Article 4(3) of the law common to the parties' residences will rectify a drafting defect in Article 4(2). It also seems arguable that Article 4(3) may properly be used to make the law of the place of injury prevail over the law of the common residence where there would otherwise be an unacceptable discrimination between plaintiffs who are resident in different countries but are injured in the same incident. But beyond these cases it seems unlikely that Article 4(3) can properly be used to overcome the arguably excessive width of Article 4(2), so as to apply the law of the place of injury, despite a common residence of the parties, whenever it seems clear that the law of the place of injury has a substantial interest in the application of its rules which favour recovery in accident cases, or which regulate the deliberate use of physical force within its borders.

The second sentence of Article 4(3) of the Rome II Regulation specifies that a manifestly closer connection with a country may be based in particular on a pre-existing relationship between the parties, such as a contract, that is closely connected with the tort in question. The Explanatory Memorandum[79] indicates that the pre-existing relationship need not consist of an actual contract. It may take the form of a contractual relationship which is only contemplated, as in the case of the breakdown of negotiations or of annulment of a contract, or it may be a family relationship. But it is considered implicit that where the pre-existing relationship consists of a consumer or employment contract, and the contract contains a choice-of-law clause, Article 4(3) of the Rome II Regulation cannot have the effect, in relation to torts, of depriving the weaker party of the protection of the law which protects him, as regards

---

[78]   Provisions resembling Restatement Second were proposed in the resolution on first reading adopted by the European Parliament on 6th July 2005; see JUSTCIV 132, 13th July 2005. This specified as factors which may be taken into account as manifestly connecting a tort with another country: (a) as far as loss-distribution and legal capacity are concerned, the fact that the defendant(s) and the claimant(s) have their habitual residence in the same country, or that the relevant laws of the country of habitual residence of the defendant(s) and of the country of residence of the claimant(s) are substantially identical; (b) a pre-existing legal or factual relationship between the parties, such as a contract, which is closely connected with the tort in question; (c) the need for certainty, predictability and uniformity of result; (d) protection of legitimate expectations; and (e) the policies underlying the foreign law to be applied and the consequences of applying that law. It also proposed the inclusion of recitals explaining that the need for legal certainty must always be subordinate to the overriding need to do justice in individual cases, and consequently that the courts must be able to exercise discretion; and referring to the reasonable expectations of the parties, and the needs of international trade and transactions.

[79]   Note 16 above, at pp. 12–13.

contracts, under Articles 6 and 8 of the Rome I Regulation. In enabling a tort claim to be subjected to the law which governs a pre-existing contract between the same parties, Article 4(3) accords with the pre-existing English law, which used s 12 of the 1995 Act in a similar way.[80]

## Agreements Choosing the Applicable Law

It has been seen that, under Article 4(3) of the Rome II Regulation, a tort claim may in some cases be governed by the law which applies to a contract between the same parties, concluded before the events constituting the tort occurred, on the basis that the tort claim is manifestly most closely connected with the country whose law governs the contract.

In addition, Article 14 of the Regulation enables parties to make an agreement, choosing the law applicable to a tort claim between them.[81] This does not apply to claims for unfair competition, restriction of competition, or infringement of an intellectual property right.[82] By Article 14(1), the agreement may be entered into after the event giving rise to the damage has occurred. Where all the parties are pursuing a commercial activity, and the agreement is freely negotiated, the agreement may also be entered into before the event giving rise to the damage has occurred.[83] The requirement of commercial activity appears to exclude agreements with a consumer or an employee. The choice must be expressed or demonstrated with reasonable certainty by the circumstances of the case, and is not to prejudice the rights of third parties (such as liability insurers).[84] Article 14(2) adds that where all the elements relevant to the situation at the time when the event giving rise to the damage occurs are located in a country other than the country whose law has been chosen, the choice of the parties is not to prejudice the application of provisions of the law of that country which cannot be derogated from by agreement.[85] Finally Article 14(3) specifies that where all the elements relevant to the situation at the time when the event giving rise to the damage occurs are located in one or more of the EU Member States, the parties' choice of a law other than that of a Member State is not to prejudice the application of provisions of European Union law, where appropriate as implemented in the Member State of the forum, which cannot be derogated from by agreement.[86]

---

[80]    See *Johnson v Coventry Churchill International* [1992] 3 All ER 14; *Glencore v Metro* [2001] 1 Lloyd's Rep 284; *Base Metal Trading Ltd v Shamurin* [2005] 1 All ER (Comm) 17 (CA); and *Trafigura Beheer v Kookmin Bank* [2006] 2 Lloyd's Rep 455 (Aikens J).

[81]    See also Recital 31, which explains that, to respect the principle of party autonomy and to enhance legal certainty, the parties should be allowed to make a choice as to the law applicable to a non-contractual obligation. It adds that this choice should be expressed or demonstrated with reasonable certainty by the circumstances of the case; and that, where establishing the existence of the agreement, the court has to respect the intentions of the parties. It also recognises that protection should be given to weaker parties by imposing certain conditions on the choice.

[82]    See Articles 6(4) and 8(3).

[83]    In contrast, in Turkey, Article 34(5) of Act 5718 of 27th November 2007 on Private International Law and International Civil Procedure enables parties explicitly to choose the law applicable to a tort, but only after the tort has been committed.

[84]    This substantially accords with Article 3(1)-(2) of the Rome I Regulation. See also the Explanatory Memorandum, note 16 above, at p. 22.

[85]    This substantially accords with Article 3(3) of the Rome I Regulation.

[86]    This substantially accords with Article 3(4) of the Rome I Regulation.

Since Article 14 of the Rome II Regulation imposes conditions on the effectiveness of an agreement on the law applicable to a possible future tort, such as that the agreement must have been freely negotiated, it is possible that a choice of law clause contained in a substantive contract and designed to extend to torts connected with the contract could be effective in designating the proper law of the contract under the Rome I Regulation, but ineffective in relation to connected torts under Article 14 of the Rome II Regulation. It is thought that in such a case the chosen law could be applicable to such torts under the provision on pre-existing relationships and closest connection specified by Article 4(3) of the Rome II Regulation.

**Public Policy and Overriding Rules**

Article 26 of the Rome II Regulation makes a classic saving for the stringent public policy of the law of the forum. It specifies that the application of a provision of the law of any country specified by the Regulation may be refused if such application is manifestly incompatible with the public policy ('ordre public') of the forum.[87] Recital 32 adds that, in particular, the application of a provision of the law designated by the Regulation which would have the effect of causing non-compensatory, exemplary or punitive damages of an excessive nature to be awarded may, depending on the circumstances of the case and the legal order of the forum State, be regarded as being contrary to the public policy ('ordre public') of the forum. As the Explanatory Memorandum noted,[88] the mechanism of the public policy exception allows the court to disapply rules of the foreign law designated by a conflict rule, and to replace it by the lex fori, where the application of the foreign law in a given case would be contrary to the public policy of the forum because its content is repugnant to the values of the forum.

In addition, Article 16 of the Rome II Regulation makes provision for overriding mandatory rules contained in the lex fori. It specifies that nothing in the Regulation shall restrict the application of the provisions of the law of the forum in a situation where they are mandatory irrespective of the law otherwise applicable to the tort or restitutionary obligation. This resembles Article 9(2) of the Rome I Regulation, and the saving by s 14(4) of the (UK) Private International Law (Miscellaneous Provisions) Act 1995 for any rule of law which has effect notwithstanding the rules of private international law applicable in the particular circumstances. But the Regulation contains no provision resembling Article 7(1) of the Rome Convention, or Article 9(3) of the Rome I Regulation, in favour of overriding mandatory rules of a country other than the forum. In the context of tort, it is difficult to discern any need for provisions dealing with overriding mandatory rules, even ones contained in the lex fori.

## SOME PARTICULAR TORTS

Particular rules for certain torts are laid down by Articles 5–9 of the Rome II Regulation. The relevant torts are product liability; unfair competition; restriction of competition; infringement of intellectual property; environmental damage; and industrial action. The particular

---

[87]   This accords with Article 21 of the Rome I Regulation.
[88]   Note 16 above, at pp. 24–5 and 28.

rules derogate to a varying extent from the main rules laid down by Article 4 of the Regulation. This approach contrasts with the traditional English law, under which these torts were governed, along with other torts, by the normal rules specified in ss 11 and 12 of the 1995 Act.

## Product Liability[89]

Article 5 of the Rome II Regulation is entitled 'product liability'. It provides:

1. Without prejudice to Article 4(2), the law applicable to a non-contractual obligation arising out of damage caused by a product shall be:

(a) the law of the country in which the person sustaining the damage had his or her habitual residence when the damage occurred, if the product was marketed in that country; or, failing that,
(b) the law of the country in which the product was acquired, if the product was marketed in that country; or, failing that,
(c) the law of the country in which the damage occurred, if the product was marketed in that country.

However, the law applicable shall be the law of the country in which the person claimed to be liable is habitually resident if he or she could not reasonably foresee the marketing of the product, or a product of the same type, in the country the law of which is applicable under (a), (b) or (c).

2. Where it is clear from all the circumstances of the case that the tort/delict is manifestly more closely connected with a country other than that indicated in paragraph 1, the law of that other country shall apply. A manifestly closer connection with another country might be based in particular on a pre-existing relationship between the parties, such as a contract, that is closely connected with the tort/delict in question.

Recital 18 explains that the conflict rule in matters of product liability should meet the objectives of fairly spreading the risks inherent in a modern high-technology society, protecting consumers' health, stimulating innovation, securing undistorted competition and facilitating trade. It declares that the creation of a cascade system of connecting factors, together with a foreseeability clause, is a balanced solution in regard to these objectives.

Article 5 of the Regulation as adopted departs very substantially from the version contained in the initial Proposal presented by the EC Commission on 22nd July 2003.[90] Its

---

[89] On choice of law for product liability in the United States, see Symeonides, 'Choice of Law for Products Liability: The 1990s and Beyond' 78 Tulane Law Review 1247 (2004), who analyses eighty reported decisions of American courts, given between 1990 and 2003, dealing with such problems. See also Stone, 'Product Liability under the Rome II Regulation', in Ahern and Binchy (eds), *The Rome II Regulation on the Law Applicable to Non-Contractual Obligations* (Martinus Nijhoff, 2009), pp. 175–97.

[90] See COM(2003) 427 final. This Proposal specified that, without prejudice to the general provisions on common habitual residence and closest connection, the law applicable to a non-contractual obligation arising out of damage or a risk of damage caused by a defective product should be that of the country in which the person sustaining the damage was habitually resident, unless the person claimed to be liable could show that the product was marketed in that country without his consent, in which case the applicable law would be that of the country in which the person claimed to be liable was habitually resident.

provisions are complex and ambiguous.[91] The ultimate version of Article 5 was substituted, with little explanation, in the EC Council's Common Position 22/2006 of 25th September 2006,[92] for a much simpler provision contained in the EC Commission's initial Proposal of 22nd July 2003 and its amended Proposal of 21st February 2006.[93] Moreover, the resolution of the European Parliament, adopted on first reading on 6th July 2005,[94] had sought to omit any special rule for product liability, and to extend the normal rules applicable to most torts to this matter.

In the circumstances, it seems proper to proceed, but with some caution, in seeking guidance on the scope of Article 5 from the EC Commission's Explanatory Memorandum[95] which accompanied its initial Proposal, and from the Hague Convention of 2nd October 1973 on the Law Applicable to Products Liability. As regards the concept of a product, it seems proper to follow the suggestion in the Explanatory Memorandum[96] that this has the same meaning in Article 5 of the Rome II Regulation as in EC Directive 85/374 (as amended),[97] which has partially harmonised the substantive laws of the Member States in respect of product liability.[98] Thus, as specified by Article 2 of the Directive, 'product' means any movable, even if incorporated into another movable or into an immovable, and includes electricity. Accordingly, the concept extends to a raw material or a component which has been used or

---

[91]    In Turkey, a simpler rule on product liability is laid down by Article 36 of Act 5718 of 27th November 2007 on Private International Law and International Civil Procedure. The plaintiff may choose between the law of the habitual residence or place of business of the defendant, and the law of the country of acquisition. But the law of the place of acquisition is excluded if the defendant proves that the product entered that country without his consent.

[92]    [2006] OJ C289E/68.

[93]    See COM(2006) 83 final. The amended Proposal specified that, without prejudice to the general provisions on common habitual residence and closest connection, the law applicable to a non-contractual obligation arising out of damage caused by a defective product should be that of the country in which the person sustaining the damage was habitually resident at the time when the damage occurred, unless the person claimed to be liable could show that the product was marketed in that country without his consent, in which case the applicable law would be that of the country in which the person claimed to be liable was habitually resident.

[94]    See JUSTCIV 132, 13th July 2005.

[95]    See COM(2003) 427 final, especially at pp. 13–15.

[96]    At p. 13.

[97]    Directive 85/374 on the approximation of the laws, regulations and administrative provisions of the Member States concerning Liability for Defective Products, [1985] OJ L210/29; as amended by Directive 1999/34, [1999] OJ L141/20.

[98]    Even as regards liability, the substantive harmonisation effected by Directive 85/374 is incomplete. For example, Article 13 of the Directive preserves any rights which an injured person may have according to the rules of the law of contractual or non-contractual liability or a special liability system existing at the moment when the Directive was notified. In addition, Article 15 gives each Member State an option to eliminate the state of the art defence provided for by Article 7(e), which enables a producer to escape liability under the Directive by proving that the state of scientific and technical knowledge at the time when he put the product into circulation was not such as to enable the existence of the defect to be discovered. This option to abolish the state of the art defence, and thus make the producer liable for development risks, has been exercised (in some or all cases) by France, Germany, Luxembourg, Spain and Finland; see the EC Commission's Report on the Application of Directive 85/374, 31st January 2001. Moreover, the Directive does not attempt to harmonise the national laws on questions relating to the assessment of damages.

incorporated in a finished product, as well as to the finished product itself,[99] and also extends to an agricultural product (whether primary or processed).[100]

The Explanatory Memorandum indicates that in other respects the scope of Article 5 of the Regulation is wider than that of the Directive. In particular, Article 5 applies whether the claim is based on strict liability or on fault.[101] But, although (unlike the initial Proposal) the Regulation as adopted does not refer to a 'defective' product, the analogy of the Directive indicates that the focus is on safety,[102] and this consideration is supported slightly by the reference in Recital 18 of the Regulation to the protection of consumers' health. Thus Article 5 should probably be construed as limited to claims in respect of physical injury to (or death of) a person, or of physical damage to property other than the product itself; and as not extending to claims for purely economic loss, not arising from physical injury or damage.[103] On the other hand, there is no obvious reason to limit Article 5 to claims made by a purchaser or a consumer of the product, or even by an individual. It seems designed to extend, for example, to a claim against the manufacturer of an unsafe car by a corporate owner of a lorry damaged in a collision with the car.[104]

In contrast with Directive 85/374, Article 5 of the Regulation is silent as to the character of the defendants to whose liability it applies. It seems clear, in view especially of the emphasis placed by its provisions on the marketing of the product, that Article 5 does not apply to claims against a current user or possessor of a product at the time of the incident from which the claim arises. Similarly, it does not extend to claims against the employer of, or anyone else who is vicariously liable for the conduct of, such a person. Thus where a car is involved in a traffic accident, Article 5 does not extend to claims by injured pedestrians against the driver or his employer, even if the car was unsafe owing to a defect which existed when it left the manufacturer. On the other hand, it seems proper to construe Article 5 as extending to claims based on the unsafe condition of a product against any other defendant than the current user or possessor of the product (or his employer or other principal). Accordingly, Article 5 applies to claims against a manufacturer or producer of a finished product, or of a raw material used or

---

[99] See also the Explanatory Memorandum, note 95 above, at p. 15; Directive 85/374, Article 3(1); and the Hague Convention 1973, Articles 2(a) and 3(1).

[100] See Directive 1999/34, Article 1 (amending Directive 85/374, Article 2). See also the Hague Convention 1973, Articles 2(a) and 3(2).

[101] See the Explanatory Memorandum, note 95 above, at p. 13.

[102] Article 6 of Directive 85/374 specifies that a product is defective when it does not provide the safety which a person is entitled to expect, taking all circumstances into account, including: (a) the presentation of the product; (b) the use to which it could reasonably be expected that the product would be put; (c) the time when the product was put into circulation.

[103] Somewhat similarly, Article 9 of Directive 85/374 limits the damage for which the Directive imposes liability to (a) damage caused by death or by personal injuries; (b) damage to, or destruction of, any item of property other than the defective product itself, with a lower threshold of 500, provided that the item of property: (i) is of a type ordinarily intended for private use or consumption, and (ii) was used by the injured person mainly for his own private use or consumption. It adds that this is without prejudice to national provisions relating to non-material damage. In contrast, Article 2(b) of the Hague Convention 1973 defines 'damage' as injury to the person or damage to property as well as economic loss; but excluding damage to the product itself and economic loss consequential thereon, unless associated with other damage.

[104] This solution contrasts with Article 9 of Directive 85/374, but accords with the Hague Convention 1973. See note 103 above.

a component incorporated in a product.[105] It extends also to claims against an importer[106] or a supplier of a product,[107] or against other persons (such as designers, repairers and warehousemen) involved in the commercial chain of preparation or distribution of a product.[108] It further extends to claims against agents or employees of persons to whose liabilities it applies.[109]

In any event, it is clear from the inclusion of Article 5 in Chapter II of the Regulation that the liability must be in tort. On the other hand, even where there is a contract between the parties for the supply of the product, Article 5 applies to a tort claim between them.[110] But in this situation the exception specified by Article 5(2) will usually mean that the tort claim will be governed by the law which governs the contract, or (where relevant) by the law which provides mandatory protection to the plaintiff as consumer, under the Rome I Regulation.

Article 5(1) lays down a cascade of five choice-of-law rules, which are applied in order. If the first rule fails to supply an applicable law, one moves to the second, and so on. All five rules are subject to the exception made by Article 5(2) in favour of the law of a manifestly more closely connected country.

The five rules and the exception may be restated as follows:

*Rule 1* If both the victim and the defendant were habitually resident in the same country at the time when the injury occurred, the applicable law is that of the common habitual residence.[111]

*Rule 2* Otherwise the applicable law is that of the country in which the victim was habitually resident when the injury occurred, if the product was marketed in that country, and unless the defendant could not reasonably have foreseen the marketing of the product, or a product of the same type, in that country.[112]

*Rule 3* Otherwise the applicable law is that of the country in which the product was acquired, if the product was marketed in that country, and unless the defendant could not reasonably have foreseen the marketing of the product, or a product of the same type, in that country.[113]

---

[105] See the Explanatory Memorandum, note 95 above, at p. 15; Directive 85/374, Article 3(1); and the Hague Convention 1973, Article 3(1) and (2).

[106] See the Explanatory Memorandum, note 95 above, at p. 15; Directive 85/374, Article 3(2); and the Hague Convention 1973, Article 3(3) and (4).

[107] See the Explanatory Memorandum, note 95 above, at p. 15; Directive 85/374, Article 3(3); and the Hague Convention 1973, Article 3(3).

[108] See the Hague Convention 1973, Article 3(4).

[109] See the Hague Convention 1973, Article 3, final clause.

[110] This contrasts with the Hague Convention 1973, whose application to a claim is excluded by Article 1(2) where the property in, or the right to use, the product was transferred to the claimant by the defendant.

[111] See the opening phrase of Article 5(1).

[112] See Article 5(1)(a), and the last clause of Article 5(1).

[113] See Article 5(1)(b), and the last clause of Article 5(1).

*Rule 4*   Otherwise the applicable law is that of the country in which the injury occurred, if the product was marketed in that country, and unless the defendant could not reasonably have foreseen the marketing of the product, or a product of the same type, in that country.[114]

*Rule 5*   Otherwise the applicable law is that of the country in which the defendant was habitually resident.[115]

*Rule 6*   But, by way of exception to the foregoing rules, where it is clear from all the circumstances of the case that the tort is manifestly more closely connected with a country other than the country whose law would be applicable under those rules, the law of that other country applies.[116]

It seems proper to refer to 'the victim', rather than 'the plaintiff', as a synonym for 'the person sustaining the damage', since the analogy of Article 4(1) indicates that the relevant person, on the claimant's side, is the person who suffers the immediate injury, rather than an associated person who claims for a consequential loss. Thus in the case of a fatal accident, the relevant person is the deceased, rather than the family members who claim for their grief or loss of financial support. On the defendant's side, the relevant person is the one whose liability is in question.

In situations where numerous parties are involved in the same incident, Article 5 on product liability (like Article 4 on most types of tort) requires the applicable law to be determined separately for each pair of parties. Thus if a car crashes into a bus queue because of the failure of a tyre as a result of a defect which arose in the course of manufacture, a claim by an injured pedestrian against the car-manufacturer may be subject to a different law from the same pedestrian's claim against the tyre-manufacturer; and a claim by one pedestrian against one of the manufacturers may be subject to a different law from a claim by another pedestrian against the same manufacturer. It would not be surprising if on occasion such severance gives rise to unsatisfactory results.

The definitions of habitual residence provided by Article 23[117] extend to product liability. As regards a company, Article 23(1) specifies that its place of central administration must be treated as its habitual residence; but that where the event giving rise to the damage occurs, or the damage arises, in the course of operation of a branch, agency or other establishment, the location of that establishment must be treated as its habitual residence. In the context of product liability, particular difficulty arises in situations where several establishments of a defendant manufacturer have been involved in the manufacture and marketing of the product. In view of the emphasis in Article 5 on the marketing of the product, it seems proper to focus on the defendant's establishment by which the product was sold to an independent purchaser. But it is also arguable that one must look to the place of central administration whenever more than one of the defendant's establishments has been involved in the manufacture or marketing of the product.

---

[114]   See Article 5(1)(c), and the last clause of Article 5(1).
[115]   See the last clause of Article 5(1).
[116]   See Article 5(2).
[117]   See p. 379 above.

Difficulties may also arise in relation to the concept of marketing. The place of marketing of the item of product complained of, and the place of foreseeable marketing of that product or products of the same type, are relevant under Rules 2, 3 and 4. The application of the law of the victim's residence, the place of acquisition, or the place of injury is made subject to conditions that the actual item of product complained of was marketed in that country, and that the defendant could reasonably have foreseen the marketing either of that item of product, or of a product of the same type, in that country. In view of the European Union rules on the free movement of goods, and the increasing globalisation of trade under the WTO Agreements, it seems unlikely that the foreseeability proviso will often have significance. But the requirement of actual marketing of the particular item of product in the country of the victim's residence, the place of acquisition, or the place of injury is designed to offer real protection to a manufacturer against the application of an unexpected law, and in any event is likely not infrequently to have real effect.

It seems reasonably clear that marketing refers to the supply of a product by a supplier who is acting for commercial purposes, and that the supply may be by way of sale, hire or similar contract, or probably by way of a gift (for example, of a sample) made for promotional purposes. It also seems clear that the marketing need not be effected by the defendant itself; any actual and foreseeable supply through normal commercial channels will do, however many resales have intervened between the sale by the defendant and the ultimate supply in question. It also seems clear that the relevant supply transaction must have been completed by delivery, and that the reference is normally to the final supply to the end-user (the final acquirer, who acquires for use, rather than resale).[118] But it is far from clear whether the marketing is to be regarded as occurring at the place where the goods were delivered to the end-user, or at the establishment of the supplier which contracted with the end-user.

Further difficulties may arise in relation to the concept of acquisition, used in Article 5(1)(b) (restated as Rule 3 above). It is suggested that acquisition has the same meaning as marketing, except that acquisition is confined to a marketing which has a real connection with the victim. Thus Article 5(1)(b) should apply only where the marketing is to, and the acquisition is by, an end-user who is either the victim himself, or a person associated with the victim (such as a member of the victim's family; or his employer; or in the case of a corporate victim, another company belonging to the same group). But not where the victim is unconnected with the acquirer, as where a pedestrian is injured in a road accident caused by brake-failure in a defective car. This approach would ensure that Article 5(1)(b), like Article 5(1)(a) and (c), which refer to the victim's residence or the place of injury, always points to a country which has a substantial connection with the victim.

Despite the declaration of objectives contained in Recital 18, it is clear that the rules for product liability specified by Article 5, like the rules for most other types of tort specified by Article 4, are content-neutral. They select the country whose law is applicable, regardless of the content of its substantive rules. While they seem to give primary emphasis to connections

---

[118]   Obviously cases could arise where the injurious incident occurs before the product has been supplied to an end-user; for example, where an explosive substance explodes while in a warehouse belonging to a trader who has purchased and intends to resell. In such a case, the last supply transaction completed before the incident would have to be treated as the relevant marketing. If the product has not been supplied at all at the time when it causes injury, any tort claim would seem to fall outside the scope of Article 5.

with the victim rather than the defendant, there is no reason to suppose that the law selected will usually contain substantive rules which are more favourable to the victim than those of some other connected law. For example, in many cases Rule 2 will make applicable the law of the victim's residence, but that law will often contain substantive rules which are more favourable to the defendant than those of the defendant's residence. Conversely, in the less frequent cases where Rule 5 applies, the applicable law of the defendant's residence may well contain rules more favourable to the victim than the law of the victim's residence. Moreover, the exception under Rule 6 seems designed to focus on connections with countries, and not on the contents of their laws.

The focus on a law connected with the victim (by residence, acquisition, or injury) may, for example, subject a victim from a non-member country to a law which requires proof of negligence, imposes a short period of limitation, or makes the victim's slight contributory fault a total defence to the claim. Rules 2–4 may give the benefit of such rules of an external law to a European producer. The result may be to undermine confidence outside Europe in the quality of European products, and thereby prejudice their competitive position in external markets. Conversely, the same Rules may lead to the application against a European producer of external rules which enable the award of punitive damages, or of supposedly compensatory damages at a level which seems (by European standards) grossly disproportionate to the real injury, unless the forum is prepared to invoke its public policy under Recital 32 and Article 26.

Under Rule 1, if both the victim and the defendant were habitually resident in the same country at the time when the injury occurred, the applicable law is that of the common habitual residence. Thus a common residence of the parties prevails over the place of acquisition and injury, whether the result is to favour the victim or the defendant. In the few American cases where a common residence existed, similar results have been reached.[119] Rule 1 also accords with the rule for torts other than product liability, laid down by Article 4(2) of the Regulation, and with the Hague Convention 1973.[120]

Application of the law of the common residence in favour of the victim seems uncontroversial. It gives effect to the interest of the victim's residence in protecting his physical and financial security, and that of the defendant's residence in promoting the safety and thus the reputation of products marketed by its businesses. On the other hand, this solution seems much less compelling where it leads to the application of a rule which is more favourable to the defendant than that of the place of acquisition or injury. It is submitted that a better solution would give the victim the benefit of a more favourable rule of the country of acquisition, if the product was acquired by him or a person associated with him and the product was actually and foreseeably marketed in the country of acquisition. Similarly, where the product was not acquired by the victim or a person associated with him, it seems desirable to give the victim the benefit of a more favourable rule of the country of injury, if the product was actually and foreseeably marketed there.

---

[119]   See *Cosme v Whitin Machine Works* 632 NE2d 832 (Massachusetts, 1994), and *Lou ex rel Chen v Otis Elevator Co* [2004] WL 504697 (Massachusetts, 2004), applying the law of the common residence in favour of the victim. See also *Beals v Sicpa Securink Corp* [1994] WL 236018 (District of Columbia, 1994), applying the law of the common residence in favour of the defendant; and *General Motors Corp v Eighth Judicial District* 134 P3d 111 (Nevada, 2006), applying the law of the common residence which on some issues favoured the plaintiff and on others the defendant.

[120]   See Article 5(a) of the Hague Convention.

In the absence of a common residence of the parties, Rules 2–4 refer to the law of a country in which the product was actually and foreseeably marketed. The actual marketing must be that of the item of product involved, but the foreseeable marketing may be either of that item or of a product of the same type. Subject to these conditions as to marketing, reference is made, in order of priority, to the victim's habitual residence when the injury occurred; then to the place of acquisition of the product; and finally to the place of injury. It is clear that these rules are designed to find a law which has a substantial connection with both of the parties. The conditions as to marketing seek to ensure a sufficient connection with the defendant, while the references to the victim's residence, the place of acquisition, and the place of injury seek to establish a substantial connection with the victim. So long as one accepts that the rule referring to the place of acquisition is confined to cases where the product was acquired by the victim or a person associated with the victim, these rules appear to make reasonable sense.

To a large extent, Rules 2–4 accord with results reached in many of the American cases. Thus in the numerous cases where the victim's residence and the places of acquisition and injury were in the same country, but the defendant's residence was elsewhere, the victim was in almost all cases given the benefit of the more favourable law of his residence,[121] and that law was also applied in most of the cases where it favoured the defendant.[122]

There is, however, a minority of American decisions which give the victim the benefit of the law of the defendant's residence.[123] These cases typically involve a forum giving the

---

[121] See *Custom Products v Fluor Daniel Canada* 262 FSupp2d 767 (Kentucky, 2003); *Kramer v Showa Denko KK* 929 FSupp 733 (New York, 1996); *Eimers v Honda Motor Co* 785 FSupp 1204 (Pennsylvania, 1992); *Hoover v Recreation Equipment Corp* 792 FSupp 1484 (Ohio, 1991); *Savage Arms v Western Auto Supply Co* 18 P3d 49 (Alaska, 2001); *Tune v Philip Morris* 766 So2d 350 (Florida, 2000); *Huddy v Fruehauf Corp* 953 F2d 955 (Texas, 1992); and *Kukoly v World Factory* [2007] WL 1816476 (Pennsylvania, 22nd June 2007). Exceptionally, there are a few decisions on punitive damages which apply the law of the defendant's residence so as to prevent the award of such damages; see *Kelly v Ford Motor Co* 933 FSupp 465 (Pennsylvania, 1996); and *Aguirre Cruz v Ford Motor Co* 435 FSupp 2d 701 (Tennessee, 2006).

[122] See *Kemp v Pfizer* 947 FSupp 1139 (Michigan,1996); *Dorman v Emerson Electric Co* 23 F3d 1354 (Missouri, 1994); *Hall v General Motors* 582 NW2d 866 (Michigan, 1998); *Rutherford v Goodyear Tire & Rubber Co* 943 FSupp 789 (Kentucky, 1996), affirmed 142 F3d 436 (1998); *Burleson v Liggett Group* 111 FSupp 2d 825 (Texas, 2000); *Clark v Favalora* 722 So2d 82 (Louisiana, 1998); *Pittman v Kaiser Aluminum* 559 So2d 879 (Louisiana, 1990); *Jefferson Parish Hospital v WR Grace & Co* [1992] WL 167263 (Louisiana, 1992); *Walls v General Motors* 906 F2d 143 (Mississippi, 1990); *Hughes v Wal-Mart Stores* 250 F3d 618 (Arkansas, 2001); *Farrell v Ford Motor Co* 501 NW2d 567 (Michigan, 1993); *Vestal v Shiley Inc* [1997] WL 910373 (CD California, 1997); *Nesladek v Ford Motor Co* 46 F3d 734 (Minnesota, 1995); *Rice v Dow Chemical* 875 P2d 1213 (Washington, 1994); *Bain v Honeywell International* 257 FSupp2d 872 (Texas, 2002); *Re Eli Lilly & Co Prozac Products Liability Litigation* 789 FSupp 1448 (Indiana, 1992); *Harlan Feeders v Grand Laboratories* 881 FSupp 1400 (Iowa, 1995); *Walters v Maren Engineering Corp* 617 NE2d 170 (Illinois, 1993); *Orleans Parish School Board v US Gypsum Co* [1993] WL 205091 (Louisiana, 1993), affirmed 9 F3d 103 (1993); *Heindel v Pfizer* [2004] WL 1398024 (New Jersey, 2004); *Jones v Cooper Tire & Rubber Co* [2004] WL 503588 (Pennsylvania, 2004); *White v Crown Equipment* 827 NE2d 859 (Ohio, 2005); *Henderson v Merck* [2005] WL 2600220 (Pennsylvania, 2005); *Alli v Eli Lilly* 854 NE2d 372 (Indiana, 2006); *Rowe v Hoffman-La Roche* 917 A2d 767 (New Jersey, 2007), reversing 892 A2d 694 (2006); and *Townsend v Sears Roebuck* 879 NE2d 893 (Illinois, 2007), reversing 858 NE2d 552 (2006).

[123] See *Gantes v Kason Corp* 679 A2d 106 (New Jersey, 1996); *Mitchell v Lone Star Ammunition* 913 F2d 242 (Texas, 1990); *McLennan v American Eurocopter Corp* 245 F3d 403 (Texas, 2001); *DeGrasse v Sensenich Corp* [1989] WL 23775 (Pennsylvania, 1989); *Lacey v Cessna Aircraft Co* 932

benefit of its own rule to a foreign victim claiming against a local manufacturer. They can be explained on the basis of the interest of the defendant's residence in securing high standards of safety for products originating in its territory, and thus supporting their reputation elsewhere. It is submitted that such an approach is on balance the preferable solution. But it also seems at any rate defensible to choose, as the Rome II Regulation has chosen, to deny the victim the benefit of a favourable law where he has little connection with the country in question. Moreover, to grant to a product liability claimant in all circumstances the benefit of the more favourable law of the defendant's country might be viewed as inconsistent with the refusal of the Regulation to offer a similar advantage to claimants in the case of other torts.

Where the product was acquired by the victim (or a person associated with the victim) in one country, but the victim was resident and suffered the injury in another country, the Regulation prefers the law of the country of acquisition, since in such cases the product has not been marketed in the country of residence and injury. In contrast, the Hague Convention 1973 prefers the law of the victim's residence and the place of injury to that of the place of acquisition, unless the defendant could not reasonably have foreseen that its products of the same type would be made available in the country of the victim's residence and the injury through commercial channels.[124] Moreover, the American cases (like the Hague Convention 1973) usually apply the law of the victim's residence and the place of injury where it is more favourable to the victim.[125] In converse cases, where the law of the country of acquisition is more favourable to the victim, the American cases are closely divided; some decisions apply the law of the victim's residence and the place of injury in favour of the defendant,[126] while others give the victim the benefit of the law of the place of acquisition.[127]

It is submitted that the Regulation's preference for the law of the country of acquisition, rather than that of the victim's residence and the injury, makes good sense. If the victim chooses to acquire the product in a country other than his residence, albeit with a view to use in the latter country, the country of acquisition has a strong connection with both parties, and the application of its law, whichever party it favours, seems justifiable. In such cases, the country of acquisition has an interest in regulating the safety of products locally marketed, while the country of the victim's residence and the injury has little connection with the defendant.

---

F2d 170 (Pennsylvania, 1991); *Mahne v Ford Motor Co* 900 F2d 83 (Michigan, 1990); *Zenaida-Garcia v Recovery Systems Technology* 115 P3d 1017 (Washington, 2005); and *Jones v Winnebago Industries* 460 FSupp2d 953 (Iowa, 2006).

[124] See Articles 4(a) and 7 of the Convention.

[125] See *Smith v DaimlerChrysler Corp* [2002] WL 31814534 (Delaware, 2002); *R-Square Investments v Teledyne Industries* [1997] WL 436245 (Louisiana, 1997); and *Allstate Insurance v Wal-Mart* [2000] WL 388844 (Louisiana, 2000). Cf. *Brewer v Dodson Aviation* 447 FSupp2d 1166 (Washington, 2006).

[126] See *Denman v Snapper Division* 131 F3d 546 (Mississippi, 1998); *Egan v Kaiser Aluminum* 677 So2d 1027 (Louisiana, 1996); *Land v Yamaha* 272 F3d 514 (Indiana, 2001); *McKinnon v Morgan* 750 A2d 1026 (Vermont, 2000); and *Normann v Johns-Manville* 593 A2d 890 (Pennsylvania, 1991).

[127] See *Magnant v Medtronic* 818 FSupp 204 (Michigan, 1993); *Sanchez ex rel Estate of Galvan v Brownsville Sports Center* 51 SW3d 643 (Texas, 2001); *Long v Sears Roebuck* 877 FSupp 8 (District of Columbia, 1995); *Torrington Co v Stutzman* 46 SW3d 829 (Texas, 2000); *Mitchell v Lone Star Ammunition* 913 F2d 242 (Texas, 1990); and *Rosenthal v Ford Motor Co* 462 FSupp 2d 296 (Connecticut, 2006).

Rule 5 provides a default rule in favour of the law of the defendant's residence.[128] This makes sense, on the ground that where no country has a sufficient connection with both parties, one should ensure that the choice of law is not unfair to the defendant. Preference for defendants over plaintiffs in doubtful situations reflects a primordial legal value, and is exemplified by the normal rule which places the burden on the plaintiff of proving facts justifying his claim. Moreover, as the American case-law shows, the situation very frequently arises in which it is the law of the defendant's residence which, of all the connected laws, contains the rules most favourable to the victim.

Rule 6 overrides all of the other rules by providing an exception in favour of the law of a country which is manifestly more closely connected with the tort. One situation explicitly envisaged by Article 5(2) is where there is a pre-existing relationship between the parties, such as a contract, which is closely connected with the tort. Thus where there is a tort claim by way of product liability between parties to a contract for the supply of the product in question, Rule 6 will usually subject the tort claim to the law which governs or controls the contract of supply. In the case of a consumer contract within Article 6 of the Rome I Regulation, this will usually be the law of the habitual residence of the consumer.

Beyond cases involving a connected contract, one may expect that Rule 6 will be used to rectify the irresponsible failure of the Regulation to specify that where two countries have relevantly identical laws, they must be treated as a single country for choice-of-law purposes. Another useful potential effect of Rule 6 could be the avoidance of arbitrary discrimination, for example between victims who were involved in the same way in the same incident but had different residences. Beyond the said cases, it seems unlikely that Rule 6 will have much application. Clearly it is not intended to have a scope wide enough to undermine frequently the carefully devised structure established by Rules 1–5.

Before leaving Article 5, it may be questioned whether the complexities of the text adopted are really necessary, even on the assumption that all questions of policy have been resolved in the best possible way, and all ambiguities will be resolved by interpretation in the best possible sense. It is submitted that the substance of Article 5 could have been achieved by a much simpler provision. The existing Article 5 would have been deleted, and product liability claims would have been subjected to the main rules laid down by Article 4 for most other torts, with just one additional provision specific to product claims. The additional provision would have specified that, in applying Article 4(1) to a product liability claim brought by the acquirer of the product, or by a person associated with the acquirer of the product, reference should be made to the law of the place of acquisition, rather than the place of injury. This additional provision would not have affected claims by bystanders (such as pedestrians injured by an unsafe vehicle), and in any event would have operated subject to Article 4(2), in favour of a common residence, and Article 4(3), in favour of a manifestly closer connection.

## Unfair Competition

Article 6(1) and (2) of the Rome II Regulation deals with torts 'arising out of an act of unfair

---

    128   See also Article 7 of the Hague Convention 1973.

competition'.[129] According to the Explanatory Memorandum,[130] this covers rules prohibiting acts calculated to influence demand (such as misleading advertising or forced sales), acts which impede competing supplies (such as disruption of deliveries by competitors, enticing away a competitor's staff, or boycotts), and acts which exploit a competitor's value (such as passing off). But Article 6 does not apply to claims for infringement of an intellectual property right, since this matter is definitively regulated by Article 8. By Article 6(4), the law applicable under Article 6 may not be derogated from by an agreement under Article 14.

By Article 6(1), the law applicable to a tort arising out of an act of unfair competition is that of the country where competitive relations or the collective interests of consumers are, or are likely to be, affected. Recital 21 explains that the special rule in Article 6(1) is not an exception to the general rule in Article 4(1), but rather a clarification of it in the light of the objectives of protecting competitors, consumers and the general public, and ensuring that the market economy functions properly. In substance, Article 6(1) replaces the test of direct injury, applicable under Article 4(1) to torts in general, by a test of direct effect on the market, regarded as better suited to torts involving unfair competition. The reference is effectively to the law of the location of the market which is directly affected, and this law will also govern liability for consequential losses sustained elsewhere. But, as the Explanatory Memorandum recognises,[131] there may be direct effects in more than one market, resulting in the distributive application of the laws involved.

Where an act of unfair competition affects exclusively the interests of a specific competitor, Article 6(2) removes the claim from the special rule laid down by Article 6(1), and subjects it to the main rules laid down by Article 4 (referring to the place of injury, common residence, and manifestly closer connection). According to the Explanatory Memorandum,[132] Article 6(2) applies to cases of enticing away a competitor's staff, corruption, industrial espionage, disclosure of business secrets, or inducing a breach of contract. In such cases, the bilateral nature of the situation is regarded as justifying the application of the normal rules which apply to most torts.

**Restrictions of Competition**

Article 6(3) of the Rome II Regulation deals with torts arising out of a restriction of competition.[133] Recital 22 explains that this covers infringements of both national and EU competition law. Recital 23 adds that it covers prohibitions on agreements between undertakings, decisions by associations of undertakings and concerted practices which have as their object or effect the prevention, restriction or distortion of competition within a Member State or within the internal market, as well as prohibitions on the abuse of a dominant position within

---

[129] In Turkey, a provision on unfair competition, which has some similarity to Article 6 of the Rome II Regulation, is adopted by Article 37 of Act 5718 of 27th November 2007 on Private International Law and International Civil Procedure.

[130] Note 95 above, at p. 15.

[131] Note 95 above, at p. 16.

[132] Note 95 above, at p. 16.

[133] In Turkey, a provision on restrictions of competition, which has some similarity to Article 6 of the Rome II Regulation, is adopted by Article 38 of Act 5718 of 27th November 2007 on Private International Law and International Civil Procedure.

a Member State or within the internal market, where such agreements, decisions, concerted practices or abuses are prohibited by Articles 101 and 102 of the Treaty on the Functioning of the European Union or by the law of a Member State. No doubt it extends also to similar prohibitions under the laws of external countries, such as American anti-trust legislation.

Article 6(3)(a) lays down the basic rule that the law applicable to a tort arising out of a restriction of competition is that of the country where the market is, or is likely to be, affected. This obviously refers to the location of the market which is directly affected.

Article 6(3)(b) applies where the market is, or is likely to be, affected in more than one country. In such a case, a person seeking compensation for damage who sues in the court of the defendant's domicile may instead choose to base his claim on the law of the forum, provided that the market in that Member State is amongst those directly and substantially affected by the restriction of competition from which the tort claim arises. But where the claimant sues, in accordance with the applicable rules on jurisdiction, more than one defendant in that court, he can only choose to base his claim on the law of the forum if the restriction of competition on which the claim against each of the defendants relies directly and substantially affects (among others) the market of the forum country. Where several markets are directly affected but Article 6(3)(c) does not apply, there will have to be distributive application of the laws of the country of each market directly affected to the loss directly sustained there and any consequential loss sustained elsewhere.

In cases governed by Article 6(3), there is no saving for the law of a common residence, or the law of a manifestly more closely connected country. By Article 6(4), the law applicable under Article 6 may not be derogated from by an agreement under Article 14.

## Intellectual Property

Article 8 deals with infringements of intellectual property rights. As Recital 26 indicates, this refers to such matters as copyright (author's rights, neighbouring rights, and sui generis rights in databases) and industrial property rights (such as patents, registered trade marks, and design rights). Article 8 does not, however, extend beyond specific intellectual property rights so as to cover torts such as passing off.

Article 8(1) specifies that the law applicable to a non-contractual obligation arising from an infringement of a intellectual property right is that of the country for which protection is claimed. As Recital 26 and the Explanatory Memorandum[134] indicate, this preserves the universally acknowledged principle in favour of the lex loci protectionis, and respects the independent and territorial character of an intellectual property right granted or recognised in a given country. No exception is admitted in favour of the law of a common residence or a manifestly closer connection.

The same principle is applied by Article 8(2) in the case of infringements of a unitary European Union intellectual property right. Such Union-wide rights now exist for plant varieties,[135] registered trade marks,[136] and designs,[137] and have been (so far unsuccessfully)

---

[134]   At p. 20.
[135]   See EC Regulation 2100/94, [1994] OJ L227/1.
[136]   See EC Regulation 207/2009, [2009] OJ L78/1; replacing Regulation 40/94, [1994] OJ L11/1.
[137]   See EC Regulation 6/2002, [2002] OJ L3/1.

proposed for patents.[138] The relevant Community legislation applies; and for any question not governed by such legislation, the applicable law is that of the country in which the act of infringement was committed.

By Article 8(3), the law applicable under Article 8 may not be derogated from by an agreement under Article 14. By Article 13, Article 8 extends to restitutionary obligations arising from an infringement of an intellectual property right, so as to override Articles 10–12.

## Environmental Damage

Article 7 of the Rome II Regulation lays down a special rule for torts 'arising out of environmental damage or damage sustained by persons or property as a result of such damage'. Recital 24 provides a definition of 'environmental damage' as referring to adverse change in a natural resource, such as water, land or air, impairment of a function performed by such a resource for the benefit of another natural resource or the public, or impairment of the variability among living organisms. The concept appears to have a wide scope, especially as there is no explicit limitation by reference to the extent or duration of the change or impairment envisaged, nor to the nature of the activities giving rise to the change or impairment.

By Article 7, the law applicable to a tort arising out of environmental damage or damage sustained by persons or property as a result of such damage is the law determined pursuant to Article 4(1), unless the person seeking compensation for damage chooses to base his claim on the law of the country in which the event giving rise to the damage occurred. This amounts in substance to a rule of alternative reference, in favour of the law of the place of direct injury, or the law of the place of the defendant's conduct, whichever is more favourable to the plaintiff.[139] But the plaintiff has to elect between the two laws, at a stage in the proceedings determined by the procedural law of the forum.[140] In any event, the normal rules laid down by Article 4(2) and (3) giving priority to the law of the common residence or the law of a manifestly closer connection are excluded.

As regards the rationale for Article 7, Recital 25 refers to Article 174 of the EC Treaty, which provides that there should be a high level of protection based on the precautionary principle and the principle that preventive action should be taken, the principle of priority for corrective action at source, and the principle that the polluter pays.[141] It asserts that this fully justifies the use of the principle of discriminating in favour of the person sustaining the damage. It may, however, be doubted whether any adequate justification has been offered for departing in this context from the normal rules which under Article 4 are applicable to most other torts.

---

[138] See p. 157 above.

[139] Cf. *Ware v Ciba-Geigy Corp* [2005] WL 1563245, which involved a claim by Alabama residents against New York corporations relating to the deposit in Alabama of toxic waste which had been generated in and shipped from New Jersey. A New Jersey court rejected the claim in accordance with Alabama law, as that of the place of injury and the plaintiffs' residence.

[140] See Recital 25; and the Explanatory Memorandum, note 95 above, at p. 20.

[141] See now Article 191 of the Treaty on the Functioning of the European Union.

**Industrial Disputes**

Article 9 of the Regulation specifies that, without prejudice to Article 4(2) (on the law of a common habitual residence), the law applicable to a tort in respect of the liability of a person in the capacity of a worker or an employer or the organisations representing their professional interests, for damages caused by an industrial action, pending or carried out, is the law of the country where the action is to be, or has been, taken.

Recital 27 explains that the exact concept of industrial action, such as strike action or lock-out, varies from Member State to Member State and is governed by each Member State's internal rules. Recital 28 adds that the special rule on industrial action in Article 9 is without prejudice to the conditions relating to the exercise of such action in accordance with national law, and without prejudice to the legal status of trade unions or of the representative organisations of workers as provided for in the law of the Member States.

**Defamation and Invasion of Privacy**

Article 1(2)(g) excludes from the scope of the Rome II Regulation non-contractual obligations arising out of violations of privacy and rights relating to personality, including defamation. The exclusion is not confined to claims against the media.

Thus, for the time being, in the United Kingdom, defamation claims (for libel or slander) remain subject to the common law rules which in general require double actionability under the lex fori and the lex loci delicti, since neither the Private International Law (Miscellaneous Provisions) Act 1995,[142] nor the Rome II Regulation, extends to such claims. Moreover, the Rome II Regulation does not apply to a claim for breach of confidence or invasion of privacy by way of publication of personal information, even though in *Douglas v Hello! Ltd*[143] the English Court of Appeal characterised such a claim not as a tort claim, but as a restitutionary claim for unjust enrichment, and therefore applied a common-law conflict rule in favour of the law of the country where the publication took place and the enrichment occurred. However, the Rome II Regulation appears to be applicable to claims for slander of title, slander of goods, or other malicious falsehood, since these relate to property or commercial reputation, rather than privacy or personality.

Article 30(2) of the Rome II Regulation requires that, by the end of 2008, the Commission must submit a study on the situation in the field of the law applicable to non-contractual obligations arising out of violations of privacy and rights relating to personality, taking into account rules relating to freedom of the press and freedom of expression in the media, and conflict issues related to EC Directive 95/46 on Data Protection.[144] This review clause emerged from the conciliation committee, as a compromise between the Council's insistence on excluding these matters from the Regulation, and the Parliament's desire to include and specifically regulate them.

In view of the fact that this matter is to receive further consideration at Community level in the near future, it seems useful to mention the various rules thereon which were suggested during the legislative procedure leading to the Rome II Regulation.

---

[142]  See s 13 of the 1995 Act.
[143]  [2006] QB 125.
[144]  [1995] OJ L281/31.

### The general rule
Under the initial Proposal presented by the EC Commission on 22nd July 2003,[145] the main rules on torts (in favour of the place of direct injury, the common habitual residence, and the manifestly closer connection) would have extended to defamation and privacy. In the case of a multiple publication (for example, by newspaper), the place where the publication was commercially distributed so as to reach third parties would have counted as the place of direct injury. Thus the effect would have been to refer distributively to the law of each country of distribution as regards the injury caused by the distribution therein.[146]

In the resolution on first reading adopted by the European Parliament on 6th July 2005,[147] general rules on defamation and privacy were laid down by Article 6(1). These rules were echoed in Article 7A(1) of the resolution on second reading adopted by the European Parliament on 18th January 2007.[148] The primary rule would have referred to the law of the country in which the most significant element or elements of the loss or damage occurred or were likely to occur. But more specific rules were provided for cases where the violation was caused by the publication of printed matter or by a broadcast. In such cases, the applicable law would have been that of the country to which the publication or broadcasting service was principally directed. If that was not apparent, one would have referred to the law of the country in which editorial control was exercised. The country to which the publication or broadcast was directed would have been determined, in particular, by the language of the publication or broadcast, or by sales or audience size in a given country as a proportion of total sales or audience size, or by a combination of those factors. The same would have applied analogistically to publications via the Internet and other electronic networks.

### The right of reply and equivalent measures
In the initial Proposal, Article 6(2) would have subjected the right of reply or equivalent measures (such as the mandatory publication of a correction)[149] to the law of the country in which the broadcaster or publisher had its habitual residence.[150] The rationale appeared to be the impracticability of the distributive application to these issues of several laws under the main rules, and the inappropriateness of a reference to the law of the forum by analogy with Article 6(1).[151]

In the Parliamentary resolutions, it was to be specified that the law applicable to the right of reply or equivalent measures, and to any preventive measures or prohibitory injunctions against a publisher or broadcaster regarding the content of a publication or broadcast, would be that of the country in which the publisher or broadcaster had its habitual residence, and the

---

145   See COM(2003) 427 final.
146   See Case C-68/93: *Shevill v Presse Alliance* [1995] ECR I-415; and the Explanatory Memorandum, COM(2003) 427 final, at p. 18.
147   See JUSTCIV 132, 13th July 2005.
148   See JUSTCIV 7, 24th January 2007.
149   See the Explanatory Memorandum, at p. 18.
150   See also Article 19(3) of the initial Proposal, by which a broadcaster would have been treated as habitually resident at the place where it was established in accordance with EC Directive 89/552, on the co-ordination of certain provisions laid down by law, regulation or administrative action in Member States concerning the Pursuit of Television Broadcasting Activities, [1989] OJ L298/23, as amended by EC Directive 97/36, [1997] OJ L202/60.
151   See the Explanatory Memorandum, at p. 18.

same would have applied to a violation of privacy or of rights relating to the personality resulting from the handling of personal data. The reference to injunctive relief seems to have been intended to be limited to interim injunctions.[152]

### Freedom of expression

In the initial Proposal, Article 6(1) specified that, as regards defamation or privacy, the law of the forum would apply if the application of the law designated by the main rules would be contrary to the fundamental principles of the forum as regards freedom of expression and information. Recital 12 explained that, in view of the Charter of Fundamental Rights of the European Union and the Council of Europe Convention for the Protection of Human Rights and Fundamental Freedoms, in relation to defamation and privacy, respect for the fundamental principles that applied in the Member States as regards freedom of the press had to be secured by a specific safeguard clause. As the Explanatory Memorandum indicated,[153] Article 6(1) made it clear that the law designated by the main rules had to be disapplied in favour of the lex fori if it was incompatible with the public policy of the forum in relation to freedom of the press.[154] In the second Parliamentary resolution, a recital 25A would have explained that, as regards violations of privacy or rights relating to the personality, the Regulation would not prevent Member States from applying their constitutional rules relating to freedom of the press and freedom of expression in the media.

## VARIOUS ISSUES

### The Scope of the Proper Law

Article 15 of the Rome II Regulation provides a wide, but non-exhaustive, definition of the issues which are governed by the proper law of the tort, determined in accordance with Articles 4–9 of the Regulation. Thus the issues listed in Article 15 must be treated as substantive and referred to the proper law, but other issues may be treated as procedural and referred to the law of the forum.[155] Under Article 15, the proper law of the tort applies both to issues relating to liability, and to issues relating to damages. Its control extends to time-limitation and to the burden of proof, and it has some effect on the availability of injunctions. Some additional choice-of-law rules, relating to certain collateral matters, are specified by Articles 18–22.

As regards issues relating to liability, Article 15 of the Regulation expressly subjects to the proper law: (a) the basis and extent of liability, including the determination of persons who may be held liable for acts performed by them; (b) the grounds for exemption from liability, any limitation of liability and any division of liability; (e) the question whether a right to claim damages or a remedy may be transferred, including by inheritance; (f) persons entitled to compensation for damage sustained personally; (g) liability for the acts of another person;

---

[152]   See the Draft Report by Diana Wallis MEP, rapporteur, to the EP Committee on Legal Affairs, 2003/0168(COD), 11th November 2004.

[153]   At p. 18.

[154]   Cf. s 13 of the (UK) Private International Law (Miscellaneous Provisions) Act 1995, which preserves for defamation claims the common-law rule requiring double actionability under the lex fori and the lex loci delicti.

[155]   See the Explanatory Memorandum, COM(2003) 427 final, at p. 9.

and (h) the manner in which an obligation may be extinguished, and rules of prescription and limitation, including rules relating to the commencement, interruption and suspension of a period of prescription or limitation. In addition, Article 22(1) specifies that the proper law applies to the extent that, in matters of non-contractual obligations, it contains rules which raise presumptions of law or determine the burden of proof.

According to the Explanatory Memorandum,[156] Article 15(a) and (b) cover such issues as whether liability is strict or fault-based; the definition of fault; the causal link between the wrongful act and the injury; the persons potentially liable; any maximum amount awardable; the division of liability between defendants; the availability of defences such as force majeure, necessity, third-party fault, and fault of the plaintiff; and the admissibility of actions between spouses. It also explains that Article 15(e)–(g) covers such issues as whether an action can be brought by a deceased victim's estate to obtain compensation for injury sustained by the deceased; whether a claim is assignable, and the relationship between assignor and debtor; whether the spouse and children of a deceased victim can obtain compensation for their own grief and financial loss; and vicarious liability (including that of parents for their children and of principals for their agents). It also seems clear that Article 15(h) covers both ordinary rules on time-limitation and statutes of repose.[157]

An exception is made by Article 17 of the Regulation, which requires that, in assessing the conduct of the person claimed to be liable, account must be taken, as a matter of fact and insofar as is appropriate, of the rules of safety and conduct which were in force at the place and time of the event giving rise to the liability.[158]

The proper law also governs the admissibility and assessment of damages. By Article 15(c) of the Regulation, it determines the existence, the nature and the assessment of damage or the remedy claimed. Thus the proper law must be applied to all issues concerning the assessment of the damages to be awarded, including mere quantification, except insofar as the proper law lacks any rule on the issue which is sufficiently definite to enable a court elsewhere to apply it with reasonable confidence and accuracy.

This accords with the approach which was recently adopted under the Private International Law (Miscellaneous Provisions) Act 1995 by the English Court of Appeal in *Harding v Wealands*,[159] where it abandoned the previously accepted view that the quantification of damages (as distinct from the admissibility of heads of damage) was governed by the lex fori as a matter of procedure.[160] Unfortunately the House of Lords[161] reversed the decision and

---

[156] At COM(2003) 427 final, pp. 23–4.

[157] A statute of repose is one which eliminates product liability if the action has not been commenced within a specified period from the marketing of the goods, even if the injury has not occurred within the period. For example, Article 11 of Directive 85/374 specifies that the rights conferred upon the injured person under the Directive are extinguished upon the expiry of a period of ten years from the date on which the producer put into circulation the actual product which caused the damage, unless the injured person has in the meantime instituted proceedings against the producer.

[158] See p. 378 above.

[159] [2005] 1 All ER 415 (CA).

[160] See *Boys v Chaplin* [1971] AC 356; *Coupland v Arabian Gulf Petroleum Co* [1983] 2 All ER 434 (Hodgson J), affirmed without consideration of this point, [1983] 3 All ER 226 (CA); *Edmunds v Simmonds* [2001] 1 WLR 1003 (Garland J); *Hulse v Chambers* [2001] 1 WLR 2386 (Holland J); and *Roerig v Valiant Trawlers* [2002] 1 All ER 961 (CA).

[161] [2006] UKHL 32.

reaffirmed that all aspects of the quantification of damages are procedural, including the application of a statutory maximum amount awardable for a claim or for a head of damage.[162] It conceded, however, that questions of causation, remoteness and mitigation, as well as the admissibility of a head of damage, are substantive. In the English context, it may be considered that the most significant (and welcome) effect of the Rome II Regulation is the overruling by Article 15(c) of the decision by the Lords in *Harding v Wealands* on the characterisation of issues relating to the assessment of damages.

By way of a curious concession to pressure from the European Parliament, Recital 33 to the Regulation asserts that, according to the current national rules on compensation awarded to victims of road traffic accidents, when quantifying damages for personal injury in cases in which the accident takes place in a State other than that of the habitual residence of the victim, the court seised should take into account all the relevant actual circumstances of the specific victim, including in particular the actual losses and costs of after-care and medical attention. It is not clear what effect, if any, this declaration will have. In principle, a recital may assist in the interpretation of an operative provision, but in this case no relevant operative provision appears to exist. Moreover, the adoption at EU level of a substantive rule requiring full compensation would probably require a legal basis other than Title IV of the EC Treaty or Article 81 of the Treaty on the Functioning of the European Union. In addition, the requirement to 'take account' is cautiously expressed. It is submitted that the Recital will have no real effect where the law applicable under the conflict rules specified by the Regulation, whether it is the law of a Member State or of an external country, for any reason refuses to award full compensation in the light of the victim's actual circumstances.

By Article 15(d) of the Regulation, the proper law applies, within the limits of powers conferred on the court by its procedural law, to the measures which a court may take to prevent or terminate injury or damage or to ensure the provision of compensation. This appears to require the application of the proper law to some extent in the grant of both permanent and interlocutory injunctions against the continuance of a wrongful activity, though without actually obliging the court to order measures which are unknown in the procedural law of the forum.[163] It also extends to the making of orders for interim payments in advance of the full adjudication of the claim.

## Some Collateral Matters

Further conflict rules are established by Articles 18–22 of the Rome II Regulation in respect of the admissibility of direct actions against liability insurers, subrogation, multiple liability, and unilateral acts (such as releases).

---

[162]    See also *Maher v Groupama* [2009] EWCA Civ 1191, where the Court of Appeal (per Moore-Bick LJ) held under the 1995 Act that the existence of a firm right (not subject to judicial discretion) to recover pre-judgment interest as a head of damage is a matter of substance, governed by the law applicable to the tort, but that, whether such a substantive right exists or not, the English court has a discretionary power to award pre-judgment interest, as a procedural matter, under s 35A of the Senior Courts Act 1981. However, the factors to be taken into account in the exercise of the court's discretion under s 35A may well include any relevant provisions of the law governing the tort which relate to the recovery of interest.

[163]    See the Explanatory Memorandum, note 95 above, at p. 24.

Article 18 of the Regulation provides a special rule governing the availability to a tort victim of a direct action against the tortfeasor's liability insurer. It enables a tort victim to bring his claim directly against the insurer of the person liable to provide compensation, if either the law applicable to the tort or the law applicable to the insurance contract so provides. But the option is limited to the admissibility of the direct action, for the scope of the insurer's obligations is determined by the law governing the insurance contract.[164] In any event, Article 18 is more favourable to the victim than the traditional English rule, which refers the admissibility of a direct action to the proper law of the insurance contract.[165]

Article 19 of the Regulation deals with subrogation. It applies where a person ('the creditor') has a non-contractual claim upon another ('the debtor'), and a third person has a duty to satisfy the creditor, or has in fact satisfied the creditor in discharge of such a duty.[166] It then refers to the law which governs the third person's duty to satisfy the creditor the determination of whether, and to what extent, the third person is entitled to exercise against the debtor the rights which the creditor had against the debtor under the law governing their relationship. This applies to subrogation by a loss insurer to a claim in tort belonging to its insured.[167] Its effect appears to accord with the existing English rules, as explained by Colman J in *The Front Comor*.[168] Thus it is for the law which governs the insurance contract to determine whether the insurer has a right of subrogation to the claim. But if such a right exists under the law governing the insurance contract, its scope is limited to the rights of the insured which are available for subrogation under the law which governs the tort.

Article 20 of the Regulation deals with multiple liability. It applies where a creditor has a non-contractual claim against several debtors who are liable for the same claim, and one of the debtors has already satisfied the claim in whole or in part.[169] It then subjects the question of that debtor's right to demand compensation from the other debtors to the law applicable to that debtor's non-contractual obligation towards the creditor. This applies where one of several tortfeasors has made a payment to the victim satisfying his claim, and deals with a claim by the payer for contribution or indemnity from another tortfeasor who is also liable for the same injury. Its effect is to subject the existence of the payer's claim for contribution or indemnity to the law which governs the victim's claim against the payer.

Article 21 of the Regulation specifies that a unilateral act intended to have legal effect and relating to a non-contractual obligation is formally valid if it satisfies the formal requirements of the law governing the non-contractual obligation in question, or if it satisfies those of the law of the country in which the act is performed. Article 22(2) adds that acts intended to have legal effect may be proved by any mode of proof recognised by the law of the forum or by any of the laws referred to in Article 21 under which that act is formally valid, provided that

---

[164]   See the Explanatory Memorandum, note 95 above, at pp. 25–6.
[165]   See *The Hari Bhum* [2005] 1 Lloyd's Rep 67 (CA), affirming [2004] 1 Lloyd's Rep 206 (Moore-Bick J); and *Maher v Groupama* [2009] EWCA Civ 1191. In Turkey, a rule similar to Article 18 of the Regulation is laid down by Article 34(4) of Act 5718 of 27th November 2007 on Private International Law and International Civil Procedure.
[166]   Very similar provision in respect of legal subrogation to a contractual claim is made by Article 15 of the Rome I Regulation. See p. 337 above.
[167]   See the Explanatory Memorandum, at p. 26.
[168]   [2005] EWHC 454 (Comm).
[169]   See also Article 16 of the Rome I Regulation, which applies where the creditor's claim is contractual in character; and pp. 337–8 above.

such mode of proof can be administered by the forum.[170] These provisions may apply, for example, to a unilateral release from a tort liability.

## Pleading and Establishment of Foreign Law

As a result of pressure by the European Parliament, the way in which foreign law is treated is mentioned in Article 30(1) of the Regulation. This requires the EC Commission to submit, by 20th August 2011, a report on the application of the Regulation, accompanied if necessary by proposals for its adaptation. The Report must include a study on the effects of the way in which foreign law is treated in the different jurisdictions, and on the extent to which courts in the Member States apply foreign law in practice pursuant to the Regulation.

Thus it is contemplated that eventually some attempt may be made to harmonise by means of an EU regulation the rules of the Member States on the pleading and the proof or other establishment of the content of foreign law. At present, the matter is governed in each Member State by its own rules. Thus, where a matter is in principle governed by foreign law by virtue of a conflict rule, an English court will normally determine the matter in accordance with English internal law unless the foreign law is properly invoked by a party who relies on it. In English litigation, a party who relies on foreign law must plead the content of the relevant foreign rule, and prove such content by means of an expert witness.[171] The need for harmonisation on such procedural matters is open to serious doubt.

---

[170] These provisions to some extent resemble Articles 11(3) and 18(2) of the Rome I Regulation. See pp. 327–8 and 331–2 above.

[171] See Dicey, Morris and Collins, 14th edition (Sweet & Maxwell, 2006), Rule 18.

# 15.  Restitution

## INTRODUCTION

It is generally recognised that the law of obligations (other than familial obligations) may be divided into three branches: contract, tort, and restitution. Each serves its own underlying purpose. The law of contract aims to support legitimate expectations arising from consensual transactions. The law of tort aims to promote security from harmful interference, especially physical interference with persons and tangible property. The law of restitution aims to prevent unjustified enrichment. Thus obligations may be classified for conflict purposes as contractual obligations, tortious obligations, and restitutionary obligations. Both tortious and restitutionary obligations are non-contractual, but a restitutionary obligation differs from a tortious obligation in that a restitutionary obligation may arise without there being any wrongful act on the part of the defendant, and that a restitutionary obligation is designed to restore or transfer to the claimant a benefit which has been obtained by the defendant, rather than to compensate the claimant for an injury or loss which has been suffered by the claimant.

The Rome I Regulation deals with contractual obligations, and the Rome II Regulation deals with both torts and restitutionary obligations. Thus Recital 29 to the Rome II Regulation explains that provision should be made for special rules where damage is caused by an act other than a tort, such as unjust enrichment, *negotiorum gestio* and *culpa in contrahendo*. These additional matters are regulated primarily by Chapter III (Articles 10–13) of the Rome II Regulation.

The main provisions of the Rome II Regulation on restitutionary obligations are Article 10, which deals with unjust enrichment, and Article 11, which deals with *negotiorum gestio* (or unauthorised agency). Article 12 deals with *culpa in contrahendo*, or non-contractual obligations arising out of dealings prior to the conclusion of a contract. It appears to cover both tortious and restitutionary claims arising from contractual negotiations. Article 13 ensures that Article 8 applies to non-contractual obligations arising from an infringement of an intellectual property right, even where the claim is restitutionary rather than tortious in character.

Where Chapter III of the Regulation applies to a claim, it excludes the operation of Chapter II (Articles 4–9) on torts, except for Article 8, in respect of that claim. But Chapter I (Articles 1–3) on such matters as the material scope of the Regulation, Chapter IV (Article 14) on choice-of-law agreements, and Chapters V–VII (Articles 15–32) on such matters as the definition of habitual residence, the exclusion of renvoi, and the proviso in favour of the stringent public policy of the forum, remain applicable to claims to which Chapter III applies. By Article 2(1), for the purposes of the Regulation, damage refers to any consequence arising out of tort, unjust enrichment, *negotiorum gestio* or *culpa in contrahendo*.

There is evidently potential for overlap, and resulting problems of characterisation, in relation to situations in which a restitutionary remedy (by way of the restoration or transfer of a benefit received by the defendant) is claimed on the ground that a breach of contract or a tort has been committed by the defendant, and in other situations where a claim is made for a restitutionary remedy in the context of an existing contractual or tortious relationship between the parties. Such problems will be explored in the discussion below. But it is worthy of initial emphasis that Chapter III of the Rome II Regulation endeavours to minimise the significance of such questions by, in most cases, subjecting a claim which is within its scope but which is connected to an existing contractual or tortious relationship between the same parties to the law which governs the related contract or tort.[1]

In any event, it seems clear that insofar as a claim has a proprietary character, it does not fall within the scope of Rome II Regulation. For example, where a claimant from whom property has been wrongfully obtained seeks to establish and enforce a constructive trust against an insolvent liquidator of a person who wrongfully obtained or received the property, and relies on a proprietary right under the constructive trust to gain priority over ordinary creditors of the insolvent debtor, the Rome II Regulation may be relevant to the personal liability of the debtor, but not to whether the claim has priority in the liquidation by reason of its proprietary character. The latter issue may be affected by the conflict rules specified by the Insolvency Regulation.

## UNJUST ENRICHMENT

Article 10 of the Rome II Regulation applies to non-contractual obligations arising out of unjust enrichment.[2] Article 10(1) specifies that this includes payment of amounts wrongly received. Thus Article 10 applies, for example, to claims for repayment of amounts paid by mistake;[3] and to restitutionary claims by a principal against his agent and a contractor for recovery of a bribe paid by the contractor to the agent for assistance in the obtaining of a contract with the principal.[4] But Article 10 does not apply to restitutionary obligations arising from an infringement of an intellectual property right, since Article 13 subjects claims in respect of such infringements to Article 8, even where the claim is restitutionary rather than tortious in character. It is also clear that Article 10 does not apply to claims based on unauthorised agency, in view of the more specific provision made by Article 11 for such claims.

Article 10 distinguishes between restitutionary obligations which are closely connected with an existing relationship between the parties, and ones which are not so connected. The former are regulated by Article 10(1) and (4), and the latter by Article 10(2)–(4). It must be emphasised that it is only an existing relationship between the parties to the restitutionary claim, and not an existing relationship between one of them and a third party, which is relevant.

---

[1]    It should also be borne in mind that both Recital 7 to the Rome II Regulation, and Recital 7 to the Rome I Regulation, emphasise that there should be consistency in respect of the scope and provisions of the Rome II Regulation, the Rome I Regulation, and the Brussels I Regulation.

[2]    For a full and valuable analysis of Article 10, see Adeline Chong, 'Choice of Law for Unjust Enrichment/Restitution and the Rome II Regulation' (2008) 57 International and Comparative Law Quarterly 863.

[3]    See *Chase Manhattan Bank v Israel-British Bank* [1981] Ch 105 (Goulding J).

[4]    See *Arab Monetary Fund v Hashim* [1996] 1 Lloyd's Rep 589 (CA), affirming [1993] 1 Lloyd's Rep 543 (Evans J); and *Thahir v Pertamina* [1994] 3 SLR 257 (Singapore CA).

## Existing Relationships

Article 10(1) and (4) apply to cases where the restitutionary obligation concerns a relationship existing between the parties, such as one arising out of a contract or a tort, which is closely connected with the unjust enrichment. In such cases, Article 10(1) provides a rebuttable presumption which subjects the restitutionary claim to the law which governs the existing relationship.[5] But Article 10(4) provides an exception, which applies where it is clear from all the circumstances of the case that the obligation arising out of unjust enrichment is manifestly more closely connected with another country, and subjects the claim to the law of the country with which it is manifestly more closely connected.

It seems clear beyond doubt that Article 10 does not apply to a claim which asserts the validity of a contract and seeks its enforcement, or a remedy for its breach, even if the amount to be awarded is to be assessed by reference to a benefit received by the defendant, rather than a loss suffered by the claimant. Such a claim must be treated simply as a contractual claim, governed by the Rome I Regulation, and not as involving any non-contractual obligation within Article 10 of the Rome II Regulation. Thus the law governing the contract cannot be displaced by reference to a manifestly closer connection under Article 10(4) of the Rome II Regulation. An example of such a contractual claim would be where a buyer under a contract of sale has paid the price of goods before delivery, and then justifiably rejects the goods tendered as not complying with the contract, and now claims repayment of the price. Although the claim for repayment relies on a total failure of consideration, and the amount claimed is measured by the payment made by the claimant to the defendant, the fundamental basis of the claim is the defendant's breach of contract in failure to tender acceptable goods as promised, and it is only the remedy sought which can be regarded as in any sense restitutionary in character. Another example of such a contractual claim would be where a seller of goods delivered claims a reasonable price in accordance with an express or implied term of the contract requiring such a payment.

It seems clear from the more specific provisions of Article 12 of the Rome II Regulation that Article 10 does not apply to non-contractual obligations arising out of dealings prior to the conclusion of a contract, whether the contract was actually concluded or not. But it seems uncertain whether it is Article 10 of the Rome II Regulation, or Article 12(1)(e) of the Rome I Regulation (on the consequences of nullity of a contract), which applies where a restitutionary claim arises from the invalidity of a contract by reason of factors other than the pre-contractual negotiations; for example, where the contract is invalid by reason of incapacity or of illegal purpose. While both provisions would at least presumptively subject the restitutionary claim to the proper law of the invalid contract, under Article 12(1)(e) of the Rome I

---

5    Article 10(1) substantially accords with the traditional English law. As regards a related contract, see *The Evia Luck* [1992] 2 AC 152; *Arab Monetary Fund v Hashim* [1996] 1 Lloyd's Rep 589 (CA), affirming [1993] 1 Lloyd's Rep 543 (Evans J); *Kuwait Oil Tanker Co v Al Bader* [2000] 2 All ER (Comm) 271 (CA); and Dicey, Morris and Collins, *The Conflict of Laws*, 14th edition (Sweet & Maxwell, 2006), Rule 230(2)(a). Cf. *Baring Brothers v Cunninghame DC* [1996] WL 1093491; and *Thahir v Pertamina* [1994] 3 SLR 257 (Singapore CA). As regards a related tort, see Dicey, Morris and Collins, paras 34-015 and 34-032. As regards a related relationship involving the ownership or use of property, see Dicey, Morris and Collins, Rule 230(2)(b), and *Batthyany v Walford* (1887) 36 ChD 269.

Regulation there is no exception in favour of a manifestly closer connection with another country.[6]

In contrast, there is no real doubt that Article 10(1) and (4) of the Rome II Regulation extend to a restitutionary claim made by a buyer under a a valid contract for the sale of goods, who has by mistake paid the price to the seller twice, and now seeks repayment by the seller of the second payment. Similarly, it seems clear that Article 10(1) and (4) apply to restitutionary claims for repayment of sums paid, or payment in respect of other benefits transferred, where a valid contract has been discharged by frustration after the payment or other transfer.[7]

Article 10(1) explicitly refers also to an existing relationship between the parties arising out of a tort. No doubt the reference to a tort extends to an equitable wrong, such as dishonest assistance in a breach of fiduciary duty, or knowing receipt of property transferred in breach of a trust or other fiduciary duty. It seems that in such cases, while a claim for a compensatory award, assessed by the reference to the claimant's loss, counts as tortious and falls within Chapter II of the Rome II Regulation, a claim for a restitutionary award, assessed by reference to the benefit received by the defendant, falls within Article 10(1) and (4). Thus in such cases a restitutionary claim will be subject to the law which applies to the tortious claim, unless the restitutionary claim is manifestly more closely connected with another country. Article 10(1) also seems capable of applying to a restitutionary obligation where the unjust enrichment is closely connected with an existing relationship between the parties which relates to the ownership or use of property.

**Stand-alone Claims**

In stand-alone cases, where there is no existing relationship between the parties from which the applicable law can be derived, Article 10(2) and (3) of the Rome II Regulation create a presumption subjecting an obligation arising out of unjust enrichment to the law of the country in which both parties had their habitual residence when the event giving rise to unjust enrichment occurred, if such a common residence existed; or in the absence of such a common residence, to the law of the country in which the unjust enrichment took place. This evidently refers to the country in which the immediate benefit was received. But Article 10(4) applies where it is clear from all the circumstances of the case that the restitutionary obligation is manifestly more closely connected with another country than that indicated in Article 10(2) and (3), and subjects the claim to the law of the country with which the obligation is manifestly more closely connected.[8]

---

    [6]    On Article 12(1)(e) of the Rome I Regulation, see pp. 333–5 above.
    [7]    See also s 1 of the (English) Law Reform (Frustrated Contracts) Act 1943, which makes the 1943 Act, which deals with the consequences of frustration, applicable to contracts governed by English law.
    [8]    Apart from the insertion of a reference to the common habitual residence, these provisions broadly accord with the traditional English law. As regards the reference to the place of the immediate enrichment, see Dicey, Morris and Collins, Rule 230(2)(c) and para 34-052; *Chase Manhattan Bank v Israel-British Bank* [1981] Ch 105 (Goulding J); *Hongkong and Shanghai Banking Corp v United Overseas Bank* [1992] 2 SLR 495 (Singapore High Court); and *Thahir v Pertamina* [1994] 3 SLR 257 (Singapore CA). As regards a closer connection with another country, see Dicey, Morris and Collins, Rule 230(1) and paras 34-052 and 34-053; *Arab Monetary Fund v Hashim* [1996] 1 Lloyd's Rep 589 (CA), affirming [1993] 1 Lloyd's Rep 543 (Evans J); and *Barros Mattos v MacDaniels Ltd* [2005] EWHC 1323 Ch (Lawrence Collins J).

It may be suggested that the presumption in favour of the law of the place of immediate enrichment may readily be displaced, perhaps in favour of the law of the place where the loss was suffered by the claimant or the ultimate enrichment occurred,[9] especially as the presumption may have the effect of subjecting a fraudster's liability to the law of the location of his bank account in which the credit is received.[10] But it should be recognised that the presumption has a number of advantages. It focuses on the most important element in the claim (the enrichment itself, rather than the act giving rise to it); it designates a law which is closely connected with the defendant; and it is usually more easily identifiable and less open to manipulation than the place of ultimate enrichment. Moreover the displacement rule expressly requires a manifestly closer connection.[11]

## UNAUTHORISED AGENCY (*NEGOTIORUM GESTIO*)

Article 11 of the Rome II Regulation, which is entitled *negotiorum gestio*, deals with non-contractual obligations arising out of acts performed without due authority in connection with the affairs of another person. It resembles Article 10, except that Article 11(3) refers to the law of the country in which the unauthorised act was performed, instead of the law of the country in which the unjust enrichment took place.

Thus Article 11(1) applies where the restitutionary obligation concerns a relationship existing between the parties, such as one arising out of a contract or a tort, which is closely connected with the restitutionary obligation, and subjects the restitutionary claim to the law which governs the existing relationship. In the absence of an existing relationship, Article 11(2) and (3) subject the restitutionary claim to the law of the country in which both parties were habitually resident when the relevant event occurred; or in the absence of such a common residence, to the law of the country in which the unauthorised act was performed. Then Article 11(4) applies where it is clear from all the circumstances of the case that the restitutionary obligation is manifestly more closely connected with a country other than that indicated in Article 11(1)–(3), and substitutes the law of the country with which the restitutionary obligation is manifestly more closely connected.[12]

---

9     See Dicey, Morris and Collins, paras 34-052 and 34-053.

10     See the Wallis Report of 11th November 2004 to the European Parliament's Committee on Legal Affairs. It was for this reason that the European Parliament's resolution on first reading, adopted on 6th July 2005, and the EC Commission's amended proposal of 21st February 2006, proposed that the presumption should refer to the law of the country in which the events giving rise to unjust enrichment substantially occurred, rather than that of the country in which the enrichment occurred; see JUST-CIV 132, 13th July 2005, and COM(2006) 83 final. But this suggestion was not adopted in the Regulation as adopted.

11     See Adeline Chong, (2008) 57 ICLQ 863 at pp. 882–90.

12     See also Dicey, Morris and Collins, at para 34-053, suggesting that, in some cases of *negotiorum gestio*, the closest connection may be with the country in which the loss was sustained by the claimant.

## PRE-CONTRACTUAL DEALINGS

Article 12 of the Rome II Regulation, which is entitled *culpa in contrahendo*, applies to non-contractual obligations arising out of dealings prior to the conclusion of a contract, regardless of whether the contract was actually concluded or not. Recital 30 explains that for the purposes of the Regulation *culpa in contrahendo* is an autonomous concept and should not necessarily be interpreted in accordance with national law. It explains that the concept includes the violation of a duty of disclosure and the breakdown of contractual negotiations. But it adds that Article 12 covers only non-contractual obligations which present a direct link with the dealings prior to the conclusion of a contract. Thus if, while a contract is being negotiated, a person suffers personal injury, Article 4 or other relevant provisions of the Regulation apply.

Article 12 appears to apply whether the claim is restitutionary or tortious in character. Thus it applies to a tortious claim for damages which is based on the wrongful breaking off of negotiations,[13] or on non-disclosure of material facts (for example, in the context of insurance), or on misrepresentation (whether fraudulent, negligent, or wholly innocent). But Article 12 does not appear to apply to a claim for the annulment or rescission of a contract by reason of misrepresentation or non-disclosure, since such a claim is essentially contractual in character. It is uncertain whether Article 12 extends to a restitutionary claim which is based on the annulment or rescission of a contract and seeks the restoration of benefits transferred in pursuance of the contract. It may be that such a restitutionary claim is governed not by Article 12 of the Rome II Regulation, but by Article 12(1)(e) of the Rome I Regulation, as a consequence of the nullity of the contract. However, both provisions have the same effect, of subjecting the claim to the actual or putative proper law of the contract.[14]

Where Article 12 of the Rome II Regulation applies, Article 12(1) subjects the claim to the law which applies to the contract, or which would have been applicable to the contract if it had been entered into. This reference to the actual or putative proper law of the relevant contract is not subject to displacement by reference to a closer connection with another country.

Since the actual or putative proper law of the contract cannot always be determined, for example where the negotiations broke down because of disagreement about a proposed choice of law clause, Article 12(2) of the Rome II Regulation provides for such cases a supplementary rule. This is similar to the main rule for tort cases specified by Article 4. The supplementary rule specified by Article 12(2)(a) and (b), read in the light of Article 2(1), provides a rebuttable presumption in favour of the law of the country in which both parties were habitually resident when the event giving rise to the damage or equivalent consequence occurred; or in the absence of such a common residence, in favour of the law of the country in which the direct damage or equivalent consequence occurred. By Article 12(2)(c), this presumption is displaced where it is clear from all the circumstances of the case that the non-contractual obligation is manifestly more closely connected with another country, in favour of the law of the country which is manifestly more closely connected with the obligation.

---

[13] See Case C-334/00: *Tacconi v Wagner* [2002] ECR I-7357.
[14] On Article 12(1)(e) of the Rome I Regulation, see pp. 333–5 above.

PART IV

Family Matters

# 16.  Matrimonial proceedings

## INTRODUCTION

### The Brussels IIA Regulation

The jurisdiction of the courts of the EU Member States to entertain matrimonial proceedings, and the recognition between Member States of matrimonial decrees, is now governed by EC Regulation 2201/2003 concerning Jurisdiction and the Recognition and Enforcement of Judgments in Matrimonial Matters and the Matters of Parental Responsibility, which may conveniently be referred to as the Brussels IIA Regulation.[1] This Regulation became applicable on 1st March 2005[2] in the twenty-four then Member States other than Denmark,[3] and on 1st January 2007 in Bulgaria and Romania.[4] It is on the provisions of the Brussels IIA Regulation which deal with matrimonial jurisdiction and decrees that this chapter is focused.

Matrimonial jurisdiction and decrees had previously been regulated by EC Regulation 1347/2000 on Jurisdiction and the Recognition and Enforcement of Judgments in Matrimonial Matters and in Matters of Parental Responsibility for Children of Both Spouses, which is commonly known as the Brussels II Regulation.[5] That Regulation had entered into force on 1st March 2001 for the fourteen then Member States other than Denmark,[6] and on 1st May 2004 for the ten States which joined the European Community in 2004.[7] The entry into force of the Brussels II Regulation constituted a landmark in the harmonisation of private international law at European Union level, since it was the first EU measure to enter into force dealing with private international law in family matters (other than maintenance). The Brussels II Regulation had in turn replaced the Convention of 28th May 1998 on Jurisdiction

---

[1]    For its text, see [2003] OJ L338/1.

[2]    See Article 72. For transitional provisions, see Article 64.

[3]    For the exclusion of Denmark, see Recital 31 and Article 2(3). Provisions ancillary to the Regulation have been made in England by the European Communities (Matrimonial Jurisdiction and Judgments) Regulations 2001 (SI 2001/310), and the European Communities (Jurisdiction and Judgments in Matrimonial and Parental Responsibility Matters) Regulations 2005 (SI 2005/265); and in Scotland by the European Communities (Matrimonial Jurisdiction and Judgments) (Scotland) Regulations 2001 (SSI 2001/36), and the European Communities (Matrimonial and Parental Responsibility Jurisdiction and Judgments) (Scotland) Regulations 2005 (SSI 2005/42). See also *YNR v MN, Ireland and the Attorney General* [2005] 4 IR 552 (O'Higgins J), upholding the validity of the Brussels II and IIA Regulations in Ireland.

[4]    See the Luxembourg Act of Accession 2005, Articles 2 and 56; [2005] OJ L157.

[5]    For its text, see [2000] OJ L160/19.

[6]    For the exclusion of Denmark, see Recital 25 and Article 1(3). For this purpose, the United Kingdom includes Gibraltar; see Annexes I and II.

[7]    See the Athens Act of Accession 2003, Article 2 (and, for minor adjustments, Annex II, Part 18(A)(2)).

and the Recognition and Enforcement of Judgments in Matrimonial Matters, which is commonly referred to as the Brussels II Convention,[8] but which had not entered into force.

As from 1st March 2005 the Brussels IIA Regulation has repealed and replaced the Brussels II Regulation.[9] With regard to matrimonial proceedings and decrees, the Brussels IIA Regulation consolidates the provisions of the Brussels II Regulation without substantial alteration. Moreover, as is indicated by Recital 6 to the Brussels II Regulation and Recital 3 to the Brussels IIA Regulation, the content of the Brussels II Regulation was substantially taken over from the Brussels II Convention. Thus assistance in the interpretation of the Brussels II and IIA Regulations can be obtained from the Borrás Report on the Brussels II Convention.[10]

Both the Brussels II Regulation and the Brussels IIA Regulation deal with direct judicial jurisdiction, and the mutual recognition and enforcement of judgments, but not choice of law, in respect of divorce, separation and annulment of marriage. They also deal with jurisdiction and judgments in respect of parental responsibility for children. As regards children, the Brussels II Regulation dealt only with children of both spouses, and applied only where parental responsibility for the child was determined on the occasion of matrimonial proceedings between the parents. In contrast, the Brussels IIA Regulation deals with jurisdiction and orders in respect of parental responsibility for children in all situations, regardless of whether any marriage, divorce, separation or annulment is involved. The provisions on parental responsibility for children are examined in Chapter 17 below.

**The Rome III Proposal**

On 17th July 2006, the EC Commission presented a Proposal for a Council Regulation amending the Brussels IIA Regulation as regards jurisdiction and introducing rules concerning applicable law in matrimonial matters.[11] This is commonly referred to as the Rome III Proposal. It was designed to amend the provisions on matrimonial jurisdiction contained in Chapter II of the Brussels IIA Regulation, and to insert therein a new Chapter IIA, dealing with choice of law in matters of divorce and legal separation.

On 5th and 6th June 2008, the EC Council noted that unanimity on taking the Rome III Proposal forward had not been obtained and that insurmountable difficulties precluded unanimity then or in the foreseeable future. It also established that the objectives of the Proposal could not be attained within a reasonable period by applying the relevant provisions of the Treaties.[12] Neither the United Kingdom nor Ireland had opted to participate in the Proposal, and its opponents included Sweden and the Netherlands.[13]

---

[8] For its text, see [1998] OJ C221/1. The matrimonial project arose from German concerns arising from the lack of mutual recognition of divorces, especially between France and Germany, neither of which had become party to the Hague Convention of 1st June 1970 on the Recognition of Divorces and Legal Separations. Negotiations within a working group were opened in June 1994.

[9] See Article 71 of the Brussels IIA Regulation.

[10] For the Borrás Report, see [1998] OJ C221/27.

[11] See COM(2006) 399 final. This followed a Green Paper on applicable law and jurisdiction in divorce matters; see COM(2005) 82 final, 14th March 2005.

[12] See PV/CONS 36, JAI 311, of 10th July 2008, and JUSTCIV 150, of 18th July 2008.

[13] See press reports by Renata Goldirova in EUobserver, Luxembourg, 6th June 2008 and 25th July 2008; and by Jim Brunsden in European Voice, 25th July 2008.

On 5th and 6th June 2008, the EC Council also called for examination of the possibility of proceeding under the provisions on enhanced co-operation between Member States towards a measure applicable by the Member States which chose to participate therein.[14] The provisions on enhanced co-operation then operative were Articles 11 and 11A of the EC Treaty (as amended by the Treaty of Nice), and Articles 43–5 of the Treaty on European Union (as so amended). They required a request to the EC Commission by at least eight Member States which intended to establish enhanced co-operation between themselves; a proposal from the Commission as requested; and an authorisation to establish enhanced co-operation granted by the EC Council, acting by a qualified majority. Other Member States could choose to participate when enhanced co-operation was being established or at any subsequent time.[15]

On 24th and 25th July 2008, the Council noted that at least eight Member States intended to ask the Commission to bring forward a proposal for enhanced co-operation.[16] Such a request was subsequently made by France, Italy, Luxembourg, Spain, Austria, Hungary, Slovenia, Bulgaria and Romania, for a proposal covering only the issue of applicable law.[17] Eventually in March 2010, the EU Commission responded to these requests by presenting a proposal, based on Article 329(1) of the Treaty on the Functioning of the European Union, for a Council decision authorising enhanced co-operation in the area of the law applicable to divorce and legal separation,[18] and a proposal, based on Article 81(3) of that Treaty, for a Council regulation implementing enhanced co-operation in the area of the law applicable to divorce and legal separation.[19] Subsequently, on 12th July 2010, the EU Council adopted a Decision authorising enhanced co-operation between the 14 then requesting Member States[20] in respect of the law applicable to divorce and legal separation.[21] The proposed regulation will be confined to choice of law in respect of divorce and separation, and will not amend the provisions of the Brussels IIA Regulation on jurisdiction.

**The Regulation on External Agreements in Family Matters**

EC Regulation 664/2009, establishing a procedure for the negotiation and conclusion of agreements between Member States and third countries concerning jurisdiction, recognition and enforcement of judgments and decisions in matrimonial matters, matters of parental responsibility and matters relating to maintenance obligations, and the law applicable to

---

[14]    See PV/CONS 36, JAI 311, of 10th July 2008, and JUSTCIV 150, of 18th July 2008.

[15]    Now that the Treaty of Lisbon has entered into force, the provisions of enhanced co-operation are now contained in Article 20 of the Treaty on European Union and Articles 326–34 of the Treaty on the Functioning of the European Union.

[16]    See POLGEN 91, of 11th September 2008.

[17]    See JAI 64, COMIX 111, of 5th February 2009; and a press report by Jim Brunsden in European Voice, 19th January 2009. A similar request by Greece was later withdrawn.

[18]    See COM(2010) 104 final/2.

[19]    See COM(2010) 105 final/2.

[20]    France, Germany, Italy, Belgium, Luxembourg, Spain, Portugal, Austria, Hungary, Slovenia, Latvia, Malta, Bulgaria and Romania.

[21]    See Council Press Release 201 of 12th July 2010; and JUSTCIV 100 of 4th June 2010. For the Council's working version of the Rome III proposal, see JUSTCIV 106 of 1st June 2010.

matters relating to maintenance obligations, was adopted by the EC Council on 7th July 2009.[22] It will remain in force at least until August 2020.[23]

As Article 1(1) explains, Regulation 664/2009 establishes a procedure by which, under certain conditions, the EU Commission may authorise a Member State to amend an existing agreement with a non-member country, or to negotiate and conclude a new agreement with a non-member country. By Article 1(2), it applies to agreements concerning matters falling, entirely or partly, within the scope of the Brussels IIA Regulation or the Maintenance Regulation.[24] By Recital 9 and Articles 1(3) and 4(2), it does not apply where the European Union has already concluded an agreement with the non-member country concerned on the same subject-matter (in the sense that the agreements regulate in substance the same specific legal issues); nor where a relevant negotiating mandate with a view to concluding a European Union agreement with the non-member country concerned is specifically envisaged within the next 24 months.[25]

By Article 2(1)(a), it applies primarily to bilateral agreements between a Member State and a non-member country. By Article 2(1)(b), it also extends to multilateral agreements amending the Nordic Convention of 6th February 1931 between Denmark, Finland, Iceland, Norway and Sweden on marriage, adoption and guardianship, or the Convention of 23 March 1962 between Sweden, Denmark, Finland, Iceland and Norway on the recovery of maintenance.

Several conditions are imposed by Articles 4 and 8 before an authorisation may be granted by the Commission to the Member State, initially to open formal negotiations, and eventually to conclude a negotiated agreement. By Article 4(2)(a), at the initial stage the Member State concerned must have provided information showing that it has a specific interest in concluding the agreement due to economic, geographic, cultural, historical, social or political ties between the Member State and the third country concerned. By Article 4(2)(b), at both stages it must appear, on the basis of the information provided by the Member State, that the envisaged agreement would not render European Union law ineffective and would not undermine the proper functioning of the system established by European Union law. By Article 4(2)(c), at both stages the envisaged agreement must not undermine the object and purpose of the European Union's external relations policy as decided by the Union.

By Article 5(1), the Commission decision authorising a Member State to open formal negotiations on an agreement may be accompanied by negotiating guidelines and a request for the inclusion of particular clauses in the envisaged agreement. In any event, by Article 5(2), the agreement must contain a clause providing for either the denunciation or the direct replacement of the agreement, in the event of the conclusion of a subsequent agreement by the European Union, or the European Union and its Member States, with the same non-member country on the same subject-matter. By Article 7, the Commission may participate

---

[22]   See [2009] OJ L200/46.
[23]   See Articles 13 and 14.
[24]   Regulation 4/2009 on Jurisdiction, Applicable Law, Recognition and Enforcement of Decisions and Co-operation in Matters relating to Maintenance Obligations; [2009] OJ L7/1. See Chapter 18 below.
[25]   Such a mandate may emerge from consultations between the Commission and the Member States following the notification by a Member State seeking authorisation under the Regulation. See Recital 12 and Article 11.

as an observer in the negotiations between the Member State and the non-member country. In any event, the Commission must be kept informed of the progress and results throughout the different stages of the negotiations.

By Article 8(1), before signing a negotiated agreement, the Member State concerned must notify the outcome of the negotiations to the Commission and transmit to it the text of the agreement. By Article 8(2) and (3), if the negotiated agreement fulfils the conditions and requirements referred to in Articles 4(2)(b) and (c) and 5(2), the Commission gives a decision authorising the Member State to conclude the agreement.

## Scope

Like the Brussels I Regulation, the Brussels IIA Regulation lays down rules on direct jurisdiction and on the recognition and enforcement of judgments, but not on choice of law. By Article 1(1)(a), the Brussels IIA Regulation applies to petitions for and decrees of divorce, legal separation of spouses, and annulment of marriage.[26] But it does not apply to annulment proceedings brought after the death of a spouse.[27] By Article 1(3)(e), it does not apply to maintenance obligations, which at present remain governed by the Brussels I Regulation[28] and will eventually be governed by EC Regulation 4/2009 (the Maintenance Regulation).[29] Nor does it apply to matrimonial property, which remains uncovered by any Community measure.[30] Moreover, the recognition of a divorce does not require recognition of findings of fault, nor of ancillary personal effects (such as on the right to a name).[31]

Although Article 1(1) specifies that the Brussels IIA Regulation applies in civil matters, regardless of the nature of the court or tribunal, Article 2 extends its scope to administrative proceedings and decisions. For Article 2(1) defines 'court' as covering all the authorities in the Member States with jurisdiction in the matters falling within the scope of the Regulation;

---

[26]     By Article 1(1)(b), it also applies to applications and orders relating to parental responsibility for children. See Chapter 17 below.

[27]     See the Borrás Report, at para 27. In the case of annulment proceedings brought after the death of a spouse, in England, reg 3(5) of SI 2001/310 amends s 5(3) of the Domicile and Matrimonial Proceedings Act 1973 so that English jurisdiction exists if the surviving spouse is domiciled in England at the commencement of the proceedings, or the deceased spouse either was domiciled in England at his death or had been habitually resident in England throughout the year up to his death; but, puzzlingly, the habitual residence of the surviving spouse is ignored. See similarly, for Scotland, reg 2(2) of SSI 2001/36, amending s 7 of the 1973 Act.

[28]     Recital 11 to the Brussels IIA Regulation explains that maintenance obligations are excluded from the scope of the Brussels IIA Regulation as these are already covered by the Brussels I Regulation. It adds that the courts having jurisdiction under the Brussels IIA Regulation will generally have jurisdiction to rule on maintenance obligations by application of Article 5(2) of the Brussels I Regulation.

[29]     Regulation 4/2009 on Jurisdiction, Applicable Law, Recognition and Enforcement of Decisions and Co-operation in Matters relating to Maintenance Obligations; [2009] OJ L7/1. See Chapter 18 below.

[30]     Recital 8 to the Brussels IIA Regulation explains that, as regards judgments on divorce, legal separation or marriage annulment, the Regulation should apply only to the dissolution of matrimonial ties and should not deal with issues such as the grounds for divorce, property consequences of the marriage or any other ancillary measures.

[31]     See Recital 8 to the Brussels IIA Regulation. See also Recital 10 to the Brussels II Regulation; and the Borrás Report, at para 22.

and Article 2(2) defines 'judge' as including an official having powers equivalent to those of a judge in such matters. Thus, but for the exclusion of Denmark itself, the Regulation would have applied to the Danish divorce procedure before a district council. But purely religious procedures are excluded.[32]

By Article 60, the Brussels IIA Regulation takes precedence, as between the Member States, over certain international conventions, including the Hague Convention of 1st June 1970 on the Recognition of Divorces and Legal Separations.[33] The Hague Convention 1970 is now in force in thirteen of the EC Member States: the United Kingdom, Italy, the Netherlands, Luxembourg, Portugal, Denmark, Finland, Sweden, Cyprus, the Czech Republic, Slovakia, Poland and Estonia; and in five other countries: Norway, Switzerland, Australia, Hong Kong and Egypt. The European Union now envisages further reflection on whether it should adopt the Hague Convention 1970.[34]

Article 59(2) makes a saving enabling Finland and Sweden to continue to apply the Nordic Convention 1931 (to which Denmark, Norway and Iceland are also parties) in their mutual relations. It is envisaged that this exception will apply only when both spouses are nationals of a Nordic Member State and their usual place of residence is situated within one of those States.[35] The exception does not extend to other agreements between the Nordic countries; for example, on the recognition and enforcement of administrative decisions on the taking into care and placement of children.[36] There is another saving, made by Article 63, for the Concordats between the Holy See and certain Member States (Portugal, Spain, Italy and Malta),[37] conferring annulment jurisdiction on ecclesiastical courts in respect of canonical marriages.

**Transitional Provisions**

The Brussels II Regulation entered into force on 1st March 2001 for the fourteen existing Member States other than Denmark,[38] and on 1st May 2004 for the ten Member States which joined the European Community on that date.[39] The Brussels IIA Regulation became applicable on 1st March 2005 for the twenty-four existing Member States other than Denmark,[40] and on 1st January 2007 for Bulgaria and Romania.[41] Transitional provisions are laid down by Article 42 of the Brussels II Regulation, and by Article 64 of the Brussels IIA Regulation.

Article 42 of the Brussels II Regulation provides:

(1) The provisions of this Regulation shall apply only to legal proceedings instituted, to documents formally drawn up or registered as authentic instruments and to settlements which have been approved by a court in the course of proceedings after its entry into force.

---

32   See Recital 9 to the Brussels II Regulation; and the Borrás Report, at para 20.
33   See also, in the United Kingdom, reg 9 of SI 2001/310, reg 17 of SI 2005/265, reg 4 of SSI 2001/36, and reg 4 of SSI 2005/42, amending s 45 of the Family Law Act 1986.
34   See JUSTCIV 235, of 6th November 2008.
35   See the Borrás Report, at para 113.
36   See Case C-435/06: *C* [2007] ECR I-10141.
37   Article 63 was extended to Malta by EC Regulation 2116/2004.
38   See Article 46 of the Brussels II Regulation.
39   See the Athens Act of Accession 2003, Article 2.
40   See Article 72 of the Brussels IIA Regulation.
41   See the Luxembourg Act of Accession 2005, Articles 2 and 56; [2005] OJ L157.

(2) Judgments given after the date of entry into force of this Regulation in proceedings instituted before that date shall be recognised and enforced in accordance with the provisions of Chapter III if jurisdiction was founded on rules which accorded with those provided for either in Chapter II of this Regulation or in a convention concluded between the Member State of origin and the Member State addressed which was in force when the proceedings were instituted.

Article 64 of the Brussels IIA Regulation provides:

(1) The provisions of this Regulation shall apply only to legal proceedings instituted, to documents formally drawn up or registered as authentic instruments and to agreements concluded between the parties after its date of application in accordance with Article 72.

(2) Judgments given after the date of application of this Regulation in proceedings instituted before that date but after the date of entry into force of [the Brussels II Regulation] shall be recognised and enforced in accordance with the provisions of Chapter III of this Regulation if jurisdiction was founded on rules which accorded with those provided for either in Chapter II or in [the Brussels II Regulation] or in a convention concluded between the Member State of origin and the Member State addressed which was in force when the proceedings were instituted.

(3) Judgments given before the date of application of this Regulation in proceedings instituted after the entry into force of [the Brussels II Regulation] shall be recognised and enforced in accordance with the provisions of Chapter III of this Regulation provided they relate to divorce, legal separation or marriage annulment or parental responsibility for the children of both spouses on the occasion of these matrimonial proceedings.

(4) Judgments given before the date of application of this Regulation but after the date of entry into force of [the Brussels II Regulation] in proceedings instituted before the date of entry into force of [the Brussels II Regulation] shall be recognised and enforced in accordance with the provisions of Chapter III of this Regulation provided they relate to divorce, legal separation or marriage annulment or parental responsibility for the children of both spouses on the occasion of these matrimonial proceedings and that jurisdiction was founded on rules which accorded with those provided for either in Chapter II of this Regulation or in [the Brussels II Regulation] or in a convention concluded between the Member State of origin and the Member State addressed which was in force when the proceedings were instituted.

## Direct matrimonial jurisdiction

As regards direct jurisdiction to entertain matrimonial proceedings, the effect of the transitional provisions is quite simple. Chapter II of the Brussels IIA Regulation applies to matrimonial proceedings instituted in or after March 2005 in the twenty-four Member States other than Denmark, Bulgaria and Romania; and to matrimonial proceedings instituted in or after January 2007 in Bulgaria or Romania.

Chapter II of the Brussels II Regulation continues to apply to matrimonial proceedings instituted between March 2001 and February 2005 in the fourteen pre-2004 Member States other than Denmark; and to matrimonial proceedings instituted between May 2004 and February 2005 in the ten Member States which joined the European Community in 2004.

Neither of the Regulations applies to matrimonial proceedings instituted before March 2001; nor to matrimonial proceedings instituted before May 2004 in the ten Member States which joined the European Community in 2004;[42] nor to matrimonial proceedings instituted before January 2007 in Bulgaria or Romania.

---

[42]   See Case C-312/09: *Michalias v Ioannou-Michalia*, 17th June 2010.

**Concurrent matrimonial proceedings**

As regards concurrent matrimonial proceedings, brought in different Member States, the analogy of the ruling of the European Court in *Von Horn v Cinnamond*[43] on the transitional operation of the Brussels Convention suggests that the position is as follows.

Article 19 of the Brussels IIA Regulation applies where the second proceeding was instituted at a time when the Brussels IIA Regulation had entered into force for both States, even if the first proceeding was instituted at a time when neither the Brussels IIA Regulation nor the Brussels II Regulation had entered into force for the first State. Similarly, Article 11 of the Brussels II Regulation applies where the second proceeding was instituted at a time when the Brussels II Regulation, but not the Brussels IIA Regulation, had entered into force for both States, even if the first proceeding was instituted at a time when neither the Brussels IIA Regulation nor the Brussels II Regulation had entered into force for the first State.

But where the first proceeding was instituted at a time when neither of the Regulations had entered into force for the first State, the operation of Article 19 of the Brussels IIA Regulation, or Article 11 of the Brussels II Regulation, is modified in the light of the transitional provisions on recognition, so that the obligation of the second court to decline jurisdiction in favour of the first court is eliminated if the first court assumes jurisdiction on a ground which will prevent its eventual decree from qualifying for recognition under the Regulations.

**Recognition of matrimonial decrees**

As regards the recognition of matrimonial decrees, the effect of the transitional provisions is very complicated. Both the date on which the proceeding is instituted and the date on which the decree is granted are relevant.[44] Also relevant are the commencement dates of both the Brussels II Regulation and the Brussels IIA Regulation, and the different commencement dates for different Member States. In the case of the Brussels II Regulation, the commencement date for the fourteen pre-2004 Member States is 1st March 2001, and the commencement date for the ten Member States which joined the European Community in 2004 is 1st May 2004. In the case of the Brussels IIA Regulation, the commencement date for the first twenty-four Member States is 1st March 2005, and the commencement date for Bulgaria and Romania is 1st January 2007. Moreover in certain cases a proviso for jurisdictional review is made applicable, in a manner analogous to that applied in certain cases by Article 66(2)(b) of the Brussels I Regulation.[45]

In the light of the decision of the European Court in *Hadadi v Mesko*,[46] as well as the tentative view expressed by the English Court of Appeal in *D v D*,[47] it now seems clear that, in the context of recognition of a matrimonial decree, every reference to a commencement date of the Brussels II Regulation or the Brussels IIA Regulation must be understood as referring to

---

43   Case C-163/95, [1997] ECR I-5451; discussed at p. 198 above.
44   It seems that, where a decision at first instance granting a divorce decree (or making a custody order) is subsequently affirmed on appeal, the date of grant (or making) for the purposes of the transitional provisions is that of the decision at first instance and not that of the decision on appeal. See *D v D* [2007] EWCA Civ 1277 (CA).
45   See pp. 236–7 above.
46   Case C-168/08, [2009] ECR I-6871; especially at paras 24–8.
47   [2007] EWCA Civ 1277 (CA), especially at paras 35–40.

the date on which the relevant Regulation became applicable for *both* the State of origin *and* the State addressed. Thus in *Hadadi v Mesko*, the European Court (in agreement with Kokott AG) ruled that, in the context of the recognition in France of a Hungarian divorce, the effective date for the commencement of the Brussels II Regulation was 1st May 2004, and accordingly that Article 64(4) of the Brussels IIA Regulation applied to the recognition in France of a Hungarian decree granted in May 2004 on an application made in February 2002.

On this basis, eight types of case can be distinguished. The first type of case is where the original proceeding was instituted and the decree was granted after the commencement date of the Brussels IIA Regulation for both the State of origin and the State addressed. For example, where recognition in England is sought for a French decree granted in 2007 on a petition lodged in 2006; or for a Bulgarian decree granted in 2008 on a petition lodged in 2007. In this situation, Chapter III of the Brussels IIA Regulation is fully applicable, in accordance with Article 64(1).

The second type of case is where the decree was granted after the commencement date of the Brussels IIA Regulation for both the State of origin and the State addressed, but the original proceeding was instituted before that commencement date, and was instituted after the commencement date of the Brussels II Regulation for both of those States. For example, where recognition in England is sought for a French decree granted in 2006 on a petition lodged in 2003, or of a Hungarian decree granted in 2006 on a petition lodged in September 2004. In this situation, Chapter III of the Brussels IIA Regulation is made applicable by Article 64(2), but subject to a proviso for jurisdictional review by reference to Chapter II of the Brussels IIA Regulation, Chapter II of the Brussels II Regulation, and any conventions in force between the States in question when the original proceeding was instituted. It is worthy of note that the effect of the proviso is to reintroduce jurisdictional review in a situation where it had been suppressed by the Brussels II Regulation. Its reintroduction is, to say the least, decidedly odd.

The third type of case is where the decree was granted after the commencement date of the Brussels IIA Regulation for both the State of origin and the State addressed, but the original proceeding was instituted before that commencement date, and also before the commencement date of the Brussels II Regulation for both of those States. For example, where recognition in England is sought for a French decree granted in 2006 on a petition lodged in 2000, or of a Hungarian decree granted in 2006 on a petition lodged in 2003. This case is ignored by Article 64 of the Brussels IIA Regulation. Presumably Chapter III of the Brussels II Regulation continues to apply, in accordance with Article 42(2) thereof, which imposes a proviso for jurisdictional review by reference to Chapter II of the Brussels II Regulation, and to any conventions in force between the States in question when the original proceeding was instituted. Such continuance assumes that the repeal of the Brussels II Regulation by Article 71 of the Brussels IIA Regulation does not extend to cases to which the Brussels IIA Regulation does not apply.[48]

The fourth type of case is where the decree was granted after the commencement date of the Brussels IIA Regulation for both the State of origin and the State addressed, but the orig-

---

[48]    See *T v L* [2009] ILPr 5, where the Irish Supreme Court accepted an analogous argument for the continued operation of the Brussels Convention in cases to which the Brussels I Regulation did not apply.

inal proceeding was instituted before that commencement date, and the Brussels II Regulation had never been in force for both of those States, since one of them is Bulgaria or Romania. For example, where recognition in England is sought for a Bulgarian decree granted in 2007 on a petition lodged in 2006. In *D v D*,[49] the Court of Appeal indicated that in this situation Chapter III of the Brussels IIA Regulation would apply, subject to a proviso for jurisdictional review, in accordance with Article 64(2).

The fifth type of case is where the decree was granted before the commencement date of the Brussels IIA Regulation for both the State of origin and the State addressed, and the original proceeding was instituted after the commencement date of the Brussels II Regulation for both of those States. For example, where recognition in England is sought for a French decree granted in 2004 on a petition lodged in 2003, or of a Hungarian decree granted in January 2005 on a petition lodged in July 2004. In this situation, Chapter III of the Brussels IIA Regulation is fully applicable, in accordance with Article 64(3).

The sixth type of case is where the decree was granted before the commencement date of the Brussels IIA Regulation for both the State of origin and the State addressed, but after the commencement date of the Brussels II Regulation for both of those States, and the original proceeding was instituted before the commencement date of the Brussels II Regulation for both of those States. For example, where recognition in England is sought for a Greek decree granted in April 2001 on a petition lodged in 2000;[50] or for an Irish decree of judicial separation granted in 2002 on a petition lodged in 1999;[51] or of a Hungarian decree granted in May 2004 on a petition lodged in February 2002.[52] In this situation, Chapter III of the Brussels IIA Regulation is made applicable by Article 64(4), but subject to a proviso for jurisdictional review by reference to Chapter II of the Brussels IIA Regulation, Chapter II of the Brussels II Regulation, and any conventions in force between the States in question when the original proceeding was instituted.

The seventh type of case is where the decree was granted before the commencement date of the Brussels IIA Regulation for both the State of origin and the State addressed, and before the commencement date of the Brussels II Regulation for both of those States. For example, where recognition in England is sought for a French decree granted in 2000, or of a Hungarian decree granted in 2003. In this situation, no European Union legislation is applicable.[53]

The eighth type of case is where the decree was granted before the commencement date of the Brussels IIA Regulation for both the State or origin and the State addressed, and the Brussels II Regulation had never been in force for both of those States. For example, where recognition in England is sought for a Romanian decree granted in 2006.[54] In this situation, no European Union legislation is applicable.

In several of the eight types of case, the recognition of a decree is subjected to review by the court addressed of the jurisdiction of the original court. Thus Article 64(2) and (4) of the Brussels IIA Regulation, which apply in the second, fourth and sixth types of case, require a

---

[49]   [2007] EWCA Civ 1277 (CA), especially at paras 35–40.
[50]   See *D v D* [2006] 2 FLR 825 (Bodey J).
[51]   See *W v W* [2005] EWHC 1811 (Fam) (Singer J).
[52]   See Case C-168/08: *Hadadi v Mesko* [2009] ECR I-6871.
[53]   See *T v L* [2009] ILPr 5 (Irish Supreme Court), affirming *DT v FL* [2007] ILPr 56 (McKechnie J in the Irish High Court), on the recognition in Ireland of a Dutch divorce decree, granted in 1994.
[54]   See *D v D* [2007] EWCA Civ 1277 (CA).

decree to be recognised if jurisdiction was founded on rules which accorded with those provided for either in the Brussels IIA Regulation, or in the Brussels II Regulation, or in a convention which was in force between the State of origin and the State addressed when the original proceeding was instituted. Similarly, Article 42(2) of the Brussels II Regulation, which applies in the third type of case, requires a decree to be recognised if jurisdiction was founded on rules which accorded with those provided for either in the Brussels II Regulation, or in a convention which was in force between the State of origin and the State addressed when the original proceeding was instituted. It seems that, for the necessary accordance to be established, it is sufficient either that the original court had explicitly assumed jurisdiction on a basis similar to one applicable under a relevant Regulation or convention,[55] or that the court addressed finds that a jurisdictional base accepted by a relevant Regulation or convention had in fact existed.[56]

# DIRECT JURISDICTION

In Chapter II of the Brussels IIA Regulation, Sections 1 (Articles 3–7) and Section 3 (Articles 16–20) deal with direct jurisdiction to entertain petitions for divorce, separation or annulment.[57] Articles 3–5 create unified rules on the existence of jurisdiction. These are based mainly on the habitual residence of one or both of the spouses, but a lesser role is played by nationality or domicile. Articles 6 and 7 deal with the exclusive nature of the unified jurisdiction, and provide also for residual jurisdiction where the unified rules do not confer jurisdiction on any Member State. Articles 16–20 deal with a court's obligation to decline jurisdiction of its own motion, notification of the respondent, concurrent proceedings in different Member States, and provisional or protective measures.

## The Unified Grounds

Article 3 of the Brussels IIA Regulation creates unified rules on direct jurisdiction to entertain petitions for divorce, separation or annulment, based mainly on the habitual residence of one or both of the spouses at the date of the application. A lesser role is played by nationality; and in relation to the United Kingdom and Ireland the concept of domicile, as understood in British and Irish laws, is substituted for nationality.[58] Several jurisdictional bases are offered, and there is no prioritisation, except in favour of the court first seised. Moreover, the unified rules take no account of any agreement between the spouses as to the competent court.[59] Articles 4 and 5 extend the jurisdiction conferred by Article 3 in relation to counter-claims and to the conversion of a separation into a divorce.

---

55     See Case C-435/06: *C* [2007] ECR I-10141, treating a finding of 'residence' as similar to habitual residence.

56     See Case C-168/08: *Hadadi v Mesko* [2009] ECR I-6871, especially at paras 29–30, in which it was considered sufficient that both spouses were nationals of the State of origin. Cf. *W v W* [2005] EWHC 1811 (Fam) (Singer J).

57     These provisions echo Articles 2 and 5–12 of the Brussels II Regulation.

58     See Articles 3(1)(a)(vi), 3(1)(b) and 3(2).

59     Article 1(2) of the Rome III Proposal envisaged the insertion of a new Article 3A into the

It seems clear, and was recognised by Sheehan J in *O'K v A*,[60] that the unified rules on jurisdiction over matrimonial proceedings, specified by Articles 3–5 of the Brussels IIA Regulation, have a similar mandatory character to the unified rules specified for civil and commercial matters by the Brussels I Regulation, and thus eliminate any judicial discretion on the part of a court of a Member State on which they confer jurisdiction to decline jurisdiction in favour of a supposedly more appropriate court of a non-member country.

### Habitual residence

Article 3(1)(a) of the Brussels IIA Regulation provides for jurisdiction arising from the habitual residence of one or both of the spouses. By Article 3(1)(a)(i) and (iii), jurisdiction is conferred on the courts of the Member State in which both spouses were, or the respondent was, habitually resident at the date of the application. By Article 3(1)(a)(iv), in the case of a joint application, jurisdiction is conferred on the courts of the Member State in which either of the spouses was habitually resident at that date.

Where only the petitioner is habitually resident in the forum State at the date of the application, a further connection is required. This may take any of three alternative forms. The first alternative, specified by Article 3(1)(a)(ii), is that the last common habitual residence of the spouses was in the forum State. The second alternative, specified by Article 3(1)(a)(v), is that the petitioner had habitually resided in the forum State for at least a year immediately before the application was made. The third alternative, specified by Article 3(1)(a)(vi), is that the petitioner had habitually resided in the forum State for at least six months immediately before the application was made,[61] and in addition that the petitioner is a national of or is domiciled in the forum State; the reference to nationality applying where the forum State is a Member State other than the United Kingdom and Ireland, and the reference to domicile applying where the forum State is the United Kingdom or Ireland.

Jurisdiction based on habitual residence is available under Article 3(1)(a) even if both spouses are nationals of a non-member State,[62] and even if the marriage was celebrated in a non-member State.[63]

By Article 66(a)–(b), with regard to a Member State in which two or more systems of law or sets of rules concerning matters governed by the Regulation apply in different territorial units, any reference to habitual residence in that Member State refers to habitual residence in a territorial unit, and any reference to nationality, or in the case of the United Kingdom domi-

---

Brussels IIA Regulation, so as to provide, in proceedings for divorce and legal separation (but not annulment), for a new unified ground of jurisdiction, based on an agreement between the spouses conferring jurisdiction on a court or the courts of a Member State with which they had a substantial connection, either by virtue of a ground of unified jurisdiction accepted by Article 3, or by virtue of its being the place of their last common habitual residence for a minimum period of three years, or by virtue of one of the spouses being its national or, in the case of the United Kingdom and Ireland, having his or her domicile in its territory. Such an agreement would have had to be expressed in writing and signed by both spouses, not later than the time at which the court was seised.

[60]   [2008] IEHC 243 (Irish High Court).

[61]   There must be habitual residence, and not merely residence, for the six-month period; see per Bennett J in *Munro v Munro* [2008] 1 FLR 1613, rejecting the contrary view of Munby J in *Marinos v Marinos* [2007] 2 FLR 1018.

[62]   See *Sulaiman v Juffali* [2002] 1 FLR 479 (Munby J).

[63]   See *Kaur v Singh* [2005] SCLR 1000 (Outer House).

cile, refers to the territorial unit designated by the law of that State.[64] In the United Kingdom, the effect of Article 66, along with the ancillary British legislation,[65] seems to be that, for the purpose of the unified grounds, each territory of the United Kingdom to which the Regulation applies (that is: England and Wales; Scotland; Northern Ireland; and Gibraltar) must be treated as a separate Member State, and the jurisdiction of the courts of each such territory must be based on habitual residence and/or domicile located in that territory, rather than in the United Kingdom as a whole. Thus no court in the United Kingdom will have jurisdiction under Article 3(1)(a)(vi) where the petitioner has been habitually resident in England for between six and twelve months and is domiciled in Scotland. Although, in such a case, the Scottish courts may in some circumstances have residual jurisdiction under Article 7, this would not exist if, for example, the respondent spouse were habitually resident in France.

Neither the Brussels II Regulation nor the Brussels IIA Regulation provides an explicit definition[66] of habitual residence. The Borrás Report[66] referred to the definition given in other contexts by the European Court,[67] which looks to the place where the person had established, on a fixed basis, his permanent or habitual centre of interests, with all the relevant facts being taken into account for the purpose of determining such residence. But in Case C-523/07: *A*,[68] which involved the reference by Article 8(1) of the Brussels IIA Regulation to the habitual residence of a child as the principal basis of jurisdiction over proceedings concerning parental responsibility,[69] the European Court emphasised that the terms of a provision of European Union law which makes no express reference to the law of the Member States for the purpose of determining its meaning and scope must normally be given an autonomous and uniform interpretation throughout the European Union, having regard to the context of the provision and the objective pursued by the legislation in question. Thus determination of the meaning and scope of the concept of the habitual residence of a child must be made in the light of the context of the provisions and the objective of the Regulation, and in particular of Recital 12, which indicates that the grounds of jurisdiction were shaped in the light of the best interests of the child and the criterion of proximity. The case-law of the Court relating to the concept of habitual residence in other areas of European law could not be directly transposed in the context of the assessment of the habitual residence of children for the purposes of Article 8(1) of the Regulation.

Thus it is clear that, for the purpose of matrimonial jurisdiction under the Brussels II and IIA Regulations, the concept of the habitual residence of a spouse must be defined by European Union law, rather than referred to the law of the forum State. The European Court must devise a suitable definition, in the light of the purposes of the Regulation. With a view to facilitating this process, it seems useful to summarise the rules which have emerged from the substantial English case-law on the concept.

---

[64] Article 66 echoes Article 41 of the Brussels II Regulation.

[65] See ss 5 and 7 of the Domicile and Matrimonial Proceedings Act 1973, as amended by reg 3 of SI 2001/310, reg 3 of SI 2005/265, reg 2 of SSI 2001/36, and reg 2 of SSI 2005/42.

[66] At para 32.

[67] See Case 76/76: *Di Paolo v Office National de l'Emploi* [1977] ECR 315; Case C-102/91: *Knoch v Bundesanstalt für Arbeit* [1992] ECR I-4341; and Case C-90/97: *Swaddling v Adjudication Officer* [1999] ECR I-1075.

[68] [2009] ECR I-2805.

[69] See pp. 453–7 below.

In the context of matrimonial jurisdiction under the Brussels IIA Regulation, the English courts have in *Marinos v Marinos*[70] and *Munro v Munro*[71] adopted the definition of habitual residence proposed in the Borrás Report: the place where the person had established, on a fixed basis, his permanent or habitual centre of interest, with all the relevant facts being taken into account for the purpose of determining such residence. They have also concluded that for this purpose a person cannot have more than one habitual residence at the same time. Thus where a person divides his or her time between two countries, the real focus of his or her life will be decisive. In this respect, the Regulation departs from the traditional English approach to habitual residence in the context of matrimonial jurisdiction, under which it was accepted that an adult could have two habitual residences simultaneously, as where a spouse had two marital homes at each of which he or she spent substantial periods.[72]

In other contexts, the traditional English case-law[73] accepts that there is no difference between the habitual residence and the ordinary residence of an individual.[74] It is possible for an individual to have no habitual residence anywhere at a given time.[75] An existing habitual residence is presumed to continue unless the contrary is shown, and the burden of establishing a change in a person's habitual residence rests on the party who asserts such change.[76] More substantively, an adult[77] becomes habitually resident in a country by actually residing there for an appreciable period of time (measured in weeks),[78] voluntarily[79] and with a settled purpose of continuing to reside there, either indefinitely or for a substantial period of time (measured in years).[80] An adult abandons his existing habitual residence in a country by leav-

---

[70]   [2007] 2 FLR 1018 (Munby J).

[71]   [2008] 1 FLR 1613 (Bennett J).

[72]   See *Ikimi v Ikimi* [2002] Fam 72 (CA); *Armstrong v Armstrong* [2003] 2 FLR 375 (Butler-Sloss P); and *Mark v Mark* [2006] 1 AC 98.

[73]   For fuller discussion, see Stone, 'The Concept of Habitual Residence in Private International Law' [2000] Anglo-American Law Review 342. For a different approach to the concept, see Rogerson, 'Habitual Residence: The New Domicile?' (2000) 49 International and Comparative Law Quarterly 86.

[74]   See *Shah v Barnet LBC* [1983] 2 AC 309; *Kapur v Kapur* [1984] FLR 920; *Re F* [1992] 1 FLR 548 (CA); *Re M* [1993] 1 FLR 495 (CA); *Re M* [1996] 1 FLR 887 (CA); *M v M* [1997] 2 FLR 263 (CA); *Nessa v Chief Adjudication Officer* [1999] 1 WLR 1937 (HL); *Ikimi v Ikimi* [2002] Fam 72 (CA); and *Mark v Mark* [2006] 1 AC 98.

[75]   See *Re J* [1990] 2 AC 562; and *Mark v Mark* [2006] 1 AC 98. Cf. *Nessa v Chief Adjudication Officer* [1999] 1 WLR 1937 (HL).

[76]   See *F v S* [1993] 2 FLR 686 (CA); *Re R* [1992] 2 FLR 481 (CA); and *Re M*, 10th August 1995 (CA). See also *P v A-N* [2000] WL 33148939.

[77]   On the habitual residence of a child, see pp. 435–7 below.

[78]   See *Re J* [1990] 2 AC 562; and *Nessa v Chief Adjudication Officer* [1999] 1 WLR 1937 (HL). Cf. Case C-90/97: *Swaddling v Adjudication Officer* [1999] ECR I-1075; *Macrae v Macrae* [1949] P 397 (CA); and *Molson v Molson* [1998] ACWSJ LEXIS 47658 (Alberta).

[79]   See *Shah v Barnet LBC* [1983] 2 AC 309; *Re N* [1993] 2 FLR 124 (CA); *Ex parte Grant*, 31st July 1997; *Ponath v Ponath* 829 FSupp 363 (1993); *D v D* [1996] 1 FLR 574; and *Re A* [1996] 1 WLR 25.

[80]   See *Shah v Barnet LBC* [1983] 2 AC 309; *Re J* [1990] 2 AC 562; *M v M* [1997] 2 FLR 263 (CA); *Dickson v Dickson* [1990] SCLR 692 (Inner House); *D v D* [1996] 1 FLR 574; *Re S* [1994] Fam 70; *Re A* [1996] 1 WLR 25; and *Re M*, 10th August 1995 (CA). See also *Hamilton* [1989] Ont CJ LEXIS 416; *Feder v Evans-Feder* 63 F3d 217 (C3, 1995); and *Re PK and CK* [1994] 1 IR 250. Cf. *Rydder v Rydder* 49 F3d 369 (C8, 1995); *Mozes v Mozes* 19 FSupp2d 1108 (1998); and *Al H v F* [2001] 1 FCR 385 (CA).

ing the country or remaining absent therefrom, with a settled purpose of not returning with a view to resuming residence indefinitely or for a substantial period of time.[81] For these purposes, one month (but no shorter period) constitutes an appreciable period of time;[82] and three years (but no shorter period) constitutes a substantial period of time.[83] Moreover, for the purposes of private law, a person may be habitually resident in a country even though his presence there is illegal under its immigration law. In general such illegality will not affect the existence of an habitual residence, but in rare cases (such as that of a person who is on the run after the making of a deportation order or removal directions) it may indicate that the person lacks the requisite settled purpose.[84]

### Nationality or domicile

In addition to the unified grounds of jurisdiction based on habitual residence specified by Article 3(1)(a) of the Brussels IIA Regulation, Article 3(1)(b) confers jurisdiction on the courts of a Member State (other than the United Kingdom or Ireland) of which, at the date of the application, both spouses are nationals. As regards dual nationality, the Borrás Report explained that each State would apply its own rules, within the framework of general Community rules on the matter.[85] But in *Hadadi v Mesko*,[86] the European Court (in agreement with Kokott AG) ruled that where both spouses hold the nationality of the same two Member States, Article 3(1)(b) of the Regulation confers jurisdiction on the courts of both of those Member States, so that a spouse has the option of seising a court of either of those Member States at his or her choice. The Court rejected an argument that Article 3(1)(b) should be treated as referring to the more effective nationality, with which the spouses have the closer links. It also ruled that, in the context of jurisdictional review in transitional cases under Article 64 of the Regulation, where both spouses hold both the nationality of the Member State of origin and the nationality of the Member State addressed, the court addressed must take into account the fact that the courts of the Member State of origin could have had jurisdiction under Article 3(1)(b). The court addressed cannot treat such spouses as nationals only of the Member State addressed.

In the case of the United Kingdom and Ireland, Articles 3(1)(b) and (2) require instead that both spouses are domiciled in the forum State under its law.[87] This recognises that the

---

81 See *Re J* [1990] 2 AC 562; *Friedrich v Friedrich* 983 F2d 1396 (C6, 1993); *Re M* [1996] 1 FLR 887 (CA); *F v S* [1993] 2 FLR 686 (CA); *Re R* [1992] 2 FLR 481 (CA); and *Re M*, 10th August 1995 (CA).

82 See *Re F* [1992] 1 FLR 548 (CA); *Nessa v Chief Adjudication Officer* [1999] 1 WLR 1937 (HL); *Re B*, 24th July 1995 (CA); and *Al H v F* [2001] 1 FCR 385 (CA). See also *V v B* [1991] 1 FLR 266; *Re B* [1993] 1 FLR 993; *A v A* [1993] 2 FLR 225; *Cameron v Cameron* [1996] SLT 306 (Inner House); *D v D* [1996] 1 FLR 574; *M v M* [1997] 2 FLR 263 (CA); and *Re S* [1998] AC 750. And see, in the Family Court of Australia, *Cooper v Casey* (1995) 18 Fam LR 433, and *Casse* (1995) 19 Fam LR 474; in the United States, *Feder v Evans-Feder* 63 F3d 217 (C3, 1995); and in Canada, *Kinnersley-Turner* (1996) 140 DLR 4th 678 (Ontario CA).

83 See the cases cited in note 80 above.

84 See *Mark v Mark* [2006] 1 AC 98, affirming [2004] 1 FCR 385 (CA). Cf. *Shah v Barnet LBC* [1983] 2 AC 309.

85 See para 33.

86 Case C-168/08, [2009] ECR I-6871.

87 See, for example, *Munro v Munro* [2008] 1 FLR 1613, where Bennett J assumed divorce jurisdiction in respect of a couple who were both domiciled in England but habitually resident in Spain.

traditional Anglo-Irish concept of domicile, with its emphasis on origin and its insistence on permanent residence, intended to last for the rest of one's lifetime, amounts to nationality in disguise.[88] It is noteworthy that the requirement of joint domicile is narrower than the traditional English rule laid down by s 5 of the Domicile and Matrimonial Proceedings Act 1973, under which the domicile of either spouse at the institution of the proceedings sufficed.

By Article 66(a) and (b), with regard to a Member State in which two or more systems of law or sets of rules concerning matters governed by the Regulation apply in different territorial units, any reference to habitual residence in that Member State refers to habitual residence in a territorial unit, and any reference to nationality, or in the case of the United Kingdom to domicile, refers to the territorial unit designated by the law of that State.[89] In the United Kingdom, the effect of Article 66, along with the ancillary British legislation,[90] seems to be that, for the purpose of the unified grounds, each territory of the United Kingdom to which the Regulation applies (that is: England and Wales; Scotland; Northern Ireland; and Gibraltar) must be treated as a separate Member State, and the jurisdiction of the courts of each such territory must be based on habitual residence and/or domicile located in that territory, rather than in the United Kingdom as a whole. Thus no court in the United Kingdom will have jurisdiction under Article 3(1)(b) where the petitioner is domiciled in England and the respondent is domiciled in Scotland. Although, in such a case, both the English and the Scottish courts may in some circumstances have residual jurisdiction under Article 7, this would not exist if, for example, the respondent spouse were habitually resident in France.

**Extended jurisdiction**

The jurisdiction of a court which has been properly seised under Article 3 is extended by Articles 4 and 5, which enable it to entertain a matrimonial counterclaim, or to convert a legal separation which it has granted into a divorce, even if the connection required by Article 3 has meanwhile disappeared.

**Residual Grounds**

Articles 6 and 7 of the Brussels IIA Regulation[91] deal with the exclusive nature of the unified grounds of jurisdiction, and provide also for residual jurisdiction where no court of any Member State is competent on the unified grounds. They are modelled, rather unwisely, on Articles 3 and 4 of the Brussels I Regulation. But they depart confusingly from that model in that there is some overlap between Article 6 and Article 7, which makes their effect not entirely clear.

Article 6, on the exclusive nature of jurisdiction under Articles 3–5, provides:

---

[88]    See Stone, *The Conflict of Laws* (Longman, 1995), chapter 2. See also *Munro v Munro* [2008] 1 FLR 1613, where Bennett J reaffirmed that, to establish a change of domicile, there must be cogent evidence of an unequivocal act and an unequivocal intention.

[89]    Article 66 echoes Article 41 of the Brussels II Regulation.

[90]    See ss 5 and 7 of the Domicile and Matrimonial Proceedings Act 1973, as amended by reg 3 of SI 2001/310, reg 3 of SI 2005/265, reg 2 of SSI 2001/36, and reg 2 of SSI 2005/42.

[91]    Articles 6 and 7 of the Brussels IIA Regulation echo Articles 7 and 8 of the Brussels II Regulation.

A spouse who:
(a) is habitually resident in the territory of a Member State; or
(b) is a national of a Member State, or, in the case of the United Kingdom and Ireland, has his or her 'domicile' in the territory of one of the latter Member States, may be sued in another Member State only in accordance with Articles 3, 4 and 5.

Article 7, on residual jurisdiction, provides:

(1) Where no court of a Member State has jurisdiction pursuant to Articles 3, 4 and 5, jurisdiction shall be determined, in each Member State, by the laws of that State.
(2) As against a respondent who is not habitually resident and is not either a national of a Member State or, in the case of the United Kingdom and Ireland, does not have his 'domicile' within the territory of one of the latter Member States, any national of a Member State who is habitually resident within the territory of another Member State may, like the nationals of that State, avail himself of the rules of jurisdiction applicable in that State.

The effect of Articles 6 and 7 is probably as follows. Firstly, where the unified rules (laid down by Articles 3–5) confer jurisdiction on the courts of at least one Member State, the jurisdiction so conferred on the courts of that or those Member States is exclusive. The Regulation mandatorily deprives the courts of the other Member States of jurisdiction, and it is not open to an excluded State to confer jurisdiction on its courts on other grounds. This is the case, for example, whenever the respondent is habitually resident in a Member State. Accordingly, in *Lopez v Lopez Lizazo*,[92] the European Court confirmed that, under Articles 6 and 7 of the Brussels IIA Regulation, the courts of a Member State cannot base their jurisdiction to hear a divorce petition on their national law, if the courts of another Member State have jurisdiction under Article 3 of the Regulation, even if the respondent is not habitually resident in a Member State and is not a national of a Member State. Thus the Swedish courts lacked jurisdiction to entertain a divorce petition filed by a wife who was of Swedish nationality but had been habitually resident for over a year in France, which was also the last common habitual residence of the couple, against a husband who was a national of and was habitually resident in Cuba.

Secondly, where the unified rules do not confer jurisdiction on the courts of any Member State, but the respondent is a national of a Member State which uses nationality, or is domiciled in a Member State which uses domicile, then the State of nationality or domicile is free, but not bound, to confer jurisdiction on its courts. Further, whether the State of nationality or domicile accepts jurisdiction or not, the Regulation deprives the other Member States of jurisdiction. This applies, for example, where both spouses are habitually resident in Argentina, and the petitioner is an Argentinian national domiciled in Argentina, but the respondent is a German national domiciled in England. In those circumstances, the Regulation permits both Germany and England to confer jurisdiction on their own courts, but whether or not either does so, the Regulation deprives the French courts of jurisdiction. Moreover, the result is the same even if the petitioner has habitually resided in France for a short period, not satisfying the requirements of Article 3.

Thirdly, where the unified rules do not confer jurisdiction on the courts of any Member State, and the respondent is not a national of a Member State which uses nationality, nor

---

[92]    Case C-68/07, [2007] ECR I-10403.

domiciled in a Member State which uses domicile, then it is open to the law of any Member State to confer jurisdiction on its courts on any ground, such as the petitioner's habitual residence merely at the moment when the proceedings are commenced, or the petitioner's domicile or nationality. But a State which confers such jurisdiction on the basis of the petitioner's nationality must also do so in favour of a petitioner who is a national of another Member State and is habitually resident in the forum State. Thus, for example, where the respondent is an Argentinian national domiciled and habitually resident in Argentina, the United Kingdom is permitted to retain its traditional rule creating English jurisdiction on the basis of the petitioner's English domicile, or to introduce a rule creating English jurisdiction on the basis of the petitioner's English habitual residence at the moment of the application alone. Similarly, in the case of such a respondent, France is permitted to maintain its rule basing jurisdiction on the petitioner's French nationality, but is then required to accept as an alternative that the petitioner is a Dutch national and is habitually resident in France.

It seems very regrettable that the Regulation leaves such options to each Member State,[93] rather than establishing a fully harmonised set of jurisdictional bases. However that may be, in the United Kingdom, reg 3 of the European Communities (Matrimonial Jurisdiction and Judgments) Regulations 2001 (SI 2001/310) has ensured that the English courts will have matrimonial jurisdiction, insofar as Articles 6 and 7 of the Regulation permit, where either of the spouses is domiciled in England at the commencement of the proceedings; and reg 2 of the European Communities (Matrimonial Jurisdiction and Judgments) (Scotland) Regulations 2001 (SSI 2001/36) has made corresponding provision where either spouse is domiciled in Scotland. These provisions make the minimum changes necessary to accommodate the Regulation, and decline the opportunity offered to create English or Scottish jurisdiction based on the petitioner's habitual residence merely at the commencement of the proceedings.

The Rome III Proposal envisaged the deletion of Article 6 of the Brussels IIA Regulation, and the replacement of Article 7 by a harmonised provision. This would have applied where neither of the spouses was habitually resident in a Member State, and they did not have a common nationality of a Member State, nor a common domicile in the United Kingdom or Ireland. In such a case, the courts of a Member State would have been competent where either: (a) the spouses had had their common previous habitual residence in the forum State for at least three years; or (b) one of the spouses had the nationality of the forum State, or, in the case of United Kingdom and Ireland, had his or her domicile therein. It seems regrettable that this aspect of the Proposal has not been adopted.

### Exercise of Jurisdiction

Like the Brussels I Regulation on civil jurisdiction and judgments, Chapter II of the Brussels IIA Regulation contains (in Articles 16–20) provisions on a court's obligation to decline jurisdiction of its own motion, on notification of the respondent, on concurrent proceedings in different Member States, and on provisional or protective measures. On these issues, there are a number of departures from Articles 25–31 of the Brussels I Regulation.[94]

---

[93]    On existing bases in various Member States, which may be retained under Articles 6 and 7, see the Borrás Report at para 47.

[94]    On Articles 25–31 of the Brussels I Regulation, see Chapters 3, 6, 8 and 9 above.

## Declining jurisdiction of the court's own motion

By Article 17 of the Brussels IIA Regulation, where a court of a Member State is seised of a case over which it has no jurisdiction under the Regulation and over which a court of another Member State has jurisdiction by virtue of the Regulation, it must declare of its own motion that it has no jurisdiction. In contrast with Article 26(1) of the Brussels I Regulation, this applies even if the respondent has entered an appearance.

## Notification of the respondent

By Article 18(1) of the Brussels IIA Regulation, where a respondent habitually resident in a State other than the forum State does not enter an appearance, the court must stay its proceedings so long as it is not shown that the respondent has been able to receive the document instituting the proceedings or an equivalent document in sufficient time to enable him to arrange for his defence, or that all necessary steps have been taken to this end. This resembles Article 26(2) of the Brussels I Regulation, but applies even if the respondent is habitually resident in a non-member country.

Article 18(2) and (3) of the Brussels IIA Regulation echo Article 26(3) and (4) of the Brussels I Regulation in substituting Article 19 of EC Regulation 1393/2007 and Article 15 of the Hague Convention 1965, where relevant.[95]

## Concurrent proceedings

Article 19(1) and (3) of the Brussels IIA Regulation applies where matrimonial proceedings between the same parties are simultaneously pending in different Member States.[96] It follows the provisions of the Brussels I Regulation on similar (rather than merely related) proceedings in mandatorily requiring the court subsequently seised to stay its proceedings of its own motion until such time as the jurisdiction of the court first seised is established, and then to decline jurisdiction in favour of the first court. But it applies this obligation to matrimonial proceedings even where they do not involve the same cause of action (for example, where the first proceeding is for divorce, and the second is for annulment), and makes no separate provision for dissimilar but related proceedings.

Article 16 of the Brussels IIA Regulation follows Article 30 of the Brussels I Regulation in specifying that a court is seised at the issue, rather than the service, of the document instituting the proceedings. For this purpose, a French court is seised of non-consensual divorce proceedings at the issue of an application for leave to petition for divorce, even though this application is followed by proceedings designed to achieve reconciliation, and eventually by the issue of an actual petition for divorce, after the attempted reconciliation has failed and the court has given the leave requested.[97] Moreover, where there are concurrent proceedings in different Member States and there is a dispute as to which of the courts was first seised, it is

---

[95] See pp. 62–8 above.

[96] As in the case of Article 27 of the Brussels I Regulation, Article 19 of the Brussels IIA Regulation does not apply where the first proceeding has been terminated by a judgment determining the claim (such as a decision granting a divorce decree). See *DT v FL* [2007] ILPr 56 (McKechnie J in the Irish High Court).

[97] See *Chorley v Chorley* [2005] 2 FLR 38 (CA), reversing *C v C* [2004] EWHC 1959 (Fam). See also *YNR v MN* [2005] 4 IR 552 (O'Higgins J).

open to one of the courts involved to stay its own proceedings, pending a decision of the point by the court of the other Member State.[98]

A further provision in Article 19(3) of the Brussels IIA Regulation specifies that where the court subsequently seised declines jurisdiction in favour of the court first seised, the party who brought the subsequent proceeding may bring that claim before the court first seised. This seems certain to produce major problems, especially in cases where the second court declines jurisdiction to entertain annulment proceedings, and annulment is unknown to the law of the first country (as in Sweden and Finland). The Borrás Report suggests that in such a case the Swedish court would grant a divorce on the ground in question, but that a court of the second country could eventually declare that the decree took effect there as an annulment.[99] It is difficult to see any warrant in the wording of the Regulation, or indeed in common sense or legal principle, for that solution. Another problematic case which may, perhaps more commonly, arise is where the law of the first country (such as Ireland) provides for much narrower grounds for divorce than that of the second country (such as England). Apparently, the Irish court would be bound to grant a divorce on a foreign ground which its own legislature had deliberately refused to introduce, since no exception in favour of the stringent public policy of the forum State is specified.

### Provisional measures

Article 20 of the Brussels IIA Regulation deals with provisional, including protective, measures. By Article 20(1), the Regulation does not prevent the courts of a Member State from taking in urgent cases such provisional, including protective, measures in respect of persons or assets in the forum State as may be available under the law of the forum State, even if, under the Regulation, the courts of another Member State have jurisdiction as to the substance of the matter. Article 20(2) adds that such measures shall cease to apply when the court of the Member State having substantive jurisdiction under the Regulation has taken the measures which it considers appropriate.

Unlike Article 31 of the Brussels I Regulation,[100] Article 20 of the Brussels IIA Regulation is explicitly limited to urgent cases[101] and to measures in respect of persons or assets located in the forum State. There is a suggestion in the Borrás Report[102] that Article 20 extends to measures which affect matters outside the scope of the Regulation, such as matrimonial property; but this contradicts the European Court's rulings under the Brussels I Regulation[103] and seems difficult to accept. In Case C-523/07: *A*,[104] which involved an order for the taking of children into care, the European Court explained that under Article 20 it is for the law of the forum State to determine the types of measure which may be adopted and the detailed procedural rules for their implementation. It added that the provisional nature of

---

[98]   See *Chorley v Chorley* [2005] 2 FLR 38 (CA), reversing *C v C* [2004] EWHC 1959 (Fam).
[99]   See paras 52–7.
[100]   On Article 31 of the Brussels I Regulation, see pp. 210–13 above.
[101]   On urgency in relation to measures of child protection, see Case C-523/07: *A* [2009] ECR I-2805; *Re ML and AL* [2007] 1 FCR 475 (Mostyn QC); and pp. 462–4 below.
[102]   At para 59.
[103]   See Case 143/78: *De Cavel v De Cavel (No 1)* [1979] ECR 1055; Case 120/79: *De Cavel v De Cavel (No 2)* [1980] ECR 731; and Case 25/81: *CHW v GJH* [1982] ECR 1189.
[104]   [2009] ECR I-2805.

the measures is ensured by Article 20(2), by which they cease to apply when a court of the Member State having substantive jurisdiction has taken the measures which it considers appropriate.

## Choice of Law

The Brussels IIA Regulation regulates the jurisdiction of the courts of the EU Member States to entertain proceedings for divorce, separation or annulment of marriage. It also provides for the recognition of matrimonial decrees between the Member States. But it does not provide rules on choice of law, specifying the country whose law is to be applied in resolving the merits of an application for divorce, separation or annulment. Thus choice of law in matrimonial proceedings remains governed by the conflict rules of the forum State. In the United Kingdom, the grounds for divorce or separation are governed by the lex fori, but issues relating to the validity of a marriage are in general referred, as regards form, to the law of the place of celebration, and, as regards capacity or consent, to the law of the relevant party's domicile at the time of the marriage.[105]

If it had been adopted, the Rome III Proposal[106] would have inserted into the Brussels IIA Regulation a new Chapter IIA (Articles 20A–20E), on the applicable law in matters of divorce and legal separation (but not annulment). Article 20A would have enabled the spouses to designate the law applicable to divorce and legal separation by an agreement in writing, signed by both spouses before the court was seised. Their choice would have been limited to the laws of certain connected countries. The acceptable countries would have been: (a) the State of the last common habitual residence of the spouses, in which one of them was still habitually resident; (b) the State of the nationality of either spouse (or in the case of the United Kingdom and Ireland, the State of the domicile of either spouse); (c) the State where the spouses had resided for at least five years; and (d) the Member State in which the application was lodged.

In the absence of such a choice by the parties, Article 20B would have provided a cascade of choice-of-law rules. The primary rule would have subjected a divorce or legal separation to the law of the State where the spouses had their common habitual residence. Failing that, one would have referred to the law of the State where they had had their last common habitual residence and one of them remained habitually resident. Failing that, one would have referred to the law of the State of which both spouses were nationals (or, in the case of United Kingdom and Ireland, to the law of the State in which both had their domicile). As a last resort, one would have referred to the law of the forum State.

Article 20D would have excluded renvoi, by specifying that the application of a law designated under the Regulation meant the application of the rules of that law other than its rules of private international law. Article 20E would have made a classic saving in favour of the forum's public policy, by specifying that the application of a provision of the law designated by the Regulation could be refused if such application were manifestly incompatible with the public policy of the forum.

---

[105]   See Dicey, Morris and Collins, 14th edition (Sweet & Maxwell, 2006), Rule 77.

[106]   EC Commission Proposal for a Council Regulation amending the Brussels IIA Regulation as regards jurisdiction and introducing rules concerning applicable law in matrimonial matters, presented on 17th July 2006; COM(2006) 399 final.

In view of the failure of the Council in June 2008 to reach agreement on the Rome III Proposal, any EU measure on choice of law for divorce and separation is likely to be adopted under the provisions on enhanced co-operation, and thus to be applicable only in Member States which choose to participate therein.[107]

## RECOGNITION OF MATRIMONIAL DECREES

Chapter III (Articles 21–52) of the Brussels IIA Regulation[108] provides for the recognition in each Member State of decrees of divorce, separation or annulment granted in the other Member States,[109] and for the recognition and enforcement of orders relating to the costs of such proceedings.[110] But it does not apply to negative decisions, refusing to grant a divorce, separation or annulment;[111] nor to findings of fault made in divorce proceedings.[112] Where a divorce is recognised under Chapter III, the effect is to terminate completely the marital status in the State addressed, even if that status had arisen from a different ceremony from the ceremony from which it had arisen in the State of origin.[113]

By Article 21(1) and (4), recognition under Chapter III of the Brussels IIA Regulation is automatic and incidental, no special procedure being required. By Article 27, a court in which incidental recognition is sought may stay its proceedings if an ordinary appeal against the judgment has been lodged in the State of origin. More specifically, Article 21(2) insists that no special procedure may be required for updating the civil-status records of a Member State on the basis of a decree of divorce, separation or annulment given in another Member State, against which no further appeal lies under the law of the State of origin.

A detailed procedure for obtaining a declaration of enforceability is established by Articles 28–39 of the Brussels IIA Regulation. This procedure closely resembles the corresponding procedure provided for in the Brussels I Regulation, especially as regards the issue of certificates by the original court. By Article 21(3) of the Brussels IIA Regulation, an interested party may use the procedure established by Articles 28–39 to apply for a decision that the judgment is or is not recognised. Thus under the Brussels IIA Regulation (in contrast to the Brussels I Regulation), the enforcement procedure can be invoked with a view to obtaining a declaration of non-recognition. In *Rinau*,[114] the European Court confirmed that any interested party can apply for non-recognition of a decree, even if no application for recognition of the decision has been submitted beforehand. It added, however, that in such a situation even the initial application must be dealt with by means of an adversarial procedure, in which the party who is seeking recognition is entitled to make submissions.

---

[107]   See pp. 420–21 above.
[108]   As regards matrimonial decrees, this consolidates Chapter III (Articles 13–35) of the Brussels II Regulation.
[109]   See Articles 1(1)(a) and 2(4).
[110]   See Article 49. Chapter III also provides for the recognition and enforcement of orders relating to parental responsibility for children; see Articles 1(1)(b) and 2(4), and Chapter 17 below.
[111]   See the Borrás Report, at para 60.
[112]   See Recital 10 of the Brussels II Regulation; and the Borrás Report, at para 64.
[113]   See *D v D* [2006] 2 FLR 825 (Bodey J).
[114]   Case C-195/08-PPU, [2008] ECR I-5271.

The exceptions to the general rule in favour of recognition are defined by Articles 22–7 of the Brussels IIA Regulation. Article 26 emphasises that under no circumstances may a decree be reviewed as to its substance, and Article 24 prevents the court addressed from reviewing the jurisdiction of the court of origin. By way of exception, jurisdictional review is required by Article 64 in certain transitional cases,[115] and permitted by Article 59 in situations involving the Nordic Convention 1931, to which Denmark, Sweden, Finland and other Scandinavian countries are party.

Under Article 16 of the Brussels II Regulation, jurisdictional review was permitted in connection with agreements with external countries, analogous to those envisaged by Article 59 of the Brussels Convention, precluding the recognition of judgments based on residual grounds of jurisdiction. But the Brussels IIA Regulation omits any provision corresponding to Article 16 of the Brussels II Regulation. This omission reflects the Commission's view that pre-existing agreements are already protected in accordance with Article 351 of the Treaty on the Functioning of the European Union, and that future agreements affecting the Regulation can only be concluded by the Union.[116]

The substantive grounds for refusal of recognition of matrimonial decrees are specified by Article 22 of the Brussels IIA Regulation. By Article 22(a), recognition must be refused if it would be manifestly contrary to the public policy of the State addressed.[117] But the scope of the public policy proviso is limited by Articles 25 and 26. Not only is the court addressed precluded by Article 26 from reviewing the substance of the decree, but Article 25 prevents the refusal of recognition because the law of the State addressed would not allow divorce, separation or annulment on the same facts. The Borrás Report adds that this refers to both the internal and the private international law of the State addressed.[118] Moreover, it is not against English public policy to recognise a divorce merely because the court of origin regarded the marriage as having resulted from a different ceremony between the spouses from the ceremony from which the marriage had arisen under English conflict rules.[119]

By Article 22(b), recognition of a decree must be refused where it was given in default of appearance, and the respondent was not served with the instituting or an equivalent document in sufficient time and in such a way as to enable the respondent to arrange for his or her defence, unless it is determined that the respondent has accepted the judgment unequivocally. This accords with Article 34(2) of the Brussels I Regulation in insisting on a European Union standard for both the time and the manner of service. But, in contrast to the Brussels I Regulation, it does not require the respondent to seek redress in the State of origin where possible. Unequivocal acceptance could take the form of remarrying in reliance on the

---

[115] See pp. 424–9 above.

[116] See the Commission's Explanatory Memorandum in COM(2002) 222 final, at p. 14. See also Opinion 1/03 (on the new Lugano Convention) [2006] ECR I-1145; and EC Regulation 664/2009, establishing a procedure for the negotiation and conclusion of agreements between Member States and third countries concerning jurisdiction, recognition and enforcement of judgments and decisions in matrimonial matters, matters of parental responsibility and matters relating to maintenance obligations, and the law applicable to matters relating to maintenance obligations, [2009] OJ L200/46, considered at pp. 421–2 above.

[117] The Brussels IIA Regulation, like the Brussels I Regulation, contains no specific provision concerning incidental questions, corresponding to Article 27(4) of the Brussels Convention.

[118] See para 76.

[119] See *D v D* [2006] 2 FLR 825 (Bodey J).

divorce granted,[120] or of an express term in an agreement between the spouses settling their financial relations.[121]

Article 22(c) and (d) require that a matrimonial decree must be refused recognition in certain cases where it is irreconcilable with another judgment given in proceedings between the same parties. The other judgment may have been given in the State addressed, in which case the order in time is immaterial. Alternatively, the other judgment may have been given elsewhere, whether in another Member State or in a non-member country, and in this case it must have been given earlier than the decree in question, and it must fulfil the conditions necessary for its recognition in the State addressed. As the Borrás Report explains,[122] there is no conflict between an earlier separation decree and a subsequent divorce decree, since the separation is replaced by the divorce. On the other hand, an earlier divorce is irreconcilable with a later separation.

The Brussels IIA Regulation contains no provision corresponding to Article 11 of the Hague Convention of 1st June 1970, whereby a State which is obliged to recognise a divorce may not preclude either spouse from remarrying on the ground that the law of another State does not recognise the divorce.[123] Such a provision had been proposed by the European Parliament when consulted on the Brussels II Convention[124] and the Brussels II Regulation, and adopted by the EC Commission in a late version of its proposal for the Brussels II Regulation.[125] Its omission from the Brussels II and IIA Regulations as adopted is presumably founded on the supposition that its express inclusion was unnecessary, since recognition of a divorce necessarily implies recognition of the resulting capacity of the former spouses to remarry. But this supposition has not always been judicially accepted,[126] and the omission can hardly be viewed as other than irresponsible.

---

[120]   See the Borrás Report, at para 70.
[121]   See *D v D* [2006] 2 FLR 825 (Bodey J).
[122]   See para 71.
[123]   This provision is reflected in the United Kingdom by s 50 of the Family Law Act 1986.
[124]   See the EP Resolution of 30th April 1998; A4-131/98.
[125]   See Article 17(2) of the March 2000 version of the Commission proposal; COM(2000) 151 final.
[126]   Contrast *R v Brentwood Registrar ex parte Arias* [1968] 2 QB 956 and *Padolecchia v Padolecchia* [1968] P 314, with *Perrini v Perrini* [1979] 2 All ER 323 and *Lawrence v Lawrence* [1985] Fam 106.

# 17.  Parental responsibility

## INTRODUCTION

### The Brussels IIA Regulation

Within the European Union, proceedings and orders concerning parental responsibility for children (as well as matrimonial proceedings and decrees)[1] are now governed by EC Regulation 2201/2003, which may conveniently be referred to as the Brussels IIA Regulation.[2] The Regulation deals with direct judicial jurisdiction, and the mutual recognition and enforcement of judgments, but not choice of law.

The Brussels IIA Regulation became applicable on 1st March 2005[3] in the twenty-four then Member States other than Denmark,[4] and on 1st January 2007 in Bulgaria and Romania.[5] It has replaced EC Regulation 1347/2000, commonly known as the Brussels II Regulation,[6] which is repealed as from the date of application of the Brussels IIA Regulation.[7] The Brussels II Regulation had entered into force on 1st March 2001 for the fourteen then Member States other than Denmark, and on 1st May 2004 for the ten States which joined the European Community on that date.

As regards parental responsibility, the Brussels II Regulation had confined its scope to proceedings and orders which concerned children of both spouses, and which were instituted or made on the occasion of matrimonial proceedings between the parents.[8] In contrast, the

---

[1]   On matrimonial proceedings and decrees, see Chapter 16 above.

[2]   EC Regulation 2201/2003 concerning Jurisdiction and the Recognition and Enforcement of Judgments in Matrimonial Matters and the Matters of Parental Responsibility, repealing Regulation 1347/2000; [2003] OJ L338/1.

Provisions ancillary to the Brussels IIA Regulation have been made in England by the European Communities (Matrimonial Jurisdiction and Judgments) Regulations 2001 (SI 2001/310), and the European Communities (Jurisdiction and Judgments in Matrimonial and Parental Responsibility Matters) Regulations 2005 (SI 2005/265); and in Scotland by the European Communities (Matrimonial Jurisdiction and Judgments) (Scotland) Regulations 2001 (SSI 2001/36), and the European Communities (Matrimonial and Parental Responsibility Jurisdiction and Judgments) (Scotland) Regulations 2005 (SSI 2005/42).

[3]   See Article 72. For transitional provisions, see Article 64.

[4]   For the exclusion of Denmark, see Recital 31 and Article 2(3).

[5]   See the Luxembourg Act of Accession 2005, Articles 2 and 56; [2005] OJ L157.

[6]   EC Regulation 1347/2000 on Jurisdiction and the Recognition and Enforcement of Judgments in Matrimonial Matters and in Matters of Parental Responsibility for Children of Both Spouses; [2000] OJ L160/19. Assistance in the interpretation of the Brussels II Regulation can be obtained from the Borrás Report, [1998] OJ C221/27.

[7]   See Article 71 of the Brussels IIA Regulation.

[8]   See Articles 1(1)(b) and 13(1). This meant that the issues concerning parental responsibility

Brussels IIA Regulation is not restricted in this way, but applies to proceedings and orders concerning parental responsibility for all children, regardless of whether any marriage or divorce is involved, and even if the parties to the dispute are not parents or even relatives of the child. This expansion in scope is perhaps the most important advance made by the Brussels IIA Regulation. It is on the relevant provisions of the Brussels IIA Regulation that this chapter will be mainly focused.[9]

Another distinctive feature of the Brussels IIA Regulation is that it abolishes the need for a declaration of enforceability in respect of orders for access. In addition, as regards child abduction, it supplements the Hague Convention of 25th October 1980 on the Civil Aspects of International Child Abduction (which may conveniently be referred to as the Hague Convention 1980) by elaborating a stronger solution for cases where a child is abducted between Member States. This involves referring substantive jurisdiction to the courts of the Member State from which the child was abducted, for at least a year after the abduction in the absence of acquiescence; restricting the grounds on which the courts of the Member State to which the child was abducted may refuse to return him, and enabling their refusal to return the child on certain grounds to be overridden by a substantive decision of the courts of the Member State from which he was abducted; and making such substantive decisions to return enforceable in other Member States without the need for a declaration of enforceability.

According to Recital 33, the Brussels IIA Regulation seeks to ensure respect for the fundamental rights of the child, as set out in Article 24 of the Charter of Fundamental Rights of the European Union. But this seems to be merely aspirational, since the Regulation omits the provisions which had been proposed by the Commission[10] declaring that a child has the right to maintain on a regular basis a personal relationship and direct contact with both parents, unless this is contrary to his or her interests, and to be heard on matters relating to parental responsibility over him or her in accordance with his or her age and maturity. Indeed, Recital 19 of the Regulation explains that the hearing of the child plays an important role in the application of the Regulation, but that the Regulation is not intended to modify national procedures applicable. Recital 20 adds that the hearing of a child in another Member State may take place under the arrangements laid down in EC Regulation 1206/2001 on Co-operation between the Courts of the Member States in the Taking of Evidence in Civil or Commercial Matters.[11]

The Brussels IIA Regulation also provides, in Chapter IV (Articles 53–8), for co-operation between Member States through central authorities. Each Member State must designate a central authority to assist with the application of the Regulation.[12] The central authorities

---

had to be closely linked to the matrimonial proceedings, though they did not have to be before the same court; see Recital 11, the Borrás Report at paras 23 and 37, and *Re G* [2004] 1 FLR 378 (CA). It was clearly implied that the proceedings relating to parental responsibility had to be in a court of the same Member State as the matrimonial proceedings; see *C v FC* [2004] 1 FLR 317.

[9]    For the initiatives and proposals which led to the Brussels IIA Regulation, see the French Initiative on access to children, [2000] OJ C234/7; the EC Council's draft Programme of Further Measures for the Implementation of the Principle of Mutual Recognition of Decisions in Civil and Commercial Matters, [2001] OJ C12/1; the EC Commission Working Document of March 2001, JAI A3 / EK - 787, version 5; the EC Commission's Proposal of September 2001, [2001] OJ C332E/269; and the EC Commission's revised Proposal of May 2002, [2002] OJ C203E/155.

[10]    See Articles 3 and 4 of the revised Proposal of May 2002.

[11]    [2001] OJ L174/1. See pp. 217–21 above.

[12]    In England, the International Child Abduction and Access Unit serves as the central authority

are to communicate information on national laws and procedures and take measures to improve the application of the Regulation and strengthen their co-operation. They are also to co-operate on specific cases to achieve the purposes of this Regulation. This involves collecting and exchanging information on the situation of the child, on any procedures under way, and on decisions taken concerning the child; providing information and assistance to holders of parental responsibility seeking the recognition and enforcement of decisions on their territory, in particular concerning rights of access and the return of the child; facilitating communications between courts, in particular in relation to cases of abduction or of transfer between courts; and facilitating agreement between holders of parental responsibility through mediation or other means. Accordingly, a holder of parental responsibility may submit a request for assistance to the central authority of the Member State of his or her habitual residence, or to that of the Member State where the child is habitually resident or present. Moreover, the assistance provided by the central authorities will be free of charge, each central authority bearing its own costs.

## The Hague Convention 1996

At global level, proceedings and orders concerning parental responsibility for children are regulated by the Hague Convention of 19th October 1996 on Jurisdiction, Applicable law, Recognition, Enforcement and Co-operation in Respect of Parental Responsibility and Measures for the Protection of Children, which may conveniently be referred to as the Hague Convention 1996.[13] The Convention entered into force on 1st January 2002. It is now in force between eight EU Member States (Hungary, the Czech Republic, Slovakia, Slovenia, Latvia, Lithuania, Estonia and Bulgaria) and eight other countries (Switzerland, Monaco, Albania, Ukraine, Armenia, Morocco, Australia and Ecuador). It has been signed (but not ratified) by the remaining EU Member States except Malta, and by Croatia. The Convention deals with direct judicial jurisdiction, and the mutual recognition and enforcement of judgments, and also with choice of law. It is clear that many of the provisions of the Brussels IIA Regulation have been strongly influenced by the corresponding provisions of the Convention.

The relation between the Brussels IIA Regulation and the Hague Convention 1996 in an EU Member State which is a party to the Convention is addressed by Articles 61 and 62(1) of the Regulation. By Article 61, the Regulation displaces the Convention in two situations: (a) where the child concerned is habitually resident in a Member State; and (b) as regards the recognition and enforcement in a Member State of a judgment given in another Member State, even if the child concerned is habitually resident in a non-member country which is a contracting party to the Convention. In the first of these situations, the derogation is authorised by Article 52(2) and (4) of the Convention. By Article 62(1), the Convention continues to have effect in relation to matters not governed by the Regulation.

The current policy of the European Union is that all of the Member States (other than Denmark) should become party to the Hague Convention 1996. Accordingly, the EC Council

---

for the purposes of both the Brussels IIA Regulation and the Hague Convention 1980. Provision for co-operation through central authorities is also made by Chapter V (Articles 29-39) of the Hague Convention 1996.

[13] For its text, see (1996) 35 ILM 1391 or [2008] OJ L151/39.

has adopted Decisions 2003/93 and 2008/431,[14] authorising the Member States, in the interest of the Community, to sign and ratify or accede to the Convention. The Decisions also require each of the Member States to make a declaration that, since the Convention allows Contracting Parties a degree of flexibility in order to apply a simple and rapid regime for the recognition and enforcement of judgments, and the European Union rules provide for a system of recognition and enforcement which is at least as favourable as the rules laid down in the Convention, a judgment given in a court of a Member State, in respect of a matter relating to the Convention, will be recognised and enforced in the Member State making the declaration by application of the relevant internal rules of European Union law. The outstanding ratifications or accessions should take place simultaneously and if possible before 5th June 2010.

### Other International Conventions

By Article 60, the Brussels IIA Regulation takes precedence in relations between Member States over certain specified international conventions.[15] But, by Article 62(1), these conventions continue to have effect in relation to matters not governed by the Regulation;[16] and, by Article 62(2), they continue to produce effects between the Member States which are party thereto, except insofar as they conflict with the Regulation.

The specified conventions include the Hague Convention of 5th October 1961 concerning the Powers of Authorities and the Law Applicable in respect of the Protection of Minors, and the European Convention of 20th May 1980 on Recognition and Enforcement of Decisions concerning Custody of Children and on Restoration of Custody of Children.[17] Thus in general a custody order which falls within the scope of the Brussels II Regulation or the Brussels IIA Regulation cannot be enforced under other regimes, such as the European Convention 1980.[18] But it seems that the European Convention 1980 remains applicable to the enforcement of a custody order whose enforcement under the Regulations is prevented by a transitional provision which requires jurisdictional review.[19]

The specified conventions also include the Hague Convention of 25th October 1980 on the Civil Aspects of International Child Abduction, which may conveniently be referred to as the Hague Convention 1980. But with regard to abduction, the provisions of the Regulation are designed to supplement and strengthen, rather than displace, those of the Convention.[20]

---

[14]   See [2003] OJ L48/1 and [2008] OJ L151/36.
[15]   See, similarly, Article 37 of the Brussels II Regulation.
[16]   See, similarly, Article 38(1) of the Brussels II Regulation.
[17]   See also, in the United Kingdom, reg 7 of SI 2005/265 and reg 3 of SSI 2005/42, amending s 12 of the Child Abduction and Custody Act 1985.
[18]   See *Re G* [2004] 1 FLR 378 (CA).
[19]   See *W v W* [2005] EWHC 1811 (Fam) (Singer J), which involved an Irish order made in 2004 in proceedings instituted in 1999, and which could not be enforced under the Brussels IIA Regulation because the requirement of accordance of jurisdictional bases imposed by Article 64(4) was not satisfied.
[20]   On abduction, see pp. 464–75 below.

## Scope

In referring to parental responsibility, the Brussels IIA Regulation appears to cover all types of application or order which are contemplated by s 8 of the (English) Children Act 1989: residence orders, contact orders, prohibited-steps orders, and specific-issue orders.[21] Thus it is convenient to speak of 'custody orders' in a broad sense, referring to all orders relating to children which fall within the Brussels IIA Regulation and s 8 of the 1989 Act.

The Brussels IIA Regulation gives no indication as to the age at which a person ceases to be a child, with the result that in general the issue is remitted to the law of the forum State.[22] In contrast, the Hague Convention 1996 specifies, by Article 2, that it applies to children from the moment of their birth until they reach the age of 18 years, while the Hague Convention 1980, by Article 4, confines its scope to children under the age of 16 years. Since the provisions of the Regulation which deal with child abduction are designed to supplement the Hague Convention 1980, those provisions must similarly be confined to children under the age of 16. Otherwise the English courts will treat references in the Regulation to a child as applying to a person under the age of 18.[23]

By Article 1(1)(b), the Brussels IIA Regulation applies in civil matters relating to the attribution, exercise, delegation, restriction or termination of parental responsibility, whatever the nature of the court or tribunal involved. It extends to administrative proceedings, since Article 2(1)–(2) defines a court as including an authority of a Member State, and a judge as including an official having equivalent powers. By Article 1(2), matters relating to parental responsibility include: (a) rights of custody and rights of access; (b) guardianship, curatorship and similar institutions; (c) the designation and functions of any person or body having charge of the child's person or property, representing or assisting the child; (d) the placement of the child in a foster family or in institutional care; and (e) measures for the protection of the child relating to the administration, conservation or disposal of the child's property.[24] Thus, despite the reference in Article 1(1)(b) to civil matters, the Regulation extends to a decision ordering that a child be taken into care and placed outside his original home in a foster family or a child care unit, adopted in the context of public law rules relating to child protection.[25]

But, by Article 1(3), the Brussels IIA Regulation does not apply to: (a) the establishment or contesting of a parent-child relationship; (b) decisions on adoption, measures preparatory to adoption, or the annulment or revocation of adoption;[26] (c) the name and forenames of the child; (d) emancipation; (e) maintenance obligations;[27] (f) trusts or succession; and (g)

---

[21]   See *Re G* [2004] 1 FLR 378 (CA); and *Re A* [2004] 1 All ER 912 (Sumner J).

[22]   See per Singer J in *Re A, HA v MB* [2007] EWHC 2016 (Fam), at para 1.

[23]   See the Children Act 1989, s 105(1); and Dicey, Morris and Collins, 14th edition, Rule 95.

[24]   Articles 1(1)(b) and (2) of the Regulation resemble Article 3 of the Hague Convention 1996.

[25]   See Case C-435/06: *C* [2007] ECR I-10141; and Case C-523/07: *A* [2009] ECR I-2805.

[26]   After joining the Hague Conference on Private International Law, the European Union has indicated that it will leave to the Member States individually the adoption of the Hague Convention of 29th May 1993 on Inter-country Adoption, since the matter is regarded as of low priority for the Community; see JUSTCIV 235, of 6th November 2008. In fact, the Hague Convention 1993 is currently in force between seventy-eight countries, which include all thirty EU Member States and Lugano Convention countries, with the exception of Ireland and Greece.

[27]   Applications and orders for the maintenance of a child are at present within the scope of the Brussels I Regulation, and will instead be governed by EC Regulation 4/2009, [2009] OJ L7/1, when it enters into application. See Chapter 18 below.

measures taken as a result of criminal offences committed by children. The last limb is intended to exclude from the Regulation both criminal proceedings and subsequent civil measures of protection, such as the placement of the child in an institution.[28] Recital 10 explains further that the Regulation is not intended to apply to matters relating to social security, public measures of a general nature in matters of education or health, or to decisions on the right of asylum and on immigration.[29]

In addition, Article 2(7) defines parental responsibility as referring to all rights and duties relating to the person or the property of a child which are given to a natural or legal person by judgment, by operation of law or by an agreement having legal effect, and as including rights of custody and rights of access. By Article 2(8), a holder of parental responsibility is any person having parental responsibility over a child. By Article 2(9), rights of custody include rights and duties relating to the care of the person of a child, and in particular the right to determine the child's place of residence. By Article 2(10), rights of access include the right to take a child to a place other than his or her habitual residence for a limited period of time. By Article 2(11), custody is considered to be exercised jointly when, pursuant to a judgment or by operation of law, one holder of parental responsibility cannot decide on the child's place of residence without the consent of another holder of parental responsibility.

These definitions of parental responsibility and rights of custody and access resemble those used in the Hague Convention 1980[30] and the Hague Convention 1996.[31] But the Regulation fails to specify the law which determines whether a person holds parental responsibility, so that in general the conflict rules of the forum State remain applicable to this issue. In child abduction cases, Article 3 of the Hague Convention 1980 indicates that the relevant rights of custody must have existed under the law of the State in which the child was habitually resident immediately before the removal or retention, and since the provisions of the Regulation which deal with abduction are designed to supplement that Convention, the same must apply for the purpose of those provisions. Otherwise, however, a court applying the Regulation will determine the holders of parental responsibility in accordance with its own conflict rules, or, where the forum State is a party to the Hague Convention 1996, with the rules specified by Chapter III (Articles 15–22) of that Convention, which refer to the habitual residence of the child. Accordingly, at present, the English courts will determine the holders of parental responsibility in accordance with English internal law.[32]

By Article 16(1) of the Hague Convention 1996, the attribution or extinction of parental responsibility by operation of law, without the intervention of a judicial or administrative authority, is governed by the law of the State of the habitual residence of the child. By Article 16(2), the attribution or extinction of parental responsibility by an agreement or a unilateral act, without intervention of a judicial or administrative authority, is governed by the law of the State of the child's habitual residence at the time when the agreement or unilateral act takes effect. But where the child's habitual residence changes, Article 16(3) and (4) provide

---

[28]    See the Explanatory Memorandum to the EC Commission's revised Proposal of May 2002, COM(2002) 222 final, at p. 6.

[29]    Article 1(3) and Recital 10 of the Regulation resemble Article 4 of the Hague Convention 1996.

[30]    See Articles 3 and 5 of the Hague Convention 1980.

[31]    See Articles 1(2) and 3(b) of the Hague Convention 1996.

[32]    See Dicey, Morris and Collins, 14th edition, Rule 95.

both for the continuance of parental responsibility which exists under the law of the State of the child's former habitual residence, and in addition for the attribution of parental responsibility by operation of law in accordance with the law of the State of the new habitual residence to a person who does not already have such responsibility. By Article 17, the exercise of parental responsibility is governed by the law of the State of the child's habitual residence; and if the child's habitual residence changes, it is governed by the law of the State of the new habitual residence. Article 18 specifies that parental responsibility may be terminated, or the conditions of its exercise modified, by measures taken under the Convention. By Article 20, these provisions apply even if the law designated thereby is the law of a non-contracting State. By Article 21(1), in general the relevant law is the internal law of the relevant State, rather than its choice-of-law rules; but Article 21(2) makes an exception where Article 16 designates the law of a non-contracting State, and the choice-of-law rules of that State designate the law of another non-contracting State, and the latter State would apply its own law. By Article 22, the application of a law designated by the Chapter can be refused if such application would be manifestly contrary to public policy, taking into account the best interests of the child.

As regards the child's property, Article 1(2)(e) of the Brussels IIA Regulation specifies that the Regulation is applicable to measures for the protection of the child relating to the administration, conservation or disposal of the child's property. Recital 9 explains that in this respect the Regulation is confined to measures for the protection of the child, and that such measures relate to the designation and functions of a person or body having charge of the child's property, representing or assisting the child, and to the administration, conservation or disposal of the child's property. Thus the Regulation applies in cases where the parents are in dispute as regards the administration of the child's property. But measures relating to a child's property which do not concern the protection of the child continue to be governed by the Brussels I Regulation.[33]

## Transitional Provisions

The Brussels II Regulation entered into force on 1st March 2001 for the fourteen then Member States other than Denmark,[34] and on 1st May 2004 for the ten Member States which joined the European Community on that date.[35] The Brussels IIA Regulation became applicable on 1st March 2005 for the twenty-four then Member States other than Denmark,[36] and on 1st January 2007 for Bulgaria and Romania.[37]

The transitional provisions laid down by Article 42 of the Brussels II Regulation and by Article 64 of the Brussels IIA Regulation extend to custody applications and orders, as well as to matrimonial petitions and decrees.[38] For this purpose, where a custody application or

---

[33]    See also Article 3(g) of the Hague Convention 1996, by which the Convention applies to the administration, conservation or disposal of the child's property.

[34]    See Article 46 of the Brussels II Regulation.

[35]    See the Athens Act of Accession 2003, Article 2.

[36]    See Article 72 of the Brussels IIA Regulation.

[37]    See the Luxembourg Act of Accession 2005, Articles 2 and 56; [2005] OJ L157.

[38]    On these provisions, and their application to matrimonial petitions and decrees, see pp. 424–9 above.

order is made on the occasion of matrimonial proceedings between the child's parents, it is treated in the same way as a matrimonial petition or decree, but other custody applications and orders are treated differently.

### Direct jurisdiction over custody proceedings

As regards direct jurisdiction to entertain proceedings relating to parental responsibility, the effect of the transitional provisions is fairly simple. Chapter II of the Brussels IIA Regulation applies to custody proceedings instituted in or after March 2005 in the twenty-four Member States other than Denmark, Bulgaria and Romania; and to proceedings instituted in or after January 2007 in Bulgaria or Romania. In such cases, it is immaterial whether the custody proceedings are connected with matrimonial proceedings.

Chapter II of the Brussels II Regulation continues to apply to custody proceedings which were instituted on the occasion of matrimonial proceedings between the child's parents, if the custody proceedings were instituted between March 2001 and February 2005 in the fourteen pre-2004 Member States other than Denmark, or between May 2004 and February 2005 in the ten Member States which joined the European Community in 2004.

Neither of the Regulations applies to custody proceedings instituted before March 2001; nor to custody proceedings instituted before May 2004 in the ten Member States which joined the European Community in 2004; nor to custody proceedings instituted before March 2005 otherwise than on the occasion of matrimonial proceedings between the child's parents; nor to custody proceedings instituted before January 2007 in Bulgaria or Romania.

### Custody orders connected with matrimonial proceedings

As regards the recognition and enforcement of custody orders made in proceedings instituted on the occasion of matrimonial proceedings, Article 42 of the Brussels II Regulation and Article 64 of the Brussels IIA Regulation establish the same (extremely complicated) transitional rules as apply to the recognition of matrimonial decrees.[39]

### Custody orders not connected with matrimonial proceedings

As regards the recognition and enforcement of custody orders made in proceedings instituted otherwise than on the occasion of matrimonial proceedings, it is only the Brussels IIA Regulation which can apply, and only the transitional provisions contained in Article 64(1) and (2) which can be relevant.

Article 64(1) makes Chapter III of the Brussels IIA Regulation fully applicable to such orders where the original proceeding was instituted and the order was made[40] after the commencement date of the Regulation for both the State of origin and the State addressed. Unless the State or origin or the State addressed is Bulgaria or Romania, the relevant commencement date is 1st March 2005. If the State of origin or the State addressed is Bulgaria or Romania, the relevant commencement date is 1st January 2007.

---

[39]   See pp. 424–9 above.

[40]   It seems that, where a decision at first instance making a custody order is subsequently affirmed on appeal, the date of making for the purposes of the transitional provisions is that of the decision at first instance and not that of the decision on appeal. See *D v D* [2007] EWCA Civ 1277 (CA).

Article 64(2) applies where such an order was made after the commencement date of the Brussels IIA Regulation for both the State of origin and the State addressed, but the original proceeding was instituted before that commencement date, and after the commencement date of the Brussels II Regulation for both of those States. For example, where recognition in England is sought for a French order made in 2006 on an application lodged in 2003, or of a Hungarian order made in 2006 on an application lodged in September 2004. In this situation, Chapter III of the Brussels IIA Regulation is made applicable, but subject to a proviso for jurisdictional review by reference to Chapter II of the Brussels IIA Regulation, and to any conventions in force between the States in question when the original proceeding was instituted. It seems that, for the necessary accordance to be established, it is sufficient either that the original court had explicitly assumed jurisdiction on a basis similar to one applicable under the Brussels IIA Regulation or a relevant convention,[41] or that the court addressed finds that a jurisdictional base accepted by the Brussels IIA Regulation or a relevant convention had in fact existed.[42]

Otherwise the wording of Article 64 indicates that no Community legislation is applicable to such orders. This is certainly the situation where the order was made before the commencement date of the Brussels IIA Regulation for both of the States involved. For example, where enforcement in England is sought for a French order made in 2004, or of a Romanian order made in 2006.[43] It is almost certainly the situation where the order was made after the commencement date of the Brussels IIA Regulation for both of the States involved, but the application was lodged before the commencement dates of both the Brussels IIA Regulation and the Brussels II Regulation for both States (being States between which the Brussels II Regulation had once been in force). For example where enforcement in England is sought for a French order made in 2006 on an application lodged in 2000. But in *D v D*,[44] the Court of Appeal has suggested that, where one of the States involved is Bulgaria or Romania (in neither of which the Brussels II Regulation was ever in force), Article 64(2) should be construed widely, so as to make Chapter III of the Brussels IIA Regulation applicable, subject to a proviso for jurisdictional review by reference to Chapter II of the Brussels IIA Regulation, in cases where the order was made after 2006 on an application lodged before 2007.

## DIRECT JURISDICTION

**Structure**

In the Brussels IIA Regulation direct jurisdiction over proceedings concerning parental responsibility is dealt with by Sections 2 and 3 (Articles 8–15 and 16–20) of Chapter II. These

---

[41]   See Case C-435/06: *C* [2007] ECR I-10141, treating a finding of 'residence' as similar to habitual residence.

[42]   See Case C-168/08: *Hadadi v Mesko* [2009] ECR I-6871, especially at paras 29–30, in which it was considered sufficient that both spouses were nationals of the State of origin. Cf. *W v W* [2005] EWHC 1811 (Fam) (Singer J).

[43]   See *D v D* [2007] EWCA Civ 1277 (CA).

[44]   [2007] EWCA Civ 1277 (CA), especially at paras 35–40.

provisions establish an elaborate set of rules on the existence and exercise of jurisdiction on the part of the courts of the Member States to determine custody applications. In general, they seek to ensure that there is only one Member State whose courts have custody jurisdiction in respect of a child.

Under the Brussels IIA Regulation, the primary connecting factor used in the determination of direct judicial jurisdiction over proceedings concerning parental responsibility is the habitual residence of the child at the date of the application. But there are exceptions in favour of the child's habitual residence at an earlier time or of a court whose jurisdiction is agreed on by the parties. The courts of the State in which the child is present have jurisdiction if his habitual residence cannot be established, and in any event may take provisional measures to protect the child in urgent cases. There is also provision for residual jurisdiction in accordance with the lex fori if no Member State has jurisdiction under the unified provisions. In the case of concurrent proceedings, the court first seised normally prevails, but there is also provision for the transfer of a case between the courts of different Member States in exceptional cases where it is in the best interests of the child.

To a large extent, the provisions of the Brussels IIA Regulation on direct jurisdiction in respect of parental responsibility resemble those contained in Chapter II (Articles 5–14) of the Hague Convention 1996. But, unlike the Convention, the Regulation does not address choice of the law to be applied by a court or authority in the exercise of its jurisdiction to determine matters relating to parental responsibility. Thus the matter is left to the conflict rules of the forum State, and at present the English courts will determine such matters in accordance with English internal law.[45] In contrast, Article 15(1) of the Hague Convention 1996 specifies that, in exercising their jurisdiction to take measures directed to the protection of a child's person or property, the judicial or administrative authorities of the Contracting States shall apply their own law. But, by Article 15(2) of the Convention, insofar as the protection of the person or the property of the child requires, they may exceptionally apply or take into consideration the law of another State with which the situation has a substantial connection. By Article 15(3) of the Convention, if the child's habitual residence changes to another Contracting State, the law of that other State governs, from the time of the change, the conditions of application of the measures taken in the State of the former habitual residence.

## The Earlier Provisions

It is clear that the provisions of the Brussels IIA Regulation on direct jurisdiction in respect of parental responsibility (which will be examined in detail below) are far more satisfactory than the earlier provisions of the Brussels II Regulation.

In the Brussels II Regulation, only Article 3 dealt specifically with the existence of direct jurisdiction to entertain custody applications.[46] This provision was limited to cases where matrimonial proceedings between the child's parents were pending in a Member State in accordance with the unified rules laid down by Articles 2 and 5–6,[47] and where in addition

---

[45]    See Dicey, Morris and Collins, 14th edition, Rule 97(10).
[46]    In addition, Article 4 of the Brussels II Regulation insisted that a court exercising jurisdiction under Article 3 should respect the Hague Convention 1980 on child abduction.
[47]    These correspond to Articles 3–5 of the Brussels IIA Regulation.

the child was habitually resident in the same or another Member State.[48] Article 3(1) conferred on the courts of a Member State in which matrimonial proceedings were pending in accordance with the unified rules ancillary custody jurisdiction in respect of a child of both spouses who was habitually resident in that Member State. Article 3(2) conferred on the courts of a Member State in which matrimonial proceedings were pending in accordance with the unified rules ancillary custody jurisdiction in respect of a child of both spouses who was habitually resident in another Member State, but subject to the conditions that at least one of the spouses had parental responsibility for the child, and that such jurisdiction had been accepted by the spouses and was in the best interests of the child.

In both cases, Article 3(3) would terminate the ancillary custody jurisdiction once decisions on the matrimonial application, and on any custody application made during the pendency of the matrimonial proceedings, had become final (in the sense that no further appeal or review of any kind was possible),[49] or the matrimonial and custody proceedings had otherwise terminated (for example, by withdrawal or by the death of a spouse).[50] An order sanctioning the permanent removal of the child from the country would normally be classified as a final judgment in the custody proceedings.[51]

As regards the exercise of jurisdiction under the Brussels II Regulation, it seems that where under Article 11 the court subsequently seised of matrimonial proceedings stayed or declined jurisdiction over them in favour of the court first seised, the stay or dismissal would extend to ancillary custody proceedings in the same country. On the other hand, it seems that Article 11 did not apply where the custody proceedings in one of the countries were not ancillary to any matrimonial proceedings there.[52] In any event, Article 12 ensured that a court was never prevented by the Brussels II Regulation from taking urgent and provisional measures to protect a child present in its territory.[53]

### The Child's Habitual Residence

Under the Brussels IIA Regulation, the general rule on the existence of direct jurisdiction over proceedings concerning parental responsibility is laid down by Article 8(1), which confers jurisdiction on the courts of the Member State in which the child is habitually resident at the time when the court is seised.[54] Since the Regulation respects the normal principle of continuance of jurisdiction, once an application concerning parental responsibility has been made in accordance with Article 8(1) to a court of the child's habitual residence at the

---

[48]   No provision of the Brussels II Regulation dealt specifically with the existence of ancillary custody jurisdiction where the child was not habitually resident in any Member State; nor where the child was habitually resident in a Member State but matrimonial jurisdiction was based on a residual ground permitted by Articles 7 and 8 (which correspond to Articles 6 and 7 of the Brussels IIA Regulation). In such cases, it seems that Article 8 of the Brussels II Regulation remitted the existence of ancillary custody jurisdiction to the law of the forum State.

[49]   See the Borrás Report, at para 39. See also *A v L* [2002] 1 FLR 142 (Judge Garner), and *Re A* [2004] 1 All ER 912 (Sumner J).

[50]   See the Borrás Report, at para 39.

[51]   See *Re G* [2004] 1 FLR 378 (CA).

[52]   See *C v FC* [2004] 1 FLR 317 (Tedd QC).

[53]   See also *A v L* [2002] 1 FLR 142 (Judge Garner).

[54]   Similar provision is made by Article 5 of the Hague Convention 1996.

time of the application, the court retains jurisdiction to determine all the issues raised by the application, even if the child's habitual residence changes during the proceedings.[55] But once the court has made orders dealing fully with all the issues raised by the application, jurisdiction under Article 8(1) to entertain a new application, for example for variation of an order, will belong to the courts of the child's new habitual residence.[56]

As Article 8(2) indicates, the jurisdiction under Article 8(1) of the courts of the child's current habitual residence is excluded in the exceptional cases specified by Articles 9, 10 and 12, which in some situations confer jurisdiction on the courts of an earlier habitual residence of the child, or on courts whose jurisdiction is accepted by the parties.[57] But, as was recognised by Sheehan J in *O'K v A*,[58] Article 8 eliminates any judicial discretion by the courts of the Member State in which the child is habitually resident to decline jurisdiction in favour of a supposedly more appropriate court of a non-member country.

The Brussels IIA Regulation does not attempt to define the concept of habitual residence (whether of adults or children).[59] With regard to children, the concept of habitual residence was addressed by the European Court in Case C-523/07: *A*,[60] which involved a family who had originally lived in Finland and had then moved to Sweden and lived there for about four years. Then they travelled to Finland, originally with the intention of spending the holidays there. In Finland, they lived in a camper van on various campsites and with relatives, and the children did not go to school. After a few months, the family applied to a Finnish municipality to be allocated social housing. Soon after this a Finnish administrative body took the children into immediate care and placed them in a child care unit, on the ground that they had been abandoned, and with a view to clarifying their situation.

In response to a reference from a Finnish court, the European Court explained that for the purpose of the Brussels IIA Regulation the concept of habitual residence must be given an autonomous and uniform interpretation, determined in the light of Recital 12, by which the grounds of jurisdiction established by the Regulation are shaped in the light of the best interests of the child and the criterion of proximity. Thus the Court's case-law relating to the concept of habitual residence in other areas of EC law cannot be directly transposed in the context of the assessment of the habitual residence of children for the purposes of the Regulation.

Accordingly, the European Court defined the habitual residence of a child, for the purposes of the Brussels IIA Regulation, as corresponding to the place which reflects some degree of integration by the child in a social and family environment. In establishing the habitual residence of a child, all the circumstances specific to each individual case must be

---

55    See per Singer J in *Re A, HA v MB* [2007] EWHC 2016 (Fam), at paras 87–90. Cf. *Re ML and AL* [2007] 1 FCR 475 (Mostyn QC).
56    See also Article 14 of the Hague Convention 1996, which specifies that measures taken by a court or authority which has substantive jurisdiction remain in force according to their terms, even if a change of circumstances has eliminated the basis upon which jurisdiction was founded, so long as the competent courts or authorities have not modified, replaced or terminated such measures.
57    On Article 9, which deals with modification of an access order after a change in the child's habitual residence, see p. 457 below. On Article 10, which deals with abduction cases, see pp. 468–70 below. On Article 12, on jurisdiction accepted by the parties, see pp. 457–9 below.
58    [2008] IEHC 243 (Irish High Court).
59    On the habitual residence of an adult, see pp. 430–33 above.
60    [2009] ECR I-2805.

taken into account. Relevant factors include the duration, regularity, conditions and reasons for the stay in and the family's move to a Member State; the child's nationality; and the place and conditions of attendance at school, linguistic knowledge, and the family and social relationships of the child in the State. The child's physical presence in the Member State must not be temporary or intermittent; the child's residence must reflect some degree of integration in a social and family environment. The parents' intention to settle permanently with the child in a Member State, manifested by tangible steps such as the purchase or lease of a residence there, may constitute an indicator of the transfer of the habitual residence. Another indicator may be constituted by lodging an application for social housing with the relevant services of the State. By contrast, the fact that the children are staying in a Member State where, for a short period, they carry on a peripatetic life, may constitute an indicator that they do not habitually reside in that State.

In view of the brevity of the guidance given by the European Court, it seems useful to refer to the fuller explanation offered by Kokott AG, whose general approach seems consistent with the principles adopted by the Court. She concluded that a child should be regarded as habitually resident in the place in which the child has his or her centre of interests, assessed by reference to all the relevant factual circumstances, and in particular to the duration and stability of residence and familial and social integration.

She explained that an habitual residence must have a certain stability or regularity. Since, in the context of custody disputes, the ideas of the persons entitled to custody as to where the child is to reside may diverge, the intention of one or both of the parents to reside with the child in a particular place can only be an indication of the child's habitual residence, and not a conclusive factor. The concept of habitual residence should be understood as corresponding to the actual centre of interests of the child. The duration and regularity of residence, and the child's familial and social integration, may be significant for determining the place of habitual residence.

She further explained that, as regards duration and regularity of residence, no particular duration is prescribed, and important factors include the age of the child and the familial and social circumstances. The residence does not have to be uninterrupted, and a temporary absence of the child (for instance, during the holidays) does not call into question the continuation of habitual residence. But habitual residence will not continue if a return to the original place of residence is not foreseeable in view of the actual circumstances. In the case of a lawful move, habitual residence can shift to the new State after a very short period. An indication that the habitual residence has shifted may be the common intention of the parents to settle permanently with the child in another State, manifested by such external circumstances as the purchase or lease of a residence in the new State, notifying the authorities of the new address, establishing an employment relationship, and placing the child in a kindergarten or school.[61] Conversely, abandoning the old residence and employment and notifying the authorities of departure suggest that habitual residence in the former State is at an end. In exceptional cases, there may be a transitional stage in which there will no longer be habitual

---

[61]    See also *Re ML and AL* [2007] 1 FCR 475, where Mostyn QC explained that a child's habitual residence will change if he is permanently removed by a parent to another country pursuant to an order made by the court of his then habitual residence, and thereafter he lives in the new country for several months, even if the parent who obtained the order had then intended wrongfully to obstruct access or contact.

residence in the former State, while the status in the new State has not yet crystallised into habitual residence.

She added that, as regards the familial and social situation of the child, an overall picture must be obtained, taking account of all factors, and their relevance may vary according to the child's age. The familial situation is characterised by the persons with whom a child lives at the place of residence or is in regular contact; in other words, parents, siblings, grandparents or other close relatives. For social integration, circumstances such as school, friends, leisure activities and, above all, command of language are important.

As regards the instant case, she noted that only a holiday was originally planned, which might suggest that habitual residence in Sweden continued. Further, the moving around from campsite to campsite probably largely excluded the possibility of the children constructing permanent social bonds with persons other than their mother and stepfather, and an aggravating factor was that they did not go to school. On the other hand, the children had a command of at least one of the official languages of Finland, and the parents had probably abandoned their original intention of only spending the holidays in Finland, and intended to move into social accommodation in Finland.

It is clear from Article 13 of the Brussels IIA Regulation, and was recognised by the European Court in Case C-523/07: *A*,[62] that for the purpose of the Regulation a child may have no habitual residence anywhere at a given time. It is also clear from the wording and structure of Chapter II, and was specifically recognised by Singer J in *Re A, HA v MB*,[63] that for the purpose of the Regulation a child cannot be habitually resident in more than one country at the same time.

Since only limited guidance on the concept of a child's habitual residence has so far emerged at European level, the further development of the concept for the purposes of the Regulation may be influenced to some extent by the prior English case-law.[64] This indicates that an existing habitual residence is presumed to continue unless the contrary is shown, and the burden of establishing a change in a person's habitual residence rests on the party who asserts such change.[65] In general, the habitual residence of a child follows that of the person or persons who have parental responsibility for him and with whom he has his home.[66] More precisely, in the case of a child (as well as an adult), habitual residence is determined by reference to a combination of factual and volitional elements; but in the case of a child, while the factual element is determined by reference to the child's own actual residence, absence or departure,[67] the volitional element is determined by reference to the intentions as to the

---

62    [2009] ECR I-2805.

63    [2007] EWHC 2016 (Fam), at paras 98–102. Cf. *M v H* [2005] EWHC 1186 (Fam).

64    On the English case-law, see also Stone, 'The Concept of Habitual Residence in Private International Law' [2000] Anglo-American Law Review 342; and Rogerson, 'Habitual Residence: The New Domicile?' (2000) 49 International and Comparative Law Quarterly 86.

65    See *F v S* [1993] 2 FLR 686 (CA); *Re R* [1992] 2 FLR 481 (CA); and *Re M*, 10th August 1995 (CA). See also *P v A-N* [2000] WL 33148939.

66    See *Re P(GE)* [1965] 1 Ch 568 (CA); *Re J* [1990] 2 AC 562; *Re F* [1992] 1 FLR 548 (CA); *Re K*, 24th June 1991 (CA). See also *Friedrich v Friedrich* 983 F2d 1396 (C6, 1993); *Prevot v Prevot* 855 FSupp 915 (1994); *Rydder v Rydder* 49 F3d 369 (C8, 1995); *Nunez-Escudero v Tice-Menley* 58 F3d 374 (C8, 1995); *Feder v Evans-Feder* 63 F3d 217 (C3, 1995); *Walton v Walton* 925 FSupp 453 (1996); and *Lops v Lops* 140 F3d 927 (C11, 1998).

67    See *Re M* [1993] 1 FLR 495 (CA); *Re B*, 24th July 1995 (CA); *Re M* [1996] 1 FLR 887 (CA); *Gateshead MBC v L* [1996] Fam 55; and *Al H v F* [2001] 1 FCR 385 (CA).

child's residence of the person or persons who have parental responsibility for the child, and not to the intention of the child himself.[68] Where more than one person has parental responsibility for a child, the child's habitual residence can only be changed by or with the consent or acquiescence of all the persons who have parental responsibility for the child[69] or with the authority of an order made by a competent court.[70] Where a person who has parental responsibility for a child consents to the child living apart from him in the care of another person at the other person's habitual residence (whether or not the other person also has parental responsibility for the child), the habitual residence of the child may be affected if the consent is to the child living there for a period not less than a school-year.[71] In a situation where no-one has parental responsibility for a child, the child's habitual residence remains the same as immediately before this situation arose, at least until the child has established a stable home with a relative without opposition from other relatives (or until the child attains adulthood).[72]

## Modification of Access Orders

Article 9 of the Brussels IIA Regulation applies where, after a judgment on access rights has been issued in the Member State of the child's habitual residence, the child moves lawfully from one Member State to another and acquires a new habitual residence there.[73] In that case, by way of exception to Article 8(1), the courts of the Member State of the child's former habitual residence retain jurisdiction during a three-month period following the move for the purpose of modifying the judgment on access rights, if the holder of access rights under the judgment continues to have his or her habitual residence there. But this does not apply if the holder of access rights under the judgment has accepted the jurisdiction of the courts of the Member State of the child's new habitual residence by participating in proceedings before those courts without contesting their jurisdiction.

## Jurisdiction by Agreement

Article 12 of the Brussels IIA Regulation provides for the jurisdiction of the courts of a Member State to be created in certain cases by agreement between the parties involved. It

---

68   See *Re J* [1990] 2 AC 562; *Re M* [1993] 1 FLR 495 (CA); *Rellis v Hart* [1993] SLT 738; and *Re M* [1996] 1 FLR 887 (CA).

69   See *Re P(GE)* [1965] 1 Ch 568 (CA); *Re F* [1992] 1 FLR 548 (CA); *Re S* [1994] Fam 70; *D v D* [1996] 1 FLR 574; *Re M* [1996] 1 FLR 887 (CA); and *Laing* (1996) 21 Fam LR 24 (Family Court of Australia). See also s 41 of the Family Law Act 1986, and *B v B* [2004] EWCA Civ 681.

70   See *Re R (No 2)* [1993] 1 FLR 249; *Re G* [1993] 1 WLR 824 (CA); *Re S* [1995] 1 FLR 314; and *Emmett v Perry* (1996) FLC 92-645 (Family Court of Australia). See also *R v R* [2005] 1 FLR 687 (Baron J); and *Re V* [2005] 1 FLR 718 (Munby J).

71   See (on consent for a sufficient period): *Re K* [1995] 2 FLR 211 (CA); *Cameron v Cameron* [1996] SLT 306; *Slagenweit v Slagenweit* 841 FSupp 264 (1993); *Re S* [1991] 2 FLR 1 (CA); *Re M* [1996] 1 FLR 887 (CA); and *Mozes v Mozes* 19 FSupp2d 1108 (1998). And (on consent for an insufficient period): *Re P(GE)* [1965] 1 Ch 568 (CA); *Re A* [1988] 1 FLR 365 (CA); *Evans v Evans* [1989] 1 FLR 135 (CA); *Re A* [1991] 2 FLR 241 (CA); *P v A-N* [2000] WL 33148939; *Hanbury-Brown* (1996) 20 Fam LR 334 (Family Court of Australia); *Medhurst* [1995] Ont CJ LEXIS 3142 (Ontario); and *Snetzko* [1996] Ont CJ LEXIS 3039 (Ontario).

72   See *Re S* [1998] AC 750; and see *Re ES*, 20th November 1997 (Irish High Court).

73   There is no corresponding provision in the Hague Convention 1996.

insists, however, that the agreement must be made expressly or otherwise in an unequivocal manner, and that the jurisdiction so created must be in the best interests of the child. By Article 12(4), one situation in which such jurisdiction must be regarded as according with the child's interests is where the child is habitually resident in a non-member country which is not a contracting party to the Hague Convention 1996, and it is found impossible to hold proceedings in that country.

Article 12(1) of the Brussels IIA Regulation deals with the creation of jurisdiction by agreement in respect of custody applications which are ancillary to matrimonial proceedings.[74] It applies where the courts of a Member State are exercising matrimonial jurisdiction on a unified ground under Article 3 of the Regulation.[75] It confers ancillary jurisdiction over any matter relating to parental responsibility which is connected with the matrimonial application if the following conditions are fulfilled: at least one of the spouses must have parental responsibility in relation to the child; the ancillary jurisdiction must have been accepted expressly or otherwise in an unequivocal manner by the spouses and by the holders of parental responsibility at the time when the court is seised; and the ancillary jurisdiction must be in the best interests of the child. Article 12(1) is wider than Article 3(2) of the Brussels II Regulation,[76] since Article 12(1) extends to a child of one of the spouses involved in the matrimonial proceedings, so long as the jurisdiction has been accepted by the other parent. By Article 12(2)(a)–(b), the ancillary jurisdiction conferred by Article 12(1) ceases when a judgment allowing or refusing the matrimonial application has become final, and a judgment in any custody proceedings which were still pending on the date when the matrimonial judgment became final has also become final. By Article 12(2)(c), the ancillary jurisdiction conferred by Article 12(1) also ceases when the matrimonial and the custody proceedings have come to an end for some other reason.

Article 12(1) was considered by the English Court of Appeal in *Bush v Bush*.[77] It ruled that the filing by the respondent spouse in English divorce proceedings of a response to the petitioner's statement of arrangements for the children does not amount to an unequivocal acceptance of the jurisdiction of the divorce court in respect of parental responsibility. For the filing of the petitioner's statement of arrangements, and the filing of the respondent's response to the petitioner's statement, are merely incidents of the divorce proceedings, and the court is not seised of an application in respect of parental responsibility until the issue of an application for a residence order, a contact order, a specific issue order or a prohibited steps order. Moreover, since Article 12(1) requires that jurisdiction in respect of parental responsibility must have been accepted expressly or in an unequivocal manner, such acceptance of jurisdiction is not lightly to be inferred, and the paradigm case will be an actual agreement by the parents at the time when the matrimonial proceedings are instituted.

In *Bush*, the Court of Appeal also considered the reference in Article 12(1) to the best interests of the child. It explained that where the principal parental dispute is as to whether the children should continue their life and education in the country of their existing habitual

---

74    Somewhat similar provision to Article 12(1)–(2) of the Regulation is made by Article 10 of the Hague Convention 1996.
75    On matrimonial jurisdiction under Article 3 of the Brussels IIA Regulation, see pp. 429–34 above.
76    On Article 3 of the Brussels II Regulation, see pp. 452–3 above.
77    [2008] 2 FLR 1437 (CA).

residence, or whether they should be taken to another country for future residence and education, the court of the existing habitual residence should be regarded as the more appropriate court, having regard to the best interests of the children. An application to relocate is properly determined by the court of the child's existing habitual residence, which is in a position to receive all the evidence as to the well-settled history and as to the children's achievements in their current environment, rather than by a court exercising divorce jurisdiction in the country to which the primary carer seeks to move.

Article 12(3) of the Brussels IIA Regulation deals with the creation of custody jurisdiction by agreement in the absence of matrimonial proceedings.[78] The chosen courts must be those of a Member State with which the child has a substantial connection; for example, because one of the holders of parental responsibility is habitually resident in that State or the child is a national of that State. The jurisdiction of the chosen courts must have been accepted expressly or otherwise in an unequivocal manner by all the parties to the proceedings at the time when the court is seised; and their jurisdiction must be in the best interests of the child. There is no explicit provision as to the duration of this jurisdiction.

**The Child's Presence**

Article 13(1) of the Brussels IIA Regulation confers jurisdiction over proceedings concerning parental responsibility on the courts of the Member State where the child is present, if his habitual residence cannot be established and jurisdiction cannot be determined on the basis of agreement under Article 12. By Article 13(2), the child's presence also founds jurisdiction in the case of refugee children or children internationally displaced because of disturbances occurring in their country, even if they remain habitually resident in the country which they have left.[79]

Article 13(1) applies generally in situations where the forum concludes that the child has no habitual residence anywhere. Thus it operates to fill the gap where, for example, a child moves between Member States, losing his earlier habitual residence in the State which he has left, but without having yet acquired an habitual residence in the State to which he has moved.[80] But, except in the case of refugee or displaced children, Article 13 does not apply where the child is regarded as habitually resident in a non-member country. In any event, Article 20 enables the courts of the Member State where the child is present to take provisional measures to protect the child in urgent cases.

**Residual Grounds**

By Article 14 of the Brussels IIA Regulation, where no court of a Member State has jurisdiction under Articles 8–13 on the basis of habitual residence, agreement or presence, jurisdiction is determined in each Member State by the laws of the forum State. But, by Article

---

[78] There is no provision in the Hague Convention 1996 which corresponds to Article 12(3) of the Regulation.

[79] Provision similar to Article 13 of the Regulation is made by Article 6 of the Hague Convention 1996.

[80] See the EC Commission's Explanatory Memorandum, COM(2001) 505 final, at p. 9.

61, in a Member State which is a party to the Hague Convention 1996, the residual jurisdiction under Article 14 is restricted by that Convention in cases where the child is habitually resident in a non-member country which is also a party to that Convention.

## Transfer between Courts

Article 15 of the Brussels IIA Regulation departs from the usual approach adopted by European Union law, whereby a competent court, properly seised, is bound to determine the dispute. It provides exceptionally for the discretionary transfer of a case (or a specific part of a case) by a competent court of one Member State to a court of another Member State with which the child has a connection, where both courts consider that the receiving court is better placed to hear the case (or relevant part) in the best interests of the child.[81]

The transfer will be from a court of a Member State having substantive jurisdiction to a court of another Member State with which the child has a particular connection. By Article 15(3), such a connection may take one of five forms: (a) that the receiving State has become the habitual residence of the child after the transferring court was seised; or (b) that the receiving State is the former habitual residence of the child; or (c) that the receiving State is that of the child's nationality; or (d) that the receiving State is the habitual residence of a holder of parental responsibility; or (e) where the case concerns measures for the protection of the child relating to the administration, conservation or disposal of his property, that the relevant property of the child is located in the receiving State.

By Article 15(2), the transferring court may invoke the power either upon application from a party, or of its own motion, or upon application from a court of another Member State with which the child has a particular connection. But a transfer made of the court's own motion or on application from a court of another Member State must be accepted by at least one of the parties. By Article 15(5), for a transfer to become effective, it must be accepted by the receiving court. By Article 15(6), for these purposes, the courts must co-operate, either directly or through the central authorities.

By Article 15(1), the mechanism for transfer involves the making by the transferring court of an order staying the case (or the relevant part of the case) and inviting the parties to introduce a request before the receiving court, or an order requesting the receiving court to assume jurisdiction. By Article 15(4), an order staying the case must also set a time-limit by which the receiving court should be seised; and if the receiving court is not seised by that time, the transfer is aborted and the transferring court resumes the exercise of jurisdiction. By Article 15(5), the receiving court has six weeks from its seisure to accept jurisdiction. If the receiving court accepts jurisdiction within the six weeks, the transferring court declines jurisdiction; otherwise the transfer is aborted and the transferring court resumes the exercise of jurisdiction. Recital 13 indicates that the receiving court cannot transfer the case to a third court.

In *Re EC*,[82] Thorpe LJ explained that Article 15 is a considerable novelty as far as the civil law countries are concerned. It introduces the concept of forum conveniens, which has more resonance for courts of common law countries than for civil law countries. It is a provision

---

[81]    Somewhat similar provision for the discretionary transfer of a case between courts of different countries is made by Articles 8 and 9 of the Hague Convention 1996.
[82]    [2007] 1 FLR 57 (CA).

negotiated for the comfort of courts which have reservations about the introduction of a strict lis alibi pendens rule into family litigation. He envisaged that it would be a truly exceptional case before Article 15 was invoked by a court of a civil law country. Moreover, there can be no possibility of a transfer under Article 15 unless and until the transferring court has been engaged by the issue of proceedings. Further, the decision of Abbott J in *RGHR v LG*[83] indicates that even an Irish (or English) court, seised of a proceeding concerning parental responsibility as the court of the child's current habitual residence, is unlikely in its discretion to transfer a case elsewhere, even to a court of the child's former habitual residence in which a maintenance claim is pending.

In Case C-523/07: *A*,[84] the European Court explained that Article 15 is the only provision in the Regulation under which a court may transfer a case to a court of another Member State. Thus where a court lacks substantive jurisdiction over parental responsibility under the Regulation and accordingly declines jurisdiction, it cannot transfer the case to a court of another Member State. But where the protection of the best interests of the child so require, it should inform the competent court of another Member State, either directly or through the central authority, of its decision declining jurisdiction. Similarly, where a court lacking substantive jurisdiction over parental responsibility takes provisional or protective measures under Article 20, and the protection of the best interests of the child so requires, it should inform the competent court of another Member State, either directly or through the central authority, of its decision taking the provisional or protective measures.

## Other Provisions

Articles 16–18 of the Brussels IIA Regulation (on the time of seisin; examination of jurisdiction of the court's own motion; and notification of the respondent) apply to proceedings concerning parental responsibility in the same way as to matrimonial proceedings.[85] As the European Court explained in Case C-523/07: *A*,[86] where a court lacks substantive jurisdiction over parental responsibility under the Regulation and accordingly declines jurisdiction, it cannot transfer the case to a court of another Member State. But where the protection of the best interests of the child so requires, it should inform the competent court of another Member State, either directly or through the central authority, of its decision declining jurisdiction.

## Concurrent Proceedings

Under Article 19 of the Brussels IIA Regulation, where there are concurrent proceedings concerning parental responsibility in respect of the same child and involving the same dispute in courts of different Member States, the court subsequently seised is required of its own motion to stay its proceedings until such time as the jurisdiction of the court first seised is established, and then to decline jurisdiction in favour of the first court. Upon such declension, the applicant in the second court may bring his claim before the first court.[87] But Article 19

---

[83]   [2008] 1 IR 369.
[84]   [2009] ECR I-2805.
[85]   See pp. 436–7 above.
[86]   [2009] ECR I-2805.
[87]   On concurrent proceedings, see also Article 13 of the Hague Convention 1996.

does not apply if, before the second court is seised, the first court has disposed of all matters in issue regarding parental responsibility which had been brought before it.[88]

As the EC Commission has explained,[89] it is expected that the mechanism provided by Article 19 will rarely be used, as in general the jurisdictional regime for parental responsibility does not provide for alternative grounds of jurisdiction. But concurrent jurisdiction is not totally excluded, and Article 19 may operate where, for example, the courts of two Member States each consider that the child is habitually resident in their own territory, as may happen where the child divides his time between two homes; or where the residual provision applies because the child is not habitually resident in any of the Member States.

## Provisional Measures

Article 20 of the Brussels IIA Regulation deals with provisional measures.[90] Article 20(1) permits the courts of a Member State to take in urgent cases such provisional measures to protect a child who is present or has assets in its territory as may be available under its law, even if under the Regulation the court of another Member State has jurisdiction as to the substance of the matter. By Article 20(2), such provisional measures cease to apply when a court of a Member State which has substantive jurisdiction under the Regulation has taken the measures which it considers appropriate.

In Case C-523/07: *A*,[91] the European Court explained that Article 20(1) applies to children who have their habitual residence in one Member State but stay temporarily or intermittently in another Member State and are in a situation likely seriously to endanger their welfare, including their health or their development, thereby justifying the immediate adoption of protective measures (such as the taking into care of the children). It is for the lex fori to determine the types of measure which may be adopted, and to lay down detailed procedural rules for their implementation. The provisional nature of the measures arises from the fact that, under Article 20(2), they cease to apply when the court of the Member State having substantive jurisdiction has taken the measures which it considers appropriate. Where the protection of the best interests of the child so requires, the court which has taken provisional or protective measures must inform the court of another Member State having substantive jurisdiction, directly or through the central authority, of the measures taken.

Another example of a case in which Article 20(1) can properly be invoked, suggested by Mostyn QC in *Re ML and AL*,[92] is where a family had travelled by car from one Member State to another Member State on their summer holiday. Once arrived in the second Member State, they were victims of a traffic accident, where they were all injured. The child was only slightly injured, but both parents arrived at the hospital in a state of coma, and the authorities of the second Member State urgently needed to take certain provisional measures to protect the child, who had no relatives there. A further example suggested by Mostyn QC is where there is evidence that the children are about to be removed from a country in order to frus-

---

88    See *RGHR v LG* [2008] 1 IR 369 (Abbott J).
89    See COM(2002) 222 final, at p. 11.
90    Article 20 of the Regulation resembles Article 11 of the Hague Convention 1996. Additional provision for non-urgent cases is made by Article 12 of the Convention.
91    [2009] ECR I-2805.
92    [2007] 1 FCR 475.

trate enforcement of a contact order there, and the order under Article 20(1) prevents the removal pending enforcement of the contact order.

In *Detiček v Sgueglia*,[93] the European Court ruled that Article 20(1) of the Brussels IIA Regulation does not allow a court of a Member State to take a provisional measure granting custody of a child who is in its territory to an abducting parent, where a court of another Member State, which has substantive jurisdiction under the Regulation over the custody dispute, has already delivered a judgment provisionally giving custody of the child to the other parent, and that judgment has been declared enforceable in the territory of the first-mentioned Member State. The European Court emphasised that, as an exceptional provision, Article 20(1) must be interpreted strictly. It explained that Article 20(1) requires urgency, relating both to the situation of the child and to the impossibility in practice of bringing the application before the court with substantive jurisdiction. Moreover, it would undermine the aims of and principles underlying the Regulation to recognise a situation of urgency on the basis of a change of circumstances resulting from a gradual process such as the child's integration into a new environment, after a wrongful removal in defiance of a decision of the court with substantive jurisdiction. The European Court also indicated that Article 20(1) does not enable a measure to be taken which deprives of custody a parent who is not present in the State in which the measure is adopted, but is resident in another Member State. On the last point, however, a contrary (and, it is submitted, much more persuasive) view was subsequently adopted by Sharpston AG in *Purrucker v Vallés Pérez*;[94] she considered that it is the presence of the child alone which determines whether urgent provisional measures may be taken under Article 20 with respect to him or her.

In *Purrucker v Vallés Pérez*,[95] the European Court ruled that provisional measures relating to the custody of children are not recognisable or enforceable in other Member States under Chapter III of the Brussels IIA Regulation, where they are adopted under Article 20 of the Regulation by a court which lacks substantive jurisdiction over the custodial issues. In contrast, it accepted that provisional measures relating to the custody of children are recognisable and enforceable under Chapter III where they are adopted by a court which has substantive jurisdiction over the custodial issues under Section 2 of Chapter II. Thus where it is not clear and obvious from the terms of a decision adopting provisional measures that the court of origin had founded its jurisdiction on one of the substantive grounds specified by Articles 8–14, the decision will not be recognisable and enforceable under Chapter III. Such refusal of recognition and enforcement by the court addressed does not infringe the prohibition on jurisdictional review imposed by Article 24, since it merely involves the court addressed in seeking to identify the basis on which the court of origin accepted jurisdiction.

The Court accepted, however, that a provisional measure properly adopted in accordance with the requirements of Article 20 of the Regulation may be recognised and enforced in another Member State in accordance with the law of the State addressed or the international conventions to which it has acceded. But it insisted in this context that the defendant should have an adequate opportunity to be heard in the State of origin; and that this entails a right of appeal against the provisional order. Such an appeal must lie to a separate court, which will act

---

[93] Case C-403/09-PPU, [2010] All ER (EC) 313.
[94] Case C-256/09, at para. 147 of her opinion.
[95] Case C-256/09, 15th July 2010.

promptly, and must extend to questions relating to the existence of substantive jurisdiction and to compliance with the requirements of Article 20. Moreover, the appeal must not be treated as a submission to the substantive jurisdiction of the court of origin.

## CHILD ABDUCTION

### Introduction

The Brussels IIA Regulation respects and strengthens the provisions of the Hague Convention of 25th October 1980 on the Civil Aspects of International Child Abduction, which may conveniently be referred to as the Hague Convention 1980. All twenty-seven EU Member States, and a very large number of other countries, are party to the Convention.[96]

The Hague Convention 1980 requires the summary return of an internationally abducted child to the country of his habitual residence unless an exceptional ground is established. Its scope is confined by Article 4 to children under the age of 16. The Brussels IIA Regulation provides a more radical solution in cases of child abduction between EU Member States. This involves conferring substantive jurisdiction on the courts of the Member State from which the child was abducted for at least a year after the abduction in the absence of acquiescence; restricting the grounds on which the courts of the Member State to which the child was abducted may refuse to return him; enabling the refusal of the courts of the Member State to which the child was abducted to return the child on certain grounds to be overridden by a substantive decision of the courts of the Member State from which he was abducted; and making such overriding decisions to return enforceable in other Member States without the need for an enforcement order.

In *Vigreux v Michel*,[97] Thorpe LJ explained that the provisions relating to the return of abducted children were the most contentious and therefore the most difficult of resolution during the negotiation of the Brussels IIA Regulation. The resolution of the resulting impasse was the retention of the operation of the Hague Convention 1980 throughout the European region, but with the fortification of what were seen, in the light of nearly twenty years of operation, as weaknesses or loopholes through which abductors were escaping. The fortifications were threefold: the emphasis on protective measures to nullify a defence under Article 13(1)(b) of the Convention; the return of the case to the requesting state in the event of a refusal by the requested state; and the automatic enforcement of return orders throughout the region.

### The Hague Convention 1980

The Hague Convention 1980 requires the prompt return of an internationally abducted child to the country of his habitual residence unless an exceptional ground is established.[98] Its scope is confined by Article 4 to children under the age of 16.

---

[96] Thus, despite its recently acquired membership of the Hague Conference on Private International Law, the European Union intends to take no further steps in regard to the Hague Convention 1980; see JUSTCIV 235, of 6th November 2008. In the United Kingdom, the Convention is given effect by Part I of the Child Abduction and Custody Act 1985.

[97] [2006] 2 FLR 1180 (CA).

[98] See also Case 38273/02: *Stochlak v Poland*, 22nd September 2009, where the European Court

By Articles 3 and 4 of the Convention, an international abduction is defined as a wrongful removal of a child from, or a wrongful retention of a child outside, the territory of the Contracting State in which the child was habitually resident immediately before the removal or retention. A removal or retention is regarded as wrongful where it infringed rights of custody which existed under the law of the State in which the child was habitually resident immediately before the removal or retention,[99] and which at the time of the removal or retention were actually exercised, or would have been exercised but for the removal or retention.

By Articles 3 and 5 of the Convention, rights of custody include rights relating to the care of the child's person, and in particular the right to determine his place of residence. Rights of custody may be attributed to an individual, or to an institution or other body. They may be attributed to one person or to several persons jointly. They may arise by operation of law, or by reason of a judicial or administrative decision, or by reason of a legally effective agreement, or in some other way.

Removal occurs when a child who has previously been in the State of his habitual residence is taken away across the frontier of that State. In general, retention occurs where a child who has previously been for a limited period of time outside the State of his habitual residence is not returned to that State on the expiry of the limited period.[100] But where a parent who had no rights of custody when a child was lawfully removed and initially retained subsequently acquires such rights (under the law of the child's then existing habitual residence) and demands the return of the child, the retention may become wrongful.[101] Conversely, an initially wrongful removal probably ceases to amount to an abduction if, before the hearing of the application for return by the court of the country to which the child has been taken, the court of the country of the child's habitual residence makes a custody order in favour of the abductor.[102]

An individual has sufficient rights of custody if the relevant law prohibits the removal of the child from the territory without his consent or a court order.[103] Thus where English internal law applies as that of the child's habitual residence immediately before the removal or retention, the normal effect of ss 2–4 of the Children Act 1989 is that the mother always has sufficient rights of custody, as does a marital father, but a non-marital father does not have such rights unless he has obtained parental responsibility by order or agreement.[104] However, a court seised of a custody dispute itself constitutes an institution or body having rights of custody, and these rights can be invoked by the person who applied for the order.[105] In two

---

of Human Rights awarded damages against a State for breach of Article 8 of the European Convention on Human Rights, on respect for private and family life, by reason of the failure of its authorities to make adequate efforts to enforce a parent's right to the return of a child internationally abducted by the other parent. The Court explained that the obligations of a Contracting State under Article 8 of the European Convention on Human Rights must be interpreted in the light of the Hague Convention 1980.

[99] The reference to the law of the child's habitual residence extends to its conflict rules, rather than being limited to its internal law. See the Perez-Vera Report, in 3 Actes et Documents de la 14th Session 426 at 445–6 (1982); and *Feder v Evans-Feder* 63 F3d 217 (C3, 1995).

[100] See *Re H* [1991] 2 AC 476.

[101] See *Re S* [1998] AC 750.

[102] See *Re T and J* [2006] 2 FLR 1290 (Potter P).

[103] See *C v C* [1989] 1 WLR 654 (CA), and *Re D* [2007] 1 FLR 961 (HL).

[104] See *S v H* [1998] Fam 49.

[105] See *Re H* [2000] 2 AC 291, and *B v B* [1993] Fam 32 (CA).

very dubious decisions,[106] merely inchoate rights of an actual carer which it was thought virtually certain that a court would have protected on application have been considered sufficient. For a person who has rights of custody to be defeated by his failure to exercise them, there must be acts which constitute clear and unequivocal abandonment of the child.[107]

The key provision of the Convention is Article 12(1), which applies where a child has been internationally abducted and, at the date of the commencement of proceedings before a court of the Contracting State where the child is present, a period of less than a year has elapsed from the date of the abduction. It imposes on the court a mandatory obligation to order the return of the child forthwith. The obligation is subject only to the limited exceptions specified by Article 13 and 20.

Article 13(1)(a) provides for exceptions to the obligation to order return where the person, institution or other body which opposes return establishes that the person, institution or other body having the care of the person of the child was not actually exercising the custody rights at the time of removal or retention, or had consented to[108] or subsequently acquiesced in the removal or retention.[109] Article 13(1)(b) provides for a further exception where the opponent of return establishes that there is a grave risk that return would expose the child to physical or psychological harm or otherwise place the child in an intolerable situation.[110] Another exception, specified by Article 13(2), applies where the court finds that the child objects to being returned and has attained an age and degree of maturity at which it is appropriate to take account of his views.[111] In addition, Article 20 enables the return of the child to be refused if this would not be permitted by the fundamental principles of the requested State relating to the protection of human rights and fundamental freedoms.[112]

---

[106] See *Re B* [1994] 2 FLR 249 (CA), involving an unmarried father; and *Re O* [1997] 2 FLR 702, involving grandparents. Cf. *Re S* [1998] AC 750.

[107] See *Friedrich v Friedrich (No 2)* 78 F3d 1060 (C6, 1996).

[108] See *Re W* [1995] 1 FLR 878, where Wall J held that prior consent cannot be passive; there must be clear and compelling evidence of a positive consent to the removal of the child from the country of his habitual residence; and *Re B* [1994] 2 FLR 249 (CA), holding that a consent obtained by deliberate deception will be ignored.

[109] See *Re H* [1998] AC 72, where Lord Browne-Wilkinson emphasised that subsequence acquiescence normally requires a real subjective consent by the wronged parent to the removal of the child, and that an intention to acquiesce should not normally be inferred from attempts by the wronged parent to effect a reconciliation or to reach an agreed voluntary return of the abducted child. By way of exception, there is acquiescence where the words or actions of the wronged parent clearly and unequivocally show and have led the other parent to believe that the wronged parent is not asserting or going to assert his right to the summary return of the child and are wholly inconsistent with such return. For example, where the wronged parent signs a formal agreement that the child is to remain in the country to which he has been abducted; or takes an active part in proceedings in the country to which the child has been abducted to determine the long-term future of the child. See also *Re AZ* [1993] 1 FLR 682 (CA); *Re S* [1994] 1 FLR 819 (CA); *Re R* [1995] 1 FLR 716 (CA); *Friedrich v Friedrich (No 2)* 78 F3d 1060 (C6, 1996); and *Re T and J* [2006] 2 FLR 1290 (Potter P).

[110] For refusal based on grave risk, see *Re F* [1995] 3 All ER 641 (CA), where the risk arose from the applicant father's violence; and *Re G* [1995] 1 FLR 64, where the children were very young and it was feared that the mother's return with them might push her existing depression into psychosis. Cf. *S v B* [2005] 2 FLR 878 (Potter P). See also *Friedrich v Friedrich (No 2)* 78 F3d 1060 (C6, 1996).

[111] See *S v S* [1993] Fam 242 (CA); *Re R* [1995] 1 FLR 716 (CA); *Vigreux v Michel* [2006] 2 FLR 1180 (CA); and *Re M* [2007] 2 FLR 72 (CA).

[112] Thus, as Lady Hale explained in *Re D* [2007] 1 FLR 961 (HL), return may be refused on the

By Article 12(2), the obligation to order the return of the child remains applicable where the proceedings seeking return were commenced after the expiration of the one-year period. In this case, the obligation remains subject to the exceptions specified by Articles 13 and 20, but a further exception, provided for by Article 12(2), applies where it is demonstrated that the child is now settled in his new environment. The one-year period runs from the abduction, even if the child's whereabouts have been concealed by the abductor. But settlement involves emotional and psychological as well as physical elements, and such concealment is an important factor in negating the necessary emotional and psychological elements of settlement.[113]

By Article 18, the Convention does not limit the power of a judicial or administrative authority to order the return of the child at any time. Thus where the obligation to order return is excluded by the establishment of an exception specified by Articles 12(2) or 13, the court has a discretion whether to order the return of the child, and this discretion should be exercised with due regard to the objectives of the Convention, and not by treating the welfare of the child as paramount. Accordingly, the court should have regard to the policy of the Convention in favour of returning an abducted child and enabling the merits of the custody dispute to be determined by the courts of the original country, as well as to the particular circumstances which give rise to or are connected with the relevant exception, and to general welfare considerations where they militate strongly against return.[114]

Further, Article 16 of the Convention applies where the courts of the State to or in which a child has been removed or retained receive notice of an abduction. It precludes them from deciding on the merits of rights of custody until it has been determined that the child is not to be returned under the Convention, or unless an application under the Convention is not lodged within a reasonable time following receipt of the notice.[115] Finally, Article 19 makes clear that a decision under the Convention concerning the return of a child must not be regarded as a determination on the merits of any custody issue.

It is also worth noting that, in *Re J*,[116] the House of Lords has ruled that the principles of the Hague Convention 1980 should not be extended to, or applied by analogy in, cases where a child has been abducted to the United Kingdom from a non-contracting State. In all non-Convention cases, the United Kingdom courts must act in accordance with the welfare of the individual child. The court does have power, in accordance with the welfare principle, to order the immediate return of a child to a foreign country without conducting a full investigation of the merits. But summary return should not be the automatic reaction to any and every unauthorised taking or keeping a child from his home country. At most, the court may start from the proposition that it is likely to be better for a child to return to his home country for any disputes about his future to be decided there, and that a case against his doing so has to be made. In this context, relevant factors include the degree of connection of the child

---

ground that it would be incompatible with the right to respect for family life, or to a fair trial, as granted by the European Convention on Human Rights. See also per Lady Hale in *Re J* [2005] 2 FLR 802 (HL), at paras 42–5. On the relevance of the effect on other children involved, see *S v B* [2005] 2 FLR 878 (Potter P).

[113]   See *Cannon v Cannon* [2005] 1 FLR 169 (CA).

[114]   See *Re S* [1993] Fam 242 (CA); *Cannon v Cannon* [2005] 1 FLR 169 (CA); *Zaffino v Zaffino* [2006] 1 FLR 410 (CA); *Vigreux v Michel* [2006] 2 FLR 1180 (CA); and *Re M* [2007] 2 FLR 72 (CA).

[115]   See *R v R* [1995] Fam 209 (CA).

[116]   [2005] 2 FLR 802.

with each country;[117] the length of time he has spent in each country; and differences in the conception of welfare accepted by the legal systems involved. Thus the fact that the foreign court would be obliged to give effect to the father's wishes, or would be unable to authorise relocation of the child, may in some circumstances be decisive against return.

## The Brussels IIA Regulation

The Brussels IIA Regulation provides a more radical solution than the Hague Convention 1980 in cases of child abduction between EU Member States.[118] This involves conferring substantive jurisdiction on the courts of the Member State from which the child was abducted for at least a year after the abduction in the absence of acquiescence; restricting the grounds on which the courts of the Member State to which the child was abducted may refuse to return him; enabling the refusal of the courts of the Member State to which the child was abducted to return the child on certain grounds to be overridden by a substantive decision of the courts of the Member State from which he was abducted; and making such overriding decisions to return enforceable in other Member States without the need for an enforcement order. The procedure established by the Regulation involves close co-operation between the central authorities of the States involved, which by Article 57(3) provide their assistance free of charge. Since, as regards abduction, the Regulation is designed to supplement the Convention, it seems clear that, like the Convention, the provisions of the Regulation which deal specifically with abduction are confined to children under the age of 16.

### Substantive jurisdiction

Article 10 of the Brussels IIA Regulation deals with substantive jurisdiction (jurisdiction to determine the merits of the custody dispute) in cases of child abduction.[119] Its basic provision specifies that, in case of wrongful removal or retention of a child, the courts of the Member State where the child was habitually resident immediately before the wrongful removal or retention ('the Member State of origin') retain their jurisdiction. This applies whether the abduction was to another Member State or to an external country. Where the abduction was to another Member State, it excludes the jurisdiction of the courts of that State.[120]

To the basic rule, two exceptions are made. Neither applies unless the child has acquired an habitual residence in another Member State ('the second Member State'). The first exception, which is specified by Article 10(a), applies where two conditions are fulfilled: that the child has acquired an habitual residence in the second Member State; and that each person, institution or other body having rights of custody has acquiesced in the removal or retention.

The second exception, which is specified by Article 10(b), requires the fulfilment of four conditions. Firstly, that the child has acquired an habitual residence in the second Member

---

117   See also *M v M* [2006] 1 FLR 138 (Wilson J), where, without full investigation of the merits, the English court returned children to the country of their domicile, despite their having become habitually resident in England.

118   This contrasts with the Brussels II Regulation, which (by Article 4) had merely required a court exercising ancillary custody jurisdiction under Article 3 to respect the Hague Convention 1980.

119   Article 10 of the Regulation resembles Article 7 of the Hague Convention 1996.

120   Cf., on abduction between different parts of the United Kingdom, s 41 of the Family Law Act 1986, and *B v B* [2004] EWCA Civ 681.

State. Secondly, that the child has resided in the second Member State for a period of at least one year after the person, institution or other body having rights of custody has had or should have had knowledge of the whereabouts of the child. Thirdly, that the child is settled in his or her new environment. As Singer J explained in *Re C*,[121] Article 10(b) of the Regulation introduces the concept that time does not begin to run towards the year required before the defence of settlement can arise, until the claimant has had or should have had knowledge of the whereabouts of the child.

A fourth requirement under Article 10(b) is designed to ensure that any application for return made within the one-year period in the Member State to which the child has been abducted, and any consequential overriding proceedings in the Member State of origin, have been disposed of without the making of an order for return. Thus at least one of the following conditions must be met: (i) that, within one year after the holder of rights of custody has had or should have had knowledge of the whereabouts of the child, no request for return has been lodged before the competent authorities of the Member State where the child has been removed or is being retained; or (ii) that a request for return lodged by the holder of rights of custody has been withdrawn, and no new request has been lodged within the said year; or (iii) that a case before the court in the Member State of origin has been closed pursuant to Article 11(7), because no submissions from the parties have been received within three months of the relevant notification; or (iv) that a judgment on custody which does not entail the return of the child has been issued by the courts of the Member State of origin.

Moreover, as the European Court ruled in *Povse v Alpago*,[122] the last mentioned condition requires a final decision on custody, based on a full consideration of all relevant matters. A decision is regarded as final even if it is open to modification in the light of subsequent developments. But the condition is not satisfied by a provisional measure, which is designed to regulate the situation (for example, by authorising the child to remain with the abductor in the second Member State) until a final decision in the proceedings can be made.

It will be noted that the effect of Article 10, in the case of an abduction between Member States, is to enable the aggrieved parent, provided that he acts within the one-year period, to apply directly to the courts of the Member State of origin for an order for return. He may then enforce the order in the Member State to which the child was taken under Chapter III of the Regulation. This procedure avoids the need for an application to a court of the Member State to which the child was abducted for an order for return under the Hague Convention 1980 and Article 11 of the Brussels IIA Regulation.

The effect of Article 10 was explained by Singer J in *Re A, HA v MB*.[123] He emphasised that the rule in child abduction cases displaces the general rule by reserving jurisdiction (save obviously in relation to Hague Convention applications for the child's return) to the home country. The home country continues to have jurisdiction if the court there becomes seised. That jurisdiction endures until the child both acquires habitual residence in another Member State and one of the conditions specified in Article 10(a) or (b) is satisfied. If at that point no court in the child's home country has been seised, the jurisdiction to determine matters of parental responsibility passes to the courts of the country of the child's acquired habitual residence.

---

[121]   [2005] 1 FLR 127; reversed on other grounds as *Cannon v Cannon*, [2005] 1 FLR 169 (CA).
[122]   C-211/10-PPU, 1st July 2010.
[123]   [2007] EWHC 2016 (Fam), especially at paras 82–94.

He added that the scheme is cogent and comprehensive. The courts of the Member State away from which a child has been unlawfully removed or retained continue to have jurisdiction until the conditions specified by Article 10 are met. Thus the ability of parents (and any institution or body having rights of custody) to seise the home court notwithstanding that the child has in fact acquired habitual residence in another Member State continues (in the absence of acquiescence) for a minimum period of one year after the holder of rights of custody has or should have had knowledge of the whereabouts of the child, and the child is settled in the new environment. At what point, if at all, the parents' ability to seise the home court comes to an end depends upon the attainment of one of the conditions in sub-paragraphs (i) to (iv) of Article 10(b), which follow a logical progression.

Singer J also recognised that Article 10 presupposes that a child can acquire a changed habitual residence without the consent of both parents, contrary in some cases to the traditional English law. But he concluded that, once the jurisdiction of a court of the Member State of origin is validly engaged in accordance with Articles 8 and 10, the court remains competent even if the pre-conditions for the assumption of jurisdiction later cease to apply, and accordingly, the court retains power to make contact orders even if it does not order the child's return to its country. Conversely, the effect of Article 10 is to deprive the courts of the Member State to which a child is abducted of any jurisdiction in matters of parental responsibility, except (by Article 20) for the taking in urgent cases of provisional measures as a stop-gap to have effect only until the home court exercises jurisdiction as to the substance of the matter.

### Applications for return under the Convention as supplemented by the Regulation

Article 11 of the Brussels IIA Regulation lays down rules which supplement and strengthen the provisions of the Hague Convention 1980 in cases of abduction between EU Member States. It is noteworthy that in 2003 over half of the applications under the Convention for the return of a child from the United Kingdom were from other EU Member States to which the Brussels IIA Regulation now applies.[124] By Article 11(1) of the Regulation, these supplementary rules apply where a person, institution or other body having rights of custody applies to the competent authorities in a Member State ('the Member State requested') to deliver a judgment on the basis of the Hague Convention 1980, in order to obtain the return of a child who has been wrongfully removed or retained in a Member State other than the Member State where the child was habitually resident immediately before the wrongful removal or retention ('the Member State of origin').

By Article 11(2) of the Regulation, when applying Articles 12 and 13 of the Hague Convention 1980, it must be ensured that the child is given the opportunity to be heard during the proceedings, unless this appears inappropriate having regard to his or her age or degree of maturity. In *Re D*,[125] Lady Hale explained that Article 11(2) of the Regulation reverses the burden in relation to hearing the child. Although strictly this only applies to cases within the European Union, the principle is of universal application and consistent with international obligations under Article 12 of the United Nations Convention on the Rights of the Child 1989. Thus the principle applies, not only when a defence under Article 13 of the Hague

---

[124]    See *Vigreux v Michel* [2006] 2 FLR 1180 (CA), at para 47.
[125]    [2007] 1 FLR 961 (HL). Cf. *Re H* [2007] 1 FLR 242 (CA).

Convention 1980 has been raised, but also in any case in which the court is being asked to apply Article 12 of the Convention and direct the summary return of the child under the Convention. It erects a presumption that the child will be heard unless this appears inappropriate; though hearing the child must not be confused with giving effect to his views. The most common method of hearing the child is by way of an interview with a suitable court officer. In most cases, this should be enough. In others, and especially where the child has asked to see the judge, it may also be necessary for the judge to hear the child. Only in a few cases will full-scale legal representation be necessary. But whenever it seems likely that the child's views and interests may not be properly presented to the court, and in particular where there are legal arguments which the adult parties are not putting forward, then the child should be separately represented. In European cases, the court must address at the outset whether and how the child is to be given the opportunity of being heard, and the same approach should be adopted in non-European cases. If, having heard from the child, an issue arises under the Convention which has not been raised by either of the parties, the court is bound to consider it, irrespective of the pleadings. But the Court of Appeal has subsequently reaffirmed that it is only in very exceptional circumstances that the child will be made a party to the proceedings and allowed separate representation.[126]

By Article 11(3) of the Regulation, the court to which an application for return of a child is made must act expeditiously in proceedings on the application, using the most expeditious procedures available in national law. Except where exceptional circumstances make this impossible, the court must issue its judgment no later than six weeks after the application is lodged. The importance of compliance with this requirement was emphasised by the Court of Appeal in *Vigreux v Michel*.[127]

By Article 11(4) of the Regulation, the court cannot refuse to return a child on the basis of Article 13(1)(b) of the Hague Convention 1980 (which refers to a grave risk that his or her return would expose the child to physical or psychological harm or otherwise place the child in an intolerable situation) if it is established that adequate arrangements have been made to secure the protection of the child after his or her return. But this does not apply where the ground for refusal is the child's objection to being returned (under Article 13(2) of the Convention).[128]

By Article 11(5) of the Regulation, a court cannot refuse to return a child unless the person who requested the return of the child has been given an opportunity to be heard.

By Article 11(6) of the Regulation, where a court issues an order for non-return pursuant to Article 13 of the Hague Convention 1980, it must immediately (either directly or through its central authority) transmit a copy of the court order for non-return, and of the relevant documents (including a transcript of the hearings before the court), to the court with jurisdiction or the central authority in the Member State of origin, as determined by national law. The court should receive all such documents within one month of the date of the non-return order.

By Article 11(7) of the Regulation, unless the courts in the Member State of origin have already been seised by one of the parties, the court or central authority which receives the said information must notify it to the parties and invite them to make submissions to the court, in

---

[126]   See *Re F* [2007] 2 FLR 313 (CA).
[127]   [2006] 2 FLR 1180.
[128]   See *Vigreux v Michel* [2006] 2 FLR 1180 (CA).

accordance with national law, within three months of the date of notification, so that the court can examine the question of custody of the child. But the court must close the case if it has received no submissions within the time-limit.

By Article 11(8) of the Regulation, notwithstanding a judgment for non-return pursuant to Article 13 of the Hague Convention 1980, any subsequent judgment which requires the return of the child, issued by a court having jurisdiction under the Regulation, is enforceable in accordance with Section 4 of Chapter III of the Regulation, in order to secure the return of the child. Accordingly, by Articles 40(1)(b) and 42(1), where an order for return is made under Article 11(8) by a court of the Member State of origin, after an order for non-return had been made under Article 13 of the Hague Convention 1980 by a court of the Member State to which he was abducted, the return of a child entailed by the order must be recognised and enforceable in another Member State without the need for a declaration of enforceability, and without any possibility of opposing its recognition, if the order has been certified by the court which made the order in the Member State of origin in accordance with Article 42(2).[129] Such enforceability is not confined to the Member State to which the child had been abducted and in which return had been refused, but extends to a third Member State to which the child has been moved.[130] Moreover, as the European Court ruled in *Povse v Alpago*,[131] Article 11(8) applies to an order for return made by a court of the Member State of origin, even if that court has not yet made a final decision on the substantive custodial issues.

In *Rinau*,[132] the European Court ruled that, once an order for non-return has been issued by a court of the Member State requested, and brought to the attention of the court of the Member State of origin, it is irrelevant, for the purposes of issuing a certificate under Article 42 of the Regulation, that in the Member State requested the order for non-return has been suspended, overturned, or set aside, or has not become res judicata, or has been replaced by a decision ordering return, so long as the return of the child has not actually taken place. Where there is no doubt as to the authenticity of the certificate, and the certificate accords with the standard form set out in Annex IV to the Regulation, opposition to the recognition of the decision ordering return is not permitted, and the only course open to a court of the Member State requested is to declare the enforceability of the certified decision and to allow the immediate return of the child.

As regards the role of the court of the Member State requested, in dealing with an application for an order for return under the Hague Convention 1980 as supplemented by the Brussels IIA Regulation, Wall LJ explained in *Vigreux v Michel*[133] that, in a case of abduction to England from another European country, where there are active proceedings pending in the court of the child's habitual residence, and where that court is plainly seised of all determinative welfare considerations, Article 11(8) of the Regulation reinforces the policy of the Hague Convention 1980, and thus falls to be considered in the exercise of discretion by the English court to order return, even though a ground for refusal has been established. He added that, in sensitive international cases relating to children, where the foreign court is plainly the

---

129   Section 4 (Articles 40–45) of Chapter III is considered more fully at pp. 479–82 below.
130   See *Re A, HA v MB* [2007] EWHC 2016 (Fam) (Singer J), at para 70.
131   Case C-211/10-PPU, 1st July 2010.
132   Case C-195/08-PPU, [2008] ECR I-5271.
133   [2006] 2 FLR 1180 (CA).

right forum in which to decide the children's future, it is incumbent on English judges, if they are not going to return the child in question, not only to ensure that they are not trespassing on the foreign court's jurisdiction, but also to explain clearly both why they have decided on that course of action, and why they take the view that it is not inconsistent with comity and international judicial co-operation. Thus, in a Convention case to which the Brussels IIA Regulation applies, the English court needs to explain clearly to the foreign court why it takes the view that its decision not to return is consistent with the philosophy of the Hague Convention 1980, and is not inconsistent with the structure and philosophy of the Brussels IIA Regulation. On the other hand, in *Re T and J*,[134] Potter P held that the Regulation eliminates the obligation to order return where, before the hearing of the application for return, a court of the Member State of origin has made a custody order in favour of the abductor which is entitled to recognition under Chapter III of the Regulation.

As regards the role of the court of the Member State of origin, in dealing with custody proceedings under Article 11(6)–(8) of the Regulation after the court of the Member State requested has made an order for non-return, Singer J explained in *Re A (2006)*[135] that in such proceedings an English court will determine the substantive issues in accordance with the welfare principle, as specified by s 1 of the Children Act 1989. In *Re A, HA v MB*,[136] Singer J explained that, under Article 11(7) of the Regulation, the court of the Member State of origin is competent to deal with the substance of the case in its entirety. Its jurisdiction is not limited to deciding on the return of the child, but extends to the determination of, for example, access rights. The court should, in principle, be in the same position to exercise jurisdiction as if the abducting parent had not abducted the child, but instead had seised the court of origin to modify a previous decision on custody or to ask for authorisation to change the habitual residence of the child. On the other hand, an order for access or contact does not amount to a judgment entailing or requiring the return of the child within the meaning of Articles 10(b)(iv) and 11(8). A judgment entailing or requiring the return of the child will be given where the examination of the question of custody results in a decision that the child should live with the parent who is in the Member State of origin, rather than in an order merely requiring the other parent to make the child available in that country for the purposes of meeting the parent who is resident there. Where under Article 11(6)–(8), the court of the Member State of origin makes a residence order in favour of the abducting parent, and a contact order in favour of the innocent parent, substantive jurisdiction then passes to the courts of the child's new habitual residence. He also emphasised that English custody proceedings under Article 11(6)–(8), following a foreign order refusing to return a child, should be heard by a High Court judge of the Family Division.[137]

**Some unsolved problems concerning Article 11(6)–(8)**
It seems clear from Article 11(1) that Article 11(2)–(5) of the Regulation apply in all cases where an application for return under the Hague Convention 1980 is made to a court of a Member State, seeking the return of a child alleged to have been abducted from another

---

[134]   [2006] 2 FLR 1290.
[135]   [2006] EWHC 3397 (Fam).
[136]   [2007] EWHC 2016 (Fam), especially at paras 87–97.
[137]   At para 138.

Member State, regardless of the merits of the application or the accuracy of the facts alleged or the correctness of the legal arguments relied on.

But the scope of Article 11(6)-(8) of the Regulation, which apply where the court requested has issued an order for non-return, and endeavour to give ultimate control over the custody dispute to the courts of the Member State in which the child was habitually resident immediately before the abduction, may be more limited. Article 11(6) envisages an order for non-return pursuant to Article 13 of the Convention. Thus there is no doubt that Article 11(6)–(8) of the Regulation apply where the court requested has accepted that the child has been abducted from another Member State, but has made an order for non-return on the basis of Article 13(1)(b) of the Convention, which refers to a grave risk that return would expose the child to physical or psychological harm or otherwise place the child in an intolerable situation, or on the basis of Article 13(2) of the Convention, which refers to the child's objection to being returned where he has attained an age and degree of maturity at which it is appropriate to take account of his views. In such cases, Article 11(6)-(8) of the Regulation will ensure that substantive jurisdiction belongs to the courts of the Member State in which the child was habitually resident immediately before the abduction.

At the opposite extreme, it seems that Article 11(6)–(8) of the Regulation cannot apply where the court requested has made an order for non-return on the basis of its finding that the child had not in fact been abducted; for example, because in its view the child had not been habitually resident in the country from which he was removed, or the alleged abductor was the sole holder of custody rights over the child. Moreover, Article 26 of the Regulation appears to preclude the courts of other Member States from reviewing such findings. Thus in this situation, substantive jurisdiction will belong to the courts of the child's current habitual residence in accordance with Article 8.

Another possible situation is where the court requested has accepted that the child has been abducted from another Member State, but has made an order for non-return on the ground that the application for return was made after the expiration of the one-year period and the child is now settled in his new environment, as specified in Article 12(2) of the Convention, taken with Article 10(b) of the Regulation. In such a case it seems that Article 11(6)–(8) of the Regulation do not apply, since the order for non-return was not based on Article 13, but on Article 12(2), of the Convention. Thus in this situation, substantive jurisdiction will belong to the courts of the child's current habitual residence in accordance with Article 8 of the Regulation.

Yet another possible situation is that the court requested has accepted that the child has been abducted from another Member State, but has made an order for non-return on the basis of acquiescence in the abduction by the holder of custody rights, as specified in Article 13(1)(a) of the Convention. It seems that, in this situation, Article 11(6)–(8) of the Regulation apply, with the effect that the substantive dispute is initially returned to the courts of the Member State from which the child was abducted. But Articles 8, 10, 17 and 26 of the Regulation appear to preclude the courts of Member State of origin from reviewing the finding of acquiescence, and to require them to determine the child's habitual residence at the time of their seisure in the light of that finding. Accordingly, in this situation, the courts of the Member State of origin may be bound to decline jurisdiction in favour of the courts of the Member State in which the child had become habitually resident before the proceedings in the Member State of origin were instituted.

Finally, there is the possibility that the order for non-return was based on grounds which are not remotely consistent with the Convention and the Regulation. It seems likely, especially in view of the robust approach which the European Court adopted in *Rinau*,[138] that it would rule that Article 11(6)–(8) of the Regulation are applicable in such cases, and accordingly that substantive jurisdiction belongs to the courts of the Member State in which the child was habitually resident immediately before the abduction.

# RECOGNITION AND ENFORCEMENT OF CUSTODY ORDERS

## Scope

As well as providing for the recognition of matrimonial decrees, Chapter III (Articles 21–52) of the Brussels IIA Regulation provides for the recognition and enforcement in each Member State of orders made in the other Member States relating to parental responsibility for children.[139] The Brussels IIA Regulation goes beyond the Brussels II Regulation in extending to all child custody orders, regardless of whether the custody proceedings were connected with matrimonial proceedings.[140] Chapter III of the Brussels IIA Regulation also applies to orders for costs of proceedings within the scope of the Regulation.[141] References in the Regulation to a judgment or order are to a document containing the terms of the judge's order which is issued by the court, rather than to a record of how the judge arrived at the relevant decision.[142]

By Article 46 of the Brussels IIA Regulation, documents which have been formally drawn up or registered as authentic instruments and are enforceable in one Member State, and also agreements between the parties which are enforceable in the Member State in which they were concluded, must be recognised and declared enforceable under the same conditions as judgments. This goes beyond the corresponding provision of the Brussels II Regulation[143] in eliminating the need for the participation of a public authority in the conclusion or recording of the agreement, but the instrument or agreement must still be enforceable by the authorities of the State of origin *without the need for a confirmatory judgment.*

As in the case of matrimonial decrees, Article 21 of the Brussels IIA Regulation makes the recognition under Chapter III of a custody order automatic and incidental, no special procedure being required. This echoes Article 14 of the Brussels II Regulation. Thus a custody order made in the country of the child's habitual residence may be accorded incidental recog-

---

138  Case C-195/08-PPU, [2008] ECR I-5271.
139  Sections 1–3 and 5–6 (Articles 21–39 and 46–52) of Chapter III of the Brussels IIA Regulation largely echo Chapter III of the Brussels II Regulation. But a radical departure is made by Section 4 (Articles 40–45) of Chapter III, which provides for the enforcement (as well as the recognition) of certain orders without the need for a declaration of enforceability by a court of the Member State addressed.
140  Chapter III of the Brussels II Regulation was limited to custody orders made on the occasion of matrimonial proceedings in respect of children of both spouses; see Articles 1(1)(b) and 13(1). But it probably applied even if the matrimonial jurisdiction of the Member State of origin was not based on the unified rules specified by Chapter II, and even if the child was not habitually resident in any of the Member States.
141  See Article 49. See similarly Article 13(2) of the Brussels II Regulation.
142  See *Re A, HA v MB* [2007] EWHC 2016 (Fam) (Singer J), at paras 122–30.
143  See Article 13(3) of the Brussels II Regulation; and the Borrás Report at para 61.

nition in proceedings for the return of the child under the Hague Convention 1980 and Article 11 of the Regulation.[144]

A detailed procedure for obtaining a declaration of enforceability of a custody order is established by Articles 28–39 of the Brussels IIA Regulation. The enforcement procedure closely resembles that provided for in the Brussels I Regulation, especially as regards the issue of certificates by the original court. The provisions on the enforcement procedure largely echo Chapter III of the Brussels II Regulation. But Article 47(1) of the Brussels IIA Regulation adds that the enforcement procedure is governed by the law of the Member State addressed. This refers to the measures of actual enforcement, to be taken after any necessary declaration of enforceability has been obtained. By Article 47(2), any judgment delivered by a court of another Member State and declared enforceable in accordance with Chapter III (or certified under Section 4 of Chapter III)[145] must be enforced in the Member State addressed in the same conditions as if it had been delivered in that Member State. It is not clear whether this widens the power which, in *Re S (No 2)*,[146] Holman J derived from the Brussels II Regulation to 'phase in' an access order with a view to making the contact envisaged by the order happen as soon as could effectively be achieved.[147] But in *Povse v Alpago*[148] the European Court explained that, at least in the context of a certified judgment for the return of an abducted child, the conditions referred to in Article 47(2) are confined to the procedural methods to be used for enforcing the judgment.

Another new provision in the Brussels IIA Regulation, Article 48, enables the courts of the Member State addressed to make practical arrangements for organising the exercise of rights of access, if the necessary arrangements have not been made in the order made by the courts of the Member State having substantive jurisdiction, and provided that the essential elements of that order are respected. But such practical arrangements will cease to apply pursuant to a later order made by the courts of the Member State having substantive jurisdiction.

By Article 21(3), an interested party may use the enforcement procedure to apply for a decision that an order is or is not recognised. Thus under the Brussels IIA Regulation (in contrast with the Brussels I Regulation), the enforcement procedure can be invoked with a view to obtaining a declaration of non-recognition. In *Rinau*,[149] the European Court ruled that an application seeking a declaration of non-recognition is not permissible in the case of an order which has been certified under Section 4 of Chapter III (which applies to certain orders for return in abduction cases, and to access orders). Otherwise, it confirmed that any person interested may request the non-recognition of an order, even if a request for its recognition has not already been lodged, but added that in such a situation Article 31(1), on the ex parte character of the initial application, does not apply, and both parties are entitled to make their submissions before the court hearing the initial application.

---

144    See *Re T and J* [2006] 2 FLR 1290 (Potter P).
145    See pp. 479–82 below.
146    [2004] 1 FLR 582.
147    With regard to enforcement under the Hague Convention 1996, Article 28 of the Convention specifies that measures taken in one Contracting State and declared enforceable, or registered for the purpose of enforcement, in another Contracting State shall be enforced in the latter State as if they had been taken by the authorities of that State; and then adds that enforcement takes place in accordance with the law of the requested State to the extent provided by such law, taking into consideration the best interests of the child.
148    Case C-211/10-PPU, 1st July 2010, at para. 82.
149    Case C-195/08-PPU, [2008] ECR I-5271.

**Grounds for Refusal of Recognition and Enforcement**

The exceptions to the general rule in favour of the recognition and enforcement of custody orders are specified in Articles 23–7 of the Brussels IIA Regulation.[150] In addition, Article 28 requires that, to be enforceable in the State addressed, a custody order must be enforceable in the State of origin and must have been served. Thus, in *Purrucker v Vallés Pérez*,[151] Sharpston AG confirmed that, in view of Article 28, enforcement of a custody order under Section 2 may be refused by the court addressed where it finds that the order is not, or is no longer, enforceable in the State of origin, or that the order has not been served; and concluded that, as regards such enforceability, the certificate issued by the original court is not conclusive. Articles 26 and 31(3) emphasise that under no circumstances may a custody order be reviewed as to its substance.[152] But, as the Borrás Report recognises,[153] this does not prevent the modification of a custody order by reason of a subsequent change in circumstances.

Article 24 excludes jurisdictional review, subject to very limited exceptions for transitional cases[154] and situations involving the Nordic Convention 1931.[155] However, as regards provisional measures relating to the custody of children, the ruling of the European Court in *Purrucker v Vallés Pérez*[156] has established that such provisional measures are not recognisable or enforceable in other Member States under Chapter III of the Brussels IIA Regulation, where they are adopted under Article 20 of the Regulation by a court which lacks substantive jurisdiction over the custodial issues. In contrast, it accepted that provisional measures relating to the custody of children are recognisable and enforceable under Chapter III where they are adopted by a court which has substantive jurisdiction over the custodial issues under Section 2 of Chapter II. Thus where it is not clear and obvious from the terms of a decision adopting provisional measures that the court of origin had founded its jurisdiction on one of the substantive grounds specified by Articles 8-14, the decision will not be recognisable and enforceable under Chapter III. Such refusal of recognition and enforcement by the court addressed does not infringe the prohibition on jurisdictional review imposed by Article 24, since it merely involves the court addressed in seeking to identify the basis on which the court of origin accepted jurisdiction.

The substantive grounds for refusal of recognition of custody orders are specified by Article 23 of the Brussels IIA Regulation.[157] If one of these grounds is established, refusal of

---

[150]    These provisions largely echo Articles 15–20 of the Brussels II Regulation.

[151]    Case C-256/09, 15th July 2010, at paras 124 and 149-155 of her opinion.

[152]    This resembles Article 27 of the Hague Convention 1996, by which, without prejudice to such review as is necessary in the application of other provisions, there shall be no review of the merits of the measure taken.

[153]    At para 78.

[154]    See pp. 449–51 above.

[155]    On the Nordic Convention 1931, see p. 424 above.

In contrast to the Brussels IIA Regulation, Articles 23(2)(a) and 25 of the Hague Convention 1996 permit refusal of recognition where the measure was taken by an authority whose jurisdiction was not based on one of the grounds provided for in Chapter II of the Convention; but the authority of the requested State is bound by the findings of fact on which the authority of the State where the measure was taken based its jurisdiction.

[156]    Case C-256/09, 15th July 2010.

[157]    This largely echoes Article 15(2) of the Brussels II Regulation.

recognition is mandatory.[158] By Article 23(a), recognition is to be refused if it would be manifestly contrary to the public policy of the State addressed.[159] But the scope of the public policy proviso is limited by Article 26, which prohibits review of the substance of the order. On the other hand, Article 23(a) indicates that the assessment of public policy involves taking into account the best interests of the child. Accordingly, in *Re S (No 1)*,[160] Holman J concluded that a Belgian access order in respect of a toddler who was living with his mother in England, which provided for frequent visits to the father in Belgium for periods of up to a fortnight, although not in the best interests of the child as viewed by English standards, was not so contrary to his best interests as to render its recognition manifestly contrary to English public policy.

Similarly, in *W v W*,[161] Singer J emphasised that in this context English public policy must enshrine and give credit to the concept that the child's interests (as perceived by the court addressed) are but an element in the equation, and thus that the policy must be, save in the most exceptional of circumstances, not to allow the foreign judgment to be subverted. The court addressed must proceed on the basis that the findings and the reasoning of the original court are unassailable and that its conclusion was impeccable. Accordingly, he enforced an Irish custody order which required that the children should move to Ireland and reside there with the mother, even though, if he had been deciding the merits in the absence of any foreign order, he would have decided in favour of the continuation of their residence in England with the father. It was clear that the Irish court had searched for the outcome which best met the children's welfare. The Irish decision was well within the bounds and scope of what an English judge could and might have decided on the findings made by the Irish court. Thus its recognition was far from being manifestly contrary to English public policy.

By Article 23(c) of the Brussels IIA Regulation, recognition of an order must be refused where it was given in default of appearance, and the person in default was not served with the instituting or an equivalent document in sufficient time and in such a way as to enable that person to arrange for his or her defence, unless it is determined that such person has accepted the judgment unequivocally. In insisting on a European Union standard for both the time and the manner of service, this accords with Article 34(2) of the Brussels I Regulation. But, unlike in the Brussels I Regulation, there is no requirement to seek redress in the State of origin where possible.

Additional grounds for refusal of recognition of custody orders on account of procedural defects are specified by Article 23(b) and (d) of the Brussels IIA Regulation.[162] By Article 23(b), recognition must be refused if the order was made, except in case of urgency, without the child in question having been given an opportunity to be heard, in violation of fundamental principles of procedure of the State addressed. By Article 23(d), it must also be refused, at the request of a person claiming that the order infringes his or her parental responsibility, if it was given without such person having been given an opportunity to be heard.

---

158   See *W v W* [2005] EWHC 1811 (Fam) (Singer J), at para. 72.
159   Similar provision is made by Article 23(2)(d) of the Hague Convention 1996.
160   [2004] 1 FLR 571.
161   [2005] EWHC 1811 (Fam).
162   These resemble Article 23(2)(b) and (c) of the Hague Convention 1996.

As regards irreconcilability between judgments, Article 23(e) and (f) of the Brussels IIA Regulation require that a custody order must be refused recognition and enforcement in certain cases where it is irreconcilable with a *later* judgment relating to parental responsibility. The later judgment may have been given in the Member State addressed. Alternatively, it may have been given in another Member State, or in the non-member country of the child's habitual residence, but in these cases it must fulfil the conditions necessary for its recognition in the State addressed.[163] Thus, as the Borrás Report recognises,[164] the Regulation accepts the inherent nature of custody orders, as being open to modification by reason of a subsequent change in circumstances. But there could be irreconcilability between a custody order made in connection with a divorce and a subsequent decision denying the former husband's paternity.[165]

A further ground for non-recognition (not found in the Brussels II Regulation) is provided by Article 23(g) of the Brussels IIA Regulation: that the procedure laid down in Article 56 for the placement of a child in institutional care or with a foster family in another Member State has not been complied with. By Article 56, an order for such placement in a State where public authority intervention is required for domestic cases of child placement may be made by a court of another Member State only if the competent authority of the State of the placement has consented to the placement. Where placement in a foster family does not require public authority intervention in the State of placement for domestic cases of child placement, a court of another Member State which decides on such a placement must inform the central authority or another competent authority in the State of the placement.[166]

## Access Orders and Orders for Return

A radical departure from earlier European Union legislation is made by Section 4 (Articles 40–45) of Chapter III of the Brussels IIA Regulation. This provides for the enforcement (as well as the recognition) of certain orders without the need for a declaration of enforceability by a court of the Member State addressed. Section 4 applies to two types of order: orders granting rights of access; and certain orders for the return of an abducted child. By Article 40(2), it remains permissible for a holder of parental responsibility to seek and obtain a declaration of enforceability in respect of such orders.

Article 41 of the Regulation applies to access orders. By Article 41(1), rights of access granted in an enforceable judgment given in a Member State must be recognised and enforceable in another Member State without the need for a declaration of enforceability, and without any possibility of opposing its recognition, if the judgment has been certified in the Member State of origin in accordance with Article 41(2). Where the law of the State of origin does not provide for enforceability by operation of law of an access order, the court of origin

---

[163] See also Article 23(2)(e) of the Hague Convention 1996, which permits refusal of recognition where the measure is incompatible with a later measure which has been taken in the non-contracting State of the habitual residence of the child, and which fulfils the requirements for recognition in the requested State.

[164] At para 78.

[165] See the Borrás Report at para 73.

[166] On placement abroad, see also Articles 23(2)(f) and 33 of the Hague Convention 1996.

may declare that the judgment shall be enforceable despite any appeal.[167] By Article 41(2), the court of origin must issue a certificate using the standard form in Annex III of the Regulation, and completed in the language of the judgment. By Article 41(3), where the rights of access involve a cross-border situation at the time of the delivery of the judgment, the certificate must be issued ex officio when the judgment becomes enforceable, even if only provisionally. If the situation subsequently acquires a cross-border character, the certificate must be issued at the request of one of the parties. In *Re ML and AL*,[168] Mostyn QC indicated that where there has been a history of default in compliance with an access or contact order, a court of a Member State which is requested to enforce an order made in another Member State should be able to enforce the order in an anticipatory manner; for example, by giving a direction, capable of being implemented by its officers, to ensure that the children are delivered to the parent in the Member State of origin as prescribed in the order.

Article 42 of the Regulation deals with certain orders for the return of an abducted child. By Article 40(1)(b), the order for return must have been made under Article 11(8) by a court of the Member State from which he was abducted, after an order for non-return had been made under Article 13 of the Hague Convention 1980 by a court of the Member State to which he was abducted.[169] By Article 42(1), the return of a child entailed by an enforceable order fulfilling these conditions must be recognised and enforceable in another Member State without the need for a declaration of enforceability, and without any possibility of opposing its recognition, if the order has been certified in the Member State of origin in accordance with Article 42(2). Even if the law of the State of origin does not provide for the enforceability of such an order by operation of law, despite any appeal, the court of origin may declare the order enforceable.[170] By Article 42(2), the court of origin must of its own motion issue a certificate using the standard form in Annex IV of the Regulation, and completed in the language of the judgment. Where the court or an authority takes measures to ensure the protection of the child after his return to the State of habitual residence, the certificate must contain details of such measures.

By Articles 41(2) and 42(2) of the Regulation, the court of origin must refuse to issue the certificate under Section 4 unless the parties were given an opportunity to be heard, and unless the child was given an opportunity to be heard or a hearing was considered inappropriate having regard to his or her age or degree of maturity. It must also refuse to issue a certificate in respect of an access order which was given in default, unless the person defaulting was served with the instituting or an equivalent document in sufficient time and in such a way as to enable that person to arrange for his or her defence, or the person was served irregularly with the document and accepted the decision unequivocally. It must also refuse to issue a certificate in respect of an order for return unless it has taken into account in issuing its judgment the reasons for and evidence underlying the order issued pursuant to Article 13 of the Hague Convention 1980. In *Re A (2006)*,[171] Singer J explained that the provisions

---

[167] This provision overrides the internal law of the State of origin; see *D v D* [2007] EWCA Civ 1277 (CA).

[168] [2007] 1 FCR 475.

[169] In Case C-195/08-PPU: *Rinau* [2008] ECR I-5271, the European Court confirmed that a certificate can be issued under Article 42 only after a judgment for non-return has been issued.

[170] See *Re A* [2006] EWHC 3397 (Fam) (Singer J), at para 11.

[171] [2006] EWHC 3397 (Fam).

requiring the parties and the child to have been given an opportunity to be heard do not prevent the court from making an order and issuing a certificate under Section 4 where a parent and the child have not in fact been heard because the parent has refused both to participate on his own behalf, and to facilitate communication between the child and the child's legal representative appointed by the court, despite being given every opportunity and encouragement to do so.

By Article 43 of the Regulation, the law of the Member State of origin applies to any rectification of a certificate issued under Section 4,[172] but no appeal lies against the issuing of such a certificate. By Article 44, a certificate takes effect only within the limits of the enforceability of the judgment. By Article 45, a party seeking enforcement under Section 4 must produce an authentic copy of the judgment, and the certificate issued under Articles 41 or 42. A translation is also required of the part of the certificate dealing with the arrangements for exercising rights of access, or for implementing the measures taken to ensure the child's return. By Article 47(2), a judgment which has been certified under Section 4 cannot be enforced if it is irreconcilable with a subsequent enforceable judgment. But, as the European Court ruled in *Povse v Alpago*,[173] this provision of Article 47(2) is confined to irreconcilability of the certified judgment with a subsequent judgment given in the Member State of origin.

In *Rinau*,[174] the European Court ruled that, once an order for non-return has been issued by a court of the Member State to which the child was abducted, and brought to the attention of the court of the Member State from which the child was abducted, it is irrelevant, for the purposes of issuing a certificate under Article 42 of the Regulation, that in the Member State to which the child was abducted the order for non-return has been suspended, overturned, or set aside, or has not become res judicata, or has been replaced by a decision ordering return, so long as the return of the child has not actually taken place. Where there is no doubt as to the authenticity of the certificate, and the certificate accords with the standard form set out in Annex IV to the Regulation, opposition to the recognition of the decision ordering return is not permitted, and the only course open to a court of the Member State requested is to declare the enforceability of the certified decision and to allow the immediate return of the child.

In *Povse v Alpago*,[175] the European Court again emphasised that a certified judgment is not open to any form of attack in the State addressed. The only exception is where there is doubt as to the authenticity of the certificate, and then such authenticity must be determined in accordance with the law of the State of origin. Moreover the role of the law of the State addressed is confined to questions of procedure. Questions concerning the merits of the judgment, and even (at least in cases where it is clear that originally the child was habitually resident in and wrongfully abducted from the State of origin) questions concerning the jurisdiction of the court of origin, can only be raised in the courts of the State of origin, and the same applies to applications for modification of the judgment by reason of a change of circumstances, and to applications for a stay of execution.

---

[172]  Rectification refers to the correction of the certificate where it contains a material error as to the content of the judgment; see Recital 24 and Case C-211/10-PPU: *Povse v Alpago*, 1st July 2010, at para. 71.
[173]  Case C-211/10-PPU, 1st July 2010.
[174]  Case C-195/08-PPU, [2008] ECR I-5271.
[175]  Case C-211/10-PPU, 1st July 2010.

Section 4 appears to overlook the practical difficulties which are likely to arise from attempts to require enforcement authorities to act on a foreign judgment which has not been in some formal manner confirmed as effective by their own court. Thus the proper operation of Section 4 is effectively dependent on the expertise and wisdom of the central authorities established under the Regulation. It is therefore unfortunate that there is no provision in Section 4 instructing all other officials involved to seek advice from their central authority.

# 18. Other family matters

## INTRODUCTION

As seen in Chapters 16 and 17 above, the Brussels IIA Regulation deals with matrimonial proceedings and decrees (for divorce, separation or annulment of marriage), and with proceedings and orders relating to parental responsibility. But the Brussels IIA Regulation does not deal with maintenance obligations under family law, nor with other aspects of family law, such as matrimonial property or succession to property on death.[1]

At present, maintenance obligations under family law are governed by the Brussels I Regulation, and its operation in relation to such obligations will be discussed in this chapter.[2] But on 18th June 2011 such obligations will be removed from the scope of the Brussels I Regulation and subjected instead to a specific regime elaborated by EC Regulation 4/2009,[3] which may conveniently be referred to as the Maintenance Regulation, and which will also be examined in this chapter.[4] The Brussels I Regulation is, and the Maintenance Regulation will be, applicable to proceedings and orders relating to maintenance obligations, regardless of whether the maintenance claim is dealt with ancillarily in matrimonial proceedings or proceedings concerning parental responsibility or is the subject of a separate proceeding.[5]

In contrast, matrimonial property is not yet regulated by any Community measure, though it is among the matters listed for action in the first stage of the draft Programme of Measures for Implementation of the Principle of Mutual Recognition of Decisions in Civil and Commercial Matters.[6]

Moreover, no Community measure has yet been adopted which deals with succession to property on death. A Green Paper on Succession and Wills was issued by the EC Commission in 2005,[7] and on 14th October 2009 the Commission presented a Proposal for a Regulation of the Parliament and Council on Jurisdiction, Applicable Law, and Recognition and Enforcement of Decisions and Authentic Instruments, in Matters of Succession, and the Creation of a European Certificate of Succession.[8] The Proposal will be examined briefly in this chapter.[9]

---

[1]  See the Brussels IIA Regulation, Recitals 8 and 11 and Article 1(3)(e)–(f).
[2]  See pp. 484–8 below.
[3]  Regulation 4/2009 on Jurisdiction, Applicable Law, Recognition and Enforcement of Decisions and Co-operation in Matters relating to Maintenance Obligations; [2009] OJ L7/1.
[4]  See pp. 488–502 below.
[5]  See Article 5(2) of the Brussels I Regulation; Case 120/79: *De Cavel v De Cavel (No 2)* [1980] ECR 731; and Article 3(c) and (d) of the Maintenance Regulation.
[6]  [2001] OJ C12/1.
[7]  COM(2005) 65 final, of 1st March 2005.
[8]  COM(2009)154 final.
[9]  See pp. 502–5.

# MAINTENANCE UNDER THE BRUSSELS I REGULATION

## Scope

The tiresome distinction which is drawn by the Brussels I Regulation between maintenance, which falls within the scope of the Regulation, and matrimonial property, which is excluded from its scope, has been examined in Chapter 2 above.[10]

In any case, the scope of the Brussels I Regulation is confined by Article 1(1) to civil and commercial matters. Thus where a public body seeks to recover from a private person sums paid by the body by way of social assistance to a member of his family (such as his spouse, divorced spouse or child), the Regulation applies if the basis and the detailed rules relating to the claim are governed by the rules of the ordinary law in regard to maintenance obligations, but not if the action for recourse is founded on legislative provisions which confer on the public body a prerogative of its own. Accordingly, the Regulation does not apply to a claim for recourse under Dutch legislation which enables the public body to disregard an otherwise binding maintenance agreement lawfully entered into between former spouses and approved by a judicial decision.[11] On the other hand, the Regulation does apply to actions by a German public body against parents of recipients of education grants under the German Act on Educational Support, by way of a statutory subrogation governed by civil law.[12]

## Direct Jurisdiction

By Article 2 of the Brussels I Regulation, a maintenance claim against a defendant domiciled in a Member State may be brought in the courts of the State in which the defendant is domiciled. For this purpose, domicile is determined in accordance with Article 59, and thus refers to a stable, substantial or habitual residence, and not in accordance with the traditional English concept, referring to origin or permanent residence.[13] In *Cook v Plummer*,[14] Thorpe LJ considered that it was not entirely clear that the ruling of the European Court in *Owusu v Jackson*,[15] that Article 2 of the Brussels I Regulation prevents a court of the defendant's domicile from declining jurisdiction in favour of a supposedly more appropriate court of a non-member country, extends to maintenance claims.

Article 5(2) of the Brussels I Regulation offers a choice of other fora to an applicant seeking maintenance from a defendant who is domiciled in a Member State. The maintenance claim may alternatively be brought, at the applicant's option, in another Member State in the

---

10  See pp. 29–32 above.
11  See Case C-271/00: *Gemeente Steenbergen v Baten* [2002] ECR I-10489.
12  See Case C-433/01: *Freistaat Bayern v Blijdenstein* [2004] ECR I-981.
13  See the Brussels I Regulation, Article 59; the Civil Jurisdiction and Judgments Order 2001 (SI 2001/3929), Schedule 1, para 9; *Dubai Bank v Abbas*, 17th July 1996 (CA); *Daniel v Foster* [1989] SCLR 378; *Grupo Torras v Al-Sabah* [1995] 1 Lloyd's Rep 374; *Foote Cone & Belding Reklam Hizmetleri AS v Theron* [2006] EWHC 1585 (Ch) (Patten J); *Petrotrade v Smith* [1998] 2 All ER 346; *Cherney v Deripaska* [2007] 2 All ER (Comm) 785 (Langley J); *High Tech International AG v Deripaska* [2006] All ER (D) 330 (Dec) (Eady J); *Yugraneft v Abramovich* [2008] EWHC 2613 (Comm) (Christopher Clarke J); and pp. 69–72 above.
14  [2008] 2 FLR 989 (CA).
15  Case C-281/02, [2005] ECR I-1383.

courts for the place where the maintenance creditor is domiciled (in accordance with Article 59) or habitually resident. The maintenance claim may also be brought, at the applicant's option, in a Member State other than that of the defendant's domicile, where the matter is ancillary to proceedings concerning the status of a person, in the court which, according to its own law, has jurisdiction to entertain the proceedings concerning status, unless that jurisdiction is based solely on the nationality of one of the parties. Although Article 5(2) refers to a maintenance creditor, these provisions operate in favour of any applicant for maintenance, including a person making a maintenance application for the first time. They are not confined to claimants who have already obtained a maintenance order.[16] But Article 5(2) does not apply to an action brought by a public body, seeking reimbursement of sums paid under public law (for example, by way of an education grant) to a maintenance creditor, to whose rights it is subrogated against the maintenance debtor (for example, a parent of the maintenance creditor), even where the claim is governed by civil law and thus falls within the scope of the Regulation.[17]

In the Brussels IIA Regulation, Recital 11 explains that maintenance obligations are excluded from the scope of the Brussels IIA Regulation as they are already covered by the Brussels I Regulation. It envisages that the courts having jurisdiction under the Brussels IIA Regulation (over matrimonial proceedings or proceedings concerning parental responsibility) will generally have jurisdiction to rule on maintenance obligations by application of Article 5(2) of the Brussels I Regulation. Accordingly, in the Lugano Convention 2007, Article 5(2)(c) explicitly refers to maintenance claims made ancillarily to proceedings concerning parental responsibility, as well as to maintenance claims made ancillarily to proceedings concerning personal status.

Where the defendant to a maintenance claim is not domiciled in any EU Member State, jurisdiction is in general remitted to the lex fori by Article 4 of the Brussels I Regulation.[18] Jurisdiction over a maintenance claim can also be created by agreement between the parties under Article 23, or by the defendant's appearance without contesting jurisdiction under Article 24. Articles 27–30, on concurrent proceedings in different Member States, apply to maintenance claims in the same way as to other claims.[19]

An order in divorce proceedings for maintenance pending suit is not a provisional measure within the scope of Article 31 of the Brussels I Regulation.[20] But the English court has power to award maintenance pending suit in English divorce proceedings, even where a dispute as to its jurisdiction remains unresolved, whether the dispute relates to connecting-factors or to priority between concurrent proceedings.[21]

---

[16]    See Case C-295/95: *Farrell v Long* [1997] ECR I-1683.
[17]    See Case C-433/01: *Freistaat Bayern v Blijdenstein* [2004] ECR I-981. See also Case C-271/00: *Baten* [2002] ECR I-10489.
[18]    On the relevant English law in respect of child maintenance, see *Re S* [2005] 2 FLR 94 (CA).
[19]    See *J v P* [2007] EWHC 704 (Fam) (Sumner J).
[20]    See *Wermuth v Wermuth* [2003] 1 WLR 942 (CA).
[21]    See *Moses-Taiga v Taiga* [2006] 1 FLR 1074 (CA); *L-K v K* [2006] 2 FLR 1113 (Singer J); and *Bentinck v Bentinck* [2007] 2 FLR 1 (CA).

## Variation of Maintenance Orders

The Brussels I Regulation does not cope well with judgments which are variable by reason of subsequent changes of circumstance, as is typically the case for orders for periodical payments of maintenance. According to the Schlosser Report,[22] the power to vary a maintenance order belongs neither to the court which originally made the order, nor to a court in which enforcement of a foreign order is sought under Chapter III of the Regulation. For the purpose of jurisdiction, an application for variation must be treated as a separate proceeding, and the necessary connecting-factor under Chapter II must exist at the institution of the application for variation.[23]

Since recognition under Chapter III implies that the order must be given the same effects in the State addressed as it has in the State of origin,[24] it seems clear that a court of a Member State which is competently seised of an application to vary or supplement a maintenance order made in another Member State is precluded from doing so in a manner inconsistent with the law of the country in which the original order was made. For example, where the law of the country of origin does not permit an order to be varied by way of remitting accrued arrears, such remission should not be ordered elsewhere.[25]

## Recognition and Enforcement

Under Chapter III of the Brussels I Regulation, Article 34(3) and (4) prevent the recognition and enforcement of a judgment if it is irreconcilable either: (i) with a judgment given in a dispute between the same parties in the Member State addressed; or (ii) with an earlier judgment which was given in another Member State or in a non-member country involving the same cause of action and between the same parties, and which fulfils the conditions necessary for its recognition in the Member State addressed.

In *Hoffmann v Krieg*,[26] the European Court explained that judgments are irreconcilable with each other for this purpose where they entail mutually exclusive legal consequences. It concluded that there was irreconcilability between a German maintenance order and a subsequent Dutch divorce, as regards the period following the divorce, on the questionable assumption that the maintenance order necessarily presupposed the continued existence of a matrimonial relationship. The ruling has been followed, loyally rather than enthusiastically, by English courts in the context of Irish maintenance orders followed by English divorces.[27] Similarly the Irish Supreme Court has refused under Article 34(3) to recognise a Dutch main-

---

22    [1979] OJ C59/71 at paras 98–108. See also Gaudemet-Tallon, at para 182.
23    See also *Thurston v Thurston*, 28th October 1997 (CA).
24    See Case 145/86: *Hoffmann v Krieg* [1988] ECR 645; the Jenard Report, [1979] OJ C59/1, at p. 43; *Re the Enforcement of a Swiss Maintenance Agreement* [1988] ECC 181 at 187 (German Supreme Court); and 28 US Code § 1738. Cf. the Schlosser Report, [1979] OJ C59/71, at pp. 127–8; and *Hart v American Airlines* 304 NYS2d 810 (1969).
25    See *Heron v Heron* 703 NE2d 712 (1998), where a Massachusetts court held that the full-faith-and-credit clause of the US Constitution prevented it from modifying a Nevada maintenance order insofar as it was unmodifiable, as regards arrears, under Nevada law.
26    Case 145/86, [1988] ECR 645.
27    See *Macaulay v Macaulay* [1991] 1 WLR 179; and *Ex parte Emmett* [1993] 2 FLR 663.

tenance order, made ancillarily to a Dutch divorce decree, as being irreconcilable with an Irish decision refusing to recognise the divorce.[28]

But it seems clear that there is no irreconcilability where a subsequent maintenance order varies an earlier maintenance order, so long as the variation effected is of such a character and is based on such grounds as to be in principle permissible under the law of the country in which the original order was made.

The prohibition of substantive review under Chapter III of the Brussels I Regulation does not prevent the court addressed from holding that the Regulation is not applicable because the subject-matter of the judgment falls outside the scope of the Regulation as defined by Article 1.[29] But the Regulation omits any provision equivalent to Article 27(4) of the Brussels Convention, which prevented recognition and enforcement where the judgment involved the decision of a preliminary question of individual status or capacity, matrimonial property, or succession, in a manner inconsistent with the conflict law of the State addressed. Accordingly, such situations will now have to be evaluated under the public-policy proviso contained in Article 34(1).[30]

## The Indirect Impact of the Brussels IIA Regulation

Since the Brussels IIA Regulation does not include maintenance within its scope, it might at first sight have been assumed that it has no effect at all on maintenance claims. But such an assumption would be unjustified, especially in an English context. For in England maintenance is frequently dealt with ancillarily in matrimonial proceedings, and the effect of the Brussels IIA Regulation is sometimes to deprive the English courts of matrimonial jurisdiction in favour of a court of another Member State. This is so, for example, where a wife of English origin has recently returned to England and revived her English domicile but has not yet habitually resided in England for six months, and the husband, who is a French national and has for many years been habitually resident in France, commences divorce proceedings there. Moreover, even if in principle the English court has matrimonial jurisdiction, as where the wife has habitually resided here for a sufficient period after her return, such jurisdiction will be defeated if matrimonial proceedings are first begun in a competent court of another Member State.

The inability of the English court as a result of the Brussels IIA Regulation to entertain divorce proceedings will entail a consequent inability to entertain ancillary proceedings for maintenance, and independent English proceedings for maintenance will meet other obstacles. If the foreign divorce court is also requested to deal with maintenance, the pending

---

[28] See *T v L* [2008] IESC 48, affirming *DT v FL* [2007] ILPr 56 (McKechnie J).

[29] See Gaudemet-Tallon, at paras 319 and 333.

[30] In this respect, the Brussels I Regulation accords with the Hague Convention of 2nd October 1973 on the Recognition and Enforcement of Decisions relating to Maintenance Obligations, which does not contain a specific provision on incidental determinations of status, but leaves the problem to be dealt with under its public policy proviso contained in Article 5(1). As between the seventeen EU Member States and two other Lugano Convention countries which are party to the Hague Convention 1973, it constitutes a specialised convention whose provisions prevail over the Brussels I Regulation under Article 71, the Lugano Convention 2007 under Article 67, and the Lugano Convention 1988 under Article 57. Cf. Gaudemet-Tallon, at para 349.

maintenance application there will prevent a concurrent English application for maintenance (for example, under s 27 of the Matrimonial Causes Act 1973 on the ground of wilful neglect to maintain), since Article 27 of the Brussels I Regulation will compel the English court to decline jurisdiction in favour of the court first seised of a maintenance application.[31]

After the court of another Member State has granted a divorce and ruled on its maintenance application, an application could in some cases be made to the English court for maintenance after foreign divorce under Part III of the Matrimonial and Family Proceedings Act 1984. But on such an application the English court would have to recognise the foreign maintenance order under Chapter III of the Brussels I Regulation; and such recognition would have the effect of preventing the English court from making a maintenance order of a character or on grounds which would not accord in principle with the permissible types of and grounds for variation of the existing order under the law of the country in which the original order was made.

## THE MAINTENANCE REGULATION

### The Legislation

On 18th December 2008, the EC Council adopted Regulation 4/2009 on Jurisdiction, Applicable Law, Recognition and Enforcement of Decisions and Co-operation in Matters relating to Maintenance Obligations, which may conveniently be referred to as the Maintenance Regulation.[32] This resulted from a Proposal presented by the EC Commission on 15th December 2005.[33] Meanwhile negotiations at the Hague Conference on Private International Law had led to the adoption on 23rd November 2007 of two instruments: a Convention on the International Recovery of Child Support and Other Forms of Family Maintenance, which may conveniently be referred to as the Hague Convention 2007;[34] and a Protocol on the Law Applicable to Maintenance Obligations, which may conveniently be referred to as the Hague Protocol 2007. On 30th November 2009, the EC Council adopted Decision 2009/941,[35] approving the conclusion of the Hague Protocol 2007 by the European Community, and making the Protocol applicable within the European Union from 18th June 2011.

The Maintenance Regulation contains 76 Articles, arranged in IX Chapters, along with XI Annexes. Chapter I (Articles 1–2) deals with its scope and provides some definitions. Chapter II (Articles 3–14) deals with the direct jurisdiction of courts and equivalent authorities. Chapter III (Article 15) deals with choice of the applicable substantive law. Chapter IV (Articles 16–43) deals with the recognition, enforceability and enforcement of decisions. Chapter V (Articles 44–7) deals with legal aid.[36] Chapter VI (Article 48) deals with court

---

[31]   See *Moore v Moore* [2007] EWCA Civ 361.
[32]   For its text, see [2009] OJ L7/1.
[33]   See COM(2005) 649 final.
[34]   On 28th July 2009, the EC Commission presented a Proposal for a Council Decision on the conclusion by the European Community of the Hague Convention 2007; see COM(2009) 373 final.
[35]   See [2009] OJ L331/17.
[36]   See also Recitals 36–7; and EC Directive 2003/8, [2003] OJ L26/41.

settlements and authentic instruments. Chapter VII (Articles 49–63) deals with co-operation between Central Authorities.[37] Chapter VIII (Article 64) deals with claims by public bodies. Chapter IX (Articles 65–76) contains general and final provisions. Annexes 1–IX contain prescribed forms, and Annexes X and XI contain lists of relevant or competent authorities.

The Maintenance Regulation and the Hague Protocol 2007 will become applicable on 18th June 2011.[38] The Regulation will apply in all the EU Member States except Denmark. Although the United Kingdom failed to take part in the adoption of the Regulation, it has subsequently notified its acceptance of the Regulation, and this acceptance has been endorsed by the EC Commission in its Decision 2009/451.[39] The Maintenance Regulation will not apply to Denmark, except that it may apply the amendments made by the Maintenance Regulation to the Brussels I Regulation.[40]

Although the Maintenance Regulation will apply in the United Kingdom, its effect in relation to the United Kingdom will differ from its effect for the other Member States. Recital 20 to the Regulation envisaged that the Hague Protocol 2007 would be concluded by the Community, and Article 15 specifies that the law applicable to maintenance obligations is to be determined in accordance with the Hague Protocol 2007 in the Member States bound by that instrument. But the United Kingdom has not participated in the adoption of, nor subsequently accepted, EC Council Decision 2009/941,[41] which has approved the conclusion of the Hague Protocol 2007 by the European Community. Thus the Regulation will not affect the existing British choice-of-law rules, which largely refer issues relating to maintenance to the lex fori. In view of this derogation from Chapter III of the Regulation in relation to choice of law, Chapter IV (on the recognition, enforceability and enforcement of decisions) adopts a different regime for the enforcement in other Member States of British maintenance orders. In the case of orders made in the other Member States, which will be bound by the Hague Protocol 2007, Section 1 of Chapter IV will apply, and the need for an enforcement order in the State addressed will be eliminated. In the case of British orders, Section 2 of Chapter IV will apply, and enforcement will require the obtaining of an enforcement order in accordance with provisions similar to those contained in Chapter III of the Brussels I Regulation.

## Scope

By Article 1(1), the Maintenance Regulation applies to maintenance obligations arising from a family relationship, parentage, marriage or affinity. Recital 11 adds that the term, maintenance obligation, should be interpreted autonomously.

The Regulation often refers to the parties to a maintenance claim as the creditor and the debtor. Article 2(1)(10) defines the creditor as any individual to whom maintenance is owed

---

[37] See also Recitals 31–5 and 39.

[38] See Article 76 of the Maintenance Regulation, and Article 4 of Decision 2009/941.

[39] See Recitals 46–8 to the Regulation; and Decision 2009/451, [2009] OJ L149/73.

[40] See Recital 48 and Article 1(2) of the Maintenance Regulation; and Article 3 of the Agreement of 19th October 2005 between the Community and Denmark, extending the Brussels I Regulation to Denmark, [2005] OJ 299/62.

[41] See [2009] OJ L331/17. See also the UK Parliamentary Committee on European Scrutiny, Session 2007–08, 40th Report, part 26, 4th December 2008, and Session 2008–09, 17th Report, part 4, 8th May 2009.

or is alleged to be owed, and Article 2(1)(11) defines the debtor as any individual who owes or who is alleged to owe maintenance. Despite the prejudicial character of the terminology, as tending to presume that the claim is justified, these definitions at least make clear that both parties must be human beings, rather than corporate or similar entities.[42] They also make clear that the terms extend to situations in which no maintenance order has yet been made.[43] But they leave obscure the identity of the creditor in such cases as where one parent claims maintenance from the other parent in respect of a child. The general tenor of the Regulation perhaps suggests that it is the child who will count as the creditor in such cases.

In other respects, the precise concept of a maintenance obligation remains shrouded in obscurity. There is no definition directly specifying whether the concept is confined to a claim for periodical payments (as distinct from a lump-sum payment), or indeed whether a claim for the transfer of an asset (such as a house, or a share in a pension) is included. Nor is there any indication as to where the line between maintenance and matrimonial property should be drawn. Presumably, in these respects, maintenance should be given a wide interpretation, in accordance with the rulings of the European Court under the Brussels I Regulation.[44] A wide approach is indicated obliquely by the forms set out in Annexes I–IV to the Regulation, to be used for an Extract from a Decision, a Court Settlement or an Authentic Instrument, to be issued by the court of origin, for use in connection with enforcement in another Member State. These include entries for an amount to be paid in one sum; an amount to be paid in instalments; a sum to be paid regularly (weekly, monthly, or at some other frequency); an amount due retroactively; interest; a payment in kind; and some other form of payment.

Another potential problem is that situations exist in which parties (such as spouses) may in principle have reciprocal obligations to maintain each other, but the Regulation appears to treat these obligations in opposite directions as separate and distinct (albeit related). In short, the efforts of the Regulation to define its scope seem very unsatisfactory.

The Regulation is primarily concerned with proceedings in and decisions of courts, but Article 2(2) extends its scope to proceedings in and decisions of administrative authorities which satisfy certain requirements. It does this by defining 'courts' as including administrative authorities of the Member States with competence in matters relating to maintenance obligations, provided that such authorities offer guarantees with regard to impartiality and the right of all parties to be heard, and provided that, under the law of the Member State where they are established, their decisions may be made the subject of an appeal to or review by a judicial authority, and have a similar force and effect as a decision of a judicial authority on the same matter. Such administrative authorities are to be listed in Annex X.

---

[42]    By Article 64, a public body acting in place of an individual to whom maintenance is owed, or to which reimbursement is owed for benefits provided in place of maintenance, counts as a creditor for the purpose of enforcement of a maintenance decision under Chapter IV of the Regulation. But a public body does not count as a creditor for the purposes of direct jurisdiction or choice of law. However, the right of a public body to act in place of an individual to whom maintenance is owed, or to seek reimbursement of benefits provided to an individual creditor in place of maintenance, is governed by the law to which the body is subject.

[43]    See similarly Case C-295/95: *Farrell v Long* [1997] ECR I-1683, on Article 5(2) of the Brussels I Regulation.

[44]    See Case 120/79: *De Cavel v De Cavel (No 2)* [1980] ECR 731; and Case C-220/95: *Van den Boogaard v Laumen* [1997] ECR I-1147; and pp. 29–32 above.

By Recital 44 and Article 68(1), the Maintenance Regulation replaces the provisions of the Brussels I Regulation in respect of matters relating to maintenance obligations. This is subject to transitional provisions specified by Article 75. By Article 68(2), in matters relating to maintenance obligations, the Maintenance Regulation replaces Regulation 805/2004, on uncontested claims, except with regard to European Enforcement Orders on maintenance obligations issued in a Member State not bound by the 2007 Hague Protocol.

## Relation with international conventions

Article 69(1)–(2) of the Maintenance Regulation deals with the relation between the Regulation and existing international conventions concerning maintenance to which one or more Member States were party at the time of its adoption. These include the Hague Convention of 2nd October 1973 on the Recognition and Enforcement of Decisions Relating to Maintenance Obligations, which is in force between seventeen EU Member States[45] and five other countries.[46] In substance, the Maintenance Regulation is not to affect the application of such conventions in situations involving a non-member country which is a party to the relevant convention, but in relations between Member States the Regulation takes precedence over such conventions. Thus in the United Kingdom the Hague Convention 1973 will cease to apply to French maintenance orders, but will remain applicable to Australian maintenance orders. By way of exception, Article 69(3) permits the continued application by the relevant Member States of the Convention of 23 March 1962 between Sweden, Denmark, Finland, Iceland and Norway on the recovery of maintenance, but this must not have the effect of depriving the defendant of his protection under Articles 19 and 21 of the Maintenance Regulation.

As regards future agreements between an EU Member State and a non-member country, EC Regulation 664/2009[47] extends to agreements relating to maintenance, as well as to agreements relating to matrimonial proceedings or parental responsibility.

## Transitional provisions

Transitional provisions are specified by Article 75. The general rule, laid down by Article 75(1), is that the Regulation applies only to proceedings instituted, to court settlements approved or concluded, and to authentic instruments established after its date of application. Thus the provisions of Chapter II on judicial jurisdiction, and Chapter III on choice of law, are confined to proceedings instituted after 18th June 2011.

However, a major exception is made by Article 75(2) in relation to the recognition and enforcement of maintenance orders (and of court settlements and authentic instruments). The provisions of Chapter IV which apply to decisions given in a Member State not bound by the Hague Protocol 2007 are made applicable to decisions which were given in the Member States (and court settlements which were approved or concluded, and authentic instruments which were established, in the Member States) before the commencement date of the Regulation, and for which recognition or a declaration of enforceability is requested after that

---

[45]   The relevant Member States are the United Kingdom, France, Germany, Italy, the Netherlands, Luxembourg, Denmark, Greece, Spain, Portugal, Sweden, Finland, Poland, the Czech Republic, Slovakia, Lithuania and Estonia.
[46]   The other countries are Australia, Norway, Switzerland, Turkey and the Ukraine.
[47]   [2009] OJ L200/46. See pp. 421–2 above.

date; and also to decisions given (and court settlements approved or concluded, and authentic instruments established) after the commencement date following proceedings begun before that date; provided that such decisions, settlements and instruments fall with the scope of the Brussels I Regulation for the purposes of recognition and enforcement. But the Brussels I Regulation continues to apply to procedures for recognition and enforcement under way on the date of application of the Maintenance Regulation.

### Direct Jurisdiction

Chapter II (Articles 3–14) of the Maintenance Regulation deals with the direct jurisdiction of the courts of the Member States to entertain maintenance claims. As Recital 15 indicates, these rules on jurisdiction apply even if the defendant is habitually resident in a non-member country, and attempt an almost complete harmonisation, eliminating reference to national law. By Recital 18 and Article 2(3), references in these rules to nationality are replaced, in relation to the United Kingdom and Ireland, by references to domicile.

The main rules on the existence of jurisdiction are specified by Article 3 of the Regulation, which gives competence to several courts: (a) the court for the place where the defendant is habitually resident; (b) the court for the place where the creditor is habitually resident; and (c) where the maintenance claim is made ancillarily to proceedings concerning the status of a person or parental responsibility, a court which, according to its own law, has jurisdiction to entertain the proceedings concerning status or parental responsibility, unless that jurisdiction is based solely on the nationality (or, in the United Kingdom or Ireland, the domicile) of one of the parties. It is left to the creditor to choose between these courts. It is clear that the reference to a person's habitual residence is to his or her habitual residence at the institution of the maintenance proceedings.

Article 4 of the Regulation derogates from Article 3 by enabling the parties to a maintenance claim to make an agreement designating a court or the courts of a Member State as competent to settle any disputes which have arisen or may arise between them, except for disputes relating to a maintenance obligation towards a child under the age of 18. Recital 19 explains that the exclusion is designed to protect the weaker party. The jurisdiction conferred by a valid agreement is exclusive unless the parties have agreed otherwise. An agreement on jurisdiction must be in writing, but any communication by electronic means which provides a durable record of the agreement is treated as equivalent to writing.

The range of courts which may be chosen by agreement under Article 4 is limited. It is permissible to choose a court or the courts of a Member State in or of which one of the parties is habitually resident or is a national (or, in the United Kingdom or Ireland, is domiciled). In addition, in the case of maintenance obligations between spouses or former spouses, it is permissible to choose a court which has jurisdiction to settle a matrimonial dispute between them, or a court or the courts of the Member State of their last common habitual residence for a period of at least one year. It is enough that any of these conditions is satisfied either at the time when the agreement on jurisdiction is concluded or at the time when the court is seised.

Article 4(4) deals with the situation where the parties have agreed to attribute exclusive jurisdiction to a court or courts of a State which is a party to the Lugano Convention 2007 and which is not an EU Member State. The Lugano Convention 2007 then applies, except in the case of disputes relating to a maintenance obligation towards a child under the age of 18.

Article 5 of the Regulation provides for submission by appearance. In addition to jurisdiction derived from other provisions of the Regulation, a court of a Member State before which a defendant enters an appearance has jurisdiction, unless the appearance was entered to contest the jurisdiction.

Article 6 of the Regulation provides for a subsidiary jurisdiction, applicable where no court of an EU Member State has jurisdiction pursuant to Articles 3–5 of the Regulation, and no court of a State which is party to the Lugano Convention 2007 and which is not an EU Member State has jurisdiction pursuant to the provisions of that Convention. In such a case, Article 6 confers jurisdiction on the courts of the Member State of the common nationality of the parties (or, in the United Kingdom or Ireland, of the common domicile of the parties).

Finally, Article 7 of the Regulation provides for jurisdiction on grounds of necessity, to avoid a denial of justice. It applies where no court of a Member State has jurisdiction under Articles 3–6, and enables the courts of a Member State on an exceptional basis to hear the case if proceedings cannot reasonably be brought or conducted or would be impossible in a non-member country with which the dispute is closely connected, and the dispute has a suffi- cient connection with the Member State of the court seised. Recital 16 explains that such an exceptional basis may exist when proceedings prove impossible in the non-member country in question, for example because of civil war, or when an applicant cannot reasonably be expected to initiate or conduct proceedings in that country. It also offers as an example of a sufficient connection with the forum Member State the nationality of one of the parties.

The foregoing provisions extend to applications to modify an existing maintenance order, as well as to original applications for maintenance. An application to modify an order is treated as a separate proceeding for the purpose of determining jurisdiction to entertain it. Thus jurisdiction over an application to modify depends under Article 3 on the habitual resi- dence of the parties at the date of the application to modify, rather than that of the original application, and the court which made the order does not necessarily have power to modify it.

However, Article 8 of the Regulation restricts jurisdiction over an application by the debtor for modification. Where a decision is given in a Member State where the creditor is habitually resident, proceedings to modify the decision or to have a new decision given cannot be brought by the debtor in any other Member State as long as the creditor remains habitually resident in the State in which the decision was given. This restriction does not apply where the parties have agreed in accordance with Article 4 to the jurisdiction of the courts of another Member State; nor where the creditor submits to the jurisdiction of the courts of another Member State by appearance in accordance with Article 5.[48]

Article 9 of the Maintenance Regulation deals with the time at which a court is regarded as seised of a proceeding. It echoes Article 30 of the Brussels I Regulation and effectively refers to the date of the issue, rather than the service, of the originating document.

Article 10 of the Maintenance Regulation requires a court of a Member State, where it is seised of a case over which it has no jurisdiction under the Regulation, to declare of its own motion that it has no jurisdiction.

---

[48]    If the European Union becomes party to the Hague Convention 2007, Article 8 will extend to a maintenance order made in an external country which is also party to that Convention in respect of the relevant sphere in favour of a creditor habitually resident there, but with some additional exceptions. See Recital 17 and Article 2(1)(8) of the Regulation.

Article 11 of the Regulation deals with notification of the defendant. By Article 11(1), where a defendant habitually resident elsewhere than in the forum State does not enter an appearance, the court must stay the proceedings so long as it is not shown that the defendant has been able to receive the document instituting the proceedings or an equivalent document in sufficient time to enable him to arrange for his defence, or that all necessary steps have been taken to that end. By Article 11(2), this provision is replaced by Article 19 of EC Regulation 1393/2007, if the document instituting the proceedings or an equivalent document had to be transmitted from one Member State to another under that Regulation.[49] In addition, Article 11(3) of the Maintenance Regulation makes applicable Article 15 of the Hague Convention of 15th November 1965 on the Service Abroad of Judicial and Extrajudicial Documents in Civil or Commercial Matters, if Regulation 1393/2007 does not apply and the document instituting the proceedings or an equivalent document had to be transmitted abroad under the Convention.[50]

Articles 12–14 of the Maintenance Regulation deal with concurrent actions and provisional measures. They echo Articles 27, 28 and 31 of the Brussels I Regulation.

### Choice of Law

Article 15 of the Maintenance Regulation specifies that the law applicable to maintenance obligations is to be determined in accordance with the Hague Protocol 2007 in the Member States bound by that instrument. Recital 20 envisaged that the Hague Protocol 2007 would be concluded by the European Community, and subsequently EC Council Decision 2009/941[51] has approved the conclusion of the Hague Protocol 2007 by the Community. Accordingly, by Article 76 of the Regulation, along with Decision 2009/941, the Regulation and the Protocol will enter into application in the European Union on 18th June 2011.

The United Kingdom has not participated in the adoption of, nor subsequently accepted, EC Council Decision 2009/941.[52] Thus the Maintenance Regulation will not affect the application in the United Kingdom of the existing choice-of-law rules, which largely refer issues relating to maintenance to the lex fori.[53] But, in the twenty-five Member States other than the United Kingdom and Denmark, choice of law in respect of maintenance obligations will be governed by the rules specified in the Protocol.[54]

---

[49]  See pp. 62–6 above.

[50]  See pp. 67–8 above.

[51]  See [2009] OJ L331/17. Provision for a Regional Economic Integration Organisation, such as the European Community, to become party to the Protocol is made by Article 24 thereof.

[52]  See the UK Parliamentary Committee on European Scrutiny, Session 2007–08, 40th Report, part 26, 4th December 2008, and Session 2008–09, 17th Report, part 4, 8th May 2009.

[53]  See Dicey, Morris and Collins, 14th edition (Sweet & Maxwell, 2006), Rule 91(7) and paras 18-207 and 18-208.

[54]  By Article 18 of the Protocol, as between the Contracting States, the Protocol replaces the Hague Convention of 2nd October 1973 on the Law Applicable to Maintenance Obligations and the Hague Convention of 24 October 1956 on the Law Applicable to Maintenance Obligations towards Children. By Article 19(1), the Protocol does not affect any other international instrument to which Contracting States are or become parties, and which contains provisions on matters governed by the Protocol, unless a contrary declaration is made by the States parties to such instrument; and by Article 19(2) the same applies to uniform laws based on special ties of a regional or other nature between the States concerned.

EC Decision 2009/941 has approved the Protocol on behalf of the Community, and declared that the Community exercises competence over all the matters governed by the Protocol, so that its Member States (except for the United Kingdom and Denmark) will be bound by the Protocol by virtue of its conclusion by the Community. It makes the Protocol applicable within the European Union from 18th June 2011, even if the Protocol has not entered into force internationally on that date. Moreover, Article 5 of the Decision overrides Article 22 of the Protocol by making the Protocol applicable within the European Union to maintenance claimed in the Member States in respect of a period before 18th June 2011, in situations where proceedings are instituted, court settlements are approved or concluded, and authentic instruments are established, after that date.

By Article 2, the Protocol applies even if the applicable law is that of a non-contracting State.[55] Article 12 excludes renvoi by specifying that references to a law are to the law in force in a State other than its choice-of-law rules. Article 13 provides a conventional proviso, excluding the application of the law determined under the Protocol to the extent that its effects would be manifestly contrary to the public policy of the forum. Article 20 instructs that, in the interpretation of the Protocol, regard must be had to its international character and to the need to promote uniformity in its application.

The general rule, laid down by Article 3(1) of the Protocol, is that maintenance obligations are governed by the law of the State of the habitual residence of the creditor. Article 3(2) adds that, in the case of a change in the habitual residence of the creditor, the law of the State of the new habitual residence applies as from the moment when the change occurs.

Article 4 of the Protocol derogates from the general rule laid down by Article 3 and introduces special rules favouring certain creditors. By Article 4(1), these special rules apply in the case of maintenance obligations of parents towards their children; of children towards their parents; and of persons other than parents, spouses and ex-spouses towards persons who have not attained the age of 21 years. In such cases, Article 4(2) makes applicable the law of the forum if under the law of the creditor's habitual residence the creditor is unable to obtain maintenance from the debtor. By Article 4(3), the law of the forum also applies where the creditor sues at the debtor's habitual residence, unless the creditor is unable under that law to obtain maintenance from the debtor, in which case the law of the State of the habitual residence of the creditor applies.

In the case of the maintenance obligations specified by Article 4(1), Article 4(4) applies where the creditor is unable under the laws referred to in Articles 3, 4(2) and 4(3) to obtain maintenance from the debtor. In that case, the law of the State of their common nationality, if such exists, applies. By Article 9, a State which uses domicile as a connecting factor in family matters may elect to use its concept of domicile, in place of nationality, for this purpose. It must inform the Permanent Bureau of the Hague Conference on Private International Law of such an election. Presumably Ireland will do so.

Article 5 of the Protocol provides a special rule with respect to spouses and ex-spouses. In the case of a maintenance obligation between spouses, ex-spouses or parties to a marriage which has been annulled, Article 3 does not apply if one of the parties objects and the law of

---

[55]　See also Articles 15–17 and 26, which deal with States in which there are several legal systems applicable to maintenance (whether on a territorial or personal basis).

another State, such as that of their last common habitual residence, has a closer connection with the marriage. In that event, the law of the more closely connected State applies.

Article 6 of the Protocol supplies a special rule in favour of the defendant. It does not apply to maintenance obligations arising from a parent-child relationship towards a child, nor to maintenance obligations between spouses or ex-spouses. Otherwise, however, it enables the debtor to contest a claim from the creditor on the ground that there is no such obligation under both the law of the State of the habitual residence of the debtor and the law of the State of the common nationality of the parties, if such a common nationality exists. Again Article 9 permits a State which uses domicile as a connecting factor in family matters to elect to use its concept of domicile, in place of nationality, for this purpose.

Articles 7 and 8 of the Protocol deal with agreements between a maintenance creditor and debtor designating the applicable law. Article 7 applies where the agreement is confined to a particular proceeding in a given State, and it expressly designates the law of that State as applicable to a maintenance obligation. If the designation is made before the institution of such proceedings, it must be contained in an agreement which is signed by both parties, and which is either in writing or is recorded in some other medium whose contents are accessible so as to be usable for subsequent reference. But no further requirements are specified for its validity and effectiveness.

Article 8 deals more generally with agreements between a maintenance creditor and debtor designating the law applicable to a maintenance obligation, but imposes much more stringent requirements. By Article 8(1)–(2), an agreement designating the law applicable to a maintenance obligation may be made at any time, but it must either be in writing or be recorded in some other medium whose contents are accessible so as to be usable for subsequent reference, and it must be signed by both parties. But the range of laws from which the parties may choose is limited by Article 8(1). Only a choice of one of the following laws is permissible: (a) the law of a State of which at the time of the designation one of the parties is a national; (b) the law of a State in which at the time of the designation one of the parties is habitually resident; (c) a law which by designation of the parties or otherwise is applicable to their property regime; and (d) a law which by designation of the parties or otherwise is applicable to their divorce or legal separation. More importantly, Article 8(3) excludes the power to choose the applicable law by agreement (other than under Article 7) where the maintenance obligation is in respect of a person under the age of 18 years, or of an adult who, by reason of an impairment or insufficiency of his or her personal faculties, is not in a position to protect his or her interest. In addition, Article 8(4) insists that, despite an agreed choice of law (other than under Article 7), the question of whether the creditor can renounce his or her right to maintenance must be determined by the law of the State of the habitual residence of the creditor at the time of the designation. Finally, Article 8(5) limits the effect of an agreed choice unless at the time of the designation the parties were fully informed and aware of its consequences. Otherwise, the law designated by the parties is not to apply where its application would lead to manifestly unfair or unreasonable consequences for any of the parties. In view of its various requirements and restrictions, it may be doubted whether Article 8 has any real utility.

Article 11 of the Protocol deals with the scope of the applicable law. It subjects the following matters (among others) to the law which is applicable to the maintenance obligation: (a) whether, to what extent, and from whom the creditor may claim maintenance; (b) the extent to which the creditor may claim retroactive maintenance; (c) the basis for calculation of the amount of maintenance, and indexation; (d) who is entitled to institute maintenance proceedings, except for issues relating to procedural capacity and representation in the proceedings; and (e) prescription or limitation periods. On the other hand, it is apparent from Article 2(2) of the Protocol, and Recital 21 to the Maintenance Regulation, that it is not for the law applicable to the maintenance obligation, but for the law otherwise applicable under the forum's conflict rules, to determine the existence of any family relationship (such as marriage or filiation) from which a maintenance obligation may arise.

By Article 11(f) of the Protocol, the law which is applicable to the maintenance obligation governs the extent of the obligation of a maintenance debtor, where a public body seeks reimbursement of benefits provided for a creditor in place of maintenance. In contrast, Article 10 specifies that the right of a public body to seek reimbursement of a benefit provided to the creditor in place of maintenance is governed by the law to which the public body is subject. The combined effect seems to be that the admissibility of a claim to reimbursement by a public body is governed by the law of the country to which the body belongs, but in the determination of such a claim the debtor's liability is limited in accordance with the law applicable to the maintenance obligation.

Article 14 of the Protocol adopts the unusual course of imposing a substantive rule which overrides the law applicable to the maintenance obligation. It specifies that even if the applicable law provides otherwise, the needs of the creditor and the resources of the debtor, as well as any compensation which the creditor was awarded in place of periodical maintenance payments, must be taken into account in determining the amount of maintenance.

### Recognition and Enforcement

Chapter IV (Articles 16–43) of the Maintenance Regulation regulates the recognition, enforceability and enforcement in an EU Member State of decisions in respect of maintenance obligations given by a court (or an equivalent administrative authority) of another Member State. By Article 2(1)(1), it is immaterial what the decision is called (such as a decree, order, judgment or writ of execution), and a decision by an officer of the court determining the costs or expenses is included.

It seems that Chapter IV does not extend to a decision rejecting a maintenance claim; for example, on the ground that no family relationship exists or that the creditor has greater resources and smaller needs than the debtor. For Recital 25 emphasises that recognition in a Member State of a decision relating to maintenance obligations has as its only object to allow the recovery of the maintenance claim determined in the decision; and that it does not imply the recognition by that Member State of the family relationship, parentage, marriage or affinity underlying the maintenance obligations which gave rise to the decision.

Chapter IV distinguishes decisions given in a Member State bound by the Hague Protocol 2007 from decisions given in a Member State not so bound. Where the decision was given in a Member State bound by the Protocol, its recognition, enforceability and enforcement in the other Member States is governed by Sections 1 and 3 (Articles 17–22 and 39–43) of the Regulation. This effectively applies to decisions given in the twenty-five Member States other than the United Kingdom and Denmark. Where the decision was given in a Member State not bound by the Protocol, its recognition, enforceability and enforcement in the other Member States is governed by Sections 2 and 3 (Articles 23–43) of the Regulation. This effectively applies to decisions given in the United Kingdom. It must be emphasised that this distinction is concerned with the position in regard to the Protocol of the Member State in which the decision was given, and not with that of the State in which recognition or enforcement is sought. Thus the enforcement in England of a French maintenance order will be subject to Section 1 of Chapter IV, while the enforcement in France of an English maintenance order will be subject to Section 2.[56]

By Article 48(1), court settlements and authentic instruments which are enforceable in the Member State of origin must be recognised in another Member State and be enforceable there in the same way as decisions, in accordance with Chapter IV. Article 2(1)(2) defines a court settlement as a settlement in matters relating to maintenance obligations which has been approved by a court or concluded before a court in the course of proceedings. Article 2(1)(3)(a) defines an authentic instrument as a document relating to maintenance obligations which has been formally drawn up or registered as an authentic instrument in the Member State of origin, and of which the authenticity relates to its signature and content, and has been established by a public authority or another authority empowered for that purpose. By Article 2(1)(3)(b), an arrangement relating to maintenance obligations concluded with administrative authorities of the Member State of origin or authenticated by them also counts as an authentic instrument. Recital 13 explains that the Regulation should not affect the right of either party to a court settlement or an authentic instrument to challenge the settlement or instrument before the courts of the Member State of origin.

**Recognition and enforcement under Section 1**
By Article 17(1) of the Regulation, a decision given in a Member State bound by the Hague Protocol 2007 must be recognised in another Member State without any special procedure being required, and without any possibility of opposing its recognition.[57] By Article 17(2), a decision given in such a Member State which is enforceable in that State is made enforceable in another Member State without the need for a declaration of enforceability.[58] By Article 39, the court of origin may declare a decision provisionally enforceable, notwithstanding any appeal, even if national law does not provide for enforceability by operation of law.[59] By

---

[56]   The report on the application of the Regulation, which Article 74 requires the EU Commission to submit within five years of its entry into application, must include an evaluation of the functioning of the procedure for recognition and enforcement applicable to decisions given in a Member State not bound by the Protocol.

[57]   As regards the documentary evidence which should be produced by a party who seeks mere recognition (without enforcement), see Article 40.

[58]   Recital 9 explains that a maintenance creditor should be able to obtain easily, in a Member State, a decision which will be automatically enforceable in another Member State without further formalities. Recital 24 adds that the guarantees provided by the application of choice-of-law rules should provide the justification for having decisions relating to maintenance obligations given in a Member State bound by the Hague Protocol 2007 recognised and regarded as enforceable in all the other Member States without any procedure being necessary and without any form of control on the substance in the Member State of enforcement.

[59]   Recital 22 explains that, in order to ensure swift and efficient recovery of a maintenance obligation and to prevent delaying actions, decisions in matters relating to maintenance obligations given in a Member State should in principle be provisionally enforceable. The Regulation should therefore provide that the court of origin should be able to declare the decision provisionally enforceable even if the national law does not provide for enforceability by operation of law, and even if an appeal has been or could still be lodged against the decision under national law.

Article 18, an enforceable decision carries with it by operation of law the power to proceed to any protective measures which exist under the law of the Member State of enforcement.

Article 41(1) establishes a general rule that the procedure for the enforcement of decisions given in another Member State is governed by the law of the Member State of enforcement. It also insists that a decision given in a Member State which is enforceable in another Member State must be enforced there under the same conditions as a local decision. Article 41(2) and Recital 27 make a minor exception to the reference of enforcement procedure to the law of the State of enforcement, by exempting a party seeking the enforcement of a decision given in another Member State from any requirement to have a postal address or an authorised representative in the Member State of enforcement, but this does not otherwise affect the rules of the Member State of enforcement as to the persons competent to act in enforcement proceedings. Article 20 specifies the documentary evidence which should be provided by a party seeking enforcement.

Article 19 offers some protection, by way of a right to apply for a review in the State of origin, to a defendant who did not enter an appearance in the proceedings which led to the decision. But this right is limited by Article 19(1) to cases where the defendant was not served with the document instituting the proceedings or an equivalent document in sufficient time and in such a way as to enable him to arrange for his defence; or where he was prevented from contesting the maintenance claim by reason of force majeure or due to extraordinary circumstances without any fault on his part. Even then the right is excluded if the defendant failed to challenge the decision in the State of origin when it was possible for him to do so. The highly restrictive approach adopted towards the defendant's right to a hearing seems remarkable, but Recital 29 explains that this right to apply for a review is an extraordinary remedy granted to a defendant in default, and does not affect the application of any other extraordinary remedies laid down in the law of the Member State of origin, provided that those remedies are not incompatible with the right to a review under the Regulation.

By Article 19(2), the time-limit for applying for a review under Article 19 in general runs from the day when the defendant was effectively acquainted with the contents of the decision and was able to react. But, in any event, time begins to run at the latest from the date of the first enforcement measure having the effect of making his property non-disposable in whole or in part. The defendant is required to react promptly, and in any event within forty-five days. No extension may be granted on account of distance. By Article 19(3), if the court rejects the application for a review under Article 19 on the basis that none of the specified grounds for a review applies, the maintenance decision remains in force. If the court decides that a review is justified for a specified reason, the maintenance decision becomes null and void, but the creditor does not lose the benefits of the interruption of prescription or limitation periods, or the right to claim retroactive maintenance, acquired in the initial proceedings.

By Article 42, under no circumstances may a decision given in a Member State be reviewed as to its substance in the Member State in which recognition, enforceability or enforcement is sought. But Article 22 and Recital 25 insist that the recognition and enforcement of a decision on maintenance under the Regulation does not in any way imply the recognition of the family relationship, parentage, marriage or affinity underlying the maintenance obligation which gave rise to the decision. Recital 25 adds that recognition in a Member State of a decision relating to maintenance obligations has as its only object to allow the recovery of the maintenance claim determined in the decision.

Article 21 deals with the refusal or suspension of enforcement in the State of enforcement.

Article 21(2) and (2) make specific provision for time-limitation, irreconcilability with another decision, and review or suspension in the State of origin. But, except in these specific areas, Article 21(1) provides generally that the grounds of refusal or suspension of enforcement under the law of the Member State of enforcement apply. Although in this connection Recital 30 refers, as examples of grounds of refusal or suspension laid down in national law which are not incompatible with those listed in the Regulation, to the debtor's discharge of his debt at the time of enforcement, or the unattachable nature of certain assets,[60] it is conceivable that the operation of Article 21(1) could undermine the entire scheme of the Regulation.

As regards time-limitation, Article 21(2) requires the competent authority in the Member State of enforcement, on application by the debtor, to refuse, either wholly or in part, the enforcement of the decision of the court of origin if the right to enforce the decision of the court of origin is extinguished by the effect of prescription or the limitation of action. For this purpose, one applies either the law of the Member State of origin or that of the Member State of enforcement, whichever provides for the longer limitation period.

As regards irreconcilable decisions, Article 21(2) also enables the competent authority in the Member State of enforcement, on application by the debtor, to refuse, either wholly or in part, the enforcement of the decision of the court of origin if it is irreconcilable with a decision given in the Member State of enforcement, or with a decision given in another Member State or in a non-member country which fulfils the conditions necessary for its recognition in the Member State of enforcement. But a decision which has the effect of modifying an earlier decision on maintenance on the basis of changed circumstances is not regarded as an irreconcilable decision for this purpose.

By Article 21(3), the competent authority in the Member State of enforcement may, on application by the debtor, suspend, either wholly or in part, the enforcement of the decision of the court of origin if the competent court of the Member State of origin has been seised of an application for a review of the decision of the court of origin under Article 19. In addition, the competent authority of the Member State of enforcement must, on application by the debtor, suspend the enforcement of the decision of the court of origin where the enforceability of that decision is suspended in the Member State of origin.

By Article 43, recovery of any costs incurred in the application of the Regulation does not take precedence over the recovery of maintenance.

### Recognition and enforcement under Section 2

As regards the recognition and enforcement in other EU Member States of a maintenance decision given in a Member State which is not bound by the 2007 Hague Protocol, Section 2 of Chapter IV of the Maintenance Regulation provides a regime of substantive and procedural

---

[60]    Recital 30 explains that, in order to speed up the enforcement in another Member State of a decision given in a Member State bound by the Hague Protocol 2007, it is necessary to limit the grounds of refusal or of suspension of enforcement which may be invoked by the debtor on account of the cross-border nature of the maintenance claim; but that this limitation should not affect the grounds of refusal or of suspension laid down in national law which are not incompatible with those listed in the Regulation, such as the debtor's discharge of his debt at the time of enforcement or the unattachable nature of certain assets.

rules which closely resembles that provided for ordinary civil and commercial judgments by Chapter III of the Brussels I Regulation.[61] Only the differences will be noted here.

With regard to the refusal of recognition and enforcement by reason of irreconcilability with another decision, Article 24 of the Maintenance Regulation establishes that a decision which has the effect of modifying an earlier decision on maintenance on the basis of changed circumstances does not count as an irreconcilable decision.

As regards enforcement procedure, Article 30 of the Maintenance Regulation sets a time-limit for the making of the initial decision on an application for a declaration of enforceability. The decision must be made within thirty days of the lodging of a complete application, accompanied by the appropriate documentary evidence,[62] except where exceptional circumstances make this impossible.[63]

By Article 32(5) of the Maintenance Regulation, an appeal against a declaration of enforceability must be lodged within thirty days of service of the declaration. But if the party against whom enforcement is sought has his habitual residence in a Member State other than that in which the declaration of enforceability was given, the time for appealing is forty-five days and runs from the date of service, either on him in person or at his residence. No extension may be granted on account of distance. By Article 34, the court seised of a normal appeal against the making or refusal of a declaration of enforceability must give its decision within ninety days from the date on which it was seised, except where exceptional circumstances make this impossible.

By Article 35 of the Maintenance Regulation, a court with which a normal or a final appeal in respect of a declaration of enforceability is lodged must, on the application of the party against whom enforcement is sought, stay its proceedings if the enforceability of the decision is suspended in the Member State of origin by reason of an appeal. But there is no further power to stay proceedings (for example, because an appeal has been or may yet be lodged against the maintenance decision in the Member State of origin).

As in the case of a maintenance decision to which Section 1 applies, Article 39 of the Maintenance Regulation enables the court of origin to declare its decision provisionally enforceable, notwithstanding any appeal, even if national law does not provide for enforceability by operation of law. Similarly, Article 41(1), which subjects enforcement procedure to the law of the State of enforcement and applies the same conditions as for a local judgment, and Article 41(2), which exempts a party seeking enforcement from requirements to have a postal address or an authorised representative in the Member State of enforcement, extend to enforcement under Section 2. Article 43, by which recovery of costs does not take precedence over the recovery of maintenance, also extends to enforcement under Section 2.

---

[61] Recital 26 recognises that Section 2 is modelled on the procedure and the grounds for refusing recognition set out in the Brussels I Regulation. On Chapter III of that Regulation, see Chapters 10 and 11 above.

[62] On the documentary evidence which should accompany an application for enforcement, see Articles 28 and 29. See also Article 40, on the documentary evidence which should be produced by a party seeking recognition.

[63] Recital 26 explains that, to accelerate proceedings and enable the creditor to recover his claim quickly, the court seised should be required to give its decision within a set time, unless there are exceptional circumstances.

**Public bodies as applicants for enforcement**

Chapter VIII (Article 64) of the Maintenance Regulation deals with enforcement of a main-tenance decision on the application of a public body which is acting in place of an individual to whom maintenance is owed, or to which reimbursement is owed for benefits provided in place of maintenance. By Article 64(1), in such cases, the public body counts as a creditor for the purposes of an application for recognition and declaration of enforceability of a decision, or for the purposes of enforcement of decisions.[64] Accordingly, Article 64(3) enables the public body to seek recognition and a declaration of enforceability, or claim enforcement, of a decision given against a debtor on the application of the public body, claiming payment of benefits provided in place of maintenance; or of a decision given between an individual cred-itor and a debtor, to the extent of the benefits provided to the individual creditor in place of maintenance.

By Article 64(2), the right of a public body to act in place of an individual to whom main-tenance is owed, or to seek reimbursement of benefits provided to an individual creditor in place of maintenance, is governed by the law to which the body is subject. By Article 64(4), a public body seeking recognition and a declaration of enforceability, or claiming enforce-ment, of a decision must on request provide documentary evidence of its right to act in place of the individual creditor or to seek reimbursement under Article 64(2), and of the provision of benefits to the individual creditor.

# SUCCESSION ON DEATH

On 14th October 2009, the EC Commission presented a Proposal for a Regulation of the Parliament and Council on Jurisdiction, Applicable Law, and Recognition and Enforcement of Decisions and Authentic Instruments, in Matters of Succession, and the Creation of a European Certificate of Succession.[65] This may conveniently be referred to as the Proposal on Succession.

## Scope

Chapter I (Articles 1 and 2) of the Proposal deals with its scope and provides some defini-tions.[66] By Article 1(1), the Regulation is to apply to successions to the estates of deceased persons. But exclusions specified by Article 1(3) (along with Recitals 8 and 9) refer (among other things) to questions regarding matrimonial or comparable property regimes; to the acquisition of property other than by succession to the estate of a deceased person, such as acquisition by means of gifts inter vivos, survivorship among joint owners, pension plans, or insurance contracts; to the constitution, functioning and dissolving of trusts; and to the nature of rights in rem in respect of property, and the publication or registration of such rights.

---

[64]  Except as provided by Article 64, only an individual can count as a maintenance creditor. See pp. 489–90 above.

[65]  COM(2009)154 final.

[66]  See also Recital 28 and Article 45, which make a saving in favour of existing bilateral or multi-lateral conventions; and Article 50, which limits the Regulation to the successions of persons deceased after its date of application.

However, Article 19(2)(j) includes among the matters governed by the law applicable to a succession any obligation to restore or account for gifts, and the taking of them into account when determining the shares of heirs.

Recital 19 explains that the formal validity of dispositions of property upon death is not covered by the Proposal. For the fifteen Member States (including the United Kingdom) which have ratified it, this matter will remain governed by the Hague Convention of 5th October 1961 on the Conflicts of Laws relating to the Form of Testamentary Dispositions.

## Jurisdiction and Choice of Law

Chapter II (Articles 3–15) of the Proposal deals with direct judicial jurisdiction, and Chapter III (Articles 16–28) deals with choice of law.

By Article 19(1) of the Proposal, the law determined under Chapter III is to govern a succession as a whole, from its opening to the final transfer of the inheritance to the beneficiaries. By Article 19(2)(g), this includes the powers of heirs, executors of wills and other administrators of the succession, in particular as to the sale of property and the payment of creditors. By Article 25, a law specified by the Regulation is to apply even if it is not the law of a Member State. By Article 26, provisions of the Regulation requiring the application of the law of a State refer to the rules of law in force in that State, other than its rules of private international law. By Article 27, the application of a rule of the law applicable to a succession under the Regulation may be refused if its application is incompatible with the public policy of the forum, but this proviso cannot be invoked on the sole ground that the rules of the applicable law regarding the reserved portion of an estate differ from those in force in the forum.

The main connecting-factor used in the Proposal, in relation both to jurisdiction and to choice of law, is the habitual residence of the deceased owner at his death. Thus Article 4 confers jurisdiction on the courts of the Member State in which the deceased was habitually resident at the time of his death, and Article 16 subjects the succession as a whole to the law of the country in which the deceased was habitually resident at the time of his death. These rules extend to immovable property situated elsewhere.

There is a major exception in favour of the law and the courts of the State of the testator's nationality. Article 17 enables a testator to specify in his will that the succession as a whole shall be governed by the law of the State of which he is a national; and where such a choice of the law of a Member State has been made, Article 5 confers a discretion on the courts of the deceased's habitual residence to transfer jurisdiction to the courts of his nationality. Recital 32 explains that, where the concept of nationality serves to determine the law applicable, account should be taken of the fact that certain States whose legal system is based on common law use the concept of domicile and not nationality as an equivalent connecting-factor in matters of succession.

Where, at his death, the deceased was not habitually resident in any Member State, Article 6 confers jurisdiction on the courts of a Member State in which property of the estate is located, at least in relation to such property. In any event, Article 9 enables the courts of a Member State in which property is located to take measures under substantive law relating to the transmission of the property, or its recording or transfer in the public register, where under its law the taking of such measures requires their involvement. In addition, Article 21(2)(a) permits the application of the law of a Member State in which property is located where it subjects the administration and liquidation of the succession to the appointment of an administrator or executor via an authority located in that Member State; but in such a case the law applicable to the succession governs the determination of the persons (such as the heirs, legatees, executors or administrators) who are likely to be appointed to administer and liquidate the succession. By Recital 22 and Article 22, there is a saving for special succession regimes to which certain special categories of property (such as family farms) are subjected by the law of the Member State in which they are located on account of their economic, family or social purpose, where, according to that law, the special regime is applicable irrespective of the law governing the succession.

A substantive rule specified by Article 23 addresses the problem of commorientes. It provides that where two or more persons whose successions are governed by different laws die in circumstances which do not allow the order of death to be determined, and the laws deal with the situation through provisions which are incompatible or which do not settle it at all, none of the persons is to have any rights regarding the succession of the other party or parties.

Another specific provision, made by Article 24, deals with regalian claims to ownerless property. It applies where under the law applicable to the succession there is neither a testamentary heir or legatee, nor a natural person who is an heir by operation of law on intestacy. In such a case, the Regulation will not prevent a Member State in which property of the estate is located, or a body appointed in accordance with the law of that Member State, from seizing the property located on its territory.

**Recognition and Enforcement**

Chapters IV and V (Articles 29–35) of the Proposal deal with the recognition and enforcement of judgments, judicially approved settlements and authentic instruments. These provisions resemble the corresponding provisions of the Brussels I Regulation.[67]

**The European Certificate of Succession**

Chapter VI (Articles 36–44) of the Proposal introduces a European Certificate of Succession.[68] By Articles 36 and 37(2), the certificate constitutes proof of the capacity of the heir or legatee and of the powers of the executors or administrators. The certificate is issued by the court competent to deal with the succession under Chapter II, in accordance with the law applicable to the succession under Chapter III. The use of the certificate is not obligatory, and the certificate is not a substitute for internal procedures, but the effects of the certificate extend to the Member State whose authorities have issued it.

By Articles 37(1), 38 and 40, the certificate is issued upon application by an heir, legatee, executor or administrator. The applicant must provide relevant information, including as to the elements of fact or law which justify his right to succession or to administer the succession, and a copy of any known will of the deceased. The certificate should be issued only if the competent court considers that the facts presented as the grounds for the application are

---

[67] With regard to authentic instruments, see also Recital 26.
[68] See also Recital 27.

established. The competent court should carry out the enquiries necessary to verify the facts. It should issue the certificate promptly.

By Article 41, the certificate should contain information as to the following matters: (a) the issuing court and the basis of its competence; (b) information concerning the deceased; (c) any marriage contracts stipulated by the deceased; (d) the law applicable to the succession under the Regulation, and the basis for its application; (e) the basis for the rights or powers of heirs, legatees, executors or administrators, in terms of testate or intestate succession; (f) details of the applicant, including his relationship to the deceased; (g) where applicable, information in respect of each heir concerning the nature of the acceptance of the succession; (h) where there are several heirs, the share of each of them, and, if applicable, the rights and assets of any given heir; (i) the assets or rights for legatees in accordance with the law applicable to the succession; (j) the restrictions on the rights of the heir in accordance with the law applicable to the succession under Chapter III and/or in accordance with the provisions contained in the will; and (k) the acts which the heir, legatee, executor or administrator may perform on the property of the estate, under the law applicable to the succession.

By Article 42, the certificate must be recognised automatically in all the Member States with regard to the capacity of the heirs or legatees, and the powers of the executors or administrators. The content of the certificate must be presumed to be accurate in all the Member States throughout the period of its validity. It must be presumed that the person designated by the certificate as the heir, legatee, executor or administrator holds the right to the succession or the powers of administration stated in the certificate, and that there are no conditions or restrictions other than those stated therein. Anyone who pays or transfers property to the bearer of a certificate who is authorised to carry out such acts on the basis of the certificate will be released from his obligations, unless he knows that the contents of the certificate are not accurate. Anyone who has acquired property of the estate from the bearer of a certificate who is authorised to possess the property in accordance with the certificate will be considered to have acquired it from a person with the authority to possess the property, unless he knows that the contents of the certificate are not accurate. The certificate constitutes a valid document allowing for the transcription or entry of the inherited acquisition in the public registers of the Member State in which the property is located. Such transcription is to take place in accordance with the conditions laid down in the law of the Member State in which the register is held, and to produce the effects specified therein.

By Article 43, the original of the certificate must be retained by the issuing court, and that court is to issue one or more authentic copies to the applicant or to any person having a legitimate interest. The copies issued have the effects specified in Article 42 for a limited period of three months. Once this period has elapsed, the bearers of the certificate or any other interested persons must request a new authentic copy from the issuing court in order to assert their rights to succession. There is also provision for a certificate to be rectified, suspended or cancelled by the issuing court, and (by Article 44) for appeals against a decision to issue or not to issue, to rectify, to suspend, or to cancel a certificate.

PART V

Insolvency

# 19. Insolvency

## INTRODUCTION

On 29th May 2000 the EC Council adopted Regulation 1346/2000 on Insolvency Proceedings, which may conveniently be referred to as the Insolvency Regulation.[1] The Regulation entered into force on 31st May 2002 for the fourteen then Member States other than Denmark;[2] on 1st May 2004 for the ten States which joined the European Community on that date;[3] and on 1st January 2007 for Bulgaria and Romania.[4]

The exclusion of insolvency proceedings from the scope of the Brussels I Regulation by Article 1(2)(b) reflects the perception that, in view of their specific nature, such proceedings require special rules differing from those appropriate for ordinary civil or commercial disputes. Accordingly, negotiations under Article 220 of the EEC Treaty, aiming to establish a convention on insolvency, commenced in 1963. A Draft Convention on Bankruptcy, Winding-up, Arrangements, Compositions and Similar Proceedings, together with a Report thereon, emerged from a working group in 1980,[5] but in 1985 work thereon was suspended by the EC Council. Thereafter negotiations within the Council of Europe led to the opening for signature at Istanbul on 5th June 1990 of a Convention on Certain International Aspects of Bankruptcy,[6] but the Istanbul Convention has not been ratified by any of the EU Member States.

Eventually, negotiations at Community level were re-opened in May 1991, and these led to the opening for signature on 23rd November 1995 of a Convention on Insolvency Proceedings.[7] By Article 49, this Convention was to be open for signature by the EU Member States until 23rd May 1996, and to enter into force on the first day of the sixth month after its ratification by all the Member States. It was indeed signed by fourteen Member States by the specified date. But, apparently for reasons relating to mad-cow disease rather than insolvency,

---

[1]   For its text, see [2000] OJ L160/1.

[2]   See Recitals 32–3 and Article 47. The Regulation extends to Gibraltar, as a European territory for whose external relations the United Kingdom is responsible; see the EC Treaty (as amended), Article 299(4). For supplementary legislation in the United Kingdom, see the Insolvency Act 1986 (Amendment) (No 2) Regulations 2002 (SI 2002/1240).

[3]   See the Athens Act of Accession 2003, Article 2 (and, for minor adjustments, Annex II, Part 18(A)(1)).

[4]   See the Luxembourg Act of Accession, 25th April 2005, Articles 2 and 56; [2005] OJ L157. See also Regulation 1791/2006; [2006] OJ L363/1.

[5]   See EC Bull Supp 2/82. For a commentary on the 1980 Draft, see Lasok and Stone, *Conflict of Laws in the European Community* (Professional Books, 1987), chapter 10.

[6]   See Güneysu, 'The New European Bankruptcy Convention' (1991) 11 Yearbook of European Law 295.

[7]   See (1996) 35 ILM 1223.

the United Kingdom withheld its signature, and thus caused the project for the time being to abort.

The project was eventually revived, after the entry into force of the Treaty of Amsterdam, by a German and Finnish Initiative, submitted on 26th May 1999, proposing the adoption of a Council Regulation on Insolvency Proceedings, under Title IV of the EC Treaty (as amended).[8] The initiative eventually led to the adoption of the Insolvency Regulation. The Regulation is very similar in content to the 1995 Convention. Thus assistance on the interpretation of the Regulation can be obtained from the (unpublished) Virgos-Schmit Report[9] on the Convention, and from other commentaries thereon.[10]

## SCOPE

The Insolvency Regulation carefully defines its own scope. By Article 1(1), it applies to collective insolvency proceedings which entail the partial or total divestment of a debtor and the appointment of a liquidator. As Article 2(a) and (c) indicate, these comprise both winding-up proceedings, which involve realisation of the debtor's assets, and reorganisation proceedings, which do not necessarily involve such realisation.

In any event, the types of proceeding covered in each Member State are listed in Annexes A and B to the Insolvency Regulation (as amended).[11] The English proceedings covered as winding-up proceedings are: bankruptcy; winding-up by or subject to the supervision of the court; winding-up through administration (including appointments made by filing prescribed documents with the court); and creditors' voluntary winding-up (with confirmation by the court).[12] The English proceedings covered as reorganisation proceedings are: administration (including appointments made by filing prescribed documents with the court);[13] and voluntary arrangements under insolvency legislation.

As regards English proceedings for winding-up by the court, the Regulation is confined to proceedings based on insolvency. Thus it does not apply to an English petition presented by the Secretary of State for Trade and Industry under s 124A of the Insolvency Act 1986 to wind up a company in the public interest, for example because it is trading fraudulently, since such proceedings are not brought on grounds of insolvency but on public interest grounds.[14] Moreover, it is the Brussels I Regulation, and not the Insolvency Regulation, which applies

---

[8]    See [1999] OJ C221/8.

[9]    References herein are to the version of the Virgos-Schmit Report contained in doc 11900/1/95 rev 1.

[10]    See Dahan, (1996) 1 Developments in European Company Law 215; and Fletcher, *Insolvency in Private International Law* (Oxford University Press, 1999), especially chapter 6.

[11]    These Annexes were last amended and codified by EC Regulation 788/2008, [2008] OJ L213/1.

[12]    On creditors' voluntary winding-up with confirmation by the court, see *Re TXU Europe German Finance BV* [2005] BPIR 209 (Registrar Baister).

[13]    See *Re MG Rover Espana SA* [2005] BPIR 1162, where Norris QC suggested that an English administration order in respect of a company also operating elsewhere in Europe should contain a Schedule referring to the authoritative legislative text (Schedules B1 and 1 to the Insolvency Act 1986), and containing a summary of the principal provisions, relevant to the administration.

[14]    See *Re Marann Brooks CSV Ltd* [2003] BPIR 1159 (Patten J).

to a dispute between a creditor and a solvent company which is in members' voluntary liquidation.[15] As regards reorganisation proceedings, the Insolvency Regulation applies to an English company voluntary arrangement,[16] and to an English individual voluntary arrangement;[17] but not to an English receivership,[18] nor to an English application under s 899 of the Companies Act 2006 for the judicial approval of a scheme of arrangement.[19]

By Article 2(d) and Recital 10, for the purposes of the Insolvency Regulation, 'court' refers to a judicial or other competent body of a Member State which is empowered to open insolvency proceedings, or to take decisions in the course of such proceedings, but the Regulation is confined to proceedings which are officially recognised and legally effective in the relevant Member State. Thus for this purpose a ministerial decree may count as a decision opening an insolvency proceeding.[20] In the case of an English voluntary arrangement under the Insolvency Act 1986, the creditors' meeting at which the relevant resolution is passed counts as a competent body, and thus a court, of a Member State for the purpose of the Regulation.[21]

As Recital 9 indicates, the Insolvency Regulation applies whether the debtor is an individual or a corporation, and whether or not he is a trader. But Article 1(2) makes an exclusion for certain debtors which provide financial services: insurance undertakings;[22] credit institutions; investment undertakings which provide services involving the holding of funds or securities for third parties; and collective investment undertakings. Recital 9 explains that this reflects their subjection to special arrangements and the fact that, to some extent, the national supervisory authorities have extremely wide-ranging powers of intervention.[23] Thus the exclusion of collective investment undertakings is confined to ones which are authorised under EC Directive 85/611 as amended.[24]

As regards proceedings concerning the winding-up or reorganisation of an insurance undertaking which is regulated by an EU Member State or an EEA country under EC Directive 2001/17, on the reorganisation and winding-up of insurance undertakings,[25] the Directive confers exclusive jurisdiction on the courts of the regulating State. The Directive applies whether the insurance undertaking is solvent or insolvent; and accordingly, where the insurance undertaking is solvent, the Directive prevails over the Brussels I Regulation in

---

[15]    See *Re Cover Europe Ltd* [2002] BPIR 931.
[16]    See *Oakley v Ultra Vehicle Design Ltd* [2005] ILPr 55 (Lloyd LJ).
[17]    See *Shierson v Vlieland-Boddy* [2006] 2 BCLC 9 (CA).
[18]    See *Oakley v Ultra Vehicle Design Ltd* [2005] ILPr 55 (Lloyd LJ).
[19]    See *Re DAP Holding NV* [2006] BCC 48 (Lewison J).
[20]    See *Bank of America v Minister for Productive Industries* [2008] ILPr 25 (Italian Council of State).
[21]    See *Re Salvage Association* [2004] 1 WLR 174 (Blackburne J).
[22]    See, for example, *Re La Mutuelles du Mans Assurances* [2006] BCC 11 (Pumfrey J). But the exclusion does not extend to reinsurers; see *Re DAP Holding NV* [2006] BCC 48 (Lewison J).
[23]    See also EC Directive 2001/24, on the reorganisation and winding-up of credit institutions, which entered into force on 5th May 2001, [2001] OJ L125/15; EC Directive 2000/12, relating to taking up and pursuit of the business of credit institutions, [2000] OJ L126/1, as amended by Directives 2000/28 and 2002/87, [2000] OJ L275/37 and [2003] OJ L35/1; EC Directive 98/26, on settlement finality in payment and securities settlement systems, [1998] OJ L166/45; and EC Directive 2002/47, on financial collateral arrangements, [2002] OJ L168/43.
[24]    See *Financial Services Authority v Dobb White & Co* [2004] BPIR 479 (Moss QC).
[25]    [2001] OJ L110/28.

accordance with Article 67 of the Regulation, so that Article 22(2) of the Regulation does not apply.[26] There is also English authority that proceedings concerning a scheme of arrangement in respect of an insurance undertaking, whether it is solvent or insolvent, are outside the scope of all existing European Union legislation; neither the Insolvency Regulation, nor the Brussels I Regulation, nor Directive 2001/17 applies to such proceedings.[27]

As Recital 14 and Articles 3, 16 and 25 make clear, the Insolvency Regulation is limited to proceedings where the centre of the debtor's main interests is located in a Member State (other than Denmark).[28] Thus it avoids the unprincipled and discriminatory approach adopted by Articles 4 and 35 of the Brussels I Regulation, which consecrate the use of excessive bases of jurisdiction against 'outsiders' and require recognition and enforcement of the resulting judgments in the other Member States. But it is enough that the debtor has its centre of main interests in a Member State, even if it is a company incorporated in a non-member country. Thus the Regulation applies and creates English jurisdiction where a corporate debtor has its centre of main interests in England, even if it is incorporated in Delaware.[29]

By Article 43, the Insolvency Regulation applies only to insolvency proceedings opened after its entry into force, and acts done by a debtor before its entry into force continue to be governed by the law which was applicable to them at the time when they were done. As regards the provisions on direct jurisdiction to open an insolvency proceeding, and on the operation of an insolvency proceeding in the State in which it has been opened, the relevant date is presumably that of the entry into force of the Regulation for the forum State. But as regards the provisions on recognition and enforcement of judgments, the relevant date is presumably that of the entry into force of the Regulation for both the State of origin and the State addressed. By Article 44, the Regulation replaces existing conventions between Member States, except as regards proceedings already opened, but gives way to existing conventions with external countries and, in the case of the United Kingdom, to existing arrangements with the Commonwealth.

## PRINCIPLES AND STRUCTURE

The Insolvency Regulation accepts the principles of unity and universality by providing for main proceedings which are opened in a single Member State and have effect throughout the Community. Thus Recital 12 explains that the Regulation enables the main insolvency proceedings to be opened in the Member State where the debtor has the centre of his main interests, and that these proceedings have universal scope and aim at encompassing all the debtor's assets.

But the Regulation derogates from the principles of unity and universality by also providing for secondary proceedings, whose effect is limited to the Member State in which they are opened, and which deprive the main proceedings of effect within that State. Thus Recital 12

---

[26]    See *Re Sovereign Marine and General Insurance Co Ltd* [2007] 1 BCLC 228 (Warren J).

[27]    See *Re Sovereign Marine and General Insurance Co Ltd* [2007] 1 BCLC 228 (Warren J).

[28]    See *Re Arena Corporation* [2003] EWHC 3032 (Ch) (Lawrence Collins J); and *Re Drax Holdings Ltd* [2004] 1 BCLC 10 (Lawrence Collins J).

[29]    See *Re BRAC Rent-A-Car International* [2003] 1 WLR 1421 (Lloyd J). See also *Re Salvage Association* [2004] 1 WLR 174 (Blackburne J).

further explains that the Regulation permits secondary proceedings to be opened to run in parallel with the main proceedings; that secondary proceedings may be opened in a Member State where the debtor has an establishment; that the effects of secondary proceedings are limited to the assets located in that State; and that mandatory rules of co-ordination with the main proceedings satisfy the need for unity in the Community.

The Regulation further derogates from the principles of unity and universality by also providing for independent territorial proceedings, which may be opened in a Member State in which the debtor has an establishment *before* any main proceeding has been opened in the Member State in which the debtor's centre of main interests is located. As with a secondary proceeding, the effects of an independent territorial proceeding are limited to assets located in the Member State in which it is opened. An independent proceeding is permitted only if a main proceeding cannot be opened at the debtor's centre of main interests because of the conditions laid down by the law of that Member State, or if the independent proceeding is requested by a local creditor or a creditor of the local establishment.

# MAIN PROCEEDINGS

## Jurisdiction to Open a Main Proceeding

Article 3(1) of the Insolvency Regulation confers jurisdiction to open a main proceeding on the courts of the Member State within which the centre of the debtor's main interests is situated. Recital 13 explains that this corresponds to the place where the debtor conducts the administration of his interests on a regular basis, so as to be ascertainable by third parties. Article 3(1) also specifies that, in the case of a company or legal person, the place of the registered office must be presumed to be the centre of its main interests, in the absence of proof to the contrary.[30]

In *Eurofood IFSC Ltd*,[31] the European Court emphasised that the concept of the centre of main interests is peculiar to the Insolvency Regulation, and it therefore has an autonomous meaning and must be interpreted in a uniform way, independently of national legislation. In *Staubitz-Schreiber*,[32] the European Court ruled that the relevant date for determining the debtor's centre is that of the lodging of the application to open the insolvency proceeding, and thus that the court for the debtor's centre at the date of the petition retains jurisdiction even if the debtor subsequently moves his centre to another Member State before the proceeding

---

[30]   See also Articles 2(e), (g) and (h), 16(3) and 17(2) of Schedule 1 to the Cross-Border Insolvency Regulations 2006 (SI 2006/1030), giving effect to the UNCITRAL Model Law on Cross-Border Insolvency, adopted on 30th May 1997; and *Rubin v Eurofinance* [2009] EWHC 2129 (Ch) (Strauss QC). See also, as regards co-operation with a non-European main proceeding at common law and under s 426 of the Insolvency Act 1986, *Re HIH Casualty and General Insurance Ltd* [2008] 3 All ER 869 (HL), per Lord Hoffmann at para 31.

[31]   Case C-341/04, [2006] ECR I-3813.

[32]   Case C-1/04, [2006] ECR I-701. See also *Stojevic v Official Receiver* [2007] BPIR 141 (Registrar Jaques). Cf. *Skjevesland v Geveran Trading Co Ltd* [2003] BCC 391 (Judge Howarth), affirming [2003] BCC 209 (Register Jaques); and *Shierson v Vlieland-Boddy* [2004] EWHC 2752 (Mann J) and [2006] 2 BCLC 9 (CA).

is opened. The English courts have recognised that a person can only have one country as the centre of his main interests at a given time.[33]

### Companies and groups

Article 3(1) specifies that, in the case of a company or legal person, the place of the registered office must be presumed to be the centre of its main interests, in the absence of proof to the contrary. The Virgos-Schmit Report suggested that this rebuttable presumption should give way when the actual head office was located elsewhere.[34] But in *Eurofood IFSC Ltd*,[35] the European Court indicated that rebuttal is possible only in cases where the company is not carrying out any business in the Member State in which its registered office is situated. It also emphasised that, in the system established by the Insolvency Regulation for determining the competence of the courts of the Member States, each debtor constituting a distinct legal entity is subject to its own judicial jurisdiction. Thus the Regulation treats each company having legal personality as a separate debtor, with its own centre of main interests and possibly other establishments.[36]

The *Eurofood* case, which had been referred by the Irish Supreme Court, involved Eurofood, a company registered in Ireland, which was a wholly owned subsidiary of Parmalat, a company incorporated in Italy. In a contest between Irish and Italian jurisdiction to open a main proceeding in respect of the subsidiary company, the European Court ruled that where a debtor is a subsidiary company whose registered office and that of its parent company are situated in two different Member States, the presumption laid down in Article 3(1) of the Regulation, whereby the centre of main interests of the subsidiary is situated in the Member State where its registered office is situated, can be rebutted only if factors which are both objective and ascertainable by third parties enable it to be established that an actual situation exists which is different from that which location at that registered office is deemed to reflect. This could be so in particular in the case of a company not carrying out any business in the territory of the Member State in which its registered office is situated. By contrast, where a company carries on its business in the territory of the Member State where its registered office is situated, the mere fact that its economic choices are or can be controlled by a parent company in another Member State is not enough to rebut the presumption laid down by the Regulation.[37]

This strong affirmation of the principle that each company within a group counts as a separate debtor, with its own centre of interests, and that the control of a subsidiary by its parent is unimportant in this context, contrasts with and discredits earlier decisions of English and French courts which had sought to enhance the co-ordinating value of the Regulation by finding that subsidiary companies in whose administration the parent company had played a

---

[33] See *Shierson v Vlieland-Boddy* [2006] 2 BCLC 9 (CA); *Cross Construction Sussex Ltd v Tseliki* [2006] BPIR 888 (Lewison J); and *Stojevic v Official Receiver* [2007] BPIR 141 (Registrar Jaques).

[34] See para III:44.

[35] Case C-341/04, [2006] ECR I-3813.

[36] See also *Re BRAC Rent-A-Car International* [2003] 1 WLR 1421, at para 27.

[37] Subsequently, the Italian Council of State complied with the decision of the European Court by annulling the ministerial decree which had opened the Italian insolvency proceeding in respect of Eurofood; see *Bank of America v Minister for Productive Industries* [2008] ILPr 25.

major role had their centres of main interests at the parent company's head office.[38] The possibility of rebuttal which remains after *Eurofood* is, however, exemplified by the decision of Warren J in *Hans Brochier Holdings Ltd v Exner*[39] that a company incorporated in England had its centre of main interests in Germany, since it had never traded in England, all its trading activities had been carried out from Nuremberg, its key trading bank accounts were held with a branch of a German bank, its main creditors were located in Germany, and all or most of its employees were there.

### Individual debtors

As regards the centre of main interests of an individual debtor, the Virgos-Schmit Report indicates that in the case of an individual who is self-employed, one refers to his place of business; and in the case of an individual who is not self-employed, one refers to his habitual residence.[40] Before *Eurofood*, the Dutch Supreme Court had ruled that an individual owner of businesses could have his centre in a country where his companies operated, even if he was habitually resident elsewhere.[41] But in England the veil between a company and its individual owner is now respected, in view of the analogous ruling of the European Court in *Eurofood* in relation to groups of companies. Thus in *Stojevic v Official Receiver*,[42] Registrar Jaques ruled that an individual debtor, who was not carrying on a business in his own name, was centred in Austria, where he resided permanently with his family and spent about a quarter of his time, and not in England, where he spent nearly half of his time and conducted the business of a company which he indirectly owned and in which he acted as a shadow director.

English courts have recognised that the burden is on the petitioner to establish jurisdiction, though it is not yet settled whether the court must be satisfied on a balance of probabilities that the debtor's centre is in its country, or whether it is sufficient that this is strongly arguable (that a good arguable case for this exists).[43] It seems likely that the latter approach will be adopted by the English courts, by analogy with their approach to jurisdictional issues under the Brussels I Regulation. English courts have also recognised that the identification of the debtor's main interests requires the court to consider and compare the scale and importance of his interests administered at each potentially relevant place, from the viewpoint of the potential creditors; and that, in the case of a trader, the most important groups of potential creditor are likely to be his financiers and trade suppliers.[44]

---

[38]    See *Re Daisytek-ISA Ltd* [2004] BPIR 30 (Judge McGonigal); *Re Aim Underwriting Agencies (Ireland) Ltd* [2005] ILPr 22 (Henderson QC); *Re Parkside Flexibles SA* [2006] BCC 589 (Langan QC); *MPOTEC GmbH* [2006] BCC 681 (Nanterre Commercial Court); and *Energotech SARL* [2007] BCC 123 (Lure Court of First Instance).

[39]    [2007] BCC 127.

[40]    See para III:44. See also *Skjevesland v Geveran Trading Co Ltd* [2003] BCC 391 (Judge Howarth), affirming [2003] BCC 209 (Register Jaques); and *Stojevic v Official Receiver* [2007] BPIR 141 (Registrar Jaques).

[41]    See *X v Fortis Bank* [2004] ILPr 37 (Dutch Supreme Court).

[42]    [2007] BPIR 141 (Registrar Jaques).

[43]    See *Shierson v Vlieland-Boddy* [2006] 2 BCLC 9 (CA).

[44]    See *Re Daisytek-ISA Ltd* [2004] BPIR 30 (Judge McGonigal); *Re Aim Underwriting Agencies (Ireland) Ltd* [2005] ILPr 22 (Henderson QC); and *Re Ci4net.com Inc* [2005] BCC 277 (Langan QC).

In *Shierson v Vlieland-Boddy*,[45] which involved an English accountant who had recently moved to Spain, both Mann J (at first instance) and the Court of Appeal held that the debtor had moved the centre of his main interests to that country. Mann J accepted that it is possible for a debtor to move his centre from one country to another, even where this has the effect of defeating the expectations of existing creditors who had relied on the insolvency laws of the previous centre. But a change of centre must be real, genuine and not ephemeral. The enquiry as to the location of the debtor's centre of main interests is an overall enquiry which takes into account all relevant facts, giving to each of the facts such weight as is appropriate to the circumstances of the particular case. On appeal, Chadwick LJ stated the relevant principles as follows:

> The centre of main interests is to be determined in the light of the facts as they are at the relevant time for determination. But those facts include historical facts which have led to the position as it is at the time for determination.
>
> In making its determination the court must have regard to the need for the centre of main interests to be ascertainable by third parties; in particular, creditors and potential creditors. It is important, therefore, to have regard not only to what the debtor is doing but also to what he would be perceived to be doing by an objective observer. And it is important, also, to have regard to the need, if the centre of main interests is to be ascertainable by third parties, for an element of permanence. The court should be slow to accept that an established centre of main interests has been changed by activities which may turn out to be temporary or transitory.
>
> There is no principle of immutability. A debtor must be free to choose where he carries on those activities which fall within the concept of 'administration of his interests'. He must be free to relocate his home and his business. And, if he has altered the place at which he conducts the administration of his interests on a regular basis – by choosing to carry on the relevant activities (in a way which is ascertainable by third parties) at another place – the court must recognise and give effect to that.
>
> It is a necessary incident of the debtor's freedom to choose where he carries on those activities which fall within the concept of 'administration of his interests', that he may choose to do so for a self-serving purpose. In particular, he may choose to do so at a time when insolvency threatens. In circumstances where there are grounds for suspicion that a debtor has sought, deliberately, to change his centre of main interests at a time when he is insolvent, or threatened with insolvency, in order to alter the insolvency rules which will apply to him in respect of existing debts, the court will need to scrutinise the facts which are said to give rise to a change in the centre of main interests with that in mind. The court will need to be satisfied that the change in the place where the activities which fall within the concept of 'administration of his interests' are carried on which is said to have occurred is a change based on substance and not an illusion; and that that change has the necessary element of permanence.

### Competing claims to jurisdiction

By Articles 16(1) and 17(1) of the Insolvency Regulation, a judgment opening a main proceeding on the basis of the centre of the debtor's main interests must be recognised in the other Member States from the time when it becomes effective in the State of origin, and so as to produce the same effects in the other Member States as under the law of the State of origin. Recital 22 indicates that the principle of mutual trust provides the basis on which any dispute should be resolved where the courts of two Member States both claim competence to

---

45 [2006] 2 BCLC 9 (CA), affirming as to the centre of main interests [2004] EWHC 2752 (Mann J).

open main insolvency proceedings. Thus the decision of the first court to open proceedings should be recognised in the other Member States without those Member States having the power to scrutinise the court's decision, even as regards the finding as to the location of the centre of the debtor's main interests.[46] It follows that where applications, perhaps made by different creditors, for the opening of a main proceeding against the same debtor are simultaneously pending in courts of different Member States, the court which first opens proceedings will gain control.

The solution indicated by Recital 22 was endorsed by the European Court in *Eurofood IFSC Ltd*,[47] where it ruled that, under Article 16(1) of the Regulation, a main insolvency proceeding opened by a court of a Member State must be recognised by the courts of the other Member States, without the latter being able to review the jurisdiction of the court of the opening State. In this connection, the Court referred to Recital 22 and the principle of mutual trust; and by analogy to the Brussels I Regulation, as construed in *Gasser v MISAT*[48] and *Turner v Grovit*.[49] It added that if an interested party, taking the view that the centre of the debtor's main interests is situated in a Member State other than that in which the main insolvency proceeding was opened, wishes to challenge the jurisdiction assumed by the court which opened that proceeding, it may use, before the courts of the Member State in which it was opened, the remedies prescribed by the national law of that Member State against the opening decision.

### The opening of a main proceeding

In *Eurofood IFSC Ltd*,[50] the European Court accepted that an order of an Irish court, made in the context of a petition for the compulsory winding-up of an insolvent company, appointing a provisional liquidator with powers to take possession of the company's assets, manage its affairs, open a bank account and appoint a solicitor, and with the effect of depriving its directors of power to act, amounted to a decision opening insolvency proceedings for the purposes of Article 16(1) of the Regulation. It ruled that, for the purpose of Article 16(1), a decision to open insolvency proceedings is a decision handed down by a court of a Member State to which a corresponding application has been made, based on the debtor's insolvency and seeking the opening of proceedings referred to in Annex A, where that decision involves the divestment of the debtor and the appointment of a liquidator referred to in Annex C. Such divestment implies that the debtor loses the powers of management that he has over his assets. If these conditions are satisfied, it does not matter that the decision is not formally described as an opening decision by the legislation of the forum State, and that the liquidator referred to in Annex C is a provisionally appointed liquidator.

In this connection, the Court explained that the conditions and formalities required for opening insolvency proceedings are a matter for national law, and vary considerably from one Member State to another. In some Member States, the proceedings are opened very shortly

---

46   See also the Virgos-Schmit Report, at para III:188.
47   Case C-341/04, [2006] ECR I-3813. See also, on the exclusion of jurisdictional review, *Public Prosecutor v Segard* [2006] ILPr 32 (Versailles CA); and *French Republic v Klempka* [2006] BCC 841 (French Court of Cassation), affirming *Klempka v ISA Daisytek SAS* [2004] ILPr 6 (Versailles CA).
48   Case C-116/02, [2003] ECR I-14693. See pp. 198–9 above.
49   Case C-159/02, [2004] ECR I-3565. See pp. 205–8 above.
50   Case C-341/04, [2006] ECR I-3813.

after the submission of the application, the necessary verifications being carried out later. In other Member States, certain essential findings, which may be quite time-consuming, must be made before proceedings are opened. Under the national law of certain Member States, the proceedings may be opened 'provisionally' for several months. Thus it was necessary, in order to ensure the effectiveness of the system established by the Regulation, that the recognition principle laid down in Article 16(1) should be capable of being applied as soon as possible in the course of the proceedings. The mechanism whereby only one main set of proceedings may be opened, producing its effects in all the Member States in which the Regulation applies, could be seriously disrupted if the courts of those States, hearing applications based on a debtor's insolvency at the same time, could claim concurrent jurisdiction over an extended period. Thus a 'decision to open insolvency proceedings' for the purposes of the Regulation must be regarded as including not only a decision which is formally described as an opening decision by the legislation of the forum State, but also a decision handed down following an application, based on the debtor's insolvency, seeking the opening of proceedings referred to in Annex A to the Regulation, where that decision involves divestment of the debtor and the appointment of a liquidator referred to in Annex C to the Regulation. Such divestment involves the debtor losing the powers of management which he has over his assets. In such a case, the two characteristic consequences of insolvency proceedings, the appointment of a liquidator referred to in Annex C and the divestment of the debtor, have taken effect, so that all the elements constituting the definition of such proceedings, given in Article 1(1), are present. This remains the case even where the liquidator referred to in Annex C is a provisionally appointed liquidator.

### Provisional measures

There are further provisions in the Insolvency Regulation enabling a court which is competent to open, but has not yet opened, a main insolvency proceeding, to order provisional measures. Recital 16 recognises that a court which is competent to open a main insolvency proceeding has power, from the time of the request to open the proceeding, to order provisional and protective measures extending to assets situated in other Member States. By Article 38, where the court of a Member State which has jurisdiction to open a main proceeding appoints a temporary administrator in order to ensure the preservation of the debtor's assets, the temporary administrator is empowered to request any measures to secure and preserve any of the debtor's assets situated in another Member State which are provided for under the law of the State in which the assets are situated, for the period between the request for the opening of the insolvency proceeding and the judgment opening the proceeding.

### Ancillary disputes

In *Seagon v Deko Marty*,[51] the European Court ruled that Article 3(1) of the Insolvency Regulation confers on the courts of the Member State within which insolvency proceedings have been opened jurisdiction to decide an action to set a transaction aside by virtue of insolvency, even where it is brought against a person resident in another Member State. The case involved an application to a German court by the liquidator of a German company, in respect of which an insolvency proceeding had been opened in Germany. Shortly before the insol-

---

51 Case C-339/07, [2009] ECR I-767.

vency was opened, the German company had transferred a sum to a Dutch company. The liquidator was now seeking an order setting aside the transfer by virtue of the debtor's insolvency, and requiring the Dutch company to repay the money.

The European Court noted that the instant action to set a transaction aside was intended to increase the assets of the undertaking which was the subject of insolvency proceedings. Under German law, only the liquidator could bring an action to set a transaction aside in the event of insolvency with the sole purpose of protecting the interests of the general body of creditors. That law enabled the liquidator to challenge acts undertaken before the insolvency proceedings were opened which were detrimental to the creditors. The Court explained that such an action derived directly from the insolvency proceedings and was closely connected to them. Concentrating all actions directly related to the insolvency of an undertaking before the courts of the Member State with jurisdiction to open the insolvency proceedings was consistent with the objective of improving the effectiveness and efficiency of insolvency proceedings having cross-border effects, and accorded with Article 25 on the recognition of judgments.

## Choice of Law

The Insolvency Regulation deals with choice of law, as well as direct jurisdiction and the recognition and enforcement of judgments. The general rule, laid down by Article 4, refers insolvency proceedings and their effects, and the conditions for their opening, their conduct and their closure, to the law of the Member State in which the proceedings are opened (the lex concursus). But a number of exceptions to the rule in favour of the lex concursus are specified by Articles 5–15. Choice of law in insolvency proceedings is examined in a later section of this chapter.[52]

## Recognition of Judgments Opening a Main Proceeding

### The principle and the exceptions

Under the general rule laid down by Articles 16(1), 17(1) and 18(1), a judgment opening a main insolvency proceeding issued by a competent court of a Member State must be recognised in the other Member States from the time at which it becomes effective in the State of origin. Such recognition entails the production, without further formalities, of the same effects in the other Member States as it has in the State of origin, and enables the liquidator appointed by the original court to exercise in the other Member States the powers conferred on him by the law of the State of origin.[53] This applies even where, on account of his capacity (for example, as a non-trader), insolvency proceedings cannot be brought against the debtor in the State addressed.[54] It is also immaterial whether the judgment is final or provisional.[55] Since 'further formalities' are excluded by Article 17(1), recognition is mandatory

---

[52]   See pp. 690–98 below.

[53]   See also the Virgos-Schmit Report, at paras III:137–8. On the publication and registration in other Member States of judgments opening a proceeding and decisions appointing a liquidator, see Articles 21–3.

[54]   See also the Virgos-Schmit Report, at para III:131.

[55]   See the Virgos-Schmit Report, at para III:130.

and automatic, there is no special procedure for establishing it, and any objection to recognition (under Article 26) may be considered incidentally in any proceedings.[56] In *MG Probud*,[57] the European Court ruled that recognition of a main insolvency proceeding has the effect, in a Member State in which no secondary insolvency proceeding has been opened, of preventing a court of the recognising State from ordering, in accordance with its law, enforcement measures relating to the assets of the debtor declared insolvent that are situated in its territory, when the legislation of the State of the opening of the main insolvency proceeding does not so permit.

However, by Articles 17(1) and 18(1), the opening of a secondary proceeding in accordance with the Regulation causes the main proceeding to cease to have effects in the Member State in which the secondary proceeding is opened. The main liquidator also loses his powers to act in another Member State if a preservation measure to the contrary has been taken there further to a request for the opening of an insolvency proceeding there.

Otherwise, by Article 26, the only permissible ground for refusal of recognition is that its effects would be manifestly contrary to the public policy of the State addressed. This relates in particular to its fundamental principles or the constitutional rights and liberties of the individual. The Virgos-Schmit Report[58] emphasises that in general review as to both substance and jurisdiction are excluded, and that Article 16(1) specifically prevents refusal by reason of the debtor's capacity (for example, as a non-trader). On the other hand it accepts that the concept of public policy is open-textured, covering both substantive and procedural issues. Thus it may be infringed by a denial or obstruction of a creditor's right to participate in the preparation of a plan for re-organisation or a composition, or by a failure to notify a creditor before taking an individual decision against him.

The public policy proviso was considered by the European Court in *Eurofood IFSC Ltd*,[59] in the context of a reference by the Irish Supreme Court concerning the recognition of an Italian decision to open a main insolvency proceeding. The Irish court had found that the applicant for the Italian decision had refused, in spite of requests and contrary to an order of the Italian court, to provide a provisional liquidator of the corporate debtor, duly appointed in accordance with Irish law, with any copy of the essential papers on which the application was based. The European Court ruled that, under Article 26 of the Insolvency Regulation, a Member State may refuse to recognise insolvency proceedings opened in another Member State where the decision to open the proceedings was taken in flagrant breach of the fundamental right to be heard enjoyed by a person concerned. In this connection, the European Court followed its ruling in *Krombach v Bamberski*[60] on the Brussels I Regulation, and referred to the general principle of European Union law that everyone is entitled to a fair legal process. It emphasised that the right to be notified of procedural documents and, more generally, the right to be heard, occupy an eminent position in the organisation and conduct of a fair legal process. In the context of insolvency proceedings, the right of creditors or their representatives to participate in accordance with the equality of arms principle is of particular importance. Though the specific detailed rules concerning the right to be heard may vary

---

56   See the Virgos-Schmit Report, at paras III:134–6.
57   Case C-444/07, 21st January 2010.
58   See paras III:188–94a.
59   Case C-341/04, [2006] ECR I-3813.
60   Case C-7/98, [2000] ECR I-1935. See pp. 240–42 above.

according to the urgency for a ruling to be given, any restriction on the exercise of that right must be duly justified and surrounded by procedural guarantees ensuring that persons concerned by such proceedings actually have the opportunity to challenge the measures adopted in urgency. The Court added, however, that under Article 26 the court addressed cannot confine itself to transposing its own conception of the requirement for an oral hearing and of how fundamental that requirement is in its legal order, but must assess, having regard to the whole of the circumstances, whether or not the party was given sufficient opportunity to be heard.

In contrast, French courts have refused to invoke the public policy proviso against recognition of an English insolvency proceeding, despite arguments that English law offers less protection to the collective interests of employees than French law,[61] or (more specifically) that the employees' representatives were not heard before the decision was made to open the insolvency proceeding.[62]

## The position of the liquidator

The main effect of the recognition of a main insolvency proceeding is the recognition of the liquidator's appointment and powers in the other Member States.[63] By Article 18(1), the main liquidator may exercise in another Member State all the powers conferred on him by the lex concursus, as long as no other insolvency proceeding has been opened there and no preservation measure to the contrary has been taken there further to a request for the opening of an insolvency proceeding there. In particular, he may remove the debtor's assets from the territory of the Member State in which they are situated, subject to Articles 5 and 7 (on rights in rem and reservation of title). It is the lex concursus which defines the nature and the extent of the liquidator's powers, and also establishes his obligations.[64]

But Article 18(3) requires the liquidator, in exercising his powers, to comply with the law of the Member State in which he intends to take action, in particular with regard to procedures for the realisation of assets. It also prevents him from taking coercive measures, or ruling on legal proceedings or disputes. The Virgos-Schmit Report explains[65] that if coercive measures are required with regard to assets or persons, the liquidator must apply to the local authorities to have them adopted and implemented. Moreover, while it is for the lex concursus to determine whether the sale of immovable property can be private, if the lex concursus requires a sale by public auction, the manner of carrying out the sale is determined by the lex situs. Further, the power to remove assets is subject to restrictions which are unconnected with insolvency, such as prohibitions on the export of art treasures. The forum competent for litigation disputing the liquidator's exercise of his powers appears to depend on the ground of the complaint.[66]

Article 20 lays down rules designed to secure the equal treatment of creditors. By Article 20(1), where a creditor, after the opening of a main proceeding, obtains by any means (including

---

[61]  See *Public Prosecutor v Segard* [2006] ILPr 32 (Versailles CA).
[62]  See *French Republic v Klempka* [2006] BCC 841 (French Court of Cassation).
[63]  See the Virgos-Schmit Report, at para III:142. On proof of the liquidator's appointment, see Article 19. On proof of his powers, see the Report, at para III:156.
[64]  See the Virgos-Schmit Report, at para III:143.
[65]  See paras III:148–50.
[66]  See the Virgos-Schmit Report, at para III:152.

voluntary payment or enforcement) total or partial satisfaction of his claim on the debtor's assets situated in another Member State, he must return what he has obtained to the liquidator. This is explicitly made subject to Articles 5 and 7 (on rights in rem and reservation of title), and the Virgos-Schmit Report suggests that it is for the lex concursus to determine whether there is also an exception in favour of a creditor who acted in good faith.[67]

By Article 20(2), where a creditor has in the course of one insolvency proceeding obtained a dividend on his claim, he will share in distributions made in other proceedings only where creditors of the same ranking or category have, in those other proceedings, obtained an equivalent dividend. According to the Virgos-Schmit Report, it is for the lex concursus to determine how this operates where part of a claim is secured by a right in rem or set-off.[68] But ranking is determined in accordance with the law of the country where the later distribution is under consideration.[69]

Article 24 deals with payments to the debtor made after the opening of an insolvency proceeding. By Article 24(1), where an obligation has been honoured in a Member State for the benefit of a debtor who is subject to an insolvency proceeding opened in another Member State, when it should have been honoured for the benefit of the liquidator therein, the person honouring the obligation is discharged if he was unaware of the opening of proceedings. By Article 24(2), where such an obligation is honoured before publication of the judgment opening the insolvency proceeding has been effected in the relevant State in accordance with Article 21, the person honouring the obligation is presumed, in the absence of proof to the contrary, to have been unaware of the opening of insolvency proceedings. Conversely, where the obligation is honoured after such publication has been effected, he is presumed, in the absence of proof to the contrary, to have been aware of the opening of proceedings.

**Recognition and Enforcement of Related Judgments**

Where a judgment opening an insolvency proceeding is recognised under Article 16 of the Insolvency Regulation, certain other judgments ('related judgments') given by the same court, or in some cases by another court of the same State, must be recognised and enforced in accordance with Article 25. By Article 25(1)(i) and (iii), this applies to judgments, given by the court which opened the insolvency proceeding, which concern the course and closure of insolvency proceedings; compositions approved by that court; and judgments given by that court relating to preservation measures taken after the request for the opening of insolvency proceedings. By Article 25(1)(ii), it also applies to judgments which derive directly from the insolvency proceedings and are closely linked with them (such as judgments setting aside a transaction at the request of the liquidator, on the basis of insolvency law, in the interests of the general body of creditors), and which are given either by the court which opened the insolvency proceeding, or by another court of the same State.[70] Such related judgments must be

---

[67]   At para III:158.
[68]   See para III:161.
[69]   See para III:162.
[70]   See Case C-339/07: *Seagon v Deko Marty* [2009] ECR I-767; Case 133/78: *Gourdain v Nadler* [1979] ECR 733; and the Virgos-Schmit Report, at paras III:46 and 181. See also Case C-111/08: *SCT Industri v Alpenblume* [2009] ECR I-5655, where the European Court ruled that the exclusion specified by Article 1(2)(b) of the Brussels I Regulation applies to a judgment which invalidated a transfer of

recognised without further formalities, and are also made enforceable in accordance with the procedure established by Chapter III of the Brussels I Regulation.[71] According to the Virgos-Schmit Report,[72] this incorporates Article 38 of the Brussels I Regulation, so that, to be enforceable abroad, the judgment must be enforceable in the State of origin.

The permissible grounds for refusal of recognition or enforcement of a related judgment are very limited. As in the case of a judgment opening an insolvency proceeding, recognition or enforcement of a related judgment may be refused under Article 26 on the ground that the effects thereof would be manifestly contrary to the public policy of the State addressed, in particular to its fundamental principles or the constitutional rights and liberties of the individual. In the case of a related judgment, recognition and enforcement may also be refused under Article 25(3) on the ground that the judgment might result in a limitation of personal freedom or postal secrecy.

Article 25(2) of the Insolvency Regulation provides that the recognition and enforcement of judgments other than those referred to in Article 25(1) remains governed by the Brussels I Regulation, if it is otherwise applicable. Accordingly, in *German Graphics Graphische Maschinen GmbH v Alice van der Schee*,[73] the European Court ruled that Brussels I Regulation was applicable to the enforcement in the Netherlands, where an insolvency proceeding had been opened in respect of a buyer of goods, of a German order obtained by the seller against the buyer, seeking recovery of the goods on the basis of a reservation of title clause, since the seller's claim to ownership was not based on insolvency law and did not require the opening of insolvency proceedings or the involvement of a liquidator, even though the goods were situated in the Netherlands at the time of opening of the insolvency proceedings there, and even though the buyer's liquidator was in fact a party to the German action brought by the seller.

## SECONDARY PROCEEDINGS

### The Opening of a Secondary Proceeding

By Articles 3(2)–(3) and 27, the Insolvency Regulation provides for the opening of a secondary insolvency proceeding. The debtor's centre of main interests must be situated in one Member State, and a main proceeding must have been opened against him in that State. He must also have an establishment in another Member State, in which the secondary proceeding is to be opened. The secondary proceeding must be a winding-up proceeding, rather than a reorganisation proceeding, and its effects are restricted to the debtor's assets which are situated in the Member State in which it is opened. By Article 17(1), the opening of a secondary proceeding causes the main proceeding to cease to have effects in the State in which the secondary proceeding is opened. Thus, as was pointed out by Norris QC in *Re MG*

---

local assets by a foreign liquidator on the ground that the law of the country of origin did not recognise his power to dispose of local assets. The Insolvency Regulation was not applicable in *SCT* since the insolvency proceedings were opened before its entry into force.

[71] See Article 68(2) of the Brussels I Regulation.
[72] At para III:178.
[73] Case C-292/08, [2009] ECR I-8421.

*Rover Espana SA*,[74] the possibility arises of a main proceeding (such as an English administration proceeding) being conducted with the aim of rescuing the business as a going concern, and secondary proceedings being conducted elsewhere with the aim of immediately closing down the business and realising and distributing its assets.

Jurisdiction to open a secondary proceeding is confined by Article 3(2) to the courts of a Member State within which the debtor has an establishment. This is defined by Article 2(h) as a place of operations where the debtor carries out a non-transitory economic activity with human means and goods.[75] The Virgos-Schmit Report indicates that the concept is wider than that used in Article 5(5) of the Brussels I Regulation,[76] but insists on a minimum level of organisation and a certain stability, externally apparent.[77] In *Shierson v Vlieland-Boddy*,[78] the Court of Appeal was satisfied with the ownership, letting and managing of a unit of multi-let business premises.

Presumably the relevant time for determining the existence of an establishment is (as in the case of the debtor's centre) that of the lodging of the application to open the insolvency proceeding.[79] In *Shierson v Vlieland-Boddy*,[80] Mann J ruled that, in the case of an individual debtor, an establishment will be created only by economic activities which are conducted on his own behalf. His activities as a director of and shareholder in a company will not give rise to an establishment of his own. The Court of Appeal reversed, holding that an individual may have an establishment through a 'front' or nominee company. But, in this respect, it seems impossible to reconcile the approach adopted by the Court of Appeal with the principle that the Regulation respects corporate personality, which in the context of corporate groups was emphasised by the European Court in *Eurofood IFSC Ltd*,[81] or with the consequent decision of Registrar Jaques in *Stojevic v Official Receiver*[82] that the business of a company cannot be treated as that of its individual owner when determining his centre of main interests. In any event, it is clear that business premises of a subsidiary company cannot rank as an establishment of its parent company for the purposes of the Regulation.[83]

By Article 27, a secondary proceeding may be opened without further examination of the debtor's insolvency. By Article 29, the opening of a secondary proceeding may be requested by the liquidator in the main proceeding, or by any other person or authority empowered to request the opening of insolvency proceedings under the law of the forum State. But it has been held in France that a secondary proceeding cannot be opened by a court of its own

---

74   [2005] BPIR 1162.
75   See also Articles 2(e), (g) and (h), 16(3) and 17(2) of Schedule 1 to the Cross-Border Insolvency Regulations 2006 (SI 2006/1030), giving effect to the UNCITRAL Model Law on Cross-Border Insolvency, adopted on 30th May 1997; and *Rubin v Eurofinance* [2009] EWHC 2129 (Ch) (Strauss QC).
76   On Article 5(5) of the Brussels I Regulation, see pp. 109–10 above.
77   See paras III:39–40.
78   [2006] 2 BCLC 9 (CA).
79   See Case C-1/04: *Staubitz-Schreiber* [2006] ECR I-701. Cf. *Shierson v Vlieland-Boddy* [2004] EWHC 2752 (Mann J).
80   [2004] EWHC 2752 (Mann J); reversed, [2006] 2 BCLC 9 (CA).
81   Case C-341/04, [2006] ECR I-3813.
82   [2007] BPIR 141 (Registrar Jaques).
83   See *Telia AB v Hilcourt (Docklands) Ltd* [2003] BCC 856 (Park J).

motion.[84] Secondary proceedings will not be possible if the debtor lacks the necessary capacity (for example, as a non-trader) under the law of the country of the establishment.[85] Moreover, a French court has refused to open a secondary proceeding on the ground that the applicant had not demonstrated that it would serve a useful purpose, such as improving the protection of local interests or the realisation of assets.[86]

By Article 28, in a secondary proceeding, the local law operates as the lex concursus, but the exceptions specified by Articles 5–15 to the control of the lex concursus apply in the same way as in a main proceeding.[87]

## The Effects of a Secondary Proceeding

By Articles 3(2) and 27, the effects of a secondary proceeding are restricted to the assets of the debtor situated in the Member State in which it is opened. The location of assets for the purposes of the Regulation is defined by Article 2(g). Tangible property is situated at its actual location. Registrable property (including patents)[88] is situated in the State under whose authority the register is kept. Claims are situated at the centre of main interests of the person liable for the claim. By Article 12, a Community trade mark, plant variety right, or design, established by European Union law with effect throughout the Union, may be included only in a main insolvency proceeding.

By Articles 16(1), 17(2) and 18(2), a secondary proceeding is recognised in the other Member States, with the result that the secondary liquidator can sue in another Member State to recover assets removed from his country after the opening of the secondary proceeding there.[89] A discharge granted in a secondary proceeding is effective against local assets. But, by Article 17(2), it is effective in relation to assets situated in other Member States only against creditors who have individually given their consent.[90]

By Article 32(1) and 39, any creditor who has his habitual residence, domicile or registered office in a Member State[91] is entitled to lodge his claim in both the main proceeding and in any secondary proceedings.[92] This extends to a tax or social security authority of a Member State, and the Irish High Court has held that it enables a tax authority of another Member State to initiate, as well as to prove in, an insolvency proceeding, and overrides the common law rule against the enforcement of foreign tax claims.[93]

---

[84]   See *Eco Jet Ltd v Selafa MJA* [2005] BCC 979 (Paris CA).
[85]   See the Virgos-Schmit Report, at para III:206.
[86]   See *Public Prosecutor v Segard* [2006] ILPr 32 (Versailles CA).
[87]   On choice of law in insolvency proceedings, see pp. 528–35 below.
[88]   See the Virgos-Schmit Report, at para III:38.
[89]   See also the Virgos-Schmit Report, at paras III:140 and 151.
[90]   See the Virgos-Schmit Report, at para III:141. See also Article 34(2), on compositions.
[91]   According to the Virgos-Schmit Report, at para III:252, the right of creditors resident outside the European Union to lodge claims is governed by the lex concursus.
[92]   See also Article 40, on the duty to notify known creditors resident in other Member States; Articles 41, on the content of the lodgement of a claim; and Article 42, on languages. Failure to notify a known creditor resident in another Member State in accordance with Articles 40 and 42(1) has the effect that time does not run against the creditor for the purpose of the time-limit for lodging proof of claims under the lex fori; see *R Jung GmbH v SIFA SA* [2006] BCC 678 (Orleans CA).
[93]   See *Re Cedarlease Ltd* [2005] IEHC 67 (Laffoy J).

Article 31 imposes a general duty on the main and secondary liquidators to communicate and otherwise co-operate with each other. By Article 32(2), a liquidator must normally lodge in the other proceedings claims which have been lodged in his own proceeding. By Article 32(3), a liquidator may attend creditors' meetings in the other proceedings. By Article 33, in general the court which has opened a secondary proceeding must stay its process of liquidation if the main liquidator so requests (for example, in order to preserve assets with a view to a reorganisation).[94] By Article 34, a composition in a secondary proceeding may be proposed by the main liquidator, and in general requires his consent. By Article 35, if the liquidation of assets in a secondary proceeding enables all claims allowed in that proceeding to be met, the secondary liquidator must immediately transfer any assets remaining to the main liquidator.[95]

In *Re Nortel Networks SA*,[96] Patten J explained that the duty of co-operation between liquidators imposed by Article 31(2) incorporates or reflects a wider obligation which extends to the courts which exercise control of insolvency procedures. Accordingly, in the context of English main proceedings, he acceded to an application by the English administrators to send a letter of request to courts of other EU Member States, asking them to put in place arrangements under which the English administrators would be given notice of any application for the opening of secondary insolvency proceedings in respect of the relevant companies, and to permit the English administrators to make submissions on any such applications in respect of the potential damage which secondary proceedings might have on the interests of the estate and the creditors of the relevant companies.

As is noted by the Virgos-Schmit Report,[97] assets available in a secondary proceeding will be distributed amongst all creditors whose claims are allowed in that proceeding. Thus, since creditors are entitled to lodge claims in any proceedings, creditors who have preferential claims in the main proceeding, but are ordinary unsecured creditors in a secondary proceeding, will have an incentive to lodge their claims in the secondary proceeding, in order to have their claims met against assets there in the same way and at the same time as other ordinary unsecured creditors.

**The Rationale for Secondary Proceedings**

It is not easy, for the present writer at any rate, to see any serious justification for the admission of secondary proceedings. The introduction of secondary proceedings follows the approach adopted in the Istanbul Convention 1990, but there its main rationale and effect was to permit discrimination in favour of local creditors. In contrast, the Regulation rejects any such discrimination, recognising that it would conflict with Article 18 of the Treaty on the Functioning of the European Union.[98]

---

[94]   See the Virgos-Schmit Report, at para III:226.
[95]   See also, as regards the remission of English assets to a non-European liquidator, under the common law and s 426 of the Insolvency Act 1986, *Re HIH Casualty and General Insurance Ltd* [2008] 3 All ER 869 (HL).
[96]   [2009] All ER (D) 128 (Feb).
[97]   At para III:237.
[98]   See Articles 32 and 39–42 of the Regulation.

Recitals 11 and 19 to the Insolvency Regulation refer in this context to widely differing substantive laws, especially on security interests, preferential rights and contracts of employment, and to cases where the estate of the debtor is too complex to administer as a unit. Security interests and contracts of employment are among the matters addressed by the choice-of-law rules laid down by Articles 5–15 of the Regulation,[99] and it is difficult to see why any further need to safeguard legitimate expectations and ensure certainty in relation to security interests or contracts of employment could not have been met either by improvements to those choice-of-law rules or, if necessary, by the inclusion of uniform substantive rules on points of particular difficulty or importance. As regards complex estates, it is difficult to see how the introduction of secondary proceedings can facilitate, rather than obstruct, the administration of the insolvency.

There appear to be two real (if misguided) concerns which underlie the introduction of secondary proceedings. First, there is a general desire to respect, as against each asset, preferential rights recognised by its lex situs, whether the claim to which preference is accorded arises from a contract of employment, a consumer contract, a fiscal or other public law, or otherwise. Secondly, there is a more specific desire to enable local public authorities having tax or similar claims to retain their rights to enforce those claims, in accordance with local rules on preferences or otherwise, against local assets. Both these rationales collapse once it is recognised that, in the case of a company operating internationally, the location of assets at the moment when an insolvency proceeding is opened is often a matter of accident, and sometimes a result of fraud, and never offers a suitable basis for the organisation of a just and efficient regime of international co-operation.[100] Thus it is submitted that a better response to such concerns would have been to harmonise the substantive laws of the Member States as regards the definition and extent of preferential rights, and the admissibility and priority of public law claims of authorities of Member States.

## INDEPENDENT TERRITORIAL PROCEEDINGS

Article 3(2) and (4) of the Insolvency Regulation provide for the opening of an independent territorial insolvency proceeding where the debtor's centre of main interests is situated in a Member State, but a main proceeding has not (or not yet) been opened against him in that State. He must also have an establishment in another Member State, in which the independent territorial proceeding is to be opened, and one of two further requirements, specified by Article 3(4), must be fulfilled.

The first of these alternative requirements is that a main proceeding cannot be opened at the debtor's centre of main interests because of the conditions laid down by the law of that Member State (for example, where it does not permit an insolvency proceeding unless the debtor is a trader). In this case, the decision to permit an independent proceeding at the

---

[99]　On these choice-of-law rules, see pp. 530–35 below.

[100]　See *Re HIH Casualty and General Insurance Ltd* [2008] 3 All ER 869 (HL), at para 35, where Lord Hoffmann noted that the fact that there were assets in England of insolvent Australian insurance companies was principally the result of the companies having placed their reinsurance business in the London market, and commented that, for the purposes of deciding how the assets should be distributed, this was an entirely adventitious circumstance.

debtor's establishment is at least understandable. But a preferable solution would surely have been to adopt a harmonised substantive rule in respect of the personal characteristics of the debtor which may be relevant to the availability of insolvency proceedings; for example, a rule abolishing any requirement that the debtor must be a trader.

The second alternative is that the opening of the territorial insolvency proceeding is requested by a creditor who has his domicile, habitual residence or registered office in the Member State in which the establishment is situated, or whose claim arises from the operation of the establishment. This alternative seems to reflect a misguided idea of according some preference to local creditors in respect of local assets, even though other provisions of the Regulation (such as Article 39) endeavour to eliminate such discrimination.

In any event, Article 3(2) insists that the effects of an independent territorial proceeding are restricted to the assets of the debtor situated in the territory of the Member State in which it is opened. Like a secondary proceeding, an independent territorial proceeding is recognised in the other Member States, with the result that the liquidator can sue in another Member State to recover assets removed from his country after the opening of the secondary proceeding there.[101] Similarly, a discharge granted in an independent proceeding is effective against local assets, but not in relation to assets situated in other Member States except against creditors who have individually given their consent.[102]

Articles 36 and 37 deal with the situation where a main proceeding is opened after the opening of an independent territorial proceeding. By Article 36, the independent territorial proceeding will so far as possible be treated as a secondary proceeding with regard to communication and co-operation between the liquidators, lodging of claims, stay, composition, and surplus assets. By Article 37, if the independent proceedings were reorganisation proceedings, the competent court may convert them into winding-up proceedings if the main liquidator so requests.

## CHOICE OF LAW

### The General Rule

The Insolvency Regulation deals with choice of law, as well as direct jurisdiction and the recognition and enforcement of judgments. The general rule, laid down by Article 4, refers insolvency proceedings and their effects, and the conditions for their opening, their conduct and their closure, to the law of the Member State in which the proceedings are opened (the lex concursus). Similarly, Article 28 makes clear that in general the law applicable to secondary proceedings is that of the Member State in which the secondary proceedings are opened.

Recital 23 explains that, unless otherwise provided, the law of the Member State of the opening of the proceedings should be applicable (the lex concursus). This conflict rule should be valid both for main proceedings and for local proceedings. The lex concursus

---

[101]   See Articles 16(1), 17(2) and 18(2).
[102]   See Article 17(2).

determines all the effects of the insolvency proceedings, both procedural and substantive, on the persons and legal relations concerned. It governs all the conditions for the opening, conduct and closure of the insolvency proceedings.

More specifically, Article 4(2) lists numerous issues which are governed by the lex concursus. By Article 4(2)(a)–(c) and (g)–(l), the following issues are governed exclusively by the lex concursus: (a) against which debtors insolvency proceedings may be brought on account of their capacity; (b) the assets which form part of the estate, and the treatment of assets acquired by or devolving on the debtor after the opening of the insolvency proceedings; (c) the respective powers of the debtor and the liquidator; (g) the claims which are to be lodged against the debtor's estate, and the treatment of claims arising after the opening of insolvency proceedings; (h) the rules governing the lodging, verification and admission of claims; (i) the rules governing the distribution of proceeds from the realisation of assets, the ranking of claims, and the rights of creditors who have obtained partial satisfaction after the opening of insolvency proceedings by virtue of a right in rem or through a set-off; (j) the conditions for and the effects of closure of insolvency proceedings, in particular by composition; (k) creditors' rights after the closure of insolvency proceedings; and (l) who is to bear the costs and expenses incurred in the insolvency proceedings.

Article 4(2) also lists certain issues to which the lex concursus is applicable, but (in view of subsequent provisions) not exclusively. These are: (d) the conditions under which set-offs may be invoked; (e) the effects of insolvency proceedings on current contracts to which the debtor is party; (f) the effects of the insolvency proceedings on proceedings brought by individual creditors,[103] with the exception of lawsuits pending; and (m) the rules relating to the voidness, voidability or unenforceability of legal acts detrimental to all the creditors.

Occasionally the Regulation lays down a substantive rule, thus derogating from the lex concursus. In particular, Article 20(1) insists that a creditor who, after the opening of a main insolvency proceeding, obtains by any means (in particular through enforcement) total or partial satisfaction of his claim on the assets belonging to the debtor situated within the territory of another Member State, must return what he has obtained to the liquidator, subject to Articles 5 and 7 (on rights in rem and reservation of title). Similarly, Article 20(2) prevents a creditor who has, in the course of one insolvency proceeding, obtained a dividend on his claim from sharing in distributions made in other proceedings until creditors of the same ranking or category have, in those other proceedings, obtained an equivalent dividend.

Another substantive rule is provided by Article 24, which deals with payments to the debtor made after the opening of an insolvency proceeding. By Article 24(1), where an obligation has been honoured in a Member State for the benefit of a debtor who is subject to an insolvency proceeding opened in another Member State, when it should have been honoured for the benefit of the liquidator therein, the person honouring the obligation is discharged if he was unaware of the opening of proceedings. By Article 24(2), where such an obligation is honoured before publication of the judgment opening the insolvency proceeding has been effected in the relevant State in accordance with Article 21, the person honouring the obligation is presumed, in the absence of proof to the contrary, to have been

---

[103]   See also Case C-294/02: *Commission v AMI Semiconductor* [2005] ECR I-2175.

unaware of the opening of insolvency proceedings. Conversely, where the obligation is honoured after such publication has been effected, he is presumed, in the absence of proof to the contrary, to have been aware of the opening of proceedings.

Moreover, as the Virgos-Schmit Report explains,[104] the existence and validity of a claim remains governed by the law otherwise applicable to it, such as the proper law of the contract from which it arises. For Article 4 deals only with matters peculiar to insolvency law, and does not affect issues which can arise in the absence of insolvency.

Although, unlike the Rome I Regulation on the Law Applicable to Contractual Obligations[105] and the Rome II Regulation on the Law Applicable to Non-contractual Obligations,[106] the Insolvency Regulation contains no provision explicitly excluding renvoi, the Virgos-Schmit Report indicates that the reference by Article 4 of most issues to the lex concursus should be read as referring to its internal law.[107]

According to a nuanced approach which has been adopted by the English courts, the general rule in favour of the lex concursus, established by Article 4 of the Insolvency Regulation, does not prevent the court which has opened a main proceeding from taking some account of the laws of other Member States in which secondary proceedings have been or could be opened. Such laws may be treated as part of the relevant factual background in the context of which decisions under the lex concursus may be taken. Thus in *Re MG Rover Espana SA*,[108] which involved an English administration proceeding at the debtor's centre and actual or potential secondary proceedings at the debtor's establishments in other European countries, Norris QC noted that, in general, in striking the balance between the interests of employees, on the one hand, and the interests of finance and trade creditors on the other, English insolvency law treats the claims of employees less favourably than the law of other Member States. He accepted that, under Article 4 of the Regulation, the English administration proceedings, and the claims of European employees therein, were subject to the administration regime created by the Insolvency Act 1986, and not to any foreign law. But he held that, in order to forestall secondary proceedings which would frustrate the purpose of the main proceeding, the English administrators were at liberty to make payments to European employees greater than their strict entitlement under English insolvency law, and in line with their entitlement under their own law. He found this power in paragraph 66 of Schedule B1 to the Insolvency Act 1986, which enables an administrator to make a payment if he thinks it likely to assist achievement of the purpose of administration. This permits an administrator to depart from the strict ranking of claims if he thinks it likely to assist achievement of the broader purpose of administration.

---

[104]   See paras II:11, III:57 and III:182.
[105]   See Chapters 12 and 13 above.
[106]   See Chapters 14 and 15 above.
[107]   See para III:58; and Fletcher, at pp. 265–6.
[108]   [2005] BPIR 1162. See also *Re MG Rover Belux SA/NV* [2007] BCC 446 (Norris QC), which involved other claims which were preferential under the law of the country of the secondary establishment; and *Re Collins & Aikman Europe SA* [2007] ILPr 2 (Lindsay J), which involved the deferral of intra-group claims under the law of the country of the secondary establishment.

## Various Exceptions

Articles 5–15 of the Insolvency Regulation specify a number of exceptions to the general rule in favour of the lex concursus. Recital 11 explains that these apply to particularly significant rights and legal relationships, such as rights in rem and contracts of employment. Recital 24 adds that the exceptions are designed to protect legitimate expectations and the certainty of transactions in other Member States. Exceptions relating to proprietary rights are specified by Articles 5, 7–8, 11 and 14. Other exceptions (dealing, for example, with set-off) are specified by Articles 6, 8–10, 13 and 15.

Many (but not all) of the rules specified in Articles 5–15 are expressly limited to cases where they operate in favour of the law of a Member State. The Virgos-Schmit Report indicates, however, that it is open to each Member State, through its conflict rules, to extend these exceptions to the lex concursus so as to make corresponding concessions to the laws of non-member countries; for example, so as to respect mortgages of property situated outside the European Community.[109]

## Proprietary exceptions

*Rights in rem*   Article 5 of the Insolvency Regulation deals with rights in rem. It specifies that the opening of insolvency proceedings is not to affect the rights in rem of creditors or third parties in respect of assets belonging to the debtor which are situated in another Member State at the time of the opening of proceedings. Article 5(1) explicitly provides that the assets may be tangible or intangible; that they may be movable or immovable; and that both specific assets and collections of indefinite assets as a whole which change from time to time are covered. Article 5(2) indicates that rights in rem include a mortgage or lien. The reference in Article 5(1) to collections of indefinite assets as a whole which change from time to time makes it clear that English floating charges are included. The Virgos-Schmit Report explains that, to be a right in rem, the right must bind transferees, though it need not be binding on a bona fide purchaser.[110]

Recital 25 emphasises the particular need for a special reference diverging from the lex concursus in the case of rights in rem, since these are of considerable importance for the granting of credit. The basis, validity and extent of such a right in rem should therefore normally be determined according to the lex situs and not be affected by the opening of insolvency proceedings. The proprietor of the right in rem should therefore be able to continue to assert his right to segregation or separate settlement of the collateral security. Where assets are subject to rights in rem under the lex situs in one Member State but the main proceedings are being carried out in another Member State, the liquidator in the main proceedings should be able to request the opening of secondary proceedings in the jurisdiction where the rights in rem arise if the debtor has an establishment there. If a secondary proceeding is not opened, the surplus on sale of the asset covered by rights in rem must be paid to the liquidator in the main proceedings.

---

[109]   See paras III:7, III:76 and III:108; and Fletcher, at p. 265.
[110]   See para III:84.

Thus Article 5 goes beyond a reference of the validity and effect of rights in rem to the lex situs. It ensures that such rights are not adversely affected by the opening of insolvency proceedings in another Member State. As the Virgos-Schmit Report explains,[111] if the lex situs enables a security to be affected by insolvency, a secondary proceeding will have to be opened there to achieve this result. Moreover, this will not be possible if the debtor does not have an establishment in the relevant country. But a saving by Article 5(4) enables rights in rem to be overridden by means of actions to establish the voidness, voidability or unenforceability of legal acts detrimental to all the creditors.

*Immovable or registered property*   Article 8 of the Insolvency Regulation deals with existing contracts relating to immovable property (that is, land). It specifies that the effects of insolvency proceedings on a contract conferring the right to acquire or make use of immovable property are governed solely by the law of the Member State in which the immovable property is situated.

Article 11 deals with the effects of insolvency proceedings on the debtor's rights in property which is subject to registration. It specifies that the effects of insolvency proceedings on the debtor's rights in immovable property, or a ship or an aircraft, which is subject to registration in a public register, must be determined by the law of the Member State under the authority of which the register is kept.

In addition, to protect third-party purchasers, Article 14 deals with acts concluded after the opening of insolvency proceedings, by which the debtor disposes, for consideration, of an immovable asset, or of a ship or an aircraft which is subject to registration in a public register, or of securities whose existence presupposes registration in a register laid down by law. It subjects the validity of such an act to the law of the State within whose territory the immoveable asset is situated or under whose authority the register is kept.

*Reservation of title*   Article 7 of the Insolvency Regulation deals with reservations of title to goods sold.[112] It applies where, at the time of the opening of insolvency proceedings, the asset sold is situated within the territory of a Member State other than the State of the opening of the insolvency proceedings. In such a case, by Article 7(1), the opening of insolvency proceedings against the purchaser of the asset is not to affect the seller's rights based on a reservation of title; and, by Article 7(2), the opening of insolvency proceedings against the seller of the asset after its delivery is not to constitute grounds for rescinding or terminating the sale, nor to prevent the purchaser from acquiring title. But a saving by Article 7(3) enables these provisions to be overridden by means of actions to establish the voidness, voidability or unenforceability of legal acts detrimental to all the creditors.

## Other exceptions

*Set-off*   Set-off is dealt with by Articles 4(2)(d) and 6 of the Insolvency Regulation, which in combination enable a creditor to invoke a set-off if either the lex concursus or the law

---

[111]   See paras II:22 and III:79.

[112]   On reservation of title, see also Case C-292/08: *German Graphics Graphische Maschinen GmbH v Alice van der Schee* [2009] ECR I-8421; considered at p. 523 above.

governing the insolvent debtor's claim so permits. For Article 4(2)(d) refers to the lex concursus the conditions under which set-offs may be invoked, but Article 6(1) specifies that the opening of insolvency proceedings is not to affect the right of creditors to demand the set-off of their claims against the claims of the debtor, where such a set-off is permitted by the law applicable to the insolvent debtor's claim. Recital 26 explains that, in this way, set-off will acquire a kind of guarantee function based on legal provisions on which the creditor concerned can rely at the time when the claim arises. However, a saving by Article 6(2) enables a set-off permitted only by the law applicable to the insolvent debtor's claim to be overridden by means of actions to establish the voidness, voidability or unenforceability of legal acts detrimental to all the creditors.

*Payment systems and financial markets*    Article 9 of the Insolvency Regulation deals with payment systems and financial markets. It specifies that the effects of insolvency proceedings on the rights and obligations of the parties to a payment or settlement system or to a financial market are governed solely by the law of the Member State applicable to that system or market. There are savings for Article 5 (on rights in rem), and for any action for voidness, voidability or unenforceability which may be taken to set aside payments or transactions under the law applicable to the relevant payment system or financial market. The Virgos-Schmit Report explains that a financial market is one where securities or monetary instruments are traded in a regular manner in accordance with established rules.[113]

Recital 27 explains that special protection is needed in the case of payment systems and financial markets. This applies, for example, to the position-closing agreements and netting agreements to be found in such systems, as well as to the sale of securities, and to the guarantees provided for such transactions as governed in particular by EC Directive 98/26 on settlement finality in payment and securities settlement systems.[114] For such transactions, the only law which is material should thus be the law applicable to the system or market concerned. This provision is intended to prevent the possibility of mechanisms for the payment and settlement of transactions provided for in the payment and set-off systems or on the regulated financial markets of the Member States being altered in the case of insolvency of a business partner. Directive 98/26 contains special provisions which should take precedence over the general rules in the Insolvency Regulation.

*Current contracts*    In general, Article 4(2)(e) of the Insolvency Regulation refers to the lex concursus the effects of insolvency proceedings on current contracts to which the debtor is party; for example, as regards the liquidator's power to terminate a contract.[115] But exceptions are made by Articles 8 and 10. By Article 8, the effects of insolvency proceedings on a contract conferring the right to acquire or make use of immovable property is governed solely by the law of the Member State in which the immovable property is situated.

By Article 10, the effects of insolvency proceedings on employment contracts and relationships is governed solely by the law of the Member State which is applicable to the contract of employment. Recital 28 explains that, in order to protect employees and jobs, the

---

[113]    See para III:102.
[114]    [1998] OJ L166/45.
[115]    See the Virgos-Schmit Report, at para III:97.

effects of insolvency proceedings on the continuation or termination of employment and on the rights and obligations of all parties to such employment must be determined by the law applicable to the agreement in accordance with the general conflict rules. But that any other insolvency-law questions, such as whether the employees' claims are protected by preferential rights, and what status such preferential rights may have, should be determined by the lex concursus.

*Invalidation of detrimental acts*    Article 4(2)(m) of the Insolvency Regulation refers to the lex concursus the rules relating to the voidness, voidability or unenforceability of legal acts performed by the debtor which are detrimental to all the creditors. But Article 13 makes an exception for acts which are governed by and are unchallengeable under the law of another Member State. It applies where the person who benefited from an act detrimental to all the creditors provides proof that the act is subject to the law of a Member State other than the lex concursus, and that the law governing the act does not allow any means of challenging the act in the relevant case. The Virgos-Schmit Report explains that the act must be unchallengeable in the actual circumstances, in view of both the general law and the insolvency law of the relevant country.[116]

*Pending actions*    Article 4(2)(f) of the Insolvency Regulation refers to the lex concursus the effects of the insolvency proceedings on proceedings brought by individual creditors, with the exception of lawsuits pending. But Article 15 specifies that the effects of insolvency proceedings on a lawsuit pending concerning an asset or a right of which the debtor has been divested are governed solely by the law of the Member State in which that lawsuit is pending.

The Virgos-Schmit Report[117] indicated that Article 15 is confined to cases where, at the opening of the insolvency proceeding, there is an action pending in a court of another Member State between the debtor and another person, in which that other person is asserting that he has a better right than the debtor to a specific item of property. In such a case, it is for the law of the State whose court is seised of the lawsuit pending to decide whether or not its proceedings are to be suspended or continued, and whether any appropriate procedural modifications are needed in order to reflect the loss or restriction of the debtor's powers of disposal and administration, and the corollary intervention of the liquidator.

But in *Syska v Vivendi*,[118] Christopher Clarke J held that the exception for 'lawsuits pending' is not confined to proprietary claims relating to a specific asset, but extends to any proceedings which are brought to establish the validity of a claim which, if successful, would operate against the debtor's estate,[119] and which, at the time when the insolvency proceeding was opened, were pending either in a court of another Member State, or before an arbitral tribunal seated in another Member State. He accepted, however, that the exception does not extend to proceedings by way of execution. He explained that the purposes of the Regulation include (a) ensuring the effective and efficient administration of the insolvency and avoiding

---

116    See para III:119.

117    At para III:125.

118    [2009] 1 All ER (Comm) 244.

119    He agreed with a line of decisions of the Austrian Supreme Court of 17th March 2005, 24th January 2006, and 23rd February 2006, and disagreed with the decision of the Irish High Court in *Re Flightlease Ireland Ltd* [2005] IEHC 274.

one creditor gaining an advantage over others; and (b) protecting the legitimate expectations of parties and the certainty of transactions. To have all execution actions subject, in the event of insolvency proceedings, to the law of the state of the opening of those proceedings would promote, and allowing individual creditors to continue with executions they have started (and thus obtain direct satisfaction against the insolvent's estate) would impede, the achievement of the first objective. In contrast, to allow actions for the determination of the merits of a claim which have already commenced to continue would promote the second objective without prejudicing the effective and efficient administration of the insolvency. A litigant who may have spent very large sums in pursuing, or defending, a claim may legitimately expect that it should proceed to adjudication. If it does so, and the claim is successful, it will then rank with the other claims in the insolvency. His decision was affirmed by the Court of Appeal.[120]

Moreover, it is not open to a court of a Member State which is properly seised of a lawsuit pending in accordance with the Brussels I Regulation to decline jurisdiction on grounds of forum non conveniens in favour of a court of another Member State which has opened an insolvency proceeding in accordance with the Insolvency Regulation.[121]

---

[120] [2009] 2 All ER (Comm) 891 (CA).
[121] See *Mazur Media Ltd v Mazur Media Gmbh* [2005] 1 Lloyd's Rep 41 (Lawrence Collins J).

# Index